Microsoft Access 2013
Inside Out

Jeff Conrad

Published with the authorization of Microsoft Corporation by:
O'Reilly Media, Inc.
1005 Gravenstein Highway North
Sebastopol, California 95472

ISBN: 978-0-7356-7123-2

1 2 3 4 5 6 7 8 9 LSI 8 7 6 5 4 3

Printed and bound in the United States of America.

Microsoft Press books are available through booksellers and distributors worldwide. If you need support related to this book, email Microsoft Press Book Support at *mspinput@microsoft.com*. Please tell us what you think of this book at *http://www.microsoft.com/learning/booksurvey*.

Acquisitions and Developmental Editor: Kenyon Brown

Production Editor: Christopher Hearse

Technical Reviewer: Andrew Couch

Copyeditor: Richard Carey

Indexer: BIM Publishing Services

Cover Design: Twist Creative • Seattle

Cover Composition: Ellie Volckhausen

Illustrator: Rebecca Demarest

For my wonderful wife, Cheryl, and for Amy, Aaron, and Arica.
Thank you for your love, support, and encouragement.

—Jeff Conrad

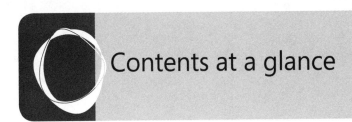

Contents at a glance

Table of contents

Part 1: Working with Access Services web apps

Introduction

Microsoft Access 2013 is just one part of Microsoft's overall data management product strategy. Like all good relational databases, it allows you to link related information easily—for example, customer and order data that you enter. But Access 2013 also complements other database products because it has several powerful connectivity features. As its name implies, Access can work directly with data from other sources, including many popular PC database programs, with many SQL (Structured Query Language) databases on the desktop, on servers, on minicomputers, or on mainframes, and with data stored on Internet or intranet web servers.

Access provides a very sophisticated application development system for the Microsoft Windows operating system. This helps you build applications quickly, whatever the data source. In fact, you can build simple applications by defining forms and reports based on your data and linking them with a few macros or Microsoft Visual Basic statements; there's no need to write complex code in the classic programming sense. Because Access uses Visual Basic, you can use the same set of skills with other applications in the Microsoft Office system or with Visual Basic.

For small businesses (and for consultants creating applications for small businesses), the Access desktop development features are all that's required to store and manage the data used to run the business. Access coupled with Microsoft SQL Server—on the desktop or on a server—is an ideal way for many medium-size companies to build new applications for Windows quickly and inexpensively. To enhance workgroup productivity, you can use Access 2013 to create an Access Services web app using Microsoft's Office 365 service or on a server with SharePoint 2013, Access Services, and SQL Server 2012. Users of your web app can view, edit, and delete data from your app directly in their web browser. For large corporations with a large investment in mainframe relational database applications and a proliferation of desktop applications that rely on personal computer databases, Access provides the tools to easily link mainframe and personal computer data in a single Windows-based application. Access 2013 includes features to allow you to export or import data in XML format (the lingua franca of data stored on the web).

Who this book is for

If you have never used a database program—including Access—you'll find Access 2013 very approachable. The Backstage view and ribbon technology makes it easy for novice users to get acquainted with Access and easily discover its most useful features. To get a new user jump-started, Microsoft provides web app and desktop database templates available for download that you can use to begin creating an application that helps solve your personal or business needs.

If you're developing a web app or desktop database application with the tools in Access 2013, *Microsoft Access 2013 Inside Out* gives you a thorough understanding of "programming without pain." It provides a solid foundation for designing web apps, desktop databases, forms, and reports and getting them all to work together. You'll learn that you can quickly create complex applications by linking design elements with macros or Visual Basic. This book will also show you how to take advantage of some of the more advanced features of Access 2013. You'll learn how to build an Access web app that you can use with Microsoft's Office 365 service offering. You'll learn all about the new design surfaces for creating objects in Access web apps and how to use apps in your web browser.

If you're new to developing applications, particularly web apps and database applications, this probably should not be the first book you read about Access. I recommend that you first take a look at *Microsoft Access 2013 Plain & Simple* or *Microsoft Access 2013 Step By Step*.

How this book is organized

Microsoft Access 2013 Inside Out is divided into eight major parts:

Part 1 shows you how to create and work with the all new Access Services web apps:

- Chapter 1, "What is Access," explains the major features that a database should provide, explores those features in Access, and discusses some of the main reasons why you should consider using database software.

- Chapter 2, "Exploring the Access 2013 web app interface," thoroughly explores the web app user interface introduced in the Access 2013 release. The chapter also explains working in the web app environment and installing web app packages.

- Chapter 3, "Designing tables in a web app," teaches you how to design web app tables and how to import and link data into web apps.

- Chapter 4, "Creating data macros in web apps," focuses on how to create data macros and work with table events to attach business logic to your tables.

- Chapter 5, "Working with queries in web apps," shows you how to build queries in web apps and work with data in query Datasheet view.

- Chapter 6, "Working with views and the web browser experience," and Chapter 7, "Advanced view design," exploree the new App Home View, show how to create all the view different view types, work with controls, and understand the properties you can use with controls in web apps. You'll also learn how to create and work with views in a web browser, and how to manage external connections.

- Chapter 8, "Automating a web app using macros," shows how to work with view and control events to automate your web app.

Part 2 shows you how to create and work with tables in a desktop database:

- Chapter 9, "Exploring the Access 2013 desktop database interface," thoroughly explores the desktop database interface. The chapter also explains content security, working with the Backstage view, ribbon, and the Navigation pane, and setting options that customize how you work with Access 2013.

- Chapter 10, "Designing tables in a desktop database," and Chapter 11, "Modifying your table design," teach you how to design desktop databases and tables and show you the ins and outs of modifying tables, even after you've already begun to load data and build other parts of your application.

The Appendix explains how to install the Office 2013 release, including which options you should choose for Access 2013 to be able to open all the samples in this book.

Part 3 through Part 8, which includes Chapter 12 through Chapter 27, can be found in the Companion Content section on the book's catalog page. The Companion Content also includes seven additional articles with important reference information.

Note

This book is current as of the general availability release date of Microsoft Access 2013 and Office 365 in February 2013. Microsoft is continually updating the Office 365 service offerings, and new features could be implemented after this release date. As a result, some of the features in the product might not exactly match what you see if you are working through the book's examples at a later date.

This book does not discuss the following deprecated features in Access 2013: Access Data Projects (ADP), PivotCharts, PivotTables, Access data collection through email, support for Jet 3.x IISAM, support for dBASE, Access 2003 toolbars and menus, Access Replication Options, Access Source Code Control, Access Three-State Workflow, and the Access Upsizing Wizard. Also, Microsoft removed the ability to create new Access 2010-style web databases with Access 2013 in favor of the new Access 2013 web apps. You can edit existing 2010-style web databases with Access 2013, but you cannot create new ones. Therefore, this book does not discuss how to create and edit 2010-style web databases. If you want to learn about Access 2010-style web databases, see *Microsoft Access 2010 Inside Out*.

Features and conventions used in this book

The following conventions are used in the syntax descriptions for Visual Basic statements in Chapter 24, "Understanding Visual Basic fundamentals," Chapter 25, "Automating your application with Visual Basic," SQL statements in Article 2, "Understanding SQL," and any other chapter where you find syntax defined. These conventions do not apply to code examples listed within the text; all code examples appear exactly as you'll find them in the sample databases.

You must enter all other symbols, such as parentheses and colons, exactly as they appear in the syntax line. Much of the syntax shown in the Visual Basic chapter has been broken into multiple lines. You can format your code all on one line, or you can write a single line of code on multiple lines using the Visual Basic line continuation character (_).

Text conventions

Convention	Meaning
Bold	Bold type indicates keywords and reserved words that you must enter exactly as shown. Microsoft Visual Basic understands key-words entered in uppercase, lowercase, and mixed case type. Access stores SQL keywords in queries in all uppercase, but you can enter the keywords in any case.
Italic	Italicized words represent variables that you supply.
Angle brackets < >	Angle brackets enclose syntactic elements that you must supply. The words inside the angle brackets describe the element but do not show the actual syntax of the element. Do not enter the angle brackets.
Brackets [ ]	Brackets enclose optional items. If more than one item is listed, the items are separated by a pipe character (|). Choose one or none of the elements. Do not enter the brackets or the pipe; they're not part of the element. Note that Visual Basic and SQL in many cases require that you enclose names in brackets. When brackets are required as part of the syntax of variables that you must supply in these examples, the brackets are italicized, as in *[MyTable].[MyField]*.
Braces { }	Braces enclose one or more options. If more than one option is listed, the items are separated by a pipe character (|). Choose one item from the list. Do not enter the braces or the pipe.
Ellipsis ...	Ellipses indicate that you can repeat an item one or more times. When a comma is shown with an ellipsis (,...), enter a comma between items.

Convention	Meaning
Underscore _	You can use a blank space followed by an underscore to continue a line of Visual Basic code to the next line for readability. You cannot place an underscore in the middle of a string literal. You do not need an underscore for continued lines in SQL, but you cannot break a literal across lines.

Design conventions

INSIDE OUT This statement illustrates an example of an "Inside Out" heading

These are the book's signature tips. In these tips, you get the straight scoop on what's going on with the software—inside information about why a feature works the way it does. You'll also find handy workarounds to deal with software problems.

Sidebar

Sidebars provide helpful hints, timesaving tricks, or alternative procedures related to the task being discussed.

Troubleshooting

This statement illustrates an example of a "Troubleshooting" problem statement.

Look for these sidebars to find solutions to common problems you might encounter. Troubleshooting sidebars appear next to related information in the chapters. You can also use "Index to Troubleshooting Topics" at the back of the book to look up problems by topic.

Cross-references point you to locations in the book that offer additional information about the topic being discussed.

CAUTION!

Cautions identify potential problems that you should look out for when you're completing a task or that you must address before you can complete a task.

> **Reader Aid**
> Notes offer additional information related to the task being discussed.

Your companion ebook

With the ebook edition of this book, you can do the following:

- Search the full text

- Print

- Copy and paste

To download your ebook, please see the instruction page at the back of the book.

About the companion content

I have included companion content to enrich your learning experience. The companion content for this book can be downloaded from the following page:

http://aka.ms/Access2013IO/files

The companion content is organized as follows:

Part 3 focuses on how to build desktop database queries to analyze and update data in your tables.

- Chapter 12, "Creating and working with simple queries," shows you how to build simple desktop database queries and how to work with data in Datasheet view.

- Chapter 13, "Building complex queries," discusses how to design desktop database queries to work with data from multiple tables, summarize information, and build queries that require you to work in SQL view.

- Chapter 14, "Modifying data with action queries," focuses on modifying sets of data with desktop database queries—updating data, inserting new data, deleting sets of data, or creating a new table from a selection of data from existing tables.

Part 4 discusses how to build and work with forms in desktop databases.

- Chapter 15, "Using forms in a desktop database," introduces you to forms—what they look like and how they work.

- Chapter 16, "Building a form," Chapter 17, "Customizing a form," and Chapter 18, "Advanced form design," teach you all about form design in desktop databases, from simple forms you build with a wizard to complex, advanced forms that use embedded forms and navigation and web browser controls.

Part 5 explains how to work with reports in desktop databases.

- Chapter 19, "Using reports," leads you on a guided tour of reports and explains their major features.

- Chapter 20, "Constructing a report," and Chapter 21, "Advanced report design," teach you how to design, build, and implement both simple and complex reports in your application.

Part 6 shows you how to make your desktop database "come alive" using macros.

- Chapter 22, "Creating data macros in desktop databases," explores the macro Logic Designer and shows how to work with events and named data macros within desktop databases.

- Chapter 23, "Using macros in desktop databases," discusses the concept of event processing in Access, provides a comprehensive list of events, and explains the sequence in which critical events occur. It also covers user interface macro design in depth and explains how to use error trapping and embedded macro features.

Part 7 shows you how to use the programming facilities in Microsoft Visual Basic to integrate your database objects and automate your desktop database.

- Chapter 24, "Understanding Visual Basic fundamentals," is a comprehensive reference to the Visual Basic language and object models implemented in Access. It presents two complex coding examples with a line-by-line discussion of the code. The final section shows you how to work with 64-bit Access Visual Basic.

- Chapter 25, "Automating your desktop database with Visual Basic," thoroughly discusses some of the most common tasks that you might want to automate with Visual Basic. Each section describes a problem, shows you specific form or report design techniques you must use to solve the problem, walks you through the code from one or more of the sample databases that implements the solution, and discusses calling named data macros.

Part 8 covers tasks you might want to perform after completing your application.

- Chapter 26, "The finishing touches," teaches you how to automate custom ribbons, create a custom Backstage view, and how to set Startup properties.

- Chapter 27, "Distributing your desktop database," teaches you tasks for setting up your application so that you can distribute it to others. It also shows you how to create your own custom Data Type Parts, Application Parts, and application templates.

The companion content includes an additional seven articles that contain important reference information:

- Article 1 explains a simple technique that you can use to design a good relational database application with little effort. Even if you're already familiar with Access or creating database applications in general, getting the table design right is so important that this article is a "must read" for everyone.

- Article 2 is a complete reference to SQL as implemented in desktop databases. It also contains notes about differences between SQL supported natively by Access and SQL implemented in SQL Server.

- Article 3 explains how to link to or import data from other sources.

- Article 4 discusses how to export data and Access objects to various types of other data formats from your Access application.

- Article 5 lists the functions most commonly used in an Access application, categorized by function type. You'll also find a list of functions that you can use with Access web apps.

- Article 6 lists common color names and codes you can use in Access.

- Article 7 lists the macro actions for both desktop databases and web apps you can use in Access.

Using the sample files

Throughout *Microsoft Access 2013 Inside Out*, you'll see references to sample Access web apps and desktop databases. To access and download the sample applications, visit:

http://aka.ms/Access2013IO/files

For detailed instructions on where to place the sample files on your local computer, see the Appendix. For information on how to install the web app samples (discussed in Part 1 of this book) in your SharePoint site, see the section "Installing app packages," in Chapter 2.

The examples in this book assume you have installed the 32-bit version of Microsoft Office 2013, not just the 32-bit version of Access 2013. You can also download versions of the sample databases that have been modified to work with the 64-bit version of Access 2013. Several examples in this book assume that you have installed all optional features of Access through the Office 2013 setup program. If you have not installed these additional features, your screen might not match the illustrations in this book or you might not be able to run the sample files. A list of the additional features you will need to run all the samples in this book is included in the Appendix.

A list of the key database files and their descriptions follows. (I have not listed all the smaller support files for the chapters or articles.)

- *Back Office Software System Restaurant Management Web App (BOSS.app).* This comprehensive web app demonstrates how a restaurant might manage food orders, maintain employee records, and create weekly work schedules. Examples of nearly all features with Access web apps are contained in this large sample web app.

- *Auctions App (Auctions.app).* This sample web app demonstrates using Access to track donated items for auctions and the users bidding on the auction items. This sample contains examples of using data macros to control the data entry by applying logic at the table level.

- *Training Tracker App (TrainingTracker.app).* This web app tracks different training courses completed by employees. You can also use the app to record employee feedback and the number of hours spent on each training.

- *Conrad Systems Contacts (Contacts.accdb and ContactsData.accdb).* This desktop database application is both a contacts management and order entry database. This sample database demonstrates how to build a client/server application using only desktop tools. You'll also find a ContactsDataCopy.accdb file that contains additional query, form, and report examples.

- *Housing Reservations (Housing.accdb).* This desktop database application demonstrates how a company housing department might track and manage reservations in company-owned housing facilities for out-of-town employees and guests. You'll also find HousingDataCopy.accdb and HousingDataCopy2.accdb files that contain many of the query, form, and report examples.

- *Back Office Software System Restaurant Management Application (BOSSDesktopDatabase.accdb).* This desktop application contains similar functionality to the BOSS.app sample web app, but this sample utilizes desktop database objects and features.

- *Wedding List (WeddingMC.accdb and WeddingList.accdb).* This application is an example of a simple desktop database that you might build for your personal use. It has a single main table where you can track the names and addresses of invitees, whether they've said that they will attend, the description of any gift they sent, and whether a thank-you note has been sent. Although you might be tempted to store such a simple list in an Excel spreadsheet or a Word document, this application demonstrates how storing the information in Access makes it easy to search and sort the data and produce reports. The WeddingMC database is automated entirely using macros, and the WeddingList database is the same application automated with Visual Basic.

Here is a list of databases that are discussed in the chapters:

Chapter	Content
Chapter 1	ContactsMap.accdb and Contacts.accdb
Chapter 2	BOSS.app
Chapter 3	RestaurantData.accdb, Contacts.app, BOSS.app, and RestaurantSample.app
Chapters 4 and 5	BOSSDataCopy.app
Chapter 6	RestaurantSampleWithData.app, BOSS.app, and ControlDefinitions.accdb
Chapter 7	RestaurantSampleChapter7.app, BOSS.app, and BOSSReportsMaster.accdb
Chapter 8	RestaurantSampleChapter8.app, BOSS.app sample app, and Auctions.app
Chapter 9	TasksSample.accdb
Chapter 10	WeddingList.accdb, Housing.accdb, and Contacts.accdb
Chapter 11	Housing.accdb, Contacts.accdb, and ContactTracking.accdb
Chapters 12, 13, and 14	ContactsDataCopy.accdb and HousingDataCopy.accdb
Chapter 15	Contacts.accdb and ContactsNavigation.accdb
Chapter 16	ContactsDataCopy.accdb
Chapter 17	HousingDataCopy.accdb and ContactsNavigation.accdb
Chapter 18	HousingDataCopy.accdb, ContactsDataCopy.accdb, and ContactsNavigation.accdb
Chapter 19	ContactsDataCopy.accdb and Housing.accdb
Chapter 20	ContactsDataCopy.accdb
Chapter 21	HousingDataCopy2.accdb
Chapter 22	BOSSDesktopDatabase.accdb
Chapter 23	WeddingMC.accdb and BOSSDesktopDatabase.accdb
Chapter 24	Contacts.accdb and Housing.accdb

Chapter	Content
Chapter 25	Housing.accdb, Contacts.accdb, and WeddingList.accdb
Chapter 26	Contacts.accdb, Housing.accdb, HousingSP.accdb, and BOSSDesktopDatabase.accdb
Chapter 27	Contacts.accdb, Housing.accdb, and ContactsNavigation.accdb

Please note that the person names, company names, email addresses, and web addresses in all the databases are fictitious. Although I pre-loaded all databases with sample data, the Housing Reservations and Conrad Systems Contacts databases also include a special form (zfrmLoadData) that has code to load random data into the sample tables based on parameters that you supply.

> **Note**
>
> All the screen images in this book were taken on a Windows 8 system with the Office theme set to White and using the Internet Explorer web browser. Your results might look different if you are using a different operating system, a different theme, or a different web browser. Also, the results you see from the samples might not exactly match what you see in this book if you have changed the sample data in the files.

System requirements

The following are the system requirements you need to install Office 2013, Access 2013, and the sample files on a Microsoft Windows–compatible computer or device.

- A gigahertz (Ghz) or faster x86-bit or x64-bit processor with SSE2 instruction set.

- Microsoft Windows 7 (32-bit or 64-bit), Microsoft Windows 8 (32-bit or 64-bit), Windows Server 2008 R2, or Windows Server 2012 operating systems.

- At least 1 gigabyte (GB) of random access memory (RAM) for 32-bit operating system environments or 2 gigabytes (GB) of RAM for 64-bit operating systems.

- A hard drive with at least 3.0 gigabytes (GB) available.

- A DirectX10 graphics card and 1024 x 576 resolution for graphics hardware acceleration.

- Microsoft Internet Explorer 8, 9, 10, or a later version; Mozilla FireFox 10.x or a later version; Apple Safari 5; or Google Chrome 17.x or a later version.

- Microsoft .NET version 3.5, 4.0, or 4.5.

- A touch-enabled device for using any multi-touch functionality in Windows 8. (However, all features and functionality are always available by using a keyboard, mouse, or other standard or accessible input device.)

- Silverlight installed together with Office 2013 is recommended to improve the online experience.

Acknowledgments

Nearly every member of the Microsoft Access development team provided invaluable technical support as I worked through the finer details in Microsoft Access 2013. The program managers, developers, and test engineers on the team helped with suggestions, tips and tricks, and reviewing my material. You folks make an author's job so much easier. But any errors or omissions in this book are ultimately mine.

A book this large and complex requires a top-notch team to get what I put into Microsoft Word documents onto the printed pages you are now holding. I had some of the best in the business at O'Reilly Media to get the job done. Many thanks go to Kenyon Brown for serving as Acquisitions and Development Editor. Special thanks to Chris Hearse and Richard Carey for handling production and copy editing and to Andrew Couch for technical reviewing. Andrew Couch was especially gifted at not only pointing out any technical mistakes I made, but he was also helpful in offering suggestions for improvement in layout, material, and presentation. Also, thanks to John Viescas for his continued mentoring and friendship. I couldn't have done it without all of you!

And last, but certainly not least, I thank my wife and soul mate, Cheryl. She not only patiently stood by me as I cranked through over 1,900 pages of manuscript, but also helped behind the scenes reviewing and editing what I did. I could not have completed this book without her support.

Support and feedback

The following sections provide information on errata, book support, feedback, and contact information.

Errata

We've made every effort to ensure the accuracy of this book and its companion content. Any errors that have been reported since this book was published are listed on our Microsoft Press site at oreilly.com:

http://aka.ms/Access2013IO/errata

If you find an error that is not already listed, you can report it to us through the same page.

If you need additional support, email Microsoft Press Book Support at:

mspinput@microsoft.com.

Please note that product support for Microsoft software is not offered through the addresses above.

We want to hear from you

At Microsoft Press, your satisfaction is our top priority, and your feedback our most valuable asset. Please tell us what you think of this book at:

http://www.microsoft.com/learning/booksurvey

The survey is short, and we read every one of your comments and ideas. Thanks in advance for your input!

Stay in touch

Let's keep the conversation going! We're on Twitter at: *http://twitter.com/MicrosoftPress.*

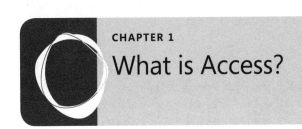

What is Access?

D ATABASE programs have been available for personal computers for a long time. Unfortunately, many of these programs have been either simple data storage managers that aren't suitable for building applications or complex application development systems that are difficult to learn and use. Even many computer-literate people have avoided the more complex database systems unless they have been handed a complete, custom-built database application. The introduction of Microsoft Access over two decades ago represented a significant turnaround in ease of use. Many people are drawn to it to create both simple databases and sophisticated database applications.

Now that Access is in its tenth release and became an even more robust product in the eighth edition, designed for 32-bit and 64-bit versions of Microsoft Windows, perhaps it's time to take another look at how you work with your personal computer and various devices to get the job done. If you've previously shied away from database software because you felt you needed programming skills or because it would take you too much time to become a proficient user, you'll be pleasantly surprised at how easy it is to work with all the new features included in Microsoft Access 2013.

With the addition of new online table templates and app templates, Access 2013 can help solve many business and personal needs. The online web app templates are fully functioning applications that can be used as is, and the table templates can be used to get a head start on creating a complete application. The key advantage to Access 2013 is the ability to quickly and easily create an Access Services web app using Microsoft SharePoint Server 2013 and SQL Server 2012 and work with your data in a web browser.

But how do you decide whether you're ready to move up to a database system such as Access? To help you decide, let's take a look at the advantages of using database application development software.

What is a database?

In the simplest sense, a database is a collection of records and files that are organized for a particular purpose. On your computer devices, you might keep the names and addresses of all your friends or customers. You might have another set of files in which you keep all your financial data—accounts payable and accounts receivable, or your checkbook entries and balances. The word processor documents that you organize by topic are, in the broadest sense, one type of database. The spreadsheet files that you organize according to their uses are another type of database. Shortcuts to all your applications on your computer device are a kind of database. Internet shortcuts organized in your Favorites folder are a database.

If you're very organized, you can probably manage several hundred spreadsheets or short-cuts by using folders and subfolders. When you do this, you're the database manager. But what do you do when the problems you're trying to solve get too big? How can you col-lect information about all customers and their orders easily when the data might be stored in several document and spreadsheet files? How can you maintain links between the files when you enter new information? How do you ensure that data is being entered correctly? What if you need to share your information with many people but don't want two people to try updating the same data at the same time? How do you keep duplicate copies of data from proliferating when people can't share the same data at the same time? Faced with these challenges, you need a database management system (DBMS).

Relational databases

Nearly all modern database management systems store and handle information using the relational database management model. In a relational database management system, sometimes called an RDBMS, the system manages all data in tables. Tables store informa-tion about a single subject (such as customers or products) and have columns (or fields) that contain the different kinds of information about the subject (for example, customers' addresses or phone numbers) and rows (or records) that describe all the attributes of a single instance of the subject (for example, data about a specific customer or product). Even when you query the database (fetch information from one or more tables), the result is always something that looks like another table.

The term *relational* stems from the fact that each table in the database contains informa-tion related to a single subject and only that subject. If you study the relational database management model, you'll find the term *relation* applied to a set of rows (a table) about a single subject. Also, you can manipulate data about two classes of information (such as cus-tomers and orders) as a single entity based on related data values. For example, it would be redundant to store customer name and address information with every order that the cus-tomer places. In an RDBMS, the information about orders contains a field that stores data, such as a customer number, which can be used to connect each order with the appropriate customer information.

You can also join information on related values from multiple tables or queries. For exam-ple, you can join company information with contact information to find out the contacts for a particular company. You can join employee information with department information to find out the department in which an employee works.

Some relational database terminology

- **Relation.**   Information about a single subject such as customers, orders, employees, products, or companies. A relation is usually stored as a table in a relational database management system.

- **Attribute.**   A specific piece of information about a subject, such as the address for a customer or the dollar amount of an order. An attribute is normally stored as a data column, or field, in a table.

- **Instance.**   A particular member of a relation—an individual customer or product. An instance is usually stored in a table as a record, or row.

- **Relationship.**   The way information in one relation is related to information in another relation. For example, customers have a one-to-many relationship with orders because one customer can place many orders, but any order belongs to only one customer. A company might have a many-to-many relationship with internal employees because an employee might be trained in more than job position, and a job position might be associated with more than one employee.

- **Join.**   The process of linking tables or queries on tables via their related data values. For example, customers might be joined to orders by matching customer ID in a customers' table and an orders table.

The architecture of Access

Access calls anything that can have a name an *object*. Within an Access desktop database, the main objects are tables, queries, forms, reports, macros, data macros, and modules. Within an Access 2013 web app, the main objects are tables, queries, views, macros, and data macros.

If you have worked with other database systems on desktop computers, you might have seen the term *database* used to refer to only those files in which you store data. However, in Access, a desktop database (.accdb) also includes all the major objects related to the stored data, including objects you define to automate the use of your data. Here is a summary of the major objects in an Access database:

- **Table.**   An object that you define and use to store data. Each table contains information about a particular subject, such as customers or orders. Tables contain *fields* (or *columns*) that store different kinds of data, such as a name or an address, and *records* (or *rows*) that collect all the information about a particular instance of the subject, such as all the information about a department named Housing Administration. You can define a *primary key* (one or more fields that have a unique value for each record) and one or more indexes on each table to help retrieve your data more quickly.

- **Query.** An object that provides a custom view of data from one or more tables. In Access, you can use the graphical query by example (QBE) facility or you can write Structured Query Language (SQL) statements to create your queries. You can define queries to select, update, insert, or delete data. You can also define queries that create new tables from data in one or more existing tables.

- **Form.** An object in a desktop database designed primarily for data input or display or for control of application execution. You use forms to customize the presentation of data that your application extracts from queries or tables. You can also print forms. You can design a form to run a macro or a Microsoft Visual Basic procedure in response to any of a number of events—for example, to run a procedure when the value of data changes.

- **View.** An object in a web app designed primarily for data input or display or for control of application execution. You use views to customize the presentation of data that your app extracts from queries or tables. Users interact with views inside a web browser. You can design a view to run macros and data macros in response to any of a number of events—for example, to run when the value of data changes.

- **Report.** An object in desktop databases designed for formatting, calculating, printing, and summarizing selected data. You can view a report on your screen before you print it.

- **Macro.** An object that is a structured definition of one or more actions that you want Access to perform in response to a defined event. For example, you might design a macro that opens a second form in response to the selection of an item on a main form. You can include simple conditions in macros to specify when one or more actions in the macro should be performed or skipped. You can use macros to open and execute queries, to open tables, or to print or view reports. You can also run other macros or Visual Basic procedures from within a macro.

- **Data Macro.** An object that is a structured definition of one or more actions that you want Access to perform on data stored in tables. Data macros can be attached directly to table events such as inserting new records, editing existing records, or deleting records. Data macros in web apps can also be stand-alone objects that can be called from other data macros or macro objects.

- **Module.** An object in desktop databases containing custom procedures that you code using Visual Basic. Modules provide a more discrete flow of actions and allow you to trap errors. Modules can be stand-alone objects containing functions that can be called from anywhere in your application, or they can be directly associated with a form or a report to respond to events on the associated form or report.

Database capabilities

An RDBMS gives you complete control over how you define your data, work with it, and share it with others. The system also provides sophisticated features that make it easy to catalog and manage large amounts of data in many tables. An RDBMS has three main types of capabilities: data definition, data manipulation, and data control.

- **Data definition.** You can define what data is stored in your database, the type of data (for example, numbers or characters), and how the data is related. In some cases, you can also define how the data should be formatted and how it should be validated.

- **Data manipulation.** You can work with the data in many ways. You can select which data fields you want, filter the data, and sort it. You can join data with related information and summarize (total) the data. You can select a set of information and ask the RDBMS to update it, delete it, copy it to another table, or create a new table containing the data.

- **Data control.** You can take advantage of features that help ensure that the right type of data goes into the correct places. In many cases, you can also define how data can be shared and updated by multiple users using the database.

All this functionality is contained in the powerful features of Access. Let's take a look at how Access implements these capabilities and compare them to what you can do with spreadsheet or word processing programs.

Access as an RDBMS

An Access desktop database (.accdb or .mdb) is a fully functional RDBMS. It provides all the data definition, data manipulation, and data control features that you need to manage large volumes of data. If you're using an Access Services web app, SQL Server serves as the RDBMS.

You can use an Access desktop database (.accdb or .mdb) either as a stand-alone RDBMS on a single workstation or in a shared client/server mode across a network. A desktop database can also act as the data source for data displayed on webpages on your company intranet. When you build an application with an Access desktop database, Access is the RDBMS.

> **Note**
>
> Access 2000, Access 2002 (XP), and Access 2003 databases use the .mdb file format, but beginning with Access 2007, Microsoft introduced a new desktop file format with an .accdb extension. To maintain maximum backward compatibility, Access 2013 can still open, run, and save .mdb databases created in the Access 2000 or Access 2002–2003 .mdb format, but to take advantage of all the features in Access 2013 for desktop databases, you need to use the .accdb file format. If you must create an Access application that will be run by users with previous versions of Access, you should use the Access 2000 or Access 2002–2003 .mdb file format. However, you'll need to take extra precautions to use only features in Access 2013 that are supported in earlier versions of Access.

Data definition and storage

As you work with a document or a spreadsheet, you generally have complete freedom to define the contents of the document or each cell in the spreadsheet. Within a given page in a document, you might include paragraphs of text, a table, a chart, or multiple columns of data displayed with multiple fonts. Within a given column on a spreadsheet, you might have text data at the top to define a column header for printing or display, and you might have various numeric formats within the same column, depending on the function of the row. You need this flexibility because your word processing document must be able to convey your message within the context of a printed page, and your spreadsheet must store the data you're analyzing as well as provide for calculation and presentation of the results.

This flexibility is great for solving relatively small, well-defined business problems. But a document becomes unwieldy when it extends beyond a few dozen pages, and a spreadsheet becomes difficult to manage as the amount of data grows. If you design a document or spreadsheet to be used by others, it's difficult to control how they will use the data or enter new data. For example, on a spreadsheet, even though one cell might need a date and another a currency value to make sense, a user might easily enter character data in error.

Some spreadsheet programs allow you to define a "database" area within a spreadsheet to help you manage the information you need to produce the desired result. However, you are still constrained by the basic storage limitations of the spreadsheet program, and you still don't have much control over what's entered in the rows and columns of the database area. Also, if you need to handle more than number and character data, you might find that your spreadsheet program doesn't understand such data types as pictures or sounds.

An RDBMS allows you to define the kind of data you have and how the data should be stored. You can also usually define rules that the RDBMS can use to ensure the integrity of your data. In its simplest form, a validation rule might ensure that the user can't accidentally store alphabetic characters in a field that should contain a number. Other rules might define valid values or ranges of values for your data. In the most sophisticated systems, you can define the relationship between collections of data (usually tables or files) and ask the RDBMS to ensure that your data remains consistent. For example, you can have the system automatically check to ensure that every order entered is for a valid customer.

With an Access desktop database (.accdb or .mdb), or Access Services 2013 web app, you have complete flexibility to define your data (as text, numbers, dates, times, currency, Internet hyperlinks, and pictures), to define how Access stores your data (string length, number precision, and date/time precision), and to define what the data looks like when you display or print it. You can define simple or complex validation rules to ensure that only accurate values exist in your database. You can request that Access check for valid relationships between files or tables in your database.

Access 2013 desktop databases include an Attachment data type that can store images and other file types within the record. The Attachment data type can handle multiple attachment files per record via the use of a concept called Complex Data. In previous versions of Access using the .mdb file format, storing images and files through OLE Object data types caused significant bloat of the database file, but Access 2013 compresses these files to minimize the size overhead. Examples of files that could be attached to a record using the Attachment data type could be a cover letter created in Microsoft Word for each business contact, a bitmap picture of the contact person, or various sales worksheets created in Microsoft Excel. Figure 1-1 shows an example of a form using the Attachment data type to display a contact picture in the Contacts Map.accdb sample desktop database. (You can download the Contacts Map.accdb desktop database loaded with sample data from the book's catalog page located at http://shop.oreilly.com/product/0790145367969.do.)

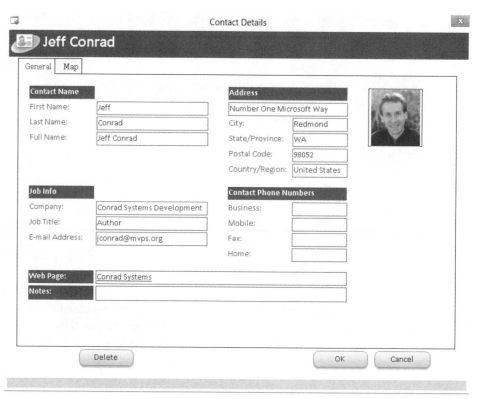

Figure 1-1 The Attachment data type displays a picture in a form.

Access can also understand and use a wide variety of other data formats, including many other database file structures. You can export data to and import data from word processing files, spreadsheets, or database files directly. You can also import and link data from these files into an Access table. In addition, Access can work with most popular databases that support the Open Database Connectivity (ODBC) standard, including SQL Server, Oracle, and DB2.

Data manipulation

Working with data in an RDBMS is very different from working with data in a word processing or spreadsheet program. In a word processing document, you can include tabular data and perform a limited set of functions on the data in the document. You can also search for text strings in the original document and, with ActiveX controls, include tables, charts, or pictures from other applications. In a spreadsheet, some cells contain functions that determine the result you want, and in other cells, you enter the data that provides the source information for the functions. The data in a given spreadsheet serves one particular purpose, and it's cumbersome to use the same data to solve a different problem. You can link to data in another spreadsheet to solve a new problem, or you can use limited search capabilities to copy a selected subset of the data in one spreadsheet to use in problem solving in another spreadsheet.

An RDBMS provides you with many ways to work with your data. For example, you can search a single table for information or request a complex search across several related tables. You can update a single field or many records with a single command. You can write programs that use RDBMS commands to fetch data that you want to display and allow the user to update the data.

Access uses the powerful SQL database language to process data in your tables. Using SQL, you can define the set of information that you need to solve a particular problem, including data from perhaps many tables. But Access simplifies data manipulation tasks. You don't even have to understand SQL to get Access to work for you. Access uses the relationship definitions you provide to automatically link the tables you need. You can concentrate on how to solve information problems without having to worry about building a complex navigation system that links all the data structures in your database. Access also has an extremely simple yet powerful graphical query definition facility that you can use to specify the data you need to solve a problem. Using pointing and clicking, dragging, and a few keystrokes, you can build a complex query in a matter of seconds.

Figure 1-2 shows a complex query used in the Conrad Systems Contacts desktop database. You can find this query in the Contacts.accdb sample database in the Contacts folder, which can be downloaded from the book's catalog page. Access displays field lists from selected tables in the upper part of the window; the lines between field lists indicate the automatic links that Access will use to solve the query.

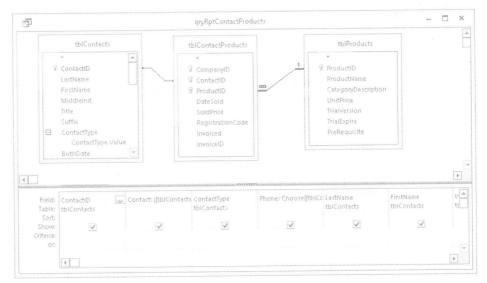

Figure 1-2 This query will retrieve information about products owned by contacts in the Conrad Systems Contacts sample application.

To create the query, you add the tables containing the data you need to the top of the query design grid, select the fields you want from each table, and drag them to the design grid in the lower part of the window. Choose a few options, type in any criteria, and you're ready to have Access select the information you want.

You don't need to be an expert to correctly construct the SQL syntax you need to solve your problem, but you can learn a lot about SQL in the article "Understanding SQL," which can be downloaded from the book's catalog page. For certain advanced types of queries, you'll need to learn the basics of SQL.

Figure 1-3 shows the result of asking the query to return the data.

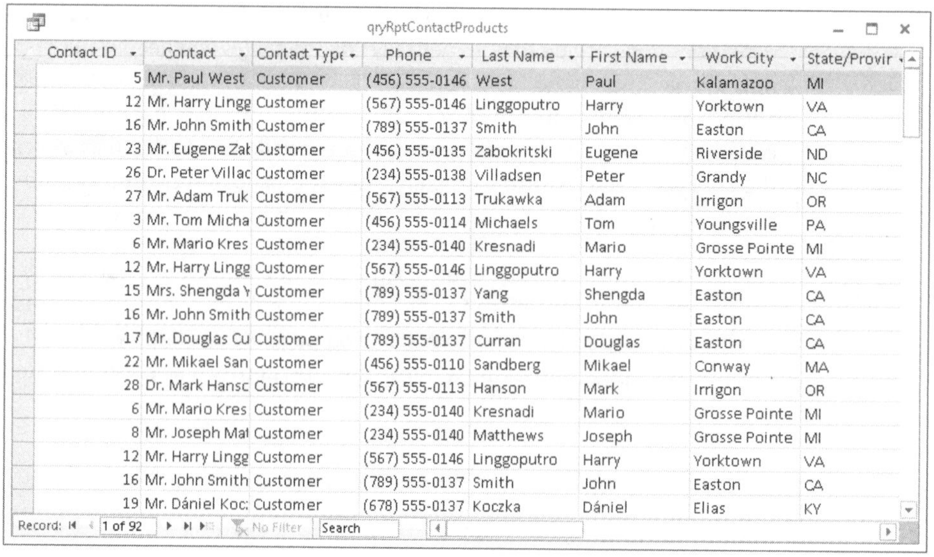
qryRptContactProducts

Contact ID	Contact	Contact Type	Phone	Last Name	First Name	Work City	State/Provir
5	Mr. Paul West	Customer	(456) 555-0146	West	Paul	Kalamazoo	MI
12	Mr. Harry Lingg	Customer	(567) 555-0146	Linggoputro	Harry	Yorktown	VA
16	Mr. John Smith	Customer	(789) 555-0137	Smith	John	Easton	CA
23	Mr. Eugene Zak	Customer	(456) 555-0135	Zabokritski	Eugene	Riverside	ND
26	Dr. Peter Villac	Customer	(234) 555-0138	Villadsen	Peter	Grandy	NC
27	Mr. Adam Truk	Customer	(567) 555-0113	Trukawka	Adam	Irrigon	OR
3	Mr. Tom Micha	Customer	(456) 555-0114	Michaels	Tom	Youngsville	PA
6	Mr. Mario Kres	Customer	(234) 555-0140	Kresnadi	Mario	Grosse Pointe	MI
12	Mr. Harry Lingg	Customer	(567) 555-0146	Linggoputro	Harry	Yorktown	VA
15	Mrs. Shengda Y	Customer	(789) 555-0137	Yang	Shengda	Easton	CA
16	Mr. John Smith	Customer	(789) 555-0137	Smith	John	Easton	CA
17	Mr. Douglas Cu	Customer	(789) 555-0137	Curran	Douglas	Easton	CA
22	Mr. Mikael San	Customer	(456) 555-0110	Sandberg	Mikael	Conway	MA
28	Dr. Mark Hansc	Customer	(567) 555-0113	Hanson	Mark	Irrigon	OR
6	Mr. Mario Kres	Customer	(234) 555-0140	Kresnadi	Mario	Grosse Pointe	MI
8	Mr. Joseph Mat	Customer	(234) 555-0140	Matthews	Joseph	Grosse Pointe	MI
12	Mr. Harry Lingg	Customer	(567) 555-0146	Linggoputro	Harry	Yorktown	VA
16	Mr. John Smith	Customer	(789) 555-0137	Smith	John	Easton	CA
19	Mr. Dániel Koc:	Customer	(678) 555-0137	Koczka	Dániel	Elias	KY

Record: 1 of 92 No Filter Search

Figure 1-3 The query returns a list of contacts and the products they own.

Data control

Spreadsheets and word processing documents are great for solving single-user problems, but they are difficult to use when more than one person needs to share the data. Although spreadsheets are useful for providing templates for simple data entry, they don't do the job well if you need to perform complex data validation. For example, a spreadsheet works well as a template for an invoice for a small business with a single proprietor. But if the business expands and several salespeople are entering orders, the company needs a database. Likewise, a spreadsheet can assist employees with expense reports in a large business, but the data eventually must be captured and placed in a database for corporate accounting.

When you need to share your information with others, true RDBMSs give you the flexibility to allow multiple users to read or update your data. An RDBMS that is designed to allow data sharing also provides features to ensure that no two people can change the same data at the same time. The best systems also allow you to group changes (a series of changes is sometimes called a *transaction*) so that either all the changes or none of the changes appear in your data. For example, while confirming a new order for a customer, you probably want to know that both the inventory for ordered products is updated and the order confirmation is saved or, if you encounter an error, that none of the changes are saved. You might also want to be sure that no one else can view any part of the order until you have entered all of it.

Because you can share your Access data with other users, you might need to set some restrictions on what various users are allowed to see or update. Access 2013 has greatly improved the ability to share data with secured SharePoint lists and SQL Server to ensure data security. With SharePoint-to-Access integration, users can take advantage of workflow support, offline SharePoint lists, and a Recycle Bin to undo changes. Access 2013 desktop databases also have strong data encryption with tougher encryption algorithms. Access automatically provides locking mechanisms to ensure that no two people can update an object at the same time, and Access also understands and honors the locking mechanisms of other database structures (such as SQL databases) that you attach to your database.

Access as an application development system

Being able to define exactly what data you need, how it should be stored, and how you want to access it solves the data management part of the problem. However, you also need a simple way to automate all the common tasks you want to perform. For example, each time you need to enter a new order, you don't want to have to run a query to search the Customers table, execute a command to open the Orders table, and then create a new record before you can enter the data for the order. After you've entered the data for the new order, you don't want to have to worry about scanning the table that contains all your products to verify the order's sizes, colors, and prices.

Advanced word processing software lets you define templates and macros to automate document creation, but it's not designed to handle complex transaction processing. In a spreadsheet, you enter formulas that define what automatic calculations you want performed. If you're an advanced spreadsheet user, you might also create macros or Microsoft Visual Basic procedures to help automate entering and validating data. If you're working with a lot of data, you've probably figured out how to use one spreadsheet as a "database" container and use references to selected portions of this data in your calculations.

Although you can build a fairly complex application using spreadsheets, you really don't have the debugging and application management tools you need to construct a robust data management application easily. Even something as simple as a wedding guest invitation and gift list is much easier to handle in a database. (See the Wedding List sample desktop database in the Wedding folder, which can be downloaded from the book's cata- log page.) Database systems are specifically designed for application development. They give you the data management and control tools that you need and also provide facilities to catalog the various parts of your application and manage their interrelationships. You also get a full programming language and debugging tools with a database system.

When you want to build a more complex database application, you need a powerful RDBMS and an application development system to help you automate your tasks. Virtually all database systems include application development facilities to allow programmers or users of the system to define the procedures needed to automate the creation and manipu- lation of data. Unfortunately, many database application development systems require that you know a programming language, such as C, to define procedures. Although these languages are very rich and powerful, you must have experience working with them before you can use them properly. To really take advantage of some database systems, you must learn programming, hire a programmer, or buy a ready-made database application (which might not exactly suit your needs) from a software development company.

Fortunately, Access makes it easy to design and construct database applications without requiring that you know a programming language. Although you begin in Access by defin- ing the relational tables and the fields in those tables that will contain your data, you will quickly branch out to defining actions on the data via forms, reports, macros, and Visual Basic.

You can use forms and reports to define how you want to display the data and what addi- tional calculations you want to perform—very much like spreadsheets. In this case, the format and calculation instructions (in the forms and reports) are separate from the data (in the tables), so you have complete flexibility to use your data in different ways without affecting the data. You simply define another form or report by using the same data.

When you want to automate actions in a simple application, Access provides a macro definition facility to make it easy to respond to events (such as clicking a button to open a related report) or to link forms and reports. Access 2013 makes using macros easy by letting you embed macro definitions in your forms and reports. When you want to build something a little more complex (like the Housing Reservations desktop database, which can be downloaded from the book's catalog page), you can quickly learn how to create simple Visual Basic event procedures for your forms and reports. If you want to create more sophisticated applications, such as contact tracking, order processing, and reminder sys- tems (see the Conrad Systems Contacts sample desktop database), you can employ more advanced techniques using Visual Basic and module objects. If you want to create a com- plex web app to help manage various aspects of managing a restaurant (see the BOSS web app), you can use user interface and data macro logic to automate the data flow in the app.

Access provides advanced database application development facilities to process not only data in its own database structures but also information stored in many other popular database formats. Perhaps Access's greatest strength is its ability to handle data from spreadsheets, text files, and any SQL database that supports the ODBC standard. This means that you can use Access to create a Windows-based application that can process data from a network server running SQL Server or from a mainframe SQL database.

Deciding to move to database software

When you use a word processing document or a spreadsheet to solve a problem, you define both the data and the calculations or functions you need at the same time. For simple problems with a limited set of data, this is an ideal solution. But when you start collecting lots of data, it becomes difficult to manage in many separate document or spreadsheet files. Adding one more transaction (another contact or a new investment in your portfolio) might push you over the limit of manageability.

If you need to change a formula or the way certain data is formatted, you might find that you have to make the same change in many places. When you want to define new calculations on existing data, you might have to copy and modify an existing document or create complex links to the files that contain the data. If you make a copy, how do you keep the data in the two copies synchronized?

Before you can use a database program such as Access to solve problems that require a lot of data or that have complex and changing requirements, you must change the way you think about solving problems with word processing or spreadsheet applications. In Access, you store a single copy of the data in the tables you design. Perhaps one of the hardest concepts to grasp is that you store only your basic data in database tables.

You can use the query facility to examine and extract the data in many ways. This allows you to keep only one copy of the basic data yet use it over and over to solve different problems. In a sales database, you might create one form to display vendors and the products they supply. You can create another form to enter orders for these products. You can use a report defined on the same data to graph the sales of products by vendor during specified time periods. You don't need a separate copy of the data to do this, and you can change either the forms or the report independently, without destroying the structure of your database. You can also add new product or sales information easily without having to worry about the impact on any of your forms or reports. You can do this because the data (tables) and the routines you define to operate on the data (queries, forms, reports, macros, or modules) are completely independent of each other. Any change you make to the data via one form is immediately reflected by Access in any other form or query that uses the same data.

Chapter 1

Reasons to switch to a database

Reason 1: You have too many separate files or too much data in individual files. This makes it difficult to manage the data.

Reason 2: You have multiple uses for the data—detailing transactions (for example, invoices) and analyzing summaries (such as quarterly sales summaries) and "what if" scenarios. Therefore, you need to be able to look at the data in many different ways, but you find it difficult to create multiple "views" of the data.

Reason 3: You need to share data. Access locks the row of a desktop table being edited by one person so that no conflicting changes can be made by another user, while still permitting many other users to access or update the remaining rows of the database table. In this way, each person is working from the same data and always sees the latest saved updates made by any other user.

Reason 4: You must control the data because different users access the data, because the data is used to run your business, and because the data is related (such as data for customers and orders). This means you must control data values, and you must ensure data consistency.

If you're wondering how you'll make the transition from word processing documents and spreadsheets to Access, you'll be pleased to find features in Access to help you out. You can use the import facilities to copy the data from your existing text or spreadsheet files. You'll find that Access supports most of the same functions you have used in your spreadsheets, so defining calculations in a form or a report will seem very familiar. Within the Help facility, you can find "how do I" topics that walk you through key tasks you need to learn to begin working with a database, and you can find "tell me about" and reference topics that enhance your knowledge. In addition, Access provides powerful wizard facilities to give you a jump-start on moving your spreadsheet data to an Access desktop database or web app, such as the Import Spreadsheet Wizard and the Table Analyzer Wizard to help you design database tables to store your old spreadsheet data.

INSIDE OUT
Design considerations when converting from a spreadsheet to a database

You can obtain free assistance from many Microsoft Most Valuable Professionals (MVPs) in the Access online forums. Some of the most difficult problems arise in databases that have been created by copying spreadsheet data directly into an Access table. The typical advice in this situation is to design the database tables first and then import and split up the spreadsheet data.

You can go to the Microsoft Answers website directly at *http://answers.microsoft.com/ en-us/office/forum*, or you can go to the Access Developer's Forum at *http://social.msdn. microsoft.com/Forums/en-US/accessdev/threads*. In these forums, you can post questions and read answers to questions posted by others.

Extending the power of Access to the web

The World Wide Web, built from simple low-cost servers and universal clients, has revolutionized computing. Not so long ago, the very concept of a common global information network was unthinkable. Today, the concept of living without the web is just as unthinkable. Database applications were among the last to appear on the web, but today, they are arguably the fastest growing type of web application. The prospect of distributing data to or collecting it from, literally, a world of clients—potentially geographically separated, working on disparate computers, devices, and operating systems, and not requiring software distribution other than the ubiquitous browser—is simply too compelling to resist for long.

As Microsoft looked at the long-term direction of Access, it was clear that the Access development team needed a way to make it easier for Access developers to move their applications to the web—a *cloud*. In our new global economy, Access developers need an easier way to share their databases and still maintain a single point of maintenance. In fact, if you look at the types of questions Access developers post into newsgroups and support forums, one of the most common questions in the last few years has been: "How do I move my database to the web so that users who do not have Access can use my application?"

Access 2007 laid the foundation of using SharePoint lists as a data platform for Access databases; however, there were still many limitations to using SharePoint lists to store your data. Access developers wanted better data integrity—relationships, validation rules, and the ability to enforce required and uniqueness for fields. Developers also wanted better performance when running against large data sets in SharePoint and the ability to design forms and reports that run in a web browser.

Access 2010 continued to build on this foundation by making it easier to provide access to your data and objects over your company's local intranet or on the web by using SharePoint Server 2010, Enterprise Edition. With Access 2010, you could publish your web database to a server running SharePoint Server 2010 and Access Services to make a fully functional web application. Access Services in Access 2010 was a set of features and services running on top of the SharePoint Server platform. After you published your web database to a server running SharePoint Server and Access Services 2010, your forms and reports could be viewed in a web browser. You could edit and view data from your web browser, in addition to editing your data from within Access 2010. Creating an Access Services 2010 web application with your data and objects stored in a SharePoint site allowed you to tap into the security, backup, and collaboration capabilities built into the SharePoint Server platform.

Access 2013 continues with web integration even further by building on the momentum of the previous two releases. Access Services in Access 2013 is built directly on SQL Server for the data storage. One drawback for Access developers with 2010 web databases was that data was stored in SharePoint lists. Although SharePoint lists offer deep integration with other features inside the SharePoint platform, they are not designed to handle as many records as larger Access applications contain. Most Access developers creating web databases in Access 2010 wanted to store their data directly in SQL Server tables that could easily process millions of records. Access 2013 web apps now fulfill this need by storing all data directly within SQL Server tables where developers can take advantage of the rich feature set of SQL Server. The views that you create for Access 2013 web apps also use HTML, CSS, and JavaScript, which are more standard for today's web apps.

Access 2013 web apps can also be created within Microsoft Office 365. You can take advantage of all the many features contained within Office 365 and also create Access web apps within your Office 365 sites and subsites. When you use Office 365 to host your Access web apps, you do not need to know how to install and configure a server with all the needed required components and services—Microsoft takes care of everything for you.

Take a long look at the kind of work you're doing today. The sidebar, "Reasons to switch to a database," earlier in this chapter, summarizes some of the key reasons why you might need to move to Access. Is the number of files starting to overwhelm you? Do you find yourself creating copies of old files when you need to answer new questions? Do others need to share the data and update it using only a web browser? Do you find yourself exceeding the limits of your current software? If the answer to any of these questions is yes, you should be solving your problems with an RDMS like Access.

In Figure 1-4, you can see an example of an Access Services 2013 web app, created entirely within Access 2013, hosted on a server running SharePoint Server 2013 and running in a web browser. The data for the application is in SQL Server, user interface macros that control the flow of the app in the browser are converted to JavaScript, and data macros that control the logic of the app at the data layer are procedures and triggers stored in SQL Server.

Figure 1-4 Access Services 2013, running on a server running SharePoint Server 2013, allows you to create a web app and view it in a web browser.

The topic of web apps in Access 2013 is a very broad subject—certainly not a topic I can fully cover in just one chapter. In fact, most of the Access development team at Microsoft worked solely on all the various features of web apps during the Access 2013 development cycle. The process of developing a web app in general is very much the same as developing a desktop application—you identify the tasks you want to accomplish with the application, chart the flow of tasks, identify the data elements, organize the data elements, design a user interface for the application, construct the application, and then test and refine the application. I've organized this book to closely follow the application building process for both web apps and desktop databases. We'll start by building the fields and tables of an application and then continue with building data macros, queries, forms, views, reports, macros, and modules throughout the various chapters in the context of web apps and desktop databases.

In Chapter 2, "Exploring the Access 2013 web app interface," I'll start the topic of web apps by first giving you an overview of the design environment for web apps. In Chapter 3, "Designing tables in a web app," you'll begin the process of developing your first web app with Access 2013 by creating fields and tables—the foundation of your web app. You'll learn how you should design your web app and its data structures. Building a solid foundation makes creating the views, queries, and macros for your app easy.

Exploring the Access 2013 web app interface

B EFORE you explore the many features of Microsoft Access 2013 web apps over the next several chapters, it's worth spending a little time looking it over and "kicking the tires." Like a new model of a favorite car, this latest version of Access has changes to the body (user interface) as well as new functionality under the hood. In this chapter, we'll explore the user interface for web apps, show you how to navigate through the Microsoft Office Backstage view, and discuss the various components of a web app and how they interact.

Working with web apps

Before we start the discussion of web apps, we should first discuss some terminology you'll be seeing throughout this chapter and subsequent chapters to follow. A web app is an Access application that is hosted on a SharePoint 2013 server running Access Services. If you are on a corporate domain, your IT department might already have a SharePoint server installed and running Access Services. You should check with your network administrator to see whether this is the case. If you do not want to take the time and expense to set up and install a SharePoint Server within your business, you can also use a third party that offers SharePoint hosting services. There are many third-party companies, including Microsoft, which can host your Access Services web apps, such as Microsoft Office 365. If your Access Services web app is hosted in an online service like Office 365, the app is said to be "in the cloud" because all of the application components are hosted in data centers and accessible from any connected computer or device. If your Access Services web app is hosted on a SharePoint Server within your organization, the app is said to be hosted "on premises" because the application components are stored locally.

A desktop database can be in the .mdb or .accdb file format and can be created in Access 2013 or earlier versions. A desktop database is a file that is usually stored locally on your computer or in a shared folder on a server. However, with a web app, your entire application is stored within an SQL Server database and is hosted inside a SharePoint site. When you are designing and working with a web app, you must have an active Internet or intranet connection with your Access Services site.

The tables in a web app, also called the *schema* of the database, are actually SQL Server tables inside an SQL Server database. You are allowed to have links to other SharePoint lists inside the same SharePoint site as your Access Services web app. However, linked Share-Point lists in your web app are read-only—you cannot make inserts, updates, or deletes to the data from those external data sources.

When you work with your web app that is hosted on a SharePoint server, such as Office 365, you use the rich Access desktop program for all of your designing tasks. The run-time experience of using your web app is all within a web browser. This differentiation between the design and run-time experience is a departure from the typical desktop database model. In desktop databases, your design and run-time experience is all contained within Access. However, in a web app, you can design your various objects only within Access; for example, you cannot view your objects in Access and interact with your data and controls in a run-time experience. The only exception to this rule for web apps is that you can open table and query datasheets within Access.

If you're already familiar with creating desktop databases in previous versions of Access, you're well on your way to understanding how to create web apps. In general, web apps have less functionality than desktop databases, so when you are designing web apps, Access 2013 presents design surfaces that show only options, properties, controls, and other design mechanisms that are supported for this class of application.

Opening Access for the first time

The first time you open Access 2013, you are presented with the Privacy Options dialog box shown in Figure 2-1. This dialog box lists three radio buttons, which are not selected by default. The Use Recommended Settings radio button, when selected, turns on several features of your Microsoft Office 2013 installation. Your computer will periodically check Microsoft's website for any product and security updates to your Office, Windows, or other Microsoft software. If any updates are detected, your computer will install these updates automatically for you. Selecting this radio button also allows Access to search Office.com's vast resources for content relevant to your search. Access downloads this information to your local computer for faster searching when you search for items in the Help section. Selecting this option means that you will have the latest Help information at your disposal. When you choose Use Recommend Settings, Office downloads a special diagnostic tool that interfaces with the Office 2013 system. You can use this tool to help identify problems with your Office installation. Although not required to run Office 2013 or Access 2013, this tool might assist you with locating the cause of any unforeseen system crashes. Selecting Use Recommend Settings also allows you to sign up for Microsoft's Customer Experience Improvement Program. This utility tracks various statistics while you use Access 2013 and

Office 2013 and sends that information to Microsoft. By tracking how customers are using their products, Microsoft can improve Office for future releases. Note that this option does not send any personal information to Microsoft. Click the Learn More link in the lower-left corner to read Microsoft's privacy statement.

Figure 2-1 You can choose the Privacy Options dialog box when you first start Access 2013.

The second radio button in the Privacy Options dialog box, Install Updates Only, performs a subset of the features for Use Recommend Settings. When you select this option, your computer will check Microsoft's website only periodically for any product and security updates to your Office, Windows, or other Microsoft software and install them. (You must have an active connection to the Internet to use the first two options.)

The last radio button, Ask Me Later, makes no changes to your Office 2013 installation. However, selecting this option could leave your computer at risk because your computer will not download and install product or security updates. After you make your selection in the Privacy Options dialog box, click Accept. Note that you can always alter these settings later.

CAUTION

If you are in a corporate network environment, before making selections in the Privacy Options dialog box, you should check with your Information Technology (IT) department to determine whether your company has established guidelines.

After selecting your options in the Privacy Options dialog box and clicking Accept, you will see an Office welcome dialog, as shown in Figure 2-2. This dialog appears only the first time you open Access 2013 or any other Office 2013 application. Click Next, and you'll see a short video presentation by Microsoft showcasing some of the highlights of Office 2013.

Figure 2-2 The first time you use an Office 2013 application, you'll see an Office welcome dialog.

> **Note**
>
> The dialog pages you see the first time you open an Office 2013 application might differ from what you see outlined here in the next few pages, depending on how you install Office. For example, if you are using Office 2013 through a subscription, you might see some differences in the welcome dialog from what is outlined here.

After the video finishes, you'll see the third page of the welcome dialog. On this page, you'll see information about the Microsoft SkyDrive cloud storage service, as shown in Figure 2-3. You can store your Office documents in a SkyDrive folder and access those files from any computer that has an active connection to the Internet. If you want to watch the video again, you can click the Back To Video link in the lower-left corner of the dialog. Click Next to continue to the next page of the welcome dialog.

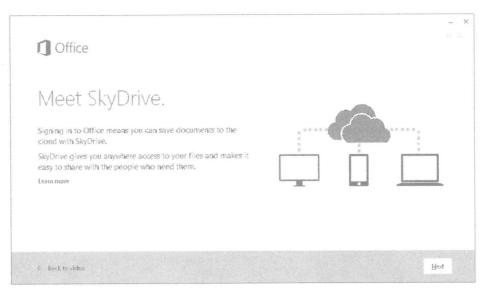

Figure 2-3 The third page of the welcome dialog displays information about Microsoft SkyDrive service.

On the fourth page of the Office welcome dialog, you can select a background scheme for your Office 2013 applications, as shown in Figure 2-4. You can choose from a selection of ten backgrounds or no background at all. The Office 2013 applications display these background schemes in the upper-right corner of the application windows and in the Backstage view. When you open Access 2013 and other Office 2013 applications from different devices using the same login information, the background scheme you select here will be the same across all of those devices. Click Next to continue to the next page of the welcome dialog.

Figure 2-4 Select a background scheme on the fourth page of the Office welcome dialog.

The fifth page of the Office welcome dialog, shown in Figure 2-5, includes an option for you to review some of the new features included with Office 2013. Click the Take A Look button to open a Microsoft PowerPoint 2013 presentation that details how to log in to Office applications, use the Microsoft SkyDrive service, and how to share your Office applications with other users. Click Next (or No Thanks, if you prefer not to watch the presentation) to continue to the last page of the welcome dialog.

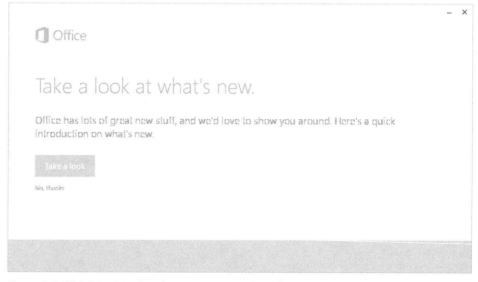

Figure 2-5 Click Take A Look to learn more about the Office 2013 applications.

The last page of the Office welcome dialog, shown in Figure 2-6, displays comments indicating that you're ready to start using Office 2013. Click All Done to begin using Access 2013 and the other Office 2013 applications.

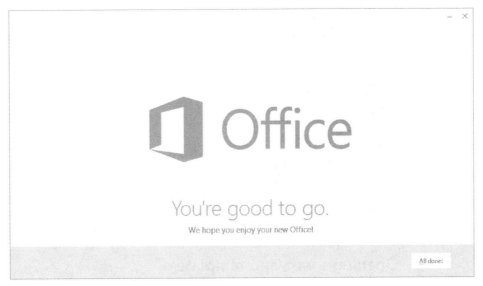

Figure 2-6 Click All Done to begin using Access 2013.

Getting started with Access 2013

If you are a seasoned developer and have used previous versions of Access, the user interface of Access 2013 for desktop databases should be familiar to you. However, if you are creating a web app, be prepared for quite a shock when you first open Access 2013. Microsoft revamped the entire look and feel of the user interface in Access 2013 for web apps. (You'll learn about the user interface for working in desktop databases in Part 2, "Creating tables in a desktop database."). We'll begin our study of Access by working with web apps, because this is the main focus for this release of Access by the development team at Microsoft.

On first starting Access, you'll see a new Office Start screen on the Backstage view, as shown in Figure 2-7. We will discuss all the elements of this New tab and the Backstage view as it pertains to web apps in greater detail in "Exploring the Microsoft Office Backstage view," later in this chapter.

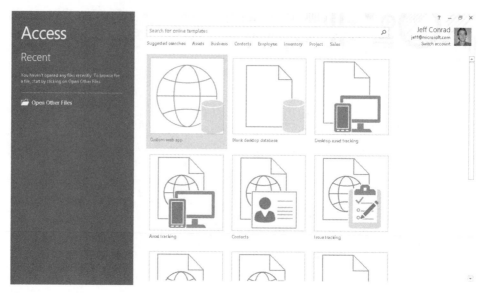

Figure 2-7 When you open Access 2013, you can see the new Office Start screen.

Opening a web app template

To showcase the new user interface for web apps, let's take one of the web app templates out for a test drive. If you're a beginner, you can use the web app templates included with Access 2013 to create one of several common applications without needing to know any-thing about designing database software. You might find that one of these apps meets most of your needs right away. As you learn more about Access, you can build on and cus-tomize the basic application design and add new features. Even if you're an experienced developer, you might find that the web app templates save you lots of time in setting up the basic tables, queries, and views for your app.

On the Office Start screen tab of the Backstage view, you can access the web app templates by clicking one of the template icons in the center of the screen. The five web app tem-plates available in Access 2013 are called Project Management, Asset Tracking, Contacts, Issue Tracking, and Task Management. On the Office Start screen, you'll also see desktop database templates. You can identify whether a template on the Office Start screen is a desktop database by looking for the text "Desktop" in the template name. (You'll learn more about desktop database templates in Part 2.)

When you click one of the web app template graphics on the Office Start screen, Access displays additional detailed information about the purpose of the web app in a pop-up dialog. Click the Projects Management web app template in the middle of the screen to see detailed information about the Project Management web app template, as shown in Figure

2-8. You can work with all web app templates from the Office Start screen in the same way. The following example will show you the steps that are needed to build a Project Management web app.

> **Note**
>
> For the following sections, you'll need to sign in to Access with your Microsoft or organizational account.

Chapter 2

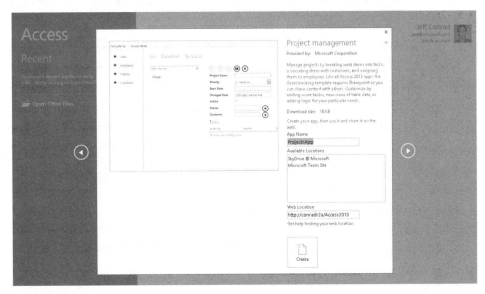

Figure 2-8 When you choose one of the web app templates in the center of the Office Start screen, Access shows you information about the app in a dialog.

Access displays a preview graphic on the left side of the dialog so that you can see what the completed web app looks like in a web browser. Access also shows you the template download size and the rating given this template by other users. Access suggests a name for your new web app in the App Name text box and a location to create the app in the Available Locations text box.

The options you see listed in the Available Locations text box might vary from what you see in Figure 2-8, based on your organizational installation setup and the location where you are trying to create the web app. You can modify the name of this web app by typing in the App Name text box. If you want to change the suggested create location, you can manually type the URL of a SharePoint server running Access Services in the Web Location text box.

If the location where you want to create your web app is listed in the Available Locations text box but is not the default, you can click the link in the Available Locations text box and Access enters that URL in the Web Location text box. If you are using Office 365, you should select the option for your Team Site or a subsite within your Team Site. Office 365 might also list an option for Personal Apps within the Available Locations text box. If you choose this option, Access creates the web app within a Personal folder on your Office 365 site. Click the Get Help Finding Your Web Location link below the Web Location text box if you need help understanding the URL to use to create new web apps.

If you decide at this point not to create the web app, click the close button near the top right of this dialog to stop the process and return to the main Office Start screen.

In Figure 2-8, you'll also notice there are left and right arrow buttons on either side of the pop-up dialog. When you click these buttons, Access displays the details about the next desktop or web app template. You can shuffle through the various templates displayed on the Office Start screen by using these buttons.

Provide a name for your new web app, provide a URL in the Web Location text box, and then click Create, and Access begins the process of creating this new web app. If you are creating your web app on a SharePoint Server inside a corporate domain, you might need to contact your SharePoint administrator to know which URL to use in the Web Location text box. You might also be prompted for your login credentials if you are using a hosting service, such as Office 365, before Access begins creating your web app. A progress bar appears on the screen asking you to wait while Access creates the web app. After a few seconds of preparation, Access opens the new Project Management web app and displays the Add Tables screen, as shown in Figure 2-9.

Backstage view

Quick Access Toolbar

Ribbon

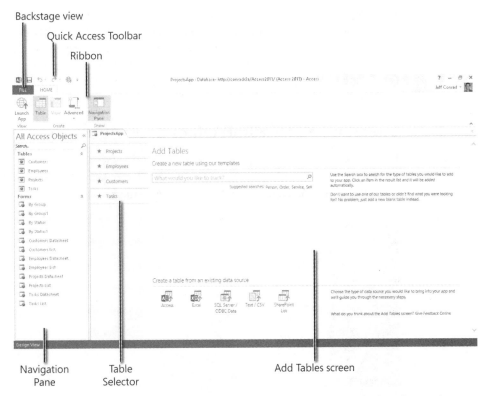

Navigation
Pane

Table
Selector

Add Tables screen

Figure 2-9 After you create the Project Management template, Access displays the user interface for web apps.

We will discuss each of the Access 2013 user interface elements for web apps in greater
detail in the following sections, but for now, here is a brief overview of the different elements. The upper-left corner of the screen contains a tab called File, which is the Backstage
view. Above this tab are a few smaller buttons on what is called the Quick Access Toolbar.
This toolbar holds frequently used commands within Access. Beneath the Quick Access
Toolbar is a tab called Home that contains many commands, options, and drop-down list
boxes. This tab, and other contextual tabs that appear based on your current context, are
located on what Microsoft refers to as the Office Fluent ribbon. You will interact heavily
with the ribbon when developing and using Access web apps because most of the commands you need are contained on it.

On the left side of the screen is the Navigation pane where you can find all the various
database objects for this web app (tables, queries, views, and so on). Notice that in Figure
2-9, I clicked the Navigation Pane button on the Home tab to toggle the visibility of the
Navigation pane, which is hidden by default.

To the right of the Navigation pane when you first create a web app is the Add Tables screen, where you create new tables for your web app, import data from data sources, or link to other SharePoint lists within your SharePoint site. Just beneath the Navigation pane and main object window is the status bar. The status bar displays text descriptions from field controls, various keyboard settings (Caps Lock, Num Lock, and Scroll Lock), and object view buttons.

Exploring the Microsoft Office Backstage view

The Microsoft Office Backstage view in Access 2013 displays a collection of commands by clicking the File tab from within any web app or desktop database. Figure 2-10 shows you the available commands on the Info tab of the Backstage view for web apps.

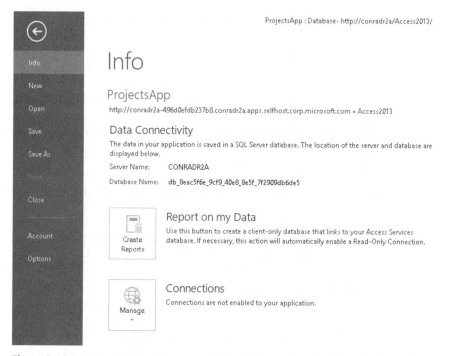

Figure 2-10 You can view many commands by clicking the File tab to open the Backstage view.

The Backstage view contains information and commands that apply to an entire web app. The eight main tabs and commands of the Backstage view for web apps are Info, New, Open, Save, Save As, Close, Account, and Options. Commands and information displayed on these tabs can change depending on the current state of your application or whether you are using a web app versus a desktop database. In Chapter 9, "Exploring the Access 2013 desktop database interface," you'll learn all about the various Backstage options available in desktop databases.

Info tab

Let's first explore the Info tab, previously shown in Figure 2-10. The Info tab displays the name of your web app and the full URL of its location. Beneath the URL, you'll see connection information about your web app, such as the server name hosting your web app and the specific SQL Server database name used for your web app. You can use this information, for example, to connect to the data tables in your web app from other data sources. Beneath the Data Connectivity section, you'll see a Create Reports button. Click this button to create a new desktop database with links to the tables in your web app. You can use this desktop database to build reports to summarize the data in your web app. The last button on the Info tab, Manage, presents various connection options that you can set on your web app to enable read and write connections. (You'll learn more about these processes in Chapter 7, "Advanced view design.")

New tab

The New tab, shown in Figure 2-11, is the first tab shown in the Backstage view when you open Access. This tab displays the Office Start screen where you can create new web apps, new desktop databases, or a new application using one of the templates available from Office.com. Access provides a scroll bar for you to scroll up and down to see the complete list of online templates. (You must be connected to the Internet to see and download any templates shown in the Office Start screen.) These templates were created by the Access development team and developers in the Access community. The templates represent some of the more common uses for a database and are therefore presented to you first.

Microsoft is continually adding and modifying the selections available on the Office Start screen, so the list you see might be different from that shown in Figure 2-11. Be sure to check this screen from time to time to see whether a new template exists for your specific needs. You can also search for a template on the Office.com website by typing your search criteria in the Search Online Templates text box.

Chapter 2

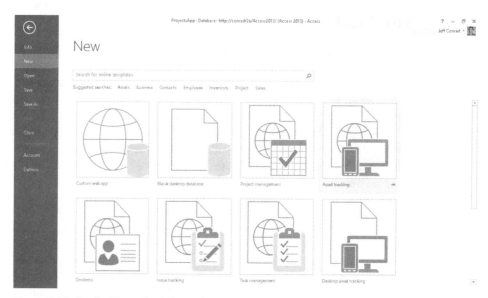

Figure 2-11 On the New tab of the Backstage view, you can create a database from a template, create a new blank custom web app or desktop database, or search for a database file to open.

Just below the Search for Online Templates text box are two buttons to create new blank applications. The first button on the left is labeled Custom Web App. You use this button to start the process of creating a new empty web app with no objects. The button on the right, Blank Desktop Database, starts the process of creating a new empty desktop database with no objects. (See Chapter 10, "Designing tables in a desktop database," for details about how to create a new blank desktop database.)

The remaining buttons on the Office Start screen are all web app and desktop database templates that you can download to get a jump-start on creating your next application. When you highlight a template file name, you'll see a pushpin button to the right of the template file name. (In Figure 2-11, you can see the pushpin next to the highlighted Asset Tracking template.) Click this toggle button to alternatively pin or unpin the selected template file to the displayed list of templates on the Office Start screen. Note that when you unpin the template file, you're not deleting the template from your computer; you are only unpinning its relative displayed position in the list of templates on the Office Start screen.

Open tab

The Open tab, shown in Figure 2-12, displays a list of the web apps and desktop databases that you previously opened. If the number of apps and databases that you open exceeds the space to display them, Access provides a scroll bar for you to scroll up and down to see the complete list. The Open tab also displays your recent web apps and desktop databases in different categories—Recent, <Your Company Name>, SkyDrive, and Computer. The last option in the left pane of the Open tab, Add A Place, allows you to add locations to make it easier to save applications to cloud services, such as Office 365.

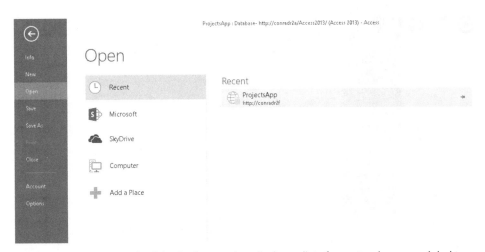

ProjectsApp : Database- http://conradr2a/Access2013/ (Access 2013) - Access

Open

Info

New

Open | Recent

Save | Microsoft

Save As | SkyDrive

Close | Computer

Account | Add a Place

Options

Recent

ProjectsApp
http://conradr2f

Figure 2-12 The Open tab of the Backstage view displays a list of recent web apps and desktop database files that you opened from various locations.

To the right of each database file name, you'll see a pushpin button. Click this toggle button to alternatively pin or unpin that specific database file to the displayed list of recent databases displayed.

Right-click any of the recent web apps or desktop databases displayed, and Access provides a shortcut menu with five options, as shown in Figure 2-13. Select Open from the list, and Access opens the highlighted web app or desktop database. Select Copy Path To Clipboard, and Access copies the full URL of the web app, or the full file path if it is a desktop database, to the Windows clipboard. When you select the Pin To List option, Access pins that specific web app or desktop database file to the displayed list of recent databases. When you select the fourth option, Remove From List, Access removes that web app or desktop database file from the list of recent databases. Note that when you remove the database file from the list, you're not deleting the web app or desktop database from your computer; you are only removing it from this list on the Backstage view.

When you select the last option on the list, Clear Unpinned Items, Access prompts you for confirmation that you want to remove all unpinned items from the list. Click Yes in the confirmation dialog box, and Access removes all web apps and desktop database files from the list of recent database files that you have not pinned. You can use this option to quickly clear files from your list of recent databases that you might have deleted and no longer want to use.

Chapter 2

ProjectsApp : Database- http://conradr2a/Access2013/ (Access 2013) - Access

Figure 2-13 Right-click a web app or database file to see additional options that you can use to manage your list of recent databases.

Save command

The Save option is not actually a tab like the other Backstage tabs; it is, in fact, a direct command. Clicking the Save command here on the Backstage view saves any pending design changes for the database object that is open and has the focus in the Navigation pane.

Save As tab

The Save As tab for web apps, shown in Figure 2-14, displays a command to save your web app as an app package. When you click the Save As Package command, Access saves your entire web app as a single file with a .app file extension. You can upload this app package to the Office Apps Marketplace, where other users in the public community can purchase and use your web app. You can also upload this app package to an internal corporate SharePoint catalog where other members of your organization can create new web apps based on your completed package. (You'll learn more about app packages, the Office Marketplace, and SharePoint corporate catalogs later in this chapter.)

> **Note**
>
> The Save Object As command on the Save As tab is dimmed and unavailable for web apps; this command is available only when you are working in desktop databases.

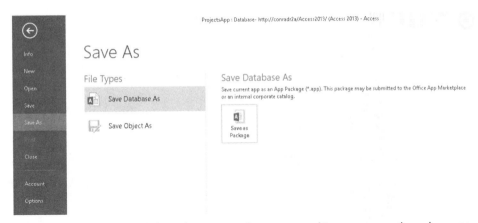

Figure 2-14 The Save As tab for web apps contains a command to save your entire web app as an app package.

Close command

The Close command, like the Save command, is not actually a tab like the other Backstage tabs; it is a direct command. Clicking the Close command closes the currently open web app.

Account tab

The Account tab of the Backstage view, shown in Figure 2-15, displays helpful information concerning Access 2013 and the Office 2013 software as well as connections to other online services and application backgrounds and themes. The connection options listed under Connected Services might differ from what you see in Figure 2-15, based on your Office installation and your organization's internal settings.

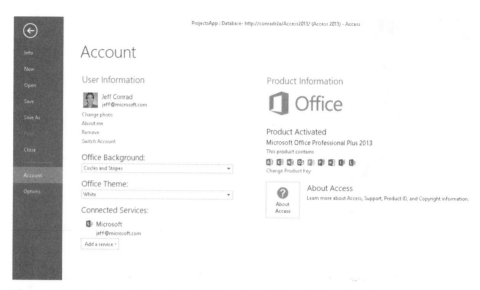

Figure 2-15 The Account tab on the Backstage view displays information about Access and Office 2013 applications.

Under the User Information category, you'll see your user name and e-mail address for the account you are currently using. Click the Change Photo link to change the photo and name on your account. Click the About Me link to view your account information. To remove your account, click the Remove link. To log in to Access under a different account, click the Switch Account link. Access then opens the Sign In To Office dialog, as shown in Figure 2-16.

Click the Microsoft Account button to sign into Access using a Microsoft account, or click the Organizational Account button on the Sign In To Office dialog to sign in to Access using an ID provided by your business or school. Click the Learn More link at the bottom of this dialog to open a webpage on Microsoft's website that discusses the sign-in process. Click the Privacy Statement link at the bottom of the Sign In To Office dialog to open a webpage that discusses Microsoft's privacy information concerning Office 2013.

After you sign in under a different account, Access refreshes the user name and e-mail address displayed on the Account tab of the Backstage view. You can also log in under a different account by clicking your user name link in the upper-right corner of the Access application window and then clicking Switch Account. If you have difficulties signing in with your account information, you might need to talk with your organization's account administrator.

Figure 2-16 Click your user name link on the Account tab to sign in to Office under a different account using this dialog box.

Beneath the user information on the Account tab, you can select a background to use for Access and your other Office applications from the Office Background combo box, and you can select either a White, Light Gray, or Dark Gray theme from the Office Theme combo box. Under Connected Services, Access displays different services that you are connected to from your current account. Click the Add A Service button, and Access displays three categories of services—Storage, Other Sites, and Office Store—as shown in Figure 2-17. You can select from these various options to connect to other online services for your Office applications. The services options listed in this menu might differ from what you see in Figure 2-17, based on your Office installation and your organization's internal settings.

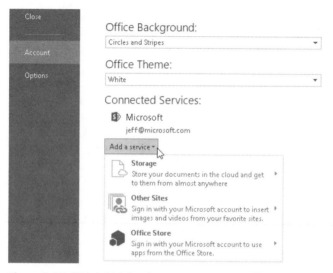

Figure 2-17 Click Add A Service to connect your Office applications with online services.

On the right side of the Account tab, you'll see information about your Access 2013 and Office 2013 installed programs. Click the Change Product Key link, previously shown in Figure 2-15, to open the Microsoft Office setup dialog box to change your product key for your installation. If you're using a subscription service through Office 365, you won't see the Change Product Key link. Click the About Access button to open the Access About dialog box to view the copyright information of your Access and Office installations.

Options command

In addition to all the various commands and options available on the Backstage view and ribbon, Access has one central location for setting and modifying global options for all your Access database files or for only the database currently open: the Access Options dialog box. The Options command, unlike the other Backstage view tabs and commands, is a direct command that opens a dialog box. To open the Access Options dialog box, click Options on the Backstage view. Figure 2-18 shows the General category of the Access Options dialog box.

Figure 2-18 Click the Options command on the Backstage view to open the Access Options dialog box.

The Access Options dialog box for web apps contains three categories in the left pane to organize the various options and settings. The first category, General, has settings that apply both to Access 2013 and to any other Office 2013 programs you might have installed. From here, you can choose to display ScreenTips, disable hardware graphics acceleration, and select a background and Office scheme for the application window. In the Creating Databases section, you can choose a default file format for new desktop databases that you create in Access. By default, the file format is set to create all new desktop databases in Access 2007- 2013 format.

The Language category, shown in Figure 2-19, contains options for controlling the language settings for your Access and Office programs. Under Choose Editing Languages, you can select a default editing language for Access. If you have installed additional language packs, you can choose to change your default language to a different language. Under Choose Display And Help Languages, you can change what display language and what Help language to use when working with Access. You will need to close your current session of Access and reopen the program to see these changes. If you click the arrow next to View Display Languages Installed for each Microsoft Office Program, a list expands beneath the arrow that shows all of the Office applications that you have installed and their display languages.

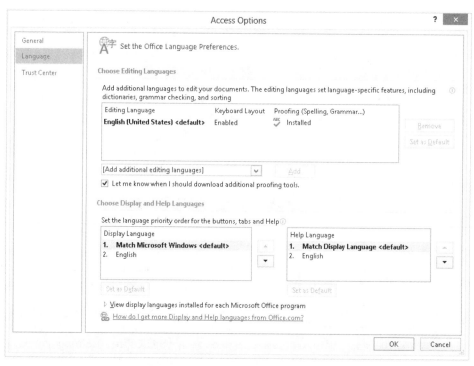

Figure 2-19 The Language category has settings for changing your editing, display, and Help language for Access and other Office programs.

The Trust Center category, shown in Figure 2-20, is the last category in the Access Options dialog box for web apps. This category is where you access Trust Center options for handling security, controlling all aspects of macro security, and defining trusted locations and documents. This category also has links to online privacy and security information. In Chapter 9, we'll discuss all the aspects concerning the Trust Center in more detail.

Figure 2-20 The Trust Center category has links to privacy and security information and displays the Trust Center Settings button, which allows you to view more options.

> **Note**
>
> The Access Options dialog box contains many more categories, commands, and options when you are working with desktop databases. In Chapter 9, we'll discuss all the additional options and settings in the Access Options dialog as they pertain to desktop databases.

> **INSIDE OUT**   Closing the Backstage view
>
> You can close the Backstage view quickly by pressing the Esc key. When you do this, Access returns focus to where you were before opening the Backstage view.

Taking Advantage of the Quick Access Toolbar

Above the Backstage view is the Quick Access Toolbar. This special toolbar gives you "quick access" to some of the more common commands you will use in Access 2013. Here are the default commands available on the Quick Access Toolbar for web apps:

- **Save.** Saves any changes to the currently selected web app object.

Chapter 2

- **Undo.**   Undoes the last change you made to an object or a record.

- **Redo.**   Cancels the last Undo change you made to an object or a record.

- **Launch App.**   Opens your web app in your default web browser.

At the right end of the Quick Access Toolbar is a small arrow. Click that arrow, and you'll see the Customize Quick Access Toolbar menu, as shown in Figure 2-21.

Figure 2-21 The default Quick Access Toolbar for web apps contains the Save, Undo, Redo, and Launch App commands, and the command to customize the toolbar.

The menu displays two additional commands that you might want to add to the Quick Access Toolbar—Hide/Show Navigation Pane and Touch Mode. Notice that the four default commands—Save, Undo, Redo, and Launch App—have check marks next to them. You can click any of these to clear the check mark and remove the command from the Quick Access Toolbar. You can click the other two commands to add them to the right end of the Quick Access Toolbar. If you click the Hide/Show Navigation Pane option, Access toggles showing the Navigation pane. If you click the Touch Mode option, Access increases the space around the various commands and options in the application window so that you can more easily tap the commands when you are on a touch-enabled device. The Show Below The Ribbon option at the bottom of the menu allows you to move the Quick Access Toolbar above or below the ribbon, depending on your preference.

INSIDE OUT   **Adding a command to the Quick Access Toolbar with two mouse clicks**

If you notice that you are using a command on the ribbon quite often for web apps, Access 2013 provides a very quick and easy way to add this command to the Quick Access Toolbar. To add a command on the ribbon to the Quick Access Toolbar, right-click the command and click Add To Quick Access Toolbar. This adds the command to the Quick Access Toolbar for all web apps you open. Alternatively, you can remove an item from your custom Quick Access Toolbar quickly by right-clicking the command and clicking Remove From Quick Access Toolbar.

Understanding the Office Fluent ribbon

The Office Fluent ribbon, shown in Figure 2-22, is a context-rich strip displaying all the program functions and commands, with large icons for key functions and smaller icons for less-used functions. Access displays a host of different controls on the ribbon to help you build and edit your applications. Note that Access displays fewer options on the ribbon when you work with web apps compared to the options you'll see in desktop databases. (You'll learn about all the ribbon options available in desktop databases in Part 2.)

Figure 2-22 The ribbon interface displays program functions and commands.

The ribbon in Access 2013 web apps consists of one main tab called Home. This tab is visible at all times when you are working in a web app. Other tabs, called contextual tabs, appear and disappear to the right of the Home tab when you are working with specific web app objects and in various views. (We will discuss in detail the various web app objects and the contextual tabs that appear when working with each in the chapters that follow.)

Each tab on the ribbon has commands that are further organized into groups. The name of each group is listed at the bottom, and each group has various commands logically grouped by subject matter. To enhance the user experience and make things easier to find, Microsoft has labeled every command in the various groups. If you rest your mouse pointer on a specific command, Access displays a ScreenTip that contains the name of the command and a short description that explains what you can do with the command. Any time a command includes a small arrow, you can click the arrow to display options available for the command.

The Home tab for web apps has the following groups:

- **View.** You can use the Launch App command to open your web app in your default browser.

- **Create.** You can use the commands in this group to create various objects in your web app.

- **Show.** You can use the Navigation Pane command to toggle the visibility of the Navigation pane.

INSIDE OUT   Collapsing the entire ribbon

If you need some additional workspace within the Access window, you can collapse the entire ribbon by double-clicking any of the tabs. All the groups disappear from the screen, but the tabs are still available. You can also use the keyboard shortcut Ctrl+F1 to collapse the ribbon, or you can click the Minimize The Ribbon button next to the Help button in the upper-right corner of the application window. To see the ribbon again, simply click any tab to restore the ribbon to its full height, press Ctrl+F1 again, or click the Expand The Ribbon button.

Working with the Navigation pane

The Navigation pane is a window that is located on the left side of the screen that displays a list of all the objects, grouped together by type, in your web app, as shown in Figure 2-23. Any open objects appear to the right of the Navigation pane. If the list of objects in a particular group is quite extensive, Access provides a scroll bar in each section so that you can access each object.

Figure 2-23 The Navigation pane displays all of the objects in your web app.

INSIDE OUT   Jumping quickly to a specific object in the Navigation pane

Click an object in one of the groups in the Navigation pane to highlight it, and then press a letter key to jump quickly to any objects that begin with that letter in that particular group.

«

Shutter bar
Open/Close
button

You can expand or contract the width of the Navigation pane easily by positioning your pointer over the right edge of the Navigation pane and then clicking and dragging the edge in either direction to the width you want. Keep in mind that the farther you expand the width, the less screen area you have available to work with your objects, because all objects open to the right of the Navigation pane. To maximize the amount of screen area available to work with open objects, you can collapse the Navigation pane by clicking the double-arrow button in the upper-right corner, called the Shutter Bar Open/Close button. When you do this, the Navigation pane disappears from view, as shown in Figure 2-24.

Chapter 2

After you have closed the Navigation pane, click the Navigation Pane button on the Home ribbon tab to reopen the Navigation pane to its previous width. Access 2013 remembers the last width that you set for the Navigation pane. The next time you open a web app, the width of the Navigation pane will be the same as when you last had the database open. Pressing the F11 key alternately toggles the Navigation pane between its collapsed and expanded views.

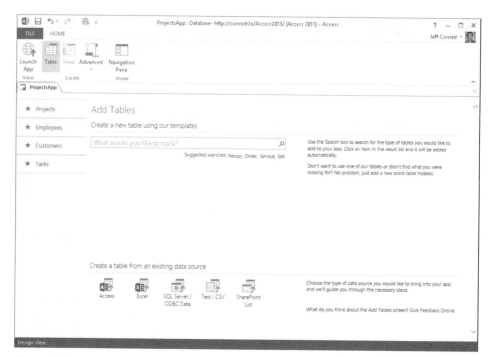

Figure 2-24 You can collapse the Navigation pane to give yourself more room to work on open objects.

We will discuss the various objects and their purposes within an Access web app in this chapter and the chapters following.

INSIDE OUT   Collapsing an entire group in the Navigation pane

If you click the header of each object type in the Navigation pane where the double arrow is located, Access collapses that part of the Navigation pane. For example, if you want to hide the tables temporarily, you can collapse that section by clicking the double arrow next to the word Tables. To bring the table list back to full view, simply click the double arrow that is now pointing downward, and the tables section expands to reveal all the table objects.

Searching for web app objects

In web apps with a large number of objects, locating a specific object can be difficult, so Access 2013 includes the Search Bar feature to make this task easier. By default, this feature is turned on; however, if the feature is turned off for your Access installation, you must turn it on through the Navigation pane. You can enable this feature by right-clicking the top of the Navigation pane (where you see the text All Access Objects) and then clicking Search Bar, as shown in Figure 2-25.

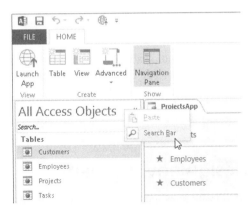

Figure 2-25 Click the Search Bar command to display the Search Bar.

Select the Show Search Bar check box, and then click OK. Access displays a Search Bar near the top of the Navigation pane, as shown in Figure 2-26.

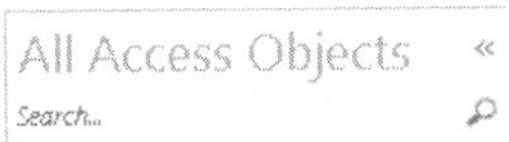

All Access Objects   «
Search...   🔎

Figure 2-26 The Search Bar in the Navigation pane helps you find specific web app objects.

Rather than "search" for objects that match what you type in the search box, Access filters the list in the Navigation pane. As you begin to type letters, Access filters the list of objects to those that contain the sequence of characters you enter anywhere in the name. For example, if you want to find an object whose name contains the word Employees, type the word **employees** in the Search Bar. As you enter each letter in the Search Bar, Access begins filtering the list of objects for any that contain the characters in your search string. With each successive letter you type, Access reduces the list of objects shown in the Navigation pane, because there are fewer objects that match your search criteria. Notice that as soon as you have typed the letters **emp**, Access reduces the list to three objects—Employees, Employees Datasheet, and Employees List. The names of these objects contain the letters *emp*.

After you finish typing the entire word *employees* in the Search Bar, the Navigation pane should look like Figure 2-27. Access collapses any group headers if it does not find any objects that meet your search criterion. In this case, Access located three objects with the word *employees* in its name. To clear your search string if you need to perform another object search, either delete the existing text using the Backspace key or click the Clear Search String button on the right side of the Search Bar. Clearing the search box or clicking the Clear Search String button restores the Navigation pane to show all displayable objects.

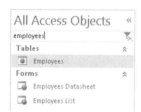

Figure 2-27 The Search Bar collapses any groups if it does not find any objects in that group that meet your search criterion.

Working in the web app design environment

The design environment for working with web app objects includes many new elements that differ substantially from working with objects in desktop databases. We'll briefly discuss these new elements and their purpose in this section, and then we'll explore each of these elements in more detail in this chapter and subsequent chapters.

Add Tables screen

Everything to the right of the Navigation pane in the main application window in web apps is actually an HTML page hosted inside the Access client shell framework. The Add Tables screen, shown again in Figure 2-28, is your starting point for creating new tables in web apps.

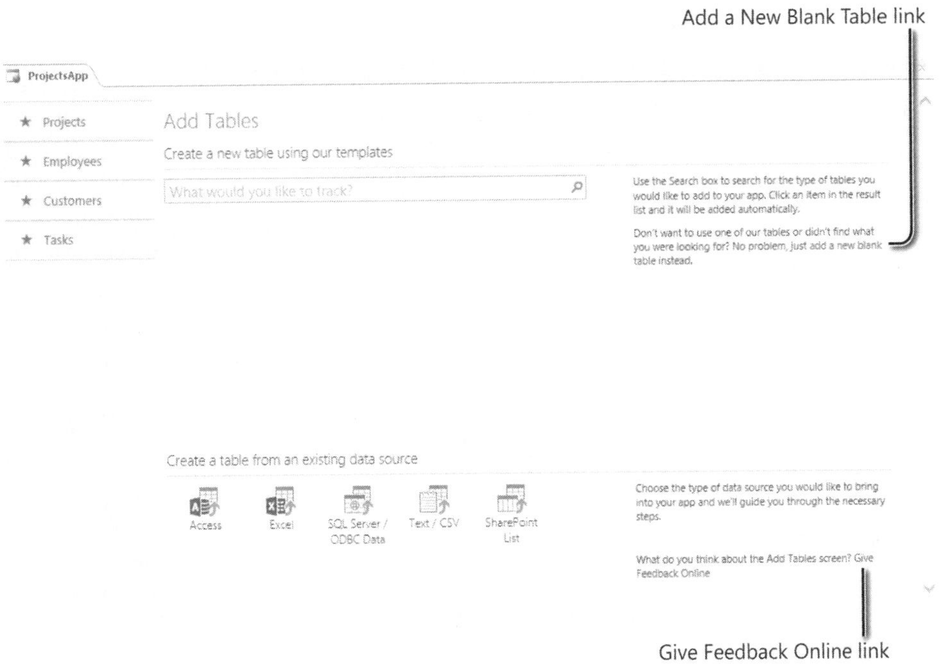

Add a New Blank Table link

Give Feedback Online link

Figure 2-28 You can create new blank tables, use a table template, or import data into your web app from the Add Tables screen.

On the Add Tables screen, you'll see a search box where you can search for a table template you'd like to add to your web app. Each table template contains one or more table definitions with data types, relationships, and field properties already prepared for you to begin data entry. If you want to start from scratch and create your own blank table, you can click the Add A New Blank Table link on the right side of the Add Tables screen.

At the bottom of the Add Tables screen, you'll see five buttons—Access, Excel, SQL Server/ODBC Data, Text/CSV, and SharePoint List—which you can use to import data into your web app. When you import data from another data source into a web app, Access creates a new table in your web app for each data source. The last button, SharePoint List, creates a read-only link to SharePoint lists within the same SharePoint site as your Access web app. At the lower-right corner of the Add Tables screen, you can click the Give Feedback Online link to provide feedback to the Access development team about your experiences with using this screen.

Chapter 2

Table Selector

To the left of the Add Tables screen and to the right of the Navigation pane, if you have it expanded, is the Table Selector. Access displays the name of each table in your web app in the Table Selector, along with a small default icon to the left of the name. Next to the selected table name in the Table Selector, Access displays two floating buttons called *charms*. You can click these buttons to open property callouts with different options and actions on the selected table. We'll discuss these options in the next chapter.

Figure 2-29 The Table Selector displays a list of all tables in your web app.

At the bottom of the Table Selector, Access displays the Add New Table button. When you click this button, Access displays the Add Tables screen again in the application window, where you can create new tables in your web app. If the Add Tables screen is currently displayed in the main application window, Access hides the Add New Table button in the Table Selector. You can also toggle displaying the Add Tables Screen at any time within Access by clicking the Table button in the Create group on the Home tab of the ribbon.

App Home View

Whenever you click on any table in the Table Selector, Access closes the Add Tables screen and then displays the full App Home View, as shown in Figure 2-30. Microsoft refers to the

App Home View as a framework consisting of several elements—the Table Selector, the View Selector, and any views associated with the selected table. When you are working within Access, you see the App Home View in design mode. When you open your web app in a web browser, you see the App Home View in run-time mode.

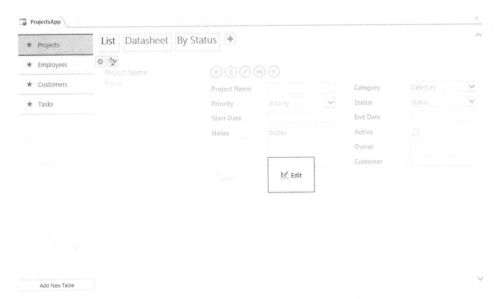

Figure 2-30 The App Home View displays tables and views in your web app.

View Selector

The View Selector displays horizontally, across the top of the App Home View window, a list containing each view attached to the selected table in the Table Selector, as shown in Figure 2-31. A *view* in an Access web app is an HTML page that users of the application use to interact with the data in your app in a web browser. In Figure 2-31, you can see that there are three views attached to the Projects table in the Projects Management web app template—List, Datasheet, and By Status. Whenever you click a view in the View Selector, Access displays a single charm button next to the view name that you can click to take different actions on that selected view. On the far right of the View Selector is the Add New View button. You can use this button to create a new view attached to the currently selected table in the Table Selector. We'll explore the view options and creating views later in Chapter 6, "Working with views and the web browser experience," and in Chapter 7.

Figure 2-31 The View Selector lists all views attached to a table.

Chapter 2

View preview window

Beneath the View Selector, Access displays a preview of the selected view, as shown in Figure 2-32. In the preview window, you can see that Access displays a preview of all the controls and layout for the currently selected List view. All of the controls in preview mode appear dimmed because you cannot edit them in this state. In the center of the view pre-view window, Access displays an Edit button. You can click the Edit button to open the selected view in Design view to make changes to that view. Whenever you click a view in the View Selector, Access changes the preview image in the view preview window to match the selected view.

Figure 2-32 You can see a preview of the controls for each selected view in the center of the application window.

Viewing your web app in a web browser

So far in this chapter, you've looked at your web app from a design perspective within Access. You created a new web app by using the Projects Management template, but you've been working with the app only within Access. Let's take a quick look at what this web app looks like in a web browser.

Click the Launch App button in the View group on the Home tab of the ribbon. Access opens your web app in your default browser and displays the App Home View in run-time mode, as shown in Figure 2-33. Now, you can begin to see how all of the pieces of the web app fit together. The tables in your web app are displayed in the Table Selector along the left, the views associated with each table are shown at the top of the App Home View in the View Selector, and each view used for data entry is displayed beneath the View Selector. (You'll learn about the runtime experience for web apps in the next few chapters.)

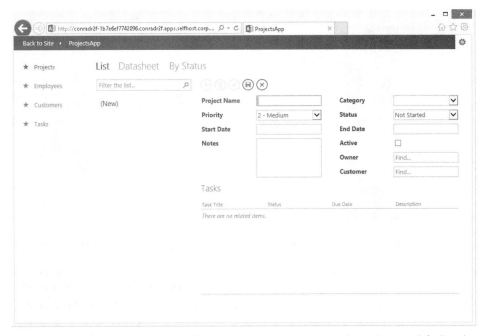

Figure 2-33 Clicking the Launch App button in Access opens your web app in your default web browser.

Saving a web app as an app package

If you want to save a copy of your web app, perhaps as a backup or to move your web app to a different SharePoint server, Access 2013 includes the ability to save a copy of your entire web app into a file called an *app package*. An Access app package has the .app file extension and contains all of the objects and the definition of your web app and even data, if you choose to include it. After you save your web app into an app package, you can upload and install that app into your company's internal SharePoint corporate catalog, where other people in your organization can install a copy of your web app. App packages can be reused to create additional, identical copies of an Access web app. You can also upload Access app packages into the Office App Marketplace or SharePoint Store where people in the community can purchase and install a copy of your web app for their own use.

Let's create an app package out of the Project Management web app that you've been using so that you can see how this process works. To create an app package of any completed web app, click the File tab on the Backstage view, click the Save As tab, click Save Database As under File Types, and then click Save As Package, as shown in Figure 2-34.

Figure 2-34 Click Save As Package on the Save As tab of the Backstage view.

Access opens the Create New Package From This App dialog box, as shown in Figure 2-35. Enter a name for your new app package in the Title text box. For this example, enter **My Projects** as the name of your app package. If you want to include all data from the tables in your app package, select the Include Data In Package check box (cleared by default).

Figure 2-35 Enter a name for your new app package, and select the check box to include data.

Click OK, and Access opens the Save Package dialog box where you can browse to a location to save the file, as shown in Figure 2-36. You can select the drive and folder where you want to save your app package by clicking the links on the left and browsing to your destination folder. If you decide at this point not to create the app package, click the Cancel button to stop the process. After you select the specific folder to which you want to save this app package, click OK, and Access begins the process of creating this new app package.

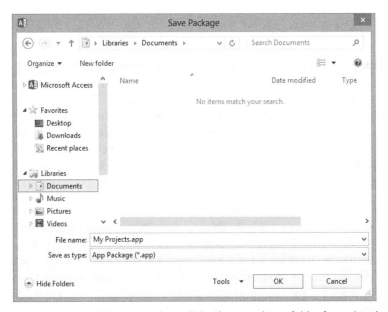

Figure 2-36 Use the Save Package dialog box to select a folder for saving the new app package.

Access displays a progress bar on the screen asking you to wait while Access 2013 creates the app package, as shown in Figure 2-37. When completed, Access closes all the dialogs and returns focus to the application window. You should now find your app package in the location you provided earlier.

Figure 2-37 Access displays a progress bar while creating your app package.

INSIDE OUT   Including a custom app icon in your app package

Each app package includes a default Access app package icon. When you install an Access app package in your SharePoint site, SharePoint displays the package icon on the Site Contents page. (You'll learn how to install app packages in the next section.) If you'd like to replace the default Access icon with your own, you can open the app package and swap out the default app icon with your own before uploading and installing the app. You can find examples of custom app icons in some of the sample app packages included with this book, which can be downloaded from the book's catalog page located at *http://shop.oreilly.com/product/0790145367969.do*.

To include your own custom app package icon, change the app package file extension from .app to .zip, using Windows Explorer. (If you haven't set options in Windows Explorer to show file name extensions, you won't see the .app extension next to your app package.) Next, extract all the contents from the zip file into a file folder. Inside the folder, you'll see an image file called accessapp.png. Create your own 96x96 pixel-sized .png image file, and then replace the default icon with your image in this folder using the same file name. Finally, save all the contents with the new icon to a zip file, and then change the file extension from .zip back to .app. When you install the app package in your SharePoint site, SharePoint displays your custom app package icon on the Site Contents page.

Installing app packages

In addition to creating a new web app by using Access, you can create Access web apps by installing Access web app packages on a server running SharePoint 2013 and Access Services. The app package can either be a package already existing on the server or an app package that you upload yourself. You can install an app package on the server even if you don't have Access installed on your local computer.

Note

Throughout the next few chapters, you'll be using web app sample files, which can be downloaded from the book's catalog page. To use these samples to follow along with the written text, you'll need to upload the samples into the corporate catalog of your SharePoint 2013 site, install the samples, and then download the apps into Access. You can also upload and install Access app packages directly into a SharePoint site through the Site Contents page. The rest of this chapter walks you through these processes, so you can always refer back to this section whenever you need to use a sample web app.

Uploading an app package to a SharePoint corporate catalog

If your organization has a server running SharePoint 2013 with Access Services and you have appropriate permissions, you can install Access app packages that are available in the SharePoint corporate catalog for your company. To install an app package that you've created, you first need to upload it to your company's SharePoint corporate catalog. (You'll need to ask your company's SharePoint administrator for the specific URL of your internal corporate catalog for use in the next step.) Open your web browser, and navigate to the corporate catalog URL for your organization. On the left side of the corporate catalog page, click the Apps For SharePoint link, as shown in Figure 2-38.

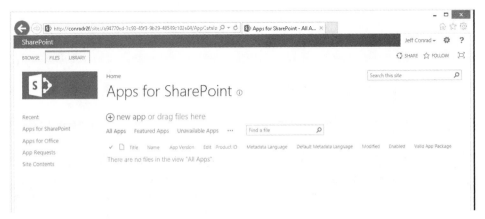

Figure 2-38 Navigate to your company's SharePoint corporate catalog page using your web browser.

INSIDE OUT   Locating the SharePoint corporate catalog on Office 365

If you are using Office 365 to host your Access 2013 web apps, the location of the SharePoint corporate catalog might not be easily discoverable. The SharePoint corporate catalog on Office 365 can usually be found by typing **/sites/AppCatalog** directly in your web browser's address bar URL after the team site name. For example, if your Office 365 team site URL is *https://MyCompany.sharepoint.com*, to navigate to your SharePoint corporate catalog on Office 365, type the following into your web browser's address bar: **https://MyCompany.sharepoint.com/sites/AppCatalog**. You might be directed to a page where you'll first need to activate the SharePoint corporate catalog.

In the middle of the Apps For SharePoint page, click the New App link. SharePoint opens the Add A Document dialog box, as shown in Figure 2-39.

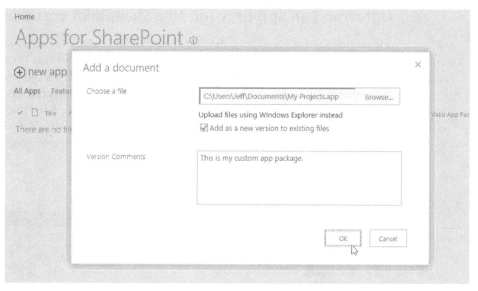

Figure 2-39 You can enter the location of your saved local app package in the Add A Document dialog box.

Enter the location of your saved app package in the Choose A File text box, or click the Browse button to help you navigate to the location of your app package. You can option-ally enter any comments about this version of the app package in the Version Comments text box. After you enter the file path to your app package, click OK to begin uploading your app package. After a few moments, SharePoint opens the Apps For SharePoint dialog box, as shown in Figure 2-40.

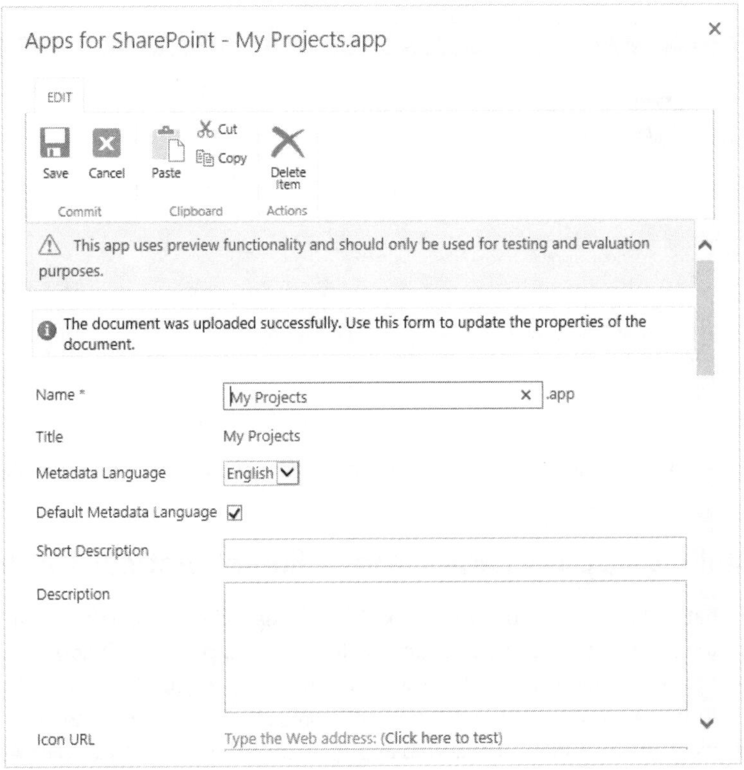

Figure 2-40 Click Save on the Apps For SharePoint dialog box to complete the upload process of your app package.

You can enter additional information about your app package in the Apps For SharePoint dialog box. None of these options is required, other than the app package name, to save your app package. Click Save to complete the upload process. SharePoint returns you to the Apps For SharePoint page and displays the name of your app package, as shown in Figure 2-41.

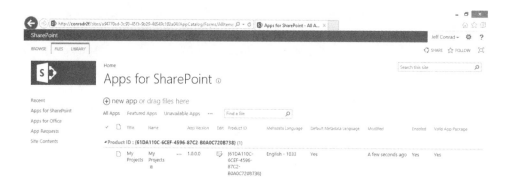

Figure 2-41 SharePoint displays your uploaded app package on the Apps For SharePoint corporate catalog page.

Installing app packages from a SharePoint corporate catalog

Now that you have your custom app package uploaded to the corporate catalog on your company's SharePoint server, you can install the web app in your SharePoint site. To install an app package, open your web browser and navigate to your SharePoint 2013 team site. You might need to navigate up to the parent site of your SharePoint server if you are currently viewing an existing Access web app in your web browser. Next, click Add Lists, Libraries, And Other Apps, as shown in Figure 2-42.

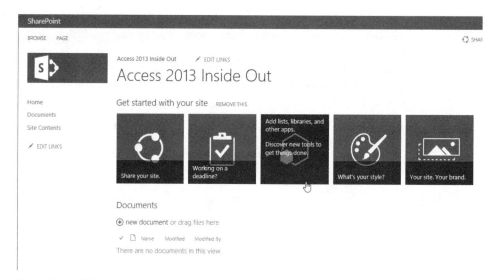

Figure 2-42 Click Add Lists, Libraries, And Other Apps to install new Access web apps in your SharePoint site.

SharePoint navigates to the Site Contents Your Apps page, as shown in Figure 2-43. On the left side of this page, click the Apps You Can Add link (if it isn't already selected).

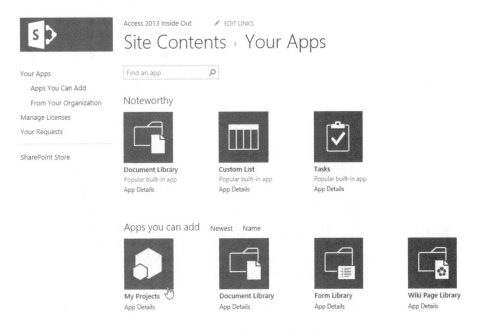

Figure 2-43 Select your web app from the list of apps to install.

Under the Apps You Can Add section of this page, you should see the app package you uploaded earlier. By default, SharePoint displays the most recent uploaded apps first. Click the Name link at the top of the Apps You Can Add section to have SharePoint sort the apps in alphabetical order by the name of the app. If there are more apps to display than there is space on the page, SharePoint displays links to navigate to additional pages of apps at the bottom of the webpage. Click the App Details link below your app package, and SharePoint navigates to a page with information about the specific app. To install your Access web app, click the app button icon. SharePoint now opens a dialog box where you must confirm that you trust the app, as shown in Figure 2-44.

Figure 2-44 Click Trust It to create an Access web app from an app package.

If you do not want to install the web app at this point, click Cancel. To install the web app, you must agree to allow the app to access information from the SharePoint site. Click Trust It to continue installing the web app. SharePoint next navigates to the Site Contents page of your SharePoint site and displays a message next to a new icon while it installs your app. Until SharePoint finishes installing your new app, you won't be able to click the icon to open your web app. When SharePoint finishes installing your web app, you'll see your app name and a default Access web app icon, as shown in Figure 2-45.

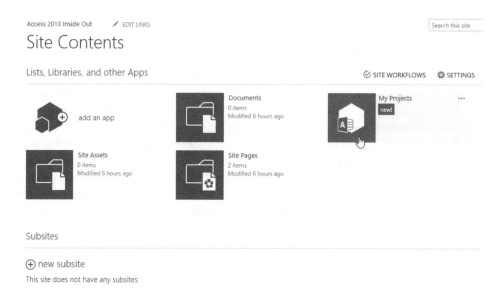

Figure 2-45 SharePoint displays your installed web app on the Site Contents page.

To the right of the web app name, SharePoint displays a link with three dots (...). Click this link, and SharePoint opens a small dialog above the web app name, as shown in Figure 2-46. In this dialog, you can see the web app name and the version number.

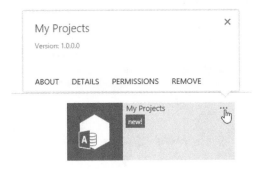

Figure 2-46 Click the three dots link to view additional options for your web app.

At the bottom of the information dialog, SharePoint displays four links—About, Details, Permissions, and Remove. Click About, and SharePoint navigates to a page with information about your web app, such as name, description, version number, and release date. Click Details, and SharePoint navigates to a page with information about usage data and any potential errors encountered in the web app. Click Permissions, and SharePoint navigates to a page where you can verify that you trust the app, such as when you are encountering issues accessing basic information with the app. Click Remove, and SharePoint prompts you for confirmation that you want to remove the web app.

CAUTION

If you click OK on the confirmation dialog to remove your web app, you cannot undo this action. SharePoint removes your web app, including all data, from the SharePoint server. If you want to save your data before removing the web app, you should save your web app as an app package first.

To navigate to your Access web app after installing it from the SharePoint corporate catalog, click the app icon on the Site Contents page. SharePoint navigates to your completed web app, as shown in Figure 2-47. You can now use your app and view, add, and edit data.

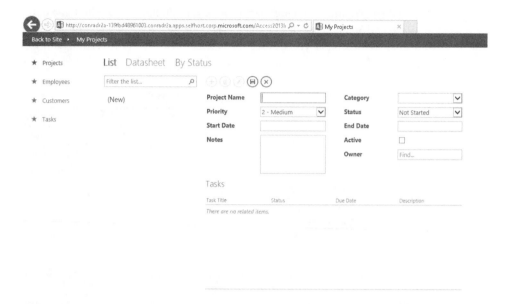

Figure 2-47 After you upload and install an Access web app from a SharePoint corporate catalog, you can begin using the app.

> **Note**
>
> You can install only one instance of a specific Access web app in a SharePoint site. If you have multiple SharePoint sites and subsites, you can install a web app from the same app package into each of those sites; however, you are restricted to one instance of a specific Access web app in each site.

Installing apps from the SharePoint Store

In addition to installing Access web apps that you and other people in your organization upload into an internal SharePoint corporate catalog, you can also install Access web apps from the SharePoint Store. Individuals, developers, and companies in the community can upload app packages to the SharePoint Store. To install an app package from the Share-Point Store, open your web browser and navigate to your SharePoint 2013 team site. You might need to navigate up to the parent site of your SharePoint server if you are currently viewing an existing Access web app in your web browser. Next, click Add Lists, Libraries, And Other Apps, as shown in Figure 2-48.

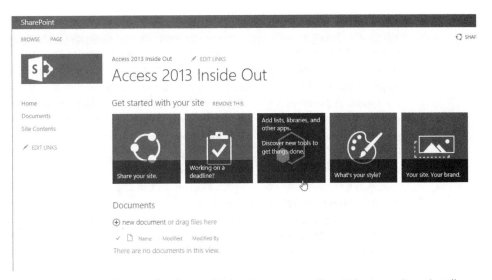

Figure 2-48 Click Add Lists, Libraries, And Other Apps on your SharePoint team site to install a new app package.

> **Note**
>
> If you are in a corporate network environment, you should check with your Information Technology (IT) department to determine whether your company has established guidelines regarding installing Access web apps from the SharePoint Store.

SharePoint then navigates to the Site Contents - Your Apps page for your team site. Click the SharePoint Store link on the left side of this page, as shown in Figure 2-49.

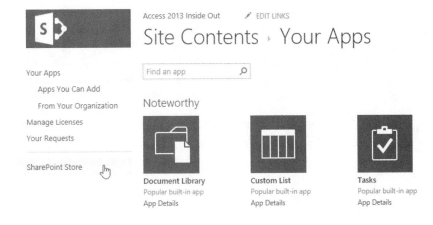

Figure 2-49 Click the SharePoint Store link on the Site Contents - Your Apps page.

Chapter 2

SharePoint now navigates to the SharePoint Store page, as shown in Figure 2-50. On the left side of this page, you'll see links under the Price and Categories headings. Under the Price link, SharePoint groups apps under All or Free headings, depending on whether the developer or company set a price for the app. Under Categories, SharePoint groups apps together serving a common purpose, such as Communication, Content Management, or Education. In the center of the SharePoint Store page, you'll see a heading, labeled Featured Apps, with several highlighted apps listed. Under the featured app icons, you'll see sorting options for the apps in the SharePoint Store. You can choose to sort apps by Most Relevant, Highest Rating, Most Downloaded, Lowest Price, Name, or Newest. Click any of these sorting option links to change the current sort option displayed. Beneath each app icon, you'll see the name of the app, a rating for the app, and the price of the app. If there are more apps to display than there is space on the page, click the right arrow or left arrow links in the upper-right portion of the page to navigate to additional pages of apps in the SharePoint Store. You can also search for a specific app by typing a search term in the Search box in the upper-right corner of the SharePoint Store page.

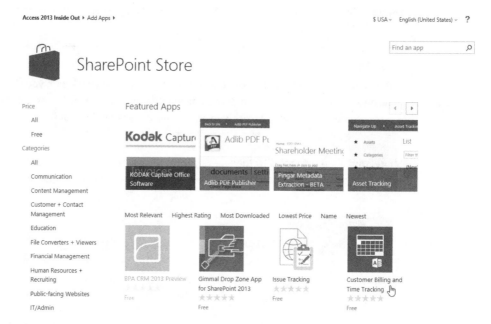

Figure 2-50 The SharePoint Store includes many different types of apps that you can install in your SharePoint site, including Access web apps.

> **Note**
>
> Microsoft frequently updates the SharePoint Store page, and apps are continually being added and removed from the store, so the options, apps, and layout you see in Figure 2-50 might differ from what you see when you visit the page.

As you hover your mouse over an app icon, SharePoint displays a short description beneath the app icon. If an app cannot be installed on your server, the icon appears dimmed and you'll see a description informing you that the app cannot be installed in your location. To find out additional information about an app, click the app icon. SharePoint navigates to a page with information about the specific app. For example, click the Customer Billing And Time Tracking icon to view more information about this app, as shown in Figure 2-51.

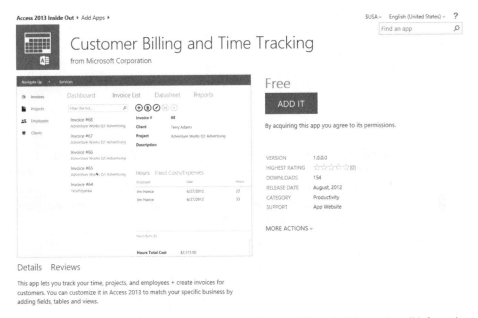

Figure 2-51 You can read information about a specific app before deciding to install it from the SharePoint Store.

SharePoint displays the app icon, the name of the app, and the name of the company who created the app—in this case, Microsoft Corporation—at the top of the page. On the app information page, you'll also a see a preview graphic of what the app looks like after you install it. Beneath the preview graphic, you can click the Details link to see a short description of the web app. Click the Reviews link to read reviews from people who have previously installed and used this specific app. On the right side of the app information page, you'll see the price of the app, version number, overall rating for the app, number of downloads, release date, category information, and links to support and permission details. In the lower-right corner of the page, you can click More Actions to view information about licensing and violations. If you want to install the web app, click the Add It button. Share-Point displays a confirmation page, as shown in Figure 2-52.

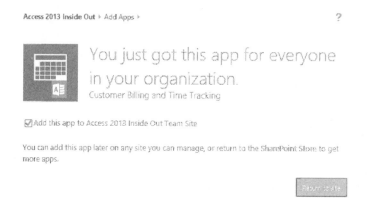

Figure 2-52 Click Return To Site to continue installing your web app.

On the confirmation page, SharePoint informs you that you now have the web app available for anyone in your organization. If you want to continue installing the web app, select the Add This App To *<your site name>* check box (selected by default), and then click the Return To Site button. SharePoint opens a dialog box where you must confirm that you trust the app, as shown in Figure 2-53.

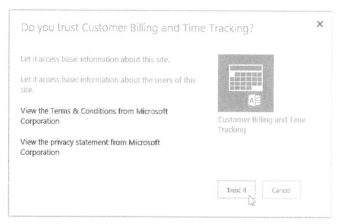

Figure 2-53 Click Trust It to install the web app from the SharePoint Store.

If you do not want to install the web app at this point, click Cancel. To install the web app, you must agree to allow the app to access information from the SharePoint site. Click Trust It to continue installing the Access web app. SharePoint navigates to the Site Contents page of your SharePoint site and displays a message next to a new icon while it installs your app. When SharePoint finishes installing your Access web app, SharePoint displays your app name and a default Access web app icon. When you click your new installed web app from the SharePoint Store, you might see a dialog containing terms and conditions for using the app, as shown in Figure 2-54.

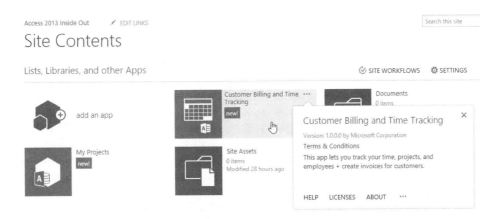

Figure 2-54 You can view terms and conditions information about the web app on this dialog.

After your web app is installed, you can click the app icon to view the new completed Access web app in your web browser, as shown in Figure 2-55. You can now use your app and view, add, and edit data from within your web browser.

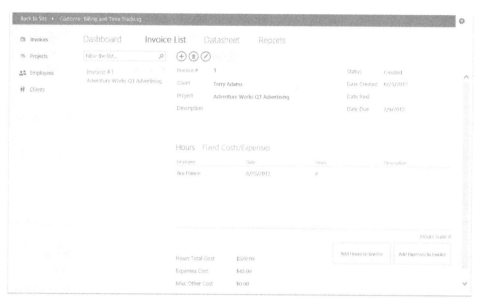

Figure 2-55 After you install an Access web app from the SharePoint Store, you can begin using the app.

Installing apps directly into a SharePoint site

Access apps stored in the SharePoint corporate catalog can be installed multiple times within different SharePoint sites. However, in some cases, you might want to install an Access web app as a one-time operation without needing the extra steps of going through the SharePoint corporate catalog. You can install Access web apps directly into a SharePoint Site without using the SharePoint corporate catalog. To do this, open your web browser and navigate to your SharePoint 2013 site. You might need to navigate up to the parent site of your SharePoint server if you are currently viewing an existing Access web app in your web browser. Next, click Add Lists, Libraries, And Other Apps, as shown in Figure 2-56.

Figure 2-56 Click Add Lists, Libraries, And Other Apps on your SharePoint site to install a new app package.

SharePoint navigates to the Site Contents Your Apps page, as shown in Figure 2-57. Under the Apps You Can Add section of this page, look for a button labeled Access App. By default, SharePoint displays the most recent uploaded apps in the SharePoint corporate catalog first on this page, so you might not see the Access App option. Click the Name link at the top of the Apps You Can Add section to have SharePoint sort the apps in alphabetical order, which should bring the Access App icon onto the first page of the list of apps you can add.

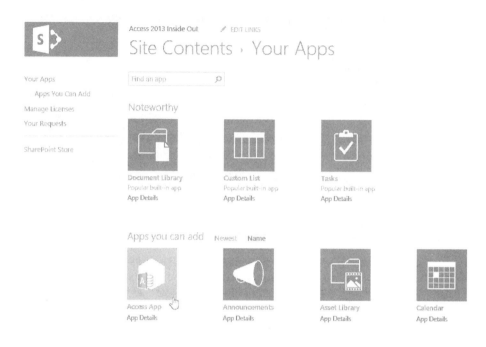

Figure 2-57 Select Access App from the list of apps to install.

Click the Access App link, and SharePoint opens the Adding An Access App dialog, as shown in Figure 2-58. In this dialog, you can choose either to create a new blank Access web app in your current SharePoint site or upload an existing Access app package.

Figure 2-58 Click the Or Upload An Access App Package link to upload an existing app package.

The default option on the Adding An Access App dialog is to create a new blank Access web app. (You'll see how to create a blank Access web app using this dialog in the next section.) To upload an Access app package, click the link labeled Or Upload An Access App Package. Access changes the elements in the dialog after you click the link, as shown in Figure 2-59. If you change your mind and want to create a blank Access web app instead of uploading an Access web app package, you can click the Or Create A New Access App From Scratch link on this dialog. Clicking this link acts like a toggle switch, swapping out the dialog elements to either create a blank web app or upload an existing Access web app package. If you do not want to install a web app at this point, click the Cancel button.

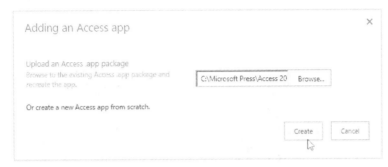

Figure 2-59 Browse to a location of an existing Access app package you want to install.

In the File Name text box on this dialog, you can type the file path and file name of your Access web app package (.app). You can also click the Browse button to open a Choose File To Upload dialog to navigate to and select the Access web app you want to upload. In Figure 2-59, I am selecting the BOSS.app sample Access web app package from the folder in which you installed the sample web apps and desktop databases:

C:\Microsoft Press\Access 2013 Inside Out

> **Note**
>
> All the sample web apps, desktop databases, and other files can be downloaded from the book's catalog page, but to follow along with the examples, you must place them in the directory mentioned above on your computer or device. For more information about the sample files, see the section titled "Using the sample files," in the book's introduction.

After you select the Access web app package by using the Browse button, or type the location and file name in the File Name text box, click the Create button. SharePoint navigates to the Site Contents page of your SharePoint site and displays an installing app message next to a new icon while it installs your app. While SharePoint is installing your new web app, you won't be able to click the icon to open your web app. When SharePoint finishes installing your web app, you'll see your app name and a default Access web app icon (or a custom icon if the package includes one), as shown in Figure 2-60. Notice the custom icon I created for the BOSS.app web app package, which can be seen in Figure 2-60.

Figure 2-60 SharePoint displays your installed web app on the Site Contents page.

To navigate to your Access web app after installing it into your SharePoint site, click the app icon on the Site Contents page. SharePoint navigates to your completed web app, as shown in Figure 2-61. You can now use your app in a web browser and view, add, and edit data.

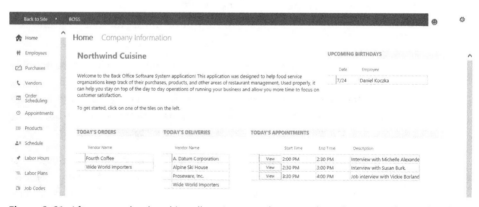

Figure 2-61 After you upload and install an Access web app package into your SharePoint site, you can begin using the app.

> **Note**
>
> You can install only one instance of a specific Access web app package in a SharePoint site. If you have multiple SharePoint sites and subsites, you can install a web app from the same app package into each of those sites; however, you are restricted to one instance of a specific Access web app in each site.

Creating a blank Access web app

You can create a blank Access web app directly into a SharePoint Site by using your web browser. In this case, you do not even need to have Access installed on your local computer or device. You'll still need to use Access 2013 to design the web app, but you can use your web browser as a starting point for creating the web app just as easily as you can from within Access.

To install an app package directly into a SharePoint site, open your web browser and navigate to your SharePoint 2013 site. You might need to navigate up to the parent site of your SharePoint server if you are currently viewing an existing Access web app in your web browser. Next, click Add Lists, Libraries, And Other Apps, shown previously in Figure 2-56. SharePoint navigates to the Site Contents Your Apps page, shown previously in Figure 2-57. Under the Apps You Can Add section of the Site Contents Your Apps page, look for a button labeled Access App. By default, SharePoint displays the most recent uploaded apps first on this page, so you might not see the Access App option. Click the Name link at the top of the Apps You Can Add section to have SharePoint sort the apps in alphabetical order, which should bring the Access App icon onto the first page of the list of apps you can add. Click the Access App link, and SharePoint opens the Adding An Access App dialog, as shown in Figure 2-62.

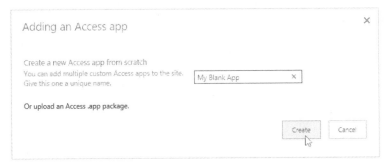

Figure 2-62 Enter a name for your blank web app into the App Name text box.

In the App Name text box, enter a name for your new blank Access web app and then click Create to begin creating your new web app. SharePoint navigates to the Site Contents page of your SharePoint site and displays an installing message next to a new icon while it creates your blank web app. While SharePoint is installing your new app, you won't be able to click the icon to open your blank web app. When SharePoint finishes, you'll see your app name and a default Access web app icon, as shown in Figure 2-63.

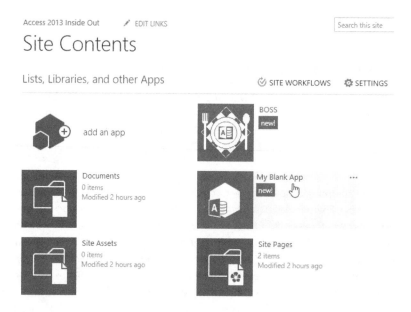

Figure 2-63 SharePoint displays your new blank web app on the Site Contents page.

To navigate to your new blank Access web app, click the app icon on the Site Contents page. SharePoint navigates to your new web app and displays a welcome page, as shown in Figure 2-64. You'll see this welcome page in your web browser whenever you navigate to any Access web app that does not contain tables. (Because you created this new blank web app from the Site Contents SharePoint page, there are currently no tables in the web app.)

Well done! You've successfully created an Access app. Now it's time to start designing. Start by adding some tables in Access.

Open this app in Access to start adding tables.

Need some help?
Check out Access online help.
Don't have Access? Download the free trial of Access on Demand.

Figure 2-64 You'll see this welcome page when you navigate to a new empty Access web app.

Included in this welcome page is a link to open the web app in Access. Your new Access web app contains no objects or data, so it is not of much use to you at this moment. To add tables and other objects to your new web app, click the Open This App In Access To Start Adding Tables link to open the web app in Access and begin customizing it. If you need help understanding how to use Access web apps, click the Check Out Access Online Help link at the bottom of the welcome page. SharePoint navigates you to an Office support page where you can search for information about Access web apps. If you do not have Access 2013 installed on your computer or device, you can click the Download The Free Trial link on the welcome page. SharePoint navigates you to an Office page with pricing, plans, and feature information about Office and Access.

Downloading a web app into Access

Gear button

When you install Access web apps from an internal SharePoint catalog or from the Share-Point Store, you can immediately start using the app inside a web browser. However, if you want to make design changes to your web app, you must open the web app within Access. The run-time experience for your web app is in a web browser, but your design experience is also contained within Access. To open a web app in Access, navigate to your web app URL using your web browser, click the gear button in the upper-right corner of the web-page, and then click Customize In Access, as shown in Figure 2-65.

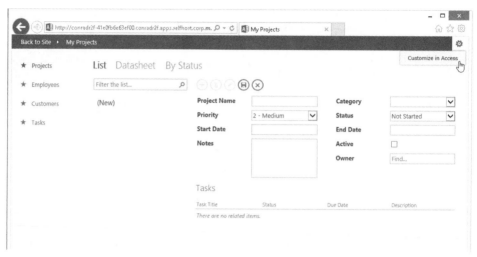

Figure 2-65 Click Customize In Access to open your web app in Access.

Access Services opens the File Download dialog box, as shown in Figure 2-66. Click Open, and Access Services downloads—or *rehydrates*—a copy of your Access web app to your computer and opens the app in Access. Click Save to download an Access web app short-cut to your local computer. An Access web app shortcut has an .accdw file extension. This shortcut is merely a pointer to the Access web app URL. You can send this .accdw file via email to other people who need to work with your Access web app from within Access.

When a user double-clicks the .accdw file, Access opens and downloads a copy of the web app to his or her local computer or device and synchronizes any server changes with their local copy of the app. If the user has a local copy of the web app already, Access opens the existing local app and synchronizes any server changes into that copy. Click Cancel on the File Download dialog box to close the dialog box without downloading anything to your computer or device.

Figure 2-66 In the File Download dialog box, you can open the web app from within Access or save a shortcut to the web app.

After Access opens and before you can design your web app, Access displays a warning dialog, as shown in Figure 2-67. Since you are downloading content from the Internet or intranet, you'll need to click OK to confirm that you want Access to download this content. Access displays this message each time you download a web app onto your computer. If you do not want to see this message each time you want to work with a web app in Access, select the Don't Show This Message Again check box (cleared by default) and then click OK. Click Cancel if you do not want to open the web app in Access.

Figure 2-67 Click OK to confirm downloading your web app into Access.

Click OK on the confirmation dialog, and Access displays a progress dialog while it downloads the web app. When Access completes the process of downloading your web app, you can view the app design surface and make any changes to the app, as shown in Figure 2-68.

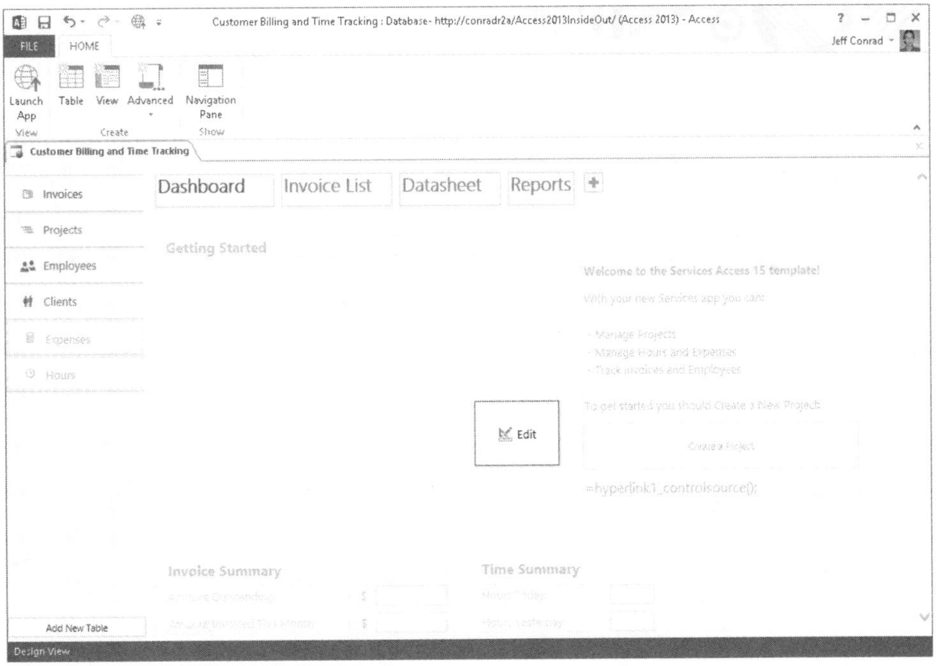

Figure 2-68 You can now see your web app in Access and make any design changes you want.

In this chapter, you've had a chance to take a look at the user interface for web apps in Access 2013. You've been introduced to web app templates and how they can quickly get you started designing web apps to meet specific business or personal needs. Finally, you've learned how to save an Access web app into an app package and install web apps from an internal SharePoint corporate catalog, from the SharePoint Store, and from the SharePoint Site Contents page. Perhaps the most important aspect of building a web app is designing the tables that will support your app. In Chapter 3, "Designing tables in a web app," you'll learn how to design the tables in your web app. Building a solid foundation makes creating the queries and views for your app easy.

Designing tables in a web app

THE process of defining tables in an Access 2013 web app is very easy. In general, you create the fields you need, assign properties to those fields, and create relationships between the tables. In this chapter, I'll show you how to begin creating your first custom web app by starting with the tables. You'll learn how to:

- Create a new web app by using a web app template.

- Create a new empty web app for your own custom application.

- Create tables using table templates.

- Define your own tables and fields from scratch by using Design view.

- Select the best data type for each field.

- Define the primary key for your table.

- Create calculated fields in your tables.

- Set validation rules for your fields and tables.

- Create lookups to other fields to define relationships between your tables.

- Optimize data retrieval by adding indexes.

INSIDE OUT   Take time to learn about table design

You could begin building a web app in Access 2013 much as you might begin creating a simple single-sheet solution in a spreadsheet application such as Microsoft Excel—by simply organizing your data into rows and columns and then inserting formulas where you need calculations. If you've ever worked extensively with a database or a spread-sheet application, you already know that this unplanned approach works in only the most trivial situations. Solving real problems takes some planning; otherwise, you end up building your application over and over again. One of the beauties of a relational database system such as Access is that it's much easier to make midcourse corrections. However, it's well worth spending time up front designing the tasks you want to per-form, the data structures you need to support those tasks, and the flow of tasks within your database application.

To teach you all you might need to know about table design would require another entire book. The good news is that Access 2013 provides many examples of good table design in the templates available with the product and online. If you want to learn at least the fundamentals of table and application design, be sure to read Article 1, "Designing your database application," which can be downloaded from the book's cata-log page.

Creating a new blank web app

To begin creating a new blank web app when you start Access 2013, click the Custom Web App button on the Office Start Screen, as shown in Figure 3-1.

Note

For the following sections, you'll need to sign in to Office 365 or your corporate Share-Point site with your Microsoft or organizational account.

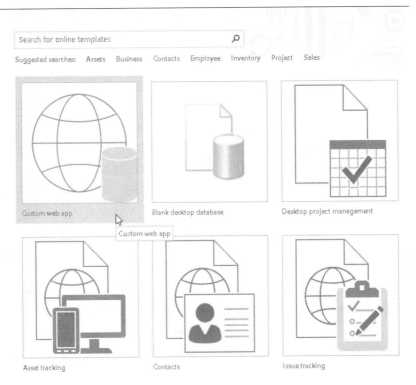

Figure 3-1 On the Office Start screen, click Custom Web App to begin creating a new blank web app.

Access opens the Custom Web App pop-up dialog, as shown in Figure 3-2, and displays a generic web app graphic on the left side of the dialog. For this new blank web app, type **Task Tracking** in the App Name text box, provide a URL to your Access Services site in the Web Location text box, and then click Create. If you are creating your web app on a Share-Point server inside a corporate domain, you might need to contact your SharePoint administrator to know what URL to use in the Web Location text box. Click the Get Help Finding Your Web Location link below the Web Location text box to open a webpage for possible assistance on choosing a URL.

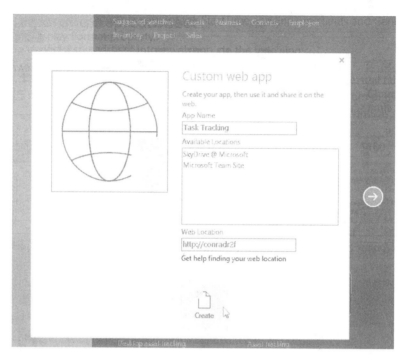

Figure 3-2 Provide an app name and URL for your new web app on the Custom Web App dialog.

A progress bar appears on the screen asking you to wait while Access 2013 creates your new web app. After a few seconds of preparation, Access opens the new web app and displays the Add Tables screen, shown in Figure 3-3, which you learned about in Chapter 2, "Exploring the Access 2013 web app interface." If you encounter a warning message during this stage indicating that the site is being created and not ready for use, navigate to the site in your browser and then click the option to customize the app in Access.

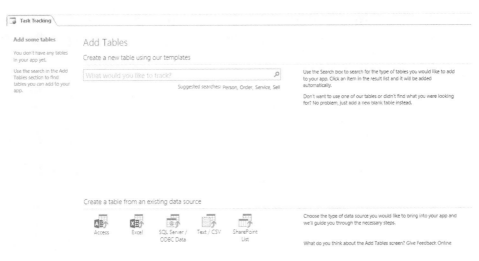

Figure 3-3 The Add Tables screen appears immediately after creating a new blank web app.

Because this is a new web app with no objects, the application is not of much use to you yet without any tables. The following sections provide various methods for creating new tables.

Creating tables using table templates

> **Note**
>
> If you'd like to follow along with the examples in the next sections, you can download the Contacts.app and BOSS.app sample web apps from the book's catalog page at *http://shop.oreilly.com/product/0790145367969.do*. For more information about the sample files, see the section titled see the section titled "Using the sample files, " in the book's introduction.

If you look in the Contacts sample web app (Contacts.app), you'll find it to be very simple, with one main table to store contact information. Most applications and databases are usually quite a bit more complex. For example, the built-in Project Management sample web app template you saw in Chapter 2 contains four main tables, and the Back Office Software System sample web app (BOSS.app) on the catalog page contains nearly two dozen tables. If you had to create every table manually, it could be quite a tedious process.

Fortunately, Access 2013 comes with a feature called table templates to help you build many common tables in your web apps. Table templates represent some of the more common types of table structures found in databases. To build new tables using table templates, enter a search term into the Search box on the Add Tables screen. For this example, let's create a new table to track tasks. Type **tasks** into the Search box, and then press Enter. Access displays several options beneath the Search box in the search results box, as shown in Figure 3-4.

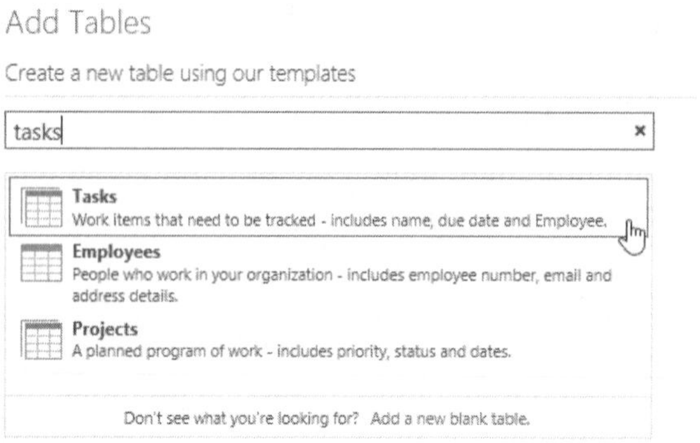

Add Tables

Create a new table using our templates

tasks   ×

Tasks
Work items that need to be tracked - includes name, due date and Employee.

Employees
People who work in your organization - includes employee number, email and address details.

Projects
A planned program of work - includes priority, status and dates.

Don't see what you're looking for?   Add a new blank table.

Figure 3-4 You can use the Search box to search for different types of table templates to use in your web apps.

In the search results for tasks, the first option Access displays contains an exact match to the **tasks** word you provided. You might be wondering why Access also returned an employees and projects table template as well. Access returned these two table templates, because they could potentially be related to tasks.

You'll also notice in Figure 3-4 that Access displays an icon with two tables next to the Tasks and Projects table templates and an icon with a single table next to the Employees table template. Some of the table templates Access provides contain only one table, while other table templates contain more than one related table. Whenever you see a single icon next to a table template in the search results, that specific table template contains only one table. If the icon displays two tables, the table template contains more than one table.

To clear the current search results, click the clear search button, denoted with an X, on the right side of the Search box. If Access cannot find any suitable table templates to your search criteria or if you're not satisfied with the search results, you can click the Add A New Blank Table link at the bottom of the search results box to start creating a new table from scratch.

> **Note**
> Microsoft is continually adding new table templates to their online content, so the results returned by your search on the word **tasks** on the Add Tables screen might differ from what you see in Figure 3-4.

Click Tasks in the search results box, and Access begins the process of creating your new table template. Access displays a progress bar while creating your table. After a brief time, Access displays two new tables in the Table Selector, as shown in Figure 3-5. You can use the tasks table for keeping track of various tasks and projects needing completion.

To complement the tasks table, Access also created a table to track employees. Tasks can be assigned to employees, so this specific table template includes a related table. Other table templates might include five or even six related tables. Next to each table caption on the Table Selector, Access displays a default icon (a star, in this case).

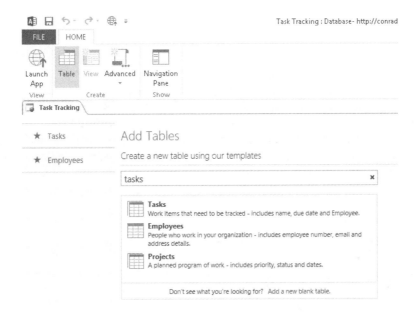

Figure 3-5 The Tasks table template contains two related tables for tracking tasks to complete.

Click the Tasks table in the Table Selector, and Access closes the Add Tables screen and displays the App Home View, as shown in Figure 3-6. In addition to creating two tables with this table template, Access also creates three views for each table for data entry. The captions for the three views for the tasks table are List, Datasheet, and By Status in the View Selector. The captions for the three views for the Employees table are List, Datasheet, and By Group. (You'll learn more about views in Chapter 6, "Working with views and the web browser experience.")

Figure 3-6 Access creates three views for each table in the Tasks table template.

To view the fields and field properties of the tasks table, you need to open the table in Design view. To do this, click the tasks table in the Table Selector and then click the gear charm button. Access displays a pop-up menu with five options—View Data, Edit Table, Hide, Rename, and Delete—as shown in Figure 3-7.

Figure 3-7 Click Edit Table to open a table in Design view.

The first option on the pop-up menu for tables in the Table Selector, View Data, opens the selected table in Datasheet view where you can add new records to your table, edit existing records, or delete records. The second option, Edit Table, opens the selected table in Design view where you can edit the structure of the table. The third option, Hide, moves the selected table to the bottom of the list of tables in the Table Selector. Access also dims the font color of the table caption to indicate the table is hidden. When you view your web app in a web browser, you will not see hidden tables in the Table Selector or views attached to that table. (If you already have a table hidden, the pop-up menu displays the text Unhide. Clicking Unhide moves the selected table above any hidden tables in the Table Selector, and you can then view that table and its associated views in your web browser.) The fourth option, Rename, allows you to rename the table caption shown in the Table Selector. Renaming the caption here does not rename the underlying table shown in the Navigation pane. Use this option if you want to present a different caption than your exact table name. The last option, Delete, deletes the underlying table from your web app (including all data in that table), deletes any views associated with the table that are shown in the View Selector, and removes that table option from the Table Selector. Note that you cannot undo a delete table operation.

INSIDE OUT   Four other ways to open the table design window

Besides clicking Edit Table on the pop-up menu, you can also open a table in Design view by double-clicking the table caption in the Table Selector, right-clicking the table name in the Navigation pane and clicking Design view, double-clicking the table name in the Navigation pane, or by highlighting the table in the Navigation pane and pressing Ctrl+Enter.

Click Edit Table to see the complete table structure for the tasks table. Access opens the Design view window for the tasks table, as shown in Figure 3-8. Notice that Access created 11 fields to identify the data elements for this tasks table. This tasks table includes fields such as Task Title, Priority, Description, Start Date, Due Date, Percent Complete, Assigned To (a lookup field to the employees table), and so on to identify a single subject—a task. The Tasks table template also defines a data type for each of these fields automatically.

Chapter 3

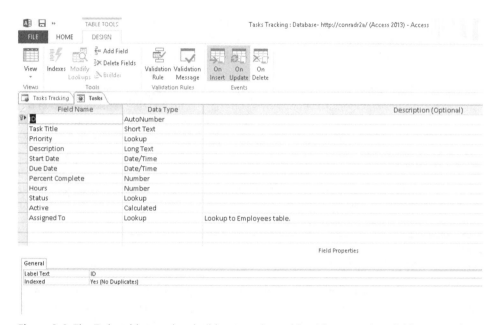

Figure 3-8 The Tasks table template builds a complete table with appropriate field types and supporting objects.

You can save time creating tables in web apps by using table templates even if the table structure that Access creates does not exactly match your needs. You can rename fields, add new fields, and delete unneeded fields to customize the table to your specific app needs. When you use a table template to help you create a table, you also get the added benefit of Access creating other supporting views and, in some cases, related tables to work with that table. In the next section, you'll learn all about the table Design view window. Close this tasks table window now, and then close Access so that you can continue with the next section.

Starting with a blank table

You could continue to use table templates to build tables; however, you'll find that in some cases you need to create your schema from scratch to meet your specific app needs. To begin creating a new blank table, let's start with a new, empty web app.

Click the Custom Web App button on the New tab of the Backstage view, name your new web app **Restaurant App**, provide a URL to your Access Services site, and then click Create on the Custom Web App dialog box. Access then displays the Add Tables screen. Click the Add A New Blank Table link, as shown in Figure 3-9, to begin creating a new blank table.

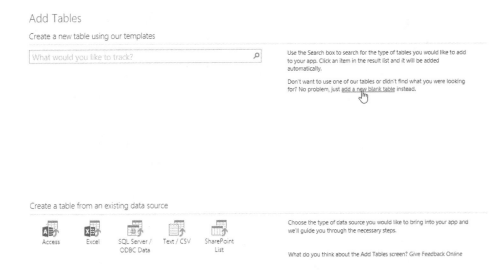

Figure 3-9 Click the Add A New Blank Table link on the Add Tables screen to create a new table.

Access 2013 displays a blank Table window in Design view, as shown in Figure 3-10. In Design view, the upper part of the Table window displays columns in which you can enter the field names, the data type for each field, and a description of each field. After you select a data type for a field, you can set field properties in the lower-left section of the Table window. In the lower-right section of the Table window is a box in which Access displays information about fields or properties. The contents of this box change as you move from one location to another within the Table window.

For details about data type values, see the section "Understanding web app data types," later in this chapter.

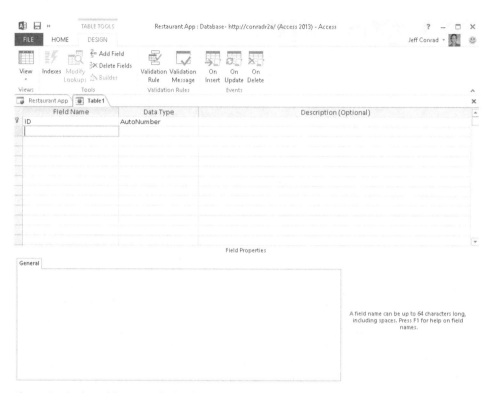

Figure 3-10 The Add A New Blank Table link opens a new table in Design view.

By default, Access creates a field called ID with an AutoNumber data type. All Access web apps must include an AutoNumber data type. You can rename this field to something else, such as EmployeeID or VendorID, but you cannot delete this field.

Defining fields in web apps

Now you're ready to begin defining some of the fields and tables in this new empty web app that you can find in the Back Office Software System sample web app (BOSS.app) on the catalog page.

The Back Office Software System sample web app is used to track various facets of a restaurant business, such as purchases, employee file maintenance, scheduling, and so forth. To understand how to create tables like the ones you can find in the Back Office Software System, we'll start by creating a new table from scratch to use for a vendor list.

You should still have your new table open in Design view that Access created when you clicked the link on the Add Tables screen. Let's start by renaming the ID field to something more useful. Put your insertion point in the first row of the Field Name column, press the Backspace or Delete key to remove the existing ID text, and then type **VendorID**, as shown in Figure 3-11.

Figure 3-11 Rename the existing ID field to VendorID.

Now move your insertion point to the second row of the Field Name column, and then type the name of the second field, **VendorName**. Press Tab once to move to the Data Type column. A button with an arrow appears on the right side of the Data Type column. In Access 2013, this type of button signifies the presence of a list. Click the arrow, or press the Alt+Down Arrow to open the list of data type options, as shown in Figure 3-12. In the Data Type column, you can either type a valid value or select from the values in the list. Select Short Text as the data type for VendorName. In the Description column for each field, you can enter a descriptive phrase to describe the purpose of this field. Type **Vendor's Name** in the Description column for the VendorName field.

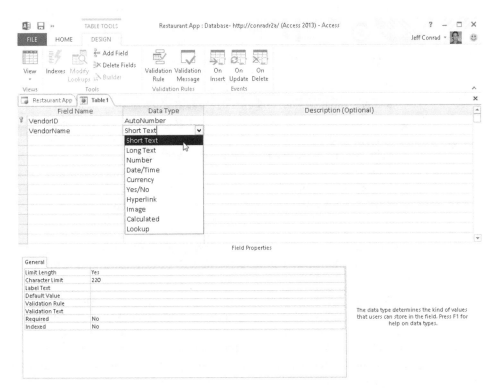

Figure 3-12 You can choose the data type for a field from a list of data type options.

INSIDE OUT   Why setting the description property is important

Entering a Description property for every field in your table helps document your web app. If another person needs to manage this web app in the future, having descriptions next to each field can be very useful in understanding the structure of the app.

Choosing field names in web apps

Access 2013 gives you lots of flexibility when it comes to naming your fields in web apps. A field name can be up to 64 characters long and can include any combination of letters, numbers, spaces, and special characters except a period (.), exclamation point (!), square brackets ([]), leading space, leading equal sign (=), or nonprintable character such as a carriage return. The name also cannot contain any of the following characters: / \ : ; * ? "" < > | # <TAB> { } % ~ &. In general, you should give your fields meaningful names. You should avoid using field names that might also match any name internal to Access. For example, all objects have a Name property, so it's a good idea to qualify a field containing a name by calling it VendorName or CompanyName. You should also avoid names that are the same as built-in functions, such as Date, Time, Now, or Space. See Access Help for a list of all the built-in function names.

Although you can use spaces within your field names in a web app, you should try to create field names without embedded spaces. If you use reserved words or function names for field names, Access 2013 catches most of these and displays a warning message. This message warns you that the field name you chose, such as Name or Date, is a reserved word and that you could encounter errors when referring to that field in other areas of the web app. Access still allows you to use this name if you choose, but take note of the problems it could cause. To avoid potential conflicts, we recommend that you avoid using reserved words and built-in functions for field names.

Move your insertion point to the third row of the Field Name column, and then type the name of the third field, **CustomerNumber**. Press Tab once to move to the Data Type column, and select Short Text from the drop-list of data type choices. (We're using a text data type for this field because the customer number can contain alphanumeric characters.) Press Tab to move to the Description column, and enter **Customer Number used by vendor** for this field. After you enter several rows of data, it's a good idea to save your table. You can do this by clicking the Save button on the Quick Access Toolbar or by clicking the File tab and then clicking Save. Access 2013 displays a Save As dialog box, as shown in Figure 3-13.

Figure 3-13 Access displays the Save As dialog box when you first save a new table so that you can specify a table name.

Name this new table **Vendors** in the Save As dialog box. Access briefly displays a progress dialog letting you know that it is saving your current table changes. Your table up to this point should now look like Figure 3-14.

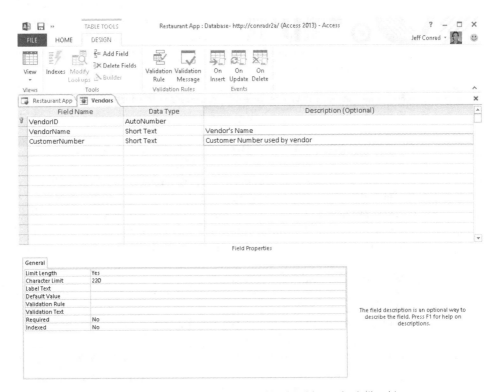

Figure 3-14 Your changes for your new Vendors table should now look like this.

Choosing table names in web apps

Access 2013 gives you lots of flexibility when it comes to naming your tables in web apps; however, there are some restrictions to be aware of. A table name can be up to 64 characters long, can include any combination of letters, numbers, spaces, and special characters except a period (.), exclamation point (!), square brackets ([]), leading space, leading equal sign (=), or nonprintable character such as a carriage return. The name also cannot contain any of the following characters:` / \ : ; * ? " ' < > | # <TAB> { } % ~ &. In general, you should give your tables meaningful names.

After you select a data type, Access displays some property boxes in the Field Properties section in the lower part of the Table window. These boxes allow you to set *properties*—settings that determine how Access handles the field—and thereby customize a field. The properties Access displays depend on the data type you select; the properties appear with some default values in place, as shown previously in Figure 3-12.

For details about the values for each property, see the section "Setting field properties," later in this chapter.

Understanding field data types in web apps

Web apps in Access 2013 support 10 types of data, each with a specific purpose. You can see the details about each data type in Table 3-1. Access also gives you an 11th option, Lookup, to help you define the characteristics of foreign key fields that link to other tables. (You'll learn about the Lookup option later in this chapter.) Included in Table 3-1 is information about the data types created in SQL Server when you define your fields in web apps.

TABLE 3-1   Access web app data types

Data type	Usage	SQL Server data type
AutoNumber	Unique value generated by Access for each new record.	int
Short Text	Alphanumeric data.	nvarchar with length from 1 to 4000
Long Text	Alphanumeric data—sentences and paragraphs.	nvarchar(max) to store large amounts of text, $2^{30}-1$ bytes in SQL Server 2012.
Number	Numeric data.	Whole number no decimal places (int), Floating-point number (double) and Fixed-point number (decimal(28,6), 6 decimal places).

Data type	Usage	SQL Server data type
Date/Time	Dates and times.	Date (date); Time (time(3)); Date with Time (datetime2(3)).
Currency	Monetary data.	decimal(28,6).
Yes/No	Boolean (yes/no) data.	bit (default is False).
Hyperlink	A link "address" to a document or file on the Internet or on an intranet.	nvarchar(max).
Image	Picture data.	Binary Image data varbinary(max). $2^{31}-1$ bytes in SQL Server 2012.
Calculated	You can create an expression that uses data from one or more fields. You can designate different result data types from the expression.	Calculated field using SQL Server functions. Storage depends on expression.
Lookup	The Lookup entry in the Data Type column in Design view is not actually a data type. When you choose this entry, a dialog opens to help you define a lookup field. A lookup field uses the contents of another table or a value list to validate the contents of a single value per row.	Creates a foreign key lookup. If lookup is to another table for foreign key, data is stored as integer (int). If lookup field is a value list, the data is stored as nvarchar with default of 200 length.

Chapter 3

For each field in your table, select the data type that is best suited to how you will use that field's data. For character data, you should normally select the Short Text data type. You can control the maximum length of a Short Text field by using a field property, as explained later. Use the Long Text data type only for long strings of text that might exceed 4000 characters or that might contain formatting characters such as tabs or line endings (carriage returns).

When you select the Number data type, you should think carefully about what you enter as the Number Subtype property because this property choice will affect precision as well as length. (For example, the Whole number option does not have decimals.)

The Date/Time data type is useful for calendar or clock data and has the added benefit of allowing calculations in seconds, minutes, hours, days, months, or years. For example, you can find out the difference in days between two Date/Time values.

INSIDE OUT   Understanding what's inside the Date/Time data type

Use the Date/Time data type and the three subtypes—Date, Time, and Date with Time—to store any date, time, or date and time value. It's useful to know that Access 2013 stores the date as the integer portion of the Date/Time data type and the time as the fractional portion—the fraction of a day, measured from midnight, that the time represents, accurate to seconds. For example, 6:00:00 A.M. internally is 0.25.

Use the Currency data type for storing money values. Currency has the precision of integers and includes a currency symbol.

The AutoNumber data type is specifically designed for automatic generation of primary key values. You can include only one field using the AutoNumber data type in any table. Whenever you create a new table in a web app, Access automatically creates an ID field for you because tables in web apps require it. You can rename the AutoNumber field in your table, but you cannot delete it.

Use the Yes/No data type to hold Boolean (true or false) values. This data type is particularly useful for flagging accounts paid or not paid, or orders filled or not filled.

The Hyperlink data type lets you store a simple "link" to an external file or document. (Internally, Hyperlink is a nvarchar(max) data type.) This link can contain a Uniform Resource Locator (URL) that points to a location on the World Wide Web or on a local intranet.

The Image data type allows you to store graphic file data. You can store graphics with .gif, .jfif, .jpe, .jpeg, .jpg, or .png file extensions. You can store one image file per field. Access stores only the raw image in the field; Access does not store other data with the image, such as file name or size. The maximum file size for images in a web app is 10 MB. The image field uses an <IMG> tag in HTML, which should allow all modern browsers to display the image data.

The Calculated data type allows you to create a calculated result using an expression. The expression can include data from one or more fields. For example, if you have a number field that holds quantity information for products purchased and a currency field that holds the price of a product, you can create a calculated field that multiplies the quantity and price fields. You could also create a calculated field that concatenates first name, middle name, and last name fields and stores it into a field called Full Name.

Access sets the data type result after you save a calculated field based on the data types of the fields and expression you use to generate the calculated field. After you save a calculated field, you can set different format options for the field, such as Currency for the price and quantity example previously noted. Access recalculates the value of the calculated field any time you change any of the dependent fields.

> **Note**
>
> You cannot reference image fields in a calculated field expression.

Setting field properties

You can customize the way Access 2013 stores and handles each field in web apps by setting specific field properties. These properties vary according to the data type you choose. Table 3-2 lists all the possible properties that can appear on a field's General tab in a table's Design view for web apps, and the data types that are associated with each property.

TABLE 3-2   Field properties on the General tab

Property	Data Type	Options, Description
Limit Length	Short Text	You can choose to impose a limit to the number of characters allowed in the field. Choosing Yes imposes a limit to the number of characters, and choosing No does not impose a limit. When you choose No, Access hides the Character Limit field property.
	Long Text	Default for Long Text is No for Limit Length.
Character Limit	Short Text	Text can be between 1 and 4000 characters, with a default length of 220 characters.
	Long Text	By default, Access hides this property for Long Text fields. If you change the Limit Length property to Yes, you can set a value between 1 and 4000 characters, with a default limit of 220.
Label Text	All	You can enter a more fully descriptive field name that Access displays in control labels on views. (Tip: If you create field names with no embedded spaces, you can use the Label Text property to specify a name that includes spaces for Access to use in labels associated with this field in views.)
Default Value	Short Text, Long Text, Number, Currency, Date/Time, Hyperlink, and Yes/No	You can specify a default value for the field that Access automatically uses for a new row if no other value is supplied. If you don't specify a default value, the field will be Null if the user fails to supply a value. (See also the Required property.)

Property	Data Type	Options, Description
Validation Rule	Short Text, Long Text, Number, Currency, Date/Time, and Yes/No	You can supply an expression that must be true whenever you enter or change data in this field. For example, *<100* specifies that a number must be less than 100. You can also check for one of a series of values. For example, you can have Access check for a list of valid cities by specifying "Boston" OR "Seattle" OR "Los Angeles". In addition, you can specify a complex expression that includes any of the built-in functions in Access web apps. See "Defining field validation rules for web apps" later in this chapter, for details.
Validation Text	Short Text, Long Text, Number, Currency, Date/Time, and Yes/No	You can specify a custom message that Access displays whenever the data entered does not pass your validation rule.
Required	All except AutoNumber, Boolean, and Calculated	If you don't want to allow a Null value in this field, select this property.
Indexed	All except Hyperlink and Image	You can ask that an index be built to speed access to data values.
Number Subtype	Number	**Fixed-point number (6 decimal places).** This is the default. Stored as decimal (28.6) in SQL Server.
		Whole number (no decimal places). Stored as int data type in SQL Server.
		Floating-point number (variable decimal places). Stored as float data type in SQL Server.
Display Format	Number	**General Number** (default). No commas or currency symbols; the number of decimal places shown depends on the precision of the data.
		Fixed. At least one digit and two decimal places.
		Standard. Two decimal places and separator commas.
		Percent. Moves displayed decimal point two places to the right and appends a percentage (%) symbol.
	Date/Time with Subtype Date	**Short Date** (the default). Uses Short Date Style from Regional And Language Options (for example, 7/1/2013).
		Long Date. Uses Long Date Style from the Regional And Language Options item in Control Panel (for example, Thursday, July 1, 2013).
	Date/Time with Subtype Time	**Short Time** (the default). For example, 5:30 PM.
		Long Time. Uses Time Style from the Regional And Language Options item (for example, 5:30:10 PM).

Property	Data Type	Options, Description
	Date/Time with Subtype Date with Time	**General Date** (the default). Combines Short Date and time (for example, 7/1/2013 5:30:10 PM).
		Long Date. Uses Long Date Style from the Regional And Language Options item in Control Panel (for example, Thursday, July 1, 2013).
		Short Date. Uses Short Date Style from Regional And Language Options (for example, 7/1/2013).
		Long Time. Uses Time Style from the Regional And Language Options item (for example, 5:30:10 PM).
		Short Time (the default). For example, 5:30 PM.
Display Decimal Places	Number	You can specify the number of decimal places that Access displays. The default specification is to display two decimal places for the Fixed, Standard, and Percent formats and the number of decimal places necessary to show the current precision of the numeric value for General Number format. You can request a fixed display of decimal places by using the drop-down list.
Currency Symbol	Currency	[1] Currency symbol from drop-down list of regions.
Modify Expression	Calculated	The expression used to calculate the value for the column. The expression can use the value of one or more fields in the same table.
Result Type	Calculated	For calculated fields, you need to provide the data type that results from the expression you use for the field. The result type can be Short Text, Long Text, Number (Floating Decimal), Number (No Decimal), Number (Fixed Decimal), Date With Time, Date, Time, or Yes/No.

[1] Currency always displays two decimal places regardless of the number of actual decimal places in the underlying data. Access rounds any number to two decimal places for display if the number contains more than two decimal places.

Chapter 3

> # INSIDE OUT   Don't specify a validation rule without validation text
>
> If you specify a validation rule but no validation text, Access 2013 generates an ugly and cryptic message that your users might not understand in your web browser:
>
> "One or more values are prohibited by the validation rule for '*<field name here>*'. Please enter a value that the expression for this validation rule can accept."
>
> Unless you like getting lots of support calls, I recommend that you always enter a custom validation text message whenever you specify a validation rule.

Completing the fields in the Vendors table

> ### Note
> You can compare your work in this section to the tblVendors table in the Back Office Software System sample web app (BOSS.app), which can be downloaded from the book's catalog page.

You now know enough about field data types and properties for tables in web apps to finish designing the Vendors table in this example. Use the information listed in Table 3-3 to complete the table shown in Figure 3-15. In addition to the properties listed below, set the Required property of the VendorName field to Yes and the Default Value property of the Active field to Yes. Save your table changes after updating the table fields and properties.

TABLE 3-3 Field definitions for the Vendors table

Field Name	Data Type	Description	Character Limit	Label Text
VendorID	AutoNumber			Vendor ID
VendorName	Short Text	Vendor's name	50	Vendor Name
CustomerNumber	Short Text	Customer number used by vendor	50	Customer Number
ContactFirstName	Short Text	Contact person's first name	50	Contact First Name
ContactLastName	Short Text	Contact person's last name	50	Contact Last Name
ContactTitle	Short Text	Contact person's title	50	Contact Title

Field Name	Data Type	Description	Character Limit	Label Text
ContactCellNumber	Short Text	Contact person's cell phone number	30	Cell Number
Address	Short Text	Address of vendor	255	Address
Address2	Short Text	Additional address information of vendor if needed	255	Address 2
City	Short Text	City	50	City
PostalCode	Short Text	Postal/Zip Code	20	Postal Code
PhoneNumber	Short Text	Telephone number of vendor	30	Phone Number
PhoneNumberExtension	Short Text	Telephone extension if applicable	30	Extension
FaxNumber	Short Text	Fax number of vendor	30	Fax Number
EmailAddress	Short Text	Email address of contact or vendor	100	E-mail Address
Notes	Long Text	Additional notes for internal use		Notes
Website	Hyperlink	Company website		Website
Active	Yes/No	Yes/No field whether this is an active vendor		Active?

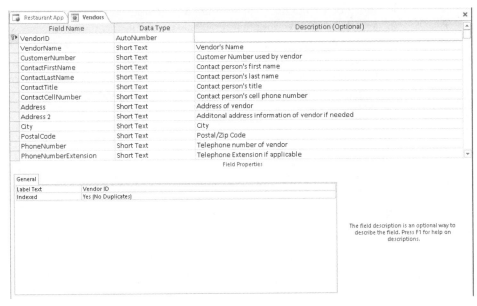

Figure 3-15 Your fields in the Vendors table should now look like this.

> **Note**
>
> When you save your additional changes to the Vendors table, Access displays a warning message that some of your data might be lost. Access displays this message whenever you reduce the Character Limit property for an existing field. You might also see a similar message about data integrity rules being changed. Access displays this message whenever you change the Required property of any existing field.

You might have noticed that we did not have you create two fields found in the tblVendors table in the Back Office Software System sample web app—ContactFullName and State. We'll discuss creating these two fields in the next sections.

Creating calculated fields

The Calculated data type allows you to create a calculated result using an expression. The expression you use can include data from one or more fields in the same table, but you cannot reference fields in other tables. For example, if you have a number field, that holds quantity information for products purchased and a currency field that holds the price of a product, you can create a calculated field that multiplies the quantity and price fields. Access recalculates the value of the calculated field any time the dependent fields are changed. If the calculation for a specific row evaluates to an error, Access displays an error message and prevents you from saving your record changes.

Calculated field expressions can reference functions and use operators that are supported in tables. You cannot use volatile (or nondeterministic) functions, such as Date() and Now(), in calculated fields, because the stored value of the field would always be incorrect. You can use a calculated field as a display column for a lookup field. You'll learn how to create relationships with lookup fields later in this chapter. In Access 2013 web apps, you can generally use calculated fields anywhere that you can use other data types in your app. You can sort, filter on, and group by calculated fields in queries and views.

Why use calculated fields?

If you are familiar with data normalization rules, you might be asking yourself why you would use a calculated field to store a value that is derived from other fields. As you'll learn in Chapter 5, "Working with queries in web apps," expressions in queries can do everything a calculated field can do and more. So why would you want to add a calculated field in your table?

Calculated fields in tables can provide potential performance gains when running large queries with the same expression. For a calculated field, the result of the expression is stored at the time Access saves the record. When you're fetching data from a table using a query, the calculated field value is fetched just like other data rather than calculated for each record. If you're running large queries against data stored in an Access Services site, you might see performance improvements by storing the value of an expression instead of calculating the value for each row.

In the Vendors table you have been building in the Restaurant App, let's add a calculated field that concatenates, or combines, the vendor contact's first and last name. Open your Vendors table in Design view, if it isn't already, and tab into the ContactTitle field. Next, click the Add Field button in the Tools group on the Design contextual tab. Access inserts a new row in the table designer above the ContactTitle field and below the ContactLastName field, as shown in Figure 3-16.

Chapter 3

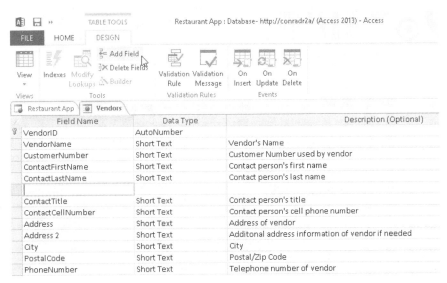

Figure 3-16 Access inserts a new blank row in the table designer when you click Add Field.

In the Field Name column, type **ContactFullName** as the name of this new field. Tab over to the Data Type column, and then select Calculated from the drop-down list of supported data types. Access opens the Expression Builder dialog box, as shown in Figure 3-17. In the upper part of the dialog box is a blank text box in which you can build an expression. You can type the expression yourself, but it's sometimes more accurate to find field names, operators, and function names in the three panes in the lower part of the dialog box.

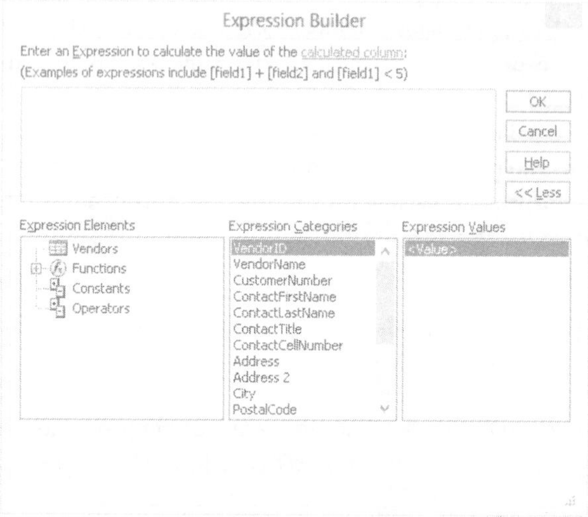

Figure 3-17 The Expression Builder dialog box helps you build simple and complex expressions.

The expression you need to build, which we'll walk you through in detail in just a moment, will look like this:

```
[ContactFirstName] + " " + [ContactLastName]
```

You can use the Expression Builder to help you correctly construct the expression you need for your new calculated field. The Expression Builder in Access 2013 includes a concept called *progressive disclosure*. In Access, the Expression Builder shows you only the elements applicable to the current context. For example, in Figure 3-17, Access shows you only the list of functions, constants, and operators you can use for calculated fields in web app tables under the Expression Elements pane on the far left. The middle pane, Expression Categories, lists all the current fields in your Vendors table that you can refer to in your calculated field. The right pane, Expression Values, shows you all possible values you can use based on the currently highlighted category selected in the middle pane. In this context, you can refer to the field value of existing fields only for new calculated fields.

Start by typing the letter **c**, which is the first letter of the ContactFirstName field in the text box at the top of the Expression Builder, as shown in Figure 3-18. Access now shows you an additional feature of the Expression Builder—the use of *IntelliSense*. IntelliSense helps you create expressions faster by showing you a drop-down list of words that match an object (such as a field or control name), function, or parameter after you type enough characters for Access to filter to the term. You can accept the suggestion that Access provides in the drop-down list by pressing Enter or Tab, or you can continue manually typing the name you want.

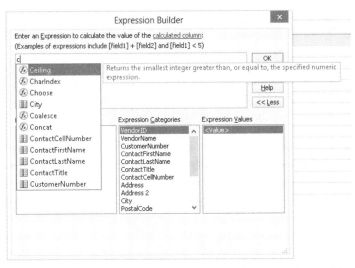

Figure 3-18 IntelliSense helps you create expressions faster by providing, as you type, a list of drop-down choices to use in your expression.

INSIDE OUT Using keyboard shortcuts to display or hide IntelliSense options

When you are working in the Expression Builder, you can press Ctrl+Space to show the IntelliSense list of available items based on where your insertion point is located. If no characters precede your insertion point, Access displays all available items. Press the Esc key to dismiss the IntelliSense list at any time.

In Figure 3-18, you'll notice that by typing the letter **c**, Access displays five functions—Ceiling, CharIndex, Choose, Coalesce, and Concat—and six fields in your Vendors tables, all of which start with the letter c. If you press Enter right now, Access selects the function Ceiling and adds that to the text box. You'll also notice in Figure 3-18 that Access displays a tooltip (also called a *ScreenTip*) for the Ceiling function. (You can find a list of the most useful functions and their descriptions in Article 5, "Function Reference," which can be downloaded from the book's catalog page.)

Chapter 3

INSIDE OUT Moving the Expression Builder ScreenTip

If the ScreenTip beneath the expression obstructs your view, you can move it to a different location on the screen. When you place the mouse pointer over the ScreenTip, the pointer changes to a four-arrow cross-hair, and you can then drag the ScreenTip to a new location.

To select the ContactFirstName field from the drop-down list, you can use the down arrow key to highlight the field and then press Enter or Tab, or you can double-click the field name in the drop-down list. Alternatively, you can continue typing the letters **contactf**, as I did, until that is the only option in the drop-down list, as shown in Figure 3-19. Notice that Access displays the field's description in the ScreenTip next to the field. Press Enter or Tab now to add the ContactFirstName field to the text box. (You could also simply double-click the field name you want to use in the Expression Categories pane to add the field to the top text box.)

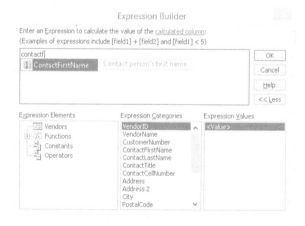

Figure 3-19 Access displays descriptions next to the field names in the IntelliSense drop-down list.

INSIDE OUT   Increasing the font size in the Expression Builder

If the font size in the upper part of the Expression Builder seems too small for you to read, you can adjust the size of the font by holding down the Ctrl key and then scrolling with your mouse wheel. When you scroll up, Access increases the font size, and when you scroll down, Access decreases the font size. Access returns the font size to the default size whenever you open the Expression Builder dialog box.

You'll notice that after you select the field, the Expression Builder pastes [ContactFirstName] into the expression area, as shown in Figure 3-20. The Expression Builder adds brackets ([ ]) around all field names in case they might have embedded spaces in their names. If you design your field names without any blank spaces, you can leave out the brackets, but it's always good practice to include them.

Figure 3-20 The Expression Builder automatically places brackets around field names after you add them to the text box area.

Continue with the rest of the expression we need by typing **+ " " +** and then adding the ContactLastName field by typing it manually, using the IntelliSense drop-down list as you type the letters, or double-clicking the field name in the Expressions Categories pane. Your completed expression should now look like Figure 3-21.

Figure 3-21 Your completed expression for the new Calculated field should now look like this.

Click OK to save your expression changes and dismiss the Expression Builder dialog box. Access returns focus to the Vendor design view and moves your insertion point to the Description column. Let's give our new Calculated field a proper description. Type **Contact full name** in the Description column. Click Save on the Quick Access Toolbar to save your new field changes. Your new Calculated field in the table design window should look like Figure 3-22.

Field Name	Data Type	Description (Optional)
VendorID	AutoNumber	
VendorName	Short Text	Vendor's Name
CustomerNumber	Short Text	Customer Number used by vendor
ContactFirstName	Short Text	Contact person's first name
ContactLastName	Short Text	Contact person's last name
ContactFullName	Calculated	Contact full name
ContactTitle	Short Text	Contact person's title
ContactCellNumber	Short Text	Contact person's cell phone number
Address	Short Text	Address of vendor
Address 2	Short Text	Additonal address information of vendor if needed
City	Short Text	City
PostalCode	Short Text	Postal/Zip Code
PhoneNumber	Short Text	Telephone number of vendor

Field Properties

General

Expression	[ContactFirstName]+" "+[ContactLastName]
Result Type	Short Text
Label Text	
Indexed	No

The field description is an optional way to describe the field. Press F1 for help on descriptions.

Figure 3-22 Your Vendors table should now look like this.

You'll notice in Figure 3-22 that Access displays the expression for this Calculated field in the Expression property under the General tab near the bottom of the table design window. You can modify the expression Access uses for the Calculated field by typing a new expression in this property line, or you can click the Builder button in the Tools group on the Design contextual tab to open the Expression Builder again.

Your new Calculated field will now concatenate the first and last names of the vendor contact with a space between the two names for each record automatically. For example, if the contact's first name is Jeff and the contact's last name is Conrad, Access displays the text Jeff Conrad in your ContactFullName field. Note that all Calculated fields are read-only— you cannot type anything into these fields, nor can you adjust their data through any other means such as using macros. Remember that Access recalculates the Calculated field whenever any dependent field values are changed.

CAUTION

Don't use the ampersand sign (&) for string concatenation in web apps. Traditional Access desktop databases support the use of both the ampersand (&) and the plus sign (+) for concatenation of strings. However, web apps support only the use of the plus (+) for string concatenation. If you attempt to use the ampersand sign (&) in an expression with string values, you'll receive an error when you attempt to save the expression. Be aware that this also means that if you enter just one part of a contact name (for example, Jeff for the first name) and leave the last name part blank, the result of the contact name is blank, because + NULL = NULL in this case. You can work around this issue by using the Coalesce function as follows: Coalesce([ContactFirstName],")+" "+Coalesce([ContactLastName],").

Defining field validation rules for web apps

To define a simple check on the values that you allow in a field in a web app, you can enter an expression in the Validation Rule property for the field. Access won't allow you to enter a field value that violates this rule. Access performs this validation for data whenever you attempt to save data changes to the entire record. In general, a field validation expression consists of an operator and a comparison value. If you do not include an operator, Access assumes you want an "equals" (=) comparison. You can specify multiple comparisons separated by the Boolean operators OR and AND.

It is good practice to always enclose text string values in quotation marks. If one of your values is a text string containing blanks or special characters, you must enclose the entire string in quotation marks. For example, to limit the valid entries for a City field to two of the largest cities in the state of Washington, enter **"Seattle"** or **"Tacoma"**. If you are comparing date values, you must enclose the date constants in pound sign (#) characters, as in #07/1/2013#.

You can use the comparison symbols to compare the value in the field to a value or values in your validation rule. Comparison symbols for web apps are summarized in Table 3-4. For example, you might want to ensure that a numeric value is always a positive number. To do this, enter **>0**. You can use one or more pairs of comparisons to ask Access to check that the value falls within certain ranges. For example, if you want to verify that a number is in the range of 100 through 200, enter **>=100 AND <=200** or **Between 100 AND 200**. Another way to test for a match in a list of values is to use the IN comparison operator. For example, to test for states surrounding California, enter **[YourFieldName] IN ("Oregon", "Nevada", "Arizona")**. If all you need to do is ensure that the user enters a value, you can use the special comparison phrase **IS NOT NULL**.

TABLE 3-4 Comparison symbols used in validation rules for web apps

Operator	Meaning
NOT	Use before any comparison operator except IS NOT NULL to perform the converse test. For example, [FieldName] NOT IN ("Seattle") is equivalent to [FieldName]<>"Seattle".
<	Less than.
<=	Less than or equal to.
>	Greater than.
>=	Greater than or equal to.
=	Equal to.
<>	Not equal to.
IN	Test for equal to any member in a list; comparison value must be a comma-separated list enclosed in parentheses.
BETWEEN	Test for a range of values; comparison value must be two values (a low and a high value) separated by the AND operator.
LIKE	Test a Text field to match a pattern string.
IS NOT NULL	Requires the user to enter a value in the field.

> **Note**
>
> In the initial release of Access 2013, to use the NOT operator against a literal value, you need to also use the IN comparison operator. For example, the expression [City] NOT "Seattle" does not work. Instead, use the expression [City] NOT IN ("Seattle") to test that the data in a City field is not Seattle.

If you need to validate a Text field against a matching pattern (for example, a postal code or a phone number), you can use the LIKE comparison operator in web apps. You can provide a text string as a comparison value that defines which characters are valid in which positions. Web apps understand two wildcard characters, characters that you can use to define positions that contain any single character or zero or more characters. These characters are shown in Table 3-5.

TABLE 3-5   LIKE wildcard characters

Character	Meaning
_ (underscore)	Any single character.
%	Zero or more characters; use to define leading, trailing, or embedded strings that don't have to match any specific pattern characters.

You can also specify that any particular position in the Text field can contain only characters from a list that you provide. You can specify a range of characters within a list by entering the low value character, a hyphen, and the high value character, as in [A-Z] or [3-7]. If you want to test a position for any characters except those in a list, start the list with a caret symbol (^). You must enclose all lists in brackets ([ ]). In the following table, you can see examples of validation rules using LIKE in web apps.

Validation Rule	Tests For
LIKE "[0-9] [0-9] [0-9] [0-9] [0-9]"	A U.S. 5-digit ZIP Code
LIKE "[0-9] [0-9] [0-9] [0-9] [0-9]-[0-9] [0-9] [0-9] [0-9]"	A U.S. 9-digit ZIP+ Code
LIKE "[A-Z][0-9][A-Z] [0-9][A-Z][0-9]"	A Canadian postal code
LIKE "[0-9] [0-9] [0-9]- [0-9] [0-9]-[0-9] [0-9] [0-9] [0-9]"	A U.S. Social Security number
LIKE "Conrad%"	A string that begins with Conrad[1]
LIKE "%conrad[0-9][0-9]%"	A string that contains conrad followed by two numbers, anywhere in the string
LIKE "%%00[0-9] [0-9] [0-9] [0-9]"	An eight-character string that contains any first two characters followed by exactly two zeros and then any four digits
LIKE "[^0-9BMQ]%[0-9][0-9][0-9][0-9]"	A string that contains any character other than a number or the letter B, M, or Q in the first position and ends with exactly four digits

[1] Character string comparisons in Access 2013 web apps are case-insensitive. So, conrad, CONRAD, and Conrad are all equal.

In the Vendors table of the Restaurant App you've been building, the EmailAddress field could benefit from the use of a validation rule. Open the Vendors table in Design view, if it isn't already open, click into the EmailAddress row, click into the Validation Rule property for this field, and then click the Builder button in the Tools group on the Design contextual tab. Access opens the Expression Builder dialog box, as shown in Figure 3-23. In the EmailAddress field, we want to be sure that the email address provided by the user appears to be a valid email address. We can verify that the email address meets most standards of valid syntax by using a combination of the LIKE operator and wildcard characters in a field validation rule. In the blank text box at the top of the Expression Builder dialog box, type **[EmailAddress] Is Null Or (([EmailAddress] Like "%@%.%") And ([EmailAddress] Not Like "%[,;]%"))** for the field validation rule, as shown in Figure 3-23. This field validation rule ensures that every email address provided by the user starts with at least one character followed by the @ symbol, contains at least one more character following the @ symbol, and contains the dot symbol followed by at least one more character after the dot symbol. Also, this field validation rule does not allow a space, a comma, or a semicolon anywhere in the email address.

Figure 3-23 Type your field validation rule into the Expression Builder dialog box.

Note

In web apps, you must provide the field name in the validation rule expression. If you do not include the field name in the expression, Access in some cases inserts the field name into the expression when you save the table changes or tab off the Validation Rule property line. Access does not always include the field name in more complex expressions, usually ones that include the AND or OR operators. If your expression does not function as you expect, make sure you've included the field name as the preceding example shows.

Click OK to save your changes to the field validation rule and dismiss the Expression Builder dialog box. You should now add an appropriate custom validation text to display to users if they provide data to the EmailAddress field that does not pass your new field validation rule. Move your focus to the Validation Text field property line. Type the following custom message into the field property: **The e-mail address you provided does not appear to be valid.** You now have a completed field validation rule and message for the EmailAddress field that will be enforced whenever you add or edit data into this table. Be sure to click the Save button on the Quick Access Toolbar to save this latest change to your table definition. Your field validation rule and message on the property lines should match Figure 3-24.

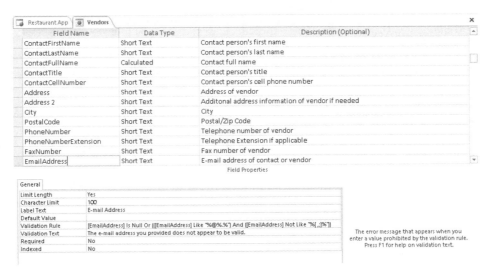

Figure 3-24 Your completed field validation rule and custom message for the EmailAddress field should look like this.

Defining a table validation rule for web apps

Table validation rules are handy when the values in one field are dependent on what's stored in another field. You need to wait until the entire row is about to be saved before checking one field against another.

In the Restaurant App you have been creating, we need an Appointments table to track day to day appointments of managing the restaurant. This table requires a table validation rule. Click the Table button in the Create group on the Home ribbon tab to get started. On the Add Tables screen, click the Add A New Blank Table link to begin creating a new table in Design view. Define that table now using the specifications in Table 3-6. Be sure to rename the ID field Access provides for you to **AppointmentID**, and then save the table and name it **Appointments** when you're finished. Be sure to also set both the StartTime and EndTime fields as required fields by selecting the Required property. Make sure you select Date and

Time for the Subtype property of the StartTime and EndTime fields and General Date for the Display Format property.

TABLE 3-6 Field definitions for the Appointments table

Field Name	Data Type	Description	Character limit	Display format
AppointmentID	ID	Unique appointment identifier		
AppointmentDescription	Short Text	Description of appointment	100	
StartTime	Date/Time with Date and Time Subtype	Start time of appointment		General Date
EndTime	Date/Time with Date and Time Subtype	End time of appointment		General Date
Notes	Long Text	Extended notes from appointment		

To define a table validation rule in a web app, open the table in Design view and then click the Validation Rule button in the Validation Rules group on the Design contextual tab, as shown in Figure 3-25. If you want IntelliSense to help with the validation rule expressions, save the table changes you've made before proceeding further.

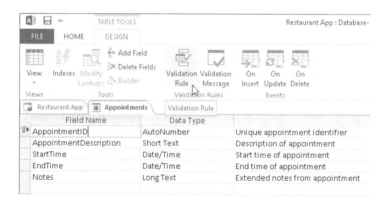

Figure 3-25 You can define table validation rules in web app tables by clicking the Validation Rule ribbon button.

Access opens the Expression Builder dialog box, as shown in Figure 3-26. For this table, we want to ensure the start time of the appointment provided by the user comes before the end time. (It certainly would not make sense to have an appointment end before it even started.) We can accomplish this by using the less than (<) operator in a table validation rule. In the blank text box at the top of the Expression Builder dialog box, type **[StartTime]<[EndTime]** for the table validation rule, as shown in Figure 3-26. This table validation rule ensures that every record in the Appointments table contains a start time that comes before the end time.

Figure 3-26 Type your table validation rule into the Expression Builder dialog box.

Click OK to save your new table validation rule and dismiss the Expression Builder dialog box. You should now add a descriptive message to display to users if they add data to a record that violates the rule in this web table. You should be careful to word this message so that the user clearly understands what is wrong. If you enter a table validation rule and fail to specify validation text, Access displays the following message when the user enters invalid data: "One or more values are prohibited by the validation rule for '*<table name>*'. Please enter a value that the expression for this validation rule can accept." Although the message does include the complete expression, it's not very pretty, is it? So I recommend that you always add a descriptive validation text to accompany your table validation rules.

To create a table validation message, click the Validation Message button in the Validation Rules group. Access now opens the Enter Validation Message dialog box, as shown in Figure 3-27. Type the following custom message into the dialog box: **The End Time for the appointment cannot be before the Start Time**. Click OK to save your changes to this property and dismiss the dialog box. You now have a completed table validation rule and message for the Appointments table. Access enforces this rule whenever you are adding or editing data in this table. Be sure to click the Save button on the Quick Access Toolbar to save this latest change to your table definition.

Chapter 3

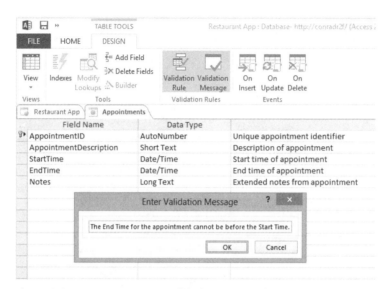

Figure 3-27 Enter your custom validation text into the Enter Validation Message dialog box.

> **Note**
>
> In Access 2013 web apps, field validation rules can refer to other fields within the same table just like table validation rules. This is a departure from previous versions of Access where field validation rules can reference only themselves in the validation expression. You might be wondering why you would use a table validation rule when field validation rules have the same functionality. If you have a validation rule that references more than one field, I recommend using a table validation rule so that you can separate out the logic from field validation rules that traditionally refer to only one field.

Defining a primary key for web apps

Every table in a relational database should have a primary key, and web apps are no exception. You'll learn later in this book that in desktop databases, you have many options available to use for a primary key. However, in web apps, you must follow a predetermined requirement that only allows the ID AutoNumber field as the primary key. From a certain perspective, this makes defining a primary key in a web app quite simple—Access creates the primary key field, the ID field, for you automatically whenever you create a new table. You cannot delete this field from your table, but you can rename the ID field to something more to your liking, such as VendorID or InvoiceID.

If you're an experienced Access developer, you might find the ID primary key restriction to be very limiting. What if you want to create a multifield primary key and set it to be unique, as you can for desktop databases? While it's true that you cannot define a unique multifield primary key in web app tables, you can create multifield indexes and enforce uniqueness across that multifield index. We'll discuss indexes in the next section.

Adding indexes

The more data you include in your tables, the more you need indexes to help Access 2013 search your data efficiently. An index is simply an internal table that contains two columns: the value in the field or fields being indexed and the physical location of each record in your table that contains that value. Access uses an index similarly to how you use the index in this book—you find the term that you want and jump directly to the pages containing that term. You don't have to leaf through all the pages to find the information you want.

Let's assume that you often search your Vendors table by city. Without an index, when you ask Access to find all the contacts in the city of Seattle, Access has to search every record in your table. This search is fast if your table includes only a few vendors but very slow if the table contains thousands of vendor records collected over many years. If you create an index on the City field, Access can use the index to find more rapidly the records for the vendors in the city you specify.

Single-field indexes

Most of the indexes you'll need to define will probably contain the values from only a single field. Access uses this type of index to help narrow the number of records it has to search whenever you provide search criteria on the field—for example, City = Seattle or PostalCode = 98101. If you have defined indexes for multiple fields and provided search criteria for more than one of the fields, Access uses the indexes together to find the rows that you want quickly. For example, if you have created one index on City and another on LastName and you ask for City = Seattle and LastName = Conrad, Access uses the entries in the City index that equal Seattle and matches those with the entries in the LastName index that equal Conrad. The result is a small set of pointers to the records that match both criteria.

Creating an index on a single field in a table is easy. Open the Vendors table in the Restaurant App you've been creating so far in Design view, and select the field for which you want an index—in this case, City. Click the Indexed property box in the lower part of the Table window, and then click the arrow to open the list of choices, as shown in Figure 3-28.

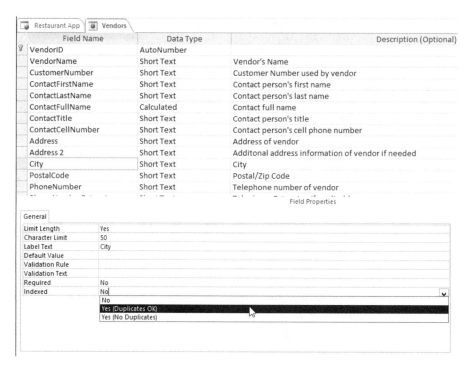

Figure 3-28 You can use the Indexed property box to set an index on a single field.

When you create a table from scratch (as you did for this Vendors table), the default Indexed property setting for all fields except the primary key is No. If you use a web app template or a Table Template to help create a table (as you did for the Tasks table earlier in this chapter), the web app template or Table Template indexes fields that might benefit from an index. If you followed along earlier using the tasks Table Template to build the Tasks table, you will find that the template built an index for the primary key (the ID field), the Task Title field, and the Assigned To field.

If you want to set an index for a field in a web app, Access offers two possible Yes choices. In most cases, a given field will have multiple records with the same value—perhaps you have multiple vendors in a particular city or multiple products in the same product category. You should select Yes (Duplicates OK) to create an index for this type of field. By selecting Yes (No Duplicates), you can have Access enforce unique values in any field by creating an index that doesn't allow duplicates. Access always defines the primary key index with no duplicates because all primary key values must be unique.

> **Note**
>
> You cannot define an index using a Hyperlink or Image field in web apps.

Multiple-field indexes

If you often provide multiple criteria in searches against large tables, you might want to consider creating a few multiple-field indexes. This helps Access narrow the search quickly without having to match values from two separate indexes. For example, suppose you often perform a search for your vendor contacts by last name and first name. If you create an index that includes both of these fields, Access can satisfy your query more rapidly.

To create a multiple-field index, you must open the Table window in Design view and open the Indexes window by clicking the Indexes button in the Tools group of the Design contextual tab on the ribbon. You can see the primary key index and the index that you defined on City in the previous section. Each of these indexes comprises exactly one field.

To create a multiple-field index, move the insertion point to an empty row in the Indexes window and type a unique name. In this example, you want a multiple-field index using the ContactLastName and ContactFirstName fields, so **FullName** might be a reasonable index name. Select the ContactLastName field in the Field Name column of this row. To add the other field, skip down to the next row and select ContactFirstName without typing a new index name. When you're done, your Indexes window should look like the one shown in Figure 3-29. Close the Indexes window when you're finished, and then click Save on the Quick Access Toolbar to save your table design changes.

> ## INSIDE OUT   Inserting new rows in the Indexes window
>
> To insert a row in the middle of the list in the Indexes window, right-click in the Index Name column and then choose Insert Rows from the shortcut menu.

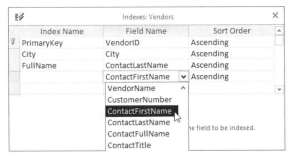

Figure 3-29 The FullName index includes the ContactLastName and ContactFirstName fields.

You can remove an existing single-field index by changing the Indexed property of a field to No on the field's property list. The only way to remove a multiple-field index is via the

Indexes window. To remove a multiple-field index, select the rows (by holding down the Ctrl key as you click each row selector) that define the index and then press Delete. Access saves any index changes you make when you save the table definition.

If you want to make a multiple-field index unique across all records, select the first field in the Indexes window that is part of the multiple-field index and then change the Unique Property in the lower-left corner of the window to Yes. You can find an example of this type of multiple-field index in the tblInvoiceHeaders table in the Back Office Software System web app (BOSS.app). In that table, you'll find a unique multiple-index that ensures there can be a specific invoice number defined only one time for each vendor. You'll learn how to create that table in the next section.

Access can use a multiple-field index in a search even if you don't provide search values for all the fields, as long as you provide search criteria for consecutive fields starting with the first field. Therefore, with the FullName multiple-field index shown in Figure 3-29, you can search for contact last name or for contact last name and contact first name. There's one additional limitation on when Access can use multiple-field indexes: only the last search criterion you supply can be an inequality, such as >, >=, <, or <=. That is, Access can use the index shown in Figure 3-29 when you specify searches such as these:

ContactLastName = "Smith"
ContactLastName > "Franklin"
ContactLastName = "Buchanan" And ContactFirstName = "Steven"
ContactLastName = "Conrad" And ContactFirstName >= "Aaron"

But Access will not use the FullName index shown in Figure 3-29 if you ask for

ContactLastName > "Davolio" And ContactFirstName > "John"

because only the last field in the search (ContactFirstName) can be an inequality. Access also will not use this index if you ask for

ContactFirstName = "John"

because the first field of the multiple-field index (ContactLastName) is missing from the search criterion.

Creating value list lookup fields in web apps

If you've been following along in this chapter, creating the Vendors table in your Restaurant App, you'll remember we are still missing one more field found in the tblVendors web table in the Back Office Software System sample web app—the State field. We defined the State field in this table to be a lookup field. A lookup field can generally be classified as one of two types—a field that "looks up" its data from a predefined list stored with the field itself or a field that looks up its data from a different table. The State field in the tblVendors table looks up its data from a predefined list I provided when I created the field. Microsoft also uses the term *value list* to describe this type of field because the field gets its data from a list of values.

Let's create this State lookup field in the Vendors table that you've been working on. Open the Vendors table in Design view if you closed it. Next, select the PostalCode field so that the focus is in that field. (Remember that Access creates the new field above the field that currently has focus.) Now, click the Add Field button in the Tools group on the Design contextual tab to insert a new blank field row. Enter **State** in the Field Name column, and then select Lookup from the drop-down list of options in the Data Type column, as shown in Figure 3-30.

INSIDE OUT Inserting new rows in the table design window

In addition to the ribbon command to insert new fields into the table design window, you can also add new fields by right-clicking a row and then clicking Insert Rows on the shortcut menu.

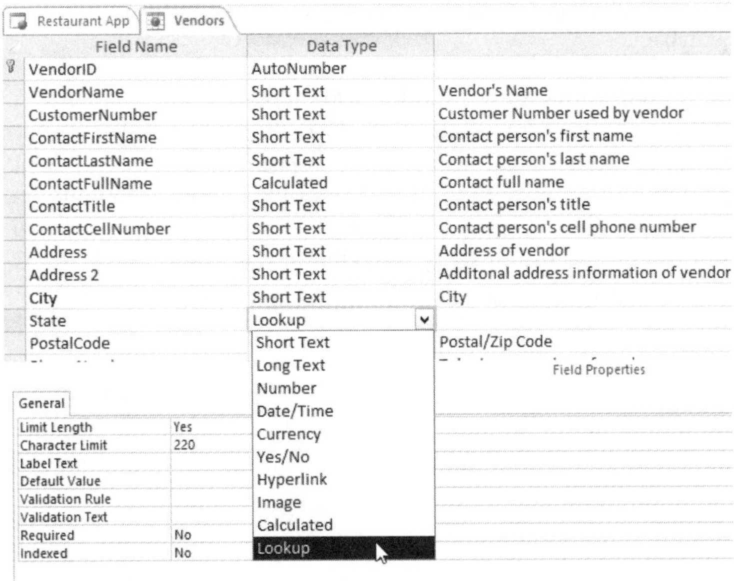

Figure 3-30 Select Lookup from the Data Type column to start creating your lookup field.

Access opens the Lookup Wizard, shown in Figure 3-31, and displays the first page. You must use this wizard if you want to create lookup fields in web apps. The first page of the wizard needs to know where you want to get the values for the field. You can either choose to have the values come from another table or query or type in the values yourself. (We'll discuss the first option in the next section of this chapter.) Select the second option—I Will Type In The Values That I Want.

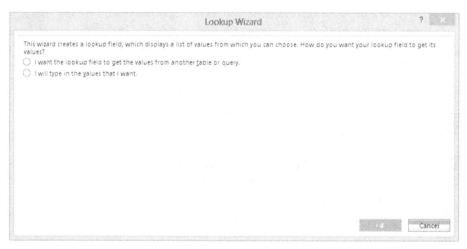

Figure 3-31 The Lookup Wizard walks you through the steps necessary to create a lookup field for your table.

Access now displays a large text box in the lower portion of Lookup Wizard, as shown in Figure 3-32. Access needs to know what values specifically you want displayed for this field. By default, Access shows one column in the drop-down list of choices for the lookup field. In the middle of the dialog, Access displays a text box where you can type in the specific values you need—one per row. In Figure 3-32, you'll notice that I typed in the first five state abbreviations in alphabetical order. Enter several state abbreviations now, and then click OK to save your lookup values and dismiss the Lookup Wizard.

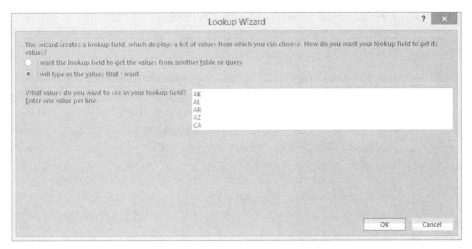

Figure 3-32 Type in values on the Lookup Wizard to display as choice options for your lookup field.

Access returns you to the table design window. Tab over to the Description column, and enter **State** for the description of this new field. The Data Type column displays Lookup, which means you cannot see the list of values available for this field. To view the list of options for this lookup field again, click anywhere on the State row and then click the Modify Lookups button in the Tools group on the Design contextual tab. Access reopens the Lookup Wizard, where you can make adjustments to your available options and save the changes for your value list lookup field. Be sure to click the Save button on the Quick Access Toolbar to save this latest change to your table definition.

Working with data in preview datasheets

You've now completed creating all of the fields and field properties necessary in your vendors table. To view, change, insert, or delete data in a table from within Access, you can use the table's Datasheet view. A datasheet is a simple way to look at your data in rows and columns without any special formatting.

Whenever you create a new web table, Access automatically creates two views that you can start using immediately for data entry in your web browser. These two views have captions of List and Datasheet, respectively, in the View Selector. The datasheet view that Access creates and displays in the View Selector is not the same datasheet you see when you open a table in Datasheet view within Access. These two views are distinct objects within Access. When you open a table in Datasheet view, you can add, edit, and delete records directly within Access instead of using a web browser. (Internally, Microsoft refers to a table datasheet as the *preview* datasheet.) You cannot make any design changes, such as adding additional controls, to a table's preview datasheet. Whenever you add or remove fields from your table, Access regenerates the table preview datasheet to include those schema changes. (You'll learn all about the two views Access creates when you add a new table in Chapter 6.)

You can open a table's preview datasheet by right-clicking the table name in the Navigation pane and selecting Open from the shortcut menu. You can also click the table name in the Table Selector, click the gear charm, and then select View Data from the shortcut menu. When you open a table in Design view, such as the Vendors table you've been working on, you can also switch to the preview datasheet view of this table, shown in Figure 3-33, by clicking the arrow in the Views group on the ribbon and clicking Datasheet View from the list of available views. Likewise, when you're in a preview datasheet, you can return to Design view by clicking the arrow in the Views group and clicking Design View from the available options. Switch to the preview datasheet of the vendors table now using one of these methods.

> **Note**
>
> Access does not display Image data types in a table preview datasheet.

Figure 3-33 Use the View button on the ribbon to switch from Design view to Datasheet view.

INSIDE OUT   Switching views from object tabs

You can also switch between Design view and Datasheet view for tables by right-clicking the object tab at the top of the application window and then clicking either Design View or Datasheet View on the shortcut menu.

As in Design view, you can move from field to field in the Table window in a preview data-sheet by pressing Tab, and you can move up and down through the records using the arrow keys. You can also use the scroll bars along the bottom and on the right side of the window to move around in the table. You can click the Refresh button in the ribbon to see the most recent changes made to the data by other users accessing the data.

You can start entering data in a new record by clicking the Add Action Bar button in the upper-left corner of the datasheet view. To delete a record, highlight the record by clicking the record selector on the left side of the row, or click in any field in the record, and then click the Delete Action Bar button. You can also delete a record by right-clicking the record selector for a specific row and then clicking Delete on the shortcut menu or by clicking the record selector for a specific row and then pressing the Delete key. Access prompts you for confirmation before deleting any records from the preview datasheet.

INSIDE OUT   Selecting multiple rows in preview datasheets

If you want to select multiple contiguous rows in the preview datasheet, click the row selector for the first row in the group and scroll until you can see the last row in the group. Hold down the Shift key, and click the row selector for the last row in the group. The first and last rows and all rows in between will be selected. Release the Shift key. You can extend the selection to multiple contiguous fields by holding down the Shift key and pressing the Up and Down Arrow keys to select multiple rows.

If you want to select multiple rows that are separated from each other in sequential order, hold the Ctrl key and click each row selector that you'd like to select. Access high-lights each row as you click the row selector. Release the Ctrl key when finished. When a row or several rows are highlighted in the preview datasheet, pressing Ctrl+C copies the contents of the row to the Clipboard. You can also press Ctrl+X to delete the row and copy the contents to the Clipboard.

When you tab or click into the State field for the vendors table, Access displays a down arrow on the right edge of the field. When you click that arrow, Access displays all the state abbreviations you typed into the Lookup Wizard, as shown in Figure 3-34.

Figure 3-34 Your completed lookup field now displays the list of values you provided in the Lookup Wizard.

If you open the tblVendors table in the Back Office Software System web app (BOSS.app), switch to see the preview datasheet, and then tab to the State field, you'll notice that Access displays a drop-down list of states, as shown in Figure 3-35.

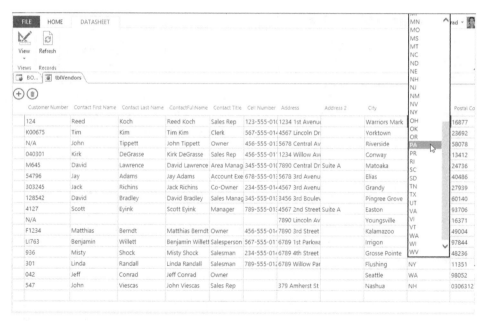

Figure 3-35 The State field in the tblVendors table is a Lookup Field that displays a list of state abbreviations.

Creating relationships using lookup fields

The process of creating relationships between tables in web apps is different from creating relationships in desktop databases. In desktop databases, you generally create all the tables and fields you need and then create relationships between the various tables using the Relationship window. However, in web apps, you do both of these steps at the same time through the Lookup Wizard. What this means to you as an Access developer is that you cannot fully complete child tables before you complete the parent tables. For example, in a desktop database, you could create a vendor field in an invoice table to hold the vendor ID even before you created the vendor table itself. After you create the vendors table, you could then link the invoice and vendor tables on the appropriate fields using the Relationship window. In a web app, the vendor table must exist before you can actually create fields in child tables (the invoice or other tables) that you intend to link to the vendor table. You cannot add relationships to existing fields in web apps; you must create the relationship at the time you create the field.

Thus far in this chapter, you have seen how to build one of the main subject tables of the Back Office Software System web apps—Vendors. You also created a generic Appointments table in your Restaurant App. To show you how to create relationships in web apps, we first need to create another main subject table—Report Groups—and then a parent and child table—Invoice Headers and Invoice Details—to track the invoices that list all our food purchases.

We'll first create all the fields for these three tables and then add the linking field last. Table 3-7 shows you the fields you need to create for the Report Groups table that holds the information for the report groups we use to track all the various expenditures for the restaurant. Click Table on the Home ribbon tab to open the Add Tables screen, and then click the Add A New Blank Table button to begin creating your new table. In addition to the definitions listed in Table 3-7, set the Required property for both the ReportGroupName and AccountNumber fields to Yes and the Indexed property to Yes (No Duplicates). Notice that we are using a Short Text data type for the AccountNumber field because the account numbers could contain alphanumeric characters.

TABLE 3-7   Field definitions for the Report Groups table

Field Name	Data Type	Description	Field Size
ReportGroupID	ID	ID Field (AutoNumber)	
ReportGroupName	Short Text	Report Group name	50
AccountNumber	Short Text	Account Number for accounting purposes	50
AccountDescription	Short Text	Optional description for additional information	255

The Report Groups main table has all the fields we need, but the Invoice Details table depends on this table, so you need to create this Report Group table first. After you define all the fields, save the table as **Report Groups**.

Table 3-8 shows you the fields you need to define for the Invoice Headers table that holds the parent information about each invoice the restaurant receives. In addition to the

Chapter 3

definitions listed in Table 3-8, set the Required property for the InvoiceDate, InvoiceNumber, and InvoiceNumber fields to Yes and the Indexed property of the InvoiceDate field to Yes (No Duplicates).

TABLE 3-8   Field definitions for the Invoice Headers table

Field Name	Data Type	Description	Field Size	Display Format
InvoiceID	ID			
InvoiceDate	Date/Time with Date Subtype	Date of the invoice		Short Date
InvoiceNumber	Short Text	Invoice number shown on invoice	50	
InvoiceAmount	Currency	Total Invoice amount		
Comments	Long Text	Any additional comments		
IsBalanced	Yes/No	Invoice balanced?		

The Invoice Headers table needs to know from which vendor this invoice came. We'll create that field and relationship to the Vendors table in just a moment. Save this table as **Invoice Headers** after you create the necessary fields and field properties.

You need one last table, the Invoice Details table, to track the invoices for the Restaurant App. Table 3-9 shows the fields you need to create. This table needs the InvoiceID from the Invoice Headers table and the ReportGroupID from the Report Groups table to track all the line items from the invoice. We'll create those fields in just a moment. Save this last table as **Invoice Details**.

TABLE 3-9   Field definitions for the Invoice Details table

Field Name	Data Type	Description	Required
InvoiceDetailsID	ID		
ReportGroupAmount	Currency	Amount for this Report Group	Yes

Defining a restrict delete relationship

Now you're ready to start defining relationships between these tables. Each vendor in our Restaurant App can have more than one invoice. This means Vendors and Invoice Headers have a one-to-many relationship. To create the relationship you need, open the Invoice Headers table in Design view and place the focus in the InvoiceDate field so that the new field will appear above the InvoiceDate field. Next, click the Add Field button in the Tools group on the Design contextual tab to insert a new row above the InvoiceDate field. In the Field Name column, enter **VendorIDFK** (the FK is a just a shorthand way of saying foreign key) and then select Lookup from the drop-down list of options in the Data Type column. Access opens the Lookup Wizard dialog box, as shown in Figure 3-36.

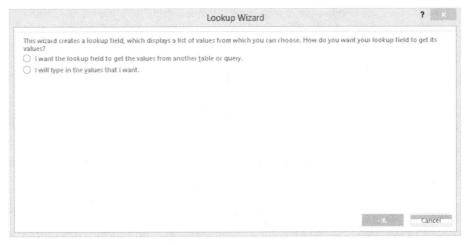

Figure 3-36 To create a new lookup field with a relationship to another table, you need to select the first option on the Lookup Wizard.

When the wizard first opens, Access needs to know where you want to fetch the values for this new lookup field. To create a new field that has a relationship between a different table in a web app, select the first option—I Want The Lookup Field To Get The Values From Another Table Or Query, as shown in Figure 3-37.

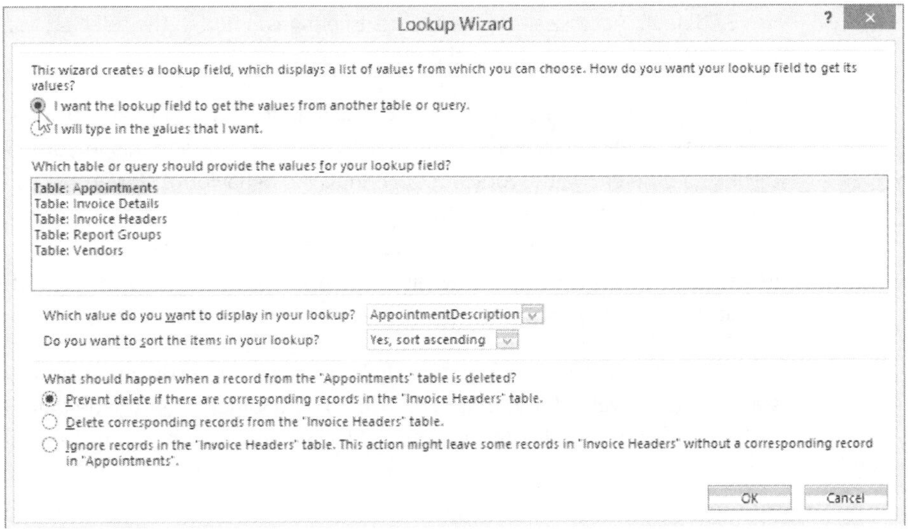

Figure 3-37 Access displays additional options after you select the first option in the lookup Wizard.

Access now displays new options in the wizard below the options for selecting a data source. Access needs to know which table or query you want to use to provide the values for your new lookup field. We want to store the vendor who produced the invoice in the Invoice Headers table, so select the Vendors table from the list, as shown in Figure 3-38.

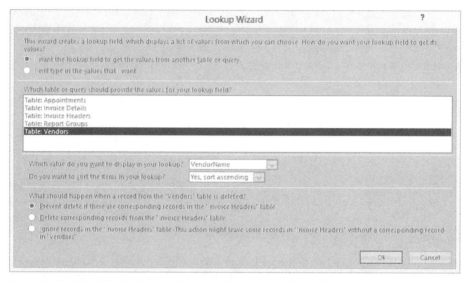

Figure 3-38 Select the Vendors table to provide a source of data for your new lookup field.

After you select the Vendors table, you can select which field to use as a display value for your lookup field in the Which Value Do You Want To Display In Your Lookup drop-down list. By default, Access selects the first text field it can find in the selected table. Leave the selected field, VendorName, as the display value.

When you create a lookup field that gets its data from another table or query in a web app, Access stores the AutoNumber ID field from the related table in your lookup field but displays a different value. You cannot change the behavior of storing the ID field, but you can choose what field you want to display in the lookup field. Access enforces the relationships on the server through the ID field. Note that you can set the ID field to be the display value; however, users of your database will find it much easier to choose, for example, a vendor name from a list rather than just a list of vendor ID numbers.

In the Do You Want To Sort The Items In Your Lookup drop-down list, you can choose to sort the display value for your lookup field in ascending order (the default), descending order, or no sort at all. For this lookup field, leave the default setting, Yes, Sort Ascending.

INSIDE OUT   Self join relationships are supported in web apps

If you want to create a self join relationship in a web app, select the same table that you are creating the new lookup field in on the Lookup Wizard. You can then select another field you want to use for the display value for your new lookup field. For example, a self join relationship could be useful when you have a table of employees and one of the fields contains the name of the employee they report to in the organization.

At the bottom of the Lookup Wizard, you'll see three options pertaining to how Access should behave if you delete a record in the related table—the Vendors table, in this case. Your decision here determines the type of relationship created between the two tables with this lookup field and whether to enforce referential integrity. If you select the default first option—Prevent Delete If There Are Corresponding Records In The "Invoice Headers" Table, Access ensures that you cannot delete any records from the Vendors table if they have invoices still defined. Also, Access ensures that you can't add a row in the Invoice Headers table containing an invalid VendorID. This type of relationship is a *restrict delete* relationship, because you cannot delete a record in a parent table if there are records using that value in a child table.

If you select the second option—Delete Corresponding Records From the "Invoice Headers" Table—Access deletes child rows (the related rows in the *many* table of a one-to-many relationship) when you delete a parent row (the related row in the *one* table of a one-to-many relationship). For example, if you remove a vendor from the Vendors table, Access removes all the related Invoice Header rows. This type of relationship is a *cascade delete* relationship, because Access removes related records in the child table when you delete a record in the parent table.

If you select the last option to ignore records at the bottom of the Lookup Wizard, Access takes no action on any records in the Invoice Headers when you delete a record in the Vendors table. Selecting this option means Access does not enforce any referential integrity between the two tables. In this situation, you could have records in the Invoice Headers containing a VendorID that no longer exists in the Vendors table.

In this design, when you delete a vendor, you don't want to remove all invoices for accounting purposes, so leave the default option set, which creates a restrict delete relationship. Click OK to complete the steps necessary to create your lookup field with a relationship to the Vendors table, and close the Lookup Wizard. Access returns you to the Table Design window. You'll notice that Access sets the Indexed property for the lookup field to Yes (Duplicates OK). Enter **Foreign Key From Vendors** in the Description column, enter **Vendor** in the Label Text property, and then set the Required field property to Yes.

Chapter 3

In Figure 3-39, you can see the completed VendorID lookup field in the Invoice Headers table. Click the Save button on the Quick Access Toolbar to save these latest definition changes.

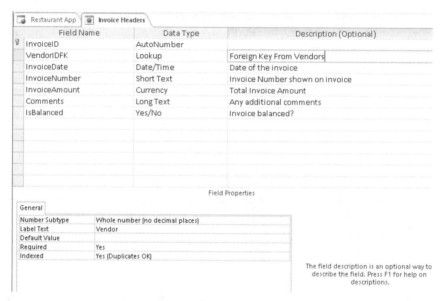

Figure 3-39 You can create a lookup field to the Vendors table and enforce referential integrity for the data.

> **Note**
> When you save your changes to the Invoice Headers table after adding the lookup field, Access might prompt you with a message indicating that data integrity rules changed. Click Yes to let Access check your data and complete saving your changes.

If you need to modify this lookup field or its relationship, you can highlight the field in Design view and click the Modify Lookups button in the Tools group on the Design contextual tab. Access opens the Lookup Wizard where you can adjust the properties of the lookup field and then save the changes.

You now know enough to define the additional one-to-many restrict delete relationship that you need in the Invoice Details table. You need to include the ReportGroupID field from the Report Groups table in the Invoice Details table, so open the Invoice Details table in Design view and set the focus on the ReportGroupAmount field.

Follow this procedure to build your restrict delete relationship:

1. Click the Add Field button in the Tools group on the Design contextual tab to insert a new row above the ReportGroupName field. Enter **ReportGroupIDFK** in the Field Name column, and then tab to the Data Type column.

2. Start the Lookup Wizard by selecting Lookup from the drop-down list of data types in the Data Type column.

3. Select the I Want The Lookup Field To Get The Values From Another Table Or Query option.

4. Select the Report Groups table from the list of tables and queries.

5. Select the ReportGroupName field as the display field for your new lookup field.

6. From the drop-down list of sorting options, keep the default setting Yes, Sort Ascending.

7. Leave the default relationship option Prevent Delete If There Are Corresponding Records In The Invoice Details Table selected. This option prevents you from deleting a record in the Report Groups table if there are corresponding related records in the Invoice Details.

8. Click OK to complete the new field and relationship, and close the Lookup Wizard.

9. Enter **Foreign Key from Report Groups** in the Description column, enter **Report Group** in the Label Text property, and set the Required property to Yes.

10. Finally, save your changes to the Invoice Details table.

Defining a cascade delete relationship

There's one last relationship you need to define in the Restaurant App between Invoice Details and Invoice Headers. The relationship between these two tables requires a cascade delete relationship. When an invoice is deleted in the Invoice Headers table (the *one* side of the relationship), you want to ensure that all corresponding child records in the Invoice Details table (the *many* side of the relationship) are deleted. Open the Invoice Details table in Design view again if you've previously closed it.

Follow this procedure to build your cascade delete relationship:

1. Click the Add Field button in the Tools group on the Design contextual tab to insert a new row above the ReportGroupIDFK field. Enter **InvoiceIDFK** in the Field Name column, and then tab to the Data Type column.

2. Start the Lookup Wizard by selecting Lookup from the drop-down list of data types in the Data Type column.

3. Select the I Want The Lookup Field To Get The Values From Another Table Or Query option.

4. Select the Invoice Headers table from the list of tables and queries.

5. Select the InvoiceNumber field as the display field for your new lookup field. We'll use the invoice numbers to display because that will be easier for users of the app to reference.

6. From the drop-down list of sorting options, keep the default setting Yes, Sort Ascending.

7. Change the default relationship to Delete Corresponding Records From The Invoice Details table, as shown next. This option instructs Access to delete all related child records in the Invoice Details table when you delete a record from the Invoice Headers table.

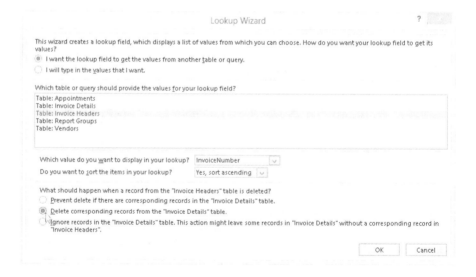

8. Click OK to complete the new field and relationship, and close the Lookup Wizard.

9. Enter **Foreign Key from Invoice Headers** in the Description column, enter **Invoice** in the Label Text property, and set the Required property to Yes.

Your completed Invoice Details table should now look like Figure 3-40.

Figure 3-40 You now have two lookup fields to two different tables in your Invoice Details table.

> **Note**
>
> If you want to compare the results of your work, the sample web app called Restaurant-Sample.app, which can be downloaded from the book's catalog page, contains all the tables you created in this chapter. To use this prepared sample app, you'll need to upload the app to the SharePoint corporate catalog, install the app, and then download the app into Access. See the section "Installing app packages," in Chapter 2, if you need help with any of those steps.

Importing and linking data into web apps

You can certainly enter from scratch all the data into your empty tables in a new web app; however, in many cases, you'll have some of the data you need already stored in other files or applications. For example, you might have an employee list in a spreadsheet or a text file, or your list of products might be in an Access desktop database. Access includes import wizards to help you bring the data into your new web app. You can import data into a web app that's in text files, spreadsheets, other Access desktop databases, SharePoint lists, and any SQL database that supports the Open Database Connectivity (ODBC) software standard. You can also create read-only links to SharePoint lists inside the same SharePoint farm where your Access Services web app resides.

In Access web apps, you can import tables and data only from the data sources mentioned above, and the only data sources you can link to are SharePoint lists. (In Article 3, "Importing and linking data," which can be downloaded from the book's catalog page, you will learn how to import tables, objects, and data into Access desktop databases and to link to different data sources.) There is overlap between the topic of importing and linking with web apps and desktop databases, but there are also many important differences. Access uses the same wizard dialog screens for importing both in desktop databases and in web apps. However, Access, in general, presents fewer options and different messages on the wizard dialog screens when you are working with web apps.

As you read through the material here in the following sections concerning importing and linking with web apps, I recommend you read through Article 3 because that article goes deeper into topics such as preparing data for import from other sources and creating data source name (.dsn) files, which can also be helpful when you are importing from ODBC data sources into web apps.

Considerations for importing lookups

When you're importing fields with relationships from a desktop database into Access web apps, you should be aware of some important considerations. Access attempts to create lookup fields with relationships whenever possible, but depending on various rules and how you set up the relationships in the source desktop database, Access might not be able to create lookup fields or create relationships during the import process.

To successfully import a lookup field into a web app and preserve any enforced relationships, the bound field of the lookup in the source desktop database table *must* be the primary key of the table and be an AutoNumber data type. If the bound field of the lookup from the source table is any other data type besides AutoNumber, Access does not create a corresponding lookup field in the web app.

In general, Access defines a lookup field and its relationships during an import process in the following order:

1. If the column is a lookup field with an enforced relationship, Access creates the lookup and drops any other relationships on the column.

2. If the column is a lookup field without an enforced relationship, Access attempts to create a lookup field. If Access encounters an error creating the field, Access does not create the lookup and all other relationships on that column are dropped.

3. If Access encounters a column with an enforced relationship, Access converts the column to a lookup field and sets appropriate properties.

4. If Access does not detect any enforced relationships on the column, no attempt is made to define a lookup or to create a relationship on the field in the web app.

When Access creates a lookup field during an import process, it must choose a display field to use from the list of fields in the same table. Access uses three rules here in deciding which column to use as the display field. Access first attempts to use the existing display field defined for the lookup in the source desktop database table. If Access cannot use that field, because of restrictions in web app tables, Access then tries to use the first text field it can find in the source table. If Access cannot find a suitable field using any of those attempts, Access defaults to using the bound field of the lookup as the display field.

> **Note**
>
> If you import a value list lookup from a desktop database table into a web app, Access creates a matching value list lookup field in the web app table with appropriate values. You can modify the values after the import process by clicking the Modify Lookups command on the ribbon.

When importing a lookup field from a desktop database table that is in a relationship with another table, you must import both tables at the same time for Access to successfully create an enforced lookup field in the web app. For example, when you import only the child table that includes an enforced relationship from the source desktop database, Access creates a field with the same data type as the source field in the web app and imports the data but does not create a relationship. Similarly, if you have already imported the parent table and then run a separate import operation to import the child table, Access does not create the relationship between the child and parent table.

If you create a lookup field in a desktop database table that looks up its values from a query, by default, Access does not enforce referential integrity. When you import this type of a field into a web app, Access imports the field as a lookup field and attempts to use the source table that the query was based on for the data in the lookup field. However, in this scenario, Access does not define any relationship in the web app lookup field because the lookup field in the desktop database table does not have a relationship defined. You can define a relationship after the import process completes by opening the table in Design view and clicking the Modify Lookups command in the ribbon.

Chapter 3

INSIDE OUT Understanding the workflow during import

Access follows a specific pattern when importing lookups and relationships behind the scenes. Access first imports the table schemas from the source file into its own data engine and then creates the matching schemas on the server. Next, Access imports the data from the source file into its own data engine and then uploads the data to the server in batches of up to a thousand records at a time. Finally, Access imports any relationships and lookup properties into its own data engine from the source tables and then sends those properties and relationships to the server for processing. During the last step of this process, if Access receives any notification of errors from the server concerning relationships, Access converts the field that had an error into a non-lookup field.

Importing Access desktop database tables

If you have data in an Access desktop database, you can import data from any of the local tables contained in the desktop database. You cannot import linked tables from desktop databases into web apps. If you need to import a linked table from a desktop database, you'll need to open that data source separately and then have Access import the table and data directly from that data source. Table 3-10 includes information about the data types Access creates when you import tables from desktop databases, specific notes about formatting issues you should be aware of, and the data type Access creates in the SQL Server database that stores your web app.

TABLE 3-10 Access desktop database data type import conversions

Data Type	Details	SQL Server data type created
AutoNumber	Access creates its own ID field AutoNumber with each new table, so when you import this field, Access creates a Number field to hold this data.	Int
Text	Access imports Text fields as Short Text in web apps.	nvarchar with length from 1 to 4000
Memo	Access imports Memo fields as Long Text in web apps. Access does not import any Rich Text formatting from Memo fields into web apps.	nvarchar(max)

Data Type	Details	SQL Server data type created
Number	Access imports all Number fields from desktop databases as Number in web apps, except for Number fields formatted as ReplicationID. For Number fields with ReplicationID formatting, Access creates a Short Text data type in the web app table.	Long Integer, Byte, and Integer formatted Number fields become int; Single, Double, and Decimal formatted Number fields become float; ReplicationID formatted Number fields become Short Text nvarchar(60)
Date/Time	Access imports all Date/Time formats as Date/Time from desktop databases. If you have Time only formatted Date/Time fields, Access preserves the zero date of 12/30/1899 during the import process.	Date with Time (datetime2(3))
Currency	Access imports Currency fields in desktop databases as Currency data types in web apps. If you have a Euro format Currency field, Access sets the Currency Symbol property to Euro during the import process.	decimal(28,6)
Yes/No	Access imports Yes/No fields from desktop databases as Yes/No data types in web apps. Access web app Yes/No fields do not accept NULL values, so Access sets these values to No during the import process.	Bit
Hyperlink	Access imports Hyperlink fields from desktop databases as Hyperlink data types in web apps. If you have display text embedded in the hyperlink data, Access preserves the display text.	nvarchar(max)
Calculated	Access does not import Calculated fields from desktop databases as Calculated data types in web apps, because the expression syntax between desktop databases and web apps differs. As a result, Access imports the calculated display data but does not import the expression. Access creates a data type in the web app that matches the result type of the Calculated field from the desktop database. After Access imports the data, you can re-create a new Calculated field with an expression compatible with web apps.	Depends on the result type of the incoming data

Chapter 3

Data Type	Details	SQL Server data type created
Lookup	Access imports value list lookup fields from desktop databases as Lookup data types in web apps. Access preserves the available lookup options, and you can view those options by opening the Lookup Wizard. Access imports Lookup fields to tables as Lookup data types. Web apps do not support Multi-Value Lookup fields. If you import this type of field from a desktop database, Access creates a Long Text data type and stores a semicolon-delimited list of values from the Multi-Value Lookup field. If you import a Lookup field that looks up the data from a saved query object instead of a table, Access attempts to create a Lookup data type based on the table that serves as the source for the query in the desktop database.	Depends on the type of lookup. Value List Lookups become nvarchar and Multi-Value List Lookups become nvarchar(max). Lookups to related tables become int.

> **Note**
>
> Access web apps do not support OLE Object and Attachment data types. If you attempt to import tables from a desktop database that contain these data types, Access excludes those fields and displays an error when the import process completes. You'll see an error on the import result page informing you that OLE Object and Attachment fields are not supported in web apps.

In nearly all cases, Access does not import field and table properties from desktop database tables into web apps. For example, Access does not import default values, required properties, field validation rules, and indexes. Access also does not import table level validation rules and any data macro logic attached to table events. (You'll learn about data macros in Chapter 4, "Creating data macros in web apps.") However, Access does import field descriptions and captions from desktop database tables and assigns those values to the properties on the new fields created in the web app tables.

Troubleshooting

Why did my field names change after I imported them?

Access web app field names do not allow many special characters or combination of characters to be used in field names. However, it is possible that you might have field names that include special characters in desktop databases and other data sources. During the import process, if Access finds any special characters in field names, it replaces each special character with an underscore (_). The special characters and combination of characters that Access replaces with an underscore are the following: / \ : * ? " < > | # { } % ~ & <TAB> ; '.

You can import data into an existing Access web app or a new, blank Access web app. In the following importing sections, you might consider creating a new, blank web app if you want to follow along. To import data from an Access desktop database into a web app, perform the following steps:

1. Click the Table button in the Create group on the Home contextual tab to display the Add Tables screen. Next, click the Access button at the bottom of the Add Tables screen in the Create A Table From An Existing Data Source section, as shown here.

Add Tables

Create a new table using our templates

What would you like to track?

Suggested searches: Person, Order, Service, Sell

Use the Search box to search for the type of tables you would like to add to your app. Click an item in the result list and it will be added automatically.

Don't want to use one of our tables or didn't find what you were looking for? No problem, just add a new blank table instead.

Create a table from an existing data source

Access   Excel   SQL Server /   Text / CSV   SharePoint
ODBC Data   List

Import data from an Access client database.

Choose the type of data source you would like to bring into your app and we'll guide you through the necessary steps.

What do you think about the Add Tables screen? Give Feedback Online

2. Access opens the Get External Data - Access Database dialog box, shown here.

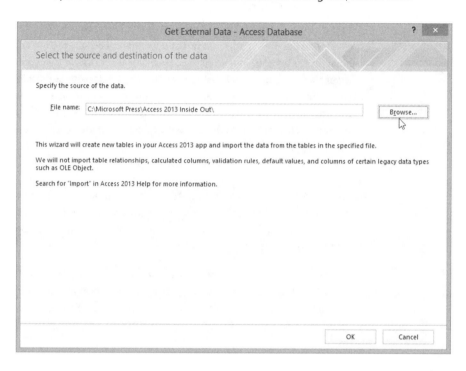

3. Click Browse to open the File Open dialog box, shown next. Select the folder and the name of the .accdb, .mdb, .mda, .accda, .mde, or .accde file containing the data that you want to import, and then click Open. If you want to follow along with this example, select the RestaurantData.accdb desktop database file found in the online sample files.

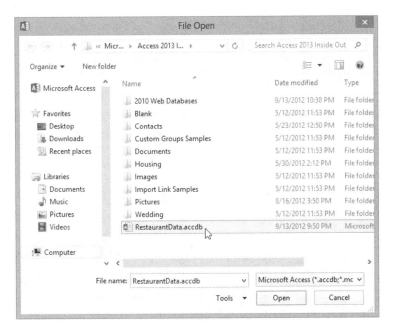

4. Access returns you to the Get External Data - Access Database dialog box with the file path to the Access desktop database file that you need in the File name box. Click OK. Access opens the Import Objects dialog box, shown here, which provides a list of all the tables in the desktop database you selected. Select the specific table you want to import.

If you select a table in error, you can click the name again to deselect it. If you want to import all tables, click Select All. You can import multiple tables by clicking each table name in turn that you want to import.

You can also click the Options button (which I clicked in the preceding illustration) to select additional options. If you import any tables from the source desktop database, you can select the option to import the table relationships (if any) defined for those tables in the source desktop database. You can also select the option to import the table structure (the table definition) only or to import the structure and the stored data. Click OK to import the tables you selected into the current web app.

5. Access displays a message that informs you of the result of the import procedure, as shown here.

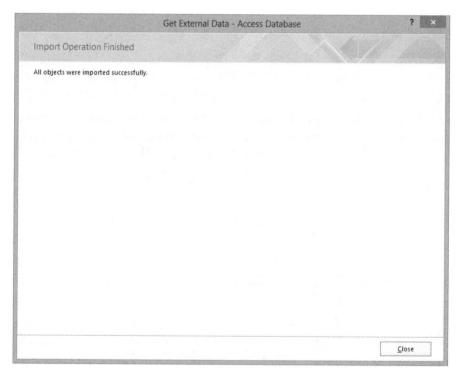

6. If the import procedure is successful, each new table in your web app you imported will have the name of the table you selected in the desktop database. If Access finds a duplicate name, it generates a new name by adding a unique integer to the end of the name.

7. Click Close to dismiss the message that confirms the import procedure.

8. Access creates a new tile and two new views—a list detail and datasheet view—for each table you import from the desktop database, as shown below. Access also imports the data from your desktop database table into the new web app table if you previously selected to include the Definition and Data—the default option.

Chapter 3

Note

If the source Access desktop database is a secured .mdb or.mde file created in a previous version of Access, you must have at least read permission for the database and read data permission for the tables to import the tables.

INSIDE OUT   Handling gaps in AutoNumber fields

If you have AutoNumber ID fields in desktop databases, in many cases you'll probably have gaps in the number sequence from records that you've deleted or records that you've started and then canceled before saving. When you import a table from a desktop database that has an ID AutoNumber field, Access imports the raw data into the default AutoNumber ID field first and then sets the auto numbering properties on the field. What this means is that the ID values are preserved through the import process, including any gaps to maintain data integrity with any related tables.

Importing a spreadsheet

To import a spreadsheet into a web app, do the following:

1. Click the Table button in the Create group on the Home contextual tab to display the Add Tables screen. Next, click the Excel button at the bottom of the Add Tables screen in the Create A Table From An Existing Data Source section, as shown here.

2. Access opens the Get External Data - Excel Spreadsheet dialog box, shown next.

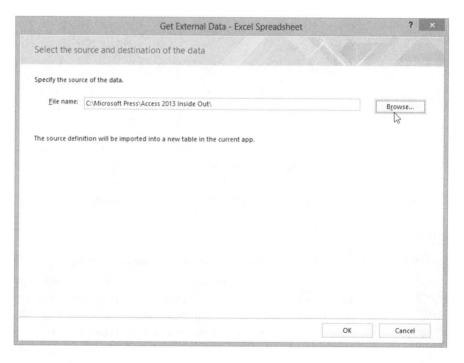

3. Click Browse to open the File Open dialog box shown in the previous import example. Select the folder and the name of the spreadsheet file that you want to import, and click Open to return to the Get External Data - Excel Spreadsheet dialog box. If you want to follow along with this example, select the Companies.xlsx file found in the online sample file folder called Import Link Samples.

4. If the spreadsheet contains multiple worksheets or any named ranges, Access shows you the first window of the Import Spreadsheet Wizard, as shown in the following illustration. (If you want to import a range that isn't yet defined, exit the wizard, open your spreadsheet to define a name for the range you want, save the spreadsheet, and then restart the import process in Access.) Select the worksheet or the named range that you want to import, and click Next to continue.

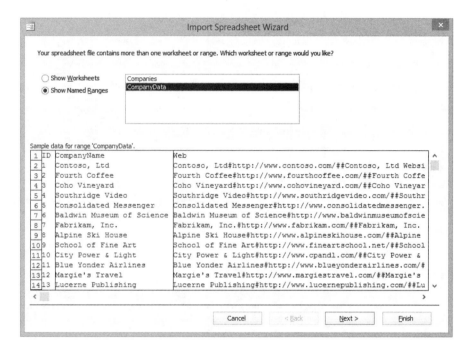

5. After you select a worksheet or a named range, or if your spreadsheet file contains only a single worksheet, the wizard displays the following page.

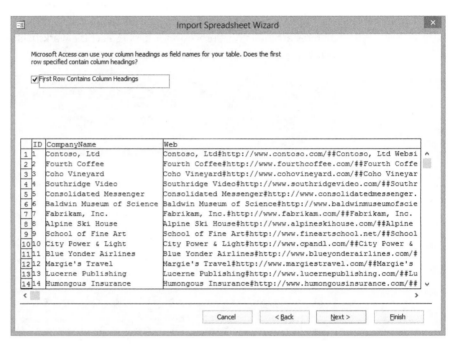

Select the First Row Contains Column Headings check box if you've placed names at the tops of the columns in your spreadsheet. Click Next to go to the next step.

6. On the next page, you can scroll left and right to the various fields and tell the wizard what field names you want to use, what data types to use, and which fields you want to import or skip.

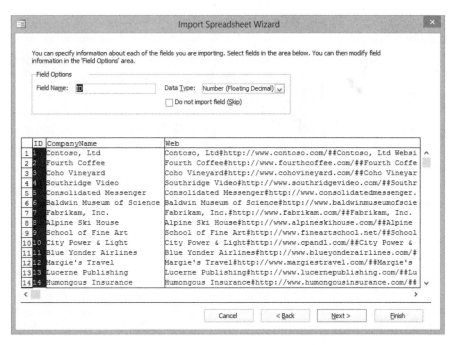

As you move from field to field, the Data Type box displays the data type that the wizard chooses for each field (based on the data it finds in the first few rows). If what you see here is incorrect, click the arrow and select the correct data type from the list. Access allows you to select the correct data type on this page of the Import Spreadsheet Wizard. Notice that Access creates an AutoNumber field called ID in each new web app table automatically. If you already have a field called ID in your spreadsheet, as is the case in this example, Access generates a new name for the default ID field by adding a unique integer to the end of the name. You can also choose to eliminate certain columns that you don't want to appear in the final table. For example, it's quite common to have intervening blank columns to control spacing in a spreadsheet that you print. You can eliminate blank columns by scrolling to them and selecting the Do Not Import Field (Skip) check box. Click Next to go to the next step.

7. Click Next to go to the final page of the wizard, where you can change the name of your new table. (The Import Spreadsheet Wizard uses the name of the spreadsheet or the named range you chose in step 4.) If you enter the name of an existing table, Access asks whether you want to replace the old table. Access deletes any views associated with that existing table as well.

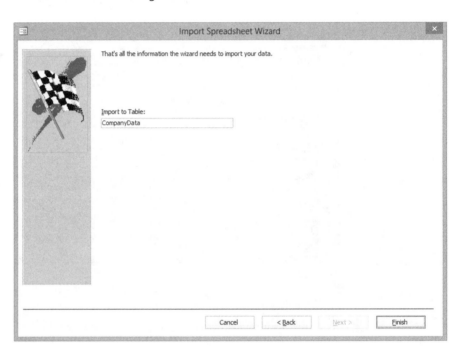

8. Click Finish on the last page to import your data. Access opens a dialog box that indicates the result of the import procedure. If the procedure is successful, the new table will have the name you entered in the last step. If Access found errors importing the data, Access displays detailed information about any data it could not import, as shown below, using this example data.

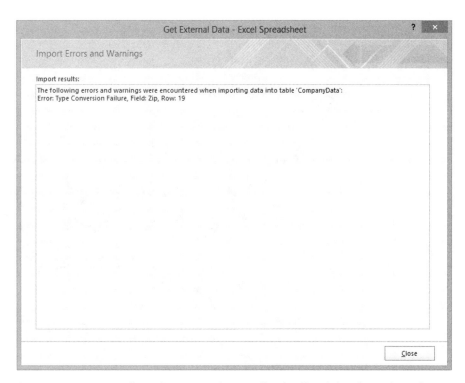

Access creates a new tile and two new views—a list detail and datasheet view—for each worksheet or a named range in your spreadsheet.

Importing SQL tables

To import a table from another database system that supports ODBC SQL (such as SQL Server or Oracle), you must first have the ODBC driver for that database installed on your computer. Your computer must also be linked to the network that connects to the computer running SQL Server from which you want to import data, and you must have an account on that server. Check with your system administrator for information about correctly connecting to the computer running SQL Server.

To import data from a SQL table, do the following:

1. Click the Table button in the Create group on the Home contextual tab to display the Add Tables screen. Next, click the SQL Server/ODBC Data button at the bottom of the Add Tables screen in the Create A Table From An Existing Data Source section, as shown here.

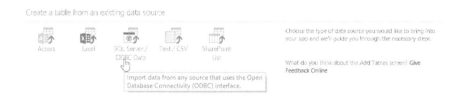

2. Access opens the Get External Data - ODBC Database dialog box, shown here. This dialog displays information about ODBC data sources. Click OK to continue.

3. Access opens the Select Data Source dialog box, shown here, from which you can select the data source that maps to the computer running SQL Server that contains the table you want to import. You can select a data source name (.dsn) file that you've created previously, or click the Machine Data Source tab, as shown here, to see data sources that are already defined for your computer.

If you don't see the data source you need, see the section "Creating a data source to link to an ODBC database," in Article 3, which can be downloaded from the book's catalog page for instructions. After you select a data source, click OK.

4. When Access connects to the server, you'll see the Import Objects dialog box, which lists the available tables on that server, as shown here.

Chapter 3

5. From the list of tables or list of files, select the ones you want to import. If you select a table name in error, you can click it again to deselect it or you can click the Deselect All button to start over. Click OK to import the SQL tables you selected.

6. If the import procedure is successful, the new table will have the name of the SQL table. If Access finds a duplicate table name, it will generate a new name by adding a unique integer to the end of the name, as explained earlier. Access creates a new tile and two new views—a list detail and datasheet view—for each table you import from the SQL Server database.

Importing a text file

Before you can import a text file, you'll probably need to prepare the data for Access. In Article 3, you can learn about this process in the section "Preparing a text file." After you do that, you can import the text file into an Access web app by doing the following:

1. Click the Table button in the Create group on the Home contextual tab to display the Add Tables screen. Next, click the Text / CSV button at the bottom of the Add Tables screen in the Create A Table From An Existing Data Source section, as shown here.

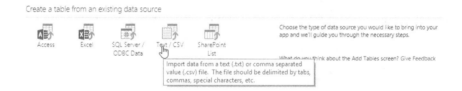

2. Access opens the Get External Data - Text File dialog box, shown here.

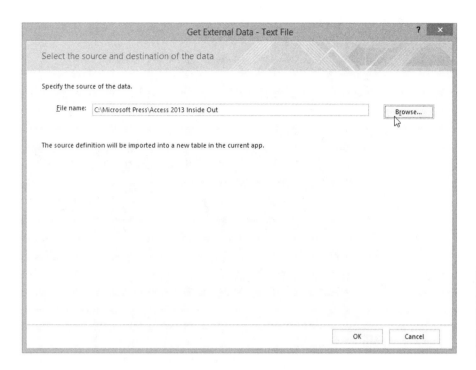

3. Click Browse to open the File Open dialog box, shown previously in the first import example. Select the folder and the name of the text file that you want to import, and click Open to return to the Get External Data - Text File dialog box. If you want to follow along with this example, select the CompaniesTab.txt file found in the online sample file folder called Import Link Samples.

4. Access starts the Import Text Wizard and displays the first page of the wizard, shown next.

On this page, the wizard makes its best estimation about whether the data is delimited or fixed-width. It displays the first several rows of data, which you can examine to confirm the wizard's choice. If the wizard has made the wrong choice, your data is probably formatted incorrectly. You should exit the wizard and fix the source file as suggested in "Preparing a text file," in Article 3. If the wizard has made the correct choice, click Next to go to the next step.

5. If your file is delimited, the Import Text Wizard displays the following page:

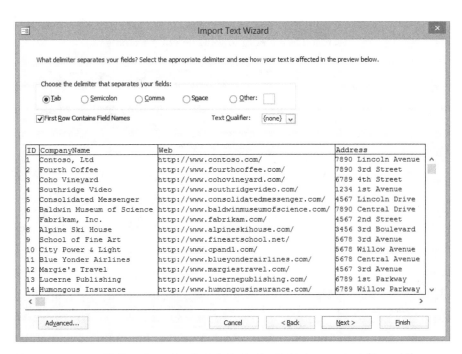

Here, you can verify the character that delimits the fields in your text file and the qualifier character that surrounds text strings. When you save a delimited text file from a spreadsheet program, the field delimiter is usually a tab character, and you'll find quotation marks only around strings that contain commas. If the wizard doesn't find a text field with quotation marks in the first few lines, it might assume that no text is surrounded by quotes, and therefore, it might set the Text Qualifier field to {none}. You might need to change the Text Qualifier field from {none} to " if this is the case. Also, be sure to select the First Row Contains Field Names check box if your file has column names in the first row. If you don't do that, the wizard assigns generic field names (Field1, Field2, and so on) and might misidentify the field data types.

If your file is in fixed-width format, the wizard displays the following page. (I have scrolled to the right to show one of the problems.)

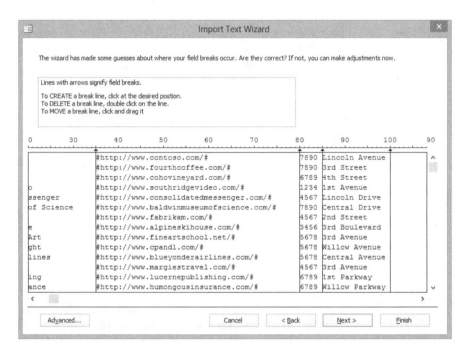

Instead of showing delimiting characters, the wizard offers a graphic representation of where it thinks each field begins. To change the definition of a field, you can drag any line to move it. You can also create an additional field by clicking at the position on the display where fields should be separated. If the wizard creates too many fields, you can double-click any extra delimiting lines to remove them. In the example shown in the preceding illustration (using the CompaniesFIX.txt file, which can be downloaded from the book's catalog page), the wizard assumes that the address number is separate from the name of the street. (For example, 7890 and Lincoln Ave, in the first row, should not be separated into two fields.) It also assumes that the State and zip fields are one field. Because many of the spaces in the sample Comments field line up, it splits this field into several fields. You can double-click the line following the street number to remove it. You can click between the state and zip data to separate those into two fields. Finally, you can double-click all the extra lines the wizard inserted in Comments to turn that into one field. Click Next to go to the next step.

6.   The wizard displays the next page shown here. Use this page to specify or confirm field names (you can change field names even if the first row in the text file contains names), select field data types, and set indexed properties. If you're working in a fixed-width text file, you should provide the field names; otherwise, Access names the fields Field1, Field2, and so on. Click Next to continue.

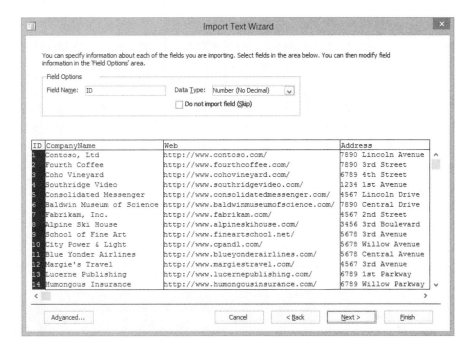

7.   On the final page of the wizard, you confirm the name of the new table. If you enter the name of an existing table, Access asks whether you want to replace the old table. Click Finish to import your data. Access displays a confirmation message at the top of the Get External Data - Text File dialog box to show you the result of the import procedure. If the wizard encounters an error that prevents any data from being imported, it displays information about the import errors on the import results dialog. Access creates a new tile and two new views—a list detail and datasheet view—for the text file.

Importing a list from a SharePoint site

In Microsoft SharePoint terminology, a table is referred to as a list that stores information about a single subject. In a list, you have columns (fields) that contain the different kinds of information about the subject. To import or link to a list from a SharePoint site into an Access web app, you need to have appropriate permissions to the SharePoint site. Contact your SharePoint administrator to give you permissions if you are having trouble accessing the SharePoint list.

Importing a list from a Microsoft SharePoint site works in much the same way as importing a table from other data sources, such as text files, spreadsheets, other Access desktop databases, or SQL databases. In this case, you are downloading data from a Microsoft SharePoint site and saving a local copy of the data in an Access web app table.

To import data from a SharePoint list into a web app, do the following:

1. Click the Table button in the Create group on the Home contextual tab to display the Add Tables screen. Next, click the SharePoint List button at the bottom of the Add Tables screen in the Create A Table From An Existing Data Source section, as shown here.

2. Access opens the Get External Data - SharePoint Site dialog box, shown here.

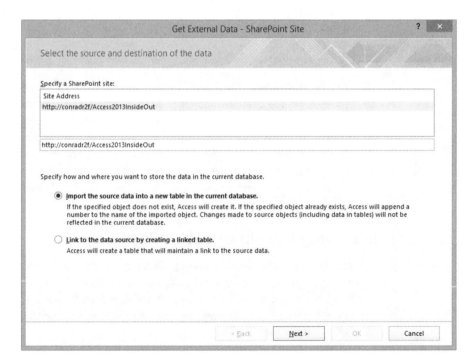

You can use this wizard to either import or link to SharePoint Services lists. (We'll discuss linking in the next section.) Under Specify A SharePoint Site, enter a valid address to a SharePoint Services site or subdirectory. If you're using Office 365, you can enter the URL to your team site or subsite where your Access web app is stored. Any SharePoint Services sites that you have previously imported from, linked to, or exported to are displayed in a list box. If one of these sites is the location from which you want to import the table, you can click that address and Access fills in the address text box below the list with that link. Enter a valid SharePoint Services address in the text box, or select a previously visited SharePoint Services address from the list box. Select the first option, Import The Source Data Into A New Table In The Current Database, to import the list and records to a local table, and then click Next.

3. The second page of the wizard, shown in the following illustration, displays all the lists found in the SharePoint Services site directory that you specified on the previous page. Select the check box in the Import column to specify which list to import into your web app. The Type column displays icons representing the different types of lists. The Name column displays the names of the lists on the SharePoint site. The fourth column, Items To Import, shows a list of views. If the list has more than one view defined in SharePoint, you can select which specific view you want to import. The default view, All Items, is the only view defined in the example Products List I'm importing. The last column, Last Modified Date, displays the date the list was last modified.

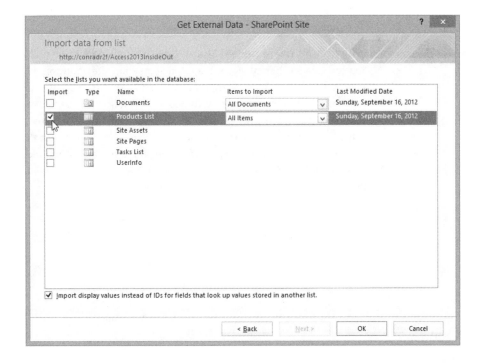

Near the bottom of this page is an option to import the display values from any lookup fields instead of the actual lookup field ID. If you think a list has one or more related lookup lists and you want to fetch the linking ID instead of the lookup value, clear this check box so that you fetch the actual ID value. For example, if an Orders list is related to a Customers list, clearing this check box fetches the Customer ID instead of the customer name that might be defined in a lookup. If you leave this item selected, you'll see the customer name imported in the Customer ID field. In this case, there are no related or lookup tables for my sample Products List, so this option does not apply. If you are unsure whether a list has more than one related lookup list, you can browse to the SharePoint site and check the field properties for the list columns.

4. Select the check box for the list you want to import, leave the other options set to their defaults, and then click OK to begin the import process. Access creates a new local table in your web app, imports the records, and then also creates a default list detail and datasheet view to accompany your new table. After Access completes the import process, Access displays the import operation result on the last page of the wizard. A message at the top of this page indicates whether the import process was a success or whether any problems were encountered. Click Close to dismiss the wizard. Remember that you've made a copy only of the data stored on the SharePoint site. Any changes you make to the local copy in your web app won't be reflected in the SharePoint site list.

Troubleshooting

Why doesn't my imported SharePoint list include all the records?
You can create different views of a list in SharePoint sites. You can define filters, include only certain columns, and assign sort orders to a custom view. If your custom view restricts the number of records returned, Access follows those rules and imports only those specific records. For example, if you define a custom view that shows only products whose price is less than one hundred dollars and then import that view into your web app, the only records imported are ones where the product price is less than one hundred dollars. If you need to import all the records into your web app, make sure that you import a view that returns all the records in the list.

Linking a SharePoint list into a web app

You can also link to a SharePoint list so that you can process it with queries and views in your web app. You can read the data only if you link to a SharePoint list. This ability to link data is especially important if the data is continually changing in the source SharePoint list.

INSIDE OUT   Linked SharePoint lists become SQL Server views

If you link to a SharePoint list in your web app, Access creates a SQL Server view instead of a logical table in the SQL Server database to represent that element. A SQL Server view is not the same thing as a view in an Access web app. A view in SQL Server is a virtual table much like what a query is in Access. In Access web apps, you work with different view types to add, edit, and delete data from within your web browser.

To link to a SharePoint list from a web app, do the following:

1. Click the Table button in the Create group on the Home contextual tab to display the Add Tables screen. Next, click the SharePoint List button at the bottom of the Add Tables screen in the Create A Table From An Existing Data Source section, as shown here.

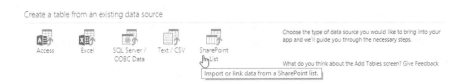

2. Access opens the Get External Data - SharePoint Site dialog box, shown here.

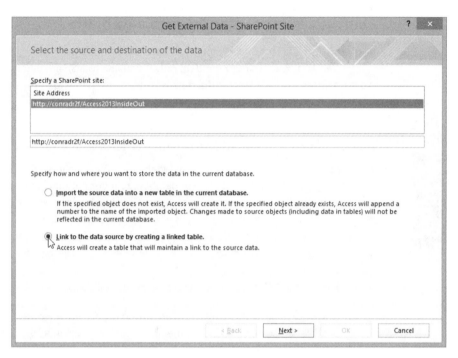

This particular wizard is the same one you used for importing lists from a SharePoint site in the previous section. Enter a valid SharePoint address in the address text box below the list of previously visited sites, or select a previously visited SharePoint address from the list box. Select the second option, Link To The Data Source By Creating A Linked Table, to link to an existing list on a SharePoint site, and then click Next.

3. The second page of the wizard, shown in the following illustration, displays all the lists found in the SharePoint site directory that you specified on the previous page. Select a check box in the Link column to specify which list you want to link to your web app. The Type column displays icons representing the type of list. The Name column displays the names of the lists on the SharePoint site. The last column, Last Modified Date, displays the date the list was last modified. When you are linking to SharePoint lists, Access links only to the default view created for the list. You cannot link to other views of the list as you can with importing lists. Select the Link check box next to the list that you want to link to, and then click OK to start the linking process.

INSIDE OUT   Link to Document Libraries

If you link to a SharePoint Document Library in your web app, Access displays the document name as a hyperlink when you open the view for the table in your web browser. When you click the link in your web browser, Windows attempts to open the document with the associated program.

4. On the third page of the wizard, shown next, Access needs you to confirm that you trust the SharePoint list. To link to the SharePoint list, you must agree to allow the web app to access information from the SharePoint site. Click Trust It to continue linking to the SharePoint list. You'll see a consent message like this for each list that you attempt to link to in the SharePoint site.

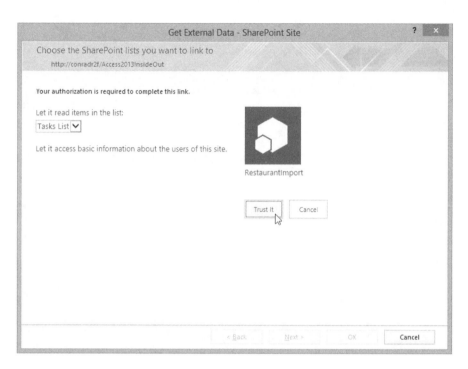

5. Access creates a new linked table in your web app and also creates a default list detail and datasheet view to accompany your new linked table. If Access finds a duplicate name, it generates a new name by adding a unique integer to the end of the name, as described earlier. Note that you've made a linked table to the data stored on the SharePoint site. The link is read-only, so you will not be able to make inserts, edits, or deletes to the records in this list from inside the web app. However, you can use the values in the linked list as a basis for lookup fields in other tables in your web app.

When you link to a SharePoint list in your web app, Access also displays ID, Created, Created By, Modified, and Modified fields in the views that it creates for the new linked table. These fields are internal fields included with each SharePoint list. Share-Point automatically fills in values for these fields as records are added or updated in the SharePoint list. If the SharePoint list you link to in your web app includes a Choice field, Access displays the data in your web app for this field as a semicolon delimited list of values in a text box control.

Access displays a maximum of 15,000 records from any linked SharePoint list inside an Access web app. This is a hard limit that cannot be changed. Also, if you create a query to return records from a linked SharePoint list, Access returns a maximum of 10,000 records in your web app. If your query returns more than 10,000 records, Access displays an error message when you attempt to execute the query.

INSIDE OUT   Refresh a linked list to see schema changes

If you add, edit, or delete columns in a linked SharePoint list, you won't see the updates from your Access web app. To see the latest schema and data changes to a linked SharePoint list, open the linked table in Datasheet view in Access and then click the Refresh button in the Records group on the Datasheet contextual ribbon. For all other table and query datasheets, clicking Refresh refreshes only the data, but when you use click Refresh with a linked SharePoint list, Access refreshes any schema changes as well. Access also updates the quick created list details and datasheet views for the linked list with any schema changes.

Troubleshooting

Why do my linked SharePoint lists not work after installing them from an app package?

In Chapter 2, you learned how to save a web app into an app package, which you can then upload and install on your SharePoint server. If you package up a web app with linked SharePoint lists, those linked tables will not work after you create a new web app from the app package. To have the links work in the new web app you created from the app package, you'll need to delete the linked tables, relink them, and confirm that you trust the links to the SharePoint lists again.

In this chapter, you've taken the first steps to learn how to create a web app. You've learned how to create a web app from scratch and create your schema and relationships between different tables. You've also learned how to import data from other sources into a web app and link to SharePoint lists. In the next chapter, you'll learn how to add logic to tables by creating data macros and attaching them to table events.

Creating data macros in web apps

IN Microsoft Access 2013, you can define a data macro to respond to different types of table events that would otherwise require the use of writing macros attached to view and control events. The unique power of data macros in Access 2013 is their ability to automate responses to several types of table events without forcing you to learn a programming language. The event might be a change in the data, the creation of a new record, or even the deletion of an existing record. Within a data macro, you can include multiple actions and define condition checking so that different actions are performed depending on the values in your table fields or criteria you specify.

> **Note**
>
> The examples in this chapter are based on the backup copy of the Back Office Software System sample web app (BOSSDataCopy.app), which can be downloaded from the book's catalog page at *http://aka.ms/Access2013IO/details*. To use the sample, you'll need to upload the app into your corporate catalog or Office 365 team site and install the app. Review the instructions at the end of Chapter 2, "Exploring the Access 2013 web app interface," if you need help with those tasks.

In this chapter, you will:

- Learn about the various types of actions that you can define in data macros and the table events that you can use.

- Tour the logic designer facility and learn how to build both a simple data macro and a data macro with multiple defined actions.

- Learn how to create local variables in data macros to store values temporarily or calculate a result.

- See how to define parameters and use them inside data macro actions.

- Learn how to create return variables in data macros to return data to the calling macro.

- See how to add conditional statements to a data macro to control the actions that Access performs.

- Learn how to create named data macros and execute them from other data macros or table events.

- Understand some of the actions automated with data macros in the Back Office Software System sample web app.

Uses of data macros

Access 2013 provides various types of data macro actions that you can attach to table events as well as inside named data macro objects to automate your web app. With data macros, you can do the following:

- Verify that an invoice is balanced with the invoice detail line items before saving the record.

- Mark an employee as inactive after you create a termination record.

- Prevent any data from being edited, added, or deleted from a table.

- Create new schedule records based on the previous week's schedule or a labor plan template.

- Delete all schedule records within a specific time frame.

As you'll learn in Chapter 8, "Automating a web app using macros," Access 2013 supports *user interface macros* to control application flow in your views and to respond to user actions. You can also utilize user interface macros to enforce complex business logic that might not be covered by table relationships, unique properties, validation rules, and required properties. However, the potential problem with using user interface macros to enforce complex business logic is that you don't always have complete control over how users interact with the data in your tables. For example, users can add, update, and delete data through table and query datasheets. (You'll learn about queries in Chapter 5, "Working with queries in web apps.") Users can also link to the tables in one Access app from an Access desktop database and add, update, and delete data from that database. In both of these examples, users can bypass your complex business logic rules normally stored in user interface macros.

Access 2013 web apps include data macros to provide a place for Access developers to centralize all their business logic and rules. Data macros get translated to triggers and stored procedures in Microsoft SQL Server, and they allow you to attach business logic directly to table events. Because data macros are translated into SQL Server triggers and stored procedures, they are performed within a transactional context—each operation is separate. Data macros attached to table events respond to data modifications, so no matter how users edit data in the web app, SQL Server enforces those rules. This means that you can write business logic in one place, and all the data entry views that update those tables inherit that logic from the data layer. After you create a data macro for a table event, Access runs the data macro no matter how you change the data.

Data macros in Access 2013 can be used in both web apps and desktops databases. However, the events, actions, and expressions that you can use in data macros are not identical between web apps and desktop databases. The Access database engine enforces data macros when you work with a desktop database. When you are using a web app, SQL Server enforces data macros on the server through the use of triggers and stored procedures. (In Chapter 22, "Creating data macros in desktop databases," which can be downloaded from the book's catalog page, you'll learn how to create data macros in desktop databases.)

Touring the Logic Designer

Install the Back Office Software System backup copy sample web app (BOSSDataCopy.app) on your team SharePoint site, and then download the app into Access so that you can follow along with all of the examples in this chapter.

To create data macros, you first need to open a table in Design view. To display all the tables in your BOSSDataCopy web app, click the Navigation Pane button in the Show group on the Home ribbon tab. Double-click the table called tblCompanyInformation to open it in Design view, and then click the Design contextual ribbon tab to see the data macro events, as shown in Figure 4-1.

Chapter 4

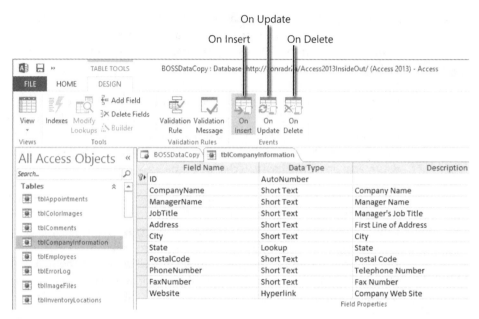

Figure 4-1 Data macro events are listed on the Design contextual ribbon tab under Table Tools in web apps.

You can attach data macros to the On Insert, On Update, and On Delete events of tables. In Figure 4-1, in the Back Office Software System sample web app, you can see that Access highlighted the On Insert and On Delete buttons on the Design contextual ribbon tab. When you create and save a data macro for a table event, Access highlights that event button in the ribbon as a visual cue for you to show that a data macro already exists for that event. To create a new data macro for a table event or edit an existing one, you click the corresponding event button in the ribbon.

Let's explore the existing data macro that I defined for the On Insert event in the tblCompanyInformation table to show you the Logic Designer for creating macros. Click the On Insert button on the Design contextual ribbon tab, and Access opens the Logic Designer, as shown in Figure 4-2.

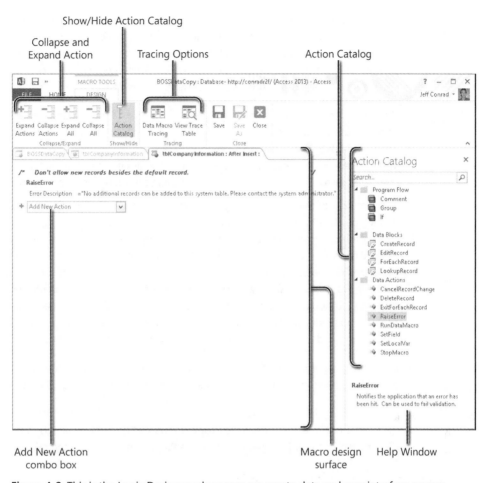

Figure 4-2 This is the Logic Designer, where you can create data and user interface macros.

Whenever you need to create or edit data macros or user interface macros in Access 2013, this is the design surface that you use. You'll notice that Access automatically collapsed the Navigation pane to show you more of the macro design surface. Access also opens the Logic Designer window modally, which means that you cannot open any other database objects until you close the designer window.

As you can see in Figure 4-2, the Logic Designer layout looks more like a Visual Basic code window in desktop databases. The Expand Actions, Collapse Actions, Expand All, and Collapse All buttons in the Collapse/Expand group selectively expand or collapse the actions listed in the macro design surface. In the Show/Hide group on the Design tab, you can choose to hide the Action Catalog shown on the right side of the Logic Designer window by clicking the Action Catalog toggle button. In the Tracing group, Access displays options to turn on data macro tracing and to display the tracing table to analyze any issues you might have executing your data macro logic. In the Close group, you can click Save to save any changes to your data macro. Click Close to close the Logic Designer window. If you attempt to close the Logic Designer window with unsaved changes, Access asks whether you want to save your changes before closing the window.

On the right side of the Logic Designer window is the Action Catalog. The Action Catalog shows a contextual list of the program flow constructs, data blocks, and data actions that are applicable to the data macro event you are currently viewing. (When you create user interface macros, the Action Catalog similarly displays actions that you can use for user interface macros.) We'll discuss the Action Catalog in more detail in the next section.

In the middle of the Logic Designer window is the main macro design surface where you define your data macro. You add program flow constructs, macro actions, and arguments to the design surface to instruct Access what actions to take for the data macro. If you have more actions than can fit on the screen, Access provides a scroll bar on the right side of the macro design surface so that you can scroll down to see the rest of your actions. You'll notice in Figure 4-2 that Access displays any arguments directly beneath the action. Access displays a combo box called Add New Action at the bottom of the macro design surface. This combo box displays a list of all the actions you can use for the type of data macro you are creating and the specific context of where you are in the data macro logic.

In the lower-right corner of the Logic Designer window is the Help window. Access displays a brief help message in this window, depending on where the focus is located in the Action Catalog.

Click the Close button in the Close group on the Design contextual tab to return to the Design view of the tblCompanyInformation table, and then close the table.

Working with table events

As I mentioned in the previous section, you can attach data macros to the On Insert, On Update, and On Delete table events. In the following sections, you'll learn about each of these events, create new data macros attached to events, and examine other data macros attached to these events in the Back Office Software System sample web app.

In On Insert and On Update events, you can look at the incoming values in the current record and compare them with a record in other tables using the LookupRecord data block. You can use the SetField data action to alter data before Access commits the changes but only on the incoming row of data, not on a record returned from the LookupRecord data block. In all table events, you can prevent a record from being saved or deleted and display custom error messages to the user using the RaiseError data action.

Using On Insert events

The On Insert event fires whenever you add new records to a table. Let's create a new data macro attached to the On Insert event of the tblWeekDays table to illustrate the process of creating, saving, and testing a new data macro. Open the tblWeekDays table in Design view, click the Design contextual tab under Table Tools, and then click the On Insert button in the Events group to open the Logic Designer, as shown in Figure 4-3.

Figure 4-3 Click the On Insert button on the ribbon to begin creating your data macro.

> **Note**
>
> You might have noticed in Figure 4-3 when you started your new On Insert data macro that the caption on the top of the object window displays After Insert. The Logic Designer for data macros is shared between web apps and desktop databases. Although you're seeing a different caption, you are, in fact, creating an On Insert table event data macro.

Troubleshooting

Why can't I add data macros to linked SharePoint lists?

In Chapter 3, "Designing tables in a web app," you learned how to link SharePoint lists into your web app. In web apps, tables linked to SharePoint lists are read-only and cannot be opened in Design view. Therefore, you cannot attach data macros to any table events for linked SharePoint lists. You also cannot reference linked SharePoint lists in any LookupRecord, CreateRecord, or ForEachRecord data blocks attached to other web app table events or in any named data macros.

In the Action Catalog on the right side of the Logic Designer, you can see three options under Program Flow, four options under Data Blocks, and eight options under Data Actions. In web apps, program flow options (Comment, Group, and If), data blocks, and data actions are available in all data macro table events. (In Chapter 22, you'll learn that the options under Data Blocks and Data Actions change based on whether you are using a before event or an after event in desktop databases.) Table 4-1 summarizes the data blocks and data actions that you can use in the table events in web apps.

TABLE 4-1   Data blocks and data actions available in table events

Element	Name	Description
Data blocks	CreateRecord	Creates a new record in a table.
	EditRecord	Allows Access to edit a record. This data block must be used in conjunction with a ForEachRecord or LookupRecord data block.
	ForEachRecord	Iterate over a recordset from a table or query.
	LookupRecord	Instructs Access to look up a record in the same table, a different table, or a query.
Data actions	CancelRecordChange	Cancels any record changes currently in progress. You can use this action to break out of CreateRecord or EditRecord changes.
	DeleteRecord	Deletes the current record from the table. Access determines the current record based on the scope of where the action is called. For example, if you are inside a LookupRecord data block, Access deletes the record found in the Where condition argument.
	ExitForEachRecord	Exits the innermost ForEachRecord loop. You can use this action when you want to break out of a long-running loop if a condition is met.

Element	Name	Description
	RaiseError	Displays a custom message to the user interface level and cancels the event changes. You can use this action to manually throw an error and cancel an insert, update, or delete.
	RunDataMacro	Runs a saved named data macro. You can optionally pass parameters to the named data macro and return values.
	SetField	Changes the value of a field. For example, you can use the SetField action to change the value of another field in the same record before committing the changes.
	SetLocalVar	Creates a temporary local variable and lets you set it to a value that you can reference throughout the data macro execution. The value of the variable stays in memory as long as the data macro runs or until you change the value of the local variable by assigning it a new value. When the data macro completes, Access clears the local variable.
	StopMacro	Stops the current data macro.

The tblWeekDays table contains seven records, each record listing the name of a day of the week. This table helps build a linking table between the tblVendors table and the tblVendorOrderDays table. Each vendor in the app can have more than one day that they accept orders, and each weekday can be used by more than one vendor. Similarly, the tblWeekDays table also serves as a linking table between tblVendors and tblVendorDeliveryDays. For the purposes of this app, I consider tblWeekDays to be a system table: a table used by other parts of the app, but one in which I don't ever need to add, change, or delete data. (I can't foresee the names of the weekdays changing any time soon.) To prevent new records from being added to this table, we'll create a data macro in the On Insert event and include a RaiseError data action to stop the insert.

Including comments

To start creating your data macro in the On Insert event of the tblWeekDays table, let's first add a comment to the macro design surface. Comments are useful for documenting the purpose of your data macro and the various data actions within it. Access ignores any comments as it executes the actions within your data macro. Click the Comment element under the Program Flow node in the Action Catalog, hold the mouse key down, drag the Comment element onto the macro design surface, and then release the mouse button, as shown in Figure 4-4.

Chapter 4

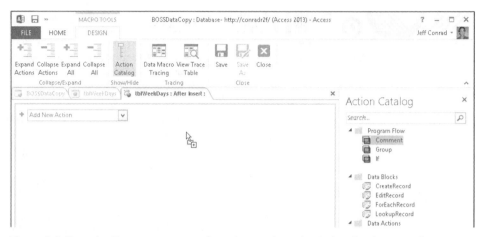

Figure 4-4 Drag the Comment program flow element from the Action Catalog onto the macro design surface.

Access creates a new Comment block on the macro design surface, as shown in Figure 4-5. If your cursor is not in the Comment block and you do not have any comments typed into the Comment block, Access displays the text Click Here To Type A Comment. You'll notice in Figure 4-5 that Access moved the Add New Action box below the Comment block. You'll also notice that Access places a delete button to the far right of the Comment block. (The delete button is a symbol shaped like an X.) If you want to remove the Comment block, click the delete button and Access removes the Comment block from the macro design surface. If you delete the Comment block in error, click the Undo button on the Quick Access Toolbar to restore the Comment block.

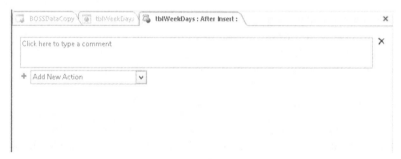

Figure 4-5 Access creates a new Comment block when you drag a Comment program flow onto the macro design surface.

Click inside the Comment block, and type the following text:

We don't want to allow additional records into this system table. If a new record is being added, raise an error and inform the user.

Click outside the Comment block onto the macro design surface. Access collapses the size of the Comment block to just fit the text you typed and displays the text in green, as shown in Figure 4-6. The /* and */ symbols mark the beginning and end of a block of comments. Access designates anything written between those symbols as a comment, which is there only to provide information about the purpose of the data macro or particular action to follow.

Figure 4-6 Access displays any comments inside comment block characters.

Chapter 4

INSIDE OUT   Take the time to include comments

You might be asking yourself whether it's really worth your time including comments in your data macros. While it's true that it takes additional time to include comments as you're creating your data macros, the investment of your time now pays off in the future. If you need to modify your app at a later date, you'll find it much easier to understand the purpose of your data macros if you include comments. This is especially true if someone else needs to make changes to your app. Trust me; it's worth your time to include comments when you design data macros.

Grouping macros

When you're creating data macros, you can use a program flow construct called Group. You use a Group construct to group a set of actions together logically to make your data macro actions easier to read. When you group macro actions inside a Group construct, you can also expand or collapse the entire group easily to see more of the macro design surface. It's not required to use the Group construct when you're creating data macros; however, grouping macro actions can be especially helpful if you have many disparate actions inside the same event or named data macro.

To add a Group construct to your data macro, click the Group element in the Action Catalog, hold down the mouse key, and drag the Group element to just beneath the comment block that you inserted previously. As you get close to the comment block, you'll notice that Access displays a horizontal bar across the macro design surface, as shown in Figure 4-7. This horizontal bar is your insertion point for the new program flow, data block, or data action. If you want to drop your new Group above the comment block, position your mouse pointer above the comment block and Access displays the horizontal bar above the comments to indicate where it will drop your new Group. We want to have this Group positioned below the comment block, so place your mouse pointer below the comment block and then release the mouse.

Figure 4-7 Access displays a horizontal bar on the macro design surface when you drag items from the Action Catalog.

Access displays a new Group block on the macro design surface, as shown in Figure 4-8. You need to provide a name for your new Group block, so type **PreventNewRecords** in the text box provided. You are limited to 256 characters, including any spaces, for the name of any Group block.

In Figure 4-8, you'll notice that Access denotes the end of the Group block by placing the words End Group at the bottom of the Group block. When you click on the Group block, Access highlights the entire block as a visual cue to indicate where the starting and ending points of the block are. You'll also notice that Access placed another Add New Action combo box inside the Group block when you dropped the Group construct onto the design surface. You can use this combo box to add new actions inside the Group block. (We'll do that in just a moment.) Next to the delete button on the right side of the Group block is a green up arrow button. Click this button if you want to move the entire Group block above the Comment block that you created earlier. For now, leave the Group block where it is.

Figure 4-8 You can use a Group block to group a set of actions together logically.

Raising errors in data macros to cancel events

In Chapter 8, you'll learn that user interface macros can interact heavily with the user's experience working with views. With user interface macros, you can display message boxes, open pop-up views, and dynamically change properties on a view. Data macros, on the contrary, are limited to the data layer and cannot interact with the user interface level. For example, in a data macro you cannot display a custom message box to the user and perform different steps based on how the user responds to your message. The only tool you can use in data macros to display information to the user is the RaiseError data action.

You can use the RaiseError data action whenever you need to force an error to occur and display a non-actionable message to the user manually. When you use the RaiseError action in a data macro, Access cancels the pending insert, update, or delete if it reaches this action during the macro execution.

In the On Insert event that you've been building for the tblWeekDays table, we don't want to allow new records to be created in this table. To add a RaiseError action inside the Group block that you previously created, you could drag the RaiseError data action from the Action Catalog onto the macro design surface and place the insertion point inside the Group block. You've already done this type of procedure twice before when creating the Comment and Group blocks, so let's show you an alternative way of adding new elements to the macro design surface. Click the Add New Action combo box inside the Group block, and Access displays a context-sensitive drop-down list of all the program flow constructs, data blocks, and data actions that you can use, based on where your insertion point is located. Click the RaiseError option from the drop-down list, as shown in Figure 4-9, to add a RaiseError data action to the macro design surface.

Chapter 4

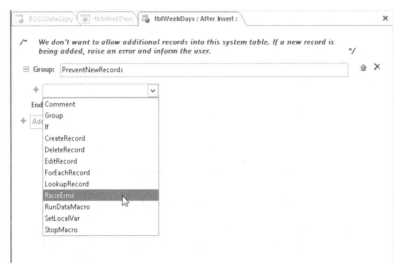

Figure 4-9 Select the RaiseError option from the Add New Action combo box inside the Group block.

Instead of using your mouse to select program flow constructs, data blocks, and data actions from the Add New Action combo box, you can also tab into the control and start typing the first letter or two of the element you want. Access highlights the first construct, data block, or data action that matches the letters you type. You can press Enter at any time, and Access adds the selected element to the macro design surface. (The macro design surface is flexible to allow you to use the mouse for selecting actions or just the keyboard if you prefer.) After you select RaiseError from the Add New Action combo box, Access displays the RaiseError data action inside the Group block, as shown in Figure 4-10.

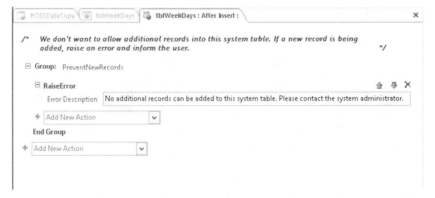

Figure 4-10 Use the RaiseError data action when you need to cancel an insert, update, or delete.

The RaiseError data action has one required argument—Error Description. The Error Description argument is the message displayed to the user if the RaiseError action is hit during execution of the data macro. You can type any custom message you want, up to 256 characters in length. You can also use an expression for the Error Description by typing the equal sign (=) as the first character. In the example earlier in this chapter, the text string started with an equal sign (=) and was enclosed within quotation marks. You're not required to use this technique with simple text strings. However, if you use an expression, you must start the expression with the equal sign (=) and enclose any text string within quotation marks. If you type an equal sign (=) at the beginning of the Error Description argument, Access displays the Expression Builder button on the far right of the text box if you need assistance creating your expression. (You'll see an example of using an expression in a RaiseError action later in this chapter.) For this example, you'd like to display a simple message to the user informing them that they cannot enter new records into this table. Type the following message, previously shown in Figure 4-10, into the Error Description argument:

No additional records can be added to this system table. Please contact the system administrator.

If you do not provide an error description in your RaiseError data action, Access displays an error message when you try to save your data macro logic, as shown in Figure 4-11. You must provide a message in the Error Description to save your data macro.

Figure 4-11 Access displays an error message if you leave the Error Description argument empty.

INSIDE OUT Pause over elements to see Help information

A very useful feature of the Logic Designer window is the ability to view Help information quickly no matter where you are. When you place your mouse over any element on the macro design surface, Access displays a tooltip with specific Help information covering the program flow, data block, data action, or argument that you are currently on. Similarly, Access displays tooltips with Help information when you pause over the elements displayed in the Action Catalog. This feature is especially useful as you are learning your way around the Logic Designer.

Testing your data macro

You've now completed all the steps necessary to prevent any new records from being added to the tblWeekDays table. To test the data macro that you've created so far, you first need to save your changes to the On Insert event. Click the Save button in the Close group on the Design contextual tab under Macro Tools, or click the Save button on the Quick Access Toolbar. Now click the Close button in the Close group to close the Logic Designer window, and return to the Design view of the tblWeekDays table. To test this On Insert event, you need to create a new record in this table. Switch to Datasheet view by right-clicking the tblWeekDays table in the Navigation pane and selecting Open from the shortcut menu or right-clicking the object tab at the top of the application window and selecting Datasheet view from the shortcut menu. Click in the WeekDayText field on the new record line of the table datasheet, enter any text other than one of the existing weekday names, and then tab or click outside of the new record line. Access displays the custom error that you created in the RaiseError data action, as shown in Figure 4-12.

Figure 4-12 Access prevents you from adding new records with the data macro that you created for the On Insert event.

The On Insert event fires because you are inserting a new record into this table. In this event, Access checks to see what data macro logic, if any, to execute when you are creating new records. In this case, the RaiseError data action fires, Access displays the custom message that you created, and then Access cancels the insert. When you click OK in the message box, Access displays a pencil icon in the row selector on the left to indicate the new record is not saved yet. You now need to right-click the row selector and select Delete to remove that uncommitted record from the datasheet. You can also choose to close the table datasheet with this uncommitted record or click the Refresh command on the ribbon. Access prompts you that you have pending changes, as shown in Figure 4-13.

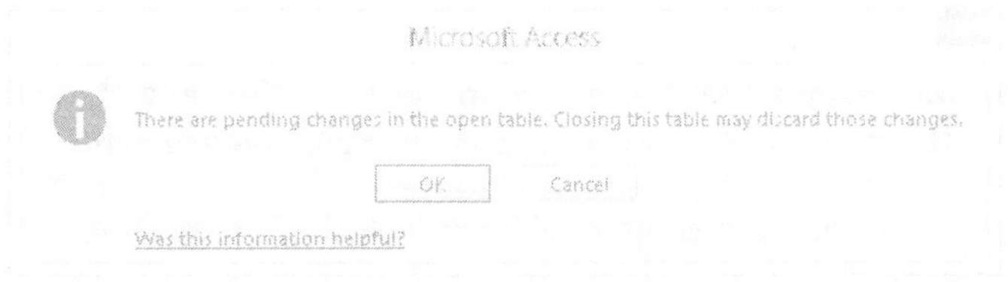

Figure 4-13 Access prompts you when you have unsaved records.

Access attempts to save any record changes when you move off a record or close the table datasheet, but in this case, Access cannot save your record changes because of the RaiseError action in the On Insert event. If you click OK on the pending changes dialog, Access cancels any pending records updates or inserts and then closes the table datasheet. If you click Cancel, Access stops the table datasheet from closing and returns focus to the datasheet; however, your record inserts or updates are still not saved. There is no way that you can add records to this table unless you remove the data macro that you defined in the On Insert event of the table. Access enforces this restriction no matter what the entry point is for creating a new record. As you can see, data macros are a very powerful feature in Access 2013 web apps.

Using If blocks to create conditional expressions

You can define more than one action within a data macro, and you can specify which actions get executed or not by adding conditional expressions into your data macro logic. For example, you might want to update a field in the same record, but only if a specific field was changed. Or, you might want to prevent an update to a record if a value in another field is a higher or lower value than you expect. In the preceding section, you designed a simple data macro in the On Insert event of the tblWeekDays table to prevent new records from being added to the table using a single action. In this section, we'll create data macro logic in the On Insert event of the tblEmployees table to update an image field each time you add a new employee record, using a conditional expression and multiple actions.

Open the tblEmployees table in Design view, click the Design contextual tab under Table Tools, and then click the On Insert button in the Events group to open the Logic Designer.

Chapter 4

The employees table includes an image field—EmployeePicture—that I use to store the picture of each employee in our restaurant management app. If the data entry person entering a new employee record into the app does not currently have a picture for the new employee, we want to save a default generic picture for the new employee record to indicate that we don't have a current picture.

Let's begin creating our data macro logic by first adding a new Comment block to the macro design surface. Click inside the Add New Action combo box on the macro design surface, type **Comment**, and then press Enter to create a new Comment block. Type the following text into the Comment block to identify easily the logic that we are going to add to this data macro:

If no picture was assigned for this new employee, use the generic default image instead from tblImageFiles. First check to see if the EmployeePicture field is Null.

Your changes to the On Insert event should now look like Figure 4-14.

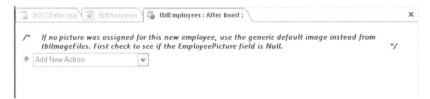

Figure 4-14 Add a Comment block to the macro design surface to document the purpose of this set of actions.

INSIDE OUT   Shortcut keys to adding Comment blocks

To add a new Comment block onto the macro design surface quickly, you can simply type two forward slashes (//) when you are in any Add New Action combo box and press Enter. Alternatively, you can type a single apostrophe (') when you are in an Add New Action combo box and press Enter. In both cases, Access creates a new Comment block on the macro design surface.

In the Add New Action combo box, type **If** and press Enter to create a new If block. Access creates a new If block under the Comment block, as shown in Figure 4-15. The text box next to If is where you type your conditional expression. Each condition is an expression that Access can evaluate to True or False. A condition can also consist of multiple comparison expressions and Boolean operators. If the condition is True, Access executes the action or actions immediately following the Then keyword. If the condition is False, Access evaluates the next Else If condition or executes the statements following the Else keyword, whichever occurs next. If no Else or Else If condition exists after the Then keyword, Access executes the next action following the End If keyword.

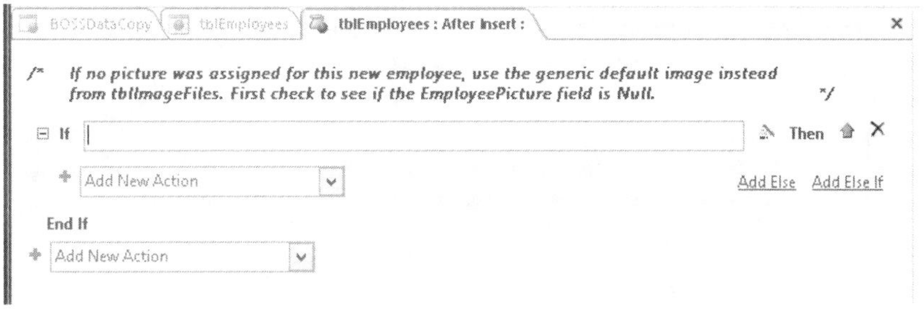

Figure 4-15 Use an If block when you want to execute actions only if a certain condition is met.

If you need help constructing your conditional expression, you can click the button that looks like a magic wand to the right of the expression text box. When you click this button, Access opens the Expression Builder, where you can build your conditional expression. (You learned about the Expression Builder in Chapter 3.) To the right of the word Then, Access displays a green up arrow. You can click this button if you want to move the position of the If block. (If there are actions below the If block, Access also displays a green down arrow.) If you move a block in error, you can click the Undo button on the Quick Access Toolbar. If you want to delete the If block, you can click the Delete button to the right of the up arrow. Below the arrow button are two links—Add Else and Add Else If. If you click the Add Else link, Access adds an Else branch to the If block, and if you click the Add Else If link, Access adds an Else If branch to the If block. (We'll explore these two conditional elements in just a moment.)

For the On Insert data macro that you have been building, we can use the Is Null phrase in our conditional expression to test whether the EmployeePicture field in the tblEmployees table has a value, an image file in this case, before Access saves the new employee record. In the conditional expression text box in the If block, type the letters **tblE** and notice that Access provides IntelliSense options for you, as shown in Figure 4-16.

Figure 4-16 Access provides IntelliSense options whenever you are writing expressions in data macros.

You can continue to type tblEmployees, or use the down arrow to highlight the tblEmployees option from the IntelliSense drop-down list and then press Tab or Enter. Notice that after you select tblEmployees, Access adds brackets around the table name. Now type a period, and IntelliSense provides a list of all the field names in the tblEmployees table, as shown in Figure 4-17.

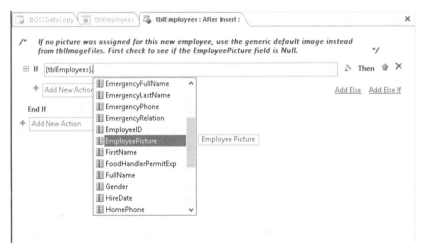

Figure 4-17 Access displays a list of all the fields in the tblEmployees table by using IntelliSense.

You can continue to type **EmployeePicture**, or use the down arrow to highlight the EmployeePicture field name from the IntelliSense drop-down list and then press Tab or Enter. Access also adds brackets around the EmployeePicture field name after you select it from the drop-down list. (Because our table name and field name contain no spaces, the brackets are not required, but its good practice to include them anyway.) Complete the entire expression by typing **Is Null**. Your completed expression should be [tblEmployees].[EmployeePicture] Is Null, as shown in Figure 4-18. Note that I also like to include the table name so that I know exactly what I'm referencing in my data macro logic, and I also get the benefit of being able to use IntelliSense.

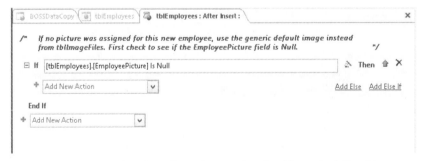

Figure 4-18 Your completed conditional expression should now look like this.

With your completed conditional expression for the If block, Access executes actions after the Then keyword and before the End If keywords only, if any employee record contains no data in the EmployeePicture image field.

Using LookupRecord data blocks to find records

The next step in our logic for the On Insert event of tblEmployees is to find a specific record in the tblImageFiles table where a default picture graphic is stored. To do this, tab or click into the Add New Action combo box that is inside the If block you completed in the previous section, type **LookupRecord**, and press Enter to add this data block inside the If block, as shown in Figure 4-19.

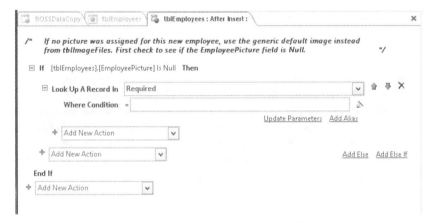

Figure 4-19 Add the LookupRecord data block inside the If block.

The LookupRecord data block takes four arguments:

- **Look Up A Record In.**   Required argument. The name of a table or query to look up a record in.

- **Where Condition.**   Optional argument. The expression that Access uses to select records from the table or query.

- **Update Parameters.**   Optional argument. If you're looking up records in a query that requires parameters, you can provide them here.

- **Alias.**   Optional argument. A substitute or shorter name for the table or query.

The only required argument for the LookupRecord data block is Look Up A Record In. Access provides a drop-down list for this argument that includes the names of all tables and saved query objects in your web app. If you want Access to look up a specific record in the specified table or query, you must provide a valid Where clause expression to find the record. If you leave the Where Condition argument blank, Access finds the first record in the specified table or query. You can click the button with the magic wand on it to open the Expression Builder to assist you with creating a Where clause if you'd like. The Update Parameters and Alias optional arguments are accessible through two links below the Where Condition argument on the right side. When you click these links, Access displays additional text boxes for you to enter these arguments. If you are looking up a record in a table, clicking the Update Parameters link does nothing, because tables do not contain parameters.

Before Access enters the LookupRecord block, the default data context is the incoming or changed record. The incoming record is either a new record or changes to an existing record. Within the LookupRecord block, Access creates a new data context. Access evaluates the Where condition of a data block with the same default context as when you are inside the data block. This means that if you do not use an alias as the table qualifier for field names in the Where condition argument, you are referring to a field within the new data context that you just created by using the data block.

Understanding alias and context

Using an alias is required when using a LookupRecord, ForEachRecord, EditRecord, or CreateRecord data block or DeleteRecord action, if you are trying to refer to a different data context other than the default. LookupRecord, ForEachRecord, and CreateRecord data blocks always create a new data context. EditRecord and DeleteRecord use only the current data context, unless you specify a different context to use. Consider the following example data macro logic:

```
ForEach Record in TableA Alias A
  LookupRecord in TableB Alias B WHERE B.TableBField1 = A.TableAField2
    EditRecord Alias A
      SetField TableAField3 = "Something"
```

In this example, the EditRecord's default context is on TableB's qualified row, so you have to use an alias to specifically indicate that the EditRecord is targeting TableA's looped row. You also need to use an alias to differentiate the data context for the same table. Consider the following example data macro logic:

```
On Insert Table1
  LookupRecord in Table1 Alias Lookup
    WHERE Lookup.ID <> Table1.ID AND Lookup.UserName = Table1.UserName
      RaiseError The user has already been added.
```

In this example, Table1 is the alias for the newly inserted row, while Lookup is the alias for the row being looked up in Table1.

Here are some considerations when working with data blocks:

- When inside a LookupRecord or ForEachRecord data block, the default context is the active row in the looped table.

- When inside a CreateRecord data block, the default context is the new row Access is creating.

- In On Insert event data macros, the default data context, outside any data block, is the row that Access is inserting.

- In On Update event data macros, the default data context, outside any data block, is the new value of the updated row.

- In On Delete event data macros, the default context, outside any data block, is the row that Access is deleting.

The tblImageFiles table is a system table that I use in this web app to hold any image files that I want to use in the app. In the On Insert event macro, you want to look up a record in this table, so click inside the Look Up A Record In argument and select tblImageFiles from the drop-down list. Currently, this table contains only one image file, but more images could be added over time. The specific image file you need for this example is the first record with ID=1. To make sure you look up the correct record, you should provide a Where clause that locates the first record every time. To do that, enter `[tblImageFiles].[ID]=1` in the Where Condition argument, as shown in Figure 4-20. When you start typing, IntelliSense helps you along and you can easily see and select the correct field name that holds the ID value. In this example, you already know that the default image needed is in the record that has ID=1. You could also use a Where clause that looks up the specific image description provided in the ImageDescription field.

Chapter 4

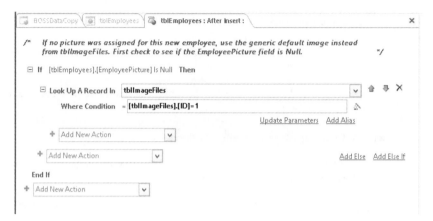

Figure 4-20 Add a Where clause to find a specific record using LookupRecord.

Using local variables

You can use a local variable in data macros to store a value that can be used throughout the execution of the data macro. Local variables are very useful when you need Access to calculate values during the execution of the data macro or remember something for later use in the data macro. You can think of a local variable in a data macro as writing yourself a note to remember a number, a name, or an email address so that you can recall it at a later time in the data macro. All local variables must have a unique name in the context of the data macro. To fetch, set, or examine a local variable, you reference it by its name. Local variables stay in memory until the data macro finishes executing, you assign it a new value, or until you clear the value.

In the previous section, you added logic for Access to look up a specific record in the tblImageFiles table. We now need to copy the contents of the image field, ImageFile in this case, to a local variable so that we can use it later in the event. The reason for this is because the code in this block is now executing in a different context and when Access finishes, we cannot make the outer code block refer to this context. Creating a local variable here allows us to pass a value back to a different context during the data macro execution. To create a local variable, click or tab into the Add New Action combo box that is inside the LookupRecord block, enter **SetLocalVar**, and press Enter to add this action inside the LookupRecord block, as shown in Figure 4-21.

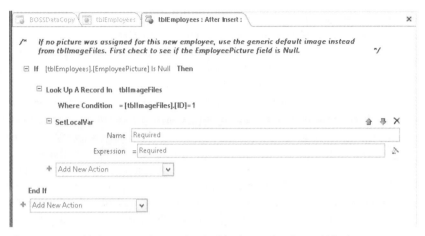

Figure 4-21 Add the SetLocalVar action inside the LookupRecord block.

The SetLocalVar action takes two required arguments:

- **Name.**   Required argument. The name of the local variable you want to use to refer to during data macro execution.

- **Expression.**   Required argument. The expression that Access uses to define the local variable.

For the Name argument, you can enter a name up to 64 characters. For the Expression argument, you can click the button that looks like a magic wand to open the Expression Builder to assist you with creating an expression. In this example, enter **varImage** into the Name argument and then enter **[tblImageFiles].[ImageFile]** into the Expression argument, as shown in Figure 4-22.

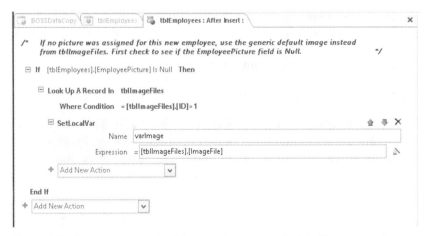

Figure 4-22 Enter a name and valid expression into the SetLocalVar arguments.

Chapter 4

Choosing variable names in web apps

Access 2013 gives you lots of flexibility when it comes to naming your local variables, parameters, and return variables in web apps. (You'll learn about parameters and return variables later in this chapter.) A variable name can be up to 64 characters long and can include any combination of letters, numbers, and special characters except a period (.), exclamation point (!), square brackets ([]), leading equal sign (=), or nonprintable character such as a carriage return. You cannot use spaces in any part of variable names in web apps. The name also cannot contain any of the following characters: / \ : ; * ? "" < > | # <TAB> { } % ~ &. In general, you should give your variables meaningful names. You should also avoid using variable names that might match any name internal to Access. For example, all objects have a Name property, so it's a good idea to qualify a variable containing a name by calling it varVendorName or varCompanyName. You could also preface the variable name with the data type, such as strVendorName for text and imgEmployeeImage for image data types. You should also avoid names that are the same as built-in functions, such as Date, Time, Now, or Space. See Access Help for a list of all the built-in function names.

When Access finds the record in the tblImageFiles table where the ID field equals 1, it creates a local variable named varImage, reads the current value in the ImageFile field for that specific record, and then assigns the value of that field (a picture file, in this case) to the local variable. You can now reference and use this value in other areas of this same table event by referencing the variable by its name. We'll do that in just a moment. Let's save the logic we've created so far by clicking the Save button on the Quick Access Toolbar.

Note

You cannot save any data macro logic if any If, Else If, Or Else blocks are empty and have no actions inside them.

Collapsing and expanding actions

Now that you have the varImage local variable currently storing the contents of an image file, it's time to save that data to the EmployeePicture field in the tblEmployees table. To do this, you'll use the EditRecord data block. The tricky part of this next procedure though is to make sure you place the EditRecord data block in the correct place on the macro design surface. If you click anywhere on the LookupRecord data block you currently have on the macro design surface, you'll notice there are three Add New Action combo boxes near the bottom of the screen, as shown in Figure 4-23.

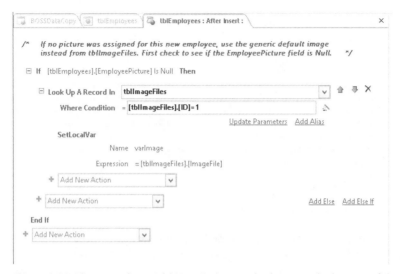

Figure 4-23 There are three Add New Action combo boxes at the bottom of the macro design surface.

We want to place the EditRecord data block outside and below the LookupRecord data block. Because you have the LookupRecord data block selected right now, it's a little easier to tell that the topmost Add New Action combo box is inside the LookupRecord data block, but if you did not have it selected, you might find it more difficult trying to decide where to place your next action. For example, compare the screen shots in Figure 4-22 and Figure 4-23 shown previously. In Figure 4-22, I selected the SetLocalVar data action and you'll notice that you can see only two Add New Action combo boxes. In Figure 4-23, I selected the LookupRecord and you can see three Add New Action combo boxes.

When you have complex data macros with many program flow constructs, data blocks, and data actions, you might find it harder to understand everything happening with the structure of your data macros, especially if you have to scroll the macro design surface to see everything. Fortunately, the Logic Designer includes features that can make these tasks easier.

To the left of the LookupRecord data block and the If block on the macro design surface, you'll notice that Access displays a box with a dash inside. If you place your mouse over the SetLocalVar data action, you can also see a similar box. (For data actions, Access shows this box only when you hover over the action.) You can use this box to expand and collapse the group or action. By default, the Logic Designer displays all group blocks and data actions in expanded mode so that you can see all actions and arguments. To collapse the LookupRecord data block, click inside the box. Access changes the dash inside the box to a plus symbol and then collapses the data block onto two lines, as shown in Figure 4-24.

Chapter 4

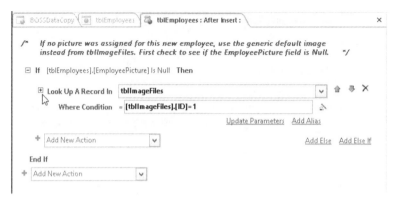

Figure 4-24 Click the box next to an action to collapse it.

Access displays the data block on two lines, and all actions contained inside the data block are hidden. It is much easier now to distinguish that the Add New Action combo box, directly below the highlighted LookupRecord data block, is outside that block. If you collapse a data action, such as the SetLocalVar action, Access displays the action without the argument names—Name and Expression for SetLocalVar—and separates the argument values with a comma. By collapsing data blocks and data actions, you can see more of the macro design surface. To expand the data block or data action again, click inside the box, now displaying a plus symbol, and Access expands the data block or data action.

You can collapse an entire Group block or If block as well using the same technique. If you want to collapse all data actions showing on the macro design surface at the same time, you can click the Collapse Actions button in the Collapse/Expand group on the ribbon. Click the Expand Actions button in the Collapse/Expand group on the ribbon to expand all data actions showing on the macro design surface.

For the maximum amount of space on the macro design surface, click the Collapse All button in the Collapse/Expand group on the ribbon. Access collapses all groups onto one line, as shown in Figure 4-25. You can't see very much with this view, of course. However, you can then selectively expand Groups, If blocks, and Data Blocks one at a time to work on specific parts of the data macro. Click the Expand All button on the ribbon to expand all Group blocks, If blocks, Data Blocks and Data Actions.

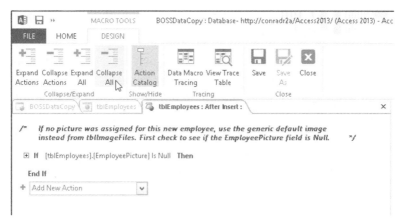

Figure 4-25 When you click the Collapse All button, Access collapses everything on the macro design surface except Comment blocks.

INSIDE OUT   Viewing super tooltips

If you hover your mouse over a collapsed data action, Access displays a super tooltip with all the arguments. You can then view all the argument values of the data action easily, without having to expand the data action.

Note

When you expand or collapse Group blocks, If blocks, Data Blocks, or Data Actions, Access marks the macro design surface as dirty, even if you did not make any other changes. If you attempt to close the Logic Designer window, Access prompts you to save your changes. Access remembers the state of any expanded or collapsed elements when you save changes and reopen the data macro. Also, when you click Expand All after previously clicking Collapse All, Access displays all Comment blocks in a narrower box than before you collapsed everything. After you close and reopen the macro design surface, the width of the Comment blocks return to their normal size.

Now that you've collapsed the LookupRecord data block, let's continue adding our EditRecord data block. Click inside the Add New Action combo box below the LookupRecord data block, type **EditRecord**, and then press Enter. Access adds a new EditRecord data block onto the macro design surface, as shown in Figure 4-26.

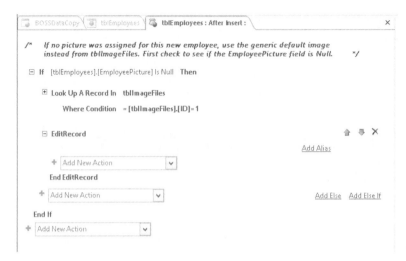

Figure 4-26 Add an EditRecord data block beneath the LookupRecord data block.

Whenever you want to change data in a table, you must use the SetField data action inside an EditRecord data block. Because our EditRecord data block is not inside any other data block such as ForEachRecord or LookupRecord, the context of the EditRecord block acts on the new record being created in the current table. For our example, we want to change the EmployeePicture field of the new employee record being created in tblEmployees to the local variable we defined earlier—varImage. Click inside the Add New Action combo box that is inside the EditRecord data block, type **SetField**, and then press Enter to add this new action to the macro design surface, as shown in Figure 4-27.

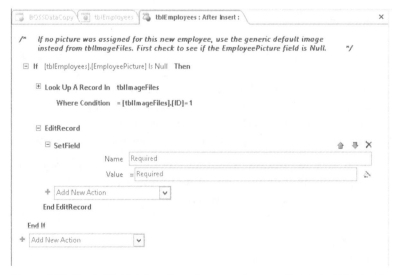

Figure 4-27 The SetField data action allows you to commit data to fields inside data macros.

The SetField action takes two required arguments, Name and Value. In the Name argument, we use the full table name and field name to clearly indicate which field we want to update. Enter **[tblEmployees].[EmployeePicture]** into the Name argument, and enter **[varImage]** into the Value argument. Notice that when you start typing the table name in the Name argument, Access provides IntelliSense to help you pick the correct table and field name you want. Also, you'll notice that Access does not add brackets around the table name and field name when using IntelliSense in this context, but it's a good idea to always include them even if you don't have spaces in your table and field names. If you do not provide brackets around the local variable name in the Value argument, Access adds them when you save and re-open the macro design window.

Click Save on the Quick Access Toolbar to save your changes to the On Insert event. Your completed changes to the data macro should now match Figure 4-28. Notice that, in Figure 4-28, I expanded all the actions again by clicking Expand All button in the ribbon.

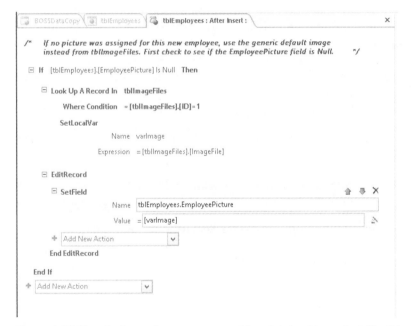

Figure 4-28 Your On Insert data macro up to this point should now look like this.

The data macro logic you've now defined instructs Access to check every new employee record entered into this table. If no picture is provided in the EmployeePicture at the time you create a new employee record, Access looks up a record in the tblImageFiles table where the ID value equals 1, stores the value of the ImageFile default picture into a local variable called varImage, and finally saves that default picture into the EmployeePicture field for that new record using the local variable. Note that datasheets do not support displaying image fields, so you would have to verify this using your web browser and a List Details or Blank view.

Moving actions

As you design data macros or user interface macros in the Logic Designer, you might find that you need to move actions around as the needs of your application change. In the On Insert event for the tblEmployees table you've been working on, it would be good to add in some comments for the extra actions you just finished. As with many areas of Access, there is usually more than one way to accomplish a task. You could drag a Comment block from the Action Catalog onto the macro design surface, or you could add comments any-where on the macro design surface and then move them into different positions. The Logic Designer makes the task of moving data blocks, data actions, and all other elements around the macro design surface very easy.

Open the tblEmployees table in Design view if you closed it, click the Design contextual ribbon tab under Table Tools, and then click the On Insert button in the Events group. You should now see the data macro that you created previously for saving a default picture graphic for each new employee record if you don't provide one. Click into the Add New Action combo box at the bottom of the macro design surface, type **Comment**, and then press Enter to add a new Comment block to the macro design surface. Type the following text into the Comment block to identify one of the tasks in this data macro:

It is Null so lookup the default image in tblImageFiles and set a local variable to the picture.

Add one more new Comment block as well to the bottom of the macro design surface using the same technique, and then type the following text into this new block:

Now update the EmployeePicture field with that image data.

Your macro logic should now match Figure 4-29.

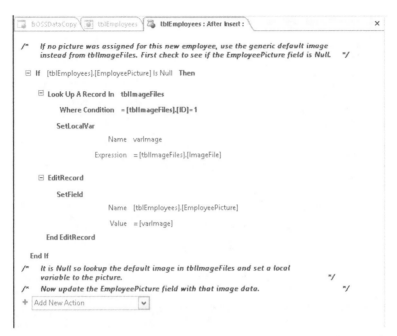

Figure 4-29 Your macro logic should now have two Comment blocks at the bottom of the macro design surface.

We want to move the first Comment block above the LookupRecord block and below the If condition line. To move the first Comment block you just added, click anywhere on the Comment block, hold the mouse key down, drag the Comment block up above the LookupRecord block until Access displays a horizontal bar above the LookupRecord block, as shown in Figure 4-30, and then release the mouse.

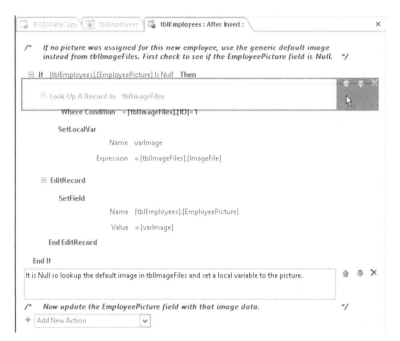

Figure 4-30 Drag the Comment block up above the LookupRecord block.

Access places the Comment block inside the If block and above the LookupRecord block. Instead of using the drag technique, you could also click the up arrow button on the far side of the Comment to move it up into the correct position. When you click the up arrow button, Access moves the selected action up one position in the macro design surface. In our example, it would take seven clicks of the up arrow to move the first Comment block action up above the LookupRecord block.

INSIDE OUT   Creating a duplicate copy of logic

To duplicate any logic on the macro design surface, you can hold the Ctrl key down and then drag to a different location. Access creates an exact copy of the program flow construct, data block, or data action, including any argument information.

You might find it easier to use the keyboard rather than the mouse to move actions around the macro design surface. Table 4-2 lists the keyboard shortcuts for working inside the Logic Designer.

TABLE 4-2 Keyboard shortcuts for logic designer

Keys	Action
Ctrl+F2	Opens the Expression Builder dialog box if you are in an expression context
Ctrl+Space	Calls up IntelliSense in expression contexts
Ctrl+Up arrow	Moves selected action up
Ctrl+Down arrow	Moves selected action down
Shift+F2	Opens the Zoom Builder dialog box
Shift+F10	Opens a context-sensitive shortcut menu
Left arrow	Collapses action
Right arrow	Expands action

Now that you've moved the first new Comment block to the correct position, let's move the last Comment block as well. Highlight the Comment block at the bottom of the macro design surface, hold the mouse key down, drag the Comment block up above the EditRecord, and then release the mouse. Your completed data macro should now look like Figure 4-31.

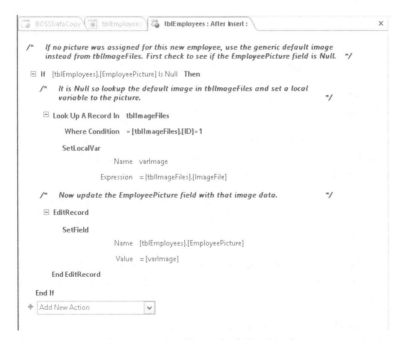

Figure 4-31 Your data macro should now look like this after you move the last Comment block.

You've now successfully revised the data macro logic by adding in more Comment blocks and moving them around the macro design surface. You've completed all the steps necessary to ensure that every new employee record added to this table contains an image in the EmployeePicture field. If the user creating a new employee record provides an image for the EmployeePicture field, Access evaluates the If block condition as False and then takes no action. If the new record does not contain an image for the EmployeePicture field, Access reads the contents of the tblImageFiles table and copies an image from that table into the new employee record. Save your changes, and then close the Logic Designer window.

Studying other On Insert events

The Back Office Software System sample web app includes On Insert events attached to other tables besides the two examples you've already seen. You can explore the data macros attached to these events for additional examples.

- **tblAppointments.**   Syncs two time display fields with values from the tblTimeLookups table. This breaks normalization, but it is needed to work around some user interface limitations.

- **tblCompanyInformation.**   Prevents additional records from being added to this system table.

- **tblEmployees.**   Ensures that each new employee record contains an employee picture. Uses LookupRecord to insert a default image if no picture exists.

- **tblInventoryLocations.**   Finds the next highest sort order number and sets the SortOrder field to that value for the new record.

- **tblInvoiceDetails.**   Checks to see whether the invoice is balanced with the invoice details after each new record is created. Uses a RunDataMacro action to execute a named data macro and passes in a parameter with each new record.

- **tblLaborPlanDetails.**   Syncs two time display fields with values from the tblTimeLookups table. This breaks normalization, but it is needed to work around some user interface limitations.

- **tblSchedule.**   Syncs two time display fields with values from the tblTimeLookups table. This breaks normalization, but it is needed to work around some user interface limitations.

- **tblSettings.**   Prevents additional records from being added to this system table.

- **tblTerminations.**   Whenever a new termination record is created for an employee, this data macro marks the employee record as inactive. The data macro logic looks up the employee's record in the tblEmployees table and sets the Boolean Active field to False for that specific employee.

- **tblTimeLookups.**   Prevents additional records from being added to this system table.

- **tblTrainedPositions.**   Ensures that each employee has only one trained position marked as their primary position. Uses a RunDataMacro action to execute a named data macro and passes in two parameters with each new record.

- **tblWeekDays.**   Prevents additional records from being added to this system table.

Using On Update events

The On Update event fires whenever Access completes the operation of committing changes to an existing record in a table. In the tblTerminations table, I have a data macro defined in the On Insert event to mark an employee's Active field to False whenever I create a termination record. In Figure 4-32, you can see the data macro logic for the On Insert of the tblTerminations table. When you create a new termination record in the Back Office Software System web app, Access looks up the corresponding employee's record in tblEmployees using the LookupRecord data block and then changes the Yes/No Active field in that table to No using EditRecord and SetField.

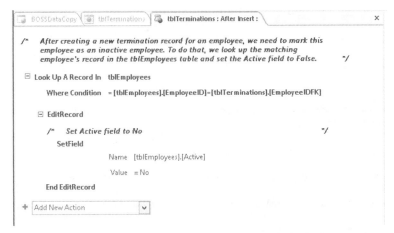

Figure 4-32 The On Insert event of tblTerminations includes logic to mark an employee inactive.

However, what happens if we accidentally select the wrong employee when we save the new termination record? We now have a situation where two employee records are inaccurate. We have one employee marked as inactive, which shouldn't be the case, and another employee still marked as active even though he or she should not be active. To fix this discrepancy manually, you would need to change the data in the existing termination record to use the correct employee, change the Active field of the employee's record to Yes for the employee to whom you first assigned the termination record, and also change the Active field to No for the employee who now has the termination record assigned to him or her. Instead of doing all these steps manually, we can use the On Update event to fix both employee records.

Open the tblTerminations table in Design view. Next, click the Design contextual tab under Table Tools, and then click the On Update button in the Events group to open the Logic Designer, as shown in Figure 4-33.

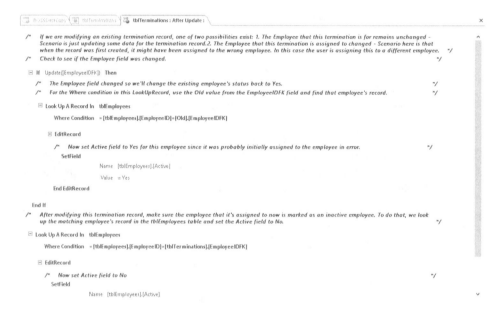

Figure 4-33 Click the On Update button on the ribbon to examine the On Update event of the tblTerminations table.

The data macro logic for the On Update event is as follows:

```
Comment Block: If we are modifying an existing termination record, one of two
possibilities exist: 1. The Employee that this termination is for remains unchanged –
Scenario is just updating some data for the termination record. 2. The Employee that
this termination is assigned to changed – Scenario here is that when the record was
first created, it might have been assigned to the wrong employee. In this case the
user is assigning this to a different employee.
Comment Block: Check to see if the Employee field was changed.
If Update([EmployeeIDFK]) Then
   Comment Block: The Employee field changed so we'll change the existing employee's
   status back to Yes.
   Comment Block: For the Where condition in this LookupRecord, use the Old value from
   the EmployeeIDFK field and find that employee's record.
   Look Up A Record In tblEmployees
```

```
    Where Condition = [tblEmployees].[EmployeeID]=[Old].[EmployeeIDFK]
      EditRecord
        Comment Block: Now set Active field to Yes for this employee since it was
        probably initially assigned to the employee in error.
        SetField
          Name: [tblEmployees].[Active]
          Value: Yes

      End EditRecord
End If
Comment Block: After modifying this termination record, make sure the employee that
it's assigned to now is marked as an inactive employee. To do that, we look up the
matching employee's record in the tblEmployees table and set the Active field to No.
Look Up A Record In tblEmployees
    Where Condition = [tblEmployees].[EmployeeID]=[tblTerminations].[EmployeeIDFK]
      EditRecord
        Comment Block: Now set Active field to No.
        SetField
          Name: [tblEmployees].[Active]
          Value: No

      End EditRecord
```

The first part of the data macro includes two Comment blocks to indicate the purpose of this event. Next, I use an If condition using the *Update* function to see whether the EmployeeIDFK field changed. The Update function takes one argument, a field name, and returns True if the field is dirty and returns False if the field is not dirty during the record update. For this On Update data macro, I can use the Update function in a conditional expression to test whether a user is attempting to change the value of the EmployeeIDFK field. If the EmployeeIDFK field changed, I know the user is assigning this existing termination record to a different employee. I then go into a LookupRecord data block and use the tblEmployees as the source. In the Where condition argument for the LookupRecord data block, I want to look up the EmployeeID in the table that matches the EmployeeIDFK field found in the tblTerminations table that Access is committing. When Access finds the matching record, it enters into the EditRecord block. Whenever you want to change data in another table in data macro events, you must use the SetField action inside an EditRecord block. For this example, I want to change the Active field of the matching employee to No to indicate that he or she is no longer an active employee in the app. In the Name argument for the SetField action, I use the table and field name, tblEmployees and Active, respectively, for the LookupRecord block. My Where condition argument for the LookupRecord uses the *Old* property. The Old property returns the value of the field before Access changed its value in the process of saving the record. My Where condition argument is therefore the following:

```
[tblEmployees].[EmployeeID]=[Old].[EmployeeIDFK]
```

To help understand this concept, imagine the value of the EmployeeIDFK field is currently 13, the record for Mario Kresnadi, in the existing termination record. If you change the EmployeeIDFK field to Jeff Conrad, EmployeeID of 31, the Old value for that field is 13 and the new value after saving the record is 31. By referencing the Old value of the EmployeeIDFK field, I can determine which employee this termination record used to be assigned to. (There is no New property available when creating data macros because the new value is simply the committed value of the field, and you can refer to it by using the field name.)

After Access finds the EmployeeIDFK that the termination record used to be assigned to, I use a SetField data action to set the Active status of that employee back to Yes. It's my assumption that if the user is assigning the termination record to a different employee, I'll error on the side of caution and assume this employee's status should be changed back to Yes.

The first part of the data macro logic is inside an If block. Based on the logic, if the user did not change the EmployeeIDFK field, Access does not change anything in the first part of the data macro. The second part of the On Update event is outside the If block, which means this part of the data macro logic runs every time a user changes anything about a termination record. I use another LookupRecord data block to look up a different employee record in the employee table. In this case, the Where condition argument is the following:

```
[tblEmployees].[EmployeeID]=[tblTerminations].[EmployeeIDFK]
```

This time, Access looks for the EmployeeID in the table that matches the now-committed value in the EmployeeIDFK field in the tblTerminations table. In the previous example, this means Access looks for the EmployeeID of Jeff's record, which is 31. Finally, I set the Active status of that employee's record to No because this termination record is now assigned to that employee.

To test this On Update event, close the Logic Designer window by clicking the Close button in the Close ribbon group. Open the tblTerminations table in Datasheet view now by right-clicking the tblTerminations object tab in the application window and selecting Open from the shortcut menu or clicking the View button in the Views ribbon group and selecting Datasheet view from the drop-down menu. Find the existing termination record in this table—the one assigned to Mario Kresnadi. Tab over to the EmployeeIDFK for this record (the datasheet caption of the field displays Employee), type **Conrad** into the control where it currently says Mario Kresnadi, and then select Jeff Conrad from the drop-down list of employee names displayed in the EmployeeIDFK field, as shown in Figure 4-34. Now, click or tab off the record, and Access saves the record with Jeff Conrad's EmployeeIDFK number.

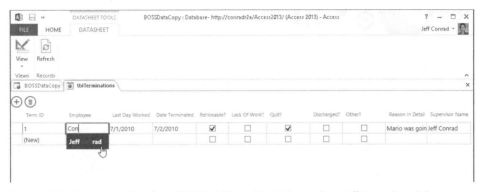

Figure 4-34 Change the EmployeeIDFK field from Mario Kresnadi to Jeff Conrad, and then save the record.

The control in the datasheet shown in Figure 4-34 for the EmployeeIDFK field is an autocomplete control, which is new in Access 2013. You'll learn more about this control in Chapter 6, "Working with views and the web browser experience."

To see the effects of this On Update event, open the tblEmployees table in Datasheet view by right-clicking the tblEmployees object in the Navigation pane and selecting Open from the shortcut menu. After you have the tblEmployees table open in datasheet view, scroll down to the record for the employee record for Mario Kresnadi. You'll notice that the Active field for Mario Kresnadi is now set to Yes, as shown in Figure 4-35. You'll also notice that Jeff Conrad's record shows his Active status is now set to No. In Figure 4-35, Mario's record is the record at the top (the highlighted record) and Jeff's record is at the bottom (where the mouse cursor is pointing).

Chapter 4

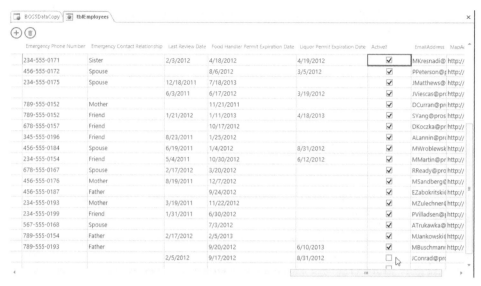

Figure 4-35 Access changes the Active field for both Jeff's and Mario's records from the On Update event of the tblTerminations table.

With the data macro logic that we have defined in the On Update event, Access automatically maintains the Active status of the employee records. If the user assigns the termination record to a different employee, Access changes the Active status of two different employees. If the user changed information other than the EmployeeIDFK field, Access marks that employee as inactive again just to be safe.

The Back Office Software System sample web app includes On Update events attached to ten tables. You can explore the data macros attached to these events for additional examples of using the On Update event.

- **tblAppointments.** Syncs two time display fields with values from the tblTimeLookups table. This breaks normalization, but it is needed to work around some user interface limitations. It uses the Update function to determine whether the time fields changed.

- **tblEmployees.** Ensures that each employee record contains an employee picture. Uses Update function and LookupRecord to insert a default image if you remove the existing employee picture.

- **tblInvoiceDetails**. Checks to see whether the invoice is balanced with the invoice details after any record changes. Uses a RunDataMacro action to execute a named data macro and passes in a parameter with each record update.

- **tblInvoiceHeaders.**   Checks to see whether the invoice is balanced with the invoice details but only if the InvoiceTotal field is changed by using the Update function. Uses a RunDataMacro action to execute a named data macro and passes in a parameter with each record update.

- **tblLaborPlanDetails.**   Syncs two time display fields with values from the tblTimeLookups table. This breaks normalization, but it is needed to work around some user interface limitations. It uses the Update function to determine whether the time fields changed.

- **tblSchedule.**   Syncs two time display fields with values from the tblTimeLookups table. This breaks normalization, but it is needed to work around some user interface limitations. It uses the Update function to determine whether the time fields changed.

- **tblTerminations.**   Ensures that the correct employee records are marked as active or inactive if the existing record is assigned to a different employee.

- **tblTimeLookups.**   Prevents any changes to existing records in this system table.

- **tblTrainedPositions.**   Ensures that each employee has only one trained position marked as their primary position. Uses a RunDataMacro action to execute a named data macro and passes in two parameters with record change.

- **tblWeekDays.**   Prevents any changes to existing records in this system table.

Using On Delete events

The On Delete event fires whenever Access attempts the operation of deleting a record from the table. There are many entry points for deleting a record when you are working with Access web apps. For example, you can delete a record in a table or query datasheet from within Access, you can run a named data macro that deletes a record, you can delete a record when using a view in your web browser, or you can delete records using user interface macros. When you attach a data macro to the On Delete event, Access runs the data macro logic no matter where the entry point is for deleting a record.

Earlier in the chapter, you created a data macro attached to the On Insert event of the tblWeekDays system table for the Back Office Software System sample web app data copy (BOSSDataCopy.app). The data macro you created prevents any additions to this system table. There is data macro logic attached to the On Update event that prevents any changes to the existing data as well. You can also lock tables down further by preventing any records from being deleted by using a data macro attached to the On Delete event.

Chapter 4

For this example, open the tblCompanyInformation table in Datasheet view, click the Design contextual tab under Table Tools, and then click the On Delete button in the Events group to open the Logic Designer, as shown in Figure 4-36. This table contains only one record to hold important company information. We don't want any new records added to this table, and we also don't want to delete the existing record.

Figure 4-36 Click the On Delete button on the ribbon to open the Logic Designer.

We should first add a Comment block to this data macro so that anyone looking at it can understand the purpose of the logic in this On Delete event. You should now be familiar with the different methods of adding a new Comment block to the macro design surface. Drop a new Comment block onto the macro design surface, and enter the following text:

Don't allow the default record to be deleted.

Now add a RaiseError data action below the Comment block. For the Error Description argument, enter the following text:

You cannot delete the record from this system table; it is used in other areas of the application.

Your completed changes to the On Delete event should match Figure 4-37.

Figure 4-37 Your completed On Delete event logic should match this.

Seems almost too simple doesn't it? Simple, yes, but completely effective. We don't need to test for any special conditions for our scenario; we just need to throw an error if this event ever occurs. To try this, save the changes to this data macro by clicking the Save button in the Close group or the Save button on the Quick Access Toolbar. Next, close the Logic Designer window by clicking the Close button in the Close group. Finally, click the record selector next to the existing record in the tblCompanyInformation table in Datasheet view and press Delete. Access first displays a confirmation dialog asking you to confirm that you want to delete the record. Click Yes to confirm the deletion, and then Access displays the custom message in the RaiseError data action, as shown in Figure 4-38.

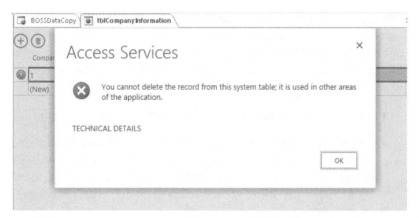

Figure 4-38 When you attempt to delete a record in the tblCompanyInformation table, Access displays your error message.

> **Note**
>
> In the On Delete event example we just discussed, the tblCompanyInformation table contains no relationships to other tables. If you have a Restrict Delete relationship enforced on any related tables, such as the tblWeekDays table has with other tables, Access prevents deletes and displays an internal message about not being able to delete the record. In this case, Access does not even show your On Delete RaiseError message. You might be asking why this is even necessary to put an On Delete data macro to prevent deletes if a Restrict Delete relationship is enforced on any related tables. You are correct that Access prevents deletes in this case; however it is possible that for a specific record in tblWeekDays, no related records exist in the other tables. In that case, a user could still delete a record from a static table that you don't want modified. Also, you might have other tables in your web app that do not have relationships with other tables and want to prevent any records from being deleted. Both the tblCompanyInformation and tblSettings tables in the Back Office Software System sample web app are two such examples where no relationships exist with other tables, but I want to prevent any record deletions.

The Back Office Software System sample web app includes On Delete events attached to other tables that use this same technique to prevent records from being deleted as well as other scenarios involving updating other tables when you delete records. You can explore the following data macros attached to these events for additional examples of using the On Delete event.

- **tblCompanyInformation.** Prevents deletion of existing records.

- **tblInvoiceDetails.** Checks to see whether the invoice is balanced with the invoice details after any record changes. Uses a RunDataMacro action to execute a named data macro and passes in a parameter with each record update. Uses the Old property to determine the ID of the invoice during the delete and passes that into the named data macro.

- **tblSettings.** Prevents deletion of existing records.

- **tblTerminations.** Ensures that the employee record is marked as active when deleting the termination record. Uses the Old property to determine the ID of the employee during the delete and finds the correct record using a LookupRecord data block.

- **tblTimeLookups.** Prevents deletion of existing records.

- **tblWeekDays.** Prevents deletion of existing records.

Deleting table events

If you want to delete a table event in a web app, you'll have to manually delete all of the data macro logic yourself. In Chapter 22, you'll learn that desktop databases include a dialog where you can quickly view all of the table events attached to tables in your application and delete any table event using this dialog. However, Access 2013 web apps do not include a similar type of dialog. To delete a table event in a web app, you need to open the table in Design view, delete each program construct, data block, and data action, and then save and close the Logic Designer. When you remove everything from the macro design surface for the specific table event, Access no longer executes that table event. Although it might seem tedious to delete each element on the macro design surface one by one, you can select everything currently displaying on the macro design surface by pressing Ctrl+A, as shown in Figure 4-39. When you have all data macro logic selected, press the Delete key to remove all logic from the macro design surface in one quick step. Now that you have everything removed, you can then save and close the Logic Designer.

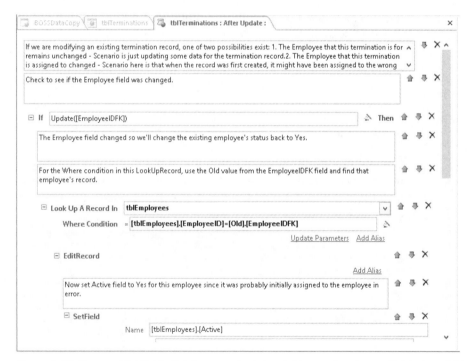

Figure 4-39 You can highlight all data macro logic in a table event and press Delete to quickly remove a table event.

Working with named data macros

So far in this chapter, you've been studying data macros attached to specific table events. Access also supports creating named data macros in web apps. A named data macro appears in the Navigation pane under the Macros group and is not attached directly to a specific table event. Named data macros in web apps execute only when called from another data macro or a user interface macro. Logic that is in a named data macro can interact with data in any table, require parameters before executing, and return data to the calling data macro or user interface macro. The Back Office Software System sample web app includes more than a dozen named data macros in the Navigation pane. In the next sections, you'll explore a few of these named data macros, as well as create a new named data macro.

Creating named data macros

In the Back Office Software System sample data copy web app (BOSSDataCopy.app), a table called tblTrainedPositions is used to track all the job positions each specific employee is trained to perform. A multiple-field index on this table ensures that each employee cannot be listed as trained in the same job position more than once. However, we also want to ensure that each employee has only one position marked as their primary job position. We can create a named data macro for this purpose, which can then be called from other areas of the app. To accomplish this goal, we'll create a new named data macro not attached to any table event and then call this named data macro from both the On Insert and On Update events of the tblTrainedPositions table.

Open the BOSSDataCopy.app sample web app within Access by downloading it from the Access Services site if you've closed the app. Now click the Advanced button in the Create group on the Home ribbon, and then click the option called Data Macro in the drop-down list, as shown in Figure 4-40.

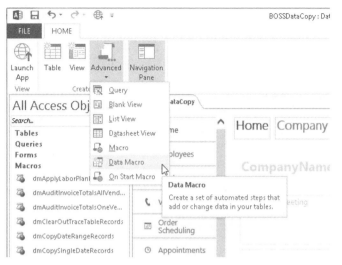

Figure 4-40 Click the Data Macro option under the Advanced button to start creating a new named data macro not attached to any table.

In Chapter 5, "Working with queries in web apps," you'll learn how to use the Query option in the drop-down list under the Advanced button in the ribbon. In Chapter 7, "Advanced view design," you'll learn how to work with the Blank View, List View, and Datasheet View options in this drop-down list. Finally, in Chapter 8, "Automating a web app using macros," you'll learn how to use the Macro and On Start Macro options under the Advanced button.

Access opens the Logic Designer with an empty macro design surface, as shown in Figure 4-41. You'll notice several differences on the macro design surface immediately that you did not see when creating data macros attached to table events in the preceding sections. When you're creating named data macros, the Logic Designer window is not modal. What this means is that you can see the Navigation pane and the App Home View, and you can interact with other objects without having to close the Logic Designer. Also, at the top of the macro design surface, you can see a section called Parameters. Named data macros allow you to create parameters, which you can use to pass information into the data macro. Creating parameters for named data macros is optional, but Access always displays the Parameters block at the top of the macro design surface whenever you are working with named data macros. The list of program flow constructs, data blocks, and data actions that you can use in named data macros is the same for table events except with the addition of one more data action called SetReturnVar. (We'll discuss the SetReturnVar action later in this chapter.) See Table 4-1 if you want to review the list of elements available in table events.

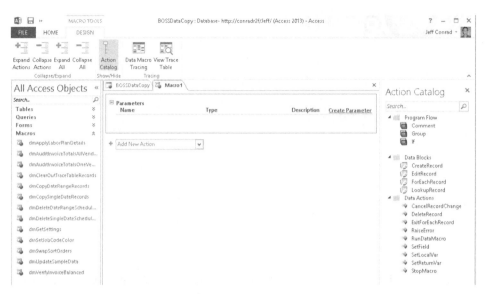

Figure 4-41 When you create named data macros, Access displays a Parameters block at the top of the macro design surface.

Let's first add a couple of Comment blocks to this named data macro to document its purpose. Drag a Comment block from the Action Catalog onto the macro design surface. Enter the following text into the new Comment block:

In this named data macro we want to make sure that only one job code is marked as the primary position for a specific employee. It is OK to not have any assigned primary positions for an employee but we do not want multiple primary positions defined.

Drag another Comment block onto the macro design surface below the first one, and enter the following text into this second Comment block:

This named data macro will run on the On Insert and On Update event for the tbl-TrainedPositions table. The employee and job code of the new or updated record will get passed in as parameters here. In the Where condition we will skip over the newly added or updated record and only touch the possible one other record that is marked as the primary position for the specific employee.

These two Comment blocks should give you an idea already of the type of logic we need to add to this named data macro as well as the reasoning behind the logic we will add.

Using parameters

In named data macros, you can define parameters to pass in information to the named data macro and use them in the data blocks and data actions. With parameters, you can pass in information to the named data macro from other data macros, views, and user interface macros. In the Back Office Software System sample web app, many of the named data macros include parameters. For the named data macro you are currently creating, we need to define two parameters—one for the employee we want to check and the second for the job code of the current record.

To create a new parameter in a named data macro, click the Create Parameter link on the right side of the macro design surface, as shown in Figure 4-42. You need to select the Parameters section to see the Create Parameter link. Access expands the Parameters section at the top of the macro design surface and inserts one new row for a parameter.

Figure 4-42 Click the Create Parameter link to create new parameters in named data macros.

Each parameter takes three arguments:

- **Name.**   Required argument. The name of the parameter you want to use to refer to during named data macro execution.

- **Type.**   Required argument. The data type that Access uses to define the parameter.

- **Description.**   Optional argument. A description for you to document the purpose of the parameter.

For the Name argument, you can enter a name up to 64 characters. The restrictions for naming parameters are the same as for local variables, which you learned about earlier in this chapter. In this example, enter **ParamEmployeeID** into the Name argument, which we'll use to denote the ID of the employee to search for in the named data macro. For the Type argument, you can choose from one of ten data type options—Short Text, Long

Text, Number (Floating Decimal), Number (No Decimal), Number (Fixed Decimal), Date With Time, Date, Time, Currency, or Yes/No. In this example, select Number (No Decimal) from the drop-down list of data type options. The employee ID values that we will be passing into this named data macro should not have any decimal places, because they are ID values, so the Number (No Decimal) data type should suffice for this named data macro parameter. For the Description argument, enter **Employee ID record to look for** into the text box to describe the purpose of this parameter value. Your completed changes for the first parameter should now match Figure 4-43.

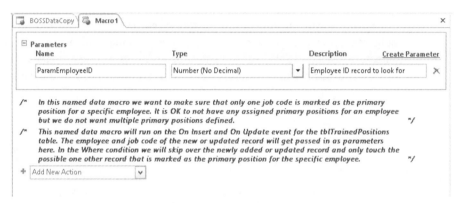

Figure 4-43 Enter the parameter information into the three arguments.

We need to define one additional parameter for this named data macro to track the job code ID of the record just created (the On Insert case) or the record just updated (the On Update case). To define another parameter, click the Create Parameter link again on the right side of the macro design surface in the Parameters section. Access inserts a new parameter row beneath the existing one. For this second parameter, enter **ParamJobCodeID** in the Name text box, select Number (No Decimal) from the drop-down list in the Type argument, and enter **Job Code ID to ignore** in the Description text box. Your completed two parameters should match Figure 4-44.

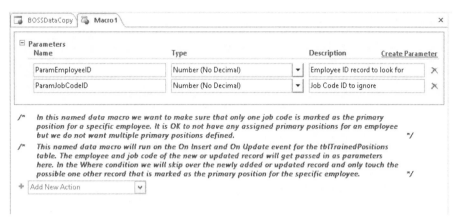

Figure 4-44 You should have two completed parameters defined in the new named data macro.

Note

If you need to delete an existing parameter, click the delete button to the far right side of the specific Parameter row. The delete button has a symbol shaped like an X.

Now that you've defined the two parameters we need, it's time to add the actions necessary to perform our task. In this named data macro, we want to loop through records in the tblTrainedPositions table looking for specific records. You've previously seen how the LookupRecord data block searches for a specific record in a table or saved query. In this case, we need to use the ForEachRecord data block to search through more than one record potentially. Drag a ForEachRecord data block from the Action Catalog to beneath the two Comment blocks, or select ForEachRecord from the Add New Action box at the bottom of the macro design surface. Access creates a new ForEachRecord block, as shown in Figure 4-45.

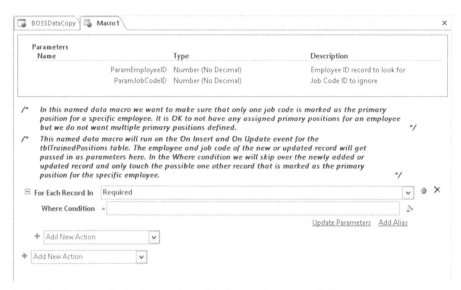

Figure 4-45 Drag a ForEachRecord data block onto the macro design surface.

The ForEachRecord data block takes four arguments:

- **For Each Record In.** Required argument. The name of a table or query to look up a record in.

- **Where Condition.** Optional argument. The expression that Access uses to select records from the table or query.

- **Update Parameters.** Optional argument. If you're looking up records in a query that requires parameters, you can provide them here.

- **Alias.** Optional argument. A substitute or shorter name for the table or query.

The only required argument for the ForEachRecord data block is For Each Record In. Access provides a drop-down list for this argument that includes the names of all tables and saved query objects in your web app. If you want Access to find a subset of specific records in the specified table or query, you must provide a valid Where clause expression to find the records. If you leave the Where Condition argument blank, Access loops through all records in the specified table or query. You can click the button with the magic wand on it to open the Expression Builder to assist you with creating a Where clause if you'd like.

The Update Parameters and Alias optional arguments are accessible through two links below the Where Condition argument on the right side. When you click these links, Access displays additional text boxes for you to enter these arguments. If you are running a ForEachRecord data block against a table, clicking the Update Parameters link does nothing, because tables do not contain parameters. If you are using a query for your data source that includes parameters, you can update the parameters using this link.

The tblTrainedPositions table contains one record for each job code that a specific employee is trained to perform. Each employee could have multiple records in this table. In an extreme case, one employee could be trained in every position in the restaurant, so that person could have one record in the tblTrainedPositions table for each job code in the app. The PrimaryPosition field in this table is a Yes/No data type that denotes whether the specific job code is the employee's primary position. In this scenario, we need to use the ForEachRecord data block instead of the LookupRecord data block to search over each record for a specific employee, so click inside the For Each Record In argument and select tblTrainedPositions from the drop-down list.

To make sure we are searching for all correct matches in the tblTrainedPositions table, we need to utilize the values passed in from the parameters in the Where condition argument. The final expression I used to accomplish this task, which you'll build in a moment, is as follows:

```
[tblTrainedPositions].[EmployeeIDFK]=[ParamEmployeeID] And [tblTrainedPositions].
[JobCodeIDFK]<>[ParamJobCodeID] And [tblTrainedPositions].[PrimaryPosition]=Yes
```

This expression contains three distinct clauses all joined together with AND operators. In the first part of the expression, we are trying to find all records where the EmployeeIDFK field in tblTrainedPositions matches the parameter ParamEmployeeID that we will pass in to this named data macro. Enter the first part of this expression into the Where condition argument. When you start typing the parameter name, IntelliSense helps you along and displays all parameter names so that you can easily see and select the parameter name that holds the employee ID value, as shown in Figure 4-46.

Chapter 4

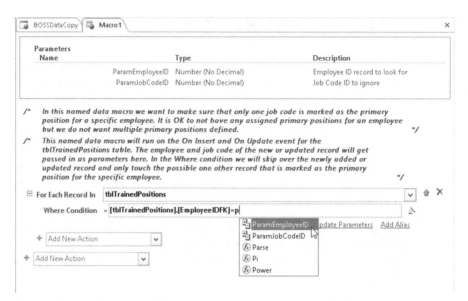

Figure 4-46 IntelliSense provides parameter names when you are building expressions in named data macros.

After you type the first part of the expression, add a space, type **And**, and then enter the second part of the expression:

```
[tblTrainedPositions].[JobCodeIDFK]<>[ParamJobCodeID]
```

In the second part of this expression, we are instructing Access to exclude records where the JobCodeIDFK field matches the parameter ParamJobCodeID that we will pass in to this named data macro. You might be wondering why we want to do this. As you'll learn in the next few sections, whenever we create new records in this table or update existing ones, we will pass in the job code of the record just created or the record just updated but only if that record is designated to be the primary position. Because this new or revised record will now be the primary position, there is no need to inspect this current record during the ForEachRecord loop.

After you type the second part of the expression, add a space, type another **And**, then enter the last part of the expression:

```
[tblTrainedPositions].[PrimaryPosition]=Yes
```

In the last part of this expression, we are instructing Access to include only records where the PrimaryPosition Yes/No field equals Yes. During the ForEachRecord loop, Access could find several records for the employee we are looking for. We really need to identify only records where the PrimaryPosition field is already Yes, so we can then mark those records as No in the PrimaryPosition field because a user just created a new primary position record or updated an existing record. This will all make sense when we complete all the tasks later in this section.

Now that you have the correct expression in place for the Where condition argument, we need to add one last step in this named data macro to update the PrimaryPosition field to No for any records Access finds during the ForEachRecord loop. To update the field, you need to use the SetField data action inside an EditRecord data block. Click inside the Add New Action combo box inside the ForEachRecord data block, type **EditRecord**, and then press Enter. Access adds a new EditRecord data block onto the macro design surface inside the ForEachRecord block. Next, click inside the Add New Action combo box inside the EditRecord data block, type **SetField**, and then press Enter to add this new action to the macro design surface. Finally, in the Name argument for the SetField action, enter **[tblTrainedPositions].[PrimaryPosition]** and No into the Value argument. Your completed changes to the named data macro should now match Figure 4-47.

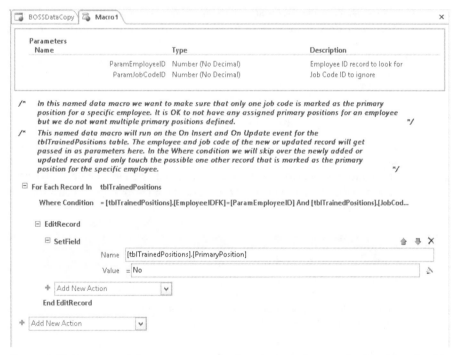

Figure 4-47 Your named data macro to maintain only one primary trained position should now look like this.

> **Note**
> You might be wondering why I used a ForEachRecord data block in the named data macro, given that the expression in the Where condition argument should return only one record. You're correct that Access should find only one record based on the logic I've put in place. I'm being extra careful to make sure that only one job position is marked as the primary position by using a ForEachRecord data block to cover the off chance that two records for a specific employee are marked as primary positions.

Saving named data macros

You've completed creating your first named data macro, but now you need to save it and give it a name. Unlike data macros attached to table events, named data macros require you to provide a unique name. To save your new named data macro, click the Save button on the Quick Access Toolbar. Access opens the Save As dialog box, as shown in Figure 4-48. Save the named data macro with the name **dmEnforceOnlyOnePrimaryPosition**.

Figure 4-48 Provide a unique name for your new named data macro in the Save As dialog box.

If you attempt to save a named data macro with the same name as an existing named data macro in the Navigation pane, Access displays an error message, as shown in Figure 4-49.

Figure 4-49 Access displays an error message if you try to save a named data macro with the same name as an existing named data macro.

Calling named data macros

I mentioned earlier that named data macros must be called for Access to execute them. If you want to test out a named data macro, you must therefore call a RunDataMacro action from a table event or from a user interface macro. In Chapter 8, you'll learn how to call named data macros from user interface macros and in Chapter 25, "Automating your desktop database with Visual Basic," which can be downloaded from the book's catalog page, you'll learn how to call named data macros from Visual Basic.

Close the Logic Designer, if you still have it open, and then open the tblTrainedPositions table in Design view. We need to call the named data macro in both the On Insert and On Update events, so let's begin with the On Insert event. Click the On Insert button in the Events group on the Design contextual tab to open the Logic Designer. Start by adding a new Comment block to the macro design surface, and enter the following text into the Comment block:

After we commit this new record we need to make sure we do not have more than one primary position designated for the same employee. Run the named data macro if this new record is marked as primary to clear out any other possibilities.

When you enter a new record in the tblTrainedPositions, we don't need to run the named data macro if you set the PrimaryPosition field to No. Remember, we want to enforce only one primary position so that if the new record is not set as a primary position, we don't need to do any extra work. To account for this possibility, add an If block beneath the Comment block onto the macro design surface. In the conditional expression text box, enter **[tblTrainedPositions].[PrimaryPosition]=Yes**. Access does not run the next action we add inside the If block if the new record has the PrimaryPosition field set to No.

To call the named data macro to run, you need to use the RunDataMacro action. Click in the Add New Action combo box inside the If block, type **RunDataMacro**, and then press Enter. Access displays the RunDataMacro on the macro design surface, as shown in Figure 4-50.

Figure 4-50 Add a RunDataMacro action inside the If block.

The only required argument for the RunDataMacro data action is Macro Name. Access provides a drop-down list for this argument that includes the names of all saved named data macros in your web app. Click in the Macro Name box, and select the named data macro you created earlier from the drop-down list—dmEnforceOnlyOnePrimaryPosition. After you select the named data macro, Access displays the parameters you defined earlier in the named data macro. Access displays the two parameters in the underlying named data macro—ParamEmployeeID and ParamJobCodeID—as parameter boxes at the bottom of the action, as shown in Figure 4-51. You can enter a value you want to use for each parameter by typing the value into the parameter box or using an expression to derive that parameter value.

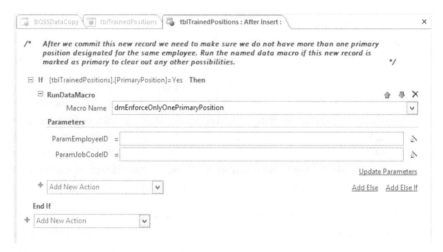

Figure 4-51 Access displays Parameter boxes on the macro design surface for any named data macros that require parameters.

The two parameters we need to pass into the named data macro come directly from the record Access just inserted. In the ParamEmployeeID parameter text box, enter **[tblTrainedPositions].[EmployeeIDFK]**, and in the ParamJobCodeID parameter text box, enter **[tblTrainedPositions].[JobCodeIDFK]**, as shown in Figure 4-52. When you create a new record in this table and set the PrimaryPosition field to Yes, Access takes the data stored in the EmployeeIDFK and JobCodeIDFK fields and passes those values into the named data macro you created earlier. Click Save in the Close group on the Design contextual tab, or click the Save button on the Quick Access Toolbar to save your changes to this On Insert table event but leave the Logic Designer window open.

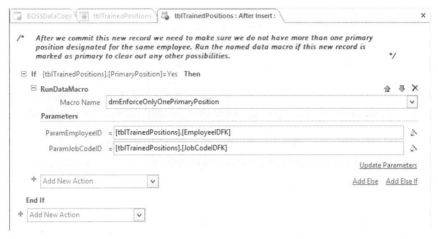

Figure 4-52 Enter field names into the parameter boxes in the RunDataMacro action.

We also need to add the same data macro logic to the On Update event of the tblTrainedPositions as well account for users of the app changing existing records. You should be very familiar now with adding data blacks, data actions, and filling in parameters in data macros manually, but this time we'll use a different technique. Because the logic currently showing in the On Insert event is the same as what we want to add to the On Update event, we can simply copy the data macro logic to the Windows Clipboard and then paste the contents into the On Update event. To do this, click inside the Logic Designer on the macro design surface, away from any commands, and then press Ctrl+A to highlight all of the logic currently showing in the On Insert table event, as shown in Figure 4-53.

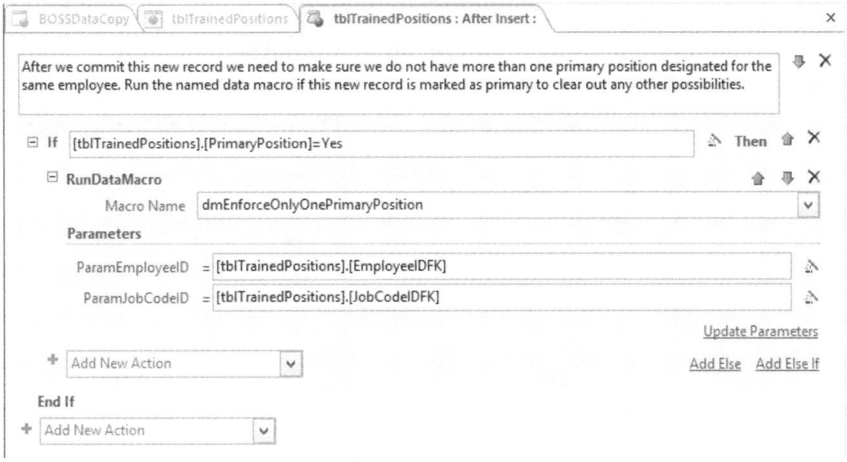

Figure 4-53 Press Ctrl+A to highlight all the data macro logic on the macro design surface.

Now that you have all the data macro logic highlighted, press Ctrl+C to copy all the Comment blocks, data blocks, and data actions to the Windows Clipboard. Next, click Close in the Close group on the Design contextual tab to close the On Insert table event. You should see the tblTrainedPositions table still open in Design view. Click the On Update button in the Events group on the Design contextual tab to open the Logic Designer window for this table event. Finally, click anywhere on the macro design surface and then press Ctrl+V. Access pastes all the data macro from the Windows Clipboard onto the macro design surface, as shown in Figure 4-54. As you can see, copying and pasting the data macro logic from the On Insert event to the On Update event using this technique is much faster than adding all of the actions manually one by one.

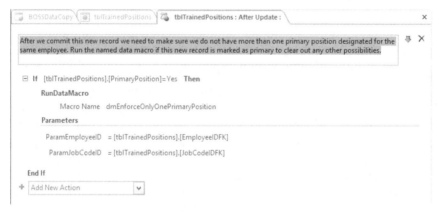

Figure 4-54 Press Ctrl+V to paste all the data macro logic from the Windows Clipboard into the On Update event of the tblTrainedPositions.

To test out the named data macro, save the changes to this On Update event and then close the Logic Designer. Switch to Datasheet view for the tblTrainedPositions table by clicking the View button in the Views group on the Design contextual tab, and then click Datasheet view on the drop-down menu. The first three records in this table display the trained positions for the employee with the last name of Sousa, as shown in Figure 4-55.

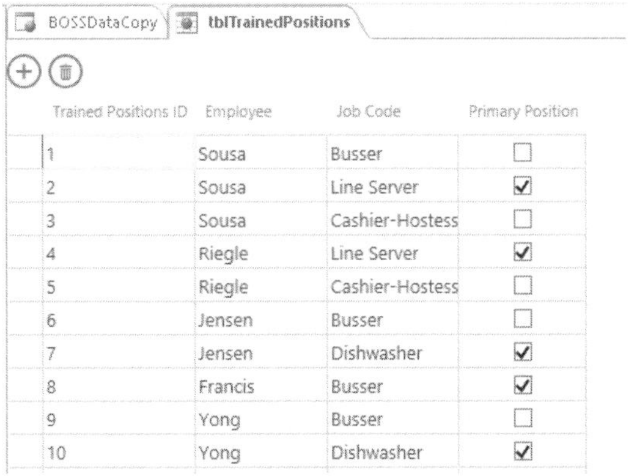

Trained Positions ID	Employee	Job Code	Primary Position
1	Sousa	Busser	☐
2	Sousa	Line Server	☑
3	Sousa	Cashier-Hostess	☐
4	Riegle	Line Server	☑
5	Riegle	Cashier-Hostess	☐
6	Jensen	Busser	☐
7	Jensen	Dishwasher	☑
8	Francis	Busser	☑
9	Yong	Busser	☐
10	Yong	Dishwasher	☑

Figure 4-55 In Datasheet view, you can see each trained position for the employees in the web app.

In Figure 4-55, you can see that the employee named Sousa is trained to be a Busser, a Line Server, and a Cashier-Hostess, with their primary position being the Line Server position. Change this employee's primary position to Busser by clicking into the first record and selecting the Primary Position check box, and then tab or click into a different record to commit the record update. Initially, you won't see any changes in any other records because Access caches the data locally. To see the most recent updates to other records, click the Refresh button in the Records group on the Datasheet contextual tab. (If you were using a view within your web browser, you would see the changes refreshed in the records.)

You'll now notice Access changed the second record after you updated the first record, as shown in Figure 4-56. Access automatically ran the named data macro after you changed the PrimaryPosition field to Yes in the first record. Access passed in the employee ID for Sousa, passed in the job code ID for the Line Server position, and then updated the second record by changing the PrimaryPosition in that record to No to maintain our goal of only one primary position for each employee. Access also runs the same named data macro whenever you add new records to this table and set the PrimaryPosition to Yes.

Chapter 4

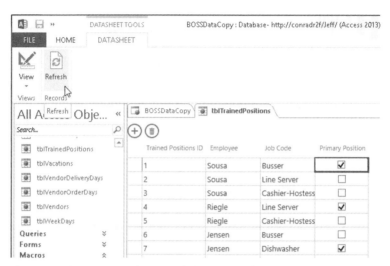

Figure 4-56 Access runs the named data macro after you update any record in the tblTrainedPositions table.

Renaming and deleting named data macros

When you need to rename or delete named data macros, you must do so from the Navigation pane. If you want to rename a named data macro, right-click the named data macro in the Navigation pane and select Rename from the shortcut menu, as shown in Figure 4-57.

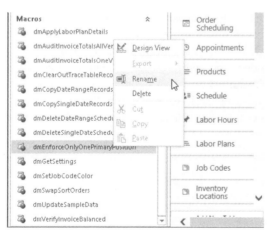

Figure 4-57 Click Rename on the shortcut menu to rename named data macros.

Access highlights the name of the named data macro in the Navigation pane and allows you to enter a new name for the named data macro, as shown in Figure 4-58. You must enter a unique name for your named data macro. If you enter the name of an existing named data macro, Access displays a warning message indicating that there is already an object in the web app with the same name.

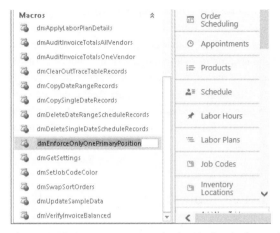

Figure 4-58 Enter a new name in the Navigation pane for the named data macro.

If you want to delete a named data macro, right-click the named data macro in the Navigation pane and select Delete from the shortcut menu. Access opens a confirmation message box, as shown in Figure 4-59. Click Yes if you want to permanently delete the named data macro.

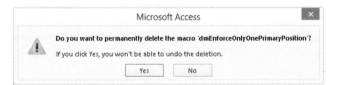

Figure 4-59 In the confirmation message, click Yes to delete the named data macro.

> **Note**
> You cannot rename table event data macros because they are attached directly to the table event.

CAUTION

If you rename a named data macro or delete a named data macro, you must adjust any other areas of your web app that reference that named data macro; otherwise, you might encounter errors using areas of your web app that reference that named data macro. For example, if you rename or delete the dmEnforceOnlyOnePrimaryPosition named data macro you created earlier, Access displays an error whenever you add or edit existing records to the tblTrainedPositions, because Access cannot find the named data macro. You won't be able to add or edit any data in that table until you remove the reference to the named data macro in both the On Insert and On Update table events for tblTrainedPositions.

Working with return variables

You can use a return variable in data macros to return data to the object that called the named data macro. In a sense, you can think of a return variable as the opposite of a parameter. You use parameters to push data into a named data macro, and you use return variables to pull data out of named data macros. Return variables are very useful when you need Access to read values from a table or query during the execution of the named data macro and perhaps perform different steps based on that value. Return variables can even be returned from the data layer up to the user interface level. All return variables have a unique name. To fetch, set, or examine a return variable, you reference it by its name. Return variables stay in memory until the data macro finishes executing, you assign it a new value, or until you clear the value. You can set return variables only in named data macros; however, you can retrieve them from table events, other named data macros, or user interface macros.

Let's examine a named data macro that uses return variables so that you can understand how this works. Open the dmGetSettings named data macro in Design view from the Navigation pane. Access opens the Logic Designer and displays the logic that I created for this named data macro, as shown in Figure 4-60.

Figure 4-60 The dmGetSettings named data macro uses return variables to return data to the caller.

The logic for the dmGetSettings named data macro is as follows:

```
Parameter Name: ParamValue
Parameter Type: Short Text
Parameter Description: What field value to return
Comment Block: This named data macro gets the current value of a field value in this
table based on a parameter and returns that back to the caller.
LookupRecord In tblSettings
  Where Condition
  Alias: TS
  If [ParamValue]="Version" Then
     Comment Block: Set ReturnVar to current value of Version field
     SetReturnVar
       Name: RVVersion
       Expression: [TS].[Version]
  Else If [ParamValue]="Range" Then
     Comment Block: Set ReturnVar to the current value of RangeLimit field
     SetReturnVar
       Name: RVRange
```

```
              Expression: [TS].[RangeLimit]
    Else If [ParamValue]="Available" Then
       Comment Block: Set ReturnVar to the current value of SiteAvailable field
       SetReturnVar
         Name: RVAvailable
         Expression: [TS].[SiteAvailable]
    Else If [ParamValue]="SendEmailOnError" Then
       Comment Block: Set ReturnVar to the current value of the
                      SendEmailForAppErrors field
       SetReturnVar
         Name: RVSendEmailOnError
         Expression: [TS].[SendEmailForAppErrors]
    Else If [ParamValue]="AdminEmail" Then
       Comment Block: Set ReturnVar to the current value of the AdminEmailAddress field
       SetReturnVar
         Name: RVAdminEmailAddress
         Expression: [TS].[AdminEmailAddress]
    Else If [ParamValue]="AllEmailInfoForErrors" Then
       Comment Block: For this parameter value, send back the settings for both the
                      SendEmailOnError and AdminEmailAddress fields so the
                      caller doesn't need to make two trips.
       SetReturnVar
         Name: RVSendEmailForError
         Expression: [TS].[SendEmailForAppErrors]
       SetReturnVar
         Name: RVAdminEmailForErrors
         Expression: [TS].[AdminEmailAddress]
    End If
```

The tblSettings table holds application-specific settings in several fields. By storing these settings in the table, we can then use data macros to retrieve these values at any time. The dmGetSettings named data macro uses a large If block inside a LookupRecord data block. The If/Else If conditions check the value of the parameter ParamValue being passed in from the caller. We then use the SetReturnVar data action to define a new return variable. The SetReturnVar action takes two arguments:

- **Name.** Required argument. The name of the return variable.

- **Expression.** Required argument. The expression that Access uses to define the return variable.

I set a unique name for each return variable inside the various Else If condition blocks. For the Expression argument of each SetReturnVar action, I use an alias of the table name and read the data from a specific field. In the last Else If condition block, I return data from two fields with two different return variables to save the caller from having to make two RunDataMacro calls for related application settings. I could optionally create a named data macro that returns all data from the fields with return variables in one call, but I didn't want to be passing around data when it would not be needed. By itself, this named data macro does not do anything more than read values from the tblSettings table. However, the real power of the return variables is the ability of the object calling this named data macro to use these values.

To see how this data in return variables can be used, close the Logic Designer for this named data macro. Now open in Design view the dmAuditInvoiceTotalsOneVendor named data macro. Access opens the Logic Designer and displays the logic that I created for this named data macro, as shown in Figure 4-61. This named data macro audits all invoice records for a specific vendor within a given date range. The named data macro starts by running a different named data macro to retrieve a date range number from a system table. The named data macro then loops through each invoice detail record for each invoice within the desired date range, adds up the total amount of the line item details, and compares it to the invoice total. If the line item details match the invoice total, Access marks the invoice balanced. If the line item details do not match the invoice total, Access marks the invoice as unbalanced. Finally, Access returns the total number of unbalanced invoices, if any, to the calling macro.

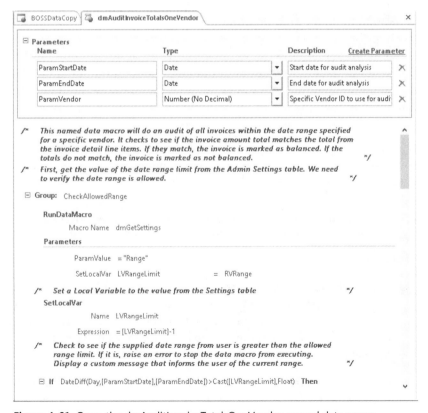

Figure 4-61 Open the dmAuditInvoiceTotalsOneVendor named data macro.

This named data macro is quite lengthy, so I'll break up our discussion of the logic behind this named data macro into several parts. The logic for the first part of the named data macro is as follows:

```
Parameter Name: ParamStartDate
Parameter Type: Date
Parameter Description: Start date for audit analysis
Parameter Name: ParamEndDate
Parameter Type: Date
Parameter Description: End date for audit analysis
Parameter Name: ParamVendor
Parameter Type: Number (No Decimal)
Parameter Description: Specific Vendor ID to use for audit analysis
Comment Block: This named data macro will do an audit of all invoices within the date
range specified for a specific vendor. It checks to see if the invoice amount total
matches the total from the invoice detail line items. If they match, the invoice is
marked as balanced. If the totals do not match, the invoice is marked as not
balanced.
Comment Block: First, get the value of the date range limit from the Admin Settings
table. We need to verify the date range is allowed.
Group: CheckAllowedRange
  RunDataMacro:
    Macro Name: dmGetSettings
    Parameters:
      ParamValue: "Range"
      SetLocalVar: LVRangeLimit = RVRange
  Comment Block: Set a Local Variable to the value from the Settings table
  SetLocalVar
    Name: LVRangeLimit
    Expression: [LVRangeLimit]-1
  Comment Block: Check to see if the supplied date range from user is greater than
  the allowed range limit. If it is, raise an error to stop the data macro from
  executing. Display a custom message that informs the user of the current range.
  If DateDiff(Day,[ParamStartDate],[ParamEndDate])>Cast([LVRangeLimit],Float)=True
    Raise Error:
      Error Description: =Concat("You have attempted to run an invoice audit with a
      date range larger than the allotted number of days. Please restrict your date
      range to ",(Cast([LVRangeLimit],Float)+1)," days.")
  End If
End Group
```

The dmAuditInvoiceTotalsOneVendor named data macro includes three parameters. I pass in all three of these values from a user interface macro to know what date range I want to audit invoice records and the specific vendor records to audit. Inside the Group block, I use the RunDataMacro action. For the Macro Name argument of the RunDataMacro action, I use the dmGetSettings named data macro, which you saw in the previous section.

You'll notice in Figure 4-61 that Access displays a Parameters section beneath the Macro Name argument. When you add a named data macro that includes parameters to the macro design surface, Access shows those parameters to you by providing a text box to enter the parameters. In our example, I pass in the Range parameter to get the value of the RangeLimit text field from the tblSettings table. Beneath the parameter value on the macro design surface, Access displays a SetLocalVar action for each return variable in the dmGetSettings named data macro. When Access returns the variable, or potential variables as the case might be, back to the calling macro, you can assign a local variable to each of the return variables and use them during the execution of the named data macro. In our example, because I'm getting one return variable back, you see only one SetLocalVar action displayed on the macro design surface. After you save and close the named data macro, Access displays only SetLocalVar actions inside the Parameters block for variables you set to handle the return variables. If you click the Update Parameters link, Access displays a SetLocalVar action for each return variable. For our example, I set a local variable called LVRangeLimit, which holds the RVRange return variable received from the dmGetSettings named data macro.

After the RunDataMacro action completes and returns back the needed data through the return variable, Access subtracts one number from the local variable previously set by the return variable. In the If condition that follows, I define an expression to calculate the difference in days from the start date and end date parameters. In the second part of the If condition, I check to see whether that value exceeds the date range limit previously defined using the *Cast* function. If the date range exceeds the limit, I use a RaiseError data action to inform the user that the date range is too large and stop the named data macro from executing any further. The message I display to the user in the RaiseError action uses the *Concat* function to display a custom text message that includes the number of days they are allowed to use for the date range.

In Figure 4-62, you can see the second section of the dmAuditInvoiceTotalsOneVendor named data macro. In Figure 4-62, I collapsed the Parameters block so that you can see more of the logic.

Chapter 4

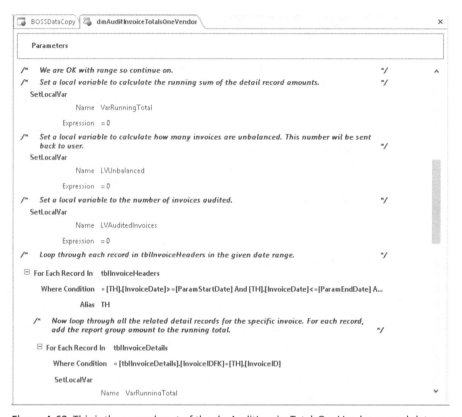

Figure 4-62 This is the second part of the dmAuditInvoiceTotalsOneVendor named data macro.

The logic for the second section of the dmAuditInvoiceTotalsOneVendor named data macro is as follows:

```
Comment Block: We are OK with range so continue on.
Comment Block: Set a local variable to calculate the running sum of the detail record
amounts.
SetLocalVar
  Name: VarRunningTotal
  Expression: 0
Comment Block: Set a local variable to calculate how many invoices are unbalanced.
This number will be sent back to user.
SetLocalVar
  Name: LVUnbalanced
  Expression: 0
Comment Block: Set a local variable to the number of invoices audited.
SetLocalVar
  Name: LVAuditedInvoices
  Expression: 0
Comment Block: Loop through each record in tblInvoiceHeaders in the given date range.
ForEachRecord In tblInvoiceHeaders
```

```
Where Condition = [TH].[InvoiceDate]>=[ParamStartDate] And
            [TH].[InvoiceDate]<=[ParamEndDate] And [TH].[VendorIDFK]=[ParamVendor]
Alias: TH
Comment Block: Now loop through all the related detail records for the specific
    invoice. For each record, add the report group amount to the running total.
ForEachRecord In tblInvoiceDetails
  Where Condition = [tblInvoiceDetails].[InvoiceIDFK]=[TH].[InvoiceID]
  SetLocalVar
   Name: VarRunningTotal
   Expression: [VarRunningTotal]+[tblInvoiceDetails].[ReportGroupAmount]
```

In this section of the named data macro, I define three local variables—VarRunningTotal, LVUnbalanced, and LVAuditedInvoices. The VarRunningTotal local variable tracks the running sum of the total invoice details line items for each specific invoice. The LVUnbalanced local variable tracks how many unbalanced invoices Access finds during the course of the named data macro execution. The LVAuditedInvoices local variable tracks how many invoices Access audits within the given parameters of data macro execution.

The named data macro then executes a ForEachRecord data block to loop through all records in the tblInvoiceHeaders table. For this ForEachRecord data block, I use TH as an alias to represent the name of the tblInvoiceHeaders table for brevity in subsequent areas of the named data macro. The expression I use in the Where condition argument for the ForEachRecord data block is as follows:

```
[TH].[InvoiceDate]>=[ParamStartDate] And [TH].[InvoiceDate]<=[ParamEndDate] And [TH].
[VendorIDFK]=[ParamVendor]
```

The Where condition restricts Access to look for invoice records between the start date and end dates passed in from the parameters. Access further restricts the records to loop through by looking for the specific vendor ID also passed in as a parameter.

Inside the ForEachRecord data block for tblInvoiceHeaders, I use another ForEachRecord data block to then loop through the invoice details records in the tblInvoiceDetails table for each invoice that Access finds in the first ForEachRecord data block. The expression I use in the Where condition argument for this second ForEachRecord data block is as follows:

```
[tblInvoiceDetails].[InvoiceIDFK]=[TH].[InvoiceID]
```

Inside the second ForEachRecord data block, I set a local variable called VarRunningTotal, previously set to zero, to increment itself by the line item total found in the ReportGroupAmount field. On each pass through tblInvoiceDetails table for each specific invoice, Access then keeps a running total of the amount spent on each invoice in this child table.

In Figure 4-63, you can see the third section of the dmAuditInvoiceTotalsOneVendor named data macro.

Figure 4-63 This is the third part of the dmAuditInvoiceTotalsOneVendor named data macro.

The logic for the third section of the dmAuditInvoiceTotalsOneVendor named data macro is as follows:

```
Comment Block: Now compare the running total amount to the current invoice amount. If
they match, mark the IsBalanced boolean field as Yes (balanced). If they don't match,
mark it as No (unbalanced).
  EditRecord
    If [VarRunningTotal]=[TH].[InvoiceAmount] Then
      Comment Block: Invoice is balanced.
      SetField
        Name: [TH].[IsBalanced]
        Value: Yes
    Else
      Comment Block: Invoice is not balanced.
      SetField
        Name: [TH].[IsBalanced]
        Value: No
    Comment Block: Increment the counter of unbalanced invoices by 1
    SetLocalVar
      Name: LVUnbalanced
      Expression: =[LVUnbalanced]+1
    End If
  End EditRecord
```

After Access finishes calculating the total from all the invoice details for one invoice, I then have an EditRecord block inside the first ForEachRecord data block. Inside the EditRecord block, I use an If block to test whether the running invoice total, tracked by the VarRunningTotal local variable, equals the amount stored in the InvoiceTotal field in the tblInvoiceHeaders table. If the two amounts match, I use a SetField data action to instruct Access to update the IsBalanced field in tblInvoiceHeaders to Yes. If the two amounts do not match, Access goes into the Else block and then uses SetField to change the IsBalanced field to No. Inside the Else block, I also increment the LVUnbalanced local variable, which is tracking the number of unbalanced invoices, by one.

In Figure 4-64, you can see the last section of the dmAuditInvoiceTotalsOneVendor named data macro.

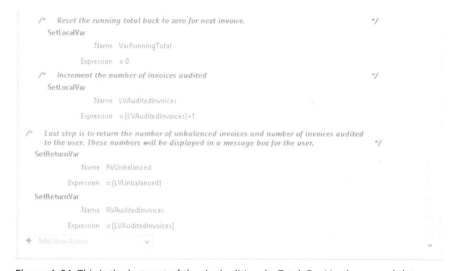

Figure 4-64 This is the last part of the dmAuditInvoiceTotalsOneVendor named data macro.

The logic for the last section of the dmAuditInvoiceTotalsOneVendor named data macro is as follows:

```
Comment Block: Reset the running total back to zero for next invoice.
SetLocalVar
  Name: VarRunningTotal
  Expression: 0
Comment Block: Increment the number of invoices audited
SetLocalVar
  Name: LVAuditedInvoices
  Expression: [LVAuditedInvoices]+1
```

Comment Block: Last step is to return the number of unbalanced invoices and number of invoices audited to the user. These numbers will be displayed in a message box for the user.

```
SetReturnVar
  Name: RVUnbalanced
  Expression: [LVUnbalanced]
SetReturnVar
  Name: RVAuditedInvoices
  Expression: [LVAuditedInvoices]
```

Now that we've completed checking one invoice inside the first ForEachRecord data block, we need to update two local variables before moving on to the next invoice. First, I need to update the VarRunningTotal local variable back to zero so that it is ready to start calculating the next invoice. Second, I need to update the LVAuditedInvoices local variable by one to account for the number of invoices Access audited. After this point, Access moves back to the beginning of the first ForEachRecord data block and completes the same steps previously outlined if another invoice exists within the given parameters. Access continues auditing each invoice one by one and updating all of the local variables as appropriate.

After Access completes auditing all invoices, the final piece of this named data macro is to set two return variables. As you might recall, this named data macro began with running a different named macro that used a return variable to bring data into this named data macro. I now end the logic in this named data macro by setting two return variables that any calling macro can use to see the results of this auditing macro. I set the first SetReturnVar data action—RVUnbalanced—equal to the local variable LVUnbalanced, which tracked the total number of unbalanced invoices. I set the second SetReturnVar data action—RVAuditedInvoices—equal to the local variable LVAuditedInvoices, which tracked the total number of audited invoices. In Chapter 7, you'll learn how to call this named data macro from a user interface macro and use the return variables in a message box.

As you can see, return variables are a very useful feature with data macros. When you use them in conjunction with parameters, you can create some very complex business logic at the data layer and even pass information back up to the user interface layer.

INSIDE OUT   Utilizing the Retrieve ID return variable

When you use the CreateRecord data block, Access displays a Retrieve ID link on the right side of the macro design surface. If you want to know the ID AutoNumber of the record Access creates inside a CreateRecord data block, you can click this link to retrieve the ID as a return variable. Access displays a SetLocalVar action inside a Parameters block where you can provide a name for the local variable. You can then use that local variable, passed from Access through the Retrieve ID return variable, in further actions of your data macro logic.

Studying other named data macros

The Back Office Software System sample web app includes many named data macros to automate various aspects of the app. Table 4-3 lists all the named data macros in the web app with a short description of their purpose. You can explore these samples for additional examples of how to design and use named data macros. In Chapter 7, you'll learn how to call some of these named data macros from user interface macros.

TABLE 4-3   Named data macros in the BOSS web app

Macro Name	Description
dmApplyLaborPlanDetails	Loops through all the labor plan details for a specific Labor Plan and creates new schedule records in tblSchedule.
dmAuditInvoiceTotalsAllVendors	Audits all invoices within a given date range.
dmAuditInvoiceTotalsOneVendor	Audits all invoices within a given date range for a specific vendor.
dmClearOutTraceTableRecords	Deletes all records from the Trace table.
dmCopyDateRangeRecords	Loops through all the schedule records within a date range and creates new schedule records in tblSchedule with the same information. The new schedule date to use comes from a parameter.
dmCopySingleDateRecords	Loops through all the schedule records for a specific date and creates new schedule records in tblSchedule with the same information. The new schedule date to use comes from a parameter.
dmDeleteDateRangeScheduleRecords	Deletes all records in tblSchedule within a given date range.
dmDeleteSingleDateScheduleRecords	Deletes all records in tblSchedule for a given date.
dmEnforceOnlyOnePrimaryPosition	Ensures that only one job code is marked as the primary position for a specific employee. This named data macro is called from both the On Insert and On Update tblTrainedPositions table events.
dmGetSettings	Gets application settings data from the tblSettings table.
dmSetJobCodeColor	Sets color choices in the tblJobCodes table from parameters passed in from user interface macros.
dmSwapSortOrders	Swaps sort order positions in the tblInventoryLocations table for two records. Uses saved query objects to find the highest and lowest values in the SortOrder field.

Chapter 4

Macro Name	Description
dmUpdateSampleData	Adjusts date values of all sample data to work easily with data around the current time frame.
dmVerifyInvoiceBalanced	Checks to see whether a specific invoice is balanced.

Debugging data macros with the Trace table

You're likely to encounter unexpected errors or unintended results when you're designing data macros attached to table events and complex named data macros for the first time. You might even be wondering whether Access is even executing your data macros at all if you see no visible results. In Chapter 24, "Understanding Visual Basic fundamentals," which can be downloaded from the book's catalog page, you'll learn that you have several tools available in the Visual Basic Editor for debugging Visual Basic code in desktop databases. Data macros, unfortunately, do not have as rich a set of tools available for debugging purposes. For example, you cannot set breakpoints on data macro logic to halt execution. You also cannot single-step through the macro logic as you can with user interface macros in desktop databases.

Access can run into errors while you are in the development phase of creating, testing, and debugging your data macros. The best tool you have for debugging data macro logic is a special system table called the *Trace* table. Access manages any errors it encounters executing data macros through this system table. This Trace table serves two purposes:

- Access uses it to log any data macro failures that it encounters while executing data macros attached to table events and named data macros.

- You can use the table for debugging purposes when designing and testing data macros by viewing a history of everything Access executes while running your data macros in this table.

Earlier in this chapter, you studied the data macro logic attached to the On Update event of the tblTerminations table. When you update a termination record and assign the termination record to a different employee, the On Update logic looks up the previous employee's record in the tblEmployees table and sets the Active field back to Yes. In the first LookupRecord data block, I used the Old property to refer to the EmployeeID that Access just finished updating. In the second LookupRecord data block, Access sets the Active field to No for the employee you just selected. Our data macro logic, again, is as follows:

```
Comment Block: If we are modifying an existing termination record, one of two
possibilities exist: 1. The Employee that this termination is for remains unchanged -
Scenario is just updating some data for the termination record. 2. The Employee that
this termination is assigned to changed - Scenario here is that when the record was
first created, it might have been assigned to the wrong employee. In this case the
```

```
user is assigning this to a different employee.
Comment Block: Check to see if the Employee field was changed.
If Update([EmployeeIDFK]) Then
  Comment Block: The Employee field changed so we'll change the existing employee's
  status back to Yes.
  Comment Block: For the Where condition in this LookupRecord, use the Old value from
  the EmployeeIDFK field and find that employee's record.
  Look Up A Record In tblEmployees
    Where Condition = [tblEmployees].[EmployeeID]=[Old].[EmployeeIDFK]
      EditRecord
        Comment Block: Now set Active field to Yes for this employee since it was
        probably initially assigned to the employee in error.
        SetField
          Name: [tblEmployees].[Active]
          Value: Yes

      End EditRecord
End If
Comment Block: After modifying this termination record, make sure the employee that
it's assigned to now is marked as an inactive employee. To do that, we look up the
matching employee's record in the tblEmployees table and set the Active field to No.
Look Up A Record In tblEmployees
    Where Condition = [tblEmployees].[EmployeeID]=[tblTerminations].[EmployeeIDFK]
      EditRecord
        Comment Block: Now set Active field to No.
        SetField
          Name: [tblEmployees].[Active]
          Value: No

      End EditRecord
```

When you set up complex table events and named data macros like this example, you'll find it helpful to debug your logic to make sure everything is working just the way you want. For example, if you have only a few sample records in your tables, you might find it relatively easy to spot and fix any issues in your data macros with such a small data set. However, if your tables have many records, you might find it more difficult to spot any issues, or you might have a more difficult time tracking down what data Access updates. To help debug your data macro logic, you can take advantage of the built in Trace table.

For this specific On Update event example, it would be helpful to know which employee records, if any, Access updates during this table event. To start using the Trace table, the first thing that you need to do is to turn on data macro tracing for your web app. To do this, open any table event for any table in your web app or open any named data macro in Design view. After Access opens the Logic Designer, click the Data Macro Tracing button in the Tracing group on the Design contextual tab, as shown in Figure 4-65.

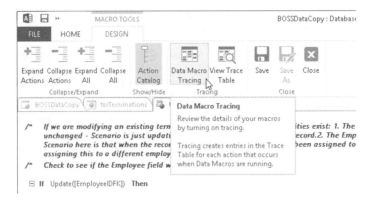

Figure 4-65 Click the Data Macro Tracing button to activate data macro tracing in your web app.

When you activate data macro tracing, Access records information to the Trace table. To see how useful the Trace table can be, let's change the existing termination record in the tblTerminations table. Switch to Datasheet view for the tblTerminations table. Next, find the existing termination record in this table—the one assigned to Mario Kresnadi. Next, tab over to the EmployeeIDFK for this record (the datasheet caption of the field displays Employee), type **Conrad** into the control where it currently says Mario Kresnadi, and then select Jeff Conrad from the drop-down list of employee names displayed in the Employee-IDFK field, as shown in Figure 4-66. Finally, click or tab off the record, and Access saves the record with Jeff Conrad's EmployeeIDFK number. (If you changed this record to Jeff Conrad previously in this chapter, change the value back to Mario Kresnadi. You'll be able to see results in the Trace table in either case.)

Figure 4-66 Change the EmployeeIDFK field from Mario Kresnadi to Jeff Conrad, and then save the record.

> **Note**
>
> Each web app you create includes the Trace system table, which is a hidden table. Therefore, you cannot create any table in your web app and name it Trace. If you do, Access informs you that an existing object with that name already exists in the web app.

To see the effects of this On Update event in the Trace table, switch to Design view for the tblTerminations table and then open any of three table events in Design view. After Access opens the Logic Designer, click the View Trace Table button in the Tracing group on the Design contextual tab, as shown in Figure 4-67.

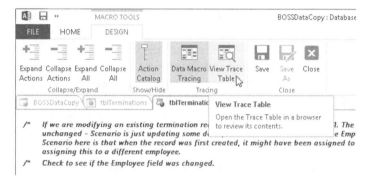

Figure 4-67 Click the View Trace Table button to open the data macro Trace table in your web browser.

Access opens the Trace table datasheet in your default web browser, as shown in Figure 4-68. The Trace table contains the following fields: ID, MacroName, ActionName, Operand, Output, TargetRow, Timestamp, and RuntimeErrorMessage. When you have data macro tracing turned on, Access creates a record in the Trace table for every action it runs during any table event or named data macro. Depending on the complexity of your data macro logic for a given table event or named data macro, you could see just a few new records in the Trace table or perhaps hundreds of new records. The Trace table holds a maximum of 1000 records. If the number of records in the Trace table exceeds 1000, Access begins deleting the oldest records as it creates new entries.

> **Note**
>
> In Figure 4-68, I resized several of the Trace table columns so that you could see more of the data in the various records. To resize a column in the Trace table, hover over the right edge of a column header until you see a double-sided arrow, click and hold your mouse, and drag the column to the right until you have the size you want.

Figure 4-68 Access opens the Trace table in your web browser so that you can examine how your data macro logic executes.

The ID field in the Trace table is the AutoNumber field Access uses for this table. The MacroName field lists the name of the table and the specific event Access executed or the name of the named data macro Access executed. The ActionName field lists the name of the program construct, data block, or data action Access executed. In the Operand field, Access lists any conditional expressions or table and field references in the case of SetField data actions. In the Output field, Access lists data values it commits into a field. In the TargetRow field, Access lists identifying information about what record it is writing data to, such as the ID values. In the TimeStamp field, Access enters the current date and time of the specific action. In the RuntimeErrorMessage field, Access displays a SQL exception message if it encounters an error while performing the specific action. Access also logs any RaiseError messages that you define into the RuntimeErrorMessage field. Table 4-4 summarizes the important information Access logs to the Trace table.

TABLE 4-4 Trace table logging information

Action Name	Operand	Output	Target Row
If	Conditional expression		
Else If	Conditional expression		
CreateRecord	Table name		
EditRecord			
ForEachRecord	Table name, Where condition		Record identifiers
LookupRecord	Table name, Where condition		Record identifiers
CancelRecordChange			
DeleteRecord			
ExitForEachRecord			
RaiseError			

Action Name	Operand	Output	Target Row
RunDataMacro	Macro name	Computed expression value	
SetField	Table and field name	Computed expression value	
SetLocalVar	Variable name	Computed expression value	
SetReturnVar	Variable name	Computed expression value	
StopMacro			

In our example On Update event, you can see that Access logged nine records carrying out all the actions in the On Update table event. In the first record, Access displays the If block and the conditional expression. In the second record, you can see that Access displays the LookupRecord in the ActionName column along with the table name and Where condition in the Operand field. In the third record, Access repeats the LookupRecord data block but this time displays the ID values of the record it found that match the Where condition. In the fourth record, Access lists EditRecord, which indicates it is now entering this data block because it found a matching record in the Where condition of the LookupRecord data block. In the fifth record, Access displays the SetField action along with the table name and field in the Operand field. In the Output field for this record, Access displays 1, which, in this case, indicates a Yes value for the Active Boolean field. In the remaining four records in the Trace table, Access lists similar information detailing the second LookupRecord actions outlined in the On Update event of the tblTerminations table. In the SetField record, you can see that Access set the Active field to 0, which indicates No for the Boolean field.

Chapter 4

INSIDE OUT Clearing the Trace table records

When you view the Trace table records in your web browser, you can delete the records if you no longer want to see them by highlighting the records and pressing the Delete key. Depending on how many records you have in your Trace table, this could be a tedious task. You can alternatively write a named data macro to perform the task very quickly. The Trace table is a hidden table in your web app, and therefore you cannot use the Trace table directly in a ForEachRecord or LookupRecord data block. However, you can create a saved query object that uses the Trace table as its source. You can then create a named data macro that includes a DeleteRecord action inside a ForEachRecord data block with the saved query as the source, which causes Access to delete all records in the Trace table when you call the named data macro.

In the Back Office Software System web app, I've included a saved query called qryTraceTable and a named data macro called dmClearOutTraceTableRecords that perform this task. If you have data macro tracing turned on while running that named data macro, Access records all the delete operations into the Trace table, which effectively cancels out what you're trying to do! To work around that issue, you must turn off data macro tracing first and then execute the named data macro to clear out all records in the Trace table using this technique.

Let's examine a different example of a table event that triggers a named data macro so that you can see how Access logs this type of scenario to the Trace table. Earlier in this chapter, you studied the On Update event of the tblTrainedPositions table. Open this table in Datasheet view within Access, and then change either the first or second record such that you've changed the primary position of the first employee listed in the table. After you update the record, refresh the Trace table in your web browser. In Figure 4-69, you can see the six records Access adds to the Trace table while executing the data macro logic in the On Update event.

10	tblTrainedPositions:On Update	If	[tblTrainedPositions].[PrimaryPosition]=Yes		9/12/2012 10:39
11	tblTrainedPositions:On Update	RunDataMacro	dmEnforceOnlyOnePrimaryPosition		9/12/2012 10:39
12	dmEnforceOnlyOnePrimaryPosition	ForEachRecord	tblTrainedPositions;WHERE [tblTrainedPositi		9/12/2012 10:39
13	dmEnforceOnlyOnePrimaryPosition	ForEachRecord		[TrainedPositionsID] = 2 ; [PrimaryPosition] = 1	9/12/2012 10:39
14	dmEnforceOnlyOnePrimaryPosition	EditRecord			9/12/2012 10:39
15	dmEnforceOnlyOnePrimaryPosition	SetField	[tblTrainedPositions].[PrimaryPosition] 0		9/12/2012 10:39
(New)					

Figure 4-69 Refresh the Trace table in your browser to see new logging records Access adds to the table.

If you follow the information that Access displays in the Trace table after you updated the record, you can see that Access first indicates it fired the On Update event in tblTrainedPositions and then executes the named data macro called dmEnforceOnlyOnePrimaryPosition, which you created earlier. You can see that Access executed the ForEachRecord data block in the named data macro, found a specific record that matched the Where condition, and then used a EditRecord with SetField action to update the PrimaryPosition field.

After Access finishes executing your data macro logic, you can examine the values of your local variables and return variables in the Trace table at different points in time to help determine what Access is doing during the data macro execution. You can use this information to assist with debugging your logic. For example, you can examine which record Access might be editing or attempting to find by looking at the values in the TargetRow column.

INSIDE OUT   Turn off data macro tracing in production apps

The Trace table can be very useful when you are designing and testing the logic in your table events and named data macros. When you have everything working just the way you want, you should turn off data macro tracing before putting your app in production for people to use. If you leave data macro tracing turned on in a production environment, Access continually logs information for all data macro logic. You'll see a slight improvement in app performance by turning this feature off in production, because Access does not need to spend extra time writing data to the Trace table for all of your actions.

To turn off data macro tracing, open any table event or named data macro in Design view and click the Data Macro Tracing button in the Tracing group on the Design contextual ribbon tab. This button is essentially a toggle button. When you have data macro tracing turned on in your web app, you'll see this button highlighted in the ribbon. Just click the button in the ribbon again to deselect it and turn off data macro tracing. If you are encountering errors in your production apps, you can turn the data macro tracing back on temporarily, diagnose the issues, fix the issues, and then turn it back off when your data macro logic is working again as you expect.

Note

If you save your web app as an app package, Access includes the Trace table, and any records included in it, into the app package.

Understanding recursion in data macros

When you're designing data macros, you have the potential to run into a recursion issue. Access runs into a recursion issue when it tries to execute the same data macro logic over and over in a repeated loop. For example, suppose that you created data macro logic attached to the On Update event of a table that changed data in the current record of the same table. Access makes the field changes and then commits the data. Access then fires the On Update again because data in the table changed. The On Update event fires again, changes the data, and the cycle begins again. Access is now in a perpetual loop executing the data macro in the On Update event. Access could also get into a loop, for example, when working with two tables that have On Update events that update each other, or even with complex named data macros that end up repeating themselves.

Data macros are limited to 32 levels of recursion, which means Access stops the data macro execution after 32 iterations through a recursive loop. If Access falls into a recursive loop, you'll see a runtime error message indicating that an endless loop was detected, as shown in Figure 4-70. Access logs a SQL Exception error into the RuntimeErrorMessage field of the Trace table if you have data macro tracing turned on. In the Trace table, you'll see essentially the same records getting updated over and over again by Access.

Figure 4-70 Access displays an error message if it gets into a data macro recursion loop.

In most cases, you can correct recursive calls by using the Update function to determine which field or fields Access changed in the last record update. You can add conditional logic with If blocks to determine whether a field was changed and perform different actions, or no actions, based on the evaluation of the condition. As you are designing and testing your data macro logic, it's a good idea to check the Trace table continually to help spot potential problems with recursion.

Sharing data macro logic

The Logic Designer in Access includes a very useful feature for sharing and reusing data macro logic. To illustrate this feature, open the tblTerminations table in the Back Office Software System data copy sample web app (BOSSDataCopy.app) in Design view. Next, click the On Insert button in the Events group to open the Logic Designer. You've already explored the data macro logic attached to this table event earlier in this chapter. Press Ctrl+A to highlight all the logic on the macro design surface, and then press Ctrl+C to copy the logic to the Windows Clipboard. Now open Notepad (or a different text editor), and then press Ctrl+V to paste all the logic into Notepad.

As you can see in Figure 4-71, Access copies the data macro logic from the Logic Designer as Extensible Markup Language (XML). You can send this XML to someone else, and that person can copy and paste the XML directly into a Logic Designer window for a data macro in his or her Access 2013 web app. This feature can be especially useful if you are trying to help someone else write or debug data macro logic, such as in an Access forum or newsgroup. You can create the logic for the person you're helping and explain how you structured the program flow constructs, data blocks, and data actions.

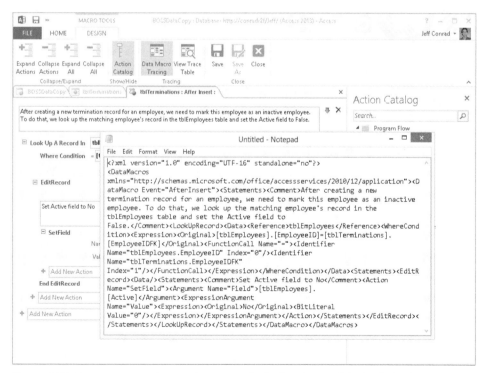

Figure 4-71 You can copy and paste data macro logic directly out of the Logic Designer.

Chapter 4

You now have all the information that you need to modify and maintain your web app table definitions. You know how to build tables, modify them, import data and link them, and create data macros to automate them. In the next chapter, you'll learn how to extract data from tables by building queries.

Working with queries in web apps

N the last two chapters, you learned how to create tables, modify them, and link or import tables from other data sources in web apps and to create data macros attached to table events. Although you can certainly build views that get their data directly from your tables, most of the time you will want to sort or filter your data or display data from more than one table. For these tasks, you need queries.

When you define and run a *select query*, which selects information from the tables and queries in your web app, Microsoft Access 2013 creates a *recordset* of the selected data. In most cases, you can work with a recordset in the same way that you work with a table: you can browse through it, select information from it, and even update the data in it. But unlike a real table, a recordset doesn't actually exist in your database. Access 2013 creates a recordset from the data in the source tables of your query at the time you run the query.

As you learn to design views in the next chapter, you'll find that queries are the best way to focus on the specific data you need for the task at hand. You'll also find that queries are useful for providing choices for combo boxes and autocomplete controls, which make entering data in your web app much easier.

Queries are essential to desktop database as well. Access uses the same query design window both for web apps and for desktop databases, but in general, Access displays fewer options for web apps. Desktop databases also include a special kind of query object called an *action query*. In Part 3, "Building queries in desktop databases," you'll learn about creating queries in desktop databases, but for now, let's focus on designing and working with queries in web apps.

Note

The examples in this chapter are based on the tables and data from the backup copy of the data for the Back Office Software System sample web app (BOSSDataCopy.app), which can be downloaded from the book's catalog page at *http://shop.oreilly.com/ product/0790145367969.do*. You'll need to upload the app into your corporate catalog or Office 365 team site and install the app to use the sample. Review the instructions at the end of Chapter 2, "Exploring the Access 2013 web app interface," if you need help with those tasks. The query results you see from the sample queries you build in this chapter might not exactly match what you see in this book if you have changed the sample data in the web app.

To begin your study of queries, download the Back Office Software System backup sample web app (BOSSDataCopy.app) from your SharePoint site into Access.

To open an existing query in Design view, make sure you have the Navigation pane expanded. If the Navigation pane is collapsed, click the Navigation Pane button in the Show group on the Home ribbon tab. You can open the query you want in Design view by selecting the query in the Navigation pane and then pressing Ctrl+Enter. You can also right-click a query name in the Navigation pane and click Design View from the shortcut menu. Figure 5-1 shows the list of queries for the Back Office Software System web app. Please note that the figure shows you only some of the queries in the web app. Use the scroll bar in the Navigation pane to see the complete list of queries available in the web app.

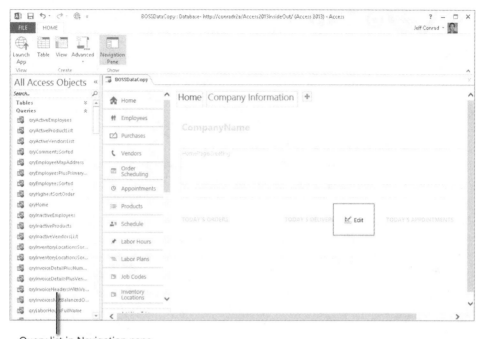

Query list in Navigation pane

Figure 5-1 The Navigation pane has been filtered to show all the queries in the Back Office Software System web app.

Figure 5-2 shows a query that has been opened in Design view. The upper part of the Query window contains field lists, and the lower part contains the design grid.

Field list of tables or
queries used in this query

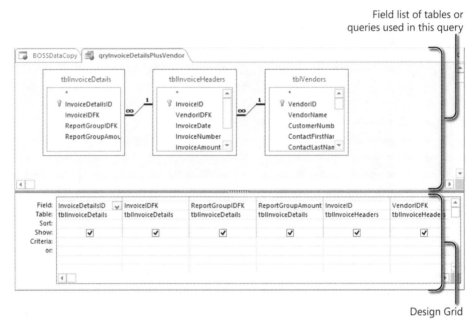

Design Grid

Figure 5-2 A query open in Design view shows the tables and field lists.

Selecting data from a single table

One advantage of using queries is that they allow you to find data easily in multiple related tables. However, queries are also useful for sifting through the data in a single table. All the techniques you use for working with a single table apply equally to more complex multiple-table queries. This section shows you how to build a query to select data from a single table. Later in this chapter, we'll create more complex queries with multiple tables, totals, parameters, and more.

To start building a query on a single table in a web app, click the Advanced button on the Home ribbon tab and then click Query in the drop-down list of options, as shown in Figure 5-3.

Figure 5-3 Click Advanced, and then click Query to start creating a new query.

In Chapter 8, "Automating a web app using macros," you'll learn how to use the Macro and On Start Macro options on the Advanced button.

Access 2013 displays the Show Table dialog box on top of the query design grid, as shown in Figure 5-4.

Figure 5-4 The Show Table dialog box allows you to select one or more tables or queries to build a new query.

Select tblEmployees on the Tables tab of the Show Table dialog box, and then click Add to place tblEmployees in the upper part of the Query window. Click Close in the Show Table dialog box to view the window shown in Figure 5-5.

Figure 5-5 The Query window in Design view for a new query on tblEmployees shows the table with its list of fields in the top part of the window.

As mentioned earlier, the Query window in Design view has two main parts. In the upper part, you find field lists with the fields for the tables or queries you chose for this query. The lower part of the window is the design grid, in which you do all the design work. Each column in the grid represents one field that you'll work with in this query. As you'll see later, a field can be a simple field from one of the tables or a calculated field based on several fields in the tables.

You use the first row of the design grid to select fields—the fields you want in the resulting recordset, the fields you want to sort by, and the fields you want to test for values. As you'll learn later, you can also generate custom field names (for display in the resulting recordset), and you can use complex expressions or calculations to generate a calculated field.

The second row shows you the name of the table from which you selected a field. This isn't too important when building a query on a single table, but you'll learn later that this row provides valuable information when building a query that fetches data from more than one table or query.

In the Sort row, you can specify whether Access should sort the selected or calculated field in ascending or descending order. In the Show row, you can use the check boxes to indicate the fields that will be included in the recordset. By default, Access includes all the fields you place in the design grid. Sometimes you'll want to include a field in the query to allow you to select the records you want (such as employees born in a certain date range), but you won't need that field in the recordset. You can add that field to the design grid so that you can define criteria, but you should clear the Show check box beneath the field to exclude it from the recordset.

Finally, you can use the Criteria row and the row(s) labeled Or to enter the criteria you want to use as filters. After you understand how a query is put together, you'll find it easy to specify exactly the fields and records that you want.

Specifying fields

The first step in building a query is to select the fields you want in the recordset. You can select the fields in several ways. Using the keyboard, you can tab to a column in the design grid and press Alt+Down Arrow to open the list of available fields. (To move to the design grid, press F6.) Use the Up Arrow and Down Arrow keys to highlight the field you want, and then press Enter to select the field.

Another way to select a field is to drag it from one of the field lists in the upper part of the window to one of the columns in the design grid, or you can double-click the field name. In Figure 5-6, the LastName field is being dragged to the design grid. When you drag a field, the mouse pointer turns into a small rectangle.

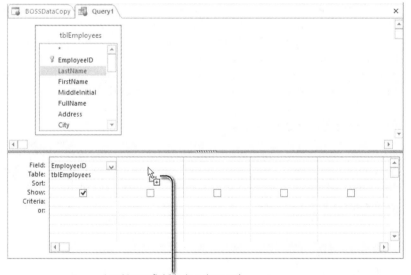

LastName field being dragged
and dropped in the design grid

Figure 5-6 You can drag a field from the table field list to a column in the design grid.

At the top of each field list in the upper part of the Query window (and also next to the first entry in the Field drop-down list in the design grid) is an asterisk (*) symbol. This symbol is shorthand for selecting "all fields in the table or the query" with one entry on the Field line. When you want to include all the fields in a table or a query, you don't have to define each one individually in the design grid unless you also want to define some sorting or selection criteria for specific fields. You can simply add the asterisk to the design grid to include all the fields from a list. You can add individual fields to the grid in addition to the asterisk to define criteria for those fields, but you should clear the Show check box for the individual fields so that they don't appear twice in the recordset.

INSIDE OUT   Another way to select all fields

Another easy way to select all the fields in a table is to double-click the title bar of the field list in the upper part of the Query window—this highlights all the fields. Then click any of the highlighted fields, and drag them as a group to the Field row in the design grid. While you're dragging, the mouse pointer changes to a multiple rectangle icon, indicating that you're dragging multiple fields. When you release the mouse button, you'll see that Access has copied all the fields to the design grid for you.

For this exercise, select EmployeeID, LastName, FirstName, State, and Birthdate from the tblEmployees table in the Back Office Software System web app. You can select the fields one at a time by dragging them to the design grid. You can also double-click each field name, and Access will move it to the design grid into the next available slot. Finally, you can click on one field you want and then hold down the Ctrl key as you click on additional fields, or you can hold down the Shift key to select a group of contiguous fields. Grab the last field you select, and drag them all to the design grid.

Viewing query results

If you want to see the results of your query, you must first save the query. Click the Save button on the Quick Access Toolbar, press Ctrl+S, or right-click the query object tab near the top of the application and select Save from the shortcut menu. Access opens the Save As dialog, as shown in Figure 5-7.

Figure 5-7 Click Save, and then provide a name for your new query.

For this test query, enter **qryEmployeeBirthdays** as the name of this new query object in the Save As dialog box and then click OK. Now that you've saved your query, you can switch to Datasheet view to view the results of this query. To switch to Datasheet view from the Design view you are currently working in, click the View button in the Results group on the Design tab under Query Tools and then click Datasheet View on the drop-down menu, as shown in Figure 5-8. Alternatively, you can right-click the query object tab and select Datasheet view from the shortcut menu to switch into Datasheet view for your saved query.

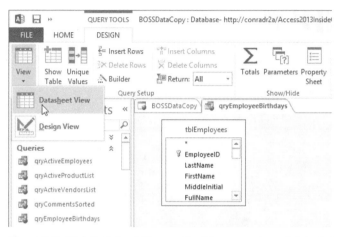

Figure 5-8 Click Datasheet View on the View menu to switch to Datasheet view.

> ## Note
>
> If you attempt to switch to Datasheet view for a new query or a query that you have changed, Access prompts you that you must save the query first. To view a query datasheet in Access, the query must not have any unsaved changes. When you're viewing a query in Datasheet view, the view is much like viewing a table in Datasheet view. In both cases, these views are intended for working with your web app data from within Access. Microsoft refers to these types of views as preview datasheets. Throughout the remainder of this chapter, I'll generally refer to viewing a query in Access as Datasheet view instead of a preview Datasheet, but remember that they are essentially the same.

Access now switches to Datasheet view, executes the query, and displays the results of your query, as shown in Figure 5-9. In this example, Access displays the data from the five fields across all 31 records in the tblEmployees table. Access does not display a record count in Datasheet view for queries displayed in web apps. (In Chapter 12, "Creating and working with simple queries," you'll learn that Access displays record counts in desktop database queries.) Later in this chapter, you'll learn how to navigate around in Datasheet view for queries, but for now, switch back to Design view for this query to continue. To do this, click

Chapter 5

the View button in the Views group, which you can see in Figure 5-9, and then click Design View on the drop-down menu.

Figure 5-9 In query Datasheet view, you can see the results of the query definition you created.

Troubleshooting

Why does my query on a large linked SharePoint list just display an error?
Access returns only a maximum of 10,000 records in a query based on a linked Share-Point list. If your linked SharePoint list contains more than 10,000 records, Access displays an error when you try to view the query in Datasheet view. To display results from a large linked SharePoint list, you should enter criteria in the query to restrict the returned records to a smaller data set. You'll learn about query criteria in the next section.

Entering selection criteria

Although you can certainly design queries to return all records, in most cases you'll want to return only a subset of the data from your tables. The next step is to further refine the records you want by specifying criteria on one or more fields. The example shown in Figure 5-10 selects employees working in the state of California.

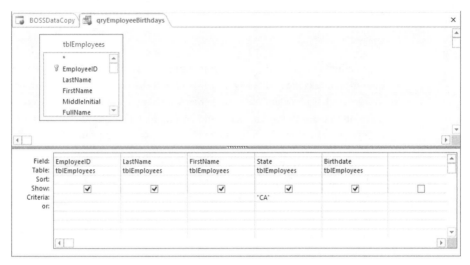

Figure 5-10 When you specify "CA" as the selection criterion in the design grid, Access returns only records with a State value equal to California.

Entering selection criteria in a query is similar to entering a validation rule for a field, which you learned about in Chapter 3, "Designing tables in a web app." To look for a single value, simply type it in the Criteria row for the field you want to test. If the field you're testing is a text field and the value you're looking for has any blank spaces in it, you must enclose the value in quotation marks. Access adds quotation marks for you around single text values. (In Figure 5-10, I typed CA, but Access replaced what I typed with "CA" after I left that column. Be aware that IntelliSense might try to be too helpful here and replace CA with the Cast function.)

If you want to test for any of several values, enter the values in the Criteria row, separated by the word *Or*. For example, specifying *CA Or NC* searches for records for California or North Carolina. You can also test for any of several values by entering each value in a separate Criteria or Or row for the field you want to test. For example, you can enter *CA* in the Criteria row, *NC* in the next row (the first Or row), and so on—but you have to be careful if you're also specifying criteria in other fields, as explained in the section "AND vs. OR," later in this chapter.

Chapter 5

INSIDE OUT   Be careful when your criterion is also a keyword

You should be careful when entering criteria that might also be an Access 2013 keyword. In the examples shown here, I could have chosen to use criteria for the two-character abbreviation for the state of Oregon (OR)—but *or*, as you can see in the examples, is also a keyword. In many cases, Access is smart enough to figure out what you mean from the context. You can enter:

Or Or Ca

In the criteria under State, and Access assumes that the first Or is criteria (by placing quotation marks around the word for you) and the second Or is the Boolean operator keyword. If you want to be sure that Access interprets your criteria correctly, always place double quotation marks around criteria text. If you find that Access guessed wrong, you can always correct the entry before saving the query.

In the section "AND vs. OR," you'll see that you can also include a comparison operator in the Criteria row so that, for example, you can look for values less than (<), greater than or equal to (>=), or not equal to (<>) the value that you specify.

Working with dates and times in criteria

Access 2013 stores dates and times as 8-byte decimal numbers in web apps. The value to the left of the decimal point represents the day (day zero is January 1, 1900, in web apps), and the fractional part of the number stores the time as a fraction of a day, accurate to seconds. Fortunately, you don't have to worry about converting internal numbers to specify a test for a particular date value, because Access handles date and time entries in several formats.

You must always surround date and time values with pound signs (#) to tell Access that you're entering a date or a time. To test for a specific date, use the date notation that is most comfortable for you. For example, *#April 15, 1962#*, *#4/15/62#*, and *#15-Apr-1962#* are all the same date if you chose English (United States) in the Regional And Language Options item in the Control Panel. Similarly, *#5:30 PM#* and *#17:30#* both specify 5:30 in the evening.

INSIDE OUT   Understanding date/time criteria

You must be careful when building criteria to test a range in a date/time field. Let's say you want to look at all records between two dates in the tblTerminations table, which has a date/time field—CompletedDate—that holds the date and time the employee termination was created. For all terminations in the month of January, 2013, you might be tempted to put the following on the Criteria line under ContactDateTime.

```
>=#1/1/2013# AND <=#1/31/2013#
```

When you look at the results, you might wonder why no rows show up from January 31, 2013, even when you know that you made and recorded several termination records on that day. The reason is simple. Remember, a date/time field contains an integer off-set value for the date and a fraction for the time. Let's say you called someone at 9:55 A.M. on January 31, 2013. The internal value is actually 41,303.4132—January 31, 2013, is 41,303 days later than January 1, 1900 (the zero point), and .4132 is the fraction of a day that represents 9:55 A.M. When you say you want rows where CompletedDate is less than or equal to January 31, 2013, you're comparing to the internal value 41,303—just the day value, which is midnight on that day. For example, you won't find an 8:30 A.M. record because the value is greater than 41,303, or later in the day than midnight. To search successfully, you must enter the following:

```
>=#1/1/2013# AND <#2/1/2013#
```

Alternatively, you could also include the time portion of the ending date in the date range as follows:

```
>=#1/1/2013# AND <=#1/31/2013 11:59:59 PM#
```

AND vs. OR

When you enter criteria for several fields, all the tests in a single Criteria row or Or row must be true for Access to include a record in the recordset. That is, Access performs a logical AND operation between multiple criteria in the same row. So if you enter **CA** in the Criteria row for State and **<#1 JAN 1984#** in the Criteria row for Birthdate, the record must be for the state of California and must be for someone born before 1984 to be selected. If you enter **CA Or NC** in the Criteria row for State and **>=#01/01/1950# AND <#1 JAN 1984#** in the Criteria row for Birthdate, the record must be for the state of California or North Carolina, *and* the person must have been born between 1950 and 1983.

Figure 5-11 shows the result of applying a logical AND operator between any two tests. As you can see, both tests must be true for the result of the AND to be true and for the record to be selected.

AND	True	False
True	True (Selected)	False (Rejected)
False	False (Rejected)	False (Rejected)

Figure 5-11 When you specify the logical AND operator between two tests, the result is true only if both tests are true.

When you specify multiple criteria for a field and separate the criteria by a logical OR operator, only one of the criteria must be true for Access to select the record. You can specify several OR criteria for a field, either by entering them all in a single Criteria cell separated by the logical OR operator, as shown earlier, or by entering each subsequent criterion in a separate Or row. When you use multiple Or rows, if the criteria in any one of the Or rows is true, Access selects the record. Figure 5-12 shows the result of applying a logical OR operation between any two tests. As you can see, only one of the tests must be true for the result of the OR to be true and for Access to select the record.

OR	True	False
True	True (Selected)	True (Selected)
False	True (Selected)	False (Rejected)

Figure 5-12 When you specify the logical OR operator between two tests, the result is true if either or both of the tests is true.

INSIDE OUT   Don't get confused by AND and OR

It's a common mistake to get *OR* and *AND* mixed up when typing compound criteria for a single field. You might think to yourself, "I want all the employees in the states of Washington *and* California," and then type **WA AND CA** in the Criteria row for the State field. When you do this, you're asking Access to find rows where *(State = "WA") AND (State = "CA")*. Because a field in a record can't have more than one value at a time (can't contain both the values WA and CA in the same record), there won't be any records in the output. To look for all the rows for these two states, you need to ask Access to search for *(State = "WA") OR (State = "CA")*. That is, type **WA OR CA** in the Criteria row under the State field.

Let's look at a specific example. In Figure 5-13, you specify **CA** in the first Criteria row of the State field and **>=#01/01/1950# AND <#1 JAN 1984#** in that same Criteria row for the Birthdate field. (By the way, when you type **#1 JAN 1984#** and press Enter, Access changes your entry to #1/1/1984#.) In the next row (the first Or row), you specify **NC** in the State field. When you run this query, you get all the employees from the state of California born between 1950 and 1983. You also get any records for the state of North Carolina regardless of the birth date.

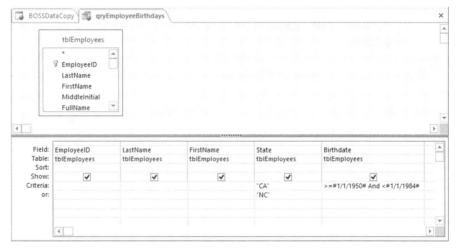

Figure 5-13 You can specify multiple AND and OR selection criteria in the design grid with additional OR lines.

In Figure 5-14, you can see the recordset (in Datasheet view) that results from running this query. Remember that you'll have to save your query changes first before switching to Datasheet view.

Chapter 5

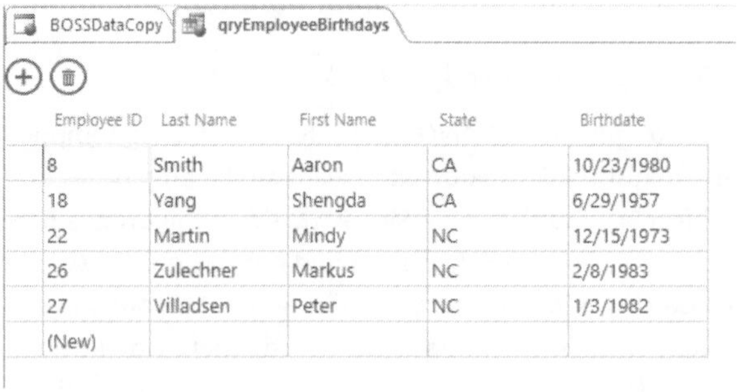

Employee ID	Last Name	First Name	State	Birthdate
8	Smith	Aaron	CA	10/23/1980
18	Yang	Shengda	CA	6/29/1957
22	Martin	Mindy	NC	12/15/1973
26	Zulechner	Markus	NC	2/8/1983
27	Villadsen	Peter	NC	1/3/1982
(New)				

Figure 5-14 The recordset of the query shown in Figure 5-13 shows only the records that match your criteria.

If you also want to limit rows from contacts in North Carolina to those who were born between 1950 and 1983, you must specify **>=#01/01/1950# AND <#1/1/1984#** again under Birthdate in the second Or row—that is, on the same row that filters for NC under State. Although this seems like extra work, this gives you complete flexibility to filter the data as you want. For example, you could include people who were born before 1960 in California and people who were born after 1980 in North Carolina by placing a different criterion under Birthdate in the two rows that filter State.

Between, In, and Like

In addition to comparison operators, Access provides three special operators that are useful for specifying the data you want in the recordset for web apps. Table 5-1 describes these operators.

TABLE 5-1   Criteria operators for queries in web apps

Predicate	Description
Between	Useful for specifying a range of values. The clause *Between 10 And 20* is the same as specifying >=10 And <=20.
In	Useful for specifying a list of values separated by commas, any one of which can match the field being searched. The clause *In ("CA", "NC", "TN")* is the same as *"CA" Or "NC" Or "TN"*.
Like[1]	Useful for searching for patterns in text fields. You can include special characters and ranges of values in the Like comparison string to define the character pattern you want. Use an underscore (_) to indicate any single character in that position. Use a percentage symbol (%) to indicate zero or more characters in that position. Include a range in brackets ([ ]) to test for a particular range of characters in a position, and use a caret symbol (^) to indicate exceptions. The range *[0-9]* tests for numbers, *[a-z]* tests for letters, and *[^0-9]* tests for any characters except 0 through 9. For example, the clause *Like"_[a-k]d[0-9]%"* tests for any single character in the first position, any character from *a* through *k* in the second position, the letter *d* in the third position, any character from *0* through *9* in the fourth position, and any number of characters after that.

[1]As you'll learn in Chapter 10, "Designing tables in a desktop database," the pattern characters supported by Access with desktop databases are different compared to when you are working in an Access web app. The pattern characters discussed here work in Access web apps only.

> **Note**
>
> **If you are creating an expression with Like in a query that uses a linked SharePoint list as its data source, Access allows up to five wildcard characters only in a single part of a WHERE clause.**

Suppose you want to find all employees in the state of North Carolina or Massachusetts who were born between 1950 and 1983 and whose first name begins with the letter M. Figure 5-15 shows how you would enter these criteria. Figure 5-16 shows the recordset of this query.

BOSSDataCopy
qryEmployeeBirthdays
tblEmployees
*
EmployeeID
LastName
FirstName
MiddleInitial
FullName
Field: EmployeeID | LastName | FirstName | State | Birthdate
Table: tblEmployees | tblEmployees | tblEmployees | tblEmployees | tblEmployees
Sort:
Show:
Criteria: Like "M%" | In ("NC","MA") | >=#1/1/1950# And <#1/1/1984#
or:

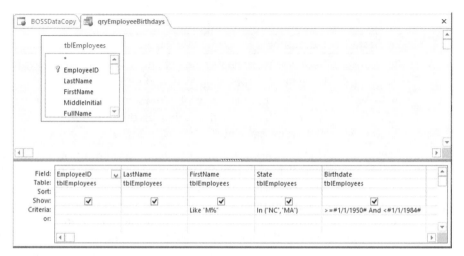

Figure 5-15 You can also restrict records by using Between, In, and Like, all in the same design grid.

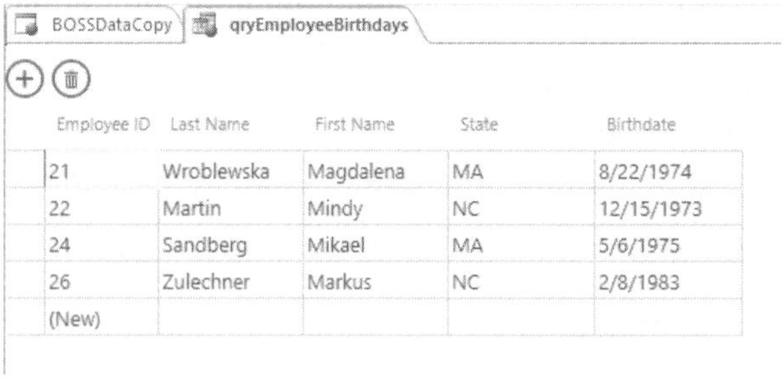

BOSSDataCopy
qryEmployeeBirthdays
Employee ID | Last Name | First Name | State | Birthdate
21 | Wroblewska | Magdalena | MA | 8/22/1974
22 | Martin | Mindy | NC | 12/15/1973
24 | Sandberg | Mikael | MA | 5/6/1975
26 | Zulechner | Markus | NC | 2/8/1983
(New)

Figure 5-16 The recordset of the query shown in Figure 5-15 shows only the records that match your criteria.

For additional examples that use the Between, In, and Like comparison operators, see "Defining field validation rules for web apps," in Chapter 3.

Using expressions

You can use an expression to combine fields or to calculate a new value from fields in your table and make that expression a new field in the recordset. You can use any of the many built-in functions for web apps that Access provides as part of your expression. You concatenate, or combine, text fields by stringing them end to end, or you use arithmetic operators on fields in the underlying table to calculate a value. Let's create a new query using the Back Office Software System web app backup copy you've been working in so far in this chapter.

CAUTION

Do not confuse a calculated expression in a query with the Calculated data type in Access. Calculated data types store the result of their expression directly in the table, but calculated expressions in queries are calculated only when Access executes the query.

Creating text expressions

One common use of expressions is to create a new text (string) field by concatenating fields containing text, string constants, or numeric data. You create a string constant by enclosing the text in double or single quotation marks. Use the addition symbol (+) between fields or strings to indicate that you want to concatenate them. For example, you might want to create an output field that concatenates the LastName field, a comma, a blank space, and then the FirstName field.

Try creating a new query on the tblEmployees table in the BOSSDataCopy.app that shows a field containing the employee last name, a comma and a blank, first name, a blank, and middle initial. You can also create a single field containing the city, a comma and a blank space, the state followed by one blank space, and the postal code. Your expressions should look like this:

```
LastName + ", " + FirstName + " " + MiddleInitial

City + ", " + State + " " + PostalCode
```

You can see the Query window in Design view for this example in Figure 5-17. I clicked in the Field row of the second column and then pressed Shift+F2 to open the Zoom window, where it is easier to enter the expression. You can click the Font button to select a larger font that's easier to read. After you choose a font, Access uses it whenever you open the Zoom window again.

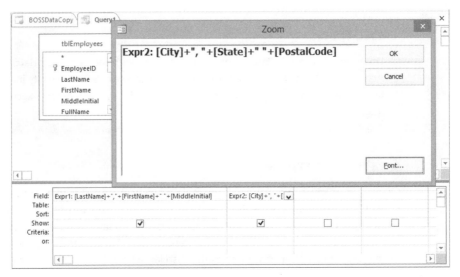

Figure 5-17 If you use the Zoom window to enter an expression, you can see more of the expression and select a different font.

> **Note**
>
> Access requires that all fields on the Field row in a query have a name. By default, the name of a simple field in a query is the name of the field from the source table. However, when you create a new field using an expression, the expression doesn't have a name unless you or Access assigns one. When you enter an expression, Access generates a field name in the form Expr*N*; that is the name that Access is assigning to your expression. Notice also that Access adds brackets around field names in expressions automatically. It does this so that the field names in the Structured Query Language (SQL) for the query are completely unambiguous. If this table had been designed with blanks in the field names, you would need to type the brackets yourself to ensure that the query designer interprets the names correctly.

When you save the query and look at the query result in Datasheet view, you should see something like the one shown in Figure 5-18. I expanded the size of the two columns so that you could see all the data in the fields.

Figure 5-18 This query is a result using concatenated text fields.

Try typing within the Expr1 or Expr2 fields in Datasheet view. Because this display is a result of an expression (concatenation of strings), Access won't let you update the data in these columns.

You've no doubt noticed by now that the Expr1 calculated field in the first row in Figure 5-18 is blank. This happened because that person has no middle initial provided in their record. In Access web apps, when you use the plus sign (+) to concatenate strings or with arithmetic expressions, as you'll learn in the next section, if a field in the expression evaluates to Null, the entire expression evaluates to Null. So, to solve this Null problem, you can use the Is Null phrase, which you've seen in previous chapters, or you can use the *Coalesce* function. Let's first learn how to solve this issue with Is Null, and then we'll discuss the Coalesce function.

Because the FirstName and LastName fields in this table are marked as required fields, we have to worry only about the MiddleInitial field containing Null values. To account for this, we can wrap the last part of our existing expression in a special built-in function called *Immediate If* (or *IIF* for short). The *IIF* function can evaluate a test in the first argument and then return the evaluation of the second argument if the first argument is true or the evaluation of the third argument if the first argument is false. You must separate each argument in the function call with commas. Note that I said *evaluation of the argument*—this means we can enter additional tests, even another IIF, in the second and third arguments. In our example, if the employee does not have a middle initial, we want to display an empty string at the end of the final concatenated string. The expression we can use to accomplish this with IIF and Is Null is as follows:

```
IIf([MiddleInitial] Is Null,"",[MiddleInitial])
```

Therefore, the first argument uses IIF to evaluate the expression `[MiddleInitial] Is Null = True`—is the value in the field named MiddleInitial Null? If this is true, IIF returns the evaluation of the second argument, which in this case results in an empty string. If the MiddleInitial field contains any value (not Null essentially), IIF evaluates the third argument. Now all we need to do is to replace the last part of our original concatenate expression with this revised expression to test for Null values in the MiddleInitial fields. The final expression you can use is as follows:

```
LastName + ", " + FirstName + "" + IIf([MiddleInitial] Is Null,
"",[MiddleInitial])
```

If you save your query changes and switch to Datasheet view, you'll see that all rows now display a concatenated name in the Expr1 calculated field. For the one employee record with no middle initial, their concatenated name just displays their last name and first name.

The Coalesce function is another option you can use to handle Null values in query expressions. The *Coalesce* function returns the first expression that is not Null from a list of arguments separated by commas. To achieve our same goal of handling possible Nulls in the MiddleInitial field, you can use the following expression:

```
Coalesce((LastName + ", " + FirstName + " " + MiddleInitial]),
(LastName + ", " + FirstName))
```

With this Coalesce function example, Access checks to see whether the first argument evaluates to Null. For any employee records that include a middle initial, Access determines that the first argument evaluates to a concatenated string of all three fields and uses that expression as the final result to display. Access does not proceed with evaluating any other arguments in the Coalesce function because it found a not Null value in the first argument. For any employee records that do not contain a middle initial, Access discovers that the first argument evaluates to a Null and then moves on to check the expression in the second argument. Access then determines that the second argument evaluates to a concatenated string of only the last name and first name fields and uses that expression as the final result to display.

If you save your query changes with the Coalesce function example above and switch to Datasheet view, you'll see that all rows now display a concatenated name in the Expr1 calculated field. For the one employee record with no middle initial, their concatenated name just displays their last name and first name.

> **Note**
>
> In the previous example, you could also handle possible Nulls in the MiddleInitial field by placing just the MiddleInitial field inside the Coalesce function as follows:
>
> ```
> LastName + ", " + FirstName + " " + Coalesce(MiddleInitial,"")
> ```

As you might imagine, when you become more familiar with building expressions and with the available built-in functions, you can create very sophisticated queries to analyze and summarize the data in your web app.

Why use Coalesce instead of Is Null?

You might be wondering under what circumstances you should use the Coalesce function over an Is Null phrase. In the preceding example, we knew only one field could potentially contain Nulls—the MiddleInitial field. For this simple case, using Is Null wrapped inside an IIF statement should suffice, and the completed expression is relatively easy to read. How would our expression differ if we had to account for the possibility that all three fields could contain Nulls? In that case, we would have to create a more complicated expression with several IIF statements. That expression would be much harder to read and understand.

The Is Null phrase accepts only two arguments, but the Coalesce function can take multiple arguments. If you have scenarios where you need to account for Nulls in multiple fields, you'll want to use the Coalesce function in your expression. With each expression argument separated by only a comma, you'll generally find the expression easier to read. As you scan through a completed Coalesce expression, you can visualize each argument as a separate entity with no relation to any other argument and potentially less complicated, nested IIF statements.

Defining arithmetic expressions

In addition to creating expressions on text fields in queries, Access provides many options for you to perform arithmetic calculations on other data types, such as Number, Currency, and Date/Time fields. Table 5-2 shows the operators you can use in arithmetic expressions in web apps. Throughout the remainder of this chapter, you'll see examples of using these types of arithmetic operators in sample queries from the Back Office Software System sample web app.

TABLE 5-2 Operators used in arithmetic expressions

Operator	Description
+	Adds two numeric expressions.
-	Subtracts the second numeric expression from the first numeric expression.
*	Multiplies two numeric expressions.
/	Divides the first numeric expression by the second numeric expression.
Mod	Rounds both numeric expressions to integers, divides the first integer by the second integer, and returns only the remainder.

When evaluating an arithmetic expression, Access evaluates certain operations before others, also known as *operator precedence*. Table 5-3 shows you the operator precedence for arithmetic operations. In an expression with no parentheses, Access performs the operations in the order listed in the table. When operations have the same precedence (for example, multiply and divide), Access performs the operations left to right.

TABLE 5-3 Arithmetic operator precedence

Access evaluates operators in the following order:	
1	Negation—a leading minus sign (-)
2	Multiplication and division (*, /)
3	Modulus (Mod)
4	Addition and subtraction (+, -)

Access evaluates expressions enclosed in parentheses first, starting with the innermost expressions. (You can enclose an expression in parentheses inside another expression in parentheses.)

The tblVacations table tracks the employee vacations in the restaurant management app. Let's say you want to want to find out the length of time for each employee's vacation. You can use a handy built-in function called *DateDiff* to calculate the difference between two Date/Time values in seconds, minutes, hours, days, weeks, months, quarters, or years. In this case, you want the difference between the start date and the end date of the vacation in days.

The syntax for calling DateDiff is as follows:

```
DateDiff(<DatePart>, <date1>, <date2>)
```

The function calculates the difference between <date1> and <date2> using the interval you specify and returns a negative value if <date1> is greater than <date2>. Table 5-4 explains the values you can supply for the *interval* in the DateDiff function.

> **Note**
> You can also use the settings you find in Table 5-4 for the *interval argument* in the
> DatePart function (which extracts part of a Date/Time value) and DateAdd function
> (which adds or subtracts a constant to a Date/Time value)

TABLE 5-4   Interval settings for DateDiff function

Setting	Description
Year	Calculates the difference in years. DateDiff subtracts the year portion of the first date from the year portion of the second date, so `DateDiff(Year, #31 DEC 2013#, #01 JAN 2014#)` returns 1.
Quarter	Calculates the difference in quarters. If the two dates are in the same calendar quarter, the result is 0.
Month	Calculates the difference in months. DateDiff subtracts the month portion of the first date from the month portion of the second date, so `DateDiff(Month, #31 DEC 2013#, #01 JAN 2014#)` returns 1.
Day	Calculates the difference in days, so `DateDiff(Day, #31 DEC 2013#, #02 JAN 2014#)` returns 2.
Week	Calculates the difference in weeks. When the first day of the week is Sunday (the default), DateDiff counts the number of Sundays greater than the first date and less than or equal to the second date. For example, March 19, 2014, is a Wednesday, and March 24, 2014, is a Monday, so `DateDiff(Week, #19 MAR 2014#, #24 MAR 2014#)` returns 1.
Hour	Calculates the difference in hours.
Minute	Calculates the difference in minutes.
Second	Calculates the difference in seconds.
Millisecond	Calculates the difference in milliseconds.

Create a new query using tblVacations as the source, and add the ID and Employee fields
from this table to the query design grid. Next, you need to enter your expression to calculate the number of days in a blank column on the Field row. Name this new column VacationDays, and then use the DateDiff function, by entering the following expression:

```
DateDiff(Day, [StartDate], [EndDate])
```

Save this new query, name the query **qryVacationDays**, and then switch to Datasheet view
for the query. In Figure 5-19, you can see the results of the query. The VacationDays calculated field displays the number of days for each employee's vacation.

Chapter 5

Figure 5-19 The *DateDiff* function calculates the difference between two Date/Time values.

So far, you have built fairly simple expressions. When you want to create a more complex expression, sometimes the Expression Builder can be useful, as discussed in the next section.

Using the Expression Builder

For more complex expressions, Access 2013 provides a utility called the *Expression Builder*. In Chapter 3, "Designing tables in a web app," you learned about the Expression Builder when you created Calculated data types and validation rules. You also learned how to use the IntelliSense feature built into the Expression Builder in Access. In this section, I'll show you additional ways the Expression Builder can help you construct expressions.

Earlier in this chapter, you created a query that returned each employee's date of birth. You also created some criteria to return records of employees who were born within a set date range. Let's say that you now want to create a query that lists the upcoming birthdays within the next thirty days for your employees. In this case, the year the employee was born is irrelevant; you want to know, based on the month and day, only which employee is having a birthday in the near future (perhaps to send a birthday greeting).

To see how the Expression Builder can help build the expression needed to accomplish your goal, start a new query using tblEmployees as the source and add the EmployeeID, LastName, FirstName, and Birthdate fields from this table to the query design grid. (If you save the query at this point, Access provides IntelliSense for the field names in the following exercise. However, you're not required to save the query to follow along.) Click in an empty field in the design grid, and then click the Builder button in the Query Setup group of the Design contextual tab. Access opens the Expression Builder dialog box, shown in Figure 5-20.

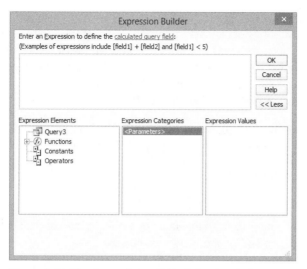

Figure 5-20 The Expression Builder dialog box helps you build simple and complex expressions.

INSIDE OUT   Opening the Expression Builder from the Field row

You can also open the Expression Builder in queries by right-clicking inside the Field row on a new column or existing column in the query design grid and then clicking Build on the shortcut menu.

In the upper part of the dialog box is a blank text box in which you can build an expression. You can type the expression yourself, but it's sometimes more accurate to find field names, operators, and function names in the three panes in the lower part of the dialog box.

In Access 2013, the Expression Builder shows the functions, constants, and operators applicable to the current context. For example, in Figure 5-20, Access shows you only the list of functions, constants, and operators you can use for expressions in a web app query under the Expression Elements pane on the far left. The middle pane, Expression Categories, changes based on what you select in the Expression Elements pane. For example, if you click Operators under Expression Elements, the Expression Categories pane lists several group names of operators you can use in your expression. The right pane, Expression Values, shows you all possible values you can use based on the currently highlighted category selected in the middle pane. The expression you need to build, which I'll walk you through in detail in the next couple of pages, will ultimately look like this:

```
DateFromParts(Year(Today()),Month([Birthdate]),Day([Birthdate]))
```

Chapter 5

You can use the Expression Builder in a couple of different ways to help you construct this expression correctly. Start by double-clicking the Functions category in the left pane, and then select Built-In Functions to see the list of function categories in the center pane and the list of functions within the selected category in the right pane. Select the Date/Time category in the center pane to narrow down the choices. Here, you can see the *DateFromParts* function as well as several other built-in functions you can use.

You can find a list of the most useful functions and their descriptions in Article 5, "Visual Basic function reference," which can be downloaded from the book's catalog page.

The syntax for calling DateFromParts is as follows:

```
DateFromParts(<year>, <month>, <day>)
```

The function returns a date value with the date portion set to the specified year, month, and day in the <year>, <month>, and <day> arguments.

Double-click the DateFromParts function in the right pane to add it to the expression text box at the top of the Expression Builder. When you add a function to your expression in this way, the Expression Builder shows you the parameters required by the function. Access also displays the parameters of the function and additional information about the DateFrom-Parts function at the bottom of the dialog box. You can click any parameter to highlight it in the text box at the top of the Expression Builder and type a value or select a value from one of the lists in the bottom panes. Click <<Year>>, and overwrite it with Year(Today()). (See Table 5-4 for a list of all the possible interval settings.) You'll notice that Access displays a ScreenTip beneath the expression as you type Year and Today, as shown in Figure 5-21. Access highlights which parameter you are currently working on in the ScreenTip.

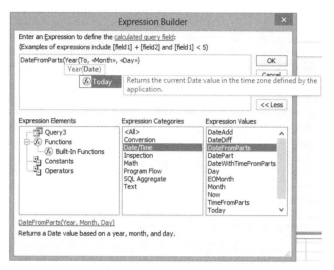

Figure 5-21 Access displays the parameters for the expression in a ScreenTip as you fill in the expression.

The *Today* function returns the current date. By wrapping the Today function inside the Year DatePart, Access returns the current year in the first part of the DateFromParts function. Note that we want to find the current year instead of the actual year the employee was born, because we want to return the date their birth date falls on within the current year.

You need to insert the month of the employee's birth date for the <<Month>> and the day of the employee's birth date for <<Day>>. Click <<Month>> to highlight it, and then type **Month([Birthdate])**. The Month DatePart returns the month number of the employee's birth date stored in the Birthdate field. Finally, click <<Day>> to highlight it, and then type **Day([Birthdate])**. The Day DatePart returns the day of the month of the employee's birth date. The Expression Builder should now look like Figure 5-22.

Chapter 5

Figure 5-22 Your completed expression should now look like this.

Click OK to paste your result into the design grid. Name this new column NextBirthdate by entering **NextBirthdate:** in front of the expression you just completed. When you save this new query (you can name it **qryEmployeeNextBirthdate**) and switch to Datasheet view, Access displays the birth date for each employee in the current year, as shown in Figure 5-23.

Employee ID	First Name	Last Name	Birthdate	NextBirthdate
1	Anibal	Sousa	3/20/1940	3/20/2012 12:00:00 AM
2	Jennifer	Riegle	3/1/1971	3/1/2012 12:00:00 AM
3	Kathleen	Jensen	11/30/1965	11/30/2012 12:00:00 AM
4	Cat	Francis	11/24/1971	11/24/2012 12:00:00 AM
5	Joe	Yong	6/20/1982	6/20/2012 12:00:00 AM
6	Harry	Linggoputro	11/28/1967	11/28/2012 12:00:00 AM
7	Mary	Gibson	6/6/1976	6/6/2012 12:00:00 AM
8	Aaron	Smith	10/23/1980	10/23/2012 12:00:00 AM
9	Tom	Michaels	2/9/1976	2/9/2012 12:00:00 AM
10	Andrew	Dixon	6/28/1983	6/28/2012 12:00:00 AM
11	Jan	Stoklasa	1/7/1988	1/7/2012 12:00:00 AM
12	Paul	West	3/10/1972	3/10/2012 12:00:00 AM
13	Mario	Kresnadi	4/15/1982	4/15/2012 12:00:00 AM
14	Palle	Peterson	3/27/1977	3/27/2012 12:00:00 AM
15	Joseph	Matthews	1/12/1970	1/12/2012 12:00:00 AM
16	John	Viescas	9/15/1977	9/15/2012 12:00:00 AM
17	Douglas	Curran	2/20/1984	2/20/2012 12:00:00 AM
18	Shengda	Yang	6/29/1957	6/29/2012 12:00:00 AM
19	Daniel	Koczka	7/31/1975	7/31/2012 12:00:00 AM

Figure 5-23 Switch to Datasheet view to see the result of your complex calculation expression.

Chapter 5

You'll notice that your new calculated expression returns the date of each employee's birth date within the current year as well as a time portion of 12:00:00 AM. These query results are close to what we want to see; however, the query results show employee records that have already had their birthday for this year. We want to display only birthdays within the next thirty days. To accomplish this, we'll need to add some criteria to the query.

Switch back to Design view for this query, and then place your cursor in the Criteria line of the calculated field you just created. Click the Builder button in the Query Setup group on the Design ribbon tab to open the Expression Builder. To restrict the records returned by Access to within the next thirty days, you can use a combination of the Today function and the *DateAdd* function.

The syntax for calling DateAdd is as follows:

```
DateAdd(<DatePart>, <number>, <date>)
```

The function returns a specified date with the given number interval added to a DatePart of that date. To find all upcoming birthdays within the next thirty days, we can use the following expression in the Criteria line:

```
>=Today() And <=DateAdd(Day,30,Today())
```

The first part of the expression before the AND operator instructs Access to find all records where our calculated field returns a date that equals the current date or any date in the future. The second part of the expression instructs to take the current date, today, and add 30 days to it. So the completed Criteria restricts records to anything equal to or greater than the current date and also less than or equal to thirty days from the current date. As you type this expression in the Expression Builder, you'll notice Access displays the list of arguments for the DateAdd function, as shown in Figure 5-24.

Chapter 5

Figure 5-24 The Expression Builder displays the list of arguments for the DateAdd function.

Click OK to paste your result from the Expression Builder into the design grid Criteria line. Save your design changes for the query, and switch to Datasheet view. Access now displays only employee birthdays within the next thirty days, as shown in Figure 5-25.

Figure 5-25 The results of your employee birthdays query show one birthday within the next thirty days.

> **Note**
>
> The results you see when you run the query might differ from what is shown in Figure 5-25. The query always starts with the current date, which most likely differs from the date I executed the query.

Sorting data

Normally, Access displays the rows in your recordset in the order in which they're retrieved from the app. You can add sorting information to determine the sequence of the data in a query. Click in the Sort row for the field you want to sort on, click the arrow in this row, and then select Ascending or Descending from the list. In the example shown in Figure 5-26, the query results are to be sorted in ascending order based on the LastName field. The recordset will list the employees in alphabetical order by last name first. The resulting Datasheet view is shown in Figure 5-27. You can find this query saved as qryEmployeesSorted in the Back Office Software System backup sample web app (BOSSDataCopy.app).

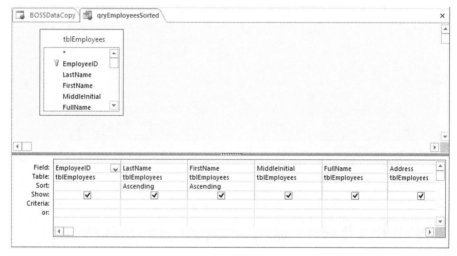

Figure 5-26 Access sorts the query on the LastName field in ascending order.

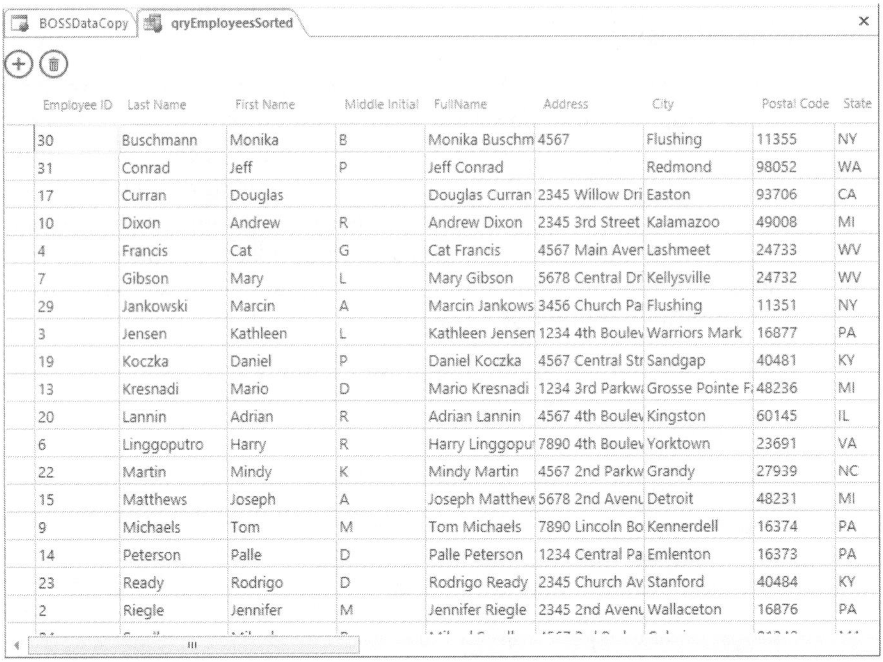

BOSSDataCopy | qryEmployeesSorted

Employee ID	Last Name	First Name	Middle Initial	FullName	Address	City	Postal Code	State
30	Buschmann	Monika	B	Monika Buschm	4567	Flushing	11355	NY
31	Conrad	Jeff	P	Jeff Conrad		Redmond	98052	WA
17	Curran	Douglas		Douglas Curran	2345 Willow Dri	Easton	93706	CA
10	Dixon	Andrew	R	Andrew Dixon	2345 3rd Street	Kalamazoo	49008	MI
4	Francis	Cat	G	Cat Francis	4567 Main Aver	Lashmeet	24733	WV
7	Gibson	Mary	L	Mary Gibson	5678 Central Dr	Kellysville	24732	WV
29	Jankowski	Marcin	A	Marcin Jankows	3456 Church Pa	Flushing	11351	NY
3	Jensen	Kathleen	L	Kathleen Jensen	1234 4th Boulev	Warriors Mark	16877	PA
19	Koczka	Daniel	P	Daniel Koczka	4567 Central Str	Sandgap	40481	KY
13	Kresnadi	Mario	D	Mario Kresnadi	1234 3rd Parkw	Grosse Pointe F	48236	MI
20	Lannin	Adrian	R	Adrian Lannin	4567 4th Boulev	Kingston	60145	IL
6	Linggoputro	Harry	R	Harry Linggopu	7890 4th Boulev	Yorktown	23691	VA
22	Martin	Mindy	K	Mindy Martin	4567 2nd Parkw	Grandy	27939	NC
15	Matthews	Joseph	A	Joseph Matthew	5678 2nd Avenu	Detroit	48231	MI
9	Michaels	Tom	M	Tom Michaels	7890 Lincoln Bo	Kennerdell	16374	PA
14	Peterson	Palle	D	Palle Peterson	1234 Central Pa	Emlenton	16373	PA
23	Ready	Rodrigo	D	Rodrigo Ready	2345 Church Av	Stanford	40484	KY
2	Riegle	Jennifer	M	Jennifer Riegle	2345 2nd Avenu	Wallaceton	16876	PA

Figure 5-27 Datasheet view shows the recordset of the query shown in Figure 5-26 sorted on the LastName field.

INSIDE OUT Why specifying sort criteria is important

When Access solves a query, it tries to do it in the most efficient way. When you first construct and run a query, Access might return the records in the sequence you expect (for example, in primary key sequence of the table). However, if you want to be sure Access always returns rows in this order, you must specify sort criteria. As you later add and remove rows in your table, Access might decide that fetching rows in a different sequence might be faster, which, in the absence of sorting criteria, might result in a different row sequence than you intended.

You can also sort on multiple fields. Access honors your sorting criteria from left to right in the design grid. For example, if you want to sort by LastName ascending and then by FirstName ascending, you should include the LastName field to the left of the FirstName field. If the additional field you want to sort is already in the design grid but in the wrong location, click the column selector box (the tinted box above the field row) to select the entire column and then click the selector box again and drag the field to its new location. If you want the field that is out of position to still appear where you originally placed it, add the field to the design grid again in the correct sorting sequence, clear the Show check box (you don't want two copies of the field displayed), and set the Sort specification. If you look closely at Figure 5-26 and Figure 5-27, shown previously, the qryEmployeesSorted query sorts by the FirstName field after the LastName field. If you'd like to see how the sort results differ, try swapping the field positions of those two columns in the query design grid and view the results.

Working in query preview Datasheet view

When you're developing a web app, you might need to work in table or query preview Datasheet view to help you load sample data or to solve problems in the queries and views you're creating. You might also decide to create certain views in your web app that display information in Datasheet view. The techniques for updating and manipulating data in views are very similar to doing so in table and query preview datasheets. Understanding how preview datasheets work will help you explain to your users how to use your web app.

Moving around and using keyboard shortcuts

Open the qryEmployeesSorted query in the Back Office Software System backup sample web app (BOSSDataCopy.app) if you've closed it. You should see a result similar to Figure 5-28. Displaying different records or fields is simple. You can use the horizontal scroll bar to scroll through a table's fields, or you can use the vertical scroll bar to scroll through a table's records.

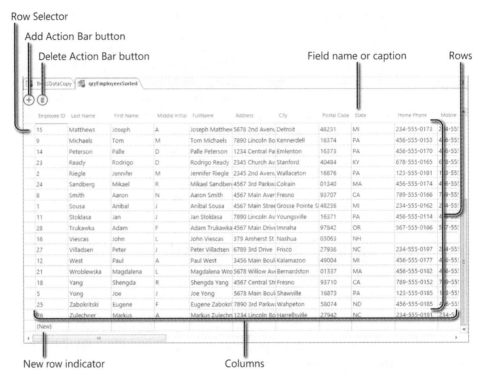

Figure 5-28 Open the Datasheet view of the qryEmployeesSorted query to begin learning about moving around and editing in a query datasheet.

You can make a record current by clicking anywhere in its row. However, you might find it easier to use the keyboard rather than the mouse to move around in a query datasheet, especially if you're typing new data. Table 5-5 lists the keyboard shortcuts you can use for working in query datasheets. These keyboard shortcuts also apply to using table preview datasheets in Access.

TABLE 5-5 Keyboard shortcuts for working in datasheets

Keys	Action
Page Up	Scroll up one page
Page Down	Scroll down one page
Tab	Move to next field
Shift+Tab	Move to previous field
Home	Move to first field, current record
End	Move to last field, current record
Enter	Move down a row

Keys	Action
Right Arrow	Move right one field
Left Arrow	Move left one field
Up Arrow	Move to current field, previous record
Down Arrow	Move to current field, next record
Ctrl+Up Arrow	Move to current field, first record
Ctrl+Down Arrow	Move to current field, last record or new record (if records can be added)
Ctrl+Home	Move to first field, first record
Ctrl+End	Move to last field, last record or new record (if records can be added)
F2	When in a field, toggles between selecting all data in the field and single-character edit mode
Spacebar	Toggles Yes/No state of a check box
Alt+Down Arrow	Opens date picker on date/time fields and the Edit Hyperlink dialog on hyperlink fields.
Shift+Down Arrow	Extend the selected field down one row
Shift+Up Arrow	Extend the selected field up one row
Shift+Page Down	Extend the selected field down one page of rows
Shift+Page Up	Extend the selected field up one page of rows
Shift+Home	Extend the selected field to the first field in a row
Shift+End	Extend the selected field to the last field in a row
Esc	Cancel current field changes
Delete	Delete current field data
Ctrl+Delete	Deletes the current row

Changing data

Not only can you view data in a query datasheet, you can also insert new records, change data, and delete records.

You might have noticed as you moved around in the datasheet that pencil icons occasionally appear on the row selector at the far left of each row. Notice also that Access highlights the current row when you click the row selector. The pencil icon indicates that you have made a change to one or more entries in this row and that Access has not committed the record changes. Access saves the changes automatically when you move to another row. If Access encounters an error and cannot save the record changes, you'll see the pencil icon in the row selector indicating that Access did not complete saving that record. Before moving to a new row, you can press Esc once to undo the change to the current cell. If someone else updates a record before you commit your changes to the same record, Access shows you a warning dialog box indicating that another user updated the data when you try to save the row. You'll need to dismiss your record changes and then click the Refresh button in the Records group on the Datasheet ribbon tab to see the latest record updates. You can then make your record changes and try to save again.

Adding a new record

As you build your web app, you might find it useful to place some data in your tables so that you can test the queries, views, and data macros that you design. If your table is empty when you open the table or a query on the table in Datasheet view, Access shows a single blank row. If you have data in your table, Access shows a blank row beneath the last record. You can jump to the blank row to begin adding a new record either by clicking the Add Action Bar button in the top-left corner of the query datasheet window above the first record or by pressing Ctrl+Down Arrow. Access places the insertion point in the blank row beneath the last record when you click the Add Action Bar button. Press the Tab key to move to the next column after you enter data in each column.

> **Note**
> You cannot enter data into the AutoNumber ID field or any Calculated data type fields in datasheets, because Access enters this data automatically.

If the data you enter in a column violates a field or table validation rule, Access displays your custom validation rule message in an error dialog as you leave the row and try to commit the record, as shown in Figure 5-29. (In Figure 5-29, I tried to enter a negative number for the employee's pay rate, which violates the existing field validation rule I defined for this field.) You must provide correct values that will pass existing validation rules before you can commit a record. If you do not provide your own message in the Validation Text field property, Access displays a generic error message if data does not pass any existing validation rules.

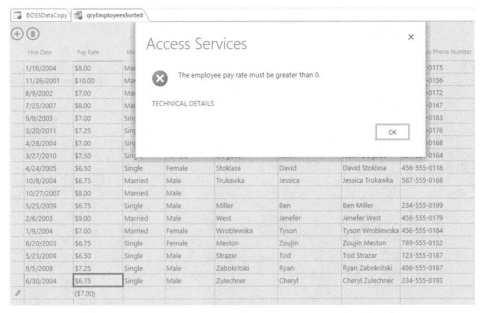

Figure 5-29 Access displays a message whenever you try to commit data that does not pass validation rules.

If the data you enter into a column violates a field property setting (other than the Validation Rule property) or if the data you enter does not match the data type for the field, Access notifies you with an error message indicating that the item was not saved when you leave the row and try to commit the record, as shown in Figure 5-30. In Figure 5-30, I tried to enter two letters into the middle initial field. The MiddleInitial field in the tblEmployees table has a Character Limit field property set to 1 to allow only one character in this field.

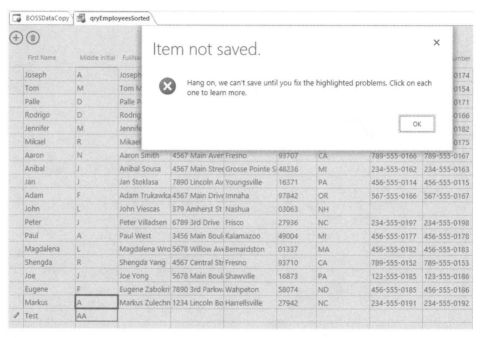

Figure 5-30 Access also displays an error message whenever you try to commit data that does not pass field property settings.

In Figure 5-30, you can also see that Access displays a red border around any field with invalid data. After you dismiss the Item Not Saved dialog shown in Figure 5-30 and click into that field, Access displays a red circle icon with an exclamation mark next to the field. Click this icon, and Access displays a message to help indicate why it cannot save the data and what you need to do to correct this. In Figure 5-31, you can see that Access displays a message indicating that you can enter only one character into the middle initial field.

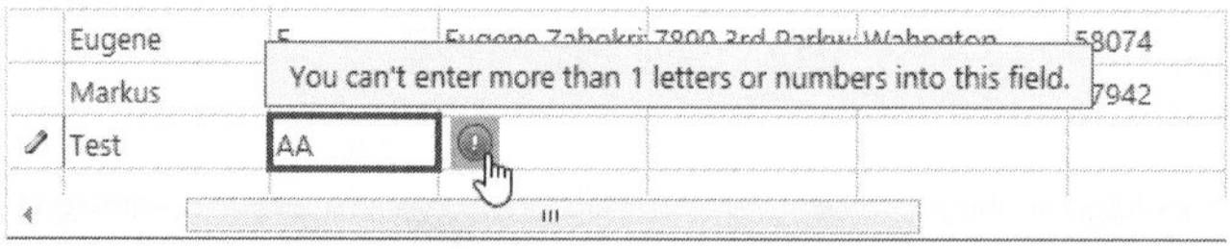

Eugene	F	Eugene Zabokri 7890 3rd Parkw Wahpeton	58074
Markus		You can't enter more than 1 letters or numbers into this field.	7942
✎ Test	AA	🔴	

Figure 5-31 Click the red circle icon to display information about why Access cannot save your data.

To save your new record, press Tab in the last column of a row to move to a new row and commit your new record to the web app. You can also use your mouse to click in any other row besides the current row to commit data changes.

> **Note**
> You cannot use the Save command on the Quick Access Toolbar to save new records or save changes to existing records when you are working with query or table datasheets. To save data in query and table datasheets, you must move your focus off the current record.

Selecting and changing data

When you have data in a table, you can easily change the data by editing it in Datasheet view. You must select data before you can change it, and you can do this in several ways, including the following:

- In the cell containing the data you want to change, click just to the left of the first character you want to change (or to the right of the last character), and then drag the insertion point to select all the characters you want to change.

- Double-click any word in a cell to select the entire word.

- Tab into a cell, and start typing. Access overwrites all the existing data in the cell.

Any data you type replaces the old, selected data. In Figure 5-32, I have single-clicked the First Name field, and Access outlines that cell. In Figure 5-33, I have changed the value to Mike but haven't yet saved the row. (You can see the cursor insertion point indicating that I'm inside this cell.) Access also selects the entire entry if you tab to the cell in the datasheet grid. If you want to change only part of the data (for example, to correct the spelling of a street name in an address field), you can shift to single-character mode by pressing F2 or clicking the location at which you want to start your change. Use the Backspace key to erase characters to the left of the insertion point, and use the Delete key to remove characters to the right of the insertion point. Hold down the Shift key, and press the Right Arrow or Left Arrow key to select multiple characters to replace. You can press F2 again to select the entire cell.

Figure 5-32 You can select the old data by clicking a cell in the datasheet.

Figure 5-33 You can then replace the old data with new data by typing the new information.

Copying and pasting data

You can copy any selected data to the Clipboard and paste this data into another field or record. To copy data in a field, tab to the cell in the datasheet grid to select the data within it. Press Ctrl+C to copy the existing data to the Clipboard. To paste the data in another location, move the insertion point to the new location, select the data you want to replace, and press Ctrl+V. If the insertion point is at the paste location (you haven't selected any data in the field), Access inserts the Clipboard data.

To select an entire record to be copied, click the row selector at the far left of the row. Press Shift+Up Arrow or Shift+Down Arrow to extend the selection to multiple rows. Press Ctrl+C to copy the contents of multiple rows to the Clipboard.

You can open another table or query and paste the copied rows at the end of the new datasheet. When you paste rows into another table or query datasheet with the same field structure, the rows you're adding must satisfy the validation rules or other field properties of the receiving table. If any validation or field properties fail, Access pastes the data as a group but then shows you an error message that it cannot commit the data. Access displays a pencil icon in the row selector next to all pasted records and highlights in red each cell with invalid data. You'll need to correct the data in each pasted record for Access to save all the changes.

Deleting rows

To delete one or more rows, select the rows using the row selectors and then press the Delete key. For details about selecting multiple rows, see the previous discussion on copying and pasting data. You can also use Ctrl+Delete to delete the current or selected row. When you delete rows in a web app, Access gives you a chance to change your mind if you made a mistake. (See Figure 5-34.) Click Yes in the message box to delete the rows, or click No to cancel the deletion. Because this web app has referential integrity rules defined between tblEmployees and several other tables, you won't be able to delete employee records using qryEmployeesSorted. (Access shows you an error message telling you that related rows exist in other tables.) You would have to remove all related records from tblLaborHours, tblSchedule, tblTerminations, tblTrainedPositions, and tblVacations first.

CAUTION

After you click Yes in the confirmation message box, you cannot restore the deleted rows. You have to reenter them or copy them from a backup if you want to restore that data.

Delete confirmation   ×

⚠   Please confirm that we should permanently delete the item(s).

                                            Yes   No

Figure 5-34 This message box appears when you delete rows.

Sorting data

When you open a table or query in Datasheet view, Access displays the rows sorted in sequence by the primary key AutoNumber field for the table. If you want to see the rows in a different sequence or search for specific data, Access provides you with tools to do that. When you open a query in Datasheet view (such as the qryEmployeesSorted sample query we're using in this chapter), you'll see the rows in the order determined by sort specifications in the query. If you haven't specified sorting information, you'll see the data in the same sequence as you would if you opened the table or query in Datasheet view.

Access provides a drop-down menu, called the AutoFilter menu, above each column with commands allowing you to quickly and easily sort the rows in a query or table datasheet in ascending or descending order. To see how this works, open the qryEmployeesSorted query, scroll the datasheet to the right until you can see the Birthdate column, and then hover your mouse over the label at the top of the column. Access displays a down arrow on the right side of the column label. Click the down arrow, and Access opens the AutoFilter menu, as shown in Figure 5-35.

Figure 5-35 Access displays AutoFilter menu options above each column for queries and tables open in Datasheet view.

At the top of the AutoFilter menu, you can click Hide Column, and Access hides the column from view. Note that this change to the query or table datasheet is not permanent. If you refresh the datasheet or close the datasheet and then reopen it, Access displays the column again. Beneath Hide Column, you can click Sort Ascending or Sort Descending to sort the records in ascending or descending order by that column. Click Sort Ascending on the AutoFilter menu above the Birthdate column. Access refreshes the query datasheet and sorts all the records by date of birth, as shown in Figure 5-36. Access displays an up arrow on the right side of the Birthdate column to indicate that this column is sorted in ascending order. If you choose Sort Descending on the AutoFilter menu, Access displays a down arrow above the column.

State	Home Phone	Mobile Number	Birthdate ↑	Hire Date	Pay Rate
MI	234-555-0162	234-555-0163	3/20/1940	3/27/2010	$7.50
CA	789-555-0152	789-555-0153	6/29/1957	8/20/2003	$6.75
WA			4/7/1960	1/26/2002	$7.50
PA	123-555-0152	123-555-0153	11/30/1965	3/10/2008	$6.50
VA	567-555-0171	567-555-0172	11/28/1967	11/20/2003	$6.65
MI	234-555-0173	234-555-0174	1/12/1970	1/16/2004	$8.00
KY	678-555-0165	678-555-0166	2/15/1971	7/25/2007	$8.00
PA	123-555-0181	123-555-0182	3/1/1971	9/9/2003	$7.00
OR	567-555-0166	567-555-0167	4/27/1971	10/8/2004	$6.75
WV	345-555-0187	345-555-0188	11/24/1971	12/10/2004	$7.75
MI	456-555-0177	456-555-0178	3/10/1972	2/6/2003	$9.00

Figure 5-36 Access sorts the records in the query based on the Birthdate column.

Note

When you choose to sort records on a Lookup data type, Access sorts the records by the display value of the Lookup data type rather than the ID value of the related record actually stored in the table.

You can also choose to sort multiple columns in query and table datasheets. When you apply sorting to multiple columns, Access displays the results of your sorting criteria from left to right. For example, in the qryEmployeesSorted query you have open, leave the sorting option for the Birthdate column intact, and then click the Sort Ascending option on the AutoFilter menu above the State column. You'll notice that Access sorts the employee records by State first and then by the Birthdate column. Remember that these sorting options are only temporary. If you want Access to sort the query results in a specific order each time you open the query, you'll need to define those sorting options in Design view.

INSIDE OUT   Opening the AutoFilter menu using a keyboard shortcut

You can open the AutoFilter menu that displays sorting and filtering options for a column by pressing Alt+\ (backslash) when your focus is in the column.

Filtering Data

Access also provides options for you to dynamically filter the results in a query or table datasheet. When you opened the AutoFilter menu above the Birthdate column in the previous section, you might have noticed specific employee birth dates listed below the sorting options. You can click one of the options in the AutoFilter menu to filter the records displayed in the datasheet to just the records that match that filter criterion. In the qryEmployeesSorted query you have opened, open the AutoFilter menu above the State column. Access displays one unique state abbreviation for each state that it finds in the existing records, as shown in Figure 5-37. You can use the scroll bar on the right side of the AutoFilter menu to scroll the list of existing state options.

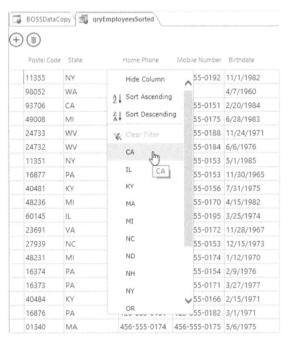

Figure 5-37 Click CA on the AutoFilter menu to filter the records in the query datasheet.

Click CA on the AutoFilter menu and Access filters the records in the query to show only the three employees who live in California, as shown in Figure 5-38. Notice in Figure 5-38 that Access displays a funnel icon above the State column. Whenever you apply a filter on a column in a query or table datasheet from within Datasheet view, Access displays a funnel icon above the column to indicate that the column is filtered and might not be displaying all records normally returned by the query.

| BOSSDataCopy | qryEmployeesSorted | | | | | | | | |

Employee ID	Last Name	First Name	Middle Initial	FullName	Address	City	Postal Code	State	Home Phone
17	Curran	Douglas		Douglas Curran	2345 Willow Dri	Easton	93706	CA	789-555-0150
8	Smith	Aaron	N	Aaron Smith	4567 Main Aven	Fresno	93707	CA	789-555-0166
18	Yang	Shengda	R	Shengda Yang	4567 Central Str	Fresno	93710	CA	789-555-0152
(New)									

Figure 5-38 Access filters the query records to show only employees in California.

You can filter by more than one option by dropping the AutoFilter menu down again and clicking another option. Access displays a check mark next to each filtered option in the AutoFilter menu for the column. Click (Blank) when you want to filter the data to show records where no value exists in that column. Click Clear Filter near the top of the AutoFilter menu to clear the filters and see all the data again.

> **Note**
>
> Depending on the data type of the column, you won't see all the options available in the AutoFilter menu. For example, Access does not display any filter options for Hyperlink fields.

INSIDE OUT   Resize and move columns in Datasheet view

You can resize the width of the columns and reposition columns when you view query and table datasheets. To resize a column, position your mouse on the right edge of the column header until your cursor becomes a two-sided arrow. Click and drag the column header to the left to decrease the width of the column, or drag the column header to the right to increase the width of the column. To move a column, position your mouse over the column header until your cursor becomes a four-sided arrow. Click and drag the entire column header to the left or right to reposition the column. Access displays a vertical I-Bar to indicate where it will place the column when you release the mouse. Note that resizing and moving columns when you view the query or table datasheet is not permanent. If you refresh the datasheet or close and then reopen the query or table datasheet, Access displays the columns at their original widths and positions.

Selecting data from multiple tables

At this point, you've been through all the variations on a single theme—queries on a single table. However, for many tasks, you'll need to build a query on multiple tables or queries (yes, you can build a query on a query!), calculate totals, and add parameters. It's easy to build on the knowledge of single table queries to retrieve related information from many tables and to place that information in a single query datasheet. You'll find this ability to select data from multiple tables very useful in designing views for your web app user interface.

Creating inner joins

A join is the link you need to define between two related tables in a query so that the data you see makes sense. If you don't define the link, you'll see all rows from the first table combined with all rows from the second table (also called the *Cartesian product*). When you use an *inner join* (the default for joins in queries), you won't see rows from either table that don't have a matching row in the other table. This type of query is also called an *equi-join query*, meaning that you'll see rows only where there are *equal* values in *both* tables. For example, in a query that joins employees and job codes, you won't see any job codes that have no employees or any employees that aren't assigned to a job code. To see how to build a query that returns all rows from one of the tables, including rows that have no match in the related table, see the next section, "Creating outer joins."

Correctly designing your tables requires you to split out (normalize) your data into separate tables to avoid redundant data and problems updating the data.

> For details about designing your tables, see Article 1, "Designing your database application," which can be downloaded from the book's catalog page.

For many tasks, you need to work with the data from multiple tables. For example, in the Back Office Software System web app, to work with employees and the job codes to which they are assigned, you can't get all the information you need from just tblEmployees. The tblJobCodes table contains the job code information for all the various positions available in the restaurant, and the tblTrainedPositions table contains a listing of each employee's trained positions that they can work in the restaurant. Separately, the tables contain the needed data to track employees and job codes; however, what if you looked at the tblTrainedPositions table and wanted to know the employee's full name for each assigned position? To view data that meets that requirement, you'll need a query that combines both tblEmployees and tblTrainedPositions.

Try the following example, in which you combine information about an employee and the positions to which they are assigned. Start by opening the Back Office Software System web app backup copy (BOSSDataCopy.app) in Access. Click the Advanced button in the Create group on the Home tab, and then click Query on the drop-down menu to begin designing a new query. Access immediately opens the Show Table dialog box. In this dialog box, you select the tables and queries that you want in your new query. Select the tblEmployees and tblTrainedPositions tables (hold down the Ctrl key as you click each table name), click Add, and then close the dialog box.

The two tables, tblEmployees and tblTrainedPositions, are directly related to each other through the EmployeeIDFK field in tblTrainedPostitions. The upper part of the Query window in Design view should look like that shown in Figure 5-39. Access first links multiple tables in a query based on the lookup fields you have defined.

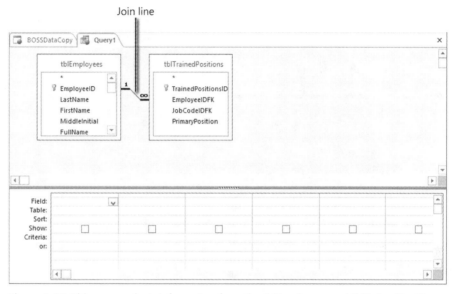

Figure 5-39 This query selects information from the tblEmployees and tblTrainedPositions tables.

Access shows the links between tables as a line drawn from the primary key in one table to its matching lookup field in the other table. As already noted, a direct relationship exists between these two tables in this example. Access sees that EmployeeID field is the primary key in tblEmployees and finds a matching EmployeeIDFK lookup field in tblTrainedPositions. Therefore, it should create a join line between the two tables on these two fields. If you don't see this line, you can click EmployeeID in tblEmployees and drag it on EmployeeIDFK in tblTrainedPositions to open the Join Properties dialog box. We'll discuss the Join Properties dialog box in the next section, "Creating outer joins."

In this example, you want to add to the query the EmployeeID, LastName, and FullName fields from the tblEmployees table and the TrainedPositionsID, JobCodeIDFK, and PrimaryPosition fields from the tblTrainedPositions table.

Chapter 5

When you save the query and switch to Datasheet view, you see the recordset shown in Figure 5-40. The fields from the tblEmployees table appear first, left to right. I resized the columns displayed in Figure 5-40 so that you can see all the data.

INSIDE OUT   A query is really defined by its SQL

The query designer converts everything you build in a query grid into SQL—the lingua franca of database queries. Access actually stores only the SQL and rebuilds the query grid each time you open a query in Design view.

Join line   Fields from tblTrainedPositions

Figure 5-40 Here you can see the recordset of the query shown in Figure 5-39.

If you type a different job code (the control for the JobCodeIDFK field in tblTrainedPositions), you can see that Access allows you to make this change. When you change the value in a foreign key lookup field (in this case, the JobCodeIDFK field in tblTrainedPositions) in a table on the *many* side of a one-to-many query (there are many trained positions for each employee), Access retrieves the related row from the *one* side (tblEmployees) to keep the data synchronized. However, to make that change, you have to include the primary AutoNumber field from the *many* side of the query—the TrainedPositionsID field in this example. You'll notice that if you remove that field from the query design grid, you can no longer update the job code field on the *many* side.

The job code control in the query datasheet shown in Figure 5-40 for the JobCodeIDFK field is an autocomplete control, which is new in Access 2013. You'll learn more about this control in Chapter 6, "Working with views and the web browser experience."

For the fields on the *one* side of the one-to-many query, you'll notice that Access prevents you from updating those fields. The FullName field is a calculated field, so you could not update data in that field in any case. However, try to change data in the LastName field in this query in Datasheet view. You'll notice that Access prevents any data updates to this field because this field is on the *one* side of the one-to-many relationship. You also cannot add any new records using this query.

You might use a query, such as the one in Figure 5-40, as the basis for a view on trained positions by employee. If you add a sort to the LastName field, Access displays each trained position grouped by the employees. If you instead sort on the JobCodeIDFK field, Access displays the results by job code first, so you can see all the employees assigned to each specific job code. In either case, combining data from related tables in queries can be very useful when it comes time to designing views based on your data. However, such a view would be even more useful if you could include the job code number and position color from tblJobCodes for each record. Switch back to Design view, click the Show Table button in the Query Setup group of the Design contextual tab, and add tblJobCodes table to the query.

INSIDE OUT   Drag tables and queries onto design grid

Instead of using the Show Table command in the ribbon to add additional tables and queries to your query design grid, you can also drag table and query objects from the Navigation pane onto the query design grid.

The JobCodeIDFK field in tblTrainedPositions is a lookup field to the tblJobCodes table, so when you add tblJobCodes to the query design grid, Access draws a join line from the JobCodeID primary AutoNumber field in tblJobCodes to the JobCodeIDFK lookup field in tblTrainedPositions. The JobCodeIDFK lookup field uses the JobTitle field from tblJobCodes as its display value. For our query, it would be useful to also include the Job-Code field, which contains job code numbers for each restaurant position and the position color assigned for each position. Drag the JobCode and PositionColor fields from tblJob-Codes to the first two empty columns in the design grid. Your query grid should now look like Figure 5-41.

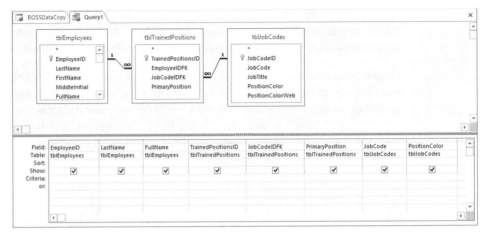

Figure 5-41 In this example, we are creating a complex query using three tables.

After you save your query changes, you can switch to Datasheet view to see the results of your work, as shown in Figure 5-42.

Employee ID	Last Name	FullName	Trained Positions ID	Job Code	Primary Position	Job Code	Position Color
1	Sousa	Anibal Sousa	1	Busser	☐	30	255
1	Sousa	Anibal Sousa	2	Line Server	☑	50	8388736
1	Sousa	Anibal Sousa	3	Cashier-Hostess	☐	70	32768
2	Riegle	Jennifer Riegle	4	Line Server	☑	50	8388736
2	Riegle	Jennifer Riegle	5	Cashier-Hostess	☐	70	32768
3	Jensen	Kathleen Jensen	6	Busser	☐	30	255
3	Jensen	Kathleen Jensen	7	Dishwasher	☑	40	8421504
4	Francis	Cat Francis	8	Busser	☑	30	255
5	Yong	Joe Yong	9	Busser	☐	30	255
5	Yong	Joe Yong	10	Dishwasher	☑	40	8421504
6	Linggoputro	Harry Linggoputro	11	Busser	☐	30	255
6	Linggoputro	Harry Linggoputro	12	Dishwasher	☑	40	8421504
7	Gibson	Mary Gibson	13	Cashier-Hostess	☑	70	32768
8	Smith	Aaron Smith	14	Cook	☐	10	8388608

Figure 5-42 In Datasheet view, you can see the recordset of the query shown in Figure 5-41.

You can now easily see data in one query datasheet from three related tables. On each row displayed in this query datasheet, you see the last name and full name of an employee, a specific job code they are trained to perform, a check box to indicate whether this is their primary position, and additional information about the job code number and the job code's position color. (You'll see how the position color is used in Chapter 7, "Advanced view design.")

Creating outer joins

Most queries that you create to request information from multiple tables will show results on the basis of matching data in one or more tables. For example, the Query window in Datasheet view, shown in Figure 5-42, contains the names of employees and their trained positions in the tblTrainedPositions table. It does not contain the names of job codes that don't have any employees assigned to them. As explained earlier, this type of query is called an equi-join query, meaning that you'll see rows only where there are equal values in both tables. But what if you want to display job codes that do not have any employees trained in those positions in the web app? Or, how do you find employees who have no trained positions? You can get the information you need by creating a query that uses an outer join. An outer join lets you see all rows from one of the tables even if there's no matching row in the related table. When no matching row exists, Access returns the special Null value in the columns from the related table.

To create an outer join, you must modify the join properties. Let's see whether we can find any job codes that don't have any employees assigned to them as trained positions. Start a new query in Access in the Back Office Software System backup web app (BOSSDataCopy.app). Add tblJobCodes and tblTrainedPositions to the query. Double-click the join line between the two tables in the upper part of the Query window in Design view to see the Join Properties dialog box, shown in Figure 5-43.

Figure 5-43 The Join Properties dialog box allows you to change the join properties for the query.

The default setting in the Join Properties dialog box is the first option—where the joined fields from both tables are equal. You can see that you have two additional options for this query: to see all job codes and only trained positions records that match or to see all trained positions and only job codes that match. If you entered your underlying data correctly, you shouldn't have trained positions for employees that aren't defined in the web app. When you create lookup fields between the tblJobCodes table and the tblTrainedPositions table, Access won't let you create any trained positions records for nonexistent job codes.

Select the second option in the dialog box. Click OK. You should now see an arrow on the join line pointing from the tblJobCodes field list to the tblTrainedPositions field list, indicating that you have asked for an outer join with all records from tblJobCodes regardless of match, as shown in Figure 5-44. For job codes that have no assigned trained positions for employees, Access returns the special Null value in all the columns for tblTrainedPositions. Therefore, you can find the job codes with no assigned trained positions by including the Is Null test for any of the columns from tblTrainedPositions. When you run this query, you should find exactly six job codes that are not assigned to any employees as trained positions, as shown in Figure 5-45. The finished query is saved as qryUnassignedJobCodes in the Back Office Software System web app.

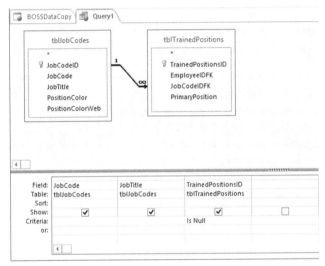

Figure 5-44 This query design finds job codes that have no employees assigned to them as trained positions.

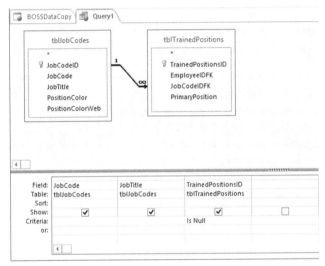

Figure 5-45 This recordset shows the six job codes that do not have any employees assigned to them as trained positions.

Summarizing information with totals queries

Sometimes you aren't interested in each and every row in your table—you'd rather see calculations across groups of data. For example, you might want the total wages for all employees for a specific week, or you might want to know the average of all purchases for each month in the last year. To get these answers, you need a totals query.

Totals within groups

If you're the restaurant manager, you might be interested in producing a weekly wage report, including any overtime wages, based on the total hours worked by employees so that you can prepare payroll paychecks. For this series of exercises, start a new query in the Back Office Software System backup copy web app (BOSSDataCopy.app) with tblEmployees and tblLaborHours in the query design grid. Include in the Field row the EmployeeID, LastName, FirstName, and PayRate fields from tblEmployees and the Hours and Tips fields from tblLaborHours.

> # INSIDE OUT   When totals queries are useful
>
> A totals query groups the fields you specify, and every output field must either be one of the grouping fields or be the result of a calculation using one of the available aggregate functions. (See Table 5-6.) Because all fields are calculated, you cannot update any fields returned by a totals query. This does not mean that learning about how to build totals queries is not useful. Totals queries are very useful for aggregating data that cannot normally be displayed in views.

To turn this into a totals query, click the Totals button in the Show/Hide group of the Design contextual tab under Query Tools to open the Total row in the design grid, as shown in Figure 5-46. When you first click the Totals button in the Show/Hide group, Access displays Group By in the Total row for any fields you already have in the design grid. At this point, the records in each field are grouped but not totaled. If you were to run the query now, you'd get one row in the recordset for each set of unique values—but no totals. You must replace Group By with an aggregate function in the Total row.

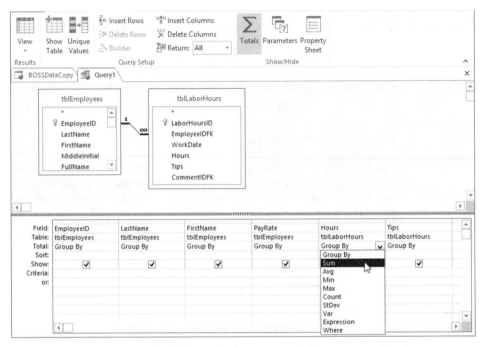

Figure 5-46 The Total row in the design grid allows you to define aggregate functions.

Access provides seven aggregate functions for your use in web app totals queries. You can choose the one you want by typing its name in the Total row in the design grid or by clicking the small arrow and selecting it from the list. You can learn about the available functions in Table 5-6.

TABLE 5-6 Total functions

Function	Description
Sum	Calculates the sum of all the values for this field in each group. You can specify this function only with number or currency fields.
Avg	Calculates the arithmetic average of all the values for this field in each group. You can specify this function only with number or currency fields. Access does not include any Null values in the calculation.
Min	Returns the lowest value found in this field within each group. For numbers, Min returns the smallest value. For text, Min returns the lowest value in collating sequence ("dictionary" order), without regard to case. Access ignores Null values.
Max	Returns the highest value found in this field within each group. For numbers, Max returns the largest value. For text, Max returns the highest value in collating sequence ("dictionary" order), without regard to case. Access ignores Null values.

Function	Description
Count	Returns the count of the rows in which the specified field is not a Null value. You can also enter the special expression COUNT(*) in the Field row to count all rows in each group, *regardless* of the presence of Null values.
StDev	Calculates the statistical standard deviation of all the values for this field in each group. You can specify this function only with number or currency fields. If the group does not contain at least two rows, Access returns a Null value.
Var	Calculates the statistical variance of all the values for this field in each group. You can specify this function only with number or currency fields. If the group does not contain at least two rows, Access returns a Null value.

Let's experiment with the query you're currently working on to understand some of the available functions. Change the Total row under Hours to Sum. Add the Hours field from tblLaborHours three more times, and choose Avg, Min, and Max, respectively, under each. Change the Total row under the Tips field to Sum. Finally, add the LaborHoursID field from tblLaborHours and choose Count in the Total row under that field. Your query design should now look like Figure 5-47.

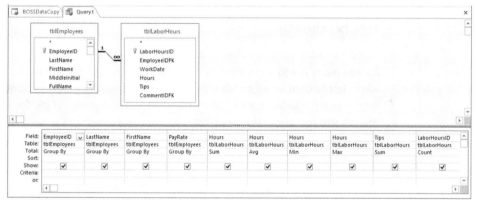

Figure 5-47 This query design explores many different aggregate functions.

Save the query design changes you've made so far (name it **qryWeekLaborHours**), and then switch to Datasheet view to see the results, as shown in Figure 5-48. The sample web app has 126 records in the tblLaborHours table, covering a week's worth of employee labor hours completed. As you look through the query results, you can see how valuable totals queries can be for analyzing your data. In this sample query, you can easily see the total number of hours worked by each employee. You can also see the average number of hours per shift for each employee, the shortest shift and longest shift for each employee, the total amount of tips, as well as the number of recorded days each employee worked.

Chapter 5

BOSSDataCopy	qryWeekLaborHours									×

Employee ID	Last Name	First Name	Pay Rate	SumOfHours	AvgOfHours	MinOfHours	MaxOfHours	SumOfTips	CountOfLaborHoursID
1	Sousa	Anibal	$7.50	20.5	4.1	3.5	5		5
2	Riegle	Jennifer	$7.00	31	5.1666666666	4.75	7		6
3	Jensen	Kathleen	$6.50	10	5	5	5		2
4	Francis	Cat	$7.75	28.75	5.75	5.5	6.5	100.5	5
5	Yong	Joe	$6.50	36	7.2	5	8		5
6	Linggoputro	Harry	$6.65	6.5	6.5	6.5	6.5		1
7	Gibson	Mary	$7.00	28	4.6666666666	4.5	5		6
8	Smith	Aaron	$7.00	41.5	6.9166666666	5	9.5		6
9	Michaels	Tom	$10.00	39	7.8	6.5	8.75	15.15	5
10	Dixon	Andrew	$7.25	15.75	7.875	7.75	8		2
11	Stoklasa	Jan	$6.50	40.25	6.7083333333	6	7.75		6
12	West	Paul	$9.00	38.25	7.65	7.25	8.25		5
13	Kresnadi	Mario	$8.50						4
14	Peterson	Palle	$7.00	28.25	4.7083333333	0	7.5		6
15	Matthews	Joseph	$8.00	36	7.2	6	7.5		5
16	Viescas	John	$8.00	17	8.5	8.5	8.5		2
17	Curran	Douglas	$7.50	10.25	5.125	5	5.25		2

Figure 5-48 Running the query in Figure 5-47 returns total hours, average hours, fewest labor hours per day, most hours per day, and count of days with labor hours by employee.

Troubleshooting

I didn't specify sorting criteria, so why is my data sorted?

A totals query has to sort your data to be able to group it, so it returns the groups sorted left to right based on the sequence of your Group By fields. If you need to sort the grouping columns in some other way, change the sequence of the Group By fields. You can also sort any of the totals fields. In the query shown in Figures 5-47 and 5-48, if you leave out the EmployeeID field from the totals query, you'll notice Access sorts the results by the employee's last names.

INSIDE OUT   Combine aggregate functions with expression setting

In the list for the Total row in the design grid, you'll also find an Expression setting. Select this when you want to create an expression in the Total row that uses one or more of the aggregate functions listed earlier. For example, you might want to calculate a value that reflects the range of hours in the group, as in the following: Max([Hours]) - Min([Hours]).

As you can with any field, you can give your expression a custom name. Notice, in Figure 5-48, that Access has generated names such as SumOfHours or AvgOfHours. You can fix these by clicking in the field in the design grid and prefixing the field or expression with your own name followed by a colon.

Let's refine the query you've created so far and focus back on our goal of calculating regular and overtime hours and wages for each employee. We'll accomplish our goal over the next few sections by modifying this existing totals query with some expressions, adding in some Where clauses, building another query on top of this totals query, and finally, adding in some parameters.

Begin by removing the extra three Hours columns (Avg, Min, and Max) from the design grid, as well as the LaborHoursID field. Now, add two expression columns to the query design grid with the following expressions:

```
TotHrs: Sum(Coalesce([Hours],0))
```

```
TotTips: Sum(Coalesce([Tips],0))
```

In the Total row for both of these expressions, select Expression as the aggregate function to use. The *Coalesce* function, as you recall, finds the first Null value in a list of parameters. Our expressions above will return a value of zero in these columns instead of Null for any employees who have no hours or tips recorded. Your query design grid should now look like Figure 5-49. When you save your query changes, you can see the results in Datasheet view in Figure 5-50.

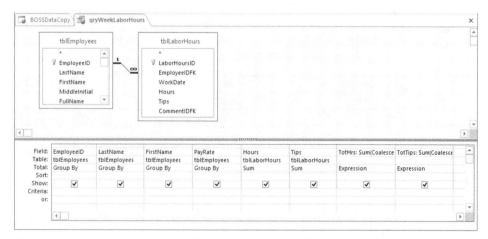

Figure 5-49 In this figure, we are adding expressions and defining custom field names in a totals query.

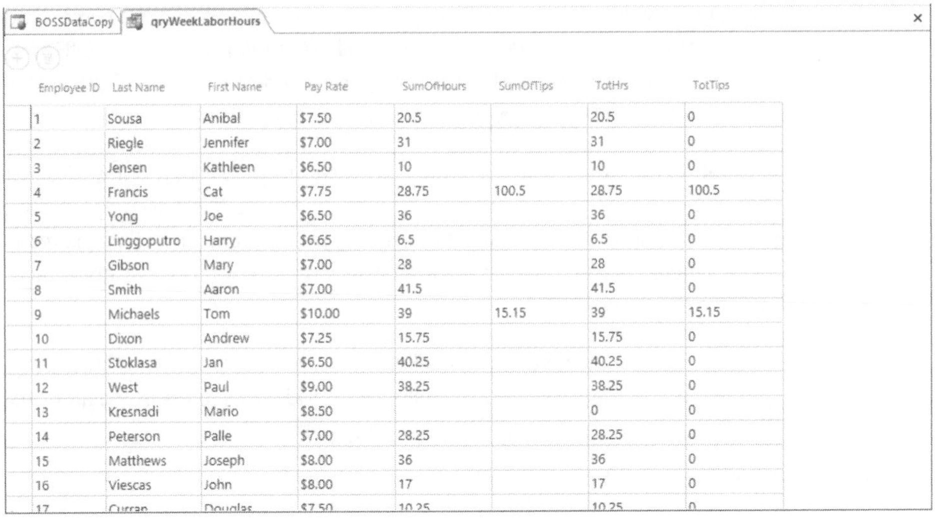

Employee ID	Last Name	First Name	Pay Rate	SumOfHours	SumOfTips	TotHrs	TotTips
1	Sousa	Anibal	$7.50	20.5		20.5	0
2	Riegle	Jennifer	$7.00	31		31	0
3	Jensen	Kathleen	$6.50	10		10	0
4	Francis	Cat	$7.75	28.75	100.5	28.75	100.5
5	Yong	Joe	$6.50	36		36	0
6	Linggoputro	Harry	$6.65	6.5		6.5	0
7	Gibson	Mary	$7.00	28		28	0
8	Smith	Aaron	$7.00	41.5		41.5	0
9	Michaels	Tom	$10.00	39	15.15	39	15.15
10	Dixon	Andrew	$7.25	15.75		15.75	0
11	Stoklasa	Jan	$6.50	40.25		40.25	0
12	West	Paul	$9.00	38.25		38.25	0
13	Kresnadi	Mario	$8.50			0	0
14	Peterson	Palle	$7.00	28.25		28.25	0
15	Matthews	Joseph	$8.00	36		36	0
16	Viescas	John	$8.00	17		17	0
17	Curran	Douglas	$7.50	10.25		10.25	0

Figure 5-50 This is the result in Datasheet view of the query shown in Figure 5-49.

In Figure 5-50, you can see how the Coalesce function has provided us with a useful zero value for any employees that had no recorded labor hours or tips.

Selecting records to form groups

You might filter out some records before your totals query gathers the records into groups. To filter out certain records from the tables in your query, you can add to the design grid the field or fields you want to filter. Then create the filter by selecting the Where setting in the Total row (which will clear the field's Show check box) and entering criteria that tell Access which records to exclude.

For example, your query so far returns records for all employees in the web app. You probably do not need to include in this query any employees that have been terminated. In Figure 5-50, you'll notice Mario (EmployeeID of 13) has no labor hours at all because he is no longer an active employee. (In Chapter 4, "Creating data macros in web apps,") I had you reassign Mario Kresnadi's termination record, which marked his status as active. If Mario's record is still marked at active, open tblTerminations and change the assigned termination record to Mario to change his Active status back to False.) To find this information, you need to add the Active field from the tblEmployees table to your query, change the Total line to Where, and add the criterion Yes on the Criteria line under this field. Your query should now look like Figure 5-51.

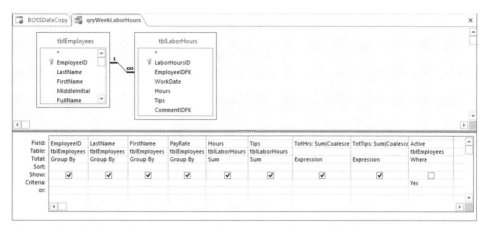

Figure 5-51 Use the Active field to select the rows that will be included in groups.

Now when you save your changes and run the query, you get totals only for active employees. After completing and saving your changes to this totals query, close the query to continue with the next section.

Building a query on a query

When you're building a very complex query, sometimes it's easier to visualize the solution to the problem at hand by breaking it down into smaller pieces. In some cases, building a query on a query might be the only way to correctly solve the problem. So far, you've created a totals query that calculates the total number of hours and tips for active restaurant employees. You've also used the Coalesce function to display a zero value instead of Null for any case where the employee has no hours or tips. We can create another query that builds on the foundation of this totals query to calculate regular and overtime wages for the employees.

Start a new query, click the Queries tab in the Show Table dialog box, select the totals query you previously saved (qryWeekLaborHours), and then click Add to add this query to the design grid, as shown in Figure 5-52.

Figure 5-52 Base your new query on the totals query you previously completed.

Include in the Field row the EmployeeID, LastName, FirstName, PayRate, TotHrs, and TotTips fields from the qryWeekLaborHours query, and then make sure to click the Totals button in the Show/Hide group of the Design contextual tab under Query Tools. We now need to create expressions for five columns that will calculate all of our needed information based on the totals data the first query provides.

For this specific example, we'll assume that if an employee works more than 40 hours in a week, they are entitled to be paid one and a half times their normal pay rate for any hours above 40. To calculate this information, we'll need to separate regular pay hours and over-time pay hours. We'll also need to then separate regular wages and overtime wages using different pay rates. Finally, we'll need a grand total of wages, which combines the regular and overtime wages. Add five expression columns to the query design grid with the following expressions:

```
RegHrs: Format(IIf([TotHrs]>40,40,[TotHrs]),"N")
```

```
OTHrs: Format(IIf([TotHrs]>40,([TotHrs])-40,0),"N")
```

```
RegWages: Format(IIf([TotHrs]>40,(40*[PayRate]),([TotHrs]*[PayRate])),"C")
```

```
OTWages: Format(IIf([TotHrs]>40,((([TotHrs]-40)*([PayRate]*1.5)),0),"C")
```

```
TotalWages:Format(IIf([TotHrs]>40,(40*[PayRate]),([TotHrs]*[PayRate]))+IIf([TotHrs]>4
0,((([TotHrs]-40)*([PayRate]*1.5)),0),"C")
```

In the first column expression, we're using the IIF function to determine whether the TotHrs field from the first totals query is greater than 40 hours. If the total hours worked is greater than 40 hours, the expression returns exactly 40. If the total hours worked is less than or equal to 40 hours, the expression returns the existing TotHrs value. The entire IIF function is then wrapped inside a Format function. The Format function works similarly to the table field Format property you learned about in Chapter 3. The first parameter is the name of the field or the expression that you want to format, and the second parameter specifies how you want the data formatted. In this case, we're asking Format to return N, which indicates a number.

In the second column expression, we're using the IIF function to determine whether the employee's hours are greater than 40. If the employee worked more than 40 hours, Access returns the total number of hours greater than 40 ([TotHrs]-40). If the employee did cross over the 40-hour threshold during the week, Access returns zero to indicate no overtime hours.

In the third column expression—RegWages—we use an IIF function similar to the one used for the RegHrs expression. If the employee worked more than 40 hours during the week, Access multiplies 40 by the employee's PayRate to determine their regular pay wages. If the employee worked less than or equal to 40 hours during the pay week, Access multiples their total hours, TotHrs, by their pay rate. Finally, the Format function wraps the entire IIF function result and displays the regular wages as currency data by using C as the format parameter.

Troubleshooting

Why can I not reference a calculated expression column in a web app query?
You might look at the five expressions used to calculate regular and overtime hours in this example and wonder why I did not just reference the previous expression instead of duplicating the logic again. If you're familiar with creating queries in desktop databases, you're probably aware that you can reference calculated expression columns in other columns. For example, in a desktop database, I could have made the **RegWages** expression much simpler by using the expression [RegHrs]*[PayRate], because the RegHrs calculated expression already returns the total number of regular hours. However, in web app queries, you cannot reference calculated expression columns in expressions used for other columns, which means you'll need to duplicate the logic in other columns.

The fourth column expression calculates the overtime wages by again checking whether the employee worked more than 40 hours. If this is true, Access calculates the number of overtime hours (the expression in the first set of parentheses) and multiplies that by the employee's overtime wage rate (the expression in the second set of parentheses). If the employee has no overtime hours, Access returns a zero for overtime wages. Access then formats the final result as currency, in this case.

The TotWages expression is a little more complicated, because it contains an IIF function nested inside another IIF function. The first part of the expression checks to see whether the employee worked over 40 hours. If this is true, the calculation is simple because we need only to multiply the employee's total hours by their pay rate. If the employee has overtime hours, we need to calculate both their regular and overtime wages separately and then add them together to get their total wages, all within the third argument of the first IIF. To accomplish this goal, we essentially repeat some of the logic that is also used in the previous wage expressions inside the third argument with a nested IIF function.

Your query design grid should now look like Figure 5-53. When you save your query changes (name the query **qryWeekLaborHoursFinalDisplay**), you'll see the results in Datasheet view in Figure 5-54.

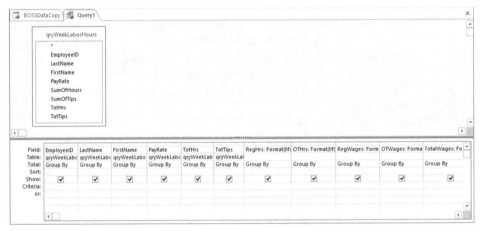

Figure 5-53 Your query design grid should include the five calculated expressions.

Employee ID	Last Name	First Name	Pay Rate	TotHrs	TotTips	RegHrs	OTHrs	RegWages	OTWages	TotalWages
1	Sousa	Anibal	$7.50	20.5	0	20.50	0.00	$153.75	$0.00	$153.75
2	Riegle	Jennifer	$7.00	31	0	31.00	0.00	$217.00	$0.00	$217.00
3	Jensen	Kathleen	$6.50	10	0	10.00	0.00	$65.00	$0.00	$65.00
4	Francis	Cat	$7.75	28.75	100.5	28.75	0.00	$222.81	$0.00	$222.81
5	Yong	Joe	$6.50	36	0	36.00	0.00	$234.00	$0.00	$234.00
6	Linggoputro	Harry	$6.65	6.5	0	6.50	0.00	$43.23	$0.00	$43.23
7	Gibson	Mary	$7.00	28	0	28.00	0.00	$196.00	$0.00	$196.00
8	Smith	Aaron	$7.00	41.5	0	40.00	1.50	$280.00	$15.75	$295.75
9	Michaels	Tom	$10.00	39	15.15	39.00	0.00	$390.00	$0.00	$390.00
10	Dixon	Andrew	$7.25	15.75	0	15.75	0.00	$114.19	$0.00	$114.19
11	Stoklasa	Jan	$6.50	40.25	0	40.00	0.25	$260.00	$2.44	$262.44
12	West	Paul	$9.00	38.25	0	38.25	0.00	$344.25	$0.00	$344.25
13	Kresnadi	Mario	$8.50	0	0	0.00	0.00	$0.00	$0.00	$0.00
14	Peterson	Palle	$7.00	28.25	0	28.25	0.00	$197.75	$0.00	$197.75
15	Matthews	Joseph	$8.00	36	0	36.00	0.00	$288.00	$0.00	$288.00
16	Viescas	John	$8.00	17	0	17.00	0.00	$136.00	$0.00	$136.00
17	Curran	Douglas	$7.50	10.25	0	10.25	0.00	$76.88	$0.00	$76.88
18	Yang	Shengda	$6.75	32	0	32.00	0.00	$216.00	$0.00	$216.00
19	Koczka	Daniel	$6.85	31.75	0	31.75	0.00	$217.49	$0.00	$217.49

Figure 5-54 This is the result in Datasheet view of the query shown in Figure 5-53.

As you can see in Figure 5-54, Access successfully calculates total hours, regular hours, overtime hours, regular pay wages, overtime pay wages, and total wages using the expressions we created and built on top of data coming from a separate totals query. This type of information is very useful for the restaurant manager to send payroll data to their accounting department.

Although I show only one example of building a query on a query, the specific user scenario on which I based this web app might have bi-weekly pay cycles. To create a bi-weekly report of total payroll, we could create two queries to handle the first week of payroll data (each overtime calculation can apply over only one week), two queries to handle the second week of the payroll cycle, and finally, create a fifth query that combines the results of the first and second week totals into a query totaling both weeks.

Using query parameters

So far, you've been entering selection criteria directly in the design grid of the Query window in Design view. However, you don't have to decide at the time you design the query exactly what value you want Access to search for. Instead, you can include a parameter in the query, and Access will prompt you for the criteria each time the query runs.

To include a parameter, you enter a name and data type in the Parameters dialog box and then match the name enclosed in brackets ([ ]) in the Criteria row instead of entering a value. What you enclose in brackets becomes the name by which Access knows your parameter. Access displays this name in a dialog box when you run the query, so you should enter a name that accurately describes what you want. You can enter several parameters in a single query, so each parameter name must be unique.

In the payroll totals queries you've been building so far, Access currently calculates the data for all of the labor hour records in the tblLaborHours table. When you run the queries, the resulting data works fine, because the sample data in this web app contains only one week's worth of labor hour records. However, if you start entering more records in the tblLaborHours table over different weeks, these queries will calculate overtime wages over a time span of several weeks. You'd be paying a lot of overtime to your employees as a result! You don't want to have to build or modify a query with specific start and end dates for the payroll cycle each time you want to calculate your payroll totals. So, you can use query parameters as a way to dynamically enter the beginning and ending dates of interest.

Open the first totals query you created early in these sections, called qryWeekLaborHours, in Design view. This query, as you recall, is the totals query that sums the amount of labor hours and tips for each employee. Now comes the tricky part. You want the query to ask for the range of dates of interest in the payroll cycle. Your query needs to find the labor hour records between a set of dates.

To define query parameters in your web app queries, click the Parameters command in the Show/Hide group of the Design contextual ribbon tab. Access then displays the Query Parameters dialog box, as shown in Figure 5-55. For each parameter in a query, you need to define the name of the parameter and the data type to expect. Access uses this information to validate the value entered. For example, if you define a parameter as a number, Access won't accept alphabetic characters in the parameter value. Likewise, if you define a parameter as a Date/Time data type, Access won't accept anything but a valid date or time value in the parameter prompt. By default, Access assigns the Text data type to query parameters.

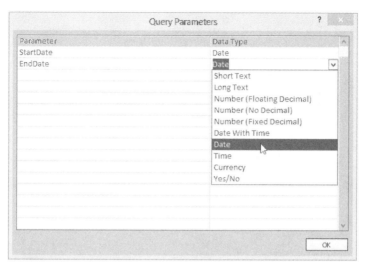

Figure 5-55 Use the Query Parameters dialog box to define names and assign data types for query parameters.

In the Parameter column, enter each parameter name you want to use in the design grid. Note that query parameters in web apps cannot contain any spaces or special characters. For this payroll totals query example, enter **StartDate** and **EndDate** as two query parameter names. In the Data Type column, select Date from the drop-down list of data types. Click OK when you finish defining all your parameters.

Now that you've defined the query parameters, you can add criteria into the query. The WorkDate field in the tblLaborHours table contains the date for each labor record for the employees. Add this field from the tblLaborHours table into the query design grid, and in the Criteria line for this field, enter **Between [StartDate] And [EndDate]**. Finally, on the Totals line for this field, select Where from the drop-down list of aggregate functions. Access clears the check box on the Show line when you do this. Your query should look like Figure 5-56.

Chapter 5

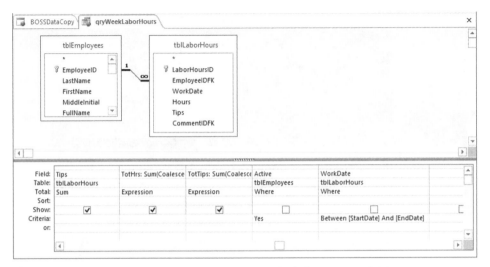

Figure 5-56 You can use query parameters to accept criteria for a range of dates.

When you save your query design changes and switch to Datasheet view, Access prompts you for an appropriate value for each parameter, one at a time, with a dialog box like the one shown in Figure 5-57. Access displays the name of the parameter that you provided in the design grid. If you enter a value that does not match the data type you specified, Access displays an error message and gives you a chance to try again. You can also click Cancel to abort running the query. If you click Cancel, Access displays an error message indicating that it could not open the query because you did not provide all the needed parameters. If you click OK without typing a value, Access returns a Null value for the parameter to the query.

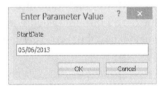

Figure 5-57 The Enter Parameter Value dialog box asks for the query parameter value.

Notice that Access accepts any value that it can recognize as a date, such as a long date or short date format. If you respond to the query parameter prompts with May 6, 2013, for the Start Date and May 12, 2013, for the End Date, you'll see a datasheet like Figure 5-58. (The sample data in this web app contains labor hour records within that week's range.)

	BOSSDataCopy		qryWeekLaborHours					×

Employee ID	Last Name	First Name	Pay Rate	SumOfHours	SumOfTips	TotHrs	TotTips
1	Sousa	Anibal	$7.50	20.5		20.5	0
2	Riegle	Jennifer	$7.00	31		31	0
3	Jensen	Kathleen	$6.50	10		10	0
4	Francis	Cat	$7.75	28.75	100.5	28.75	100.5
5	Yong	Joe	$6.50	36		36	0
6	Linggoputro	Harry	$6.65	6.5		6.5	0
7	Gibson	Mary	$7.00	28		28	0
8	Smith	Aaron	$7.00	41.5		41.5	0
9	Michaels	Tom	$10.00	39	15.15	39	15.15
10	Dixon	Andrew	$7.25	15.75		15.75	0
11	Stoklasa	Jan	$6.50	40.25		40.25	0
12	West	Paul	$9.00	38.25		38.25	0
14	Peterson	Palle	$7.00	28.25		28.25	0
15	Matthews	Joseph	$8.00	36		36	0
16	Viescas	John	$8.00	17		17	0
17	Curran	Douglas	$7.50	10.25		10.25	0
18	Yang	Shengda	$6.75	32		32	0
19	Koczka	Daniel	$6.85	31.75		31.75	0

Figure 5-58 This figure displays the recordset of the query shown in Figure 5-56 when you reply with May 6, 2013, and May 12, 2013, to the parameter prompts.

If you're already familiar with query parameters in desktop databases, you'll need to be aware of some important differences when working with query parameters in web apps. The first issue to be aware of is that if you base a query on another query that uses query parameters, you'll need to duplicate those parameters in both queries; otherwise, Access displays a parameter error message when you run the query based on the other query. For example, you've just completed adding parameters to the qryWeekLaborHours query. Remember that the second query, qryWeekLaborHoursFinalDisplay, uses qryWeekLaborHours as its source. If you try and open qryWeekLaborHoursFinalDisplay in Datasheet view now, Access prompts for both parameters. Even if you supply valid dates, Access displays an error message indicating that the parameters were not provided. To solve this issue, you'll need to open the qryWeekLaborHoursFinalDisplay query in Design view, add the tblLaborHours table to the grid, create identical parameter names and data types as you did for the qryWeekLaborHours query, add the WorkDate field to the grid, provide the same expression in the Criteria as you did before, and set the aggregate function to Where. After you save your changes, switch to Datasheet view, and provide the necessary parameters in the prompts, Access displays the payroll totals data for the given date range.

The second important issue to be aware of with query parameters in web apps is that while Access prompts you for query parameters if you open the query within Access, this behavior does not exist when you view your web app in a web browser. You cannot open a query directly from within your web browser; however, you can base views on saved query

Chapter 5

objects. To work with query parameters in your web browser at runtime, you'll need to create a view that uses the query as its source and then use an OpenDialog macro action to pass in the needed parameters for the query that serves as the data source of the view you are trying to open. You'll learn how to design views in Chapter 6, "Working with views and the web browser experience," and how to work with macro actions in Chapter 8, "Automating a web app using macros."

Troubleshooting

Why do I get an error when I use query parameters on linked SharePoint lists?

Access web apps do not support parameters in queries that use linked SharePoint lists as their data source. This is a design implementation, and you cannot work around this limitation.

Selecting specific groups

You can also filter groups of totals after the query has calculated the groups. To do this, enter criteria for any field that has a Group By setting, one of the aggregate functions, or an expression using the aggregate functions in its Total row. For example, you might want to know only the employees who had overtime hours within a given time frame. To determine this, open the qryWeekLaborHours query and enter a Criteria setting of **>40** for the TotHrs calculated field, as shown in Figure 5-59. Save the query changes, and switch to Datasheet view. The query should now return only two rows in the web app with the sample data in the dates between May 6, 2013, and May 12, 2013.

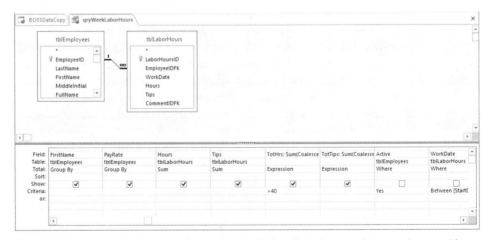

Figure 5-59 Enter a Criteria setting for the TotHrs field to limit the records to employees with overtime hours.

Working with unique values

When you run a query, Access often returns what appear to be duplicate rows in the recordset. The default in Access web apps is to return all records. You can ask Access to return only records with unique values. When you ask for unique values, you're asking Access to calculate and remove duplicate values in the returned recordset. If you want to see all possible data (including duplicate rows), leave the Unique Values property turned off. Note that the Unique Values property setting for all new queries is not turned on by default.

To understand how the Unique Values property setting works, create a new query that includes both the tblLaborHours table and the tblComments table. Let's say you want to find out which employees arrived late for their assigned shifts over a particular period of time. Include the EmployeeIDFK field from the tblLaborHours table, and include the CommentText field from the tblComments table. In the Criteria line for the CommentText field, enter **"Arrived Late"** to restrict the records to only ones where an employee was late. Also, drop in the WorkDate field from tblLaborHours, but clear the Show check box. Figure 5-60 shows a sample query with a date criterion that will display labor hour records between May 1, 2013, and May 31, 2013.

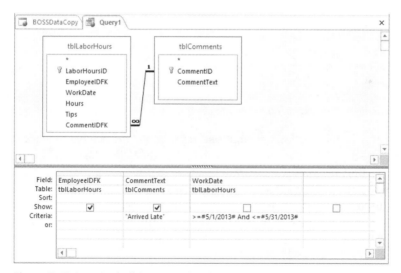

Figure 5-60 You can build a query that demonstrates leaving the Unique Values setting turned off when you're using two tables.

Chapter 5

> **Note**
> You cannot include Image data type fields in a query with the Unique Values query prop-
> erty turned on. Access displays an error message in this case and prevents you from sav-
> ing your query design changes.

If you save your query design changes and switch to Datasheet view, as shown in Figure
5-61, you can see that the query returns nine rows within our specified date range—each
row from tblLaborHours appears once for each related labor comment text that matches
the Arrived Late text between the specified days. Some of these rows come from the same
employee, and some come from different employees within the given time period.

Figure 5-61 Run your sample query to see the result of retrieving all rows.

If you want only one row per employee, regardless of the number of times the employee
was late during the date range, you can turn on the Unique Values property setting. To turn
on the Unique Values property setting, switch to Design view for the query you've been
creating. Now click the Unique Values command in the Query Setup group of the Design
contextual tab, as shown in Figure 5-62. Note that the Unique Values command in the ribbon is a toggle button. When you click this command, Access turns on the query property.
Click the command again, and Access turns off the query property.

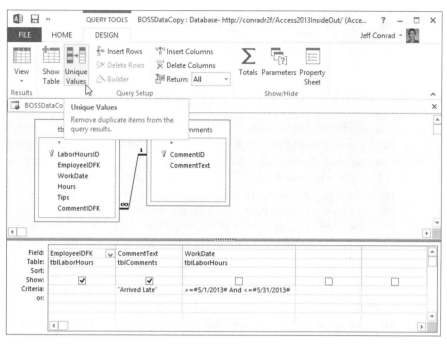

Figure 5-62 Click the Unique Values command in the ribbon to remove duplicates from your query results.

Save your query design changes, and then switch back to Datasheet view. The result is shown in Figure 5-63. This tells us that there were seven different employees who arrived late for a work shift within the date range. This information might prove useful during their next performance evaluation.

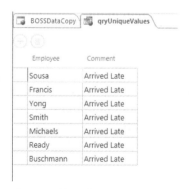

Figure 5-63 When you turn on the Unique Values property setting, Access removes all duplicate records.

> **Note**
>
> As with any calculated value in a query, fields in a unique values query can't be updated.

Using the Top Values query property

You can use the Top Values property to tell Access that you want to see the first *n* rows or the first *x* percent of the rows. If you enter an integer value, Access displays the number of rows specified. If you enter a decimal value between 0 and 1 or an integer less than 100 followed by a percent sign (%), Access displays that percentage of rows. For example, you might want to find the top 10 products you purchase or the top 20 percent of highest paid employees. In most cases, you'll need to specify sorting criteria—perhaps by count of products purchased descending or pay rate descending—to place the rows you want at the "top" of the recordset. You can then ask for the top 10 or top 20 percent to get the answers you want.

To see an example of using the Top Values property, open the qryHighestSortOrder query in the Back Office Software System backup copy web app (BOSSDataCopy.app) in Design view. You can set the Top Values property, shown in Figure 5-64, in the Return drop-down list in the Query Setup ribbon group. In Figure 5-64, you can see that I set the Top Values property to 1, which means Access returns only one record when you run this query. Because I set the query to sort Descending on the SortOrder field, Access returns the record with the highest SortOrder value in the tblInventoryLocations table whenever you run this query.

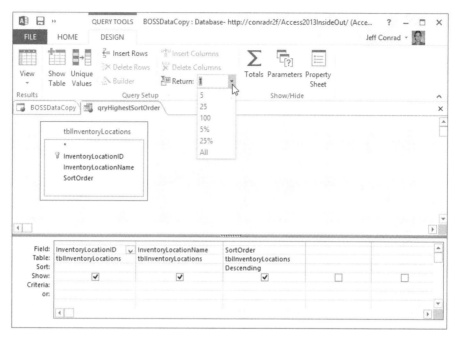

Figure 5-64 When you set the Top Values property, Access can return a specific number or percentage of records.

This query is used in the tblInventoryLocations AfterInsert table event to determine the current highest value in the SortOrder field and then insert one number higher than the current highest value for the next record. This query and a similar one, called qryLowestSortOrder, are also used in the named data macro called dmSwapSortOrders, which allows you to swap SortOrder numbers between two different records.

INSIDE OUT   Setting Top Values through the property sheet

You can also set the Top Values property by opening the query's property sheet. Click the Property Sheet command in the Show/Hide group of the Design contextual tab. Access opens the query property sheet, where you can set the Top Values property using a drop-down list. You can optionally provide a description for your query on the Description line of the property sheet.

At this point, you should have a good understanding of how you can use queries to sort, analyze, and filter the data in your web apps. Now it's time to go on to building the user interface for your Access web app using views.

Chapter 5

Working with views and the web browser experience

You've created your tables, data macros, and queries, and now you're ready to create a user interface for your web app by creating views. You might be wondering why I've waited until now to describe how to create a user interface for web apps. If you've followed along with this book up to this point, you should understand the mechanics of designing and building web app table structures, entering and viewing data in tables, creating data macros to enforce your business logic, and building queries to select and summarize your data. An understanding of tables and queries is important before you jump into views because most of the views you design will be bound to an underlying table or a query. As you'll see later in this chapter, Access automatically designs a user interface for you as you create your tables, so if you've designed your tables well, you're already on your way to having a completed user interface.

Views are the most important objects you'll build in your Access web app because they're what users see and work with every time they run the app. This chapter shows you how to design and work with the quick-created views Access generates with each table and how to use them in a web browser. You'll learn how to work with a view window in Design view to design and customize views. You'll also learn how to use controls on views to simplify data entry on your views and how to work with the Action Bar to control basic record operations.

> **Note**
>
> The examples in this chapter are based on a restaurant management sample web app called RestaurantSampleWithData.app, which can be downloaded from the book's catalog page. You'll need to upload the app into your corporate catalog or Office 365 team site and install the app to use the sample. Review the instructions at the end of Chapter 2, "Exploring the Access 2013 web app interface," if you need help with those tasks. The data you see from the sample views you build in this chapter might not exactly match what you see in this book if you have changed the sample data in the web app.

Uses of views

Views are the primary interface between users and your Microsoft Access web app. You can design views for many different purposes:

- **Displaying and editing data.**   This is the most common use of views. Views provide a way to customize the presentation of the data in your web app. You can also use views to change, delete, or add data in your web app. You can set options in a view to make all or part of your data read-only, fill in related information from other tables automatically, calculate the values to be displayed, or show or hide data based on either the values of other data in the record or the options selected by the user of the view.

- **Controlling application flow.**   You can design views that work with macros to automate the display of certain data or the sequence of certain actions. You can create special controls on your view, such as command buttons, which run a macro when you click them. With macros, you can open other views, run named data macros, restrict the data that is displayed, set values in records and views, and perform many other actions. You can also design a view so that macros run when a specific event occurs—for example, when someone opens the view, clicks an option on the view, or changes data in the view. See Chapter 8, "Automating a web app using macros," for details about using macros with views to automate your web app.

- **Accepting input.**   You can design views that are used only for entering new data in your web app or for providing data values to help automate your app.

- **Displaying messages.**   Views can provide information about how to use your app or about upcoming actions. Access also provides a MessageBox macro action that you can use to display information, warnings, or error messages.

- **Searching data.**   List detail and summary views include built-in filtering controls to allow you to easily search for specific data displayed in views.

- **Summarizing information.**   You can use the new summary views in Access 2013 web apps to group and summarize data. Users of your app can quickly see consolidated data along fields you designate.

Understanding the App Home View

To begin our discussion of views, you first need to understand all the various elements of the App Home View. Install the RestaurantSampleWithData.app web app in your SharePoint site, and then download the app into Access. This web app is the same app you created in Chapter 3, "Designing tables in a web app," when you learned how to create tables

(RestaurantSample.app). The only difference with this web app and the one you created previously is that I've added in sample data to this copy so that you can work through the upcoming sections building views with data.

Your main entry point for creating new views and editing existing views is the App Home View. Figure 6-1 shows the App Home View for this sample web app. As you might recall, the App Home View is a framework consisting of several elements—the Table Selector, the View Selector, and any views associated with the selected table. When you are working within Access, you see the App Home View in design mode. When you open your web app in a web browser, which we'll discuss later in this chapter, you see the App Home View in runtime mode. Microsoft uses the term *runtime* to refer to any use of an Access web app inside a web browser.

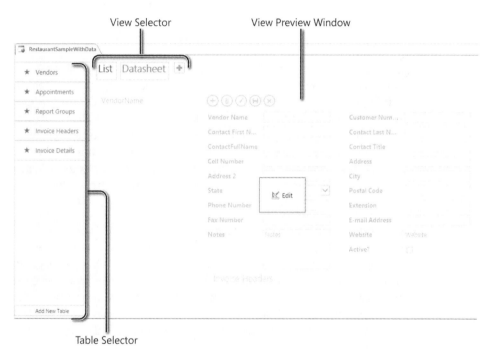

Figure 6-1 The App Home View displays tables and views in your web app.

On the left side of the App Home View is the Table Selector. Access displays the name of each table in your web app in the Table Selector along with a small default icon to the left of the name. At the very bottom of the Table Selector, Access displays the Add New Table button. When you click this button, Access displays the Add Tables screen in the application window where you can create new tables in your web app.

Across the top of the App Home View, the View Selector displays a list of each view associated to the selected table in the Table Selector. (You'll learn more about the types of views that you can create later in this chapter.) In Figure 6-1, you can see that there are two views associated to the currently selected Vendors table in this web app—List and Datasheet. You'll learn how to customize each of the view types later in this chapter.

Beneath the View Selector, Access displays a preview of the selected view. In the preview window, you can see that Access shows a preview of all the controls and layout for the currently selected view. The controls in preview mode appear dimmed, because you cannot edit them in this state. In the center of the view preview window, Access displays an Edit button. You can click the Edit button to open the selected view in Design view to make changes to that view. Whenever you click a view in the View Selector, Access changes the preview image in the view preview window to match the selected view.

Working with the Table Selector

The Table Selector is similar to the Navigation pane in that it displays a list of objects in your web app. However, in this case, the Table Selector displays only table objects. Also, the Table Selector displays at runtime in your web browser, whereas the Navigation pane does not. When you are working with the Table Selector in Access, you can create new tables, open table datasheets, open the Table Design window, hide tables, rename table captions, delete tables, and choose custom icons to display alongside your table names. When you view your web app in a web browser, you use the Table Selector to navigate to different tables so that you can see and use the views associated with the tables. (I'll show you how to do this later in the chapter.)

In Chapter 2, you learned how to use the Add New Table button at the bottom of the Table Selector to create new tables in your web app. If the Add Tables screen is currently displayed in the main application window, Access hides the Add New Table button in the Table Selector. (You can toggle the display of the Add Tables screen at any time within Access by clicking the Table button in the Create group on the Home tab of the ribbon.) When you view your web app in a web browser, Access does not show the Add New Table button in the Table Selector, because you can design objects only within Access, not your web browser.

Changing the table display order

By default, Access displays all the table names in the Table Selector as captions in the order in which you create the tables. You can keep this order if you want, or you can reorder the table captions listed in the Table Selector.

In the sample web app you have open, let's change the display order so that the Invoice Headers table is listed below the Vendors table. Click the Invoice Headers table name caption in the Table Selector, hold your mouse, and then drag the table name above the Appointments table name, as shown in Figure 6-2. As you move the Invoice Headers table up, Access swaps the table name positions with the table name you're moving. In this example, as you move Invoice Headers up, Access first moves the Report Groups table name down so that Invoice Headers is the third table listed in the Table Selector. As you continue dragging Invoice Headers up, Access moves the Appointments table name down so that Invoice Headers is now the second table listed in the Table Selector. Access shifts the table names as a visual cue to indicate where it will drop the table name. After you release the mouse, Access places the Invoice Headers table directly below the Vendors table name and lines up the controls.

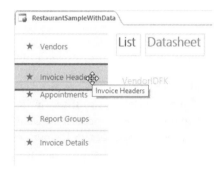

Figure 6-2 Click and drag the Invoice Headers table name caption above the Appointments table name caption.

Customizing table captions

When you create new tables in web apps, Access creates a corresponding control in the Table Selector representing the table. The table name listed in the Table Selector is just a caption. By default, Access uses the table name for the caption, but you can change the caption if you want. For example, if you analyze the Back Office Software System sample web app included with this book, you'll see that all of the table names start with the pre-fix tbl and contain no spaces, but the Table Selector in that web app displays more user-friendly captions, even some with spaces. In the sample web app you have open, let's change the caption name of the Invoice Headers table in the Table Selector to be Invoices. Click the Invoice Headers table name caption in the Table Selector. Access displays two floating buttons called *charms*, as shown in Figure 6-3. You can click these buttons to open property callout menus with different options and actions on the selected table.

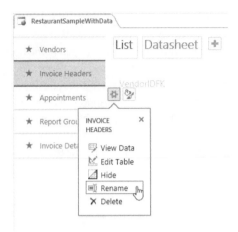

Figure 6-3 Click the gear charm button, and then click Rename to change a table caption.

Click the charm with a gear icon on it and Access displays a callout menu with five options—View Data, Edit Table, Hide, Rename, and Delete, also shown in Figure 6-3. As you might recall from Chapter 3, the first option on the callout menu, View Data, opens the selected table in Datasheet view, where you can add new records to your table, edit existing records, or delete records. The second option, Edit Table, opens the selected table in Design view, where you can edit the structure of the table. The third option, Hide, moves the selected table to the bottom of the list of tables in the Table Selector. Hidden tables do not show in the Table Selector in runtime mode. (You'll see how this works in the next section.) The fourth option, Rename, allows you to rename the table caption shown in the Table Selector. The last option, Delete, deletes the underlying table from your web app (including all data in that table), deletes any views associated with the table that are shown in the View Selector, and removes that table option from the Table Selector.

CAUTION

If you choose to delete a table from the Table Selector property callout menu or the Navigation pane, the delete operation is permanent. You cannot undo a delete operation, so be careful choosing this option. You will lose all data stored in any table you delete.

Click the Rename option on the property callout menu, and Access places your cursor inside the caption area of the selected table in the Table Selector, as shown in Figure 6-4. Access denotes the caption area with a dotted line box. Type **Invoices** into the caption here. As you enter your text, Access displays the old caption name below where you are typing the new name.

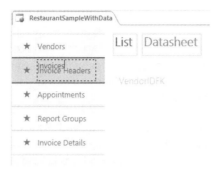

Figure 6-4 Type a new table caption into the Table Selector for the Invoice Headers table.

Press Enter after you finish typing in the new caption in the Table Selector. Access displays your new table caption for the selected table in the Table Selector, as shown in Figure 6-5. (Renaming the caption here does not rename the underlying table shown in the Navigation pane.) Access wraps any long caption names over two lines within the Table Selector. If your table caption is too long for Access to display across two lines, Access truncates any remaining text and displays three dots at the end of the display text. Access uses the three dots as a visual cue that it cannot display the entire caption. (You'll also see this visual cue for long text in other areas of the runtime later in this chapter.)

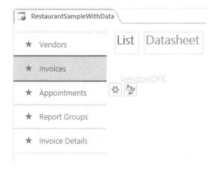

Figure 6-5 Access displays the new table caption in the Table Selector.

Hiding table captions

You can choose to hide tables in the Table Selector. For example, you might choose to hide junction tables that are part of a many-to-many relationship or hide tables you use for administrative purposes that you don't want users of your app to change. When you hide tables in the Table Selector, you'll still see the table when you view the App Home View from within Access, but you won't see hidden tables or any associated views attached to hidden tables when you view the App Home View within your web browser.

In the sample web app you have open, let's hide the Invoice Details table in the Table Selector. The Invoice Details table contains the detail records for items purchased for each invoice. Although you can add and enter data in this table by using views based directly on this table in your web browser, you'll find it more useful to enter data for this related table while also viewing the parent invoice record. (You'll see how to add and view data from related tables using controls on views later in this chapter.)

Click the Invoice Details table caption name in the Table Selector, click the gear charm button next to the table, and then click Hide on the callout property menu. Access dims the font color of the table caption and icon to indicate that the table is hidden and displays a dashed border around the table element, as shown in Figure 6-6.

Figure 6-6 Click Unhide on the property callout menu to show tables in the Table Selector.

Whenever you hide a table in the Table Selector, Access moves that table to the bottom of the display table list. Because Invoice Details in this example is already at the bottom of the display list, you won't see the table change positions. When you click Hide on the property callout menu, Access changes the callout option to Unhide, also shown in Figure 6-6. Access displays the text Unhide on the property callout menu here for all hidden tables. Click Unhide if you no longer want a table be hidden in the Table Selector. When you click Unhide, Access moves the selected table above any hidden tables in the Table Selector and you can view that table and its associated views in your web browser again.

Choosing table icons

You've probably noticed by now in the previous screen shots that Access displays an icon
next to each table caption name. The default icon Access uses next to each table caption is
a star. You can choose from a variety of other icons to display next to your table captions,
but you cannot remove an icon from the Table Selector. Let's change the table icons for
each of the four non-hidden tables in the sample app you're working on. To change the
table icon, click a table name caption in the Table Selector, and then click the charm button
with a paint can and paint brush next to the table, as shown in Figure 6-7.

Figure 6-7 Click the paint can charm button to choose table icons.

Access displays a drop-down menu of over 150 icons you can choose from for tables. In
Figure 6-7, I'm selecting the People icon to use for the Vendors table. If you open the table
icon callout menu by mistake, you can click the Close (X) button in the upper-right corner
of the callout menu to dismiss it without making any changes. (If you changed an icon by
mistake, click the Undo button on the Quick Access Toolbar.) After you change the icon for
the Vendors table, continue changing the table icons for the other non-hidden tables by

selecting the Calculator icon for Invoices, the Alarm Clock icon for Appointments, and the Document Stack icon for Report Groups. Your Table Selector should now match Figure 6-8.

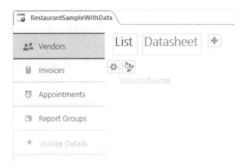

Figure 6-8 Your completed Table Selector changes with custom table icons should now look like this.

Viewing the Table Selector in a web browser

Now that you've completed some customizations to the Table Selector portion of the App Home View, let's see how your changes look in a web browser at runtime. Click Save on the Quick Access Toolbar to save your Table Selector changes, and then click the Launch App button in the View group on the Home ribbon tab or click the Launch App button on the Quick Access Toolbar. Access automatically saves changes made to the Table Selector and View Selector after a few seconds, but its good practice to save any edits each time you want to view your web app in your web browser. Access opens your default web browser and navigates to your Access web app, as shown in Figure 6-9.

Figure 6-9 You can see all of your Table Selector customizations in your web browser.

You'll notice that all of your Table Selector customizations are shown in the App Home View here in the web browser. You can see the specific display order you defined, the revised caption name for Invoices, and the custom table icons you selected. Also, you'll notice that you do not see the Invoice Details table listed, because you made this a hidden table. You can make additional changes to the Table Selector in Access at any time, save your changes, and quickly view the results in your web browser until you're satisfied with the results. If you have your web browser open to your Access web app, you can click the Refresh button in your web browser to view the most recent changes you've made to the Table Selector. Switch back to Access before continuing with the next section.

Working with the View Selector

The View Selector is another important part of the App Home View. The Table Selector, as you just learned, displays a list of all tables in your web app down the left side of the App Home View. The View Selector works in conjunction with the Table Selector. When you select a table in the Table Selector, Access displays horizontally, across the top of the App Home View window, a list of views associated to the selected table. On the right side of the View Selector is the Add New View button. You can use this button to create a new view associated to the currently selected table in the Table Selector. You'll learn more about adding new views to the View Selector in Chapter 7, "Advanced view design."

Customizing view captions

When you create a new table, Access creates two views for each table and displays them in the View Selector. By default, Access assigns captions of List and Datasheet to these views, as shown in Figure 6-10. Notice that the captions shown here for these views do not match the actual view object names. The actual view object names listed in the Navigation pane are *<name of the table>* List and *<name of the table>* Datasheet.

Figure 6-10 The View Selector displays two default view captions for each table.

Similar to the Table Selector, you can change the caption names for the views displayed in the View Selector. Let's change the caption for one of the views attached to the Vendors table. Click the Vendors table name caption in the Table Selector, and then click the view caption called List in the View Selector. Access displays a single charm button with a gear icon next to the view name that you can click to take different actions on that selected view. Click the gear charm button, and Access displays a callout menu with five options— Open In Browser, Edit, Rename, Duplicate, and Delete, as shown in Figure 6-11. The first option on the callout menu, Open In Browser, opens your default web browser, navigates to your Access web app, and then navigates to the currently selected table and view. The second option, Edit, opens the selected view in Design view, where you can edit the layout and structure of the view. The third option, Rename, allows you to rename the view caption shown in the View Selector for the selected view. The fourth option, Duplicate, allows you to create an identical copy of the selected view and associate it to the current table in the Table Selector, associate it with another table in the web app, or to make a *stand-alone* view. (A stand-alone view is a view object listed in the Navigation pane but not displayed in the View Selector for any table. You'll learn more about duplicating views and stand-alone views in upcoming sections.) The last option, Delete, deletes the underlying view from your web app and removes the current view caption shown in the View Selector.

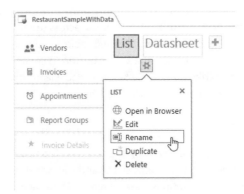

Figure 6-11 Click the gear charm button, and then click Rename to change a view caption.

Click the Rename option on the property callout menu, and Access places your cursor inside the caption area of the selected view in the View Selector, as shown in Figure 6-12. Access denotes the caption area with a dotted outline. Type **Vendor List** into the caption. As you enter your text, Access displays the old caption name above where you are typing the new name.

Figure 6-12 Type a new view caption into the View Selector.

Press Enter after you finish typing in the new caption in the View Selector. Access displays your new view caption for the selected view in the View Selector, as shown in Figure 6-13. (Note that renaming the caption here does not rename the underlying view object shown in the Navigation pane.) Access expands the space for the view caption to accommodate the increased length of the caption name. If your new view caption is shorter than the length of the current view caption, Access collapses the extra space to the right of the view caption. Access then moves any view caption names that are to the right of the edited view caption over to the left to reclaim the extra space. If your view caption is too long to fit within the design space or if there are more view captions than can be shown in the space provided, Access displays a horizontal scroll bar just beneath the View Selector so that you can scroll to the right or left to see additional view captions.

Figure 6-13 Access displays the new view caption in the View Selector.

> ## Note
> You cannot customize the font styling or font weight of the captions in the View Selector or the Table Selector; Access controls the styling for these elements. However, if you use different themes for the SharePoint site hosting your web app, you'll see different styling and colors for table and view captions. See the section "Applying themes to web app views" in Chapter 7 to learn more about themes.

Switching view caption positions

By default, Access displays the view caption names in the View Selector in the order in which you create the views. You can keep this order if you want, or you can reorder the views listed in the View Selector.

In the sample web app you have open, let's change the positions of the two views for the Vendors table. Click the Datasheet view caption name in the View Selector, hold your mouse, and then drag the view name to the left of the Vendor List view caption name, as shown in Figure 6-14. As you move the Datasheet caption to the left, Access swaps positions of the view name captions. Access displays the view caption names shifting as a visual cue to indicate where it will drop the view caption name. After you release the mouse, Access places the Datasheet view caption to the left of the Vendor List caption name and lines up the controls.

Figure 6-14 Click and drag the Datasheet view caption to the left of the Vendor List view caption name.

Duplicating views

In Access web apps, you can create (or *duplicate*, as Microsoft refers to it) identical copies of existing views for use in other areas of your app. For example, you might find it useful to create an identical copy of a view to use it as a starting point for adding on to the new view, or you might want to make a copy of a view and assign it a different *record source*. A view that displays data from your tables must have a record source. A record source can be the name of a table, the name of a query, or an embedded query. When a view has a record source, it is bound to the records in that record source—the view displays records from the record source and can potentially update the fields in the records. For example, you could create identical views and have one view display all active vendors and another view display inactive vendors only.

In the sample web app you have open, let's duplicate the view that has the caption Vendor List. Click the Vendors table in the Table Selector, click the Vendor List view caption in the View Selector, click the gear charm button, and then click the Duplicate option on the property callout menu, as shown in Figure 6-5.

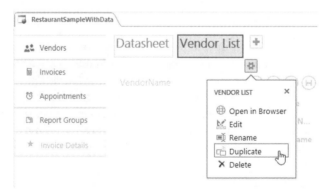

Figure 6-15 Click Duplicate on the callout menu to create an identical copy of a view.

Access opens the Duplicate View dialog, as shown in Figure 6-16. In the Name Of Duplicate text box, you enter a name for the new view object Access creates. Remember that all objects of the same type must have unique names, so you cannot create a new view, using the duplicate command, with the same name as an existing view. Enter **Vendor List New** in the Name Of Duplicate text box. In the Location For Duplicate drop-down list, Access displays a list of all table names in your web app. You can choose to associate this new duplicated view with any table in your web app. If you associate the new view with a different table than the one currently selected in the Table Selector (the default in the drop-down list), Access creates a new view caption in the View Selector for that table. If you choose the last option in the drop-down—[Standalone/Popup]—Access creates a duplicate view in the Navigation pane but it does not create any new view caption in the View Selector. Select Vendors (the default, in this example) from the Location For Duplicate drop-down list, and then click OK on the Duplicate View dialog box.

Figure 6-16 In the Duplicate View dialog box, provide a unique name for the view and associate it with a table.

Access creates a new view caption in the View Selector for the Vendors table with the same name that you provided in the Duplicate View dialog box, as shown in Figure 6-17. Access also creates a new view object with the same name in the Navigation pane under the Forms group (also shown in Figure 6-17). You now have three views associated with the Vendors table, two of which are identical views.

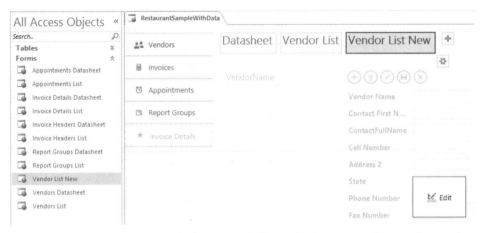

Figure 6-17 Access creates a new duplicate view in the Navigation pane and a new view caption in the View Selector.

> **Note**
>
> You might notice in Figure 6-17 that all the view objects in an Access web app are listed in the Navigation pane under a group called Forms. The Navigation pane is an Access component shared between web apps and desktop databases. In desktop databases, forms are the object type used for data entry. Instead of creating separate groups in the Navigation pane for web apps and desktop databases, Microsoft chose to use Forms as the group name even in web apps.

INSIDE OUT Duplicating views from the Navigation pane

You can also duplicate views directly from the Navigation pane by right-clicking a view name in the Navigation pane and selecting Duplicate from the shortcut menu. Access displays the same options, shown previously, for assigning the view to a table caption name in the Table Selector or creating a stand-alone view.

Using the View Selector in a web browser

Now that you've completed some customizations to the View Selector portion of the App Home View, let's see how your changes look in a web browser at runtime. Click Save on the Quick Access Toolbar to save your View Selector changes, and then click the Launch App button in the View group on the Home ribbon tab or click the Launch App button on the

Quick Access Toolbar. Access opens your default web browser and navigates to your Access web app, as shown in Figure 6-18.

Figure 6-18 You can see all of your View Selector customizations in your web browser.

You'll notice that all of your View Selector customizations are shown in the App Home View here in the web browser. You can see the Datasheet view caption listed first because you changed the view display order for the Vendors table. You can also see the revised view caption name for Vendor List and the new view caption you created through the Duplicate command. Whenever you make additional changes to the View Selector in Access, you can view the results quickly in your web browser by saving your changes in Access and then refreshing your browser window.

The Table Selector and View Selector components of the App Home View work together in the runtime, so you can navigate to different areas of your web app. In Figure 6-18, shown previously, you'll notice the font style of Vendors in the Table Selector and Vendor List New in the View Selector are bold. This bold font style indicates the table and view you are currently viewing. To navigate to a different view, simply click the view caption name in the View Selector. To navigate to a different table, click the table caption name in the Table Selector. When you click a table caption in the Table Selector, Access Services changes the View Selector element to show the view caption names associated with the selected table. Access Services then loads the first default view in the View Selector for that table. Notice that if you previously clicked on a different view caption other than the default for a table, navigate to a different table, and then navigate back in the same session, Access Services remembers the last view selected for the table and navigates you to that view rather than the default view.

Click the different tables and views in your web browser for this sample web app now so that you can become more familiar with how Access Services uses the App Home View elements for navigation. After you complete this task, switch back to Access before continuing with the next section.

Chapter 6

INSIDE OUT   Using the keyboard to navigate to different tables and views

You can also navigate to different tables and views in your web browser by using the keyboard. When your focus is on the Table Selector, you can use the Down Arrow and Up Arrow keys to highlight different table caption names. Press Enter to select the high-lighted table. To move focus to the Table Selector, press Tab or Shift+Tab until your focus is on the Table Selector. You can also use Tab or Shift+Tab to move your focus to each of the view caption names in the View Selector. Press Enter on the highlighted view caption to load that view into the App Home View.

Deleting views

If you no longer want a specific view to display in the View Selector, you can delete it from the View Selector by using the view callout menu.

Let's delete the new view you created earlier for the Vendors table. In Access, click the Vendors table name caption in the Table Selector, click the Vendor List New view caption name in the View Selector, click the gear charm button, and then click Delete on the property callout menu, as shown in Figure 6-19.

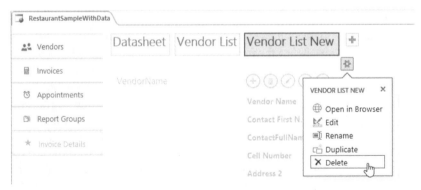

Figure 6-19 Click Delete on the property callout menu to delete views from your web app.

Access displays a warning message when you attempt to delete a view, as shown in Figure 6-20. You can click No to stop the process if you think you made a mistake. Click Yes now to proceed with the deletion of this sample view.

CAUTION

If you delete a view from the View Selector property callout menu or the Navigation pane, the delete operation is permanent. You cannot undo a delete view operation, so be careful when choosing this option.

Figure 6-20 This dialog box asks you to confirm a view deletion.

Access deletes the view object from the Navigation pane and deletes the view caption name from the View Selector, as shown in Figure 6-21.

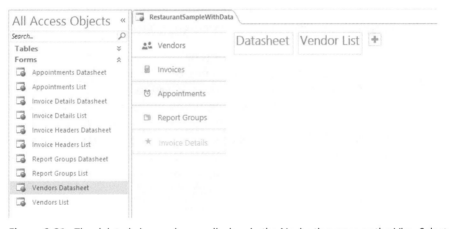

Figure 6-21 The deleted view no longer displays in the Navigation pane or the View Selector.

INSIDE OUT   Removing views only from the View Selector

It's not possible to delete a view caption name in the View Selector and keep the view object in the Navigation pane. If you want to retain a view object but remove it from the View Selector, use the duplicate view feature to first make an identical copy of the view and associate it with a different table or make it a stand-alone view. You can then delete the first view from the View Selector and Navigation pane.

Starting with quick-created views

Now that you're familiar with using the Table Selector and View Selector elements of the App Home View, it's time to start designing views. Our discussion of designing views begins with understanding the two quick-created views Access generates with each new table you create. You're not required to use these quick-created views, but they can be very helpful in designing a user interface quickly for your web app. You might find that they need little or no customization to be used for data entry by users of your web app.

Access web apps contain four types of views—List Details, Datasheet, Summary, and Blank. Each of these view types can be associated with tables in the View Selector. You can also use all of these view types as stand-alone views. (As you learned earlier in this chapter, stand-alone views are displayed in the Navigation pane but not in the View Selector for any tables.) The design surface, the controls you can use, and the properties you can assign for controls are different for each of the four types of views. Throughout the next sections in this chapter and Chapter 7, you'll learn how to design each of these types of views within Access and use them in a web browser.

Working within the web design surface

When you create new tables or import data into your web app, Access creates a List Details and a Datasheet view type for each table. Let's first explore the List Details view that Access created for the Vendors table in the sample web app you've been working on. To open this view in Design view, click the Vendors table name caption in the Table Selector, click the Vendor List view caption in the View Selector, and then click the Edit button in the middle of the view preview window, as shown in Figure 6-22. (Note that you changed the view caption of this specific view earlier in the chapter. If you had not changed the caption, this view would display List as the default caption instead.)

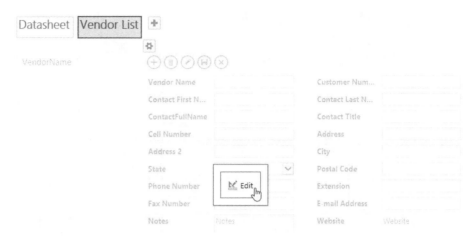

Figure 6-22 Click Edit in the middle of the window to edit the Vendor List view.

INSIDE OUT   Using other techniques to open views in Design view

You can use many different techniques to open views in Design view. You can click the gear charm button for the view in the View Selector and click Edit from the callout menu. You can double-click the specific view caption name in the View Selector. You can also double-click the view name listed in the Navigation pane, right-click a view name in the Navigation pane and click Open from the shortcut menu, or press Enter when the view is highlighted in the Navigation pane.

Access opens the view in Design view on its own object tab in the application window and provides several design tools on the Design contextual tab in the ribbon, as shown in Figure 6-23. Access also opens the Field List on the right side of the design window, by default.

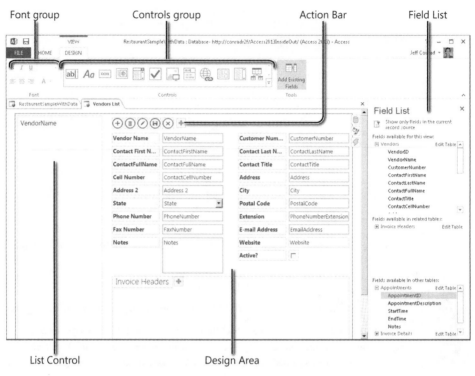

Font group   Controls group   Action Bar   Field List

List Control   Design Area

Figure 6-23 When you open a view in Design view, you can use the design grid and tools to create your view elements.

Some key view design terms

As you begin to work in designing views, you need to understand a few commonly used terms.

A view that displays data from your tables must have a *record source*. A record source can be the name of a table, the name of a query, or an *embedded query*. An embedded query is a query created within the view design Record Source property. Embedded queries are not displayed in the Navigation pane.

When a control (text box, label, multiline text box, check box, autocomplete control, combo box, image control, and hyperlink control) can display information, its *control source* defines the name of the field from the record source or the expression that provides the data to display. A control that has an expression as its control source is not updatable.

When a view has a record source, it is *bound* to the records in that record source—the view displays records from the record source and can potentially update the fields in the records. When a control is on a bound view and its control source is the name of a field in the record source, the control is bound to the field—the control displays (and perhaps allows you to edit) the data from the bound field in the current row of the record source. A control cannot be bound unless the view is also bound.

A view that has no record source is *unbound*. A control that has no control source is unbound.

When you work with a quick-created List Details or Datasheet view for the first time, Access already assigns a record source to the view and adds a control and corresponding label for each field in your record source onto the design grid.

The view design contextual tab

As you learned in Chapter 2, the ribbon provides contextual tabs when Access displays objects in various views. When a view is in Design view, a contextual tab, called Design, appears under the View heading. This contextual tab is the "command center" of view design. This tab provides all the essential controls and some of the commands you need to design and modify your views.

The Font group on the Design tab, shown in Figure 6-24, provides a quick and easy way to alter the appearance of a control by allowing you to click buttons rather than set properties. Select the control you want to format on the design grid, and then click the appropriate button in the Font group. Table 6-1 describes each of the buttons in this group.

Chapter 6

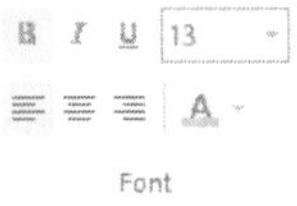

Figure 6-24 The Font group provides you with tools to change the appearance of view controls.

TABLE 6-1 Font group buttons

Button	Description
Bold	Click to set font style to bold. Click again to remove bold.
Italic	Click to set font style to italic. Click again to remove italic.
Underline	Click to underline text. Click again to remove underline.
Font Size	Use to set font size.
Align Left	Click to left-align text.
Center	Click to center text.
Align Right	Click to right-align text.
Font Color	Use to set the font color of the control.

INSIDE OUT   Using the alignment buttons

You can click only one of the alignment buttons—Align Left, Align Right, or Center—at a time. If you do not click a button, alignment is set to Align Left, except for command button controls, which have the label caption text set to Center by default.

Depending on the control you select in the design grid, the Font group options might not be available. For example, the commands in the Font group are unavailable to use with web browser controls, check boxes, image controls, subview controls, and related item controls.

At the heart of the Design contextual tab for views is the Controls group. This group contains a gallery of buttons for all the types of controls you can use when you design a view. To select a particular control to place on a view, click the control's button in the gallery. Access places the control on the design grid directly beneath the control that currently has focus on the design grid. If no control currently has focus on the design grid, Access places the control in the first available empty grid location. Note that Access might shift other controls down the design grid if the first available empty grid location is not at the bottom of the design grid. You can size a control and move it to a different location after Access places it on the grid. (You'll learn how to move and resize controls later in this chapter.)

Chapter 6

The buttons in the Controls group are described in Table 6-2, listed from left to right. The last column in the table lists the view types in which you can place a particular control type.

TABLE 6-2   Controls group buttons

Button	Description	View Type
`ab|`	Text Box. Click this button to create text box controls for displaying text, numbers, dates, and times. You can bind a text box to one of the fields in an underlying table or query. If you allow a text box that is bound to a field be updated, you can change the value in the field in the underlying table or query by entering a new value in the text box. You can also use a text box to display calculated values.	List Details, Datasheet, and Blank
Aa	Label. Click this button to create label controls that contain fixed text. By default, controls that can display data have a label control automatically attached. You can use this command to create stand-alone labels for headings and for instructions on your view. You can also bind a label to one of the fields in an underlying table or query.	List Details and Blank
xxxx	Button. Click this button to create a command button control that can activate a user interface macro. You'll learn how to create user interface macros and work with control events in Chapter 8.	List Details, Datasheet, and Blank
⊕	Web Browser Control. Click this button to add a web browser control to your view design grid. A web browser control displays the content of webpages directly inside a view. You can use a web browser control to display, for example, a map of an address stored in a table. You can bind the web browser control to a field in your view's record source by using the Control Source property of the control.	List Details and Blank
▦	Combo Box. Click this button to create a combo box control that contains a list of potential values for the control. To create the list, you can enter values for the Row Source property of the combo box. You can also specify a table or a query as the source of the values in the list. Access displays the currently selected value in the combo box. When you click the arrow to the right of the combo box, Access displays the values in the list. Select a new value in the list to reset the value in the control. If you bind the combo box to a field in the underlying table or query, you can change the value in the field by selecting a new value in the list. You can choose to select no value by selecting the blank option at the top of the list of values. You can choose to bind the combo box to one field and display values from another field in the same source. You can also choose a view to open for the related record when you are in view mode in your web browser. Combo boxes are limited to displaying 500 items in web apps.	List Details, Datasheet, and Blank

Button	Description	View Type
	Check Box. Click this button to create a check box control that holds a yes/no value. When you select a check box, its value becomes yes and a check mark appears in the box. Select the check box again, its value now becomes no, and the check mark disappears from the box. If you bind the check box to a field in the underlying table or query, you can toggle the field's value by clicking the check box.	List Details, Datasheet, and Blank
	Image. Click this button to place a picture on your view. You can bind an image control to an Image data type in the underlying table or query and then upload an image into the field or remove an existing image. You can also choose to display an image from a Uniform Resource Locator (URL) that points to a location on the Internet.	List Details and Blank
	Autocomplete Control. Click this button to create an autocomplete control that can be used to search for a specific value contained in a table or query. You must specify a table or a query as the source of the values for autocomplete controls. Access displays the currently selected value in the autocomplete control. (An autocomplete control is similar to a combo box control in that the control displays a list of potential values from its source. In runtime, it looks like a text box control.) As you type a search string into the control, Access searches through the values in the table or query for that search criteria and displays a list of possible matches. If you bind the autocomplete control to a field in the underlying table or query, you can change the value in the field by searching for a new value and choosing it from the list. You can choose to bind the autocomplete control to one field and display values from another field (the primary display value) and a second field (the secondary display value) in the same source. Autocomplete controls return up to eight items in each search. If your search returns more than eight values, you can add more values to your search criteria to refine your search and further limit the returned values to find the specific item you need. You can also choose a view to open for the related record when you are in view mode in your web browser.	List Details, Datasheet, and Blank
	Hyperlink Control. Click this button to add a hyperlink control to your view design grid. This hyperlink can contain a URL that points to a location on the Internet. If you bind a hyperlink control to a field in the underlying table or query, Access Services displays the value as a link you can click in view mode to navigate to in your web browser. Clicking this button in edit mode in runtime opens the Insert Hyperlink dialog box.	List Details, Datasheet, and Blank
	Subview Control. Click this button to embed another view in the current view. You can use the subview to show data from a table or a query that is related to the data in the main view. Access maintains the link between the main view and the subview for you.	List Details and Blank

Button	Description	View Type
	Multiline Textbox Control. Click this button to add a multiline text box control to your design grid. You can use multiline text boxes for displaying text, numbers, dates, and times. The main difference between multiline text boxes and text boxes is that multiline text boxes can display data over multiple lines. Press Enter when entering data in multiline text boxes to move to a new line. You can bind a multiline text box to one of the fields in an underlying table or query. If you allow a multiline text box that is bound to a field be updated, you can change the value in the field in the underlying table or query by entering a new value in the multiline text box. You can also use a multiline text box to display calculated values.	List Details, Datasheet, and Blank
	Related Items Control. Click this button to add a related items control to your view design grid. You can use a related items control to provide an easy way to show data from a table or query that is related to the data in the main view. A related items control provides an interface with a series of tab pages similar to a tab control in desktop databases. Each tab can display related data from a different table or query. In runtime, when a user clicks a different tab on a related items control, Access Services displays the data contained on that tab.	List Details and Blank

The Field list

The last button on the right side of the Design contextual tab for views in the Tools group is the Add Existing Fields button. This button toggles the visibility of the Field List pane to the right of the design grid. You can use the field list to place bound controls (controls linked to fields in a table or a query) on your view. If the view is bound to a table or query, Access displays the name of the underlying table or query along with all the fields available, as shown in Figure 6-25. Any tables that have relationships to the underlying table serving as the record source are displayed under Fields Available In Related Tables. The last section of the field list, Fields Available In Other Tables, lists the tables and fields from all other tables in this web app.

Click the Show Only Fields In The Current Record Source link to remove the bottom two sections of the field list. You can undock the field list by clicking the title bar and dragging it away from the right edge of the design view window. After you undock the field list, you can drag the edges of the window to resize it so that you can see any long field names. Double-click the title bar to dock the field list again. You can also drag the title bar to move the window out of the way. When the list of available field names is too long to fit in the current size of the window, you can use the vertical scroll bar to move through the list.

Chapter 6

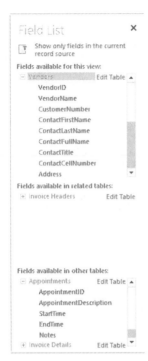

Figure 6-25 The Field List pane shows the names of the fields in the bound table or query, any related tables, and fields from all other tables in the current web app.

To use the field list to place a bound control on the view, drag the field you want from the field list and place it into position on the design grid. Access creates an appropriate display control type on the design grid to match the data type defined for the field you are dragging onto the grid. For example, if you drag an image field from the field list, Access creates an image control to represent the image field. Access also adds a corresponding label to the design grid for each field that you drag from the field list.

With quick-created views, Access already includes an appropriate control and corresponding label control to represent each field in the table's record source, so there is no need for us to add any more fields to the view you're currently working on. (You'll see how to drag controls onto the design grid later in this chapter when you learn how to customize views.)

Property callouts

The view and each control on the view have a list of properties associated with them, and you set these properties using property callouts. Each control on a view and the view itself are all objects. The kinds of properties you can specify vary depending on the object. List Details views contain three main parts—List Control, Action Bar, and Detail Section. (You'll see how all parts of a List Details view work in a web browser later in this chapter. For now, we'll focus on designing the List Control within Access.) The List Control, shown again in Figure 6-26, encompasses the entire left portion of a List Details view. In runtime, you use the List Control for record navigation. When you click a record in the List Control, Access Services displays the record information in the Detail section. When you click the List Control in Design view, Access highlights the entire List Control and displays a single charm button called Data.

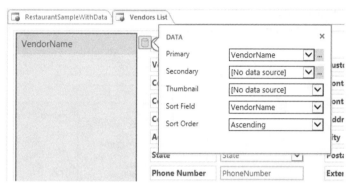

Figure 6-26 The List Control is on the left side of a List Details view, and you can set five properties for it in the Data property callout menu.

To open the property callout menu for the List Control, select it and then click the Data charm button next to it. Access opens the Data property callout menu, also shown in Figure 6-26. Property callout menus cannot be undocked, and they stay expanded until you dismiss them by clicking the Close (X) button in the upper-right corner, by clicking another object on the design surface, or by pressing Esc.

> **Note**
>
> You cannot remove the List Control from a List Details view, because it is an essential and embedded part of a List Details view structure. You can resize the List Control to a certain extent, and you can define properties for it, but you cannot remove it.

You can set five properties on the List Control for List Details views—Primary, Secondary, Thumbnail, Sort Field, and Sort Order. Each of these properties provides a drop-down list of valid values. The Primary property is a required property and designates which field in the record source you want Access to display as the primary value in the List Control. The drop-down list for the Primary property here includes a list of all field names in the record source, except for fields bound to Yes/No and Image data types. Access selected VendorName for this property in this quick-created view, because it was the first field name bound to a Short Text data type. Leave this property set as VendorName because it provides a natural choice for users to identify the vendor records at runtime.

The Secondary property is similar to the Primary property; however, the Secondary property is optional. Select a field name here if you want to Access to list the value of another field in the record source to help identify a record for navigation. In your web browser, Access displays the values defined for the Secondary property below the Primary property data values and with a smaller font. By default, Access did not select a value for this property and therefore displays the value [No data source] in Design view, which means Access shows the primary display field only at runtime. The CustomerNumber field in this table is a good choice to use as a secondary display at runtime, so click this property and select CustomerNumber from the drop-down list, as shown in Figure 6-27.

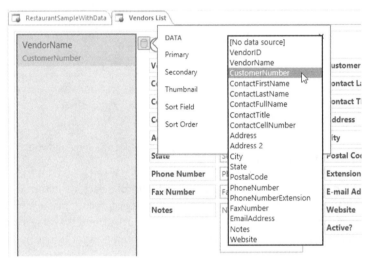

Figure 6-27 Select the CustomerNumber field for the Secondary property on the List Control.

After you select the CustomerNumber field for the Secondary property, you'll notice that Access displays that field name beneath the primary VendorName field in the List Control, also shown in Figure 6-27. Access collapses the drop-down list for the Secondary property and lists the selected field name.

Use the optional Thumbnail property when you want to display a small thumbnail image to the left of the primary and secondary display fields at runtime. The drop-down list of field names for this property displays only field names in the record source bound to Image data types. You might want to use this property if you have pictures for an employee table or products in a products table. Because no Image data type fields exist in this sample Vendors table, the only option displayed here is [No data source], which means that Access does not display images in the List Control at runtime for this view.

Use the Sort Field property to designate which field in the view's record source you want Access Services to sort by when you view the List Details view in your web browser. The list of valid field names for this property match the Primary and Secondary property data type restrictions. By default, Access selects the same field name here as it did for the Primary property. You're not required to match the Sort Field property with the Primary property. For example, you might want to display invoice numbers as the Primary property in a view that contains a list of invoices but choose to sort by an invoice date. If you do not want to apply a sort, select [No data source] for this property. If you select [No data source] for the Sort Field property, Access Services sorts the records by the AutoNumber primary field at runtime. In our example, Access selects to sort by the VendorName field, which makes it easier for users to find the vendor records they want at runtime.

The Sort Order property lists only two options—Ascending and Descending. In the Sort Order property, you can specify whether Access should sort the selected field in the Sort Field property in ascending or descending order. By default, Access always chooses Ascending for the Sort Order property in quick-created views. You might find changing this property to Descending useful if, for example, you want to display a most recent list of appointments by date or most recent orders received. For our example, leave this property set at Ascending.

> **Note**
>
> If you choose not to assign a field in the Sort Field property by selecting [No data source] from the drop-down list, Access hides the Sort Order property line from the Data property callout menu in Design view.

Build

In some cases, Access allows you to use the Expression Builder to help you create property settings for properties that can accept a complex expression. When such help is available for a property setting, Access displays a small button with an ellipsis next to the property box; this is the Build button. For the List Control in a List Details view, Access displays this small button next to the Primary and Secondary properties. If you click the Build button, Access responds by opening the Expression Builder. (You should be very familiar with working in the Expression Builder from the previous three chapters.) You might find building an expression, such as concatenating several fields of data together, useful as the primary or secondary display value in a List Control.

INSIDE OUT   Modifying the width of the List Control

You can expand or collapse the width of the List Control in List Details views. To change the width of the List Control, click the control and move your pointer over the right edge until you see your pointer turn into a double arrow. Then drag the handle to resize the control.

Chapter 6

Exploring Action Bar buttons

To the right of the List Control in the upper-left corner of the design grid is the Action Bar. The Action Bar for List Details views displays five buttons by default—Add, Delete, Edit, Save, and Cancel, as shown in Figure 6-28. When you work with a view in runtime with your web browser, the Action Bar buttons serve as your main commands for record operations.

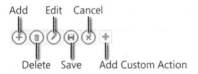

Figure 6-28 Access includes five built-in Action Bar buttons in List Details views.

The Add Action Bar button navigates to a new record in the view where you can begin creating a new record. The Delete Action Bar button deletes the currently selected record in the view. The Edit Action Bar button switches the view into Edit mode, where you can edit the data in the currently selected record. The Save Action Bar button saves any pending changes to the currently selected record in the view. The Cancel Action Bar button cancels any pending changes to an edited record and switches the view out of Edit mode and back into View mode. To the right of the Cancel button is the Add Custom Action button. You can use the Add Custom Action button to create custom Action Bar buttons that respond to user interface macros that you design. You'll see how to use the Action Bar buttons in a web browser later in this chapter.

Moving and deleting Action Bar buttons

You cannot position the Action Bar at a different location on the design grid, but you can change the positions of the buttons within the Action Bar. To move a built-in Action Bar button to a different position, click the button you want to move, hold your mouse, and then drag the button to the left or right. As you move a button to the left or right, Access swaps positions with the button next to it. Access displays the buttons shifting as a visual cue to indicate where it will drop the button within the Action Bar. After you release the mouse, Access places the button to the left or right, depending on which direction you moved the button, and lines up the button controls.

In Figure 6-29, I am moving the Add button to the right, and Access swaps positions of the Add and Delete buttons. You'll notice your cursor changes to a four-sided cross arrow when you are moving Action Bar buttons. If you haven't saved your view changes and decide to change your mind after moving an Action Bar button to a different position, you can press the Undo button on the Quick Access Toolbar or press Ctrl+Z to cancel the change.

Figure 6-29 Click and drag an Action Bar button to change the display order of the buttons.

When you're designing and modifying views for your web app, you might decide to remove a built-in button from the Action Bar. For example, you might decide not to allow new records to be created within a specific view. If you remove the built-in Add button from the Action Bar from a List Details view, users of your web app cannot create new records when they use that view in their web browser. If you want to remove a built-in button from the Action Bar, select the button and then press the Delete key. Access moves any buttons on the right side of the deleted button to the left to take up the space of the deleted button.

CAUTION

If you delete any of the built-in Action Bar buttons for any view, save your view changes, and then close the view, the deletion is permanent. Access cannot re-create built-in Action Bar buttons on existing views. If you delete any of the built-in buttons by mistake, you'll need to create a new view for Access to regenerate all default built-in Action Bar buttons for the specific view type.

Defining custom Action Bar buttons

The five built-in Action Bar buttons cannot be customized because Access controls their actions, but you can create your own custom Action Bar buttons that execute macro logic that you define. To create a custom Action Bar button, click the Add Custom Action button on the right side of the Action Bar. Access creates a new custom button and positions it along the right side of the Action Bar. When you select a custom Action Bar button, Access displays a single charm button (Data). Click this charm button, and Access opens the Data callout menu, as shown in Figure 6-30.

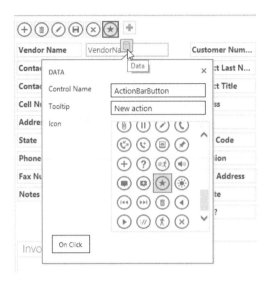

Figure 6-30 Click the Add Custom Action button to create custom Action Bar buttons.

In the Control Name text box on the Data callout menu, enter a name to identify your custom Action Bar button. Access provides a name here by default (ActionBarButton, in the example in Figure 6-30), but you can change that to another name if you want. Each control on a view, including Action Bar buttons, must have a unique name. The name you enter in the Control Name text box is not shown in the web browser at runtime; however, you can refer to this custom Action Bar button by name when using user interface macros.

In the Tooltip text box, you can optionally provide helpful text to display as a Tooltip for the custom Action Bar button at runtime. When you hover your mouse over a custom Action Bar button at runtime, Access Services displays the Tooltip text as a visual cue to indicate to users the purpose of the button. By default, Access enters the text "New Action" as the Tooltip for all new custom Action Bar buttons, but you can modify this for your needs. For example, if you're creating a custom Action Bar button to sort records in the view, you might want to provide a Tooltip with the text "Sort Records" or "Apply Sort" so that users of your web app can understand the purpose of the custom Action bar button.

Access displays a drop-down menu of 72 icon choices that you can choose from for custom Action Bar buttons beneath the Tooltip text box, shown previously in Figure 6-30. All Action Bar buttons, including custom ones, have an icon that you can see in both Design view and runtime. The default icon Access uses for custom Action Bar buttons is a star, but you can choose from a variety of other icon choices to display. Note that you cannot adjust the icons used with built-in Action Bar buttons.

Beneath the icon choices in the Data callout menu is a button labeled On Click. When you click this button, Access opens up the Logic Designer, where you can define custom macro logic to run when users of the app click a custom Action Bar button. (You'll learn how to create user interface macros in Chapter 8.) For now, leave all the default settings for the custom Action Bar button if you added one to the design grid.

Defining view properties

Each view in an Access web app includes properties that you can set to control aspects of the view itself. To see and modify the properties of a view you must first select the view. To do this, click anywhere on the design grid away from the Action Bar or controls on the grid. When you select the design grid, Access displays three charm buttons in the upper-right corner of the design grid, as shown in Figure 6-31. You can click these buttons to open property callout menus with different options and actions for the selected view. In Figure 6-31, the screen shot combines into a single screen shot each of the callout menus expanded for List Details views so that you can see all of the options at the same time. When you click these charm buttons, Access displays only one callout menu at a time.

Figure 6-31 You can choose view property options by clicking the three charm buttons shown on the right side of the design grid.

On the Data callout menu for all view types, you'll see the Record Source property. Access displays a drop-down list of the names of all tables and queries in your web app for this property. This drop-down list includes an option called [No Data Source]. Selecting this option makes the view unbound. In some cases, you might create an unbound view to display a simple message to users. Next to the Record Source property, Access displays a Build button. Clicking this button opens the query design window where you can build a query, perhaps joining two or more tables, to use as the record source for your view. When you create a query using this entry point, you're creating an *embedded query*. An embedded query is a query defined within the definition of a view. Embedded queries are not displayed in the Navigation pane and can be edited only by using the Build button entry point on the Record Source property. If you've defined an embedded query for your view's record source, Access displays [Embedded Query] for the Record Source property.

On the Formatting callout menu for List Details, Datasheet, and Blank views, you'll see the ActionBar Visible property. Access displays a drop-down list for this property with two options—Visible and Hidden—with Visible being the default option selected. (When you first open a new Blank view, the ActionBar Visible property is set to Hidden until you assign the view a record source.) When you select Visible for this property, Access displays the Action Bar and all buttons contained within it in both design and runtime mode. When you set this property to Hidden, Access hides the entire Action Bar container control from the design grid and moves all controls up on the design grid to reclaim the space of the now-removed Action Bar container. Access Services then does not display any Action Bar buttons at runtime in your web browser for this view.

If you hide the Action Bar for a view and want to have users add, edit, or delete data in their web browser, you'll have to create macro logic attached to other control events, such as clicking command buttons, for users to perform record operations. If the Record Source property for a view is set to [No Data Source], Access removes the Action Bar from the design grid and the ActionBar Visible property from the Formatting callout menu, because an unbound view cannot perform record operations.

Beneath the ActionBar Visible property on the Formatting callout menu, Access displays the Caption property. By default, Access sets the Caption property for quick-created views to the same name as the table or query used as the record source for the view. When you open a view as a pop-up window in runtime, Access displays the view on top of the main view and displays the Caption property text above the Action Bar. (You'll see how the Caption property text works in runtime later in this chapter.) You can define Caption property text for all view types.

On the Actions callout menu for all view types, you'll see two buttons—On Load and On Current. When you click these buttons, Access opens the Logic Designer where you can define macro logic for Access to execute for these two view events. You'll learn about control and view events and creating user interface macros in Chapter 8.

Sizing and moving controls

The main part of a view, the design grid, is where you can place controls for displaying and entering data, controlling application flow, accepting inputs from users, and even displaying messages. You can think of the design grid as a canvas where you can position different controls in a way that is useful and meaningful to you and the users of your web app. With quick-created views, Access completes a lot of the work of creating views for your tables for you. As you can see from the quick-created List Details view for the Vendors table you have open, the layout of the controls on the view looks professional. Notice how Access creates an appropriate control type on the view for each field in the Vendors table and an associated label with a caption for each control, and then aligns all the controls into columns, as shown in Figure 6-32. This view could still use some modification, such as moving and resizing some controls, but overall, Access has completed a lot of the hard work of creating the view. You could use this view in your web browser without any modification and begin entering data.

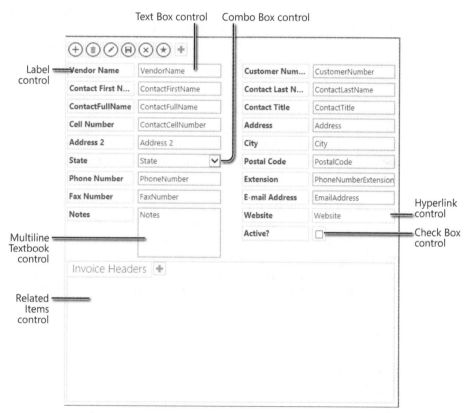

Figure 6-32 Access creates a control type and label for each field in your table for quick-created views.

Note

Access does not add the AutoNumber ID field automatically to the design grid for quick-created views. If you want to display the ID field on a view, you'll need to add this field onto the design grid from the Field List pane.

For each label control on the design grid, Access assigns the Caption property of the control to be the same text as what is defined for the Label Text field property at the table level. If you do not assign a Label Text field property when you create your fields in table Design view, Access uses the field name as the Caption property for each label control. For controls bound to fields, Access displays the name of the field within the control (except for check boxes) so that you can easily determine to which field a specific control is bound.

By default, Access makes most controls bound to fields about 1.5 inches wide (3.75 centimeters), except for check box controls, and the associated labels about 1.25 inches wide (3 centimeters). For some of the controls in this List Details view based on the Vendors table, the default widths are larger than necessary—especially with the default 13-point font size. For other controls, the width isn't large enough. In Figure 6-32, previously shown, you'll notice that some of the captions in the label controls are truncated and display three dots at the end to indicate that the text cannot fit inside the defined width. You'll also notice in Figure 6-32 that Access creates multiline text box controls with heights that are three times taller than the text box and label controls and that the related items control at the bottom of the design grid spans multiple columns. Access creates larger sizes for these controls because they usually display more data. Although Access laid out the controls in an orderly fashion by the field order in the table, you'll probably want to resize some of these controls and adjust their location.

To change a control's size or location, first click the control you want to resize or move, and Access highlights the control. When you hover your mouse over the edges of a selected control, the pointer turns into a double-arrow pointer, as shown in Figure 6-33. With the double-arrow pointer, click and drag the edge of the control to resize it. You can practice on this view by selecting the Contact First Name label control, clicking the right edge when you see the double-pointer arrow, and then expanding the label control to the right.

Figure 6-33 Access displays a double-arrow pointer around the edges of a selected control.

As you expand the width of the Contact First Name label control, Access moves the ContactFirstName text box control further to the right to make room for the wider Contact First Name label control, as shown in Figure 6-34. When you release your mouse, Access snaps the edges of the control to specific grid layout points. What this means is that as you release the mouse, you might see the control edge reduce or expand just a little more from your cursor location. You cannot see the grid layout points, so it might take a little trial and error to get the width or height of controls positioned just the way you want. If you continue to expand the Contact First Name label further to the right, Access moves the ContactFirstName text box, Contact Last Name label, and ContactLastName text box to the right as well.

Figure 6-34 Access moves the ContactFirstName text box further to the right when you expand the width of its associated label control.

You'll notice in Figure 6-34 that you can now see all of the text within the Contact First Name label after resizing the control. The downside to expanding the label width and having the text box moved to the right is that now the controls in the columns are not lined up neatly together. You certainly don't have to always display your controls in perfectly aligned columns, but it does make your view more polished to line up the controls.

To align the rest of the label and text controls, let's resize them to the same expanded width as the Contact First Name label. Click the Vendor Name label control, click the right edge when you see the double-pointer arrow, hold your mouse key down, and then expand the label control to the right to match the width of the Contact First Name label control. You could continue to resize each of the label controls in the column one by one, but that would not be very efficient. A much quicker way to resize all of the remaining label controls is to select them and resize them as a group. To do that, click the design grid beneath the Notes label so that you're no longer selecting any specific control. Click and hold your mouse key down, and then drag your mouse up and across all the label controls from the Notes label to the ContactFullName label, as shown in Figure 6-35. Access highlights all of the label controls when you perform this step.

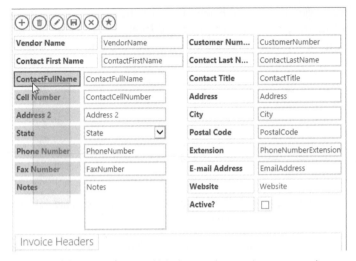

Figure 6-35 Select a group of label controls to resize or move them as a group.

Now that you've selected all of these labels as a group, you can resize all of them at the same time. Move your mouse over to the right edge of any of the highlighted labels until you see the double-pointer arrow, and then expand the label controls to the right until they are the same width as the Vendor Name and Contact First Name label controls. As you move your mouse to the right, Access expands the width of all the highlighted labels and moves other controls to the right, as shown in Figure 6-36. Your labels and controls in the first and second columns are now nicely aligned again. You can also see all of the text in each label control.

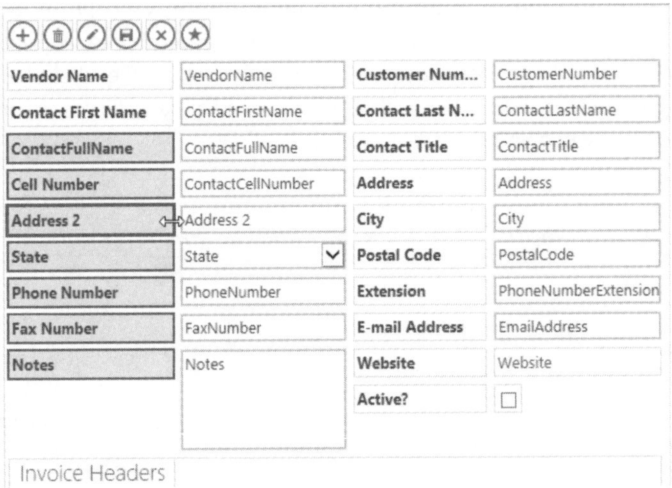

Figure 6-36 Resize the group of controls by dragging the right edge of one of the control to the right.

INSIDE OUT   Selecting a group of controls

You can also select a group of controls, even different control types, by holding down the Ctrl key and clicking each control one by one. Access highlights each control during this process, and you can then resize or move the controls as a group. If you select a control by mistake, continue holding the Ctrl key and click the control again to deselect it.

Now that you're familiar with selecting and resizing controls, expand the width for all the label controls in the third column. The first label control in the third column is the Customer Number label, which is currently too small to display all of the caption text. Expand the width of these labels in the column using the techniques you just learned. As you perform this step, Access moves the text boxes and other controls in the fourth column further to the right. It's a good idea to save the changes you've made to this view up to this point, after you've completed resizing the controls. Click the Save button on the Quick Access Toolbar to save your changes. Whenever you save view changes, Access displays a save progress dialog to indicate that it is currently in the process of saving your changes, as shown in Figure 6-37.

Figure 6-37 Access displays a progress dialog when you save view changes.

Note

If you expand or move controls over the existing boundary of the design grid, Access expands the design grid to accommodate the extra needed space. Similarly, Access contracts the design grid as you resize or move controls smaller than the current design grid boundaries. When you save a view, you might see the design grid boundaries contract to wrap around the controls horizontally and vertically. Access displays horizontal or vertical scroll bars when needed, based on the design grid size and your display settings.

On quick-created views, Access places controls on the grid left to right and top to bottom to match the field order found in the table. Access also places related items controls at the bottom of the design grid beneath all other controls. In some cases, you might find that this default order of controls suits your needs just fine. In other cases, however, you might want to change the order of the controls or perhaps add extra space in between controls.

Chapter 6

In the quick-created List Details view for the Vendors table you've been working on, let's move the Website hyperlink control and associated label to beneath the Fax Number label and text box control. You could choose to move the label and hyperlink controls separately, but you can reposition the controls quicker by moving them together as a group. To select both controls, click the label control for the Website field, press and hold the Ctrl key, and then click the Website hyperlink control. Alternatively, highlight both controls by clicking the design grid, click and hold your mouse key down, and then drag your mouse across both controls. Because the controls are so close together with other controls above and below in this example, you might find it easier in this case to select the controls by using the Ctrl key approach.

After you select both controls, position your mouse over the center of one of the controls until your mouse pointer turns into a four-arrow cross hair, as shown in Figure 6-38. You can now drag the controls to a new location. As you drag the two controls to the left beneath the Fax Number controls, Access pushes the controls for the Notes field and the related items control down one grid space to make room for the Website field controls, also shown in Figure 6-38. Release the mouse to drop the controls into their new positions. Access snaps the controls to the nearest grid location.

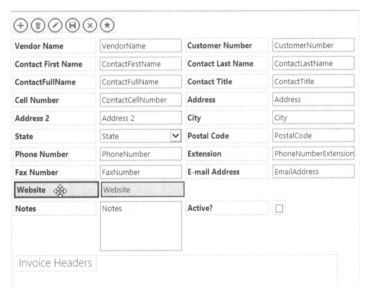

Figure 6-38 Move the Website field controls as a group to beneath the FaxNumber field controls.

Whenever you move controls on the design grid into a location currently occupied by existing controls, Access moves those controls out of the way to make room for the new controls. Depending on how and where you are moving controls into position, Access might move other controls up, down, left, or right to make room for the new controls. For example, if you started moving the two Website controls up the design grid to the top of the view now, Access moves the other controls in the columns down one grid space as you move your mouse up the column.

INSIDE OUT   Moving controls with the keyboard

You can also move controls by selecting them and then pressing the Up, Down, Left, or Right arrow keys. Access moves the control, or group of controls, if you select multiple controls, one grid space at a time in the direction you specify. You might find this technique a little easier for moving control around the design grid if you need more precise control.

Now that you moved the Website field controls over to the left side of the design grid, you should probably move the two controls for the Active field up to fill the gap left open by the previous positions of the Website controls. Select the check box control for the Active field and its associated label by clicking and dragging your mouse over both controls. (You should now be comfortable using this technique to select or "lasso" multiple controls using the mouse.) Now drag the controls up one grid space, or press the Up Arrow key once to move these controls into their new positions. Finally, let's resize the Notes multiline text box control to go across the remaining empty space on the design grid. Select the Notes multiline text box control, move your mouse over to the right edge of the highlighted control until you see the double-pointer arrow, and then expand the controls to the right until you reach the edge of the design grid space, as shown in Figure 6-39. Save the design changes you've made to the layout of the controls now by clicking the Save button on the Quick Access Toolbar.

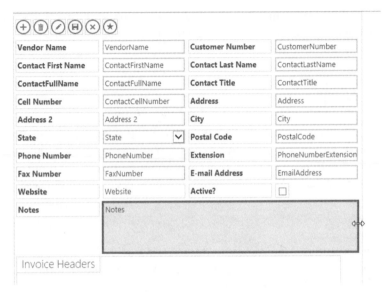

Figure 6-39 Expand the Notes multiline text box control to the right.

INSIDE OUT Deleting controls from the design grid

If you need to remove a control from the design grid, select the control and then press the Delete key. If you delete a control by mistake, press the Undo button on the Quick Access Toolbar to undo your changes. If you want to delete multiple controls at the same time, highlight the controls as a group and then press the Delete key. Notice that when you delete a control, Access does not move any controls into the now unoccupied grid position.

Defining control properties

As you've been selecting, resizing, and moving controls on the design grid, you've no doubt noticed that Access displays charm buttons next to the controls when you select them. Each control on the design grid contains a set of properties that you can set and modify to meet the specific needs of your view. Similar to the List Control and Action Bar buttons for views, which you've already explored, you can customize controls on the design grid, beyond the type of formatting options available to you in the Font group on the ribbon, through these properties. For example, you could choose to hide, disable, and display Tooltips for controls at runtime by setting their control properties in Design view. Each control type contains a specific set of properties you can set, some of which are common to many different control types.

To view the properties for a control on the design grid, you must first select it. Select the ContactFullName text box control on the design grid. Access displays three charm buttons next to the control—Data, Formatting, and Actions—as shown in Figure 6-40. Click the Data charm button, and Access opens the Data callout menu, also shown in Figure 6-40.

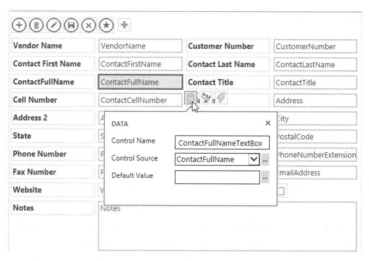

Figure 6-40 Click the Data charm button to view data properties for the ContactFullName text box.

For text box controls, Access displays three properties on the Data callout menu—Control Name, Control Source, and Default Value. For some control properties, Access displays a text box where you can type information, such as Control Name and Default Value properties. For other properties, such as the Control Source property, Access displays a drop-down list of options. The Control Source property defines the field to which the control is bound. Access displays the Build button next to the Control Source and Default Value properties. Click the Build button, and Access opens the Expression Builder dialog, where you can define an expression for these properties. By default, Access fills in the Control Name and Control Source properties for all controls on quick-created views. Each control must have a unique name in the Control Name property.

To view the formatting properties for the ContactFullName text box control, close the Data callout menu and then click the Formatting charm button. Access opens the Formatting callout menu, as shown in Figure 6-41. For text box controls bound to Short Text data types, Access displays four properties on the Formatting callout menu—Tooltip, Visible, Enabled, and Input Hint.

Figure 6-41 Clear the Enabled property for the ContactFullName text box on the Formatting callout menu.

You can define custom text in the Tooltip property that appears as a control tip when you rest your mouse pointer for a few seconds on the control at runtime in your web browser. You might find this especially useful for command buttons, to further describe the action that occurs when the user clicks the button. Leave the Tooltip property empty for this ContactFullName control, because the associated label for the control clearly identifies its purpose.

Access provides a drop-down list of two options for the Visible property—Visible and Hidden. When you specify Visible (the default), Access Services displays the control at runtime in your web browser. When you specify Hidden, Access Services hides the control at runtime in your web browser. Leave this property set at Visible for this control because we want users of the web app to see the control and its value at runtime.

The Enabled property determines whether the control can receive the focus (the user can click in or tab to the control). Because the ContactFullName field in the Vendors table is a calculated field, which a user cannot change, you should change the properties of this control to prevent it from being selected in the view at runtime. Clear the Enabled property of this control, previously shown in Figure 6-41, so that the user cannot click in or tab to the control. When you do this, Access prohibits access to the field and causes the control to appear dimmed in your web browser.

You can define custom text in the Input Hint property that appears inside the control when the control does not have focus and currently does not contain any value. In your web browser, Access Services displays Input Hint text as grayed-out text, but the text disappears when you tab to or click into the control to begin typing. Leave the Input Hint property empty for this ContactFullName control, because users won't be able to type into the control. (Remember, you cleared the Enabled property previously.)

To view the control actions for the ContactFullName text box control, close the Formatting callout menu and then click the Actions charm button. Access opens the Actions callout menu, as shown in Figure 6-42. For text box controls, Access displays two buttons on the Actions callout menu—On Click and After Update.

Figure 6-42 Click the Actions charm button to view control actions for the ContactFullName text box.

When you click one of the action buttons on the Actions callout menu for controls, Access opens the Logic Designer window, where you can create user interface macros attached to control events. (We'll discuss control events and creating user interface macros in Chapter 8.)

You can also set separate properties for the labels attached to controls. Click the label for ContactFullName to see the three charm buttons next to this control. Now click the Formatting charm button to see the Formatting property callout menu for label controls, as shown in Figure 6-43. Access assigns the field name ContactFullName to both the Caption property and the Tooltip property for this associated label, because I did not define a Label Text field property for the ContactFullName field at the table level.

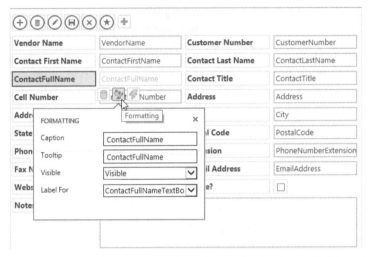

Figure 6-43 Click the Formatting charm button for the ContactFullName label control.

Compared to the captions shown in the other label controls, the caption for the ContactFullName field seems out of place, because it does not include spaces between the three words. To make this label look more professional and readable for users of the app, you should adjust these properties to include spaces within the text. Place your cursor in the Caption property text box, and insert a space between the words Contact and Full and another space between the words Full and Name. Repeat the same steps for the Tooltip property as well. (You could also copy the revised Caption property after you changed it and paste it into the Tooltip property.) After you make these changes to the two properties, you'll notice that Access displays the revised caption text within the control, as shown in Figure 6-44. Click the Save button on the Quick Access Toolbar to save your design changes for this view.

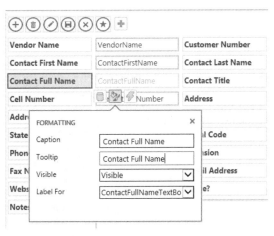

Figure 6-44 Change the Caption and Tooltip properties for the ContactFullName label control to include spaces in the text.

INSIDE OUT   Directly editing label caption properties

You can also change the Caption property for a label control by double-clicking in the label control on the design grid. Access highlights the existing text for the Caption property. You can then edit the text to something different and then press Enter to commit the changes to the Caption property.

Some of the properties for controls that can be bound to fields from your view's record source are exactly the same as those you can set in table Design view on the General tab or by clicking the Modify Lookups button in the ribbon for lookup fields. (See Chapter 3 for more details.) If you do not specify a different setting in the control, the view uses the properties you defined for the field in your table. In some cases, a particular field property setting migrates to a different property in the bound control on your view. For example, the Label Text property of a field moves to the Caption property of a bound control's associated label.

Table 6-3 describes all the control properties on views and explains their usage. The table also lists which control types use the property. The properties are listed by control type in the ribbon and by the order listed on the Data and Formatting callout menus. When you're exploring the various properties for different controls in Table 6-3, take note that some control properties appear and disappear on the callout menus based on the selections of other properties. I've called these out in the appropriate places under the description column in the table. We'll cover properties that you can define on Related Items controls later in this chapter.

TABLE 6-3 Control properties

Property	Description	Control Types
Control Name	The control name for each control on the design grid must be unique and not Null. You can use the Control Name property in user interface macros to refer to values in controls and set different properties at runtime. See Chapter 8 for more details.	All control types.
Control Source	The name of the field to which the control is bound. Access displays a drop-down list of field names with valid data types for this property. For example, with check boxes, Access displays only names of fields in your view's record source that are Yes/No data types. Access also displays the Build button next to this property so that you can open the Expression Builder dialog and create an expression to use for the Control Source property of the controls. Controls with an expression for their Control Source property are not editable in the runtime.	Text Box, Label, Web Browser, Combo Box, Check Box, Image, Autocomplete, Hyperlink, and Multiline Textbox,
Default Value	You can define a default value for a control to display whenever you are entering a new record if no other value is supplied. If you don't specify a Default Value property, the field that the control is bound to will be Null if the user fails to supply a value for new records. If you define a Default Value field property setting at the table level, Access does not display that default value in the control's Default Value property; however, Access does display the default value at runtime in your web browser. If you define a Default Value property at the table level for a field and define a different Default Value property for a control on a view bound to that field, Access uses the default value defined for the control at runtime. For check boxes, you can choose Yes or No from a drop-down list for the Default Value property. Access displays the Build button next to this property, so you can open the Expression Builder dialog and create an expression to use for the Default Value property of controls.	Text Box, Combo Box, Check Box, Autocomplete, and Multiline Textbox
Tooltip	You can enter custom text that appears as a control tip when you rest your mouse pointer on the control for a few seconds at runtime in your web browser. You might find this especially useful for command buttons to further describe the action that occurs when the user clicks the button.	Text Box, Label, Command Button, Combo Box, Check Box, Image, Autocomplete, Hyperlink, and Multiline Textbox
Visible	Specify Visible (the default) to make the control visible at runtime in your web browser. Specify Hidden to hide the control. You will find this property useful when you begin to automate your web app to display or hide controls depending on the contents of other fields. See Chapter 8 for details.	All control types

Property	Description	Control Types
Enabled	Select this property (the default) to make the control enabled at runtime in your web browser. Enabled controls allow you to change their values at runtime. Clear this property if you do not want users of your app to change the value of the control or execute any macro actions attached to the control events. Disabled controls appear dimmed in runtime mode. Note that disabled controls can still have their values changed by user interface macros. You will find this property useful when you begin to automate your web app to enable or disable controls depending on the contents of other fields. See Chapter 8 for details.	Text Box, Command Button, Combo Box, Check Box, Autocomplete, and Multiline Textbox
Format	You can use the Format property to determine how Access Services displays the data in text boxes at runtime. The Format property displays only for text boxes bound to Number or Date/Time data types or text boxes bound to Calculated data types with result types evaluating to Number or Date/Time data types. You can select General, Standard, Fixed, Percent, and Currency as format options for Number data types. You can select General Date, Long Date, Short Date, Long Time, and Short Time as format options for Date/Time data types. (See Tables 6-4 and 6-5 for detailed descriptions of each of these Format property options.)	Text Box
Decimal Places	You can specify the number of decimal places that Access Services displays for the data in a text box control at runtime. You'll see the Decimal Places property option only when you're working with a text box bound to a Currency data type field. The default specification is Auto, which means Access Services displays two decimal places for the Currency, Fixed, Standard, and Percent formats and the number of decimal places necessary to show the current precision of the numeric value for General Number format. You can also request a fixed display of decimal places ranging from 0 through 15.	Text Box
Input Hint	You can enter custom text that appears inside an input control when the control does not have focus and currently does not contain any value. In your web browser, Access Services displays Input Hint text as grayed-out text, but the text disappears when you tab to or click into the control to begin typing. You might find this property especially useful for Autocomplete controls to have users of your app enter a search term. By default, Access enters the text Find... into the Input Hint property for Autocomplete controls bound to lookup fields on quick-created views.	Text Box, Autocomplete, and Multiline Textbox

Chapter 6

Property	Description	Control Types
Label For	Use the Label For property to specify the control to which the label is associated. In runtime, label controls change their fore color text when their associated controls receive focus. Also, when you click a label control in runtime, Access Services executes any macro actions in the On Click event, if one exists, of the associated control.	Label
Caption	You can define the text displayed in labels at runtime using the Caption property. You can also dynamically change the captions of labels at runtime using user interface macros. (Tip: If you define Label Text property for your fields at the table design level, Access, by default, uses that text for the Caption property of labels associated with those fields on quick-created views.) See Chapter 8 for more details.	Label
Default URL	For web browser controls, you can define a URL to load by default when the control is unbound or its field has no value. For hyperlink controls, you can define the URL component of the default value that Access Services automatically enters in the field for new records.	Web Browser and Hyperlink
Show Scrollbars	If you want a web browser control to display scroll bars to see additional content of the webpage displayed within the control, select When Needed (the default). Select Never to not display scroll bars for the control. Note that users of your app might not easily be able to see additional content inside the web browser control if no scroll bars are shown and the content exists outside the viewable area of the page.	Web Browser
Row Source Type	For combo boxes and autocomplete controls, the Row Source Type property instructs Access that the data to display in the control comes from a table, query, or list of values. The Control Source property determines the field to which Access stores the data, but the Row Source Type property helps determine from *where* Access gets the data options to display. Select Table/Query, and Access pulls data directly from a table or from a saved query object in the web app. Select Value List if you want to provide a static list of values that you type in to display in the control.	Combo Box and Autocomplete

Property	Description	Control Types
Row Source	The Row Source property works in tandem with the Row Source Type and Control Source properties to determine what values to display in combo boxes and autocomplete controls. On the Data callout menu, the Row Source property dynamically changes based on how you define the Row Source Type property and whether the control is bound. For controls on quick-created views bound to lookup fields, Access displays a drop-down list of the table or query name defined at the table level for the lookup field and an option called [No data source]. The [No data source] means Access does not provide data, and your control would not be of much use in this case. If you're creating an unbound control and select Table/Query for the Row Source Type property, Access displays a drop-down list of all tables and saved query object names for the Row Source property. For controls bound to value list lookup fields, you won't see the Row Source property option at all on the Data callout menu, because Access pulls the values directly from the list of options defined at the table level. If you're creating an unbound control and select Value List for the Row Source Type property, Access displays the Row Source property as a multiline text box control. In this scenario, you can type each value that you want to display—one per row.	Combo Box and Autocomplete
Bound Field	The Bound Field property also works in conjunction with the Row Source Type and Row Source properties. The Bound Field property determines which field's value in the Row Source property to use as the saved value of the control. For controls on quick-created views bound to lookup fields, Access displays a drop-down list of the AutoNumber ID field name from the table or query defined in the Row Source property and an option called [No data source] for the Bound Field property. The [No data source] option means that Access does not store the ID field data. Your control is essentially unbound and won't store any values when you create new records. If you're creating an unbound control, Access displays a list of all field names (except Image data type fields) from the source table or query defined in the Row Source property. Note that you won't see the Bound Field property on the Data callout menu if you select Value List for the Row Source Type property.	Combo Box and Autocomplete

Chapter 6

Property	Description	Control Types
Display Field	The Display Field property also works in conjunction with the Row Source Type and Row Source properties. The Display Field property determines which field in the Row Source property to display in the control. Instead of displaying a usually unhelpful ID number for a related field, you can choose a field from the row source to display that users of your web app can more easily identify. (For example, a vendor name is easier to understand than a vendor ID.) For controls on quick-created views bound to lookup fields, Access displays a drop-down list of the field name matching the display value defined at the table level for the lookup field and an option called [No data source] for the Display Field property. If the control is bound to a lookup field and you select [No data source] as the Display Field, Access Services still uses the display value defined at the table level for the lookup field. If you're creating an unbound control, Access displays a list of all field names (except Image data type fields) from the source table or query defined in the Row Source property. Note that you won't see the Display Field property on the Data callout menu if you select Value List for the Row Source Type property.	Combo Box
Popup View	Use the Popup View property to designate a view that Access Services opens to display the related record when you click the value currently displayed in the control. When you provide a Popup View property, Access Services displays the value in the combo box or autocomplete as a hyperlink. You'll find this especially useful for viewing related information as well as adding new records to related tables. For the Popup View property, Access provides a drop-down list of view names that include the related table in its record source. This property is not available if you are creating controls on Datasheet views or if your control's Row Source Type property is set to Value List.	Combo Box and Autocomplete
Picture URL	For image controls, you can choose to display an image from a URL that points to a location on the Internet or your local intranet using the Picture URL property. This property is available only for image controls that are unbound. For bound image controls, Access Services displays the image stored in the field.	Image
Picture Tiling	For unbound image controls, you can optionally choose to tile a picture. The default setting, None, places one copy of the picture within the control. Choose Horizontal, Vertical, or Both if you want multiple copies "tiled" within the control. When you choose Horizontal, Vertical, or Both, you can set the Size Mode property to Clip or Zoom, and the picture should be smaller than the control. Setting Picture Tiling to an option other than None is useful if your picture is a small pattern picture. You can also choose additional tiling options using the Horizontal Alignment and Vertical Alignment properties.	Image

Property	Description	Control Types
Size Mode	For unbound image controls, you can optionally choose how to size a picture within the control. Use Zoom (the default) to stretch the picture to the dimensions of the image control without distorting it, but if the aspect ratio of the picture does not match the display space in the control, the picture won't cover the entire control. Use the Clip option to specify that the picture appears in its original resolution. If the control is larger than the picture, the picture will not cover the entire control area. If the control is smaller than the picture, you'll see only part of the picture. Use the Stretch option to stretch the picture to the dimensions of the control, but the picture might appear distorted.	Image
Horizontal Alignment	This property applies only when the Size Mode property for an unbound image control is Clip or Zoom. The default setting, Middle, centers the picture in the control area. You can also specify Left to align the picture to the left side of the control or specify Right to align the picture to the right side of the control.	Image
Vertical Alignment	This property applies only when the Size Mode property for an unbound image control is Clip or Zoom. The default setting, Middle, centers the picture in the control area. You can also specify Top to align the picture with the top of the control, or you can specify Bottom to align the picture with the bottom of the control.	Image
Primary Display Field	The Primary Display Field property for autocomplete controls performs the same function as the Display Field property performs for combo boxes. See the Display Field property for an explanation of its purpose and behavior with bound and unbound controls.	Autocomplete
Secondary Display Field	The Secondary Display Field property for autocomplete controls is an optional property that you can set to display another field value from the source table or query in the drop-down list of options presented at runtime. When you perform a search into a source table or query using an autocomplete control, Access Services displays a drop-down list of search results. By default, Access Services displays only the field values designated by the Primary Display Field property. If you also provide a Secondary Display Field property, Access Services displays the search results stacked in two rows of data—the primary on top and the secondary on the second row. You'll find this property useful, for example, to more easily identify unique records from a set of similar records.	Autocomplete

Chapter 6

Property	Description	Control Types
Default Display Text	You can define the default text displayed in hyperlinks at runtime using the Default Display Text property. If no URL is entered into the hyperlink field, you won't see the default display text for new records. You'll see this text displayed in hyperlink controls when a URL is saved in the underlying field and no display text was provided. You might find this property especially useful to further describe to users of your app the purpose of a long URL address.	Hyperlink
Open In	With hyperlinks, you can designate how Access Services navigates to a web address displayed in the control you click at runtime. Select New Window/Tab (the default), and Access Services opens the hyperlink in a new window or tab in your web browser when you click the hyperlink. If you select Same Window, Access Services navigates to the web address shown in the hyperlink control in the same window. If you use the Same Window setting, you'll navigate away from your Access web app whenever you click the hyperlink.	Hyperlink
Source Object	Use the Source Object property to define what view you want displayed inside a subview control. Access displays a drop-down list of the names of all the views in your web app for this property. You won't see the name of the view on which you are placing the subview control in the drop-down list of view names, because that would create a recursive situation in your web browser.	Subview
Link Master Field	Use the Link Master Field property in conjunction with the Link Child Field property to link a subview with a main view's displayed record. The Link Master Field property should contain the name of the related field on the outer main view. As you move from record to record in the outer main view, Access Services uses the value it finds in the field defined in the Link Master Field property as a filter against the field in the subview defined in the Link Child Field property.	Subview
Link Child Field	The Link Child Field property refers to the "child" view—the one in the subview. Enter the name of the field in the record source of the view inside the subview that should be filtered based on which row you have displayed in the outer main view.	Subview
Datasheet Caption	You can assign a caption for controls displayed in datasheet views. The caption appears as a column header above each control. Note that you'll see the Datasheet Caption property on the Formatting callout menu on the design grid only for controls in Datasheet views.	Text Box, Command Button, Combo Box, Check Box, Autocomplete, Hyperlink, and Multiline Textbox

Troubleshooting

Why do I see a red border around a property on the callout menu?

Access displays a red border around a property, typically a property that includes a drop-down list, if the saved value in the property is no longer valid. For example, the saved Label For property for a label control lists the name of its associated control. If you delete the associated control or rename it, the saved control name in the Label For property is no longer valid. You'll need to clear that Label For property or select a different control name from the drop-down list. When the property value is valid again, Access removes the red border around the property.

INSIDE OUT   Formatting a group of controls

You can change common formatting property options across multiple controls, even different control types, by selecting them as a group. When you highlight a group of controls, Access displays one charm button—Formatting. When you click the Formatting charm button, Access displays a callout menu with a list of common properties you can set across all the control types. For example, you could change the Enabled or Visible properties across all highlighted controls.

Specifying a format for numbers

If you don't specify a Format property setting for a text box control that displays a number value, Access Services displays the number in the General format. You can choose from five Format property settings for numbers in web apps, as shown in Table 6-4.

TABLE 6-4   Format property settings for text boxes bound to number data types

Format	Description
General	Displays numbers as entered, with up to 11 significant digits. If a number contains more than 11 significant digits or the control you are using to display the value is not wide enough to show all digits, Access Services rounds the displayed number first and then uses scientific (exponential) notation for very large or very small numbers (more than 10 digits to the right or to the left of the decimal point).
Standard	Displays numbers with thousands separators and with two decimal places. The number displayed is rounded if the underlying value contains more than two decimal places.

Format	Description
Fixed	Displays numbers without thousands separators and with two decimal places. The number displayed is rounded if the underlying value contains more than two decimal places.
Percent	Multiplies the value by 100, displays two decimal places, and adds a trailing percent sign. The number displayed is rounded if the underlying value contains more than four decimal places.
Currency	Displays numeric data according to the Currency setting in the Regional And Language Options section of the Control Panel. In the English (U.S.) layout, Access Services uses a leading dollar sign, maintains two decimal places (rounded), and encloses negative numbers in parentheses.

Specifying a format for date/time

If you don't specify a Format property setting for a text box control that displays a date/time value, Access Services displays the date/time in the General Date format. You can choose from five Format property settings for date/time values in web apps, as shown in Table 6-5.

TABLE 6-5 Format property settings for the date/time data type

Format	Description
General Date	Displays the date as numbers separated by the date separator character. Displays the time as hours, minutes, and seconds separated by the time separator character and followed by an AM/PM indicator. If the value has no time component, Access displays the date only. If the value has no date component, Access displays the time only. Example: 5/29/2013 06:17:55 PM.
Long Date	Displays the date according to the Long Date setting in the Regional And Language Options section of the Control Panel. Example: Wednesday, May 29, 2013.
Short Date	Displays the date according to the Short Date setting in the Regional And Language Options section of the Control Panel. Example: 5/29/2013.
Long Time	Displays the time according to the Time setting in the Regional And Language Options section of the Control Panel. Example: 6:17:55 PM.
Short Time	Displays the time as hours and minutes separated by the time separator character, using a 24-hour clock. Example: 18:17.

> **Note**
>
> Included with the sample files, which can be downloaded from the book's catalog page, is a desktop database called ControlDefinitions.accdb. This desktop database contains a list of all controls and their associated control properties found in desktop databases, 2010 style web databases, and 2013 web apps. You might find this desktop database useful as a reference for understanding the different controls and properties available in Access.

Understanding related items controls

At the bottom of the List Details view for the Vendors table you've been working on, you'll see a related items control. This control is a new control type for Access 2013 and is available only on List Details and Blank views in web apps. Whenever you have a lookup field defined in a table that looks up data to another source table, Access creates a related items control at the bottom of the design grid of the source table to display data from the related table. (If you're familiar with Access desktop databases, you can think of a related items control as similar to a combination of a tab control with embedded subforms.) If you have multiple tables with lookup fields pointing to a single source table, Access creates one related items control on the quick-created views for the source table and one tab on the control for each lookup field to represent the data from each related table.

> **Note**
>
> Related items controls can be created only on List Details and Blank views. You cannot add a related items control to Datasheet or Summary view types.

As you might recall from Chapter 3, the Invoice Headers table in this sample web app contains a lookup field to the Vendors table. Remember that each invoice created in this app is assigned to a specific vendor and that data is tracked in the VendorIDFK lookup field in the Invoice Headers table. When Access quick-creates a List Details view based on the Vendors table in this sample web app, it creates a related items control with one tab containing a caption matching the related table name, Invoice Headers, as shown in Figure 6-45. When you click the tab caption, Access displays three charm buttons—Data, Formatting, and Calculation.

Figure 6-45 Click the tab caption on related items controls to view its properties.

> **Note**
> The related items control does not expose any properties you can modify. You can modify properties only on the individual tabs contained within the related items control.

Click the Data charm button next to the selected tab, and Access opens the Data callout menu for this Invoice Headers tab, as shown in Figure 6-46. As you can see, there are quite a few properties for this callout menu. I'll describe each of the properties you can set in related items controls and their purpose in just a moment, but for now let's look at each of the property callout menus for tabs on related items controls.

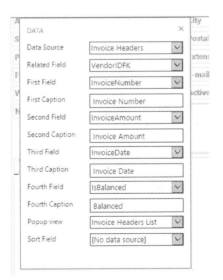

Figure 6-46 Click the Data charm button to view data properties for the Invoice Headers tab of the related items control.

To view the formatting properties on the Invoice Headers tab, close the Data callout menu and then click the Formatting charm button. Access opens the Formatting callout menu for related items controls, as shown in Figure 6-47. Caption is the only property available on the Formatting callout menu. The Caption property determines what text to display across the tab header.

Figure 6-47 Click the Formatting charm button to view the Caption property for tabs on related items controls.

To view the calculation properties of the Invoice Headers tab, close the Formatting callout menu and then click the Calculation charm button. Access opens the Calculation callout menu, as shown in Figure 6-48. Access displays five properties here on the Calculation callout menu—Calculation, Field, Calculation Caption, Calculation Visible, and Control Name.

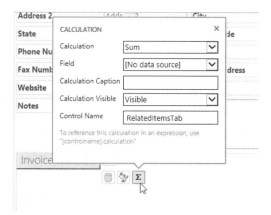

Figure 6-48 Click the Calculation charm button to view calculation properties for the Invoice Headers tab on the related items control.

Table 6-6 lists all the properties and their usage for related items control tabs. When you're exploring the various properties for the control tabs in Table 6-6, take note that some properties appear and disappear from the callout menus based on the selections of other properties. I've called these out in the appropriate places under the usage column in the table.

TABLE 6-6 Related items control tab properties

Property	Settings	Usage
Data Source	A drop-down list of related table and query names in the web app.	For the Data Source property, Access displays only a list of table names that have a lookup field to the table defined in the view's Record Source property. Access also displays query names that include the table defined in the view's Record Source property in the drop-down list. The Data Source property tells Access which related table or query to retrieve data from for display in the control.
Related Field	A drop-down list of field names that are lookups into the source table.	The Related Field property serves as the "linking" field between the main view's record and the fields displayed in the related items control. You can think of this property as similar to the Link Master Field and Link Child Field properties for subview controls. You can also select [No Data Source] in the drop-down list for the Related Field property, but Access Services won't display any data in the control in this case.
First Field Second Field Third Field Fourth Field	A drop-down list of field names from the table or query defined in the Data Source property.	You can display up to four fields of data in related items controls. Access displays a drop-down list of all the fields in the source table or query, excluding field names bound to Image data types for these properties. If you select [No Data Source] for any of these properties, Access Services does not display any data for that column. In some cases, you might want to display four fields, but in other cases, displaying fewer than four fields might work fine for your scenario.
First Caption Second Caption Third Caption Fourth Caption	You can optionally type a caption to display as the column header for each of the four display fields.	If you do not provide captions for the First Field, Second Field, Third Field, or Fourth Field properties, Access Services displays the actual field name defined in the property for the column header in the control. You might find it useful to provide a more user friendly short description as column headers instead of actual field names.
Popup View	A drop-down list of view names that include the related table in its record source.	Use the Popup View property to designate a view that Access Services opens to display the related record when you click a row displayed in the control. When you provide a Popup View property, Access Services also displays a link beneath the control at runtime that allows you to add new records into the related table using the view designated in the Popup View property. You'll find this property especially useful for viewing related information, as well as for adding new records to related tables.

Property	Settings	Usage
Sort Field	A drop-down list of field names from the table or query defined in the Data Source property.	Use the Sort Field property to designate which field in the Data Source property you want Access Services to sort by when you view the Related Items control in your web browser. The list of valid field names in the drop-down list excludes any field names bound to Image data types. You can choose to sort by a field not displayed as one of the four display columns. You're not required to define a Sort Field property, in which case you'll see [No Data Source] selected by default. If you select [No Data Source] for the Sort Field property, Access Services sorts the records by the AutoNumber primary field at runtime.
Sort Order	Ascending (default) or Descending.	The Sort Order property lists only two options—Ascending and Descending. In the Sort Order property, you can specify whether Access should sort the selected field in the Sort Field property in ascending or descending order. By default, Access always chooses Ascending for the Sort Order property. Note that you won't see this property listed on the Data callout menu until you select a field to sort by in the Sort Field property.
Caption	Access displays a text box for you to type caption text.	You can define the text displayed over each tab in a related items control using the Caption property. You cannot define an expression to use for this property.
Calculation	Sum (default), Count, or Avg.	You can optionally choose to perform aggregate functions across any of the four display fields in the control that are Number or Currency data types. If you choose Sum or Avg, you must select a field name in the Field property. Access Services performs the aggregate across the records currently displayed in the control and updates the values as you move to different records displayed in the main view. If you select Count, Access hides the Field Property on the Calculation callout menu, because you do not need to select a display field for Access to count the number of records displayed in the control.
Field	A drop-down list of field names from the table or query defined in the Data Source property that are Number or Currency fields and defined as one of the display columns for the control.	When you select Sum or Avg for the Calculation property, you need to select which of the four display fields to use in the aggregate calculation. If there are no display fields in the control that are Number or Currency data types, Access displays [No Data Source] in the drop-down list. In this case, Access does not perform the Sum or Avg aggregate functions across any fields.

Chapter 6

Property	Settings	Usage
Calculation Caption	Access displays a text box for you to type caption text.	When you choose to use one of the three aggregate calculations in the Calculation property, Access Services displays the results of the calculation beneath the control on the right side in runtime. You can optionally define the text displayed next to the calculation total. If you do not define a Calculation Caption text, Access Services displays the name of the aggregate field (if you're using Sum or Avg), a space, the type of aggregate performed, a colon, and finally, the result of the aggregate. You might find it useful to provide more descriptive text next to the calculation for users of your web app. You cannot define an expression to use for this property.
Calculation Visible	Visible (default) or Hidden.	When you choose to use one of the three aggregate calculations in the Calculation property, you can choose whether to display the results of the calculation at runtime. If you select Visible (the default), Access Services displays the results of the calculation beneath the control on the right side in runtime. If you select Hidden, Access Services does not display the results beneath the control at runtime. However, you can still refer to the results of the calculation using expressions in other controls on your main view. See the Control Name property for more information.
Control Name	Access displays a text box for you to type a control name.	When you choose to use of the three aggregate calculations in the Calculation property, you can optionally refer to the result of the aggregate calculation using expressions in other controls displayed on the main view. For example, if your Control Name property is OrdersTab, you can create an expression as the Control Source property for a text box control shown on the main view like so: `=[OrdersTab].Calculation`. You might find this property useful to refer to values on multiple tabs of a related items control and perform additional calculations using values displayed in the main view. Each tab on a related items control must have a unique Control Name.

If you want to add a new tab to an existing related items control, select the control and then click the Add New Tab button displayed to the right of the last tab. Access opens the Add New Tab callout menu, as shown in Figure 6-49. You must provide a name for your new tab in the Tab Caption property. You are allowed to have multiple tabs with the same caption, but users of your app might not understand the difference between two or more identically named tabs.

For the Data Source property, Access displays a drop-down list of only table names or query names with lookup fields to related tables. If there are no related tables to the source table, Access displays [No Data Source] in the drop-down list. After you provide a Tab

Caption text and select a Data Source property, click the Add New Tab button on the call-out menu and Access creates the new tab. You can then set your desired property settings for the new tab on the three property callout menus available for the new tab.

Figure 6-49 Click Add New Tab to create additional tabs for a related items control.

INSIDE OUT Changing the display order of tabs

If you have multiple tab pages on a related items control, you can change the display order of the tabs using a similar technique as changing the display order of views in the View Selector. Select the tab you want to move in the related items control, hold your mouse, and then drag the tab to the left or right. As you move the tab, Access swaps positions with the tab next to it.

As you'll see later in this chapter, Access displays related records from tables and queries on each tab of a related item control. Access displays the records within the height and width of the related items control. This means that the taller you have your control, the more records Access displays without needing to display vertical scroll bars. Similarly, the wider you have your control, the more space Access has available to display your column data. You cannot resize an individual tab on a related items control; all tabs display the same size in your web browser. To resize a related items control, you must first select the control instead of a specific tab within the control. To do this, click the control outline on the design grid anywhere except one of the tab pages. You'll know whether you selected the control because Access highlights the entire control, including all tab pages.

Let's resize the related items control on the view you have open to line up the right edge with the other controls on the grid. Click the related items control, click the right edge when you see the double-pointer arrow, hold your mouse, and then expand the control to the right until the right edge lines up with the other columns, as shown in Figure 6-50.

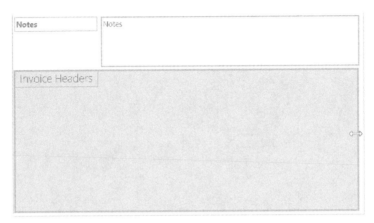

Figure 6-50 Resize the width of the related items control to line it up with the other view controls.

If you want to delete a tab off a related items control, select the tab and then press the Delete key. Access deletes the tab page from the control and also removes all properties associated with that tab. If you accidently delete a tab page by mistake and haven't yet saved your view design changes, you can click the Undo command on the Quick Access Toolbar or press Ctrl+Z to undo the deletion. If you want to delete an entire related items control, you must first select the control instead of a specific tab. After you select the entire control, press the Delete key to remove the control from the grid. Access deletes the related items control from the design grid along with all tabs contained within the control. You can press the Undo command if you delete the related items control by mistake.

Save the design changes you've made to the List Details view for the Vendors table, and close the view before moving on to the next section. You can click the Save button on the Quick Access Toolbar or press Ctrl+S to save your design changes. To close the view, click the Close button in the upper-right corner of the object window. (The Close button is denoted with an X.) You can also close a view by right-clicking the view object tab at the top of the application window and selecting Close from the shortcut menu. If you attempt to close a view with unsaved changes, Access prompts you and asks whether you want to save your changes before closing.

Customizing Datasheet views

Now that you've explored how to design a List Details view, learned about different control types, and practiced setting properties for controls, let's explore a different view type—Datasheet views. As you've already learned, when you create new tables or import data into your web app, Access creates a List Details and a Datasheet view type for each table. Open the Datasheet view that Access quick-created for the Vendors table, in the sample web app you've been working on, in Design view. To do this, click the Vendors table name caption in the Table Selector, click the Datasheet view caption in the View Selector, and then click the Edit button in the middle of the view preview window, as shown in Figure 6-51.

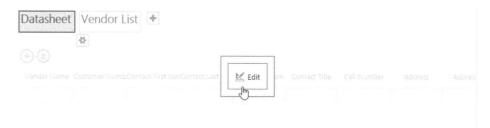

Figure 6-51 Click Edit in the middle of the window to edit the Datasheet view for the Vendors table.

Access opens the Datasheet view in Design view on its own object tab in the application window and provides several design tools on the Design contextual tab in the ribbon, as shown in Figure 6-52. Access also opens the Field List on the right side of the design window. If Access does not open the Field List, you can click the Add Existing Fields button in the Tools group on the Design contextual ribbon tab to open the Field List.

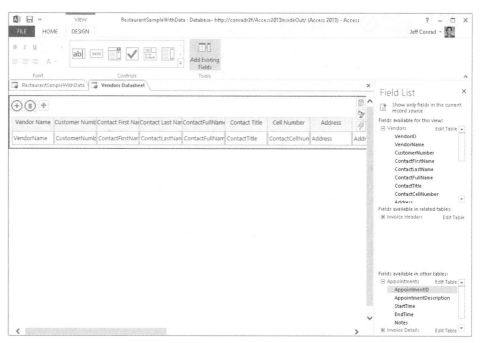

Figure 6-52 When you open a Datasheet view in Design view, you can use the design grid and tools to create your view elements.

You'll notice, in the Controls group on the Design contextual tab, that Access displays fewer control type options for Datasheet views than it does for List Details views. Access web apps support only six control types for use in Datasheet views—Text Box, Command Button, Combo Box, Check Box, Autocomplete, and Multiline Textbox. When you work with a quick-created Datasheet view for the first time, Access already assigns a record source to the view (the table name on which the selected table in the Table Selector is based). Access also adds a control and corresponding label for each field in your record source onto the design grid, except for fields bound to Image data types. Image controls are not supported on Datasheet views. If your source table or query includes a field bound to an Image data type, Access does not list that field name in the Field List pane on the right side of the application window when you work with Datasheet views.

INSIDE OUT   Adding hyperlink controls to Datasheet views

If you scroll to the right with the Datasheet view for the Vendors table you have open, you'll notice a Hyperlink control bound to the Website field in the Vendors table. How is this possible when Hyperlink controls are not listed as a control type option in the Controls group on the ribbon? While it is true Access does not provide Hyperlink controls as an option on the ribbon, you can work around this limitation by dragging a field name bound to a Hyperlink field from the Field List pane onto the view design grid. In this case, Access creates a Hyperlink control, with all appropriate control properties, on the design grid.

As you explore the design surface for Datasheet views, you'll notice similarities to working with List Details views; however, you need to be aware of some important differences. Datasheet views display data from the view's Record Source property in rows, which means all controls in this view type are lined up next to each other horizontally across the design surface. Unlike List Details views, where you can arbitrarily move, resize, and position controls anywhere within the design grid, Datasheet views are more restrictive in the positioning of controls. You can resize the width of controls on Datasheet views, but you cannot resize the height. You can change the order of the controls on Datasheet views, but you must align them along one row of the design grid.

> **Note**
>
> Because you cannot make controls taller on Datasheet views, you might find it a little more difficult to work with Multiline Textbox controls with datasheets in runtime. You can make Multiline Textbox controls wider to display more data, but if the data contains multiple lines, you'll need to use the control's scroll bars to see each separate row of data in your web browser.

You'll also notice that Datasheet views do not include a List Control along the left side of the view. List Details views are designed to show data from one record at a time and you use the List Control portion for navigating and selecting different records to view. Datasheet views show multiple records of data at the same time, so no List Control is needed for navigation. In runtime mode, it might look like you need to add controls to display the data for each row, but in reality, Access Services uses just one set of controls repeated multiple times to display all the rows of data.

Access generates only two built-in Action Bar buttons on quick-created Datasheet views—Add and Delete—compared to five Action Bar buttons on List Details views. (As you'll learn later in this chapter, the data entry experience for Datasheet views in your web browser is quite different than the data entry experience for List Details views.) You can create your own custom Action Bar buttons in addition to using the two built-in buttons. You'll learn how to define macro logic attached to custom Action Bar buttons in Chapter 8.

Datasheet views have the same view properties as List Details views, with one exception—an additional view property called Read Only, which you can find on the Data callout property menu, as shown in Figure 6-53. By default, Access clears the Read Only property when it quick-creates Datasheet views for new and imported tables. If you select the Read Only property, Access disables all controls for the datasheet when you view it in your web browser. You might find this property useful when you want to allow users of your app to view records in your datasheet only and not make data additions, editions, or deletions. Note that you can selectively disable individual controls in datasheets by clearing their Enabled property. The Read Only view property applies to all controls on datasheets and cannot be modified by user interface macros at runtime.

Figure 6-53 Select the Read Only property on Datasheet views to prevent data updates.

In general, the properties available for the supported controls on Datasheet views are the same as controls on List Details views, with a few notable exceptions. Combo Box and Autocomplete controls on Datasheet views do not include the Popup View property. As you recall from earlier in this chapter, the Popup View property allows the value in combo boxes and autocomplete controls to display as a link in runtime that you can click to open a pop-up view and displayed related data. Datasheet views do not support this property.

All controls on Datasheet views include an additional property called Datasheet Caption. The Datasheet Caption property determines what text to display in the column header above each control in your web browser. Let's change the Datasheet Caption property for the ContactFullName text box control on this view, because the caption currently displayed shows no spaces in between the three words. Select the ContactFullName text box control on the design grid, and then click the Formatting charm button. Access opens the Formatting callout menu for this control, as shown in Figure 6-54.

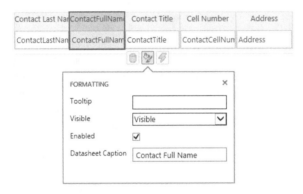

Figure 6-54 Update the Datasheet Caption property to include spaces in the displayed text.

Place your cursor in the Datasheet Caption property box, and then add a space between the words Contact and Full and add another space between the words Full and Name. Also, clear the Enabled property for this control, because the ContactFullName field is a Calculated filed and cannot be changed by the user. After you close the Formatting callout menu, Access updates the caption above the text box control with the new text. Access also dims the control to indicate that it is now a disabled control, as shown in Figure 6-55.

Figure 6-55 You can see your revised Datasheet Caption property text above the control.

By default, Access assigns the same width for all controls on the design grid for quick-created Datasheet views. You might find the default width to be suitable to display the data in a control. However, in most cases, you'll find that you need to adjust the control widths to be narrower or wider to more accurately display the data from your record source fields.

Let's resize the controls on this Datasheet view you have open so that you can see all of the Datasheet Caption property text for each control. Select the control, click the right edge when you see the double-pointer arrow, hold your left mouse key down, and then expand the label control to the right to make the control wider or collapse the control to the left to make the control narrower. You can select each control one at a time and expand the width, or you can expand a group of controls at the same time. To do so, hold down the Ctrl key while you select each control you want to resize. Hover your mouse over the right edge of one of the highlighted controls until you see the double-pointer arrow, click and hold your left mouse key down, and then expand the label controls to the right to make them all wider. In Figure 6-56, I expanded each control to see the Datasheet Caption property text.

Figure 6-56 Expand the control widths to display more data in runtime and to see the full caption text.

To add fields to the design grid of a Datasheet view, select the field name in the Field List pane along the right side of the application window and drag it onto the design grid. (If the Field List pane is not showing, you can click the Add Existing Fields command in the Tools group on the Design contextual tab to make the pane appear.) Let's add the VendorID field from the Vendors table onto this datasheet, because Access does not add the AutoNumber ID field onto quick-created Datasheet views. Select the VendorID field name in the Field List pane, hold your mouse key down, and then drag the field across the design grid and into the first position to the left of the Vendor Name text box control, as shown in Figure 6-57.

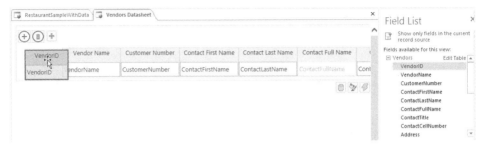

Figure 6-57 Drag the VendorID field from the Field List pane onto the design grid.

As you drag the VendorID field from the Field List across the design grid, Access displays an appropriate control for the data type and an associated label control on top of the control. Access pushes other controls to the right or left as you move controls across the design grid and into position. When you release your mouse, Access snaps the control and associated label to the design grid and lines up the controls. Access always includes an associated label for each control in Datasheet views, including command buttons. You cannot remove or add new label controls to Datasheet views, but you can change the caption or provide no caption at all.

If you want to drop a new control onto the design grid from the Controls group in the ribbon, click the control type button in the Controls group. By default, Access drops new controls from the ribbon into the last control position on right side of the screen. If you have many controls on your design grid, you might have to scroll to the right to see your new control. Save the design changes you've made to the Datasheet view for the Vendors table, and close the view before moving on to the next section.

INSIDE OUT   Mitigating scrolling with many fields in Datasheet views

If you have a lot of fields in a Datasheet view, users of your web app might need to scroll often to see and interact with the data you want to display. Depending on the number of fields you need to display, the amount of scrolling could impact the usability of your datasheets, especially if the user has scrolled so far to the right that they don't know what record they're viewing. To avoid excessive scrolling, consider placing only key fields into your Datasheet views. You can then include a command button, for example, that allows users to open a pop-up view that displays all the fields for that record in a List Details or Blank view. Using this technique, users of your app can have the benefits of seeing many records at the same time, edit data quickly in the datasheet, and view additional fields for a record in a pop-up view without having to scroll quite as much.

Working with views in a web browser

Now that you're familiar with designing quick-created List Details and Datasheet views in Access web apps, let's learn how to work with those views in a web browser. To open your app in a web browser, save any pending changes you might have to open objects and then click the Launch App command in the View group on the Home ribbon tab, as shown in Figure 6-58.

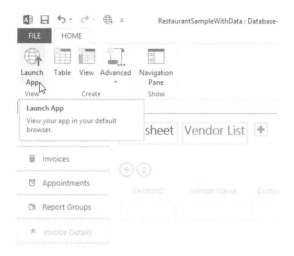

Figure 6-58 Click the Launch App button on the ribbon to open your app in your web browser.

INSIDE OUT   **Opening your web app to a specific view**

If you want to open your web app to a specific view, select the view caption name in the View Selector within Access, click the Settings/Actions charm button next to the view name, and then click Open In Browser on the shortcut menu. Access opens your default web browser and navigates to that specific view.

Access opens your default web browser and navigates to your web app, as shown in Figure 6-59. Access Services displays your App Home View in runtime, selects your first table in the Table Selector, and displays the first view attached to the selected table. By default, Access Services displays the quick-created List Details view first. However, earlier in this chapter, you swapped the display order positions of the two views attached to the Vendors table, so Access Services displays the Datasheet view first for this web app.

Figure 6-59 Access Services displays your App Home View with tables and views.

INSIDE OUT   Locating your web app URL

If you cannot remember the URL to your Access Services web app but you have the web app open in Access, you can always find the URL on the Backstage view. Click the File tab on the Backstage view, and then click the Info tab. Access displays the URL beneath the web app name. If you click the URL on the Info tab, Access displays a drop-down list with two options—Copy Link To Clipboard and Open File Location. Click Copy Link To Clipboard, and Access copies the full URL to the Windows Clipboard. You can then paste the link in your web browser to navigate to your web app. Click Open File Location to open the SharePoint site hosting your Access Services web app in your default web browser.

The App Home View in your browser functions in much the same way as in design mode within Access. For example, if you click the Invoices table caption in the Table Selector in your web browser, Access Services selects that caption, changes the view caption name in the View Selector to show the list of views attached to the Invoices table, and then loads the first view attached to the Invoices table in the app view window. Access Services also bolds the selected table caption name in the Table Selector and the selected view caption name in the View Selector to indicate which table and view currently has focus. To switch views, click a different view name caption in the View Selector. Access Services bolds the view caption text and loads the new view in the app view window.

Let's explore, in your web browser, the List Details view for the Vendors table you modified earlier in this chapter. Select the Vendors table name caption in the Table Selector, if it isn't already, and then click the Vendor List view caption text in the View Selector. Access loads the view and displays the first record, as shown in Figure 6-60.

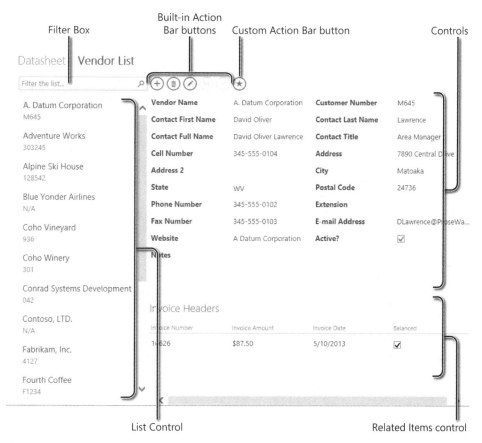

Figure 6-60 Click the Vendor List view caption in the View Selector to display the List Details view you modified previously.

We'll discuss each element of this List Details view displayed in a web browser in the following sections, but here is a brief overview of the view elements. On the left side of the view, you'll see the List Control. The List Control for this List Details view displays data from two fields in the Vendors table—VendorName and CustomerNumber. Use the List Control to navigate to different records in the Vendors table. You can use the Filter box, shown above the List Control, to search for specific records. To the right of the Filter box, you'll see the Action Bar buttons. The Action Bar for this view contains the five built-in buttons for List Details views along with one custom Action Bar button you created previously. (The custom

Action Bar button currently performs no action, because we didn't define any macro actions for the button.) Beneath the Action Bar, you'll see the various controls for the fields defined in the Vendors table. At the bottom of the view, you'll see the Related Items control. This control displays related invoices for each displayed vendor in the main view.

Navigating to records using the List Control

The List Control is an essential part of List Details views. As you learned earlier in this chapter, you can set properties on the List Control to display data from two fields in your view's record source and an optional thumbnail image from an Image data type field. The List Control for this List Details view displays data from the VendorName field in the Vendors table as the primary display field. Earlier in this chapter, you also selected to display the data from the CustomerNumber field as the secondary display field in the List Control. Access Services displays the primary display field data with a slightly larger font size than the secondary display field data, previously shown in Figure 6-60. We currently do not have an Image data type in the Vendors table, so we do not have the option of displaying thumbnail images in the List Control for this view. Access Services displays the records in ascending order of the VendorName field data in the List Control.

When you select display values in the List Control, Access Services changes the data values shown in the right side of the view to correspond with the record data selected. To practice this, click the Conrad Systems Development display text in the List Control. Access Services navigates you to this record in the view's record source and displays the data corresponding to this vendor's record in the controls, as shown in Figure 6-61.

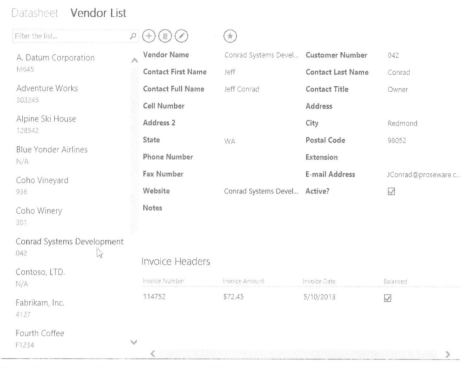

Figure 6-61 Access Services navigates to a different record when you click display text in the List Control.

Access Services displays a scroll bar along the right side of the List Control if there are more records to display than the current space allows. The number of records Access Services displays before needing to show a scroll bar depends on your screen resolution, the size of your browser window, the number of records in the view's record source, and whether Access Services shows primary and secondary display text or just primary display text.

You can also navigate to different records with the List Control by using keyboard shortcuts. You might find it easier to use the keyboard rather than the mouse to move around and select records in List Controls. Table 6-7 lists the keyboard shortcuts you can use for working in List Controls.

TABLE 6-7   Keyboard shortcuts for using List Control

Keys	Action
Page Up	Scroll up one page of display records
Page Down	Scroll down one page of display records
Home	Move to the first display field at the top of the list

Keys	Action
End	Move to the last display field at the bottom of the list
Up Arrow	Move up one record in the list
Down Arrow	Move down one record in the list

You cannot change any data displayed in the List Control; you can only view and select display text for record navigation in List Controls. To change data displayed in List Controls, you'll need to change the field values in the record source of the view using bound controls. I'll show you how to do this later in this chapter.

Filtering in views

Above the List Control in the List Detail view is the Filter box. In views that display a large number of records, locating a specific record can be difficult, so the Filter box feature makes this task easier. You can enter a search term in the Filter box, and Access Services searches across all displayed fields in the view and across all records from the view's record source. Access Services filters the list of records to those that contain the sequence of characters you enter in the displayed values. However, Access Services returns only those records where the sequence is at the beginning of a word; Access does not search for the sequence of characters within a word.

> **Note**
>
> At the time of this writing, Full Text Search is not enabled on Office 365. This means that you could see a difference of behavior in filtering on views between using an on-premise server running SharePoint 2013 and Access Services 2013 compared to Office 365. Full Text Search is enabled by default for on-premise installations. When Full Text Search is not enabled, Access Services uses a LIKE '%SearchString%' to filter the results. In this case, if you search for the text *con*, Access Services finds a record for Jeff Conrad, but searching for the text *rad* also returns a record for Jeff Conrad. With Full Text Search enabled, Access Services finds the record for Jeff Conrad using *con* but not *rad*.

Suppose you want to find a vendor record whose name contains the word Coho in this List Details view. Type the word **coho** in the Filter box. After you're finished entering your search criteria, you can either press Enter or click the Apply Filter button on the right side of the Filter box. (The Apply Filter button displays a magnifying glass icon.) Access Services finds two vendor records in this view that contain the text coho—Coho Vineyard and Coho Winery, as shown in Figure 6-62. Access Services conducts the search in a case-insensitive manner, which means Access Services returns these two records whether you searched for Coho, coho, or COHO. If you're searching across many records, you might see a loading progress message indicating that Access Services is currently executing the search and returning the filtered list of records.

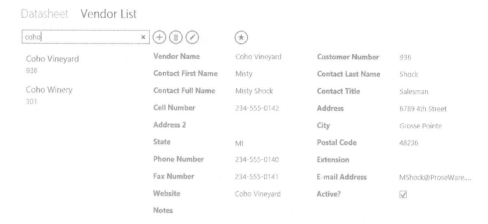

Figure 6-62 Access Services displays two records after searching for the word coho in the view's record source.

> **Note**
>
> If you have any controls bound to fields on the view with the Visible control property set to Hidden, Access Services does not use the values within those controls during its search. Access Services searches only for values displayed in the List Control and visible controls within the view.

To clear your filter string if you need to perform another record search, either delete the existing text using the Backspace key and then press Enter or click the Remove Filter button on the right side of the Filter box. Clearing the Filter box and pressing Enter or clicking the Remove Filter button restores the view to show all records from the view's record source.

> **Note**
>
> If you have lookup fields in your view that look up their values in other tables, Access Services searches across the display values of the lookup fields instead of the stored related AutoNumber ID values when you use the Filter box feature.

INSIDE OUT   Using keyboard shortcuts with the Filter box

You can quickly move the focus to the Filter box in your web browser to begin a search by pressing the forward slash key (/). Before pressing the forward slash, your focus must be either on the List Control or on a different part of the App Home View, except in an input control such as a text box in edit mode. You can also clear all existing text in the Filter box by placing your focus in the control and then pressing the Esc key. If you press Enter after pressing the Esc key, Access Services restores the view to show all records from the view's record source.

If you conduct a search using the Filter box feature, it's possible that Access Services won't find any records matching your search criteria. To see what happens in this case, clear any existing search string you might have in the Filter box for the Vendor List view you have open, type **Microsoft** into the Filter box, and then press Enter or click the Apply Filter button. Because there are no vendor names in this sample Vendors table with that name and no data in any other fields includes that text, Access Services returns no results. When your search returns no records, Access Services display two notifications, as shown in Figure 6-63. In the upper-right corner of your browser window, Access Services displays the text "No matches found" in a small pop-up notification window that appears on-screen for a few seconds and then disappears. Access Services also displays the text "There are no items to display" beneath the Action Bar. This text remains until you clear the existing search text from the Filter box, begin creating a new record, or navigate to a different view. You'll also notice in Figure 6-63 that Access Services does not display any controls or data in the List Control or in the view area if it could not find any matching records.

Figure 6-63 Access Services displays messages when it cannot find any matches for your search criteria.

INSIDE OUT   Searching over only one field

By default, Access Services searches across all fields visible in the view when you enter a search criterion into the Filter box. If you have many fields in your view, it might take Access Services a while to conduct the search because it has to check data across many fields. You can refine your search in the Filter box to search only one field instead of all visible fields by entering the field name followed by a colon and then your search criteria. For example, in the Vendor List view you have open, if you enter Proseware into the Filter box, Access Services returns all 16 vendor records because each vendor record contains the text Proseware in the email address field. But, what if you wanted to find only vendor records where the vendor name field contained the text Proseware? To do this, enter **VendorName:proseware** into the Filter box and press Enter. In this case, Access Services searches across data in the VendorName field only and returns one record whose vendor name matches the search—the Proseware, Inc. vendor record. Note that if your field name contains spaces, you must enclose the field name in quotation marks in the Filter box. For example, if your field name is Vendor Name, enter **"Vendor Name":proseware** into the Filter box to search across that one field.

If you separate your search criterion in the Filter box with spaces, Access Services searches across the view data for instances where each criterion appears. Essentially, this is the same as using the AND operator in a WHERE clause in a query. If you enter **Northwind Jay** (with the included space) into the Filter box in your current view, Access Services locates the Northwind Traders vendor record. Access Services finds the word Northwind in the vendor name field and also the word Jay in the contact first name field, even though the values are in separate fields. If you want to search for the specific text Northwind Jay as one value, enclose your search criterion within double quotation marks. Clear any existing filter you have in the Filter box and then run a new filter using **"Northwind Jay"** in the Filter box. Access Services does not locate the Northwind Traders vendor record this time, because it is searching for the text Northwind Jay together. When you enter a filter criterion within quotation marks, Access Services performs a search that matches on whole words only. Searching for "Jay" finds the record in the previous example, but searching for "North" returns no matches.

You can also use the Filter box feature to search across other data types besides text fields, such as dates and numbers. Because the Vendor List view you have open does not contain any Date/Time fields, let's switch to a different view so that you can see how the Filter box feature works with Date/Time data. Click the Invoices table name caption in the Table Selector. Access Services loads the default quick-created List Details for the Invoices table. (This view's caption name is called List in the View Selector.) This view includes a Date/Time field called InvoiceDate, which contains the date of each invoice in the sample web app.

Chapter 6

Enter **5/10/2013** into the Filter box, and press Enter. (Note that this date is May 10th in the United States.) Access Services returns two invoice records that have that date recorded in the InvoiceDate field, as shown in Figure 6-64.

Figure 6-64 Access Services displays two matching invoice records with the date 5/10/2013.

Access Services can also try to interpret your search criterion in the Filter box as a Date/Time value using other syntaxes. For example, Access Services locates the two matching records in the previous example if you enter any of the following into the Filter box: 5.10.2013, 5-10-2013, or 5/10/13. However, Access Services won't find the two matching records if you type out the date in Long Date format as May 10, 2013 into the Filter box unless you enclose the search in double quotation marks.

When you work with Date/Time fields and the Filter box, you should also be aware of time implications. If you enter a date into the Filter box, Access Services returns not only records that match that date, but also any records with Date/Time fields containing time values that occur anywhere within that date. If you enter a date and time value into the Filter box wrapped within double quotation marks, Access Services returns any Date/Time field values that match the level of precision that you specify. For example, searching for "5/10/2013 11:09 AM" (precise to the nearest minute) returns any values greater than or equal to 11:09 AM and less than 11:10 AM. In this case, Access Services finds a time value of 11:09:27. Similarly, if you specify seconds within your search, Access Services finds values that fall within that second. However, if you specify down to the millisecond in your search term, Access Services returns exact matches only. Access Services searches only time fields when you enter a time without a date in the Filter box. Note that when you specify a time in your search, Access Services defaults to AM (morning) unless you either explicitly specify PM (evening) in your search term or use 24-hour notation.

When you are using the Filter box feature to find Number and Currency data types, you need to be aware of potential rounding implications. Access Services rounds to the value you entered to the precision you used or starts with what you entered. In the Invoices List View you have open, one of the invoice records contains an invoice amount of $89.45. Access Services finds this record even if you search for the value **89.5,** because it finds numbers that either round to or begin with the search criteria. In this example, 89.45 rounds up to 89.50. The sample data for this view also includes a credit invoice entered as -5.195.

If you search for **-5.20** in the Filter box in this view, Access Services finds any values less than or equal to -5.195 and greater than -5.21. Access Services finds -5.195 with a search of -5.20 because -5.195 equals -5.20 when rounded to the nearest 1/100. Access Services therefore finds the credit invoice for the Northwind Traders when you search for -5.20. When you specify the extra significant digit of -5.20 instead of -5.2 in the previous example, Access Services returns different results. In this case, -5.2 returns results less than or equal to -5.15 and greater than -5.3.

INSIDE OUT   Using scientific notation with the Filter box

You can also use scientific notation to find matching number data in your views. One of the invoice records in the Invoices List Details view you've been using in this section contains an invoice amount of $15,202.00. If you enter **1.5e4** into the Filter box, Access Services finds that invoice record correctly during its search because 1.5e4 in scientific notation equates to 15202.

Access Services can also locate data represented as percentages. This sample app doesn't contain any numbers represented as percentages, but suppose you had the value 55% in a field. Access Services can find that record in a view if you type 55% or 0.55 into the Filter box and press Enter. You'll find the Filter box feature very useful in your List Details views to locate records quickly.

Note

Access does not display the Filter box on the design grid when you're designing your view; you'll see the Filter box only in runtime in your web browser. You cannot remove or hide the Filter box; it is part of the List Control in List Details and Summary views. (You'll learn about Summary views in Chapter 7.) The Filter box maintains the same width as the List Control, so if you reduce or increase the width of the List Control in the view, Access reduces or increases the width of the Filter box to match.

Understanding view and edit mode

When you browse to a List Details view in your web browser, Access Services displays the data in *view* mode by default. In view mode, you cannot edit data in any bound controls. Access Services displays the data in what appears to be label controls instead of the control types you defined for each field within Access. You can select and copy the data displayed to the Windows Clipboard, but you cannot change the data. You are allowed to interact with data displayed in Hyperlink, Combo Box, Autocomplete, or Related Items controls by navigating to other web addresses or opening related views, but in general, you cannot change data while in view mode. The purpose of view mode is for you to easily filter, browse, and navigate to records in your view without inadvertently changing data by mistake.

To see how view mode works, let's take a look at the List Details view based on the Vendors table again. Click the Vendors table name caption in the Table Selector, and then click the Vendor List view caption name in the View Selector. Access Services navigates to the view and displays the data from the first record in view mode, as shown in Figure 6-65.

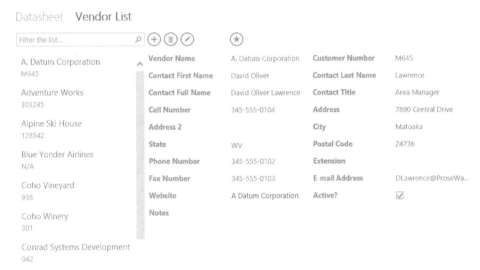

Figure 6-65 Access Services displays data in List Details views in view mode by default.

> ## Note
> **Access Services remembers the last view displayed against a selected table. If you were previously viewing the List Details view for the Invoices table and then clicked Vendors in the Table Selector, Access Services loads the Vendor List view instead of the default Datasheet view.**

You can see from Figure 6-65 that the data for each field in the vendor record displays and interacts much like a label control. However, the data in the Website field displays as a hyperlink. The Website field, as you recall, is a Hyperlink data type. In view mode, you can click the hyperlink and Access Services navigates to the web address defined in the field for the displayed record. You can activate the hyperlink for this field, but you cannot change the data in view mode.

In Figure 6-65, you'll also notice that three of the five built-in Action Bar buttons are enabled in view mode—Add, Delete, and Edit. The other two buttons, Save and Cancel, are not enabled in view mode. As you'll see in the next few sections, Access Services selectively enables or disables the built-in Action Bar buttons based on the state of the view. To add new records to your view or edit data on existing records, you must be in *edit* mode. In edit mode, Access Services displays the appropriate control type you defined for each field and enables you to add and edit data within the controls.

To switch to edit mode, you can click either the Add or the Edit Action Bar button. If you click the Add Action bar button, you can create new records in the current view. If you click the Edit Action Bar button, you can edit the existing data of the current displayed record. I'll show you how to create new records in just a moment, but for now, we'll explore edit mode on an existing record. Click the Edit Action Bar button, and Access Services switches the view into edit mode, as shown in Figure 6-66.

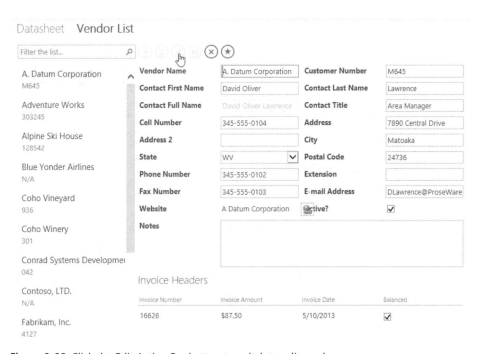

Figure 6-66 Click the Edit Action Bar button to switch to edit mode.

In addition to using your mouse to activate the five built-in Action Bar buttons, you can also activate each button using keyboard shortcuts. You might find it easier to use the keyboard rather than the mouse to activate each Action Bar button. Note that custom Action Bar buttons do not have keyboard shortcuts. Table 6-8 lists the keyboard shortcuts you can use for activating built-in Action Bar buttons.

TABLE 6-8 Keyboard shortcuts for using Action Bar buttons

Keys	Action
N	Places the view in edit mode for a new record
Delete	Deletes the current record displayed
E	Places the view in edit mode for the current record displayed
Ctrl+S	Saves any pending data changes to the current record displayed and switches the view back into view mode
Esc	Cancels any pending data changes to the current record displayed and switches the view back into view mode

When you switch to edit mode for this specific view, you'll notice several changes happen. First, the Cancel Action Bar button is enabled, but all other Action Bar buttons, excluding the custom one, are disabled. You can click the Cancel Action Bar button to cancel any pending data changes to the selected record and return to view mode. Second, you can now see the appropriate control type for each of the bound fields in the Vendors table next to their associated labels. Access quick-created these control types for this view. You can change the data in these fields now in edit mode. Finally, you'll notice that the text box for the Contact Full Name field appears dimmed. As you might recall from earlier in this chapter, you cleared the Enabled property for this control in Access. In edit mode, this control appears as a text box, but Access Services dims the control text and disallows you from changing data in this control even though you're in edit mode for the view.

Troubleshooting

Why can't I go into edit mode for my view based on a linked SharePoint list?
Views that include linked SharePoint lists in their record source are always read-only and cannot be edited. If you open a view in your web browser that includes a linked SharePoint list in the record source, Access Services disables all built-in Action Bar buttons to prevent you from entering into edit mode. If you attempt to edit data within a view that includes a linked SharePoint list in the record source through your own custom Action Bar buttons and macro actions, Access Services displays an error message and prevents the update.

Using special controls for data entry

As with table and query preview datasheets within Access, you must select a control in the view to change the data in the field in your web browser. To select a control, either tab to the control or click in the control with the mouse. (Remember, if the control contains a hyperlink, clicking in it will activate the link.) As you tab through different controls, Access Services bolds the font in the associated label control to indicate which control currently has focus. The tab order of the controls in the view is determined by the specific web browser you use. In general, the tab order is from left to right and top to bottom down the view. After you select a control, you can change the data in it by using the same techniques you used for working with data in datasheets within Access. You can type over individual characters, replace a sequence of characters, or copy and paste data from one control to another.

Combo boxes

Most of the controls in this view are text boxes bound to the various fields in the Vendors table, and their values can be changed by using the techniques just mentioned. Other controls present different input methods for data entry. Tab into the State field, which is represented by a combo box control. If you know the specific text you want to select in a combo box, you can type the value and Access Services displays that value in the control if it matches a value in the control's Row Source property. If you'd like to see all the values available in the combo box, click the down arrow on the right side of the control. To try this, click the down arrow on the right side of the combo box bound to the State field. Access Services displays a drop-down list of all state abbreviations within the United States, as shown in Figure 6-67. The default selected item, WV, matches the saved value for this vendor record.

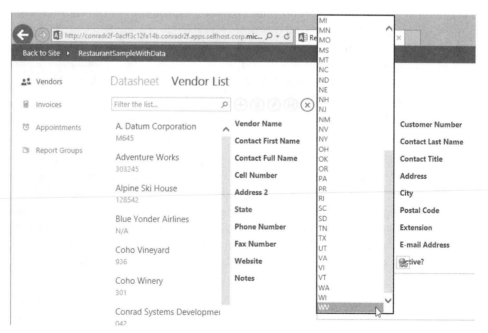

Figure 6-67 The combo box control bound to the State field displays a list of all state abbreviations.

Chapter 6

You can select a different value for this field by clicking a state abbreviation with your mouse. You can also select a value in the drop-down list by using the Up Arrow and Down Arrow keys to highlight a value up or down the list and then pressing Enter. Access Services collapses the drop-down list and displays your new selected value in the combo box. If you want to clear an existing value in a combo box, you can select the blank (or Null) option at the top of the list. If you expand the drop-down list by mistake, you can press Esc to collapse the list; however, Access Services also cancels any pending changes to other fields and switches the view out of edit mode and into view mode in this case.

INSIDE OUT   Using keyboard shortcuts to drop-down combo box values

You can also expand the drop-down list of a combo box if the control has focus by pressing Alt+Down Arrow.

Troubleshooting

Why do I not see all the values in my combo box?

Access Services supports displaying only 500 values in combo boxes. If the Row Source property defined for your control returns more than 500 values, Access Services lists the first 500 values. This means that you cannot select and save any values outside the first 500 returned. If you need to select a value from a table or query that contains more than 500 possible values, you should use an Autocomplete control instead, because that control type has no limitation on the amount of values you can potentially search for in the source table or query.

Hyperlink controls

Edit Hyperlink
button

The Vendor List view includes a hyperlink control that lets you specify the website address of the vendor. To add or edit a hyperlink, click the Edit Hyperlink button displayed to the right of the hyperlink control. (Remember that if the field contains a valid link, clicking in the control activates the link even in edit mode.) To try this, click the Edit Hyperlink button on the right side of the hyperlink control bound to the Website field. Access Services displays the Edit Hyperlink dialog box, shown in Figure 6-68, which lets you edit or define the link.

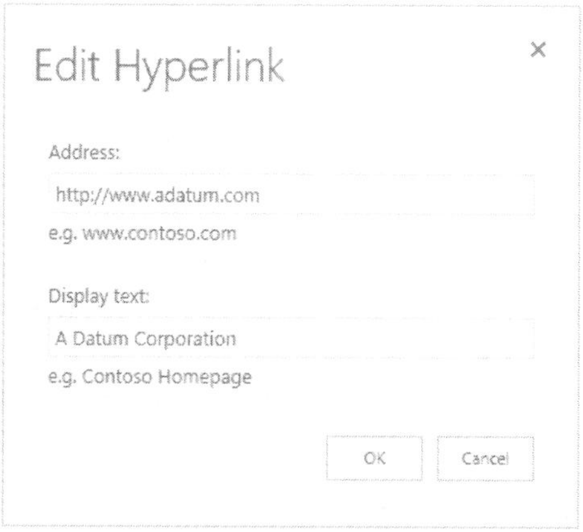

Figure 6-68 Use the Edit Hyperlink dialog to define and edit data for Hyperlink data types.

In the Address box, type the web address of the site you want Access Services to navigate to when a user of your app clicks the link. You can optionally provide a custom display text that Access Services displays in the hyperlink control in view and edit mode, instead of displaying the actual web address in the Display Text box. You might it useful to define text to display in the Display Text box if the web address in the Address box is especially long.

In Figure 6-68, you can see that this current vendor record includes a web address to the vendor's company website in the Address box. In the Display Text box, I've defined a custom display text by using the vendor's company name. After you enter your values in the Address and Display Text boxes, click OK to save and dismiss the dialog. If you do not provide display text for your hyperlink, Access Services copies the web address from the Address box and pastes the value into the Display Text box when you click the OK button to save and close the dialog. Click Cancel if you want to cancel any updates you made in the dialog and dismiss it. You can also click the Close (X) button in the upper-right corner of the dialog to cancel any updates and close the dialog.

INSIDE OUT   Moving the Edit Hyperlink dialog

By default, Access Services opens the Edit Hyperlink dialog in the middle of your browser window. You can move the dialog to a different position if you need to see data or controls beneath the dialog. To do this, position your mouse near the top of the dialog until your mouse pointer turns into a four-arrow cross hair. Click and hold your mouse, and then move the dialog to a new location within your browser window. The next time you open the Edit Hyperlink dialog, Access Services opens it in the middle of the browser window again.

Multiline text boxes

The Vendor List view includes a multiline text box control that lets you enter text about each vendor as notes. You add, edit, or delete data in multiline text boxes in the same way as you do text boxes. You can type over individual characters, replace a sequence of characters, or copy and paste data from one control to another. The main difference between a multiline text box and a text box is that when you press Enter in a multiline text box, Access Services moves your cursor to a new line in the control. If you press Enter in a text box, nothing happens. For example, you'll find multiline text boxes useful to display long descriptions of products in a products table or notes about meetings in an appointments table.

To practice using a multiline text box, tab or click into the multiline text box control bound to the Notes field in the Vendor List view. Enter the following text: **First line of notes.** Press Enter to move to the second line in the control, and then enter the following text on the second line: **Second line of notes.** Access Services displays the data over two lines in the control, as shown in Figure 6-69.

First line of notes.
Second line of notes.

Figure 6-69 Enter text onto separate lines using the Notes multiline text box control.

If the data displayed or saved in the control exceeds the height or width of the control, Access Services displays scroll bars within the multiline text box. You can use the scroll bars to view all of the data and position your cursor to a specific place in the data to make additions, edits, or deletions.

Check boxes

The Vendor List view includes a check box control to indicate whether the current vendor is an active vendor (a vendor that actively supplies you with products) or an inactive vendor (a vendor from whom you no longer purchase products). If you look at the check box bound to the Active field, you'll notice the check box for the current vendor is selected, as shown in Figure 6-70. A selected value indicates Yes for the field data, and a cleared value indicates No for the field data. To change the value of check boxes, you can either click in the control to toggle its value or tab into the control and then press the Space bar. Leave this value selected for this vendor record.

Figure 6-70 Check boxes display values from Yes/No data types.

Image controls

The Vendor List view does not include an image control, because there are no Image data types defined in the Vendors table. To familiarize you with working with image controls, let's add a new Image data type field into the Vendors table and then add this field to the Vendors List view. You'll also see how quickly you can make changes to tables and views and see the changes within your web browser.

Before we create an image field in the Vendors table, we first need to save the data changes we've made to the current vendor record. (Remember, you added data to the multiline text box bound to the Notes field.) If you have unsaved data changes to a record in a List Details view and attempt to navigate to a different record within the same List Details view using the List Control or attempt to navigate to a different view within the same web app, Access Services prompts you to save your changes with the Save Changes dialog, as shown in Figure 6-71.

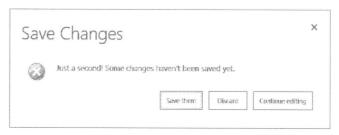

Figure 6-71 Access Services displays the Save Changes dialog when you have pending changes and attempt to navigate to a different record or view.

Click Save Them, and Access Services saves any pending data changes to the current record and continues navigating to the new view or new record to which you were navigating. If Access Services cannot save the record changes, perhaps because of a field or table level validation rule violation, Access Services stops the record update and keeps you on the same record and view. You'll need to correct any data issues before you can continue saving the record. Click Discard on the Save Changes dialog, and Access cancels any pending data updates to the current record and then continues navigating to the new view or new record to which you were navigating. Click Continue Editing, and Access Services returns focus to the current record and view with the uncommitted data changes still pending. Note that clicking the Close (X) button on the Save Changes dialog performs the same action as clicking Continue Editing.

If you attempted to navigate to a different record or view in the previous example, click Save Them to save the data changes you made to the first vendor record in the Vendor List view. If you did not attempt to navigate away, click the Save button now on the Quick Access Toolbar to save your changes. Whenever you save changes to a record, Access

Services briefly displays a notification message in the upper-right corner of your browser window, as shown in Figure 6-72.

Figure 6-72 Access Services displays a notification whenever you save changes to a record.

Now that you've saved the data changes you made to the vendor record, let's add an Image data type field to the Vendors table. To create the new Image data type field in the Vendors table and add it to the Vendor List view, do the following:

1. Switch back to Access where you have the web app open in design mode. You can keep the web browser open in the background if you want. If you have the Vendor List view open in Access, close the view before continuing.

2. Double-click the Vendors table name caption in the Table Selector to open the table in Design view.

3. Create a new field, called Company Logo, at the end of the list of fields, and select Image in the drop-down list of choices for the Data Type column. Save and close the table design view.

4. Double-click the Vendor List view caption name in the View Selector to open the view in Design view.

5. Reduce the width of the Notes multiline text box so that it has the same width as the Website field.

6. Open the Field List pane, if it isn't already open, by clicking the Add Existing Fields button on the Design contextual ribbon tab. Drag the Company Logo field from the top part of the Field List pane onto the design grid beneath the controls for the Active field. This action pushes the related items control down the grid.

7. Align the associated label for the Company Logo field with the other labels in the column, and resize the label to match the width of the other labels. Also, reduce the height of the image control by one grid height so that it matches the height of the Notes multiline text box.

8. Finally, move the related items control back up one grid height so that it is directly beneath the Notes and Company Logo controls. Save your view changes, close the view in Access, switch back to your web browser, and then use your browser's Refresh button to refresh the Vendor List view.

As you can see, making changes to your web app in Access and seeing those changes within your web browser can be very quick. You can easily make design changes to your app and try out your changes in your browser very quickly by switching between Access and your web browser. Now that you've made these design changes to the Vendors table and the Vendor List view, click the Edit Action Bar button to switch to edit mode for the Vendor List view. Your view should now look like Figure 6-73.

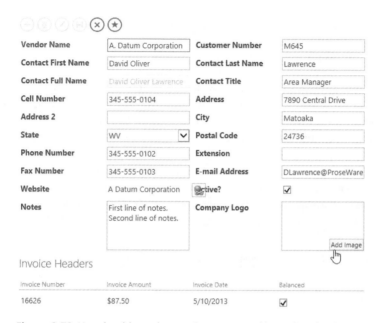

Figure 6-73 You should see the new image control bound to the Company Logo field beneath the Active field controls.

In Figure 6-73, you can see the image control you added bound to the Company Logo field. In edit mode, Access Services displays a button labeled Add Image in the lower-right corner of the control if no image is previously saved for the current record. If the field currently contains a saved image file, Access Services displays a button labeled Change Image in lower-right corner of the control. To add an image file to the current record for the Company Logo field, click the Add Image button within the image control. Access Services opens the Add Image dialog box, as shown in Figure 6-74.

Figure 6-74 Use the Add Image dialog to upload an image file into an image control on a view.

Access Services provides the Choose An Image text box for you to enter a location to upload an image file. If you know the location of the image file you want to upload, you can type the folder path and file name in the Choose An Image text box. The image file you want to upload must be less than 10 MB in size, and the file type must be a .gif, .jfif, .jpe, .jpeg, .jpg, or .png file extension. You can store one image file per field per record. Click the Remove Image link on the Add Image dialog to remove an image file previously saved in an Image data type field. If you do not know the exact folder and file path of the image file you want to upload or if you do not want to manually type in the image path, click Browse to open the Choose File To Upload dialog box, as shown in Figure 6-75.

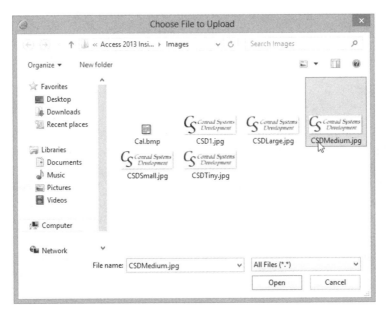

Figure 6-75 Click one of the company logo image files in the sample files folder to upload it to the Company Logo field.

You can select the drive and folder you want by clicking the links on the left and browsing to your destination folder. For this example, navigate to the Images folder of the sample files, which can be downloaded from the book's catalog page. Select the CSDMedium.jpg file in this folder. After you select the specific image file you want to upload, click Open to return to the Add Image dialog. Access Services displays your selected folder location and file name in the Choose An Image text box. If you decide not to upload the image file, click the Cancel button on the Add Image dialog to dismiss it and return to the view. Click OK on the Add Image dialog, and Access Services returns you to the view and displays the name of the image file in the image control, as shown in Figure 6-76.

Figure 6-76 After you browse for a file to upload, you'll see the name of the file listed in the image control.

Access Services displays the text Pending Upload within the image control. At this point, your image file is not saved with the record. If you click the Cancel Action Bar button now, Access Services does not upload the image, cancels any other pending data changes to the record, and switches out of edit mode and into view mode. Click the Save Action Bar button now to save your changes to this record. Access Services uploads the image file from your local hard drive and saves it into the Company Logo field. Access Services switches into view mode and displays the uploaded image in the image control, as shown in Figure 6-77.

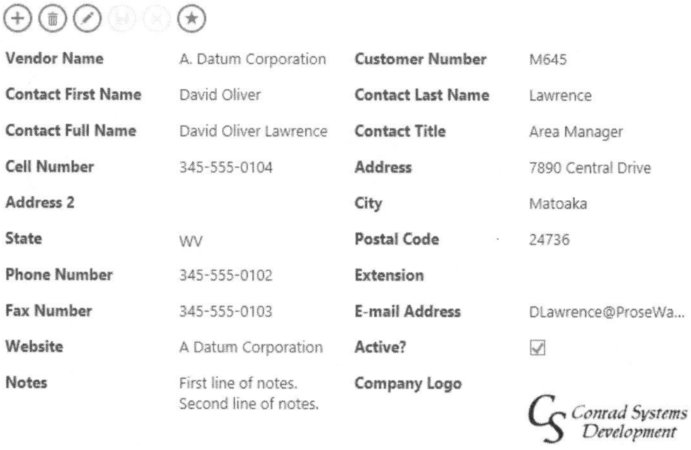

Vendor Name	A. Datum Corporation	**Customer Number**	M645
Contact First Name	David Oliver	**Contact Last Name**	Lawrence
Contact Full Name	David Oliver Lawrence	**Contact Title**	Area Manager
Cell Number	345-555-0104	**Address**	7890 Central Drive
Address 2		**City**	Matoaka
State	WV	**Postal Code**	24736
Phone Number	345-555-0102	**Extension**	
Fax Number	345-555-0103	**E-mail Address**	DLawrence@ProseWa...
Website	A Datum Corporation	**Active?**	☑
Notes	First line of notes. Second line of notes.	**Company Logo**	*CS Conrad Systems Development*

Figure 6-77 You can see your uploaded image file in view mode after saving your changes.

To remove an image field displayed in a bound image control or to change the image file stored in an existing record, you'll first need to switch into edit mode for the view. Next, click the Change Image button displayed within the image control to open the Change Image dialog. (Note that the Edit Image dialog is the same as the Add Image dialog except for a different title on the dialog.) Click the Remove Image link, and save your changes. To replace an existing image with another image, browse to a new image or type in the folder and file path with the Change Image and Choose File To upload dialogs. When you save your changes, Access Services removes the existing image and then uploads the new image into the image field.

Autocomplete controls

Now that you're familiar with using image controls, let's discuss a few other control types that you'll use frequently in Access web apps. For these next examples, we'll switch to a different view to see some different control types. (If you still have any pending changes on the Vendor List view, click the Save Action Bar button to save your changes before proceeding.)

Click the Invoices table name caption in the Table Selector to switch to the List Details view attached to the Invoices Headers table. (Previously in this chapter, you changed the table caption from Invoice Headers to Invoices. Also, notice that List is the view caption name in the View Selector for the List Details view of the Invoices Headers table.) If this view does not load by default, click List in the View Selector after you click Invoices in the Table Selector. Access Services displays the view and the first record in the Invoices Headers table in view mode, as shown in Figure 6-78.

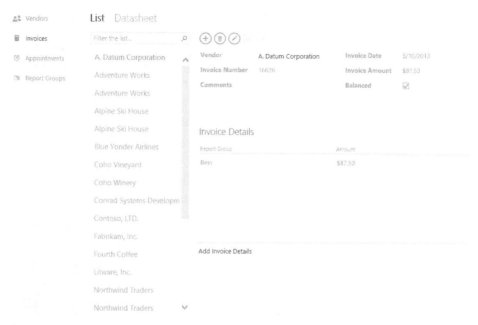

Figure 6-78 The List Details view for the Invoice Headers table displays invoice information using different control types.

> **Note**
>
> In Figure 6-78, the control and associated label with the text Vendor field is actually named VendorIDFK in the Invoices Headers table. Because I defined the Label Text field property to be Vendor at the table level for this field, Access Services uses Vendor for the Caption property of the associated control. I'll be referring to this field as Vendor in the next few sections, but remember that the field name in the table is actually VendorIDFK.

This view has two control types I haven't shown you yet in views in a web browser—autocomplete controls and date picker controls. When you create a lookup field that looks up data in another table, Access creates an autocomplete control on quick-created views to represent the field by default. Autocomplete controls function in a similar manner as combo boxes by fetching data from a table or query defined in the control's Row Source property. Autocomplete controls and combo box controls possess a unique feature that allows you to interact with their data in view mode.

The autocomplete control for the Vendor field, shown previously in Figure 6-78, displays the name of the vendor to which the invoice is assigned. Related data displayed in autocomplete controls in view mode display as a link, if you define a view name in the Popup View control property. When you click data displayed as a link in autocomplete controls (and combo boxes), Access Services opens a different view as a pop-up window so that you can see and edit data from the related table. To try this, click the A. Datum Corporation text displayed as a link in the Vendor autocomplete control for the first record in this view. Access Services opens the quick-created List Details view for the Vendors table you previously studied as a pop-up window, as shown in Figure 6-79.

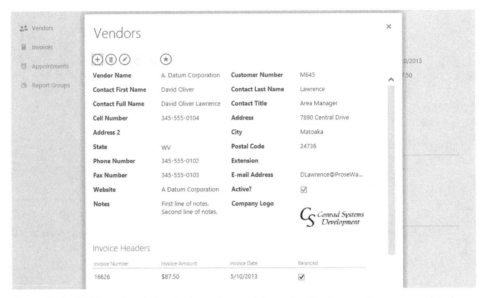

Figure 6-79 Clicking related data in the autocomplete control in view mode opens a related view as a pop-up window on top of other browser windows.

When you open a view as a pop-up window from autocomplete and combo box controls in view mode, Access Services displays the view on top of other windows. Notice, in Figure 6-79, that Access Services also dims the view displayed underneath the pop-up window. You cannot interact with any view elements on views displayed underneath other views opened as pop-up windows. To close a view opened as a pop-up window, click the Close (X) button in the upper-right corner of the view window or press Esc.

You'll recognize not only the view opened as a pop-up window in Figure 6-79, but also the specific record displayed. The vendor record displayed in the pop-up view is the A. Datum Corporation record you modified previously. The first invoice record for the Invoices List Details view is assigned to the A. Datum Corporation record, so when you click that vendor's name in the autocomplete control, Access Services opens the Vendors List Details view and navigates to that vendor's record. From the pop-up view, you can see the details of the vendor and even make changes to the record by clicking the Edit Action Bar button on the pop-up view. If you make any changes to the vendor record here, you'll see those same changes if you navigate back to the Vendors List Details view in the Table and View Selector.

The Popup View control property for autocomplete and combo box controls determines which view Access Services opens when you click the data displayed in view mode in your web browser. If you examine the Popup View control property for the autocomplete control bound to the VendorIDFK field for the Invoices List Details view within Access, you'll see that Vendors List is the name of the view defined for this property.

You might be wondering why, in Figure 6-79, you don't see the List Control portion of the List Details view. Whenever you open a List Details type view as a pop-up view for auto-complete and combo box controls from view mode, Access Services hides the List Control portion of the view. Access Services assumes that you want to view the specifics of the indi-vidual related record displayed in the control and not view all the records from the related table. You cannot override this behavior of hiding the List Control portion for List Details views opened as pop-up views through the Popup View control property. If you want to navigate to other records in this scenario, you'll need to create user interface macros, per-haps defined in custom Action Bar buttons, to navigate to different records in the view. You'll learn how to create user interface macros in Chapter 8.

> **Note**
>
> If you do not define a view name in the Popup View property for autocomplete and combo box controls, Access Services does not display related data as a hyperlink in view mode. Access Services displays the data as normal text, which means that you cannot open a view to see the related record details. You might want to leave the Popup View property blank in some cases, such as when you are viewing data that you do not want users of your app to modify.

In Figure 6-79, you'll notice that Access Services displays the text Vendors in the upper-left corner of the popup view. When you previously customized and opened this view from the Table and View Selector, Access Services did not display that text within the view. This text is defined in the view's Caption property, and Access Services displays the caption text within the view itself only when you open it as a pop-up view. If you want to change the default text Access defined for this property (the name of the source table), you can open the view in Design view from within Access and change the Caption property text.

We don't need to change any data for this vendor record displayed here in the pop-up view, so close this Vendors pop-up view by clicking the Close (X) button in the view win-dow. Access Services closes the pop-up view and returns focus to the Invoice List Details view.

To see how autocomplete controls work in the web browser in edit mode, let's create a new invoice record in this view. To create a new record in a List Details view, click the Add Action Bar button or press N if your focus is on the List Control. Access Services switches the view into edit mode for a new record and places the insertion point in the first enabled control, the autocomplete control bound to the Vendor field, as shown in Figure 6-80. Notice that, in Figure 6-80, I moved the focus to the Invoice Number text box so that you could see the default Input Hint control property text Access applied to the autocomplete control for the Vendor field.

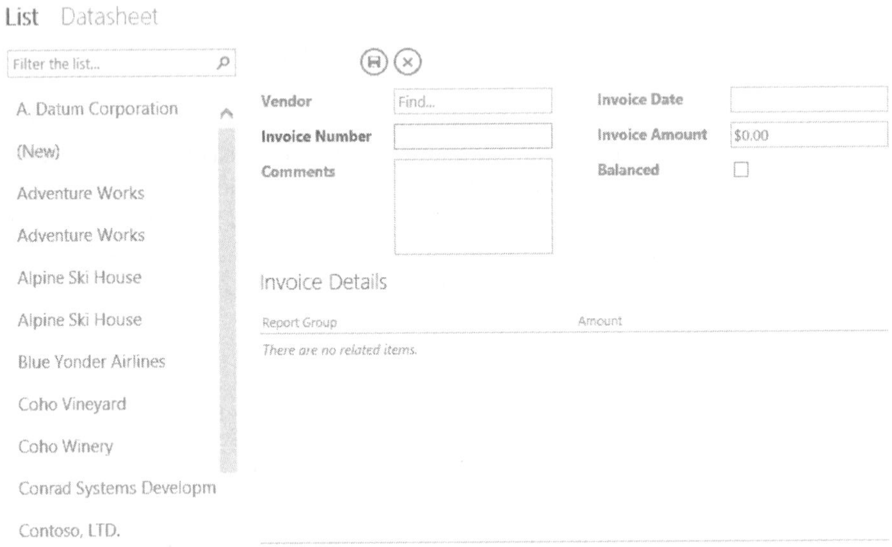

Figure 6-80 Click the Add Action bar button to begin creating a new invoice record.

Notice that when you start to create a new record in a List Details view, Access Services places a new entry in the List Control with a display value of (New) to indicate that you are on a new record. Access Services uses this placeholder to designate the new record. If you click the Cancel Action Bar button at this point, Access Services removes this placeholder from the List Control. Access Services positions this placeholder in the List Control beneath the record you viewed previously before you clicked the Add Action Bar button. Your focus was in the first record before clicking the Add Action Bar button, so the new record placeholder is shown second in the List Control display order.

> **Note**
>
> If you navigate to a bound view that has no records in the data source and the view allows record updates, Access Services opens the view to a new record in edit mode by default so that you can begin entering records.

Access Services fills in any values into the controls that have Default Value field properties or control properties defined on new records. In Figure 6-80, you'll notice that the Invoice Amount currency field displays $0.00. The Default Value field property at the table level for the InvoiceAmount field is 0. Because this field is also a Currency data type with the US dollar symbol ($) defined for the Currency Symbol field property, Access Services displays the formatted $0.00 for new records. If you save an invoice record without making changes to the value in this control, Access Services saves 0 into the InvoiceAmount field for the new record.

When opening to a new record with List Details views, Access Services displays the text, "There are no related items," in the related items control by default, if the view contains this type of control. Because you are creating a new invoice record, you haven't created any related records in the Invoice Details table for this new invoice yet. If you compare Figures 6-78 and 6-80, shown previously, you'll also notice that for an existing invoice record (Figure 6-78), Access Services displays a link labeled Add Invoice Details beneath the related items control. For a new invoice record (Figure 6-80), Access Services displays no link beneath the related items control. We'll explore how to work with related items controls later in this this chapter.

Access also defines an Input Hint control property text (the word Find followed by three dots) for the autocomplete control, but you can change the text within Access to be more descriptive. Autocomplete controls look like regular text box controls in your web browser when they don't contain data, so having a defined Input Hint property text can help users of your app distinguish that the behavior of these controls differs from text boxes.

Autocomplete controls do not display a drop-down list of potential choices until you type text into the control. Autocomplete controls have no limitation on the quantity of values they can potentially "look up" from their source table or query. (In contrast, combo boxes include a down arrow on the right side of the control, which you can click to see all available options. A combo box control is also limited to displaying 500 values.) To use an autocomplete control, type the value you want to look up in the control. After you stop typing, Access Services queries the table or query defined in the Row Source property, looking for records that contain the sequence of characters you enter anywhere in the field that is defined in the Primary Display Field control property.

To begin creating a new invoice record, we need to select a vendor from the Vendor auto-complete control. Tab into the Vendor control, and notice that Access Services removes the Input Hint text when the control receives focus. If you know the specific vendor you want to select in an autocomplete control, you can begin typing a few characters of the vendor name in the control. We'll assign this invoice record to the Conrad Systems Development vendor, so type **con** into the Vendor autocomplete control. As you enter each let-ter and pause for a moment in the control, Access Services begins returning the vendors, whose names contain the characters you entered in the search string, in a drop-down list, as shown in Figure 6-81. With each successive letter you type, Access Services reduces the list of vendor records shown in the drop-down list, because there are fewer vendor names that match your search criteria. Notice that as soon as you type the letters con, Access Ser-vices reduces the list to three vendors. The names of these vendors contain the letters *con* together somewhere in their name. If you continue to type *conrad* into the autocomplete control, Access Services displays only the Conrad Systems Development vendor.

Figure 6-81 Autocomplete controls display values after you type values to search.

Autocomplete controls display only eight items in the drop-down list. If your search text returns more than eight records, Access Services displays text at the bottom of the drop-down list, indicating that more results were found. You should continue typing more text to further reduce the list. Remember, even though autocomplete controls display up to eight items only in their drop-down list, they can search over all values from the Row Source property. If your search term returns no records, Access Services displays No Matches Found at the bottom of the drop-down list. You'll need to search with different text to find a lookup value that exists in your source table or query.

INSIDE OUT   Closing an autocomplete drop-down list

To dismiss a drop-down list displayed in an autocomplete control without making any selection, press Esc. Access Services closes the drop-down list and leaves the entered text in the autocomplete control. If you press Esc a second time, Access Services cancels all pending data changes to the current record and places the view back into view mode.

In Figure 6-81, you'll notice that the autocomplete control for the Vendor field also displays the full name of the vendor contact in smaller text beneath the vendor name. I defined the ContactFullName calculated field from the InvoiceHeaders table as the Secondary Display Field control property for this control. Access does not assign a field as the Secondary Display Field for autocomplete controls on quick-created views. If you want to use the secondary field for distinguishing between similarly named lookup values, you'll need to define this property yourself within Access in Design view. You're not required to define a Secondary Display Field property for autocomplete controls, but users of your app might find it useful to see extra information about each item in the drop-down list in some cases. When you type text into an autocomplete control, Access Services searches for matching text within the Primary Display Field text only and excludes searching within the Secondary Display Field text.

If you define a view to open in the Popup View property for autocomplete and combo box controls, Access Services displays <Add A New Item> at the bottom of the drop-down list, shown previously in Figure 6-81. If you click this option in the drop-down list, Access Services opens the view defined in the control property (Vendors List, in this case) as a pop-up window and places the view in edit mode on a new record. You can use <Add A New Item> at the bottom of the drop-down list if you want to add a record to the related table.

For example, assume that you are entering a new invoice record into this view and discover that you need to create a new vendor, because you are receiving product from this vendor for the first time. You could cancel the invoice record, navigate back to the views based on the Vendors table, create a new record for the vendor in one of those views, navigate back to the Invoices views, and finally create your new invoice record. However, a much easier method is to use the <Add A New Item> item at the bottom of the drop-down list for the Vendor autocomplete control. You can select that item, add a new vendor record in the pop-up view, save it, and then select that new vendor, without having to leave the context of the invoice record you're creating. You'll find this feature very useful especially when you just beginning to add new data to your web app.

Let's continue creating our new invoice record. Select Conrad Systems Development from the drop-down list of the Vendor autocomplete control. If the drop-down list is no longer showing, type **con** into the control again and select Conrad Systems Development before moving on to the next section.

Date Picker controls

Date Picker
button

After you've entered Conrad Systems Development into the Vendor autocomplete control, tab over to the Invoice Date field. This control is a text box control and is bound to the InvoiceDate field. The InvoiceDate field in the Invoice Headers table is a Date/Time field. Access Services displays a Date Picker button to the right of the text box control bound to any Date/Time fields. You can manually type in a date (or a date and time, if the field format is set to include a time portion) into the text box control, but in most cases, you'll find it easier to use the Date Picker control to select a date. Click the Date Picker button on the right side of the text box bound to the InvoiceDate field. Access Services displays the Date Picker control beneath the text box, as shown in Figure 6-82.

Figure 6-82 Use the Date Picker control to select a date quickly in your views.

The Date Picker control displays the dates of one month at a time as numbers in columns and rows in much the same way as the Windows Date/Time control. The top row of the control displays a single letter representing the day of the week. The remaining rows display numbers that coincide with the day in the displayed month. For example, in the United States, the first column of data represents dates falling on a Sunday within the displayed month. Depending on the displayed month and year, you might see numbers in the first or last row representing days from the previous month or next month after the displayed month. (Access Services displays previous month and next month days with a slightly lighter font color to distinguish them from the current month.) By default, Access Services opens the Date Picker to the current month and year if your field contains no date value. If your field contains a date, or date and time, Access Services opens the Date Picker to the month and year that coincides with the field value.

Access Services lists the current displayed month and year at the top of the Date Picker control. At the bottom of the Date Picker control, Access Services displays a link with the current day, month, and year. When you click this link, Access Services changes the displayed values in the Date Picker control to the current month and year no matter where your starting displayed month might have been. You'll find this link helpful to quickly navigate to and see the days from the current month.

To select a day in the Date Picker control, click the date you want or use your arrow keys to highlight the date you want and press Enter. If you need to navigate to a previous month, click the left arrow button in the upper-left corner of the Date Picker control. Access Services changes the dates displayed in the Date Picker control to the previous month. You can continue clicking the left arrow button to move back to previous months and years. Similarly, click the right arrow button in the upper-right corner of the Date Picker control to move forward one month.

INSIDE OUT   Using keyboard shortcuts with Date Picker controls

If your focus is in a text box control bound to a Date/Time field, you can press Alt+Down Arrow to display the Date Picker control. Use your arrow keys to navigate to different days within the displayed month. To select a date with the keyboard, navigate to the date you want using the arrow keys and then press Enter. You can also use Tab and Shift+Tab to navigate to different days, similar to the left and right arrow keys. If you use Shift+Tab to move focus up to the previous or next month buttons and press Enter, Access Services changes the dates displayed in the Date Picker control to the previous month or next month, respectively. To dismiss the Date Picker, press Esc or press Enter on a date.

For the invoice record you've started, select any date from the Date Picker control. (The current date is fine for this example.) Access Services closes the Date Picker control and displays your selected date in the Invoice Date text box. Access Services formats the selected date to match the format defined at the table level or at the control Format property level.

You've now provided a vendor name in the Vendor autocomplete control and a date for the invoice in the Invoice Date text box using the Date Picker control. You haven't provided data for all the fields yet, but let's see what happens when you try to save the invoice record at this point. Click the Save Action Bar button on this view, or press Ctrl+S. Access Services moves your cursor focus to the Invoice Number text box control, highlights the control with a red border, and displays a message below the control indicating that you must provide a value for this field, as shown in Figure 6-83.

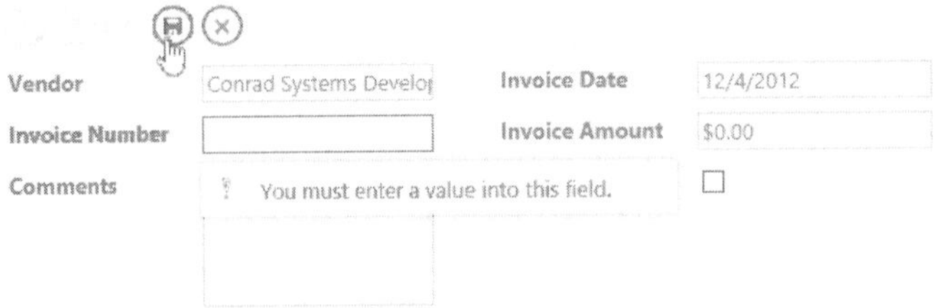

Figure 6-83 You'll see this error message when you do not provide data for required fields.

Access Services cannot save records if data for required fields is not provided. Both the InvoiceNumber and InvoiceAmount fields in the Invoice Headers table are required fields. Access Services changes the border color of the control to red as a visual cue that the data you entered (nothing, in this case) won't pass the Required field property. (The text box control bound to the InvoiceAmount contains a default value of zero, so the data in that control can pass the Required field property check.) However, because you did not specify any data in the Invoice Number control, Access Services cannot proceed with the record save.

> **Note**
> If you attempt to save data in a view that won't pass a field or table level validation rule, Access Services displays an error message in a pop-up dialog. If you define a custom message in the Validation Text property, Access Services displays your custom text in that pop-up dialog.

Let's continue with saving this invoice record by providing an invoice number. Tab or click into the text box control for the Invoice Number, and enter **Invoice A**. Next, tab or click into the Invoice Amount control, and enter **100**. Access Services displays the currency symbol in front of your value after you tab or click out of the control. The Comments field and the IsBalanced fields are not required fields, so you can leave the Comments multiline text box control and the Balanced check box empty. Click the Save Action Bar button now, and Access Services saves your new invoice record, as shown in Figure 6-84.

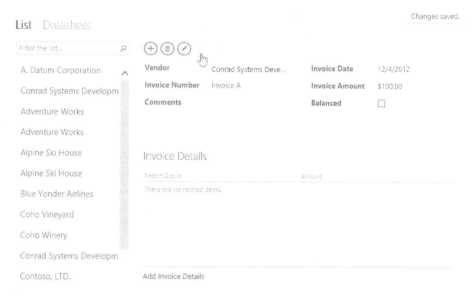

Figure 6-84 Click the Save Action Bar button to save your new invoice record.

You'll notice a few things changed in the view after you saved the invoice record. First, Access Services switched out of edit mode and into view mode where you can no longer edit the data in the displayed record. You'll need to switch back into edit mode to make further changes to the record, by clicking the Edit Action Bar button. Second, the text in the Vendor autocomplete control changed to a hyperlink, because you are now in view mode again. If you click the Conrad Systems Development link displayed in the autocomplete control, Access Services opens the Vendors List view and displays that vendor's record. Third, the List Control of the view displays the vendor name for this invoice instead of the (New) text displayed with a new record. Note that the display order here in the List Control is only temporary. If you refresh your browser or navigate to a different view and come back, Access Services sorts the List Control by the properties defined within Access. Your new record might not be in the same order that you see at this point.

Related items controls

One drawback to working with a relational database is that you often have to deal with information stored in multiple tables. That's not a problem if you're using a query to link data; however, working with multiple tables can be confusing if you're entering new data. Access web apps provide some great ways to show information from related tables, thus making data input much simpler. One of the ways Access web apps allow you to easily enter and view related data from multiple tables is through the related items control.

In the Invoices List Details view you've been working on in the previous sections, you've no doubt noticed the related items control at the bottom of the view. In Figure 6-84, shown previously, you can see that after you save the new invoice record, Access Services displays an Add Invoice Details link at the bottom of the control. Until you save a record in the main view, called the *parent* view, you cannot add new records to related table in a related items control.

Now that you've created a new invoice parent record, you can enter the specific invoice detail records, called the *child* records, using the related items control. As you recall from Chapter 3, the Invoice Details table contains a lookup field, InvoiceIDFK, to the Invoice Headers table. This lookup field forms a relationship between the two related tables. The Invoice Details table lists all the child records of the Invoice Headers table, and the child records are linked through the InvoiceIDFK lookup field. Access Services maintains the link between the main view record and the data displayed in the related items control through the Related Field property of the control. If you examine this view in Design view within Access, you'll see that when Access quick-created this List Details view, it identified the relationship between the two tables and defined the InvoiceIDFK lookup field for the Related Field property of the related items control.

To see how to add related data to another table using a related items control, click the Add Invoice Details link at the bottom of the control. Access Services opens the quick-created List Details view for the Invoice Details table as a pop-up window, as shown in Figure 6-85.

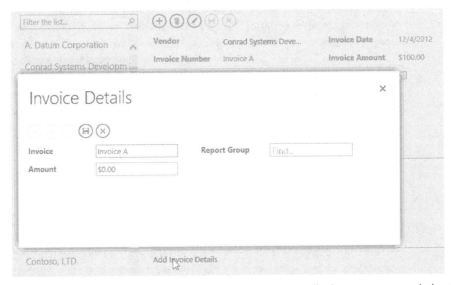

Figure 6-85 Click Add Invoice Details to open the Invoice Details view as a pop-up window from the related items control.

Similar to the autocomplete and combo box control feature when you open a view as a pop-up window from a related items control, Access Services displays the view on top of other windows. Notice, in Figure 6-85, that Access Services also dims the view displayed underneath the pop-up view. You cannot interact with any view elements on the main parent view displayed underneath, but you can move the pop-up window if you need to see data on the main view. Also, when you open a List Details view as a pop-up view from a related items control, Access Services hides the List Control portion of the view.

The quick-created List Details view for the Invoice Details table displays three controls and associated labels—Invoice, Report Group, and Amount. In Figure 6-85, you'll notice Access Services filled in Invoice A into the Invoice autocomplete control for you when it opened the view. The main view record you are looking at is the Invoice A record you previously created and saved. Because you now want to create related child records for that invoice through the related items control, Access Services assumes you want to assign these child records to that main view record and fills in the related field value for you—Invoice A, in this case. You could choose a different invoice by typing a different value into the autocomplete control, but the record won't show in the related items control after you save the record, because the main view displays a different parent record.

Let's create two detail child records for our main invoice record. Start by tabbing over to the Report Group autocomplete control. Type **bre** into the control, and then select the Bread And Rolls report group from the drop-down list, as shown in Figure 6-86.

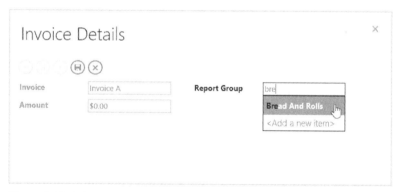

Figure 6-86 Select Bread And Rolls in the Report Group autocomplete control.

After you select the report group value, tab into the Amount text box control and enter **50** for the value. Click the Save Action Bar button to save your new record changes. Access Services saves your record changes and then switches from edit mode to view mode, as shown in Figure 6-87. You'll notice that Access Services changes the text to be links in both the Invoice and Report Group autocomplete controls. If you click these links, Access Services opens up another pop-up view on top of this pop-up view to see the related data.

You can easily and quickly view related data and return to your starting point without having to navigate to different views.

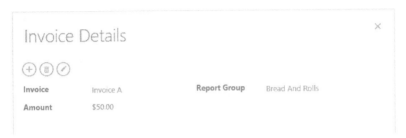

Figure 6-87 Click the Save Action Bar button to save your new record displayed in the pop-up window.

Let's create one more child detail record using this pop-up view. You could choose to close this pop-up view and then click the Add Invoice Details link beneath the related items control on the main view again; however, it's much easier to keep the pop-up view open and add more records as needed.

Click the Add Action Bar button to begin creating another record in this view. Notice that when you do this, Access Services fills in Invoice A again into the Invoice autocomplete control for you. Type **gen** in the Report Group control, select General Groceries from the drop-down list, and enter **50** into the Amount text box control. When you're finished entering your values, click the Save Action Bar button to save your changes and then close the pop-up view by clicking the Close (X) button in the upper-right corner. Access Services closes the pop-up view and then displays both of your new invoice detail child records in the related items control, as shown in Figure 6-88.

Invoice Details

Report Group	Amount
Bread And Rolls	$50.00
General Groceries	$50.00

Add Invoice Details

Figure 6-88 You can see both of your new related records displayed in the related items control.

You'll notice in Figure 6-88 that Access Services does not display the data from the linking InvoiceIDFK field in the related items control. By default, Access does not include the field defined in the Related Field property as one of the four output display fields when it quick-creates views with related items controls. You can add this field as a display field if you want, but it's not necessary because Access Services links and displays only related child records in the related items control based on the main view's parent record. When you hover over a record in a related items control, Access Services highlights the row and changes your cursor to a hand. When you click a record displayed in a related items control, Access Services opens the view defined in the Popup View property as a pop-up window and navigates to that record, where you can edit the detail record, delete the record, or add additional related records. If you do not define a view in the Popup View property, Access Services opens the related record when you click the display values in the control.

You can have more than one tab on a related items control displaying data from different related tables. If you examine some of the views found in the Back Office Software System sample web app (BOSS.app), which can be downloaded from the book's catalog page, you'll see several views containing related items controls with more than one tab. If you have more tabs defined for a control than can fit within the control's width, Access Services displays a link with three dots on the right side of the tab list at runtime, as shown in Figure 6-89. When you click this link, Access Services displays the tab names in a drop-down list. If you click one of the tab names in the drop-down list, Access Services cycles that tab into view.

Figure 6-89 Click the link with three dots to see more tabs on a related items control.

Using Datasheet views

Now that you know how to work with List Details views in your web browser, let's explore how to use Datasheet views within your web browser. Click the Invoices table name caption in the Table Selector (it should already be selected if you've been following along up to this point), and then click the Datasheet view caption name in the View Selector. Access Services loads the quick-created Datasheet view for the Invoice Headers table, as shown in Figure 6-90.

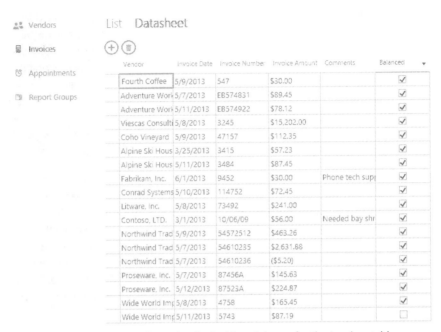

Figure 6-90 Select the Datasheet view in the View Selector for the Invoices table name caption.

Datasheet views displayed in your web browser function very much like table and query preview datasheets displayed in Access. If you've cleared the Read-Only view property for a Datasheet view (cleared by default), you can create new records, make changes to the data, and delete records within the browser window. To create a new record in a Datasheet view, you can click the Add Action Bar button or scroll to the bottom of the Datasheet view window until you see the new record line, and then enter your data on the new datasheet record. To delete a record, you can click the Delete Action Bar button or right-click the row selector on the left side of the Datasheet view, and then click Delete on the shortcut menu to remove the record. You can also use Ctrl+Delete to delete the current or selected record in a datasheet. If you attempt to delete a record in a Datasheet view, Access Services first prompts you with a message to confirm the deletion. (See Figure 6-91.) Click Yes in the message box to delete the record, or click No to cancel the deletion.

CAUTION

After you click Yes in the confirmation message box, you cannot restore the deleted records. You have to reenter the records or copy them from a backup if you want to restore the data.

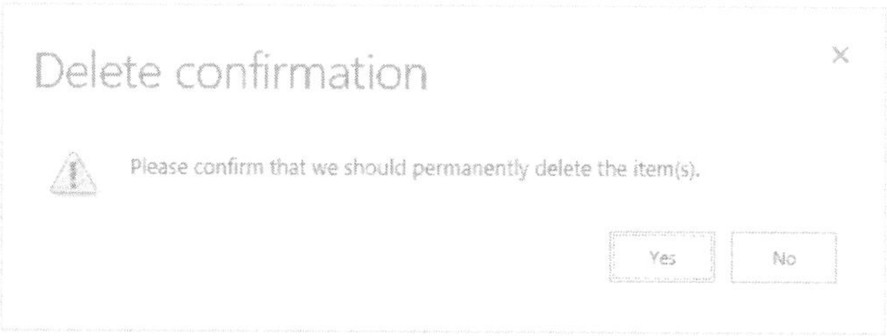

Delete confirmation   ×

⚠   Please confirm that we should permanently delete the item(s).

                                        Yes   No

Figure 6-91 This message box appears when you attempt to delete records in your web browser.

> **Note**
>
> When you attempt to delete a record that is part of a relationship through lookup fields, Access Services might prevent you from deleting the record, depending on how you set up the relationship. Access displays an error message telling you that related rows exist in other tables. For example, if you try to delete a report group record in the sample web app you've been working with in this chapter, Access Services prevents the delete if you used the report group in any records in the Invoice Details table.

You'll notice that Access Services does not display Save, Edit, and Cancel Action Bar buttons with datasheets. These Action Bar buttons are not required for datasheets, because the data interactions with datasheets differ from other views. To edit data in datasheets, you can click in a cell and edit the data. If you want to add to the existing data, select a cell and press F2 to go into edit mode for the cell, which positions your cursor at the end of the existing data. If you want to cancel any changes to the data in the cell, press Esc. (Note that unlike List Details views, you cannot undo all changes to all edited fields in a record using the Esc key. When you press Esc, Access Services reverts only the data in the current cell.) You can use the Tab and arrow keys to move around the datasheet and press Enter to move down a column. When you move to a new record, Access Services automatically attempts to save the record. When Access Services successfully saves any record changes, you'll see a Changes Saved message displayed briefly in the upper-right corner of the browser window.

Across the top of Datasheet views, you'll see column headers for each column of data. If you hover over the column header, Access Services displays a down arrow on the right side. Click the arrow button to open the AutoFilter menu. You can see that in Figure 6-92, I clicked the column header above the Vendor field to display the AutoFilter menu options available for this column.

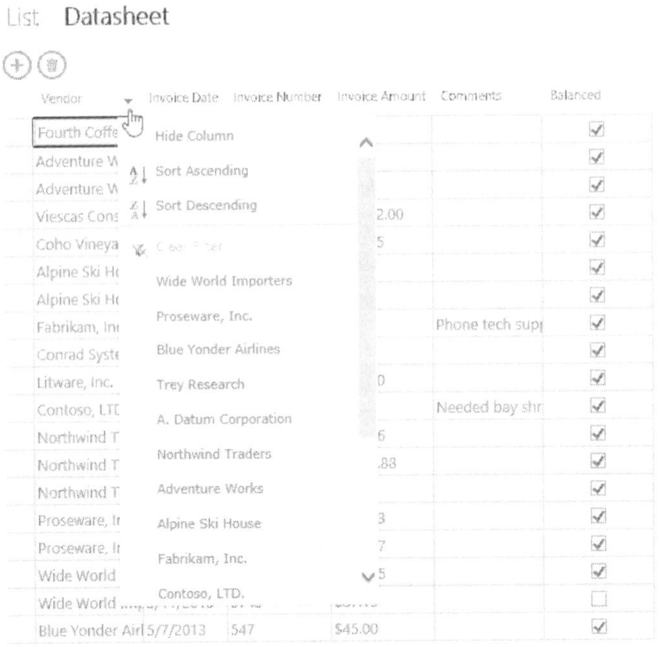

Figure 6-92 Access Services displays AutoFilter menu options for Datasheet views.

INSIDE OUT Using a keyboard shortcut to open the AutoFilter menu

You can open the AutoFilter menu above any column by pressing ALT+Backslash (\)
when you're not in edit mode for the cell.

At the top of the AutoFilter menu, you can click Hide Column, and Access Services hides
the column from view. (This change to the datasheet is not permanent. If you refresh the
browser or navigate away and come back to the view, Access Services displays the column
again.) Beneath Hide Column, you can click Sort Ascending or Sort Descending to sort the
records in ascending or descending order by that column. You can also click one of the
filter options to filter the records displayed in the Datasheet view to just the records that
match that filter criterion. You can filter by more than one option by dropping the AutoFilter menu down again and clicking another option. Click (Blank) when you want to filter the
data to show records where no value exists in that column. Click Clear Filter, near the top of
the AutoFilter menu, to clear the filters and see all the data from the view's record source.

You won't see all the options available in the AutoFilter menu, depending on the data type
of the column. For Hyperlink fields, Access Services doesn't display any filter options. When

you have a Yes/No field, Access Services displays No and Yes as the only filter options. For lookup fields that look up data in a table, Access Services displays each possible display value from the related source table as a filter option, even if they are not selected in any records.

> **Note**
>
> At the initial time of release for Access 2013, the filter options for lookup fields are displayed by ID order and are not sorted by display value order.

Troubleshooting

Why do I not see all of my possible values in the AutoFilter menu?
Access Services limits the number of filtering options to 500. If you have more than 500 unique possible values in the field, Access Services won't display all the possible options in the AutoFilter menu.

INSIDE OUT   Resize and move columns in Datasheet views

You can resize the width of the columns and reposition columns when you view datasheets in a web browser. To resize a column, position your mouse on the right edge of the column header until your cursor becomes a two-sided arrow. Click and drag the column header to the left to decrease the width of the column, or drag the column header to the right to increase the width of the column. To move a column, position your mouse over the column header until your cursor becomes a four-sided arrow. Click and drag the entire column header to the left or right to reposition the column. Access Services displays a vertical I-Bar to indicate where it will place the column when you release the mouse. Note that resizing and moving columns when you view the datasheet in a web browser is not permanent. If you refresh the browser or navigate away and then return to the view, Access Services displays the columns at their original widths and positions.

As you work with datasheets in your web browser, you'll notice that Access Services does not display data in autocomplete and combo box controls as links. The feature that exists in List Details and Blank views for opening related data in those control types does not exist in Datasheet views. If you examine autocomplete and combo box controls in Design view for datasheets, you'll see that the Popup View control property is not an option when you work with datasheets.

You should now have a good understanding of how to design and work with quick-created List Details and Datasheet views within Access as well as in the runtime using your web browser. You learned how to work with the view design surface in Access and how to navigate to different tables and views within your web browser. You should also be familiar with the different types of controls you can use in views and the different properties you can set with each control type. In Chapter 7, you'll learn how to create Summary and Blank views as well as design stand-alone views. We'll also explore the remaining control types and learn about more advanced view design topics, such as site themes and setting site permissions for your web app.

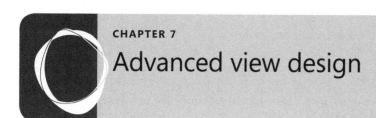

I N the previous chapter, you learned how to customize and work with quick-created List Details and Datasheet views. In this chapter, we'll discuss some more advanced view topics and how to apply these techniques to your Access web apps. You'll learn how to do the following:

- Create a Summary view that consolidates and groups information.

- Create a Blank view that displays one record at a time.

- Embed a subview in a main view so that you can work with related data from two tables or queries at the same time.

- Use web browser controls to display webpages from different sources in your views.

- Create views that are not displayed within any View Selector and can be opened only as a pop-up view.

- Apply different themes to Access web apps using SharePoint site themes.

- Understand how name fixup within Access affects your views and view controls.

- Explore some of the more complicated and advanced views defined within the Back Office Software System sample web app.

- Extend your web app with features inside Access desktop databases.

> **Note**
>
> The examples in this chapter are based on a restaurant management sample web app called RestaurantSampleChapter7.app and the BOSS.app sample, which can be downloaded from the book's catalog page at *http://aka.ms/Access2013IO/details.do*. You'll need to upload these apps into your corporate catalog or Office 365 team site and install the apps to use the samples. Review the instructions at the end of Chapter 2, "Exploring the Access 2013 web app interface," if you need help with those tasks. The data you see from the sample views you create in this chapter might not exactly match what you see in this book if you have changed the sample data in the web app.

Creating Summary views

In Chapter 6, "Working with views and the web browser experience," you learned how to customize and use List Details and Datasheet views quick-created by Access. Both of those view types allow you to not only view data, but also create, edit, and delete records. Summary views are a unique view type in Access web apps that consolidate and group data together. You cannot create new records, edit records, or delete records with Summary views; however, you'll find this very useful for grouping together common sets of records, in much the same way that reports function in Access desktop databases.

To begin our discussion of Summary views and other advanced view topics, you first need to install the RestaurantSampleChapter7.app sample web app in your SharePoint site and then download the app into Access to follow along with the examples in this chapter. If you've been following along with this book through Chapter 6, you can continue to use the sample web app you modified in Chapter 6 or install the sample app; both should be identical.

As you'll recall from Chapter 6, the Invoices table in the sample web app currently has a quick-created List Details and Datasheet view attached to it in the View Selector, as shown in Figure 7-1.

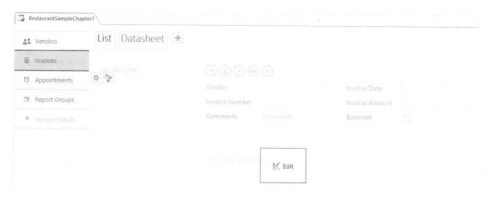

Figure 7-1 The View Selector for the Invoices table displays two quick-created views.

To create a new Summary view of the data in the Invoices Headers table, select the Invoices table name caption in the Table Selector and then click the Add New View button to the right of the Datasheet view name caption in the View Selector. (The Add New Button always displays to the right of the last view shown in the View Selector. Access Services does not display this button at runtime.) Access displays the Add New View menu, as shown in Figure 7-2. The Add New View button is your main entry point for creating new views in your app that are attached to the View Selector for selected table name captions in the Table Selector.

Figure 7-2 Click the Add New View button to create a new Summary view.

You can enter a name for the view you want to create in the View Name box. Each view name displayed in the Navigation pane must be unique. If you attempt to create a new view (any view type) with the same name as an existing view, Access displays an error message and prevents you from creating a new view. (If you opened the Add New View menu by mistake, you can click the Close (X) button in the upper-right corner of the menu to close it.) Now type **Invoice Summary** into the View Name box. Access displays a drop-down list of the four main view types in the View Type option—List Details, Datasheet, Summary, and Blank. Access, by default, selects List Details for this option whenever you use the menu to create a new view. Select Summary in this drop-down list to create a Summary view for our new view type.

In the Record Source option, Access displays a drop-down list of the table name that matches the underlying selected table caption in the Table Selector and the names of any queries that include that table in their source. Note that the table name caption in the Table Selector might not match the actual table name source. For example, in Figure 7-2 (shown previously), Access displays Invoice Headers in the drop-down list for the Record Source option. The name of the source table shown in the Navigation pane is Invoice Headers for this sample web app, but the corresponding table name caption displayed in the Table Selector is Invoices. Access always uses the actual names in the Record Source option. We don't have any queries defined in this app that use the Invoice Headers as one of its sources, so the only option Access displays in the Record Source drop-down list is the Invoice Headers table.

After you enter your view name and select Summary for the View Type, click the Add New View button on the menu. Access creates a new Summary view for your app called Invoice Summary, creates a view name caption in the View Selector that matches your selected view name, and displays a preview of the Summary view structure in the view preview window, as shown in Figure 7-3. If you do not have the Navigation pane currently expanded, you won't see the new view name listed, but you can verify that the view name exists by clicking the Navigation Pane button on the Home ribbon tab.

Figure 7-3 Access creates a new view caption name called Invoice Summary.

To open this new Summary view in Design view, click the Edit button in the middle of the view preview window. Access opens the view in Design view on its own object tab in the application window, as shown in Figure 7-4.

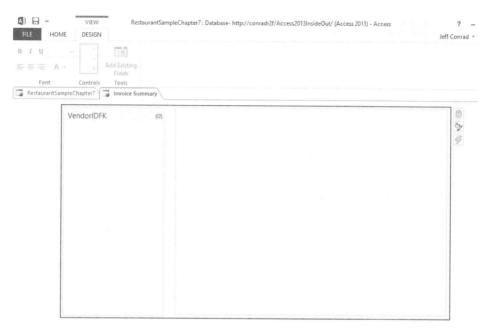

Figure 7-4 When you open a Summary view in Design view, you'll see fewer design options.

You'll notice immediately that the design surface and options available for Summary views are quite different compared to List Details and Datasheet views. On the Design contextual tab, you'll see that all options are disabled. You cannot set any formatting options on view controls, place any controls onto the design surface, or use the Field List with Summary views. If you have the Field List displayed with another view open on a different object tab, Access hides the Field List when you set focus to the Summary view object tab.

When you work with Summary views, Access displays no Action Bar buttons. Because Summary views are used for data consolidation and not data entry, Access does not create any built-in Action Bar buttons and you cannot define any custom Action Bar buttons for this view type.

In Figure 7-4, shown previously, you'll see that Access displays the three charm buttons for setting view properties along the upper-right corner of the view design window. The view properties available for Summary views are also more limited compared to other view types. The only option available on the Data property callout menu for Summary views is Record Source. Access displays the table or query name you selected when you first created the view; you cannot change the Record Source property after you create a Summary view. If you want to use a different table or query as the record source for the Summary view, you'll have to delete this Summary view and then create a new Summary view with the correct record source.

On the Formatting property callout menu, Access displays the Caption property. By default, Access sets the Caption property for Summary views to the same name as the table or query being used as the record source for the view. When you open a Summary view as a popup in runtime, Access displays the Caption property text at the top of the view.

On the Actions callout menu for Summary views, you'll see two buttons—On Load and On Current. When you click these buttons, Access opens the Logic Designer, where you can define macro logic for Access to execute for these two view events. You'll learn about control and view events and how to create user interface macros in Chapter 8, "Automating a web app using macros."

Summary views contain a List Control portion along the left side of the view similar to List Details views. The List Control for Summary views contains different properties that you can set compared to List Details views. (We'll explore those properties in just a moment.) The remaining design area of Summary views contains a control similar to a related items control. You cannot remove this control from the design area, but you can resize the control. You cannot add additional controls to the design grid for Summary views, which is why Access displays no controls in the Design contextual tab for this view type. The related items control portion on Summary views does not display tabs, and you cannot add additional tab pages to this control.

Before we make any customizations to this Summary view, let's see how the view functions in runtime so that you can understand the purpose and display of Summary views. Click the Launch App button on the Quick Access Toolbar to open the new Invoice Summary view in your web browser. Alternatively, you can click the Launch App button in the View group on the Home ribbon tab. Access opens your default web browser and navigates to the Invoice Summary view, as shown in Figure 7-5. If, instead, Access navigates to your default first table and view displayed in the App Home View, click the Invoices table name caption in the Table Selector and then click Invoice Summary in the View Selector to navigate to the correct view. (You can keep Access running in the background.)

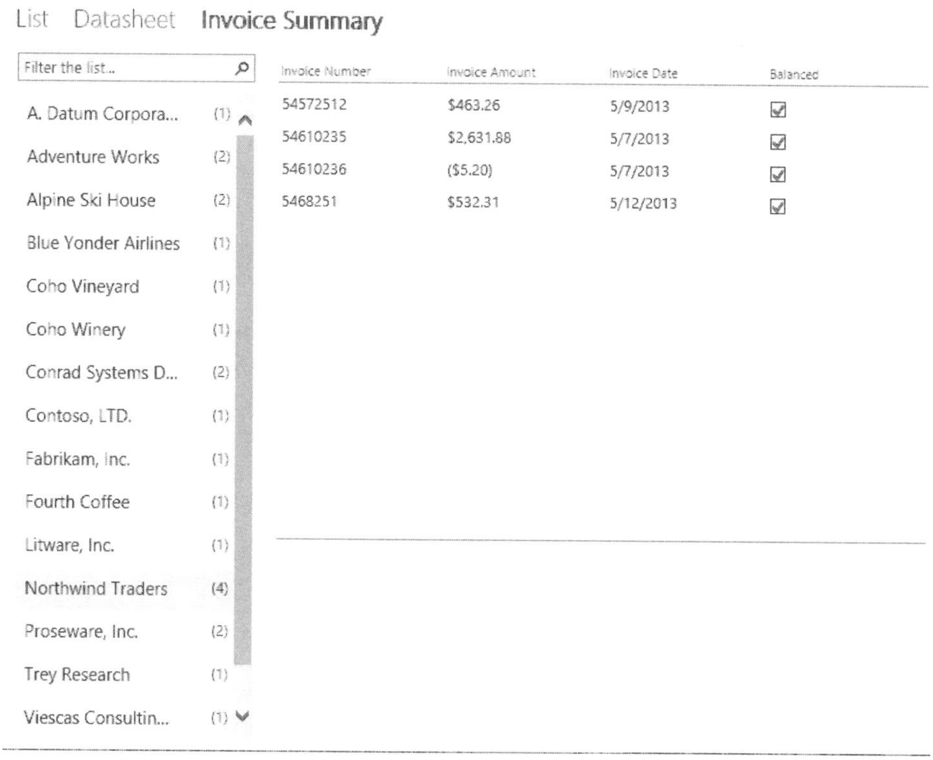

List   Datasheet   **Invoice Summary**

		Invoice Number	Invoice Amount	Invoice Date	Balanced
A. Datum Corpora...	(1)	54572512	$463.26	5/9/2013	☑
Adventure Works	(2)	54610235	$2,631.88	5/7/2013	☑
Alpine Ski House	(2)	54610236	($5.20)	5/7/2013	☑
Blue Yonder Airlines	(1)	5468251	$532.31	5/12/2013	☑
Coho Vineyard	(1)				
Coho Winery	(1)				
Conrad Systems D...	(2)				
Contoso, LTD.	(1)				
Fabrikam, Inc.	(1)				
Fourth Coffee	(1)				
Litware, Inc.	(1)				
Northwind Traders	(4)				
Proseware, Inc.	(2)				
Trey Research	(1)				
Viescas Consultin...	(1)				

Filter the list...

Figure 7-5 When you open a Summary view in your web browser, Access Services groups data from related records.

> **Note**
>
> In Figure 7-5, I clicked the Northwind Traders vendor name in the List Control after Access Services opened the view so that you could see an example of multiple related records displayed in the detail section. When Access Services opens a Summary view, it always navigates to the first displayed option in the List Control by default.

Along the left side of the Invoice Summary view, you can see the Filter box and the List Control. The functionality of these view elements mirrors the functionality you've already explored with List Details views. When you enter a search term in the Filter box, Access Services searches for a match only within the data displayed in the List Control and the possible four fields displayed in the detail section. In the List Control, Access Services displays a field value (in this case, the data from the VendorIDFK lookup field within the Invoice Headers table). When you click a display value in the List Control, Access Services displays related records in the detail section.

The List Control for Summary views, unlike List Details views, displays only one entry for each unique value in the record source. As you saw previously in Figure 7-5, Access Services displays data from four different invoice records, all assigned to the Northwind Traders vendor. (One row of data in the related items portion of the detail section equals one record in the source table or query.) If you navigate to the List Details view for the Invoices table name caption, Access Services displays the Northwind Traders vendor name four times, once for each record. Access Services groups all related records around a single field in Summary views. By clicking each unique item in the List Control, you can see the related records in the detail section at one time.

By default, Access Services displays the number of related records for each item displayed in the List Control in Summary views. In Figure 7-5, you'll notice that on the right side of the List Control, Access Services displays a number within parentheses. For example, Access Services displays the text (4) next to the Northwind Traders vendor name in the List Control, indicating four related invoice records. With the count feature turned on for the List Control in Summary views, on by default, you can quickly see the number of related records for each item displayed in the List Control without even selecting an item.

The detail section of a Summary view functions like related items controls by displaying up to four fields of data from a source table or query. Because the Summary view is based directly on the Invoice Headers table, the detail section and the List Control display data from the Invoice Headers table. When you click a row displayed in the detail section of Summary views, Access Services opens a view to display the entire record details by default. To try this, select the Northwind Traders vendor in the List Control and then click the first row displayed in the detail section. Access Services opens the List Details view for the Invoice Headers table as a pop-up view and displays the matching record details for the first row displayed in the Summary view detail section, as shown in Figure 7-6.

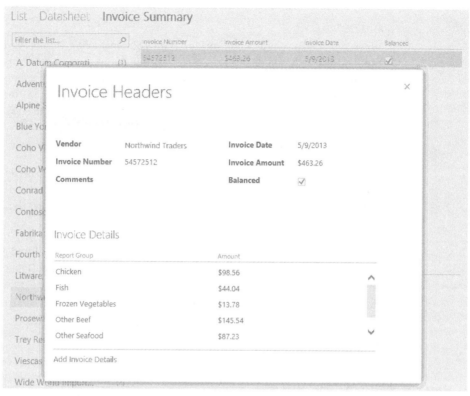

Figure 7-6 Click a record displayed in Summary views to open a pop-up view displaying the related record details.

In the pop-up view, you can see all the fields and data for the matching record highlighted in the Summary view detail section. Using the pop-up view functionality built into Summary views, you can quickly review related record data. Similar to opening pop-up views from autocomplete controls, combo boxes, and related items controls, Access Services hides the List Control for List Details views when you open that view type from Summary views. To close a pop-up view opened from a Summary view, click the Close (X) button in the upper-right corner or press Esc.

> **Note**
>
> When you open a view as a pop-up view from a Summary view, Access Services makes the view read-only and disables any built-in Action Bar buttons. You cannot change any data within a view opened as a pop-up view from a Summary view. If your pop-up view displays a related items control, as shown in the example view in Figure 7-6, you can add and edit related data through the related items control displayed in the pop-up view. However, you cannot edit data in the main view.

Although the options you can use to customize Summary views are more limited compared to other view types, you can still make adjustments to the various properties in Summary views to displayed grouped data to match your specific needs. Let's switch back to Access and make some customizations to this Summary view.

Open the Invoice Summary view in Design view, if you've previously closed it. Select the List Control on the left side of the Summary view, and Access displays the Data charm button next to the List Control. Click the Data charm button, and Access displays the Data property callout menu for the List Control, as shown in Figure 7-7.

> **Note**
>
> You cannot remove the List Control from a Summary view because it is an essential and embedded part of a Summary view structure. You can resize the List Control, to a certain extent, and define properties for it, but you cannot remove it.

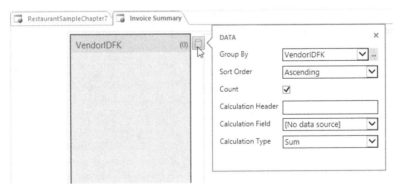

Figure 7-7 Click the Data charm button to view properties you can set for Summary view List Controls.

You can set six properties on the List Control for Summary views—Group By, Sort Order, Count, Calculation Header, Calculation Field, and Calculation Type. The Group By property is a required property and designates which field in the record source you want Access to display in the List Control and group related records around in the detail section. The drop-down list for the Group By property includes a list of all field names in the view record source, except for fields bound to Hyperlink, Yes/No, and Image data types. Access selected VendorIDFK for this property in this quick-created view, because it was the first field name bound to a lookup field. Leave this property set as VendorIDFK because it allows users to easily identify the vendor invoice records in runtime.

You're not required to use the default selection Access uses in the Group By property. You could change the existing view or create another Summary view, based on the Invoice Headers table for example, and group by the InvoiceDate field. (In this scenario, Access Services displays each unique invoice date in the List Control and then displays all invoice records for the displayed invoice date within the detail section.) Access also displays the Build button next to the Group By property. If you click the Build button, Access opens the Expression Builder where you can create a complex expression to use for the Group By property.

Understanding the default List Control selection

When you create a new Summary view or quick-create a List Details view, Access chooses one field to display as the default in the List Control. Access first performs a quick scan of all the fields and their associated data types in the view's record source. Access looks at the first field and then determines whether the next field in the display order (determined by the order at the table design level or the query output design level) is a better candidate to be the List Control display value. If there are fields bound to Short Text, Long Text, calculated fields with Short Text for the Result Type, and Lookup data types, Access chooses these fields above other fields in the record source. Access considers fields bound to Number, Currency, and Date/Time data types with less precedence than other data types for the List Control display field.

If Access cannot find any good candidates (a table of only Yes/No fields, for example), Access defaults to using the ID AutoNumber for the List Control selection. In this case, Access displays a red border around the property when you open the Data property callout menu for the List Control. If you base a view on a query, do not include the ID field in the query, and Access cannot find any good candidates for the display field, Access does not select any field for the List Control display field.

Lookup fields can look up data with different data types from other tables. If the data type in the related table is Short Text or Long Text, Access sets a higher precedence for these fields over lookup fields that look up data in Number, Currency, or Date/Time data types.

For example, assume you had a table with three fields in the following order: ID (AutoNumber), a lookup field with display text set to a Short Text field, and a Short Text field. Access defaults to using the lookup field for the List Control display. In another example, assume you had a table with three fields in the following order: ID (AutoNumber), a lookup field with display text set to a Number field, and a Short Text field. Access defaults to using the Short Text field for the List Control display.

Remember that Access uses the first good candidate field it comes across in the display order. For example, if you have two Short Text fields in your table, Access never selects the second Short Text field for the List Control display when it creates new Summary and List Details views. If you have a preference for a specific field to use in your List Controls, consider opening the table in Design view and moving that field below the ID field in the list of fields or above the field Access currently defaults to for using for the List Control display field. The next time you create a Summary or List Details view for that table, Access should select that field for the List Control candidate field.

If you are using a Table Template, tables created from these templates contain information within them that predefine what field Access uses for the List Control primary display field. In some Table Templates, Access also defines a field to use for the Secondary property of the List Control for List Details views, as well as the Group By property of the List Control for Summary views. You cannot override the defined display field values for Table Templates. You'll have to manually change these properties after Access creates the view, if you want to use a different field other than the default.

INSIDE OUT   Use a Group By expression to create a jump list

A great use for defining an expression in the Group By property for Summary view List Controls is to create a jump list, similar to what you see with a Windows phone contact list. You can create an expression that uses the Left function to display the first letter only of a field in the Group By property. For example, if you had a table of contacts with First Name and Last Name fields, you could create the following expression in the Group By property of a Summary view: =Left([Last Name],1). Access Services then displays only the last letter of the contact's last name and groups all records by the letters of the alphabet. You'll find several Summary views using this technique in the Back Office Software System sample web app (BOSS.app), which can be downloaded from the book's catalog page

The Sort Order property lists only two options—Ascending and Descending. You can specify whether Access should sort the field defined in the Group By property in ascending or descending order. By default, Access always chooses Ascending for the Sort Order property in Summary views. You might find changing this property to Descending useful if, for example, you want to display a most recent list of invoices by dates or a list of most recent orders received. Leave this property set to Ascending here.

Access displays a check box for the Count property. Selecting this property, which is selected by default, instructs Access Services to count the number of related records for each unique item displayed in the List Control at runtime. Access Services displays the number of related records within parentheses next to the data displayed for the Group By property. With the Count property selected, you can quickly see the number of related records for each item displayed in the List Control. Clear this property if you do not want to display the number of related records for each item in the List Control.

Access displays a text box for the Calculation Header property. When you choose to define a field in your record source for the Calculation Field property, Access Services displays the results of the calculation beneath the group by text in the List Control. You can optionally define the text displayed next to the calculation total. If you do not define a Calculation Header text, Access Services displays just the calculation result. You might find it useful to provide a more descriptive text next to the calculation result for users of your web app. Enter **Total:** into the Calculation Header property here.

The Calculation Field property is an optional property for the List Control that works in conjunction with the Calculation Type property in Summary views. When you select Sum or Avg for the Calculation Type property, you need to select which of the four possible display fields defined in the detail section to use in the aggregate calculation. (We'll discuss display fields in the detail section later in this section.) If no display fields defined in the detail section are Number or Currency data types, Access displays [No Data Source] in the drop-down list. In this case, Access does not perform the Sum or Avg aggregate functions across any fields. By default, Access selects [No Data Source] for the Calculation Field property whenever you create a new Summary view. In addition to the [No Data Source] option, Access displays a drop-down list of Number or Currency field names from the defined display fields in the detail section. In the sample Summary view you have open, it would be useful to have Access calculate the total amount of invoices across each vendor, so select InvoiceAmount from the drop-down list for the Calculation Field property.

You can optionally choose to perform aggregate functions across any of the four display fields in the detail area of the Summary view that are Number or Currency data types by using the Calculation Type property. If you choose Sum or Avg, you must select a field name in the Calculation Field property for Access Services to display the results of the aggregation in the List Control. Access Services performs the aggregate across the records currently displayed in the List Control and updates the values as you page up or page down to different values displayed in the List Control. Access Services displays the calculation results and any Calculation Header text beneath the group by text in the List Control. Leave the Calculation Type property set at Sum, the default.

Your changes to the List Control properties should now match those seen in Figure 7-8. Access displays the values defined for the Calculation Header, Calculation Field, and Calculation Type properties below the Group By property data value and with a smaller font in the List Control.

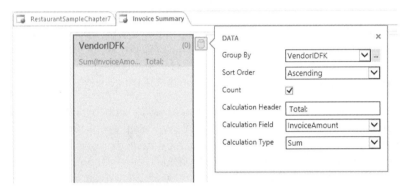

Figure 7-8 Your List Control properties should now look like this.

Now that you've set the List Control properties, let's explore the properties you can set in the detail section for Summary views. Select the detail section on the right side of the Summary view, and Access displays a single Data charm button in the upper-right corner. Click the Data charm button, and Access displays the Data property callout menu for the detail section, as shown in Figure 7-9.

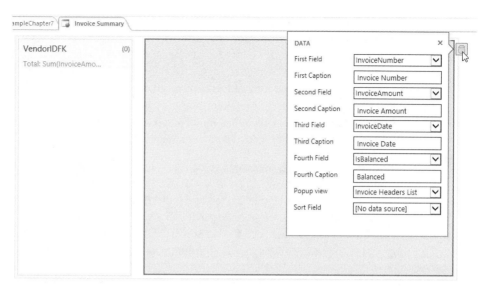

Figure 7-9 Click the Data charm button to adjust the properties for the detail section.

The properties you can set in the detail section for Summary views are very similar to what you can set for related items controls. You can select up to four fields to display in the detail section using the First Field, Second Field, Third Field, and Fourth Field properties. Access displays a drop-down list of all the fields in the source table or query, excluding field names bound to Image data types, for these properties. If you select [No Data Source] for any of these properties, Access Services does not display any data for that column in your web browser. Leave these properties set at the default selections.

If you do not provide captions for the First Field, Second Field, Third Field, or Fourth Field properties, Access Services displays the actual field names defined in the property for the column header in the control. You might find it useful to provide a more user-friendly short description as column headers, instead of actual field names, using the First Caption, Second Caption, Third Caption, and Fourth Caption properties. If you defined custom text at the table level in the Label Text field property previously, Access uses that text by default for the appropriate caption property in the Data callout menu. Leave these properties set at the default selections.

Use the Popup View property to designate a view that Access Services opens to display the related record when you click a row displayed in the detail section of a Summary view. You'll find this property especially useful for viewing related information. Access provides a drop-down list of view names that include the same table or query in its record source as the Summary view. Views opened as pop-up views from Summary views open as read-only. Leave this property set to the Invoice Headers List view name.

Use the Sort Field property to designate which field in the record source you want Access Services to sort by when you open the Summary view in your web browser. The list of valid field names in the drop-down list exclude any field names bound to Image data types. You can choose to sort by a field not displayed as one of the four display columns. You're not required to define a Sort Field property, in which case you'll see [No Data Source] selected by default for this property. Access sets this property to [No Data Source] on all new Summary views by default. In the Summary view you have opened, it would be useful to sort the invoice records by date, so select InvoiceDate for this property in the drop-down list.

The Sort Order property lists only two options—Ascending and Descending. In the Sort Order property, you can specify whether Access should sort the selected field in the Sort Field property in ascending or descending order. By default, Access always chooses Ascending for the Sort Order property. Note that you won't see this property listed on the Data callout menu until you select a field to sort by in the Sort Field property. Leave this property set at the default, Ascending, in the Summary view you have open.

Now that you've completed making some customizations to the List Control and detail section of the Invoice Summary view, let's see how your changes look in a web browser at runtime. Click Save on the Quick Access Toolbar to save your view changes, close the Invoice Summary view, and then click the Launch App button in the View group on the Home ribbon tab or click the Launch App button on the Quick Access Toolbar. Access opens your default web browser and navigates to your Access web app. If you still have the Invoice Summary view open in your web browser, you can switch to that window and then refresh the page in your browser to see the latest changes. After Access Services loads the Summary view, click the Northwind Traders vendor name displayed in the List Control, as shown in Figure 7-10.

List   Datasheet   **Invoice Summary**

Filter the list...	🔍	Invoice Number	Invoice Amount	Invoice Date	Balanced
		54610235	$2,631.88	5/7/2013	☑
Conrad Systems D...	(2) ⌃	54610236	($5.20)	5/7/2013	☑
Total: 172.45		54572512	$463.26	5/9/2013	☑
Contoso, LTD.	(1)	5468251	$532.31	5/12/2013	☑
Total: 56					
Fabrikam, Inc.	(1)				
Total: 30					
Fourth Coffee	(1)				
Total: 30					
Litware, Inc.	(1)				
Total: 241					
Northwind Traders	(4)				
Total: 3622.255					
Proseware, Inc.	(2)				
Total: 370.5					
Trey Research	(1)				
Total: 123.45					
Viescas Consultin...	(1)				
Total: 15202					
Wide World Impo...	(2)				
Total: 252.64	⌄				

Figure 7-10 Access Services displays your Summary view customizations in the List Control and detail section.

In Figure 7-10, you can see that Access Services now displays an extra line of text in the List Control beneath the vendor name. Access Services lists the Calculation Header text Total, followed by a colon, and a number representing the sum of all the assigned invoice totals for the vendor. Without clicking a vendor name in the List Control, you can browse each vendor's invoice totals by just scrolling or paging up and down the display totals in the List Control. In the detail section, you can see that Access Services sorts the assigned invoice records in ascending order by their invoice date. You can optionally customize this Summary view by increasing the width of the List Control and increasing the height and width of the detail section to display more text and data within the Summary view parts.

As you can see, you'll find Summary views extremely useful for grouping data together around a common field. With different Summary views, you can display totals and averages from your data and open up popup views to display more information about related records.

Creating Blank views

The last view type you can create in Access web apps are Blank views. Blank views are unique: Bound Blank views display one record of data at a time, but they do not include a List Control for record navigation. Blank views allow the same types of customizations available for List Details views. However, in some cases, you'll find using a Blank view more appropriate than using a List Details view. For example, a Blank view is useful when you want to create a view that's displayed as a pop-up message with display text, because you probably do not need a List Control element for this scenario. To learn about Blank views, you'll create a simple view that displays data from both the Invoice Headers and Vendors tables in the sample restaurant management app you've been working with in this chapter and then make additional customizations to the view in later sections of this chapter. Switch back to Access if you still have the web browser window open from the previous section.

To create a new Blank view attached to the View Selector for the Invoices table name caption in the Table Selector, select the Invoices table name caption in the Table Selector and then click the Add New View button to the right of the Invoice Summary view name caption in the View Selector. Access displays the Add New View menu, as shown in Figure 7-11.

Figure 7-11 Select Blank on the Add New View menu to create a new Blank view.

In the View Name box, you can enter a name for the view you want to create. In our example here, type **Invoice Blank** into the View Name box. Select Blank in the drop-down list for the View Type option to create a Blank view for our new view type.

Access displays a drop-down list of the table name that matches the underlying selected table caption in the Table Selector and the names of any queries that include that table in their source in the Record Source option. If you want to design a view that uses more than one table for a record source, you can create a query first and then select it in the Record Source drop-down list, or you can select the table as the record source and then build an embedded query within the view. If you want to design an unbound view, perhaps to use for displaying messages or gathering information from users, choose a table or query name in the Record Source drop-down and then clear the Record Source view property after

Access creates the view. We'll create an embedded query for this view, so for now, select Invoice Headers for the Record Source option in the Add New View menu.

After you enter your view name and select Blank for the View Type, click the Add New View button on the menu. Access creates a new Blank view for your app called Invoice Blank, a new view name caption in the View Selector that matches your selected view name, and displays a preview of the Blank view structure in the view preview window, as shown in Figure 7-12. If you do not have the Navigation pane expanded currently, you won't see the new view name listed. You can verify that the view name exists by clicking the Navigation Pane button on the Home ribbon tab.

Figure 7-12 Access creates a new view caption name called Invoice Blank.

To open this new Blank view in Design view, click the Edit button in the middle of the view preview window. Access opens the view in Design view on its own object tab in the application window, as shown in Figure 7-13.

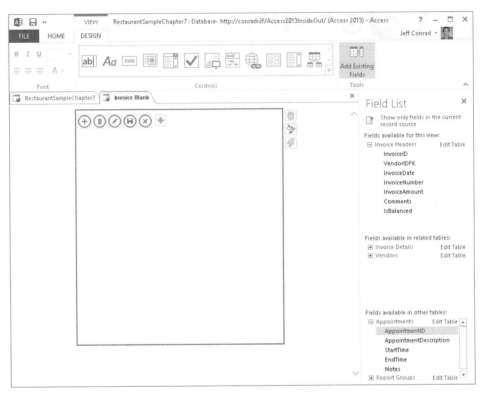

Figure 7-13 When you open a Blank view in Design view, you'll see Action Bar buttons only.

The options you'll see on the Design contextual tab for Blank views match the options you see with List Details views. You can use all control types on Blank views, and you can use the same formatting options with view controls on Blank views that you can with List Details views. On the design surface for Blank views, you'll notice that Access displays only the five built-in Action Bar buttons; you essentially start with a blank canvas. Blank views do not contain a List Control element, which means Access Services displays only one record at a time in runtime. You'll also have to build in a way to navigate to different records if your Blank view is bound to a table or a query, because Access does not provide a List Control.

The Field List on the right side of the Access application window shows the fields available from the view's record source. Access also displays fields from related tables in the middle of the pane and the names of other tables and fields in the web app at the bottom of the pane. When you first create a Blank view, Access does not drop any controls bound to fields onto the design surface. You can use the Field List to drag fields from your view's record source onto the design surface. If you drag a field from a related table onto the design surface, Access modifies the view's Record Source property and creates an embedded query to return data from the related table.

In Figure 7-13, shown previously, you'll see that Access displays the three charm buttons for setting view properties along the upper-right corner of the view design window. Blank views have the same view properties as List Details views. The only option available on the Data property callout menu for Blank views is Record Source. Access displays the table or query name you selected when you first created the view. On the Formatting property callout menu, Access displays the Action Bar Visible and Caption properties. By default, Access sets the Action Bar Visible property to Visible and leaves the Caption property empty for Blank views. If you set the Record Source property to [No Data Source], Access sets the Action Bar Visible property to Hidden and removes the Action Bar container from the design surface. On the Actions callout menu for Blank views, you'll see two buttons— On Load and On Current. When you click these buttons, Access opens the Logic Designer where you can define macro logic for Access to execute for these two view events. You'll learn about control and view events and creating user interface macros in Chapter 8.

Let's modify the record source for your new Blank view from the default setting of the Invoice Headers table to use an embedded query. As you'll recall from Chapter 6, embedded queries are queries defined at the view level and are not displayed within the Navigation pane. For the view we want to build, it would be useful to include the Website field from the Vendors table. Although you can drag fields from the field list and Access will figure out the appropriate record source for you, you have more control if you design an embedded query yourself to serve as your view's record source. To create an embedded query, click the Data charm button for the view and then click the Build button next to the Record Source property, as shown in Figure 7-14.

Figure 7-14 Click the Build button next to the Record Source property to define an embedded query.

Access displays a confirmation message, shown in Figure 7-15, asking whether you want to create a query based on the table. Access displays this message because, if you proceed with defining an embedded query, Access needs to modify the view's record source. If you click the Build button by mistake, click No to dismiss the message box. To continue defining an embedded query, click Yes to proceed.

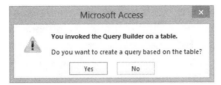

Figure 7-15 Access displays a confirmation message whenever you first define an embedded query.

Access now opens the Query window in Design view and displays the Invoice Headers table in the upper part of the Query window, as shown in Figure 7-16.

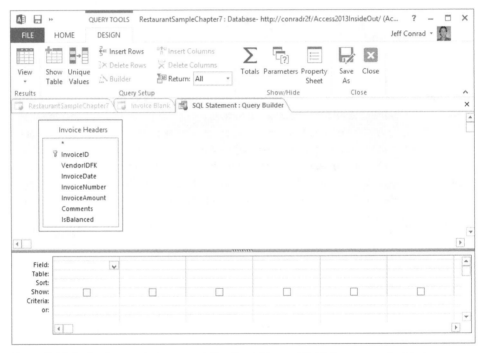

Figure 7-16 In the Query window, you define the tables and fields for your embedded query.

For the view we are creating, we first want to include all fields within the Invoice Headers table. You could drag each field from the Invoice Headers table into the lower part of the design, but let's use one of the shortcut techniques you learned previously in Chapter 5, "Working with queries in web apps." Select all the fields in the Invoice Headers table by double-clicking the title bar of the field list in the upper part of the Query window—this highlights all the fields. Click any of the highlighted fields, and drag them as a group to the Field row in the design grid. While you're dragging, the mouse pointer changes to a multiple rectangle icon, indicating that you're dragging multiple fields. When you release the mouse button, you'll see that Access copies all the fields to the design grid for you.

> **Note**
>
> For Access Services to allow data updates to a view based on a query, you must include the ID AutoNumber field as an output field from at least one of the tables. If you do not include the ID field, Access Services does not know which record to update. At runtime, Access Services disables all built-in Action Bar buttons and prevents any updates if a view is based on a query without an ID field as one of the output fields.

Now that you've added all the output fields to the design grid from the Invoice Headers table, let's sort the records by their invoice date. Click in the Sort row for the InvoiceDate field, click the arrow in this row, and then select Ascending from the list. Your changes up to this point should match Figure 7-17.

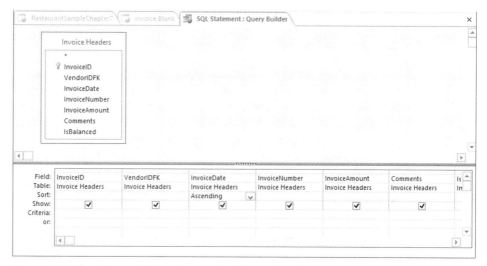

Figure 7-17 Your Query window changes should now look like this.

To also display the vendor's website in this query, we need to add the Vendors table to the Query window. Click the Show Table button in the Query Setup group on the Design contextual ribbon tab. Access opens the Show Table dialog box. Select Vendors on the Tables tab of the Show Table dialog box, and then click Add to place Vendors in the upper part of the Query window. Click Close in the Show Table dialog box to dismiss the dialog. Finally, double-click the Website field in the Vendors list of fields to add the field to the query grid at the bottom of the Query window, as shown in Figure 7-18.

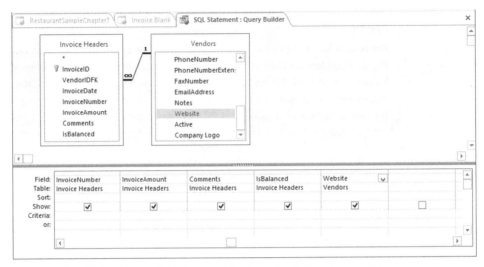

Figure 7-18 Add the Website field from the Vendors table to the design grid.

You've now completed your embedded query for the Blank view. To save the changes you've made to the embedded query and update the view's record source, click Save on the Quick Access Toolbar and then click Close in the Close group on the Design contextual tab. Note that if you click Close to close the Query window with unsaved changes, Access prompts you with a save changes confirmation message, as shown in Figure 7-19. Click Yes, and Access saves any pending changes and updates the Record Source property. Click No, and Access closes the Query window and discards any changes you made. Click Cancel, and Access prevents the Query window from closing and returns you to the Query window with the pending changes still unsaved.

Figure 7-19 Access displays this confirmation message when you attempt to close the Query window with unsaved changes.

After you save your embedded query design changes and close the Query window, Access returns you to the Blank view design grid. Access now displays [Embedded Query] for the Record Source property, as shown in Figure 7-20. Because you defined an embedded query for this view, you can click the Build button next to the Record Source to open the Query window if you need to modify the record source in the future.

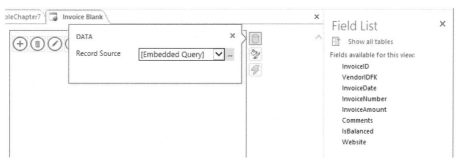

Figure 7-20 Access displays [Embedded Query] in the Record Source property after you close the Query window.

In Figure 7-20, you'll notice that Access changed the Field List to display only the field names defined within the embedded query you just created. To use the Field List to place a bound control on a view, you can either double-click a field name or click and then drag the field name you want from the Field List and place it into position on the view design grid. In both cases, Access creates an appropriate control for the field data type defined at the table level. For example, if you place a field bound to an Image data type onto the design grid, Access creates an image control to represent the bound field. If you double-click each field name in the Field List, Access adds the control one by one down the grid in a column. You can position the controls where you want on the view design grid more precisely if you drag fields from the Field List.

Let's practice using both techniques to place the fields from the view's record source onto the design grid for this Blank view. To start, double-click one at a time the InvoiceID, VendorIDFK, InvoiceDate, InvoiceNumber, and InvoiceAmount fields. Access places each appropriate control type and an associated label onto the view design grid, as shown in Figure 7-21. If you accidentally add a field twice to the design grid, select the duplicate control and then press Delete to remove the control from the design grid.

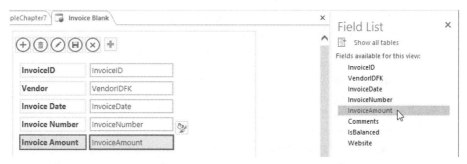

Figure 7-21 Double-click the first five fields displayed in the Field List to add them to the view design grid.

Let's drag the last three fields in the Field List (Comments, IsBalanced, and Website) from the Field List and drop them in a specific order onto the view design grid to the right of the other controls.

Follow this procedure to add the remaining fields to the design grid:

1. Select the IsBalanced field in the Field List, and then drag the controls to the right of the InvoiceID controls. Notice that Access expands the width of the design grid to accommodate the new controls when you perform this step.

2. Select the Website field in the Field List, and then drag the controls to the right of the VendorIDFK controls and beneath the IsBalanced controls. You'll see Access expand the width of the design grid again, because the hyperlink control for the Website field is wider than the check box control for the IsBalanced field.

3. Select the Comments field in the Field List, and then drag the controls to the right of the InvoiceDate controls and beneath the Website controls.

Your view design grid should now look like Figure 7-22.

Figure 7-22 Position the three remaining fields to the right of the other controls.

Note that I had you add the Comments field last, because Access creates a multiline text box that is taller than the other controls on the grid. You're not required to place fields bound to Long Text data types last onto the design grid; I wanted to line up the controls so that all the columns take up the same height on the grid.

Now that you've added all the fields from the view's record source onto the design grid, let's save the design changes and see how this view functions in a web browser. Click Save on the Quick Access Toolbar to save your Blank view design changes. When you save your changes, Access collapses the design grid boundaries to just fit around the controls. Click the Launch App button on the Quick Access Toolbar to open the new Invoice Blank view you created in your web browser. Alternatively, you can click the Launch App button in the View group on the Home ribbon tab. Access opens your default web browser and navigates to the Invoice Blank view, as shown in Figure 7-23. If Access instead navigates to your default first table and view displayed in the App Home View, click the Invoices table name caption in the Table Selector and then click Invoice Blank in the View Selector to navigate to the correct view. (You can keep Access running in the background for now.)

Figure 7-23 When you open a bound Blank view in your web browser, Access Services displays data from the first record in the record source.

> **Note**
>
> The record data you see in Figure 7-23 might not match the record data you see in your own sample view and web app. As you'll recall, I had you adjust the embedded query to sort the records for this view by the InvoiceDate field in ascending order. The first record you see when you open the Invoice Blank view might differ based on the current date in your computer or device.

Because we defined the records to be sorted by the InvoiceDate field in the embedded query, Access Services displays the record with the earliest invoice date when you navigate to the view. Access Services displays the data in the various controls in the layout you defined earlier within Access. Access Services displays the data in the Vendor autocomplete control as a link when you are in view mode, just as it does with List Details views.

You've no doubt noticed by now that no List Control element is displayed for Blank views. You can create new invoice records in this Blank view by clicking the Add Action Bar button. You can also edit the current record by clicking the Edit Action Bar button or delete the current record by clicking the Delete Action Bar button. However, at this moment, you cannot navigate to a different record within the record source; you're restricted to viewing this one record only. To navigate to different records in a Blank view, you'll need to define user interface macros attached to control events. In Chapter 8, you'll learn how to create user interface macros for custom Action Bar buttons for this specific view so that you can navigate to different records.

The controls on this Blank view could use a little more fine-tuning by adjusting their widths to be wider to display more data instead of truncating data that cannot fit within the control. You could also reduce the font size of the controls to display more text if you don't want to increase the width of the controls. Or, you can leave the controls as they are without any customizations. One of the strengths of designing views is that you can customize the controls and layout to meet the needs of your web app.

Defining subviews

If you want to show data from several tables and be able to update the data in more than one of the tables, you might need to use something more complex than a standard view. In Chapter 6, you learned how related items controls can display data from related tables on tabs. You can edit and add data to related tables from related items controls by opening views as pop-up views. Subviews can also help in this scenario. You can create a main view that displays a parent record's information and embed in it a subview that displays all the related rows from a related table.

You can embed up to seven levels of subviews within another view (a view with a subview that also has a subview, and so on), although nesting more than two levels deep might be impractical in actual use. If you try and embed more than seven levels of subviews, Access displays an error. Let's start by designing the innermost view and working outward, because you must design and save an inner view before you can embed it in an outer one.

The Invoice Headers table in the sample web app you've been working on is related to the Invoice Details table in a one-to-many relationship. The InvoiceIDFK lookup field in the Invoice Details table provides the link between the two tables. When you are viewing information about a particular invoice, you might also want to see and edit the related invoice detail information. In the previous section, you created a new Blank view that displays data from the Invoice Headers table. You could add a related items control to display related data from the Invoice Details table, but in this exercise, we'll add a subview to this Blank view to perform the same task.

Let's switch back to Access and add a subview control to the Invoice Blank view. Open the Invoice Blank view in Design view, if you closed it, and then select the associated label control for the InvoiceAmount field. Now click the Subview control button in the Controls group on the Design contextual tab. Access places a new empty subview control onto the design grid beneath the invoice amount controls, as shown in Figure 7-24. Remember that Access places new controls from the ribbon beneath the selected control on the grid (the associated label control for the InvoiceAmount field, in this case).

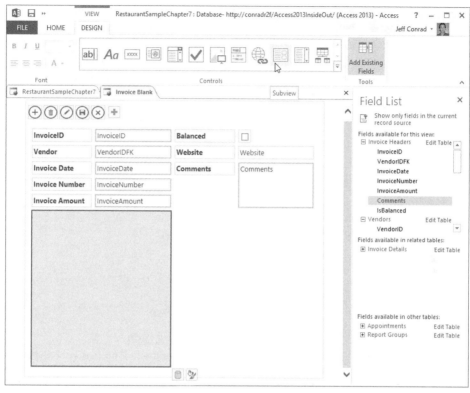

Figure 7-24 Click the Subview command to place a subview control onto the view design grid.

You'll notice that the default size that Access uses for subview controls is taller and wider than most other controls. Because subview controls display the entire contents of other views within themselves, you'll typically need to allow extra room on your view for these types of controls. If you want to display a view with only a few controls inside a subview, you can resize the subview control to be smaller than the default.

INSIDE OUT   Creating horizontal separation lines with label controls

Access web apps do not include a line control for views, but you can simulate a horizontal line by using a label control. Place a label control on the view design grid, and resize the width to the desired width. Then type the underscore character (_) in the Caption property as many times as necessary to fill the space of the label control width. You might find this technique useful to create a visual separation between different areas of your views. For example, you could use this technique to create a visual separation line between the main view controls and the subview control shown in Figure 7-24.

In Figure 7-24, you'll notice that Access displays two charm buttons next to subview controls—Data and Formatting. (Subview controls do not support any control events, so Access does not display the Actions charm button with this control type.) The Formatting property callout menu displays only one property—Visible. Set this property to Visible, the default, to display the subview at runtime in your web browser. Set the property to Hidden if you do not want to display the control at runtime. Click the Data charm button, and Access displays the Data property callout menu for subview controls, as shown in Figure 7-25.

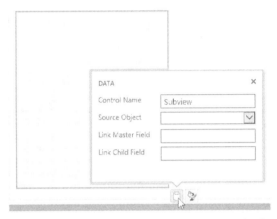

Figure 7-25 Click the Data charm button to see the four properties on the Data callout menu.

You can set four properties on the Data callout menu for subview controls—Control Name, Source Object, Link Master Field, and Link Child Field. As you learned in Chapter 6, all controls on views must have a unique name defined in the Control Name property. By default, Access uses the text Subview for the Control Name property of this new subview control. Leave the control name set at the default.

In the Source Object property, Access displays a drop-down list of the names of all views defined within the web app, except for the name of the view you currently have open. (It would not make sense to display the same view within itself inside a subview control.) You can select any view type to display within a subview control, based on what you want to display and how you want users to interact with the subview. In the Invoice Blank view you have open, you could design your own custom view to display the records from the Invoice Details table; however, Access already quick-created a datasheet view based on this table that should work perfectly for our needs—the Invoice Details Datasheet view. Click the Source Object property, and then select the Invoice Details Datasheet view from the drop-down list.

Access does not display a preview of selected views within the subview control at design time. To see how the subview looks and functions, you'll need to display the view at runtime in your web browser. Click Save on the Quick Access Toolbar to save your design

changes up to this point, and then click the Launch App button on the Quick Access Toolbar. Alternatively, you can click the Launch App button in the View group on the Home ribbon tab. Access opens your default web browser and navigates to the Invoice Blank view, as
shown in Figure 7-26. (You can keep Access running in the background for now.)

Figure 7-26 Access displays a separate Datasheet view within the Invoice Blank view.

Access Services displays the entire contents of the Invoice Details Datasheet view within the
dimensions of the subview control. Access Services also displays all invoice detail records
returned within that view's record source. You'll notice that Access Services provides a
horizontal and vertical scroll bar within the subview control so that you can scroll to see all
records within the subview. At the top of the subview, you can see the built-in Action Bar
buttons for the datasheet subview. When you interact with the Action Bar buttons within a
subview, Access applies those actions only within the context of the subview. You can add,
edit, and delete records within the subview datasheet even when the main view is in view
mode.

Although the subview, as it is currently designed, functions for data entry, it's not very useful, because you see all records in the related table. It might be more helpful if Access Services displayed only the child invoice records that relate to the main view invoice record, in
much the same way related items controls function. Fortunately, Access provides a method

to relate the main view with the subview records through the Link Master Field and Link Child Field properties.

Let's switch back to Access and make some customizations to this subview control. Open the Invoice Blank view in Design view, if you've previously closed it. Select the subview control, and then click the Data charm button again to open the Data property callout menu, shown in Figure 7-27.

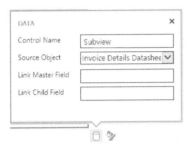

Figure 7-27 Click the Data charm button to see the four properties on the Data callout menu.

As mentioned earlier, the Invoice Details table is related to the Invoice Headers table through the InvoiceIDFK lookup field. When you view records in an outer view and you want Access to filter the rows in the subview to show only related information, you must make sure that Access knows the fields that link the two sets of data. The Link Child Field property refers to the *child* view—the one in the subview. Enter the name of the field in the record source of the view inside the subview that should be filtered based on what row you have displayed in the outer view. Likewise, the Link Master Field property should contain the name of the related field on the outer view.

Whenever you create records in the Invoice Details table, Access stores the ID value from the InvoiceID field from the Invoice Headers table into the InvoiceIDFK lookup field. These two fields form the linking information that Access needs to filter the records to the correct invoice at runtime. Enter **InvoiceID** in the text box for the Link Master Field property, and then enter **InvoiceIDFK** in the text box for the Link Child Field property, as shown in Figure 7-28.

Figure 7-28 Enter the linking field names in the property text boxes on the Data callout menu.

Save your design changes by clicking the Save button on the Quick Access Toolbar. Switch back to your web browser and refresh the Invoice Blank view. (If you previously closed your web browser, click the Launch App button on the Quick Access Toolbar to open your web app in your default browser and then navigate to the Invoice Blank view.) Your view should now look like Figure 7-29. As you move from record to record in the outer view, Access uses the value it finds in the field defined in the Link Master Field property as a filter against the field in the subview defined in the Link Child Field property.

Figure 7-29 You now have a view to display invoice information with a subview that displays the related invoice details.

> **Note**
> You won't be able to navigate to other main view records in the Invoice Blank view to see the linking occur for other records yet, because Blank views have no record navigation built-in, by default. In Chapter 8, you'll learn how to create custom Action Bar buttons on this view to navigate to different records.

In the datasheet subview, you'll notice that Access Services displays the matching invoice number text in the Invoice autocomplete control for new records. Because you properly set the linking field information for the subview controls, Access Services assumes that you want to use the same main invoice number when creating detail records in the subview datasheet. One advantage to using a subview datasheet over a related items control to work with related data is that you can add, edit, and delete related data quickly with a subview datasheet without having to open pop-up views each time. When you build and customize your web apps, you'll appreciate the flexibility of having different options and tools available within Access to fulfill your app requirements.

Using web browser controls

Access web apps include a web browser control that you can use on both List Details and Blank views. A web browser control displays the content of webpages directly inside a view. For example, you can use a web browser control to display a map of an address stored in a table or a site or page within your Office 365 site. You can optionally bind the web browser control to a field in your view's record source by using the Control Source property of the control. You can also use a web browser control to display a static webpage, such as a link to a specific website (for example, *http://www.AccessJunkie.com*), or you can use a web browser control to display a video hosted on a webpage.

The Invoice Blank view you've been working with in the last few sections includes a field bound to a Hyperlink data type in its record source. As you might recall, you defined an embedded query for this view's record source and included the Website field from the Vendors table as one of the output fields. Let's add a web browser control onto this view. Open this view in Design view, if you've closed it, and then select the Comments multiline text box. Now click the Web Browser Control button in the Controls group on the Design contextual tab. Access places a new web browser control onto the design grid beneath the Comments multiline text box control, as shown in Figure 7-30. If you don't select the Comments control, Access places the web browser control beneath the subview control you created earlier.

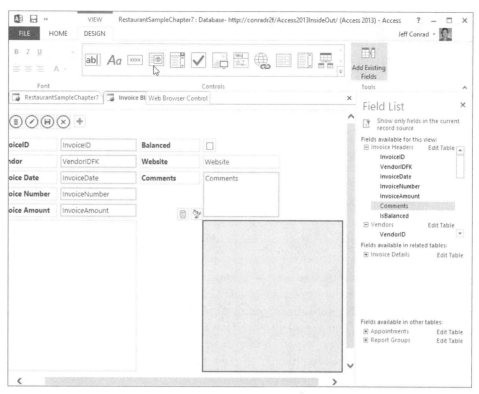

Figure 7-30 Click the Web Browser Control command to drop a web browser control onto the view design grid.

You'll notice that the default size that Access uses for web browser controls is the same size as subview controls. Because web browser controls display the entire contents of other webpages within themselves, you'll typically need to allow extra room on your view for these types of controls. Access placed the web browser control directly beneath the Comments control, which is not aligned with the associated label control for the Comments field. Drag the left edge of the web browser control to resize it and make it align with the Comments label control.

In Figure 7-30, you'll notice that Access displays two charm buttons next to web browser controls—Data and Formatting. Similar to subview controls, web browser controls do not support any control events, so Access does not display the Actions charm button with this control type. The Formatting property callout menu for web browser controls displays one property only—Visible. Set this property to Visible, the default, to display the web browser control at runtime in your web browser. Set the property to Hidden if you do not want to display the control and its contents at runtime. Click the Data charm button, and Access displays the Data property callout menu for web browser controls, as shown in Figure 7-31.

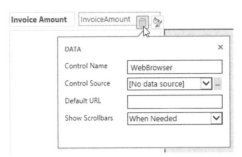

Figure 7-31 Click the Data charm button to see the four properties on the Data callout menu.

You can set four properties on the Data callout menu for web browser controls—Control Name, Control Source, Default URL, and Show Scrollbars. By default, Access uses the text WebBrowser for the Control Name property of this new web browser control. You can leave the control name set at the default.

You can bind a web browser control to a field in the view's record source by selecting a field from the drop-down list on the Control Source property. The view must be bound to bind the web browser control to a field. Access restricts the field names listed in the Control Source property drop-down list to fields bound to the following data types: Short Text, Long Text, Hyperlink, Calculated fields with result type of text, and Lookup fields with display values consisting of text or hyperlink outputs. All other data types and subtypes of Calculated and Lookup fields, including value list lookups, are not supported for web browser control sources. The default setting, [No Data Source], indicates that the control is unbound. In the view you're working on, select the Website field name from the drop-down list for this property. When you navigate to this view at runtime in your web browser, Access Services fetches the data from the Website field, sends a request to that Uniform Resource Locator (URL), and then displays the result in the web browser control.

You can enter a URL in the Default URL property that you want Access Services to navigate to when the control is unbound (no Control Source defined) or when the field defined in the Control Source property has no value. You might find this property useful if you want to display a webpage at all times, no matter what record might be currently displayed in the view. Leave this property empty for our example.

You can choose to turn off displaying scroll bars for the web browser control by changing the Show Scrollbars property from When Needed, the default, to Never. In some cases, different web browsers might still display scroll bars, even if you set this property to Never, if the web browser determines scroll bars are needed.

Save your design changes to this view now by clicking the Save button on the Quick Access Toolbar, and then close the view because we no longer need this view open. Switch back to your web browser, and refresh the Invoice Blank view. (If you previously closed your web browser, click the Launch App button on the Quick Access Toolbar to open your web app in your default browser and then navigate to the Invoice Blank view.) Your view should now look like Figure 7-32.

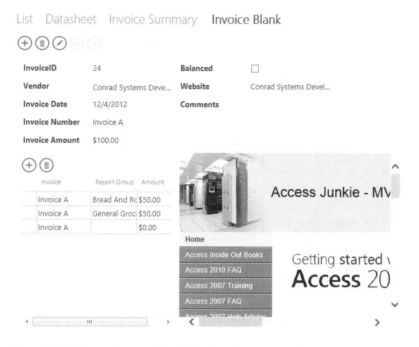

Figure 7-32 You now have a view displaying the contents of another webpage within a web browser control.

Note

The webpage displayed in the web browser control you see in Figure 7-32 might not match the webpage data you see in your sample view and web app. As you'll recall, you adjusted the embedded query to sort the records by the InvoiceDate field in ascending order for this view. The first record you see when you open the Invoice Blank view might differ based on the current date in your computer or device. As a result, Access Services loads the webpage in the web browser control defined for the vendor currently displayed in your web app copy. All of the URLs in the Website field of the Vendors table, except the Conrad Systems Development vendor, redirect to Microsoft's main home page, so you might see that page displayed in your view when you work through this example.

When you are working with web browser controls, you'll need to be aware of a special security implication that might affect displaying webpage content in your web browser controls. Due to potential security issues, content displayed in web browser controls within Access web app views cannot cross different domains and protocols. This means that if you are viewing your Access web app within a URL with an HTTPS protocol, such as with Office 365, Access Services won't display content in a web browser control that uses a different protocol or domain (for example, HTTP addresses). In Figure 7-32, the webpage for the Conrad Systems Development vendor displays correctly, because I'm using a dedicated server running Access Services using an HTTP protocol. If I instead use this sample web app within my Office 365 site (using the HTTPS protocol), Access Services won't display the URLs defined in the Website field of the Vendors table, because the data uses the HTTP protocol. In this case, Access Services displays a message within the web browser control, as shown in Figure 7-33. If you're using an Access web app within Office 365, you'll be able to view pages within your same Office 365 site only.

The URL 'http://www.accessjunkie.com' can't be loaded because it isn't secure. Only secure URLs (beginning with https) can be loaded here.

Figure 7-33 Access Services displays this message within web browser controls if the webpage crosses different domains.

Creating stand-alone views

So far in this chapter and in Chapter 6, you've explored the four different view types available in Access web apps and you've worked with views displayed within the View Selector for different tables. You can also create views that are not displayed within the View Selector. Views that are displayed only within the Navigation pane and not displayed in the View Selector for any tables are referred to as *stand-alone* views. Because stand-alone views do not display a caption that you can click in the View Selector, you must use different techniques to open them. You can only open stand-alone views at runtime in your web browser using one of these techniques:

- Create custom user interface macros that you assign to control or view events

- Use the stand-alone view name as the Popup View property for autocomplete and combo box controls displayed in List Details and Blank views

- Use the stand-alone view name as the Popup View property for related items control tabs displayed in List Details and Blank views

- Use the stand-alone view name as the Popup View property for Summary view detail sections

- Use the stand-alone view name as the Source Object property for subview controls

To create a stand-alone view, you need to use an entry point in the ribbon instead of creating the view from the View Selector. Switch back to Access, if you still have your web browser open from the previous section. Click the Advanced command in the Create group on the Home ribbon tab. Access displays a drop-down list of seven options, as shown in Figure 7-34. Clicking the View button in the Create group opens the Add New View dialog in the View Selector for the currently selected table in the Table Selector. You must click the Advanced command in the Create group to create a stand-alone view.

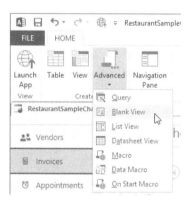

Figure 7-34 Click Blank View, List View, or Datasheet View under Advanced to create stand-alone views.

> **Note**
>
> Clicking the Query option under Advanced opens a new query window. (See Chapter 5.) Clicking the Macro or On Start Macro options under Advanced opens a new macro window, which we'll discuss in Chapter 8. Clicking Data Macro under Advanced opens a new named data macro window. (See Chapter 4, "Creating data macros in web apps.")

INSIDE OUT

Creating stand-alone Summary views

You probably noticed that under the Advanced option in the ribbon, Access does not present an option to create a stand-alone Summary view type. The only way you can create a stand-alone Summary view is to first create a Summary view attached to the View Selector for a table. Next, use the Duplicate feature you learned about in Chapter 6 to create an identical copy of the Summary view using a different name. On the Duplicate View dialog box, make sure to select Standalone/Popup in the Location Of Duplicate drop-down list. Access creates a copy of the Summary view in the Navigation pane. Finally, delete the Summary view that is attached to the View Selector.

To create a new stand-alone view, you can click Blank View, List View, or Datasheet View in the drop-down list under the Advanced command. Clicking the List View option creates a List Details view, even though the label text on this drop-down displays List only. Let's create a new stand-alone Blank view based on the Vendors table. Click the Blank View option on the drop-down list, beneath the Advanced command on the ribbon. Access opens a new unsaved Blank view in Design view on its own object tab in the application window, as shown in Figure 7-35.

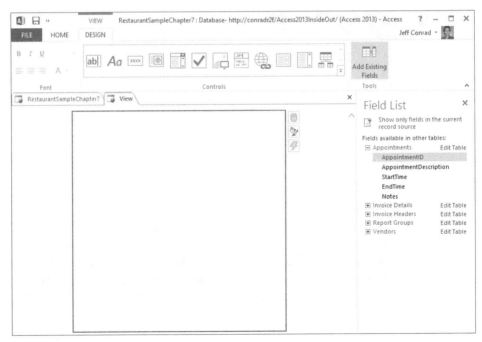

Figure 7-35 When you open a new stand-alone view, Access displays an empty design grid.

Whenever you create a new stand-alone view, Access opens the view object with an empty design grid, because Access does not define the record source for new stand-alone views. (In some cases, you might want to create unbound stand-alone views, such as message pop-up views.) If you create a new stand-alone List Details view, you'll need to define all the properties for the List Control, including the primary display value.

Follow these steps to customize the view to display data from the Vendors table:

1. Click the Data charm button for the view, and select Vendors for the Record Source property from the drop-down list. After you perform this step, Access adds the Action Bar container to the top of the design grid and displays the five built-in Action Bar buttons. Access also displays the fields defined in the Vendors table at the top of the Field List. Close the Data property callout menu for the view.

2. Click the Show Only Fields In The Current Record Source link at the top of the Field List so that Access displays only fields from the Vendors table in the Field List.

3. Double-click each of the following field names to add them in a single column down the design grid: VendorID, VendorName, CustomerNumber, ContactFirstName, ContactLastName, ContactFullName, ContactTitle, ContactCellNumber, Address, Address 2, City, State, and PostalCode. If you add a field in error or if you add the same field twice, delete those controls from the design grid before continuing.

4. Resize all the associated label controls for these first controls so that they are wide enough to display all the label text.

5. Drag the PhoneNumber field name from the Field List, and place the controls to the right of the VendorID controls to start a new column for associated labels and a new column for field controls.

6. Double-click each of the remaining field names in the following order to add them in columns beneath the PhoneNumber controls: PhoneNumberExtenson, FaxNumber, EmailAddress, Website, Active, Notes, and Company Logo.

After you've performed the preceding steps, your design grid should look like Figure 7-36.

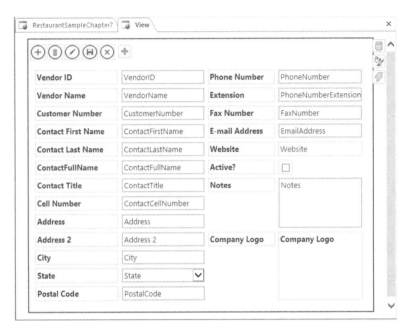

Figure 7-36 Your control layout for the new stand-alone view should look like this.

Now that you've assigned a record source and placed all the fields onto the design grid, let's save the new stand-alone view. Click the Save button on the Quick Access Toolbar. When Access prompts you for a view name, enter **Vendors Standalone** into the Save As dialog box. After you save the view, Access displays the text Vendors Standalone at the top of the object view tab. Close the new stand-alone view you just created. Notice that you don't see this new view listed anywhere in the View Selector for any selected table caption names. You can verify that the new view exists in your web app by looking in the Navigation pane. (Click the Navigation Pane button on the Home ribbon tab, if you do not have the Navigation pane currently expanded.)

If you need to edit an existing stand-alone view, you can open the view by expanding the Navigation pane and then double-clicking the view name, selecting the view and pressing Ctrl+Enter, or right-clicking the view name and selecting Open from the shortcut menu. If you want to rename an existing stand-alone view, expand the Navigation pane, select the view, and press F2, or right-click the view name and select Rename from the shortcut menu. Access places the view name in edit mode in the Navigation pane where you can type in a new view name. (Each view name in the web app must be unique, and you cannot rename a view if it is currently open in Design view.) If you want to delete an existing stand-alone view, expand the Navigation pane, select the view name, and then press Delete, or right-click the view name and then select Delete from the shortcut menu. Access prompts you for confirmation before deleting any view (or any other object type) from the Navigation pane.

You've created and saved a new stand-alone Blank view, but at the moment, you cannot see how this view looks in the runtime in your web browser. As you've learned previously, you'll have to open this stand-alone view from a user interface macro, assign the view to a Popup View property for different control types, or use it as a subview on a different main view that displays in the View Selector. Let's assign this new stand-alone view to open as a pop-up view from another control.

Open in Design view the Invoice Blank view you created and customized earlier in this chapter. Select the VendorIDFK autocomplete control, and then click the Data charm button to open the Data property callout menu. Now click the Popup View property, and select Vendors Standalone, the name of the stand-alone view you just created, from the drop-down list of supported view names, as shown in Figure 7-37.

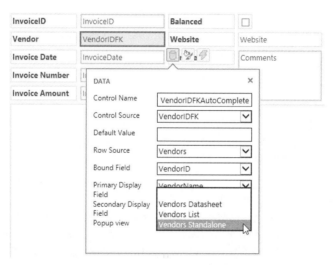

Figure 7-37 Select your new stand-alone view from the drop-down list on the Invoice Blank view.

Save your design changes to the Invoice Blank view by clicking the Save button on the Quick Access Toolbar, and then close the view because we no longer need this view open. Switch back to your web browser, and refresh the Invoice Blank view. (If you previously closed your web browser, click the Launch App button on the Quick Access Toolbar to open your web app in your default browser and then navigate to the Invoice Blank view.) After Access Services loads the Invoice Blank view, click the vendor name link in the Vendor autocomplete control. Access Services now opens the Vendors Standalone view you created as a pop-up view, as shown in Figure 7-38.

Figure 7-38 Access Services displays your stand-alone view as a pop-up view from the Vendor autocomplete control on the main view.

> **Note**
>
> The record displayed in the stand-alone popup view you see in Figure 7-38 might not match the data you see in your own sample view and web app. As you'll recall, you adjusted the embedded query to sort the records in ascending order by the InvoiceDate field for this main view. The first record you see when you open the Invoice Blank view and the subsequent record you see in the Vendors Standalone pop-up view might differ, based on the current date in your computer or device.

INSIDE OUT   Handling views that are displayed too small as pop-up views

When you save a view, Access collapses the design grid boundaries to just fit around the controls. If you have only a few controls on a view and open it as a pop-up view, Access Services displays the view smaller, compared to views with more controls. In most cases, the size of the pop-up window Access Services displays should work fine; however, in some cases, the size can be a hindrance. For example, if you have an autocomplete control at the bottom of a view with a small height, Access Services might not display all the return options in the drop-down list, because the bottom of the list might be truncated. If you encounter this issue, consider placing an additional unused control, perhaps a label or text box, further down the design grid, and then set the Visible property of the control to Hidden. Access Services displays the view with a larger window to accommodate the extra control at runtime, but you won't see the control because it is hidden.

Stand-alone views can be versatile and useful in your web apps for different scenarios. For example, you might want to create a stand-alone view that displays a message to a user or asks for confirmation before completing a step in your web app. You might also use stand-alone views placed within subview controls as a dashboard type of view displaying data from different sources.

Understanding name fixup

No matter how carefully you design your web app, you'll most likely need to change it at a later date. For example, you might find that you need to add new fields to an existing table, rename a field in a table, or rename an object in your web app. When you're working with a relational application like Access web apps, changing one element of your application, such as renaming a field, can impact many other areas of your app. It can potentially cause error messages to appear and objects to no longer function properly. Thankfully, Access includes a feature called *name fixup* that can help fix up related areas of your web app easily when you make some of these types of changes.

Adding fields

Access maintains an internal mapping of object dependencies when you're working with an Access web app. As you create and update tables, queries, and views within your web app, Access updates this internal mapping and uses it to update related objects. Whenever you make any changes to existing tables, you must have all related objects closed before attempting to save your changes. If you attempt to save table changes with related objects open, Access displays an error dialog, as shown in Figure 7-39.

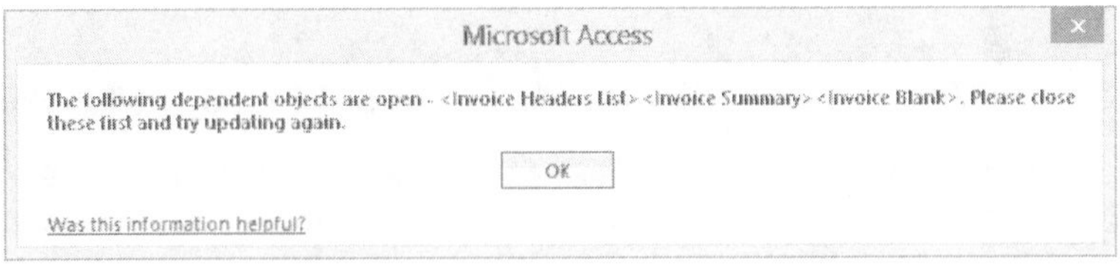

Figure 7-39 Access displays an error dialog when you attempt to save table changes with related objects open.

Access lists the names of all objects related to the table you are changing that are currently open. Access prevents you from saving any table changes until you close all the related objects listed in the error dialog. The names of the objects can be other related tables, queries, and views within the web app. In the example shown previously in Figure 7-39, Access displays the name of three views currently open that must be closed before making changes to the Invoice Headers table—Invoice Headers List, Invoice Summary, and Invoice Blank.

When you're adding new fields to existing tables, Access automatically regenerates a new quick-created List Details and Datasheet view for the table with the new field (or fields, as the case may be), if you have not made any changes to those two views. Access adds new controls bound to the new fields for the quick-created List Details and Datasheet views. If you have opened the two quick-created views, made any edits to them, and saved your changes, Access does not add new controls to those two views when you add new fields to the table. In this case, Access assumes that you made custom changes to the views previously. Therefore, Access does not regenerate new quick-created views, because your custom changes would be lost.

> **Note**
> All preview datasheets for tables opened within Access are always up to date. Access regenerates preview datasheets whenever you make any table schema changes, because you cannot make any design changes to these objects.

Access also won't add new controls to any existing views you previously created to represent new fields added to the source table. If Access adds new controls to your custom views for new fields, Access might adjust the layout of existing controls. (This also applies to any views based on queries.) If you add new fields to a table and want to have controls bound to those new fields on views you've created or modified, you'll have to open each of those views in Design view and add them to the design grid yourself. New List Details and Datasheet views you create from the Add New View dialog on the View Selector, from this point on, will include the new fields, but you'll have to adjust existing views.

Renaming fields

When you rename an existing field in an Access web app table, Access uses the name fixup feature to correct other parts of your web app where the field is referenced. (Remember that when you rename a field, you must have all related objects closed before saving your changes.) Access updates all view types, including quick-created views (changed or untouched) and views you create. When you rename a field, Access searches through the following areas of your web app and updates the property with the new name:

- Display values for lookup fields in related tables

- List Control properties on List Details and Summary views

- Control Source property for view controls bound to the field name you changed

- Display fields for autocomplete controls, combo boxes, and related items controls

- Link Master Field and Link Child Field properties for subview controls

- Display fields used in the detail section of Summary views

- Field names referenced in queries and embedded queries

However, Access won't fix up some areas of your web app when you rename existing fields. You'll need to manually update all of the areas that Access won't fix up with a revised field name. Access won't fix up the following areas when you rename fields:

- Any type of expression within tables, queries, and views. For example, if you use a field name in an expression for a calculated field within the same table, Access won't fix up the field name used in the expression. When you attempt to save your table changes, Access displays a technical details error dialog indicating that it could not find the old field name.

- Expressions used for field and table level validation rules.

- Data macros and user interface macros. Access does not search across these objects when you rename a field.

Renaming objects

Depending on the object type, many areas of your web app could potentially be affected when you rename an object. Here are the object types you can rename that are used within the name fixup feature and their affect within your web app:

- When you rename a table, Access fixes up lookup fields in related tables, queries that use the table as its source, embedded queries that use the table as its source, and view record sources. Access also updates the Row Source property for any affected autocomplete and combo box controls. In addition, Access renames the two quick-created views attached to the table so that the naming scheme remains the same. For example, when you create a table called Employees, Access quick-creates a List Details view, called Employees List, and a Datasheet view, called Employees Datasheet, by default. If you rename the Employees table to Employees New, Access renames the two quick-created views to Employees New List and Employees New Datasheet, respectively. Access renames those views even if you made design changes to them previously. However, Access won't rename the views in this scenario if you've renamed the two quick-created views from their default names. When Access renames quick-created views, it must also update other related objects.

- When you rename a query, Access fixes up other queries that use that query as its source, embedded queries that use the table as its source, and view record sources. Access also updates the Row Source property for autocomplete and combo box controls if you use a saved query object instead of a table. If you use a query as the source for a lookup field, Access updates those lookup field properties in related tables as well.

- When you rename a view, Access fixes up the View Selector, if the view is displayed in any place within the View Selector. Access maintains the link with the new name and opens the correct view at runtime. (Note that view captions displayed in the View Selector are not modified.) Access fixes up the Popup View property for autocomplete, combo box, and related items controls. In addition, Access fixes up the Popup View property for the detail section on Summary views. If you have subview controls that use the view you renamed, Access fixes up the Source Object property.

When you rename a table, query, or view object, Access searches through and fixes up all view types, quick-created and non-quick-created views, changed or untouched views, stand-alone views and views displayed within the View Selector.

> **Note**
> Access won't update any user interface macros or data macros with the name fixup feature. If you use a table, query, or view name in a user interface macro or data macro, you'll need to manually update those macros with any revised object names.

Deleting objects

The name fixup feature does not include deleting objects. If you delete an object, Access does not fix up any references to that object in your web app. You'll need to fix up any objects that reference the deleted object yourself. Depending on the object you delete, you might not be able to add, edit, or delete data in your web app until you fix up the remaining areas of your web app. For example, if you delete a table that is referenced in the After Insert, After Update, and After Delete events of a different table, you'll get an error message any time you try to update data in the source table.

> **Note**
>
> If you delete an object and do not fix up all areas of your web app that reference the deleted object, you might not be able to save your web app as an app package. If you encounter an error while attempting to save your app as an app package, make sure to take special note of the error message because it might indicate a broken object or field reference. To successfully save your app as an app package, you'll need to fix up any broken object and field references.

If you delete fields in a table, Access does fix up the two quick-created views for the table, but only if you have not modified and saved changes to the views. Remember that Access regenerates a new List Details and Datasheet quick-created view if you have not modified those views. In this case, Access does not create controls for the deleted field, so the new quick-created views won't contain any references to the deleted field. On views that you create or modify, Access Services displays an error message inside any controls bound to deleted fields at runtime, as shown in Figure 7-40. You'll need to remove any controls bound to deleted fields within your views if you encounter this type of error.

Error: Invalid control reference

Figure 7-40 Access displays this error message inside controls at runtime if it cannot find the field referenced in the Control Source property.

Applying themes to web app views

SharePoint sites allow you to change their look and appearance globally through site themes. All screen shots you've seen so far in this book concerning web app views have used the default SharePoint Office site theme. If you change the theme of the SharePoint site in which your Access web app is hosted, your Access web app inherits the look and feel of the site theme. Your views can now look much more colorful and blend in with the rest of the SharePoint site elements.

To apply a different theme to your Access web app, you must select a different theme for the SharePoint site in which your Access web app resides. First, navigate to the SharePoint site where your Access web app resides. Above the Table Selector and View Selector in your web app at runtime, you'll see a few options that appear at all times—the Back To Site link, the name of your Access web app, and the Customize In Access gear button, as shown in Figure 7-41. These elements are referred to as the *shell* of your Access Services web app site. Click the Back To Site link in the upper-left corner to navigate to the parent site of your SharePoint server where your Access web app resides. Next to the Back To Site link, you'll see the name of your Access web app—RestaurantSampleChapter7, in this example. Click this hyperlink to return to the default page of your web app at any time. Click the Customize In Access gear button if you want to open the web app in Access. Clicking this option downloads the web app into Access where you can customize the web app. (You learned how to use this button in Chapter 2.)

Figure 7-41 Click the Back To Site link in your Access web app to navigate to the parent SharePoint site.

Click the Back To Site link in the sample web app you've been working with so far in this chapter. Access Services navigates you to the parent SharePoint site in which your Access web app resides, as shown in Figure 7-42.

> **Note**
> The layout, links, buttons, and command options shown on the SharePoint main site page in Figure 7-42 might differ from what you see within your own SharePoint site. Your internal organization's SharePoint server administrator or third-party hosting services company might have configured the server you are using differently than the server I used in the figure.

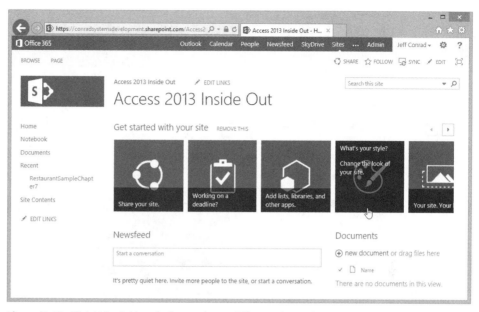

Figure 7-42 Click What's Your Style to select a different theme for your parent SharePoint site.

> **Note**
>
> A full discussion of SharePoint sites and all the features contained within them is beyond the scope of this book. This section will familiarize you with how Access web app views work in conjunction with SharePoint site themes.

Near the top of the SharePoint site page, you'll see the name of the SharePoint site—Access 2013 Inside Out, in this example. In the middle of the SharePoint site page, you'll see several large buttons for performing different tasks in your SharePoint site. Among these large buttons, you'll see one labeled What's Your Style, shown previously in Figure 7-42. Click the What's Your Style button, and SharePoint navigates you to the Change The Look page within the Site Settings section of your site, as shown in Figure 7-43.

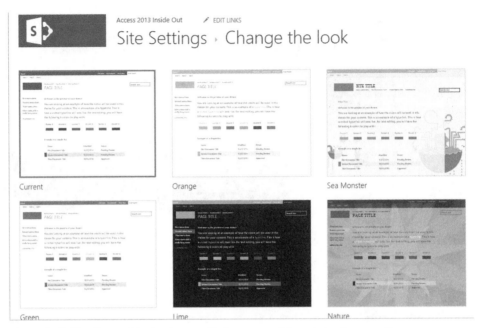

Figure 7-43 The Change The Look page displays many different site theme options you can choose from and apply to your site.

On the Change The Look page, SharePoint displays 17 different themes you can choose from to customize the look of your SharePoint site. (You can scroll down the page to see all of the theme options.) SharePoint displays your current site theme with the heading Current in the upper-left corner of the page. Your current site theme is also listed with its formal name in the list of themes, so you'll actually see 18 themes listed on the page. If you're using Access web apps inside your corporate organization's SharePoint sites, your SharePoint administrators might have created custom site themes to match their own corporate color scheme. The default site theme currently applied to the SharePoint site in Figure 7-43 is the Office site theme.

SharePoint displays a preview graphic of how each theme would look when applied to your site, as well as the different main colors used. You'll notice that some of the themes also include an image displayed as a watermark background. You can scan through the various site theme preview graphics on this page to see which theme you want to display for your Access web app. Scroll down the page now, and click the Breeze site theme preview graphic. SharePoint navigates you to a page where you can take a closer look at the Breeze site theme, as shown in Figure 7-44.

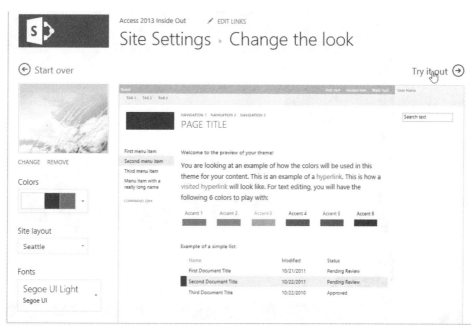

Figure 7-44 On the preview page, you can make additional customizations to the site theme.

In this preview page, SharePoint displays options along the left side where you can make additional customizations to the selected site theme. For example, you can make changes to the background image, colors for the page elements, site layout, and fonts used with the theme. In the middle of the page, SharePoint displays a sample site page layout so that you can see how your site will look with the selected theme elements and colors. If you don't want to select this theme, you can click the Start Over link in the upper-left corner of the page to navigate back to the Change The Look page with the list of all site themes, where you can select a different theme. After you make your changes or keep the default theme settings, you can click the Try It Out link in the upper-right corner of the page. For this example, leave the default Breeze site theme settings as they are and click the Try it Out link. SharePoint navigates you to the final preview page, as shown in Figure 7-45.

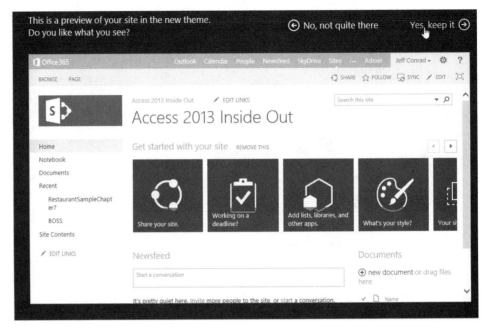

Figure 7-45 Click the Yes, Keep It link to apply the selected theme to your SharePoint site.

On this final page, SharePoint displays a preview of what your selected site theme will look like with actual page elements from your existing site page. If you do not like what this site theme looks like, click the No, Not Quite There link at the top of the page. SharePoint navigates you back to the previous page where you can make customizations to the site theme settings. If you like how the site theme preview looks, you can click the Yes, Keep It link in the upper-right corner of the page to apply the theme to your SharePoint site. SharePoint then navigates you back to the main page of your site where you can see the site theme applied. Click Yes, Keep It to apply the Breeze theme to your SharePoint site, and Share-Point navigates to your main SharePoint site page. Now navigate to your Access web app to see how applying a site theme to your parent SharePoint site affects your Access web app. In Figure 7-46, I've navigated to the Vendor List view in the sample web app we've been working on in this chapter.

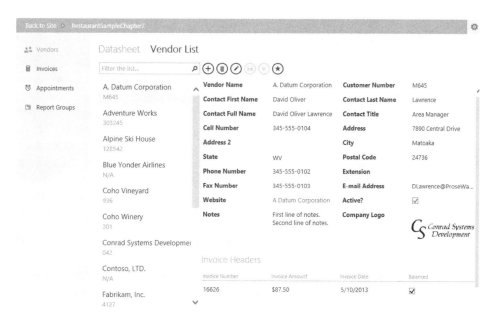

Figure 7-46 The Vendor List view in the sample web app now displays visual elements from the SharePoint Breeze site theme.

You can see how Access web app views inherit the look and feel from the SharePoint Breeze site theme when you change the theme on the SharePoint site and take on a completely new look. Although it might not appear completely obvious from the screen shot, the color of the Access Services shell elements and the Table Selector are now different shades of blue. The selected Vendor List view caption in the View Selector changed color from the previous theme. Also, the background site theme image can be seen behind the detail area controls in the view. As you navigate around the different views in both edit and view mode, you'll see how the Access web app views and view controls seamlessly blend in with the site theme. If you'd like, you can try out some of the other SharePoint site themes on your own and see how they look with your Access web app views, or you can change the site theme back to the default Office theme.

> ## Note
>
> All Access web apps hosted within a SharePoint site inherit the site theme from the parent site. If you want different Access web apps to use different site themes, you'll need to create separate SharePoint subsites within your parent site, apply different site themes to the respective sites, and then create your Access web apps within the separate subsites.

Exploring sample views in the BOSS app

Now that you've explored all the different control and view types and learned how to create and customize views, let's take a closer look at some of the sample views in the more complex Back Office Software System web app (BOSS.app), which you can download from the book's catalog page. Although showing you every view available in the Back Office Software System web app and how it was constructed is not possible due to the large number of views in the app (over 100), I encourage you to open up the various views in Design view and study how the controls and control properties are set up. You'll no doubt learn some more advanced tricks with web app views, as well as get ideas on how to create and customize different views for your own specific app needs. In this section, I'll highlight some of the more interesting views that you might want to spend extra time studying.

Download the BOSS.app sample web app from the book's catalog page, and install the app within your SharePoint site running Access Services. After you install the BOSS web app, the first view you'll navigate to is the Home view, shown in Figure 7-47. The Home view is a unique Blank view, in that it contains four subview controls, each displaying separate views.

The first subview displays a list of employee names that have birthdays within the next 30 days. The view name used in the subview control is viewUpcomingBirthdays, and the query used for the record source is qryUpcomingBirthdays. The query uses several expressions to calculate and format the display of upcoming employee birthday data. Two other subviews on the Home view display any orders and deliveries from vendors scheduled for the current day of the week. The last subview displays a list of appointments scheduled for the current day. This subview lists the start time and end time for each appointment and includes a command button control labeled View. Clicking this command button opens a stand-alone view, called viewAppointmentDetails, showing the details of the selected appointment record. The subviews on the Home view do not use the Link Master Field and Link Child Field properties of the subview control, because the queries that are used for the subviews control the data to display. The Home view serves as a dashboard type of view that quickly shows everything important for the current day.

Figure 7-47 The Home view of the BOSS web app displays four subview controls.

You'll notice in Figure 7-47 that the Table Selector displays over a dozen table name captions with different table icons. More tables exist than those seen here, because many other tables are hidden in the Table Selector and not displayed at runtime.

In the lower-right corner of the Home view, you'll see a command button labeled About. Clicking the About command button opens an unbound stand-alone Blank view, called viewAbout, as a pop-up view, as shown in Figure 7-48. This view displays copyright information for the web app. You'll notice this specific view displays no Action Bar buttons because the view is not bound to any table or query. Click the OK command button on this view to close it, or click the view Close (X) button.

Chapter 7

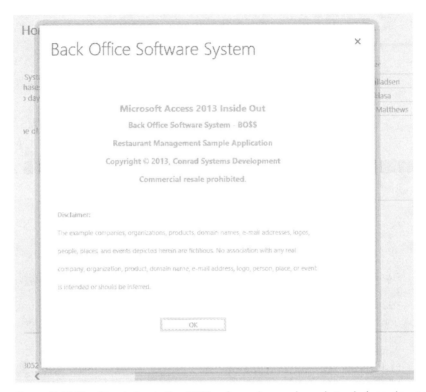

Figure 7-48 The About view in the BOSS web app is an unbound stand-alone view opened as a pop-up view.

Now let's look at Company Information view. Click the Home table name caption (it should already be selected) in the Table Selector, and then click the Company Information view caption name in the View Selector. Access Services opens the Company Information view, as shown in Figure 7-49. This Blank view uses the tblCompanyInformation table for its record source. This table contains only one record, and data macros attached to the table ensure that only one record ever exists in the table. The data in this view displays specific company information for the web app, which can be customized by clicking the Edit Action Bar button. You'll notice on this view that I've removed the Add and Delete built-in Action Bar buttons, because I don't want users to be adding new records to the view or deleting the existing record. The data shown in this view is also displayed in the Home view, shown previously. You can customize the text here to your company name and details that show in the Home view. I also include a label control with a red asterisk defined for the Caption property next to the Company Name field to indicate that field is a required field. At the bottom of the view, you'll see three command buttons used to perform additional administrative functions. I used a wide label control with the underscore character (_) for the Caption property above these command buttons to serve as a visual separation from the rest of the view controls.

Home   Company Information

Company Name	*	Northwind Cuisine	Manager Name	Jeff Conrad
Job Title		General Manager	Website	http://www.AccessJunkie.com
Address		One Microsoft Way	City	Redmond
State		WA	Postal Code	98052
Phone Number		121-212-1212	Fax Number	121-212-1213

Greeting   Welcome to the Back Office Software System application! This application was designed to help food service organizations keep track of their purchases, products, and other areas of restaurant management. Used properly, it can help you stay on top of the day to day operations of running your business and allow you more time to focus on customer satisfaction.

View Admin Settings   View Trace Table   Clear Trace Table

Figure 7-49 Use the Company Information view in the BOSS web app to customize the text displayed in the Home view.

So far, you've seen several examples of Blank views. Now I'd like to show you a complex List Details view. Click the Employees table name caption in the Table Selector, and then click the Active Employees view caption name in the View Selector. Access Services opens the Active Employees view, as shown in Figure 7-50. This List Details view uses a query for its record source to display currently active employees only.

The List Control portion of the view uses a custom expression for the Primary property of the List Control. The expression concatenates the employee's last name, a comma, and the employee's first name. The employee's hire date is used for the Secondary property of the List Control. Finally, I used the EmployeePicture field in the tblEmployees table for the Thumbnail property, so users of the app can easily recognize an employee by their picture as they scan through the records in the List Control.

Figure 7-50 The Active Employees view in the BOSS web app is a complex List Details view with information concerning employee and related records.

On the Active Employees view, I use label controls for indicating required fields and for creating a visual separation from the emergency contact information for each employee record. You'll notice, at the top of the view, a custom Action Bar button that toggles, sorting the employee records from ascending to descending. You'll learn how to create this type of custom Action Bar button with macro logic in Chapter 8.

At the bottom of the Active Employees view, you'll see a related items control, as shown in Figure 7-51. This particular related items control contains five different tabs—Labor Hours, Schedule, Trained Positions, Vacations, and Terminations. Each tab displays related records from other tables so that you can easily view, edit, and add data for the selected employee without having to navigate to other views in the app. Some of the tabs in this related items control also display calculations using the properties available on the Calculation property callout menu.

Labor Hours   Schedule   Trained Positions   Vacations   Terminations

Work Date	Hours	Tips	Comment
12/21/2012	8.00		
12/20/2012	8.00		
12/19/2012	8.00		
12/18/2012	8.00		
12/17/2012	8.00		

Add Labor Hours   Number of hours: 40.00

Figure 7-51 The related items control on the Active Employees view in the BOSS web app displays related record data for employees in the app.

Now that you've seen the Active Employees view, click the Inactive Employees view caption name in the View Selector. Access Services opens the Inactive Employees view, as shown in Figure 7-52. This view is nearly identical to the Active Employees view you saw previously. This List Details view also uses a query for its record source but, in this case, restricts the records to inactive employees only. You'll notice that I hide the Add Action Bar button on this view. You might think that I designed this view from scratch; in fact, I used the duplicate feature, which saved a lot of development time, because I knew that this view would be nearly identical to the Active Employees view. After duplicating the Active Employees view to create the Inactive Employees view, I then needed only to change the record source for the view and hide the Add Action Bar button. You'll find the duplicating view feature very useful if you're creating similar views with different record sources.

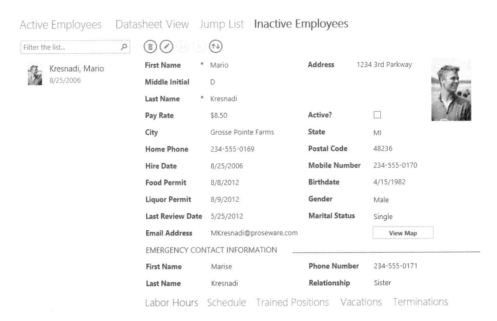

Figure 7-52 The Inactive Employees view in the BOSS web app was created by duplicating the Active Employees view.

Let's open a List Details view from a different table now. Click the Purchases table name caption in the Table Selector, and then click the Purchases - Subview view caption name in the View Selector. Access Services opens the Purchases - Subview view, as shown in Figure 7-53. This List Details view uses a saved query called qryInvoiceHeadersWithVendor as its record source. The query joins data from both the tblInvoiceHeaders and tblVendors table. (This view is similar to the Invoice Blank view you created earlier in this chapter.) The view displays invoice records, and the subview control displays related invoice detail records. To maintain the linking between the main view and subview, I use the Link Master Field and Link Child Field properties of the subview control. If the invoice total is balanced with the invoice details, the text Invoice Is Balanced is displayed in a label control in the upper-right corner of the view. I also set the background color of the label control to green and the fore color to white. If the invoice is not balanced with the invoice details, the label text displays Invoice Not Balanced with a red background color. I'll show you how to accomplish this task using macros in Chapter 8.

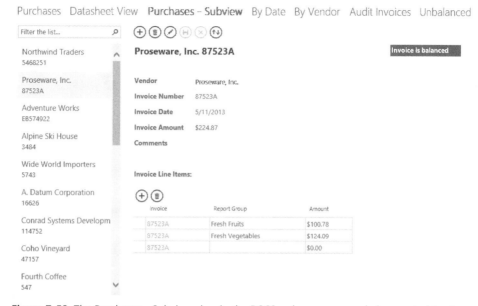

Figure 7-53 The Purchases - Subview view in the BOSS web app uses a subview control to display invoice details.

You've seen several examples of Blank views and List Details views, so let's take a look at a Summary view now. Click the By Date view caption name in the View Selector for this same table name caption. Access Services opens the By Date view, as shown in Figure 7-54. This view is a Summary view that groups all purchases by specific dates. By clicking a specific displayed date in the List Control, you can easily see all purchases for that date in the detail section of this view. The detail section displays the vendor name, invoice number, amount, and a check box control to indicate whether the invoice is balanced. The List Control in this view also displays the total amount of invoices for each displayed date.

Purchases Datasheet View Purchases - Subview **By Date** By Vendor Audit Invoices Unbalanced

Filter the list... 🔍		Vendor	Invoice Number	Amount	Balanced
12/22/2012	(2)	Coho Vineyard	47157	$112.35	☑
Amount: 757.18		Fourth Coffee	547	$30.00	☑
12/21/2012	(3)	Northwind Traders	54572512	$463.26	☑
Amount: 252.76		Trey Research	65472	$123.45	☑
12/20/2012	(2)				
Amount: 329.95					
12/19/2012	(4)				
Amount: 729.06					
12/18/2012	(4)				
Amount: 617.1					
12/17/2012	(5)				
Amount: 2898.41					
11/4/2012	(1)				
Amount: 57.23					
10/11/2012	(1)				
Amount: 56					
8/18/2012	(1)				
Amount: 30					

Figure 7-54 The By Date view in the BOSS web app is a Summary view that groups invoice records by date.

You can review the By Vendor view listed in the View Selector for the Purchases table caption to see another example of a Summary view. The By Vendor view groups all invoice records by vendor so that you can quickly see and review a purchases history for each vendor in the app.

Let's look at an example of a Datasheet view in the Back Office Software System app. Click the Products table name caption in the Table Selector, and then click the Datasheet View caption name in the View Selector. Access Services opens the Datasheet View, as shown in Figure 7-55. This view displays a list of all products in the web app (over 600 records). The products records are sorted alphabetically, by default, using a query that sorts on the ProductName field in the tblProducts table. In Figure 7-55, you can see that I clicked the column header above the Report Group field to display the AutoFilter menu options available for this column. Using the various filtering options above each column, you can quickly filter this large number of records to a much smaller subset. For example, you might want to see only products assigned to a specific report group or only products stored in a specific inventory location. You can make quick edits to multiple records by using Datasheet views in your web apps.

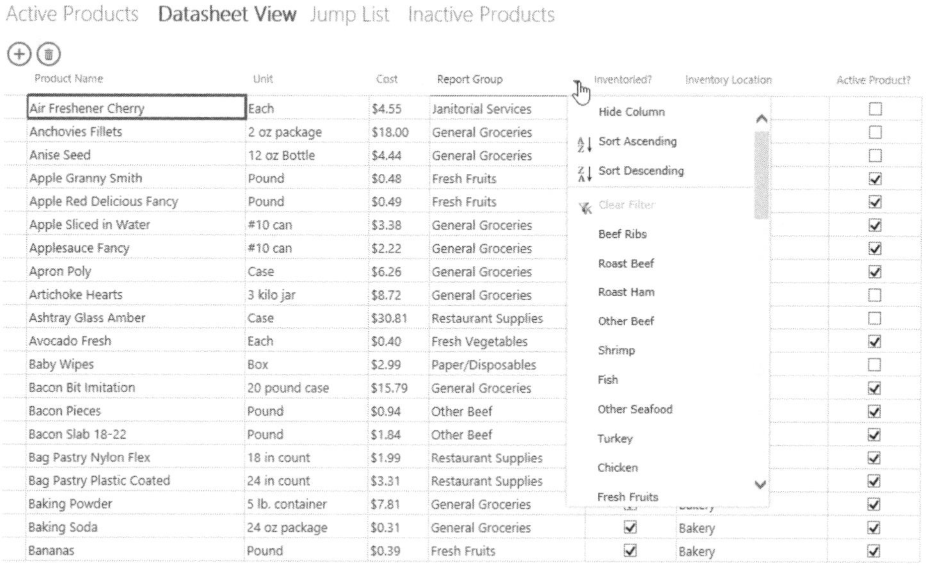

Figure 7-55 The Datasheet View in the BOSS web app displays all product records in a Datasheet view.

Switch over now to the Jump List view on this same Products table name caption. Access Services opens the Jump List view, as shown in Figure 7-56. This Summary view uses an expression for the Group By property in the List Control. The expression in the List Control groups product records by the first letter in the product name so that you can quickly review and find all product records that begin with a specific letter. The List Control also displays a count of the number of products for each letter. With the large number of product records in this sample app, you'll find using a Summary view with this type of Group By expression useful for finding records.

Active Products   Datasheet View   **Jump List**   Inactive Products

Filter the list...		Product Name	Report Group	Inventory Location	Cost
A	(11)	Air Freshener Cherry	Janitorial Services	Cleaning Closet	$4.55
		Anchovies Fillets	General Groceries	Main Cooler	$18.00
B	(82)	Anise Seed	General Groceries	Spice Shelf	$4.44
C	(131)	Apple Granny Smith	Fresh Fruits	Pantry Cooler	$0.48
		Apple Red Delicious Fancy	Fresh Fruits	Pantry Cooler	$0.49
D	(29)	Apple Sliced in Water	General Groceries	Dry Storage	$3.38
E	(13)	Applesauce Fancy	General Groceries	Dry Storage	$2.22
F	(31)	Apron Poly	General Groceries	Dry Storage	$6.26
		Artichoke Hearts	General Groceries	Dry Storage	$8.72
G	(31)	Ashtray Glass Amber	Restaurant Supplies	Dry Storage	$30.81
H	(7)	Avocado Fresh	Fresh Vegetables	Pantry Cooler	$0.40
I	(2)				
J	(8)				
K	(8)				
L	(15)				
M	(23)				
N	(3)				

Figure 7-56 The Jump List view in the BOSS web app groups product records by the first letter in the product name.

The next view I'd like to show you is the Edit Schedules view. Click the Schedule table name caption in the Table Selector, and then click the Edit Schedules view caption name in the View Selector. Access Services opens the Edit Schedules view, as shown in Figure 7-57. This Blank view uses the tblSchedule table for its record source. What makes this view unique is that the view contains a subview control; however, I'm not using a field name for the Link Master Field property of the subview control. Instead, I'm using an actual control name for this property. Access Services can still keep the main view and subview records in sync when you use a control name for the link field properties.

Edit Schedules   Copy Schedules   Delete Schedules   All Records   By Date   By Employee   By Position

Enter date to view   5/11/2013

⊕ ⊝

Schedule Date	Start Time	End Time	Employee	Job Code
5/11/2013	7:30 AM	5:00 PM	Conrad	Manager
5/11/2013	9:00 AM	3:00 PM	Smith	Pantry
5/11/2013	8:00 AM	4:00 PM	Lannin	Cook
5/11/2013	8:00 AM	5:00 PM	Viescas	Baker
5/11/2013	8:30 AM	4:30 PM	Dixon	Dishwasher
5/11/2013	10:00 AM	4:00 PM	Zulechner	Busser
5/11/2013	10:30 AM	3:00 PM	Gibson	Cashier-Hostess
5/11/2013	10:45 AM	3:30 PM	Curran	Line Server
5/11/2013	12:00 PM	7:30 PM	Trukawka	Busser
5/11/2013	12:00 PM	8:00 PM	Matthews	Cook
5/11/2013	12:30 PM	7:30 PM	Wroblewska	Cashier-Hostess
5/11/2013	2:00 PM	8:15 PM	Zabokritski	Baker
5/11/2013	2:00 PM	8:45 PM	Stoklasa	Pantry
5/11/2013	3:00 PM	8:00 PM	Jankowski	Line Server
5/11/2013	3:00 PM	8:00 PM	Buschmann	Cashier-Hostess
5/11/2013	3:00 PM	9:30 PM	Ready	Cook
5/11/2013	3:30 PM	10:00 PM	Linggoputro	Dishwasher
5/11/2013	4:00 PM	9:30 PM	Villadsen	Busser
5/11/2013	5:30 PM	9:30 PM	Jensen	Line Server
5/11/2013				

Figure 7-57 The Edit Schedules view in the BOSS web app uses an unbound text box control for the Link Master Field property of the subview control.

When the Edit Schedules view first opens, you'll see no records displayed in the subview because the only text box control visible in the main view initially contains no value. When you type in a date and press Enter, or use the date picker to select a date for the text box control at the top of the view, Access Services displays all employee schedule records that match the entered date. In Figure 7-57, shown previously, I selected a date of 5/11/2013. Access Services displays all the saved schedule records for that date. If I choose a different date, Access Services requeries the subview control and displays any matching records for the new date. Using this technique, users of the app can pick a date to enter new records or edit existing records. Access Services loads any matching records and automatically displays the selected date in the disabled Schedule Date control within the subview for new records.

Now click the Copy Schedules view name caption in the View Selector to load this view, as shown in Figure 7-58. This view is an unbound view with all unbound controls. I use this view to create new schedule records in the tblSchedule table either by copying existing schedule records from the same table and applying new schedule dates or by copying labor plan schedule template records from the tblLaborPlans and tblLaborPlanDetails tables.

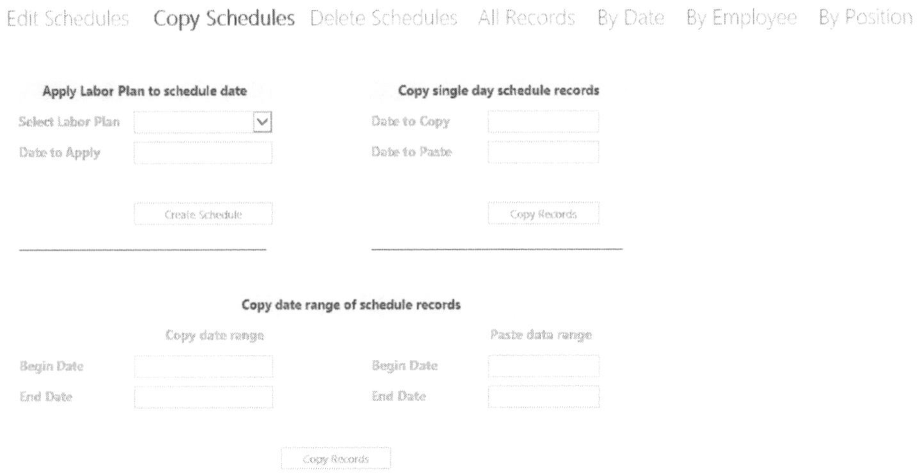

Edit Schedules   **Copy Schedules**   Delete Schedules   All Records   By Date   By Employee   By Position

Apply Labor Plan to schedule date

Select Labor Plan   [▼]

Date to Apply   [   ]

Create Schedule

Copy single day schedule records

Date to Copy   [   ]

Date to Paste   [   ]

Copy Records

Copy date range of schedule records

Copy date range   Paste data range

Begin Date   [   ]   Begin Date   [   ]

End Date   [   ]   End Date   [   ]

Copy Records

Figure 7-58 The Copy Schedules view in the BOSS web app is an unbound view used to execute named data macros.

In the first group of controls, the user selects a labor plan template that they want to use from a combo box control. The user then provides a date to apply the new records to in the Date To Apply text box. When the user clicks the Create Schedule command button, Access Services executes a named data macro and passes those view control values on to the named data macro as parameters to create new schedule records. In the other two groups of controls, the user selects either a single date or a range of dates to copy existing schedule records. Using this view and the named data macros, the restaurant manager can quickly make future daily and weekly employee work schedules by using past schedules as a base from which to start. If the user creates records in error, they can switch to the Delete Schedules view, which has a similar setup but allows deleting scheduling records in bulk.

The last view I'd like to show you is a special view I created that allows users of the app to select a color to use to assign to different job codes. Click the Job Codes table name caption in the Table Selector, and then click the Job Code List view caption name in the View Selector. Access Services opens the Job Codes List view. Click the command button, labeled Set Colors, in the upper-right corner of the view. Access Services opens a pop-up view with a caption labeled Select A Color, as shown in Figure 7-59.

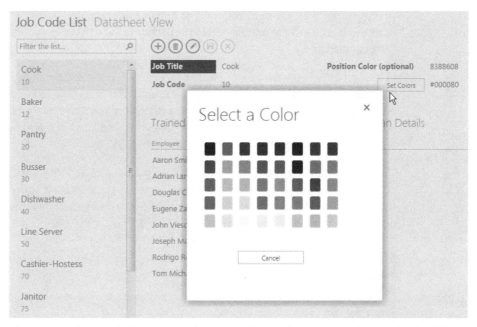

Figure 7-59 This stand-alone view in the BOSS web app allows you to select a color for different job codes.

This view is named viewColorPicker in the Navigation pane. It is a stand-alone Blank view bound to the tblColorImages table, which contains 40 image fields. The table contains only one record, with a saved color image file for each field. On the view, I placed 40 image controls, each bound to the separate fields. When the user clicks a color image, I use macros to save the selected hexadecimal color code and the RGB color code to two different fields in the tblJobCodes table. I use the hexadecimal color value for the background of the Job Title label on the Job Code List view and the RGB color code for desktop database reports linked to the web app tables. Click the command button labeled Cancel to close this pop-up view without making changes.

Although you've only seen a small sampling of various views and view types in the Back Office Software System web app, I encourage you to explore the other views in this app as well as the Auctions and Training Tracker sample web apps, which can be downloaded from the book's catalog page.

Extending your web app with desktop database reports

You can extend the capabilities of your Access web app, beyond the features included with the web app interface, by linking your web app tables to an Access desktop database. In Chapter 3, "Designing tables in a web app," you learned how to link SharePoint lists into an Access web app. You can also link the tables in a web app to an Access desktop database where you can then use all the objects and functionality available within desktop databases. Access web apps include options within the Backstage view that allow you to perform this link operation easily.

In this section, you'll learn how to create a reporting desktop database based on the Back Office Software System sample web app (BOSS.app). This reporting desktop database will include read-only links to all the tables in the BOSS app. You'll then import desktop database objects from a separate database I've already created into the reporting database so that you can open reports based on the data in the BOSS app.

To begin, open the Back Office Software System sample web app (BOSS.app) in Access. (If you closed Access after completing the previous section, open Access again and then open the Back Office Software System app.) Click the File tab on the Backstage view, and Access displays the Info tab, as shown in Figure 7-60.

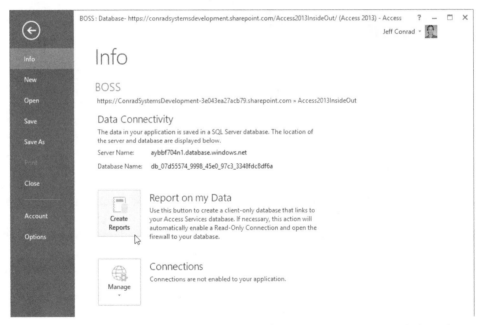

Figure 7-60 Click the Create Reports button on the Info tab to create a reporting desktop database for your web app.

As you learned in Chapter 2, the Info tab displays the name of your app, the URL to your app, the server name, and the database name where your app is stored within SQL Server. To create a reporting desktop database linked to your web app tables, click the Create Reports button in the middle of the Info tab. Depending on where you have your Access web app hosted and how the SharePoint server administrators configured the server, you might see an error message concerning connection issues after clicking the Create Reports button, as shown in Figure 7-61.

Figure 7-61 You might see this message when first attempting to click the Create Reports button with a web app.

As the message indicates, you'll need to perform an extra step before Access can successfully create links to your web app. If you see this message, you need to change an option within the Manage command list of connection options. To solve this issue, click OK to dismiss the dialog, and then click the Manage button on the Info tab of the Backstage view. Access displays a menu of nine connection options, as shown in Figure 7-62. (Note that the ninth option—From My Location—is not shown in Figure 7-62.)

Figure 7-62 Click the From Any Location connection option to enable Access to create a connection for a reporting desktop database.

I'll discuss each of these connection options in more detail later in this chapter, but for now, the only option you need to be concerned with is the From Any Location option. When you select this option, Access allows connections to the SQL Server database that contains your web app structure and data from any computer or device. This means that you can make connections from a different computer or device as long as you have appropriate permission to access the web app. Click From Any Location, and Access dismisses the list of options in the Manage button menu. Access now displays text next to the Manage button indicating that connections are enabled for your web app, as shown in Figure 7-63.

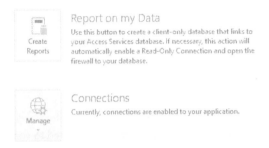

Figure 7-63 Access displays a message indicating that connections are enabled for your application.

Now that you've successfully enabled connections for this specific web app, click the Create Reports again. Access opens the Save A Local Copy dialog box, as shown in Figure 7-64. To create a reporting desktop database linked to the tables in your web app, you need to provide a location where you want to save the desktop file and a file name.

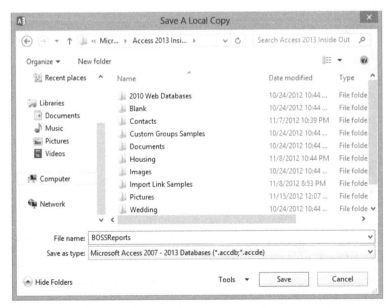

Figure 7-64 Select a destination folder, and enter a file name for the reporting database.

You can select the drive and folder you want by clicking the links on the left and browsing to your destination folder. In Figure 7-64, shown previously, I'm saving this new reporting desktop database in the Access 2013 Inside Out folder where all the sample files are stored on my local computer. You can choose this same destination folder or a different location for this example if you want. After you select the specific folder to which you want to save this new database, enter **BOSSReports** as the name for your database in the File Name text box. If you decide at this point not to create the database, click the Cancel button to return to the Info tab on the Backstage view to stop the process.

Click Save on the Save A Local Copy dialog to return to the Info tab on the Backstage view. Access then begins the process of creating this new reporting desktop database. Note that it might appear for several seconds that Access is not responding. Be patient here; Access is communicating with the SQL Server database where your web app resides, and it might take as long as 30 seconds for a response. Access then opens up another instance of itself, creates a new desktop database in your destination folder, and displays a list of links to all the tables in your web app in this new database, as shown in Figure 7-65.

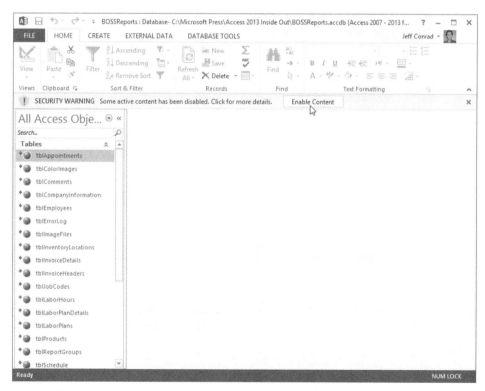

Figure 7-65 Your reporting desktop database includes read-only links to all the tables in your web app.

Access displays an icon—a blue arrow and globe—next to each linked table in the Navigation pane indicating that these are linked tables instead of local tables. If you open any of these tables, you'll see all the data stored in the corresponding web app table within the SQL Server database. Access creates these links as read-only, so you won't be able to add, edit, or delete any data in these tables from this desktop database.

You could now build query, form, and report desktop database objects into this database using the data in the web app as their source. I've already created a separate desktop database that includes these types of objects, which you can import into this reporting database. To import these objects, first click the Enable Content button in the message bar to trust the content of this database, shown previously in Figure 7-65. This step is necessary to use the reports I created. When you click Enable Content, Access closes the reporting database and then reopens it. You'll learn more about enabling content and trusting desktop databases in Chapter 9, "Exploring the Access 2013 desktop database interface."

After you enable the content in the reporting database, you'll need to import objects from a separate desktop database into this file. To do this, click the Access button in the Import & Link group on the External Data contextual ribbon tab. Access opens the Get External Data - Access Database dialog, as shown in Figure 7-66. In this dialog, enter the folder and the name of the desktop database file containing the objects that you want to import. In the Access 2013 Inside Out folder where you downloaded and installed the sample files for this book, you'll see a subfolder called Import Link Samples. Within this subfolder is a file called BOSSReportsMaster.accdb, the desktop database from which you need to import objects into your reporting database. You can either enter the path manually in the File Name text box or use the Browse button to navigate to the correct file in the sample folder.

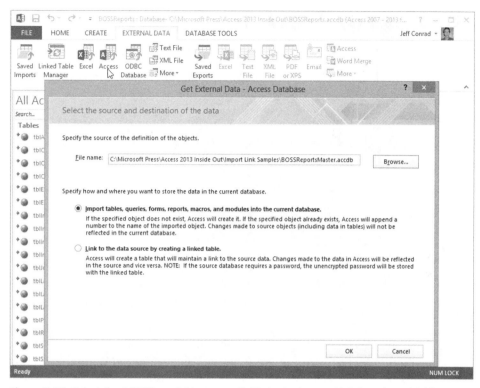

Figure 7-66 Select the BOSSReportsMaster.accdb file in the Import Link Samples subfolder.

On the Get External Data - Access Database dialog, leave the Import Tables, Queries, Forms, Reports, Macros, And Modules Into The Current Database option selected and then click OK. (You can learn about the second option—Link To A Data Source By Creating A Linked Table—in Article 3, "Importing and linking data," which can be downloaded from the book's catalog page.) Access then opens the Import Objects dialog box, shown in Figure 7-67, which provides tabs for each of the object types in the desktop database you selected.

Figure 7-67 Click Select All on each tab in the Import Objects dialog, except the Tables tab, to highlight and select all objects for import.

You do not want to import any table objects from the BOSSReportsMaster.accdb file, so do not select any tables on the Tables tab. Click the Queries tab, and then click the Select All button to highlight all of the query objects for import. Next, click the Forms tab and click Select All to highlight all the form objects. Repeat this process for the Reports, Macros, and Modules tabs so that all objects are highlighted. Remember: do not attempt to import any table objects from the BOSSReportsMaster.accdb database. After you have all the objects highlighted, except tables, click OK to begin the import process. Access imports all of the existing objects from the BOSSReportsMaster.accdb into your reporting database. This process might take a minute or two to complete. When all objects are imported, Access displays a message dialog that informs you of the result of the import procedure, as shown in Figure 7-68. Click Close to dismiss the dialog.

> **Note**
> During the import process of these objects, you might see two parameter input boxes appear. These appear due to some specific query parameters in some of the objects you are importing. When you see Access display these parameters, click Cancel for each one to continue with the import process.

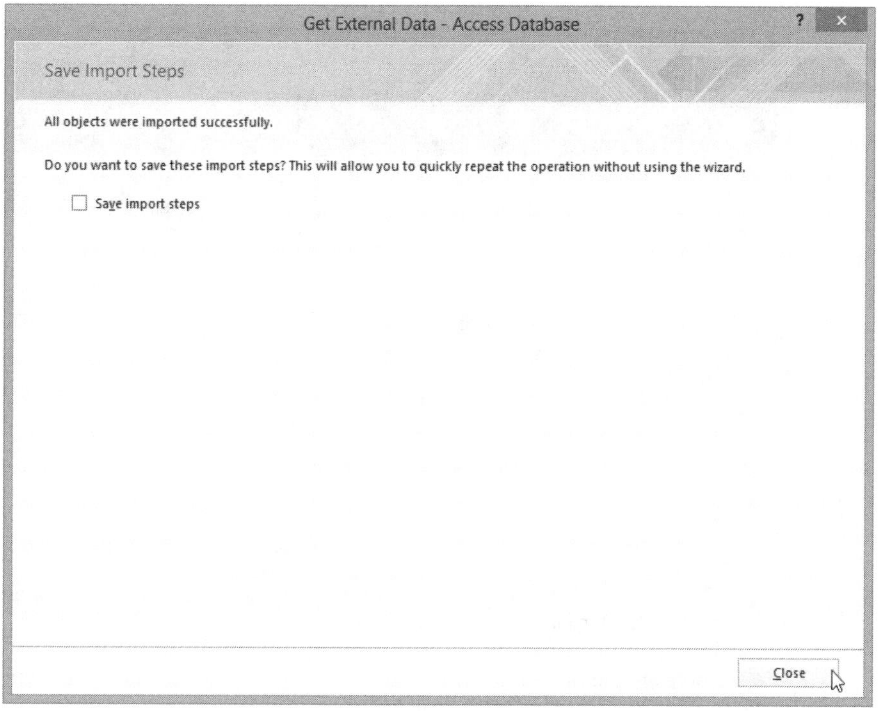

Figure 7-68 Click Close after Access successfully imports all of the objects.

The Navigation pane in your reporting desktop now has many different desktop database objects to complement the data in the Back Office Software System web app. I've included one main form that you can use to open various reports on the data in the linked tables in the database. Locate the form object called frmMainMenuClient in the Navigation pane, and then double-click it. Access opens the form, shown in Figure 7-69, and displays a similar layout to the Home view in the web app you studied previously in this chapter.

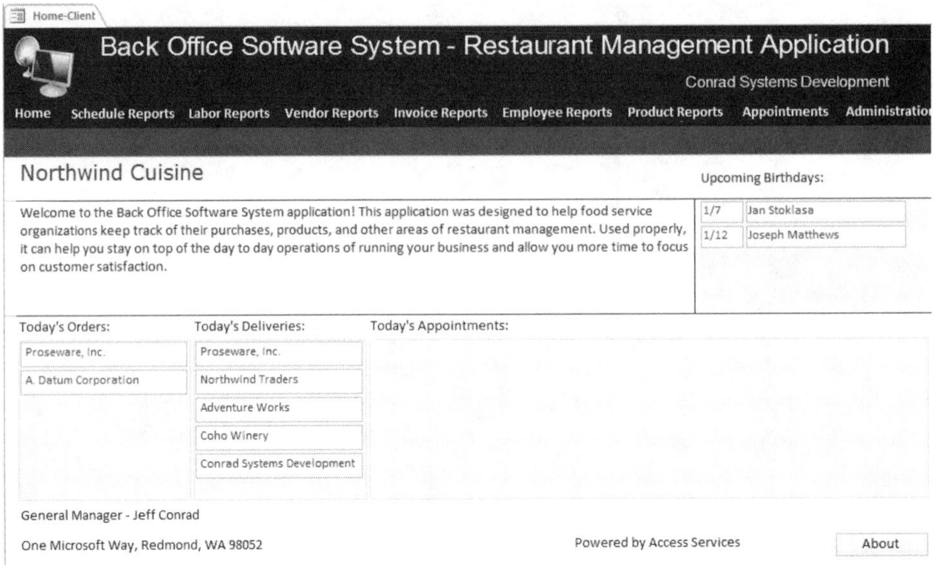

Figure 7-69 Open the frmMainMenuClient form object in the reporting database to see data from the linked tables in the web app.

To see an example of a report that you can open that uses data from the linked web app tables, click the tab labeled Schedule Reports on this form. Access changes the contents underneath the tab and displays controls that you can use to open a report with employee schedule records for a specific date, as shown in Figure 7-70. You'll learn how to create this type of form in desktop databases in Chapter 18, "Advanced form design," which you can download from the book's catalog page.

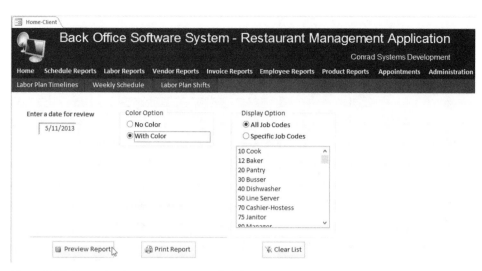

Figure 7-70 Enter the date **5/11/2013**, and click Preview Report to open a desktop database report listing data about employee schedules.

Enter the date **5/11/2013** (May 11, 2013, in the United States) into the date field text box labeled Enter A Date For Review. (If you haven't modified the sample data in the Back Office Software System web app, you should see existing schedule records with this date.) Select the With Color option, under the Color Option label, and press the command button labeled Preview Report. Access reads the data from the linked tables and displays a graphical report on each employee's assigned shift for that date, as shown in Figure 7-71.

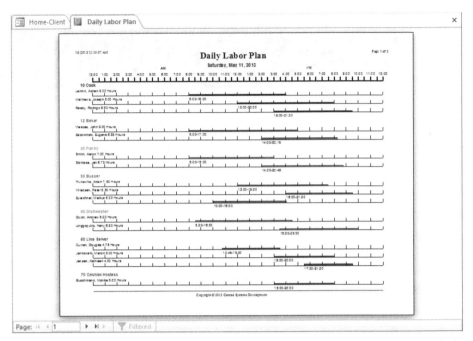

Figure 7-71 The Daily Labor Plan desktop database report displays shift data from the linked web app tables.

Although you might not be able to tell by the screen shot in Figure 7-71, each job code shift displays in a different color. These color values for each job code were assigned using the color picker custom view in the web app I showed you in the previous section. When you're finished looking at the report, you can click the Close (X) button in the upper-right corner of the application window to close the report. You can open many other reports from the various tabs on this main form. If you want, you can explore some of the other tabs and reporting option on your own. Close the reporting desktop database when you're finished reviewing the various reports.

As you can see, you can utilize additional functionality from desktop databases with the data in your web app. You can use reporting desktop databases linked up with data in Access web apps to create complex reports that summarize data and display it in different ways not available within views in your web browser.

Chapter 7

> **Note**
>
> In this section, I've shown you only a very brief look at using objects in desktop databases. The topic is too large to cover here in this section about extending your web app with desktop database functionality. Beginning in Part 2, "Building tables in a desktop database," you'll learn how to create and use all the various types of objects within desktop databases.

Managing external connections

In the previous section, you learned how to open a read-only external connection to your web app to allow Access to create a reporting desktop database linked to your web app tables. Access provides other options for managing external connections to your web app, including read-write connections, which allow you to connect your web apps tables with other programs such as Microsoft Access, Microsoft Excel, or any other SQL database that supports the Open Database Connectivity (ODBC) software standard.

To view and modify external connections for your web app, you'll need to open the app within Access first. If you still have the Back Office Software System sample web app (BOSS. app) open from the previous section, you can use this app to follow along in this section, or you can use any other web app you currently have open. Click the File tab on the Backstage view to display the Info tab, and then click the Manage button. Access displays a menu of nine connection options, as shown in Figure 7-72. Note that the first option—From My Location—at the top of the menu cannot be seen in Figure 7-72. Click the up arrow at the top of the menu or the down arrow at the bottom of the menu to scroll up or down the list to see all the options.

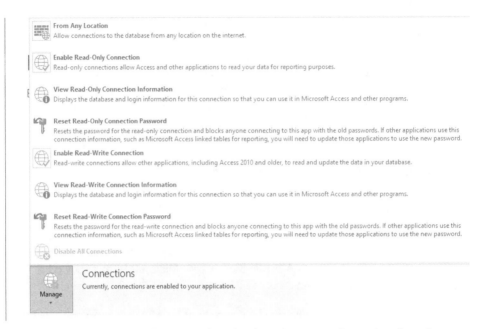

From Any Location
Allow connections to the database from any location on the internet.

Enable Read-Only Connection
Read-only connections allow Access and other applications to read your data for reporting purposes.

View Read-Only Connection Information
Displays the database and login information for this connection so that you can use it in Microsoft Access and other programs.

Reset Read-Only Connection Password
Resets the password for the read-only connection and blocks anyone connecting to this app with the old passwords. If other applications use this connection information, such as Microsoft Access linked tables for reporting, you will need to update those applications to use the new password.

Enable Read-Write Connection
Read-write connections allow other applications, including Access 2010 and older, to read and update the data in your database.

View Read-Write Connection Information
Displays the database and login information for this connection so that you can use it in Microsoft Access and other programs.

Reset Read-Write Connection Password
Resets the password for the read-write connection and blocks anyone connecting to this app with the old passwords. If other applications use this connection information, such as Microsoft Access linked tables for reporting, you will need to update those applications to use the new password.

Disable All Connections

Connections
Currently, connections are enabled to your application.

Manage

Figure 7-72 Click the Manage button on the Info tab to view connection options for web apps.

Here is a description of each of the nine options in the Manage command:

- **From My Location.** Use this option to open the firewall for the SQL Server database your Access web app uses to the IP address of the computer or device from which the request is made. This option allows ODBC connections from just your current computer or device to the SQL Server database.

- **From Any Location.** Use this option to open the firewall for the SQL Server database your Access web app uses to all IP addresses. This option allows ODBC connections from other computers and devices to the SQL Server database.

- **Enable Read-Only Connection.** Use this option to enable read-only connections from other programs to your Access web app. For example, you might want to use this type of connection for a reporting desktop database, which prevents the user from modifying any data in the web app tables.

- **View Read-Only Connection Information.** Use this option to open a dialog box in Access that displays the server name, database name, a read-only user name, and a read-only password that you can use in other programs such as Microsoft Access and Microsoft Excel. You can copy and paste the connection information displayed in this dialog to create read-only ODBC connections from other programs to your web app.

- **Reset Read-Only Connection Password.** Use this option if you want to reset the current password for the read-only connection used by other programs to connect to your web app. Any program using the old password receives a connection error message and won't be able to connect to the web app until you update the connections with the new password.

- **Enable Read-Write Connection.** Use this option to enable read-write connections from other programs to your Access web app. For example, you might want to use this type of connection for an Access desktop database, which allows users of that database to add, edit, and delete records from linked tables within your web app.

- **View Read-Write Connection Information.** Use this option to open a dialog box in Access that displays the server name, database name, a read-write user name, and a read-write password that you can use in other programs such as Microsoft Access and Microsoft Excel. You can copy and paste the connection information displayed in this dialog to create read-write ODBC connections from other programs to your web app.

- **Reset Read-Write Connection Password.** Use this option if you want to reset the current password for the read-write connection used by other programs to connect to your web app. Any program using the old password receives a connection error message and won't be able to connect to the web app until you update the connections with the new password.

- **Disable All Connections.** Use this option if you want to disable all external read-only and read-write connections for your Access web app. Any program using existing connections receives an error message and won't be able to connect to the web app. If you select this option, Access displays a confirmation dialog to make sure you want to disable all connections. Click Yes if you want to continue, or click No on this confirmation dialog to dismiss the dialog without affecting current connections. Disabling connections with this option does not affect using the web app within your web browser or designing the app within Access from your current computer or device.

You'll notice, when reviewing these connection options, that some options are dimmed and not available. The reason that some connection options are disabled is that they depend on other options being selected first. For example, the View Read-Write Connection Information and Reset Read-Write Connection Password options are not available until you select the Enable Read-Write Connection option.

In Article 3, "Importing and linking data," which can be downloaded from the book's catalog page, you'll learn much more about the ODBC standard as well as importing and linking data to Access desktop databases. You can review this article to learn how you can use the connection information found in the Manage connection dialogs to import and link data from your web app tables into Access desktop databases.

Setting SharePoint site permissions

You must grant other people appropriate permissions if you want them to use your Access web app. To grant other people permissions to your web app, you need to assign them permissions to the SharePoint site or subsite in which your Access web app resides. To do this, open your Access web app in your web browser and then click the Back To Site link above the Table Selector and View Selector. Access Services navigates to the SharePoint site in which your Access web app resides, as shown in Figure 7-73. The command options and links on the SharePoint ribbon for this page can vary based on how your internal organization's SharePoint server administrator or third-party hosting services company configured the server you are using.

Figure 7-73 Click the Share command to give permissions for people to use your Access web app.

To create, edit, and delete site permissions, click the Share button in the upper-right section of the SharePoint site page above the Search This Site text box. SharePoint opens the Share site page dialog, as shown in Figure 7-74. SharePoint displays the name of your site at the top of the dialog. In this example, Access 2013 Inside Out is the name of the site where my Access web app resides. If your site is a SharePoint subsite, it might inherit permissions from the parent site. In this case, all Access web apps contained in your subsite inherit permissions from the parent site as well. In the example shown in Figure 7-74, my site is a subsite, so SharePoint also displays the name of the parent site—Conrad Systems Development Team Site—along with a message indicating that granting permissions for someone to the subsite allows them to access the parent site.

Figure 7-74 On the Share site dialog, you can assign permissions for people to use a SharePoint site where your Access web app resides.

In the Select Users box, enter the name of a user within your organization (or their email address) to whom you want to give access to your site, as shown in Figure 7-75. In the Personal Message box, you can optionally enter a personal message that you want to send to the user with the invitation email. If you are having difficulty providing the correct user name or email address for SharePoint to recognize in the Share site dialog, you might need to talk with the appropriate SharePoint administrator in your organization for help.

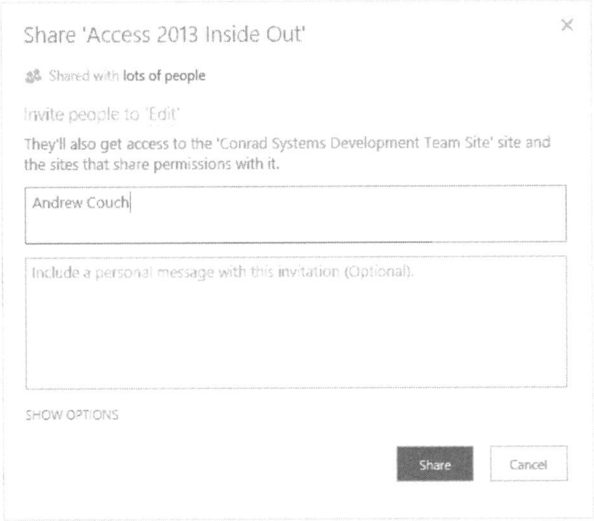

Figure 7-75 Enter the name of a person to whom you want to grant permissions to use your SharePoint site in the first text box.

Under the Personal Message box, you'll see a link labeled Show Options. Click this link, and SharePoint expands the bottom of the Share dialog and displays two additional options, as shown in Figure 7-76. Select the Send An Email Invitation check box (selected by default, if you are using Office 365) if you want SharePoint to send an email to the user, inviting them to the SharePoint site. Clear this option if you don't want SharePoint to send an email invitation. Click the Select A Group Or Permission Level combo box, and SharePoint displays a list of built-in SharePoint groups. When you assign the user to a specific group, they receive the permissions designated for that SharePoint group.

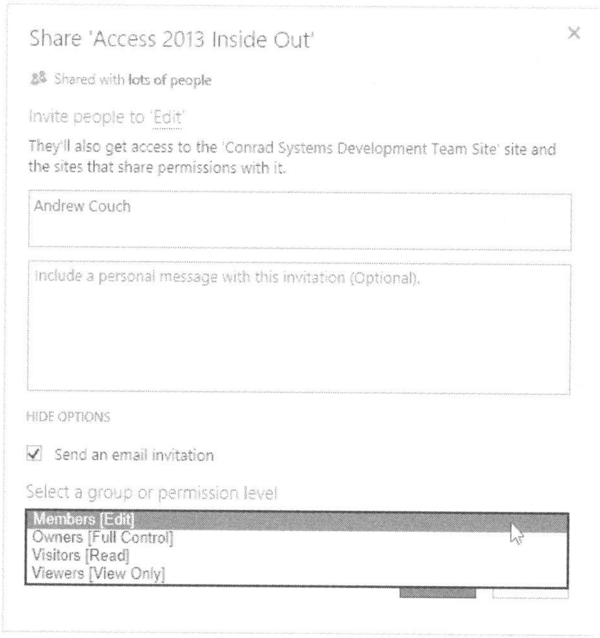

Figure 7-76 Select a SharePoint permission group to assign your user for access to your SharePoint site.

Select the Members [Edit] group to allow users to view and edit data in their web browser and make changes to the web app from within Access. Select the Owners [Full Control] group to allow users to view and edit data in their web browser, make changes to the web app from within Access, and perform other SharePoint functions. Select the Visitors [Read] group to enable users to view data in their web browser, although they cannot add new records, edit existing records, or delete records. Users in this group cannot download the web app into Access. When you select the Viewers [View Only] group, users have essentially the same permissions as the Visitors [Read] group. Note that the latter two groups have some differences when you are working with SharePoint features, but for Access web apps, the Visitors [Read] and the Viewers [View Only] groups are essentially the same. If you are using a SharePoint server within your own organization, you might see additional SharePoint groups listed in this drop-down list. Talk with your appropriate SharePoint administrator for more information about custom groups that might exist within your organization.

After you've selected a SharePoint group for the user, click Share at the bottom of the dialog to save your changes and grant permissions to the user. Click Cancel if you want to dismiss the dialog without committing any changes. The user can now navigate to your Access web app and use the app based on their permission settings. Note that the user has the same permission rights to all Access web apps hosted inside the same SharePoint site.

In this chapter, you studied some of the more advanced topics concerning views in Access web apps. You learned how to create Summary, Blank, and stand-alone views and how to use web browser and subview controls. You learned how to apply themes to your web app views using SharePoint site themes, set permissions for new users of your web app, create a reporting desktop database for your web app, and manage external connections. You also explored some of the more complex views in the Back Office Software System sample web app. In the next chapter, you'll learn how to add logic to views by creating user interface macros and attaching them to control and view events.

Automating a web app using macros

I N Chapter 4, "Creating data macros in web apps," you learned how to create data macros. Data macros interact only at the data layer and can be attached to table events or exist as named data macros. In this chapter, you'll learn about *user interface macros*. In Access web apps, you can define a user interface macro to execute tasks you would otherwise initiate with the keyboard or the mouse at the user interface level. The unique power of user interface macros in Access web apps is their ability to automate responses to different types of events without forcing you to learn a programming language. The event might be a change in the data, the opening of a view, or even changing the value of a view control. Within a user interface macro, you can include multiple actions and define condition checking so that different actions are performed depending on the values in your view controls. For the remainder of this chapter, I'll use the term *macros* only to refer to user interface macros.

In this chapter, we'll focus on the events for views and view controls and how you can attach macros to those events. You'll also learn the difference between embedded macros and stand-alone macro objects (macros that appear in the Navigation pane). I'll show you how to define macros actions to automate different elements of your web app to help users navigate through the different parts of your web app and perform automated tasks. I'll help guide you around potential pitfalls you'll encounter when trying to automate web views and offer tips to help you build a smooth interface for the users of your web app. I'll also show you how to make macros work with data macros to interact with the data layer.

> **Note**
>
> The examples in this chapter are based on the RestaurantSampleChapter8.app,
> BOSS.app sample app, and Auctions.app sample web apps. You can download these sam-
> ple web apps from the book's catalog page. You'll need to upload these apps into your
> corporate catalog or Office 365 team site and install the apps to use the samples. Review
> the instructions at the end of Chapter 2, "Exploring the Access 2013 web app interface,"
> if you need help with those tasks. The data you see from the sample views you build in
> this chapter might not match exactly what you see in this book if you have changed the
> sample data in the web app.

In this chapter, you will do the following:

- Learn about the various types of actions you can define in macros with web apps.

- Tour the Logic Designer for macros and learn how to build both a simple macro and a macro with multiple defined actions.

- See how to add conditional expressions to a macro to control the actions that Access Services performs.

- Learn about embedded macros and assigning temporary variables for use in other areas of your web app.

- Understand how to define embedded macros for both view and view control events.

- Learn how to control record navigation in views using embedded macros.

- See how to create an On Start macro that runs each time you open the app in your web browser.

- Learn how to pass parameters when opening views using macros.

- Learn how to reference other view control values in macros.

- Learn how to call data macros from the user interface level and use values returned from the data layer with return variables.

- Understand some of the actions automated with macros in the sample web apps pro- vided with this book.

The macro design surface—an overview

To begin our discussion of macros, you'll first need to install the RestaurantSampleChapter8.app sample web app in your SharePoint site and then download the app into Access to follow along with the examples in this chapter. This web app is the same app you finished modifying at the end of Chapter 7, "Advanced view design." If you've been following along with this book through Chapter 7, you can continue to use the sample web app you used in Chapter 7 or install the RestaurantSampleChapter8.app sample app; both should be identical.

Working with the Logic Designer

Open the RestaurantSampleChapter8 sample web app within Access. To create a new macro object, click the Advanced command in the Create group on the Home ribbon tab. Access displays a drop-down list of seven options, as shown in Figure 8-1.

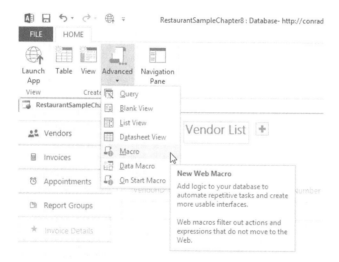

Figure 8-1 Click the Macro option under Advanced to create a new macro object.

To create a new macro object, click the Macro option in the drop-down list beneath the Advanced command. Access opens the Logic Designer for creating macros, as shown in Figure 8-2.

Chapter 8

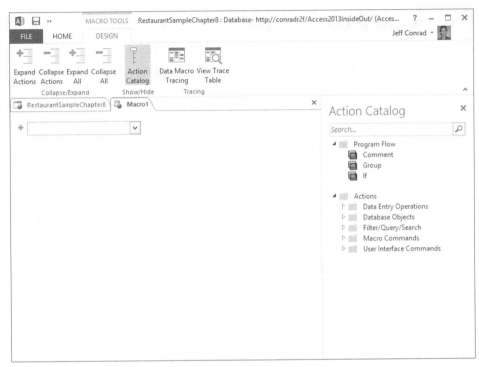

Figure 8-2 This is the Logic Designer, where you create macros in web apps.

Whenever you need to create or edit macros in Access web apps, this is the design surface that you use. On the right side, Access displays the macro actions available for macros in the Action Catalog. You'll notice that Access does not collapse the Navigation pane (if you have it expanded) when you click the Macro option under the Advanced command on the ribbon. When you are working with macro objects (macros displayed in the Navigation pane), Access does not open the Logic Designer window modally, which means that you can open other objects in your web app while working on your macro. Macro objects that appear in the Navigation pane are also referred to as *stand-alone macros*. (Later in this chapter, you'll learn that Access opens the Logic Designer modally when you're creating embedded macros.)

As you can see in Figure 8-2, the Logic Designer layout for macros is very similar to the layout you see when you work with data macros. The Expand Actions, Collapse Actions, Expand All, and Collapse All buttons in the Collapse/Expand group on the Design contextual ribbon tab selectively expand or collapse the actions listed in the macro designer surface. In the Show/Hide group on the Design tab, you can choose to hide the Action Catalog by clicking the Action Catalog toggle button. (Note that Access does not display the Close group on the Design tab as it does for data macros.) When you want to save your macro changes, you can click the Save button on the Quick Access Toolbar or press Ctrl+S. If you attempt to close the Logic Designer window with unsaved changes, Access prompts you and asks whether you want to save your changes before closing the window. Access also displays two commands in the Tracing group on the Design tab—Data Macro Tracing and View Trace Table. You learned about these two options in Chapter 4.

On the right side of the Logic Designer window is the Action Catalog. The Action Catalog shows a contextual list of the program flow constructs and macro actions that are applicable for macros in web apps. In Table 8-1, you can see a list of the 17 macro actions and their arguments available in Access web apps. The macros are organized in functional categories, as listed in the macro Action Catalog.

TABLE 8-1 Access web app macro actions

Category	Macro action	Purpose	Arguments
Data Entry Operations	DeleteRecord	Deletes the current record.	None
	EditRecord	Changes the view state into edit mode for editing records.	None
	NewRecord	Moves to a new record in the current view.	None
	SaveRecord	Saves the current record changes.	None
	UndoRecord	Undoes all changes to the current record.	None
Database Objects	GoToControl	Sets the focus to the specified control. If you are in edit mode, Access Services also switches you into view mode before moving the focus to the control.	Control Name
	GoToRecord	Moves to a different record and makes it current in the view. You can move to the first, last, next, or previous record.	Record
	SetProperty	Changes selected properties of a control on a view or selected properties of the view itself at runtime. The properties that you can change with this action are Enabled, Visible, ForeColor, BackColor, Caption and Value.	Control Name, Property, Value
Filter/Query/ Search	RequeryRecords	Refreshes the data in a view. If you provide a Where clause, you can optionally restrict the view's records displayed in the view. Setting an optional Order By applies a sort to the records displayed in the view.	Where, Order By
Macro Commands	RunDataMacro	Runs a named data macro in the app. If the named data macro has any parameters, Access displays text boxes on the macro design surface for each parameter value. Actions following this action run after the named data macro completes.	Macro Name

Category	Macro action	Purpose	Arguments
	RunMacro	Runs a named user interface macro defined in the app. Actions following this RunMacro action run after the called macro completes.	Macro Name
	SetVariable	Creates a temporary variable and lets you set it to a value that you can reference in other areas of your app at runtime. The value of the variable stays in memory as long as the browser session remains open or until you change the variable to a different value.	Variable, Value
	StopMacro	Stops the current macro.	None
User Interface Commands	ChangeView	Changes the currently displayed view in the browser to the specified table and view. The Where argument allows you to filter the records shown in the new view. You must use a syntax such as [TableName].[FieldName] when referring to field names. You can optionally use the Order By argument to sort the records displayed in the view.	Table, View, Where, Order By
	ClosePopup	Closes the current pop-up view.	None
	MessageBox	Displays an informational message in a dialog box. The user must click OK to close the dialog box and proceed.	Message
	OpenPopup	Opens the selected view on top of the current view as a pop-up view. The Where argument allows you to filter the records shown in the new pop-up view. You must use a syntax such as [TableName].[FieldName] when referring to field names. You can optionally use the Order By argument to sort the records displayed in the pop-up view.	View, Where, Order By

INSIDE OUT   Searching the Action Catalog also searches the action descriptions

When you type search criteria into the Action Catalog Search box, Access not only looks at the action name for a possible match but also searches all the action descriptions for any matching text. For example, if you type **Query** into the Search box, you'll see that Access returns the GoToRecord and RequeryRecords actions even though the word query is not in the GoToRecord action name. Access shows these results because the word query exists in the descriptions for those actions.

In the middle of the Logic Designer window is the main macro design surface where you define your macro. You add program flow constructs, macro actions, and arguments to the design surface to instruct Access what actions to take for the macro. If you have more actions than can fit on the screen, Access provides a scroll bar on the right side of the macro design surface so that you can scroll down to see the rest of your actions.

In the lower-right corner of the Logic Designer window is the Help window. Access displays a brief help message in this window, which changes based on where the focus is located in the Action Catalog. (Remember: You can always press F1 to open a context-sensitive Help topic.)

To get you accustomed to using the Logic Designer for macros, let's create a simple macro that displays a message. You use the MessageBox action to open a pop-up modal dialog box with a message in it. This is a great way to display a warning or an informative message in your web app without defining a separate view. To begin, let's add a Comment block to the macro design surface. As you learned in Chapter 4, you'll find the Comment block especially useful for documenting large macros that contain many actions. Click the word Comment under the Program Flow node in the Action Catalog, hold the mouse key down, drag the comment onto the macro design surface, and then release the mouse button, as shown in Figure 8-3.

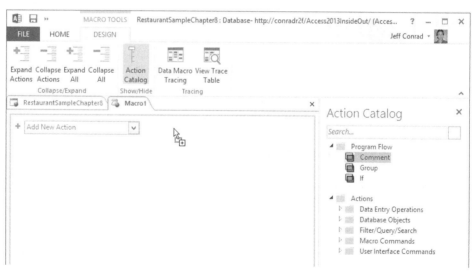

Figure 8-3 Drag the Comment program flow element from the Action Catalog onto the macro design surface.

This message will be a greeting, so click inside the Comment block and type **Greeting message**. Click outside the Comment block onto the macro design surface, and Access collapses the size of the Comment block to just fit the text you typed and displays the text in green. As you learned in Chapter 4, the /* and */ symbols mark the beginning and end of a block of comments. Access designates anything written between those symbols as a comment, which provides information about the purpose of the macro or particular action to follow only.

Click in the Add New Action combo box on the macro design surface to see the drop-down list of macro actions. In the Add New Action combo box, you can specify any of the 17 macro actions and three program flow constructs provided for Access web app macros. Select MessageBox from this drop-down list. After you select an action, Access displays argument boxes in which you enter the arguments for the specific action you chose, as shown in Figure 8-4.

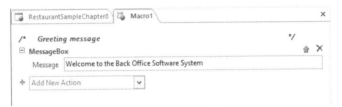

Figure 8-4 Enter arguments for a MessageBox action to display a greeting message.

You use the Message argument box to set the message that you want Access Services to display at runtime in the dialog box you're creating. Enter **Welcome to the Back Office Software System** in the Message argument box for this example.

Saving your macro

You must save a macro object before you can run it, so click the Save button on the Quick Access Toolbar, or press Ctrl+S. When you do so, Access opens the Save As dialog box shown in Figure 8-5. Enter a name for your new macro object, such as **TestGreeting**, and click OK to save your macro.

Figure 8-5 Enter a name for this test macro in the Save As dialog box.

When you save a new macro object, Access displays your new macro object under a Macros heading in the Navigation pane, as shown in Figure 8-6. (You'll need to expand the Navigation pane, if you currently have it closed, to see the new macro.) You'll notice that Access also added a new node, called In This Database, at the bottom of the Action Catalog (also shown in Figure 8-6). If you expand this node, you'll see the name of your new macro object listed under Macros.

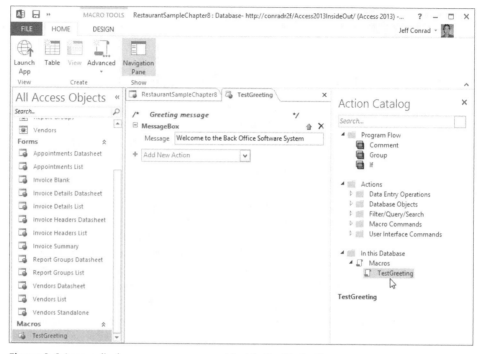

Figure 8-6 Access displays your new macro object in the Navigation pane.

You cannot run macro objects directly from the Navigation pane. To run a macro object in a web app, you must call the macro object from a view event or view control event. You'll learn how to execute macros from view events and view control events in the next few sections. For now, you can close the new macro you just created by clicking the Close (X) button for the macro design window. You'll learn how to call this macro later in this chapter.

If you want to open a macro object saved in the Navigation pane to make any additions or edits to the saved macro logic, you can open it again by double-clicking the macro in the Navigation pane, right-clicking the macro in the Navigation pane and selecting Design view from the shortcut menu, or selecting the macro in the Navigation pane and then pressing Ctrl+Enter.

If you want to rename a macro object, select the macro in the Navigation pane and press F2 to enter into rename mode, or right-click the macro in the Navigation pane and then select Rename from the shortcut menu.

To delete a macro object, select the macro in the Navigation pane and then press Delete, or right-click the macro in the Navigation pane and then select Delete from the shortcut menu. Access prompts you for confirmation before deleting any macros. If you rename or delete a macro object, you'll need to manually fix up any areas of your web app that reference the macro. Otherwise, you'll encounter errors at runtime when you try and run that macro, because Access won't be able to find the renamed or deleted macro.

Working with view and control events

To automate your web app with macros, you need to understand events with views. Similar to data macros attached to table events, views and controls on views also contain a set of events to which you can attach macros. When a view event occurs (such as opening a view) or a view control event occurs (such as clicking a command button control), Access Services executes the macro logic you defined for the specific event.

All four view types support two view events—On Load and On Current. The On Load event occurs whenever Access Services loads a view into your web browser. This event fires whether you open the view by clicking the view name caption in the View Selector, open the view as a pop-up view, or Access Services loads the view in a subview control within a separate main view. In each case, the On Load event occurs once each time the view loads. If you navigate to a different view in your web browser and then navigate back to the same view, Access Services fires the On Load event again because the view is loaded again. This event is useful if, for example, you want to initially set variables or controls to a specific value. View events do not fire when you open views in Design view within Access; they fire only at runtime in your web browser.

The On Current event fires in a bound view when the focus moves from one record to another. Access Services also triggers the On Current event when the focus moves to the first record as a view opens, even if the view is unbound. This event is most useful when you want to change values in view controls or perhaps toggle the visibility of controls based on certain conditions within each record. If you define macro logic for both the On Load and On Current events for a view, Access Services fires the On Load event first and then the On Current event once, because the focus is on the first record. If your view is bound and contains more than one record, Access Services fires the On Current event each time you move to a different record, including a new record.

> **Note**
> Preview datasheets for tables and queries opened within Access do not support any type of view or view control events.

Controls on views support two control events—On Click and After Update. However, not all control types support one or both events. Control events do not fire when you open views in Design view within Access; they fire only at runtime in your web browser. The On Click event occurs whenever you click the control on List Details, Datasheet, or Blank views at runtime in your web browser. (Summary views do not allow you to place controls onto the view design surface, so no control events are supported for this view type.) The control must be enabled and visible for Access Services to fire the On Click event. For most control types, Access Services fires the On Click event only when you are in edit mode with List Details and Blank view types. Custom Action Bar buttons, command buttons, image controls, and label controls can fire their On Click event when you are in view or edit mode with List Details and Blank views. (Datasheet views are always in edit mode, so the On Click event fires whenever you click an enabled, visible control in this view type.)

The After Update event fires after the data in the specified view control has been updated. For example, changing the value in a text box or selecting a different value from the drop-down list in a combo box triggers the After Update control event. Datasheet views do not support the After Update event, which means check boxes and combo boxes do not support control events when displayed in Datasheet views.

In Table 8-2, you can see a list of events each view control supports.

TABLE 8-2   Supported view control events

Control type	On Click	After Update
Action Bar (custom)	Supported	
Autocomplete	Supported	Supported
Check Box		Supported
Combo Box		Supported
Command Button	Supported	
Hyperlink	Supported	Supported
Image	Supported	
Label	Supported	
Multiline Textbox	Supported	Supported
Text Box	Supported	Supported

> **Note**
> Web browser controls, subview controls, and related items controls do not support any events on any view types.

Defining macros for view events

Now that you're familiar with view and control events, let's define a macro to run whenever you open one of the views in the sample test app you have open. Open the RestaurantSampleChapter8 sample web app within Access, if you previously closed it. Click the Vendors table name caption in the Table Selector, click the Vendor List view caption in the View Selector, and then click the Edit button in the middle of the view preview window. Access opens the Vendor List view in Design view, as shown in Figure 8-7.

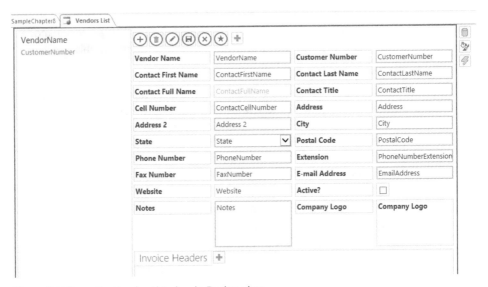

Figure 8-7 Open the Vendor List view in Design view.

As you might recall, you worked with and customized this quick-created List Details view in Chapter 6, "Working with views and the web browser experience." The view displays all the information from the Vendors table in the sample app. To attach macros to one or both of the events available for this view, you must first select the view. To do this, click anywhere on the design grid, away from the Action Bar or controls on the grid. When you select the design grid, Access displays three charm buttons in the upper-right corner of the design grid, previously shown in Figure 8-7. Click the Actions charm button, and Access opens the Actions callout menu, as shown in Figure 8-8.

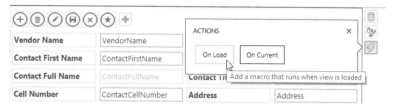

Figure 8-8 Click the Actions charm button and then the On Load button on the Actions Callout menu.

Access displays two buttons—On Load and On Current—on the Actions callout menu. To define a macro for the On Load event, click the On Load button on this callout menu. Access opens the Logic Designer, where you can define macro logic for Access Services to execute for this event at runtime, as shown in Figure 8-9.

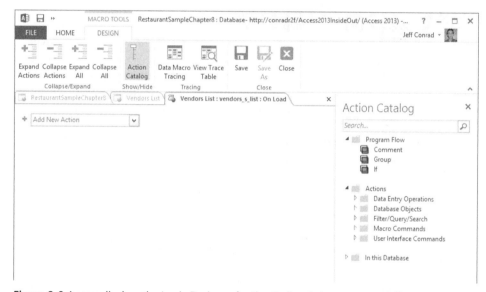

Figure 8-9 Access displays the Logic Designer for the On Load view event modally.

You'll notice Access automatically collapsed the Navigation pane, if you had it open, to show you more of the macro design surface. Access also opens the Logic Designer window modally when you are working with macros attached to view events, which means you cannot open any other web app objects until you close the designer window. When you are creating macros attached to view events and view control events, Microsoft refers to these macros as *embedded macros*. The macro object you created earlier in this chapter is a macro object that you can access from the Navigation pane. However, you save embedded macros within the event for views and view controls. You cannot see these macros listed in the Navigation pane. You can think of embedded macros as similar to data macros attached to table events. Data macros attached to table events are also not seen in the Navigation pane. Embedded macros can run saved macro objects in much the same way that data macros attached to table events can run named data macro objects that appear in the Navigation pane.

When you are designing macros attached to view events and view control events, Access displays the Close group on the Design contextual ribbon tab under Macro Tools, shown previously in Figure 8-9. Click Save to save your macro design changes attached to the view or control event. Access disables the Save As command in the Close group when you are designing embedded macros in web apps. (However, this option is enabled for desktop databases.) Click the Close command when you want to close the Logic Designer window. If you have unsaved changes to the macro design surface and attempt to close the Logic Designer, Access prompts you to save your changes.

With the Logic Designer open, you can now add macro actions to the macro design surface. Earlier in this chapter, you created and saved a new macro object called TestGreeting. Let's add a macro action in the On Load event to run that separate macro object. To run macro objects saved in the Navigation pane within view and view control events, use the RunMacro action. Now drag the RunMacro data action from the Action Catalog onto the macro design surface. (The RunMacro action is under the Macro Commands heading in the Action Catalog.) You can also click in the Add New Action combo box on the macro design surface and select the RunMacro option from the drop-down the list of macro actions. After you add the action to the macro design surface, Access displays a Macro Name argument box for this action, as shown in Figure 8-10.

Figure 8-10 Select TestGreeting for the Macro Name argument.

INSIDE OUT   Adding RunMacro to design surface with object name

You can also use another technique to add the RunMacro action to the macro design surface. Expand the In This Database node in the Action Catalog. Underneath that node, you should see another node called Macros. Expand the Macros node, and you'll see a list of all the saved macro objects in your web app. You can either double-click the macro object name you want to run or drag the macro object name onto the macro design surface. In either case, Access creates a new RunMacro action on the design grid and fills in the Macro Name argument with the name of the macro you selected in the Action Catalog. Using this technique saves the extra step of having to select the macro you want to run in the Macro Name argument.

Chapter 8

By default, Access displays RunMacro in the Macro Name argument box. However, this is not a valid choice, because no macro object called RunMacro exists in your web app. Access provides a drop-down list for this argument that displays the names of all saved macro objects in your web app. Select TestGreeting from the drop-down list for the Macro Name argument.

To test out the macro logic you've added to the On Load event, you need to save your work and then open the view in your web browser. Click Save in the Close group, press Ctrl+S, or click Save on the Quick Access Toolbar to save the macro design changes you've made. Close the Logic Designer for this event by clicking the Close button in the Close group on the Design tab. Access closes the Logic Designer and returns your focus to the view design grid with the Actions callout menu still open. You'll notice now that Access changed the background color of the On Load event button to green to indicate that macro logic is saved with that particular event, as shown in Figure 8-11. As you continue working through this chapter, you'll observe that Access follows this same pattern with control events. Whenever there is macro logic saved with a view control event, Access changes the background color of those buttons on the Actions callout menu for the control.

Figure 8-11 The On Load event button displays a different background color because you defined logic for that event.

Now that you've saved the macro logic in the On Load event, you also need to save the view itself to complete the operation. Click the Save button on the Quick Access Toolbar, or press Ctrl+S to save your view changes. To test this event in your web browser, click the Launch App button on the Home ribbon tab or click the Launch App button on the Quick Access Toolbar. (You can leave the Vendors List view open in Design view during this step, but make sure you've saved your view changes.) Access opens your default web browser, navigates to your Access web app, and then attempts to navigate directly to the Vendor List view. However, before the view loads, Access Services displays a message box with the message you defined earlier in this chapter in the MessageBox action for the TestGreeting macro object, as shown in Figure 8-12.

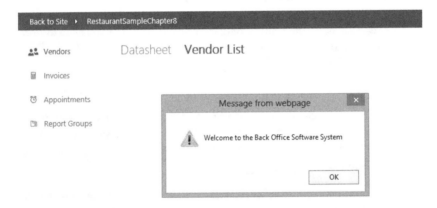

Figure 8-12 Access Services displays a message box when you navigate to the Vendor List view in your web browser.

Access Services executes the macro logic you defined in the On Load event before it displays any controls or data in the view at runtime. You must click OK on the message box for Access Services to continue loading the view. Click OK on the message dialog now and Access Services finishes loading the view, controls, and data. If you navigate to a different view and then navigate back to the Vendor List view, Access Services displays the message box dialog again. If you click to navigate a different record using the List Control within the Vendor List view, Access Services does not display the message box dialog, because you are changing only record context and not reloading the view. If you defined the On Current event for this view to also run the TestGreeting macro, Access Services displays the message box whenever you navigate to a different record.

> **Note**
>
> Access Services fires the view events within a subview control before firing the view events of the main view. For example, if you define macro logic in the On Load and On Current view events for both a main view and a subview, Access Services fires the events in the following order: subview On Load, subview On Current, main view On Load, and then main view On Current. However, if you have multiple subviews within the same main view, you cannot guarantee the order in which Access Services loads the subviews in their respective subview controls.

Defining macros for control events

The process of defining macros for view control events is essentially the same as it is for defining macros for view events. You select the control event you want to use, open the Logic Designer to design your macro logic, save your changes, and then test your logic at runtime in your web browser. In this section, I'll walk you through designing macro logic attached to the On Click control event for a custom Action Bar button. The logic we'll create in this control event will toggle the sort order of the displayed records within the Vendor List view you've been working on. Before I show you how to set up the control event macro logic, let's make a quick change to the On Load event macro logic you just completed for this view. The macro logic you'll change in the On Load will work in conjunction with the control event macro logic you'll define later.

Switch back to Access, and then open the Vendor List view in Design view again, if you previously closed it. When the view is open in Design view, click anywhere on the design grid away from the Action Bar or controls on the grid and then click the Actions charm button. When the Actions callout menu opens, click the On Load button to open the Logic Designer and see the RunMacro action you defined earlier.

We no longer need the existing RunMacro action we created earlier, so let's delete this action. To delete macro logic in an embedded macro, you select the actions you want to remove and then press the Delete key. No command or option is available that clears the macro design surface, so if you want to remove a single action or all the actions for a particular view event or view control event, you have to open the Logic Designer for the associated event and manually delete the macro actions. Select the RunMacro action on the macro design surface now, and then press Delete to remove it. You should now have an empty macro design surface again.

INSIDE OUT Quickly remove all macro logic from the design surface

If you want to remove all existing macro logic from the macro design surface, a quick way to accomplish this task is to click the macro design surface and then press Ctrl+A. Access highlights all actions, arguments, comments, and program flow constructs on the macro design surface. After Access highlights everything, press Delete, and Access removes everything from the macro design surface.

In the control event macro logic you'll define in a moment, our end goal is to toggle the current sort order of the records displayed. To know what the current sort order might be at any given time, we can define macro logic in the On Load event of the view to set a variable that saves the current sort order. Each time you navigate to the Vendor List view in your web browser, Access Services sorts the records by the Vendor Name field in ascending order as determined by the properties in the List Control. With that information, we can create a variable in the On Load to match that sort order and then refer to that variable in the On Click event of a custom Action Bar button.

To get started, add a Comment block onto the macro design surface and then enter the following text into the Comment block:

Set a variable to track the current sort order.

Your changes to the macro design surface should now match Figure 8-13.

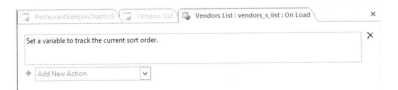

Figure 8-13 Add a Comment block to the macro design surface, and include text explaining the purpose of the macro.

You can use a variable to store a value that can be used in other macros, expressions, and queries at runtime. Variables are useful when you need Access Services to remember something for later use. You can think of a temporary variable in a macro as writing yourself a note to remember a number, a name, or a date so that you can recall it at a later time. For example, you can use a variable to store the user name of the person using the web app in their web browser. All variables must have a unique name. To fetch, set, or examine a variable, you reference it by its name. Variables stay in memory until you close your browser window, assign it a new value, or you clear the value.

To create a local variable, click or tab into the Add New Action combo box beneath the Comment block you just created, enter **SetVariable**, and press Enter to add this action to the macro design surface, as shown in Figure 8-14.

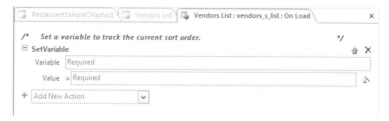

Figure 8-14 Add a SetVariable action to the macro design surface.

The SetVariable action takes two required arguments:

- **Variable.** Required argument. The name of the variable you want to refer to in macros and expressions.

- **Value.** Required argument. The expression that Access uses to define the local variable.

For the Variable argument, you can enter a name up to 64 characters. For the Value argument, you can click the button that looks like a magic wand to open the Expression Builder to assist you with creating an expression. In this example, enter **VendorSortOrder** into the Variable argument and then enter **"Ascending"** into the Value argument, as shown in Figure 8-15. You must enclose the word in quotation marks, because if you don't, Access adds brackets around the word and then attempts to set the variable to a field name called Ascending at runtime.

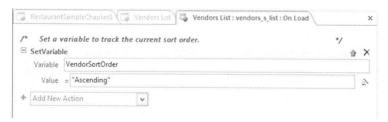

Figure 8-15 Enter a variable name and value into the SetVariable arguments.

That's all the macro logic you need to define in the On Load event for the Vendor List view. When you navigate to this view in your web browser, Access Services creates a variable in memory, called VendorSortOrder, and assigns it a text value of Ascending. You won't see anything happen at runtime when setting a variable, but you can see the effects of setting a variable by using that variable in other areas of your web app. Save your macro design changes now, and then close the Logic Designer. Access returns your focus to the Actions callout menu for the view. You can dismiss this callout menu by clicking the Close (X) button in the upper-right corner of the menu.

In Chapter 6, you learned how to create custom Action Bar buttons, and you added one to the Vendor List view you currently have open. The custom Action Bar button was not much use to you at the time, because custom Action Bar buttons don't perform any tasks unless you define macro logic in their On Click event. At the top of the Vendor List view you have open, you'll see a custom Action Bar button to the right of the five built-in Action Bar buttons. (The custom one has the default star icon.) Click the custom button, and then click the Data charm button that appears next to it. Access opens the Data property callout menu for the custom Action Bar button, as shown in Figure 8-16.

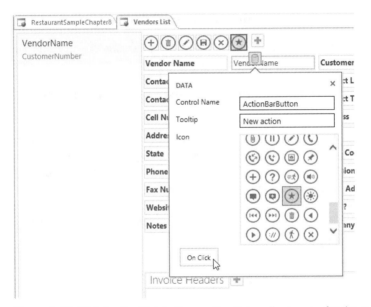

Figure 8-16 Click the On Click button on the Data callout menu for the custom Action Bar button.

Beneath the Control Name, Tooltip, and Icon properties, you'll see a button labeled On Click in the lower-left corner of the menu. Click this button, and Access opens the Logic Designer modally, where you can define macro logic for Access to execute for this control event, as shown in Figure 8-17. Notice that in the tab at the top of the macro design surface, Access displays the name of the view, the name of the control the macro is attached to, and the specific event of the control that runs the macro.

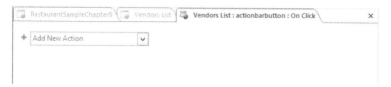

Figure 8-17 Access displays the Logic Designer for the control events modally.

Before adding the macro actions to toggle the sorting of the displayed records in this view, let's add a Comment block that explains the purpose of this macro. Click the Add New Action combo box, select Comment from the drop-down list, and then enter the following text into the Comment block:

Check the current sort order applied. Toggle the sort order using RequeryRecords macro.

You can define more than one action within a macro, and you can specify which actions get executed or not by adding conditional expressions into your macro logic, just like you can with data macros. For example, you might want to update a value in a view control but only if another view control's value was changed. Or, you might want to run a named data macro but only if the user provided all the needed values. Previously, you designed a simple macro in the On Load event of the view to set a variable indicating the current sort. You now need to test what the value of that variable is in the On Click event of the custom Action Bar button and then take different actions based on that value.

In the Add New Action combo box at the bottom of the macro design surface, type **If** and press Enter to create a new If block. Access creates a new If block under the Comment block, as shown in Figure 8-18. The text box next to If is where you type your conditional expression. Each condition is an expression that Access can evaluate to True or False. A condition can also consist of multiple comparison expressions and Boolean operators. If the condition is True, Access executes the action or actions immediately following the Then keyword. If the condition is False, Access evaluates the next Else If condition or executes the statements following the Else keyword, whichever occurs next. If no Else or Else If condition exists after the Then keyword, Access executes the next action following the End If keyword.

Figure 8-18 Use an If block when you want to execute actions only if a certain condition is met.

If you need help constructing your conditional expression, you can click the button that looks like a magic wand to the right of the expression text box. When you click this button, Access opens the Expression Builder, where you can build your conditional expression. (You learned about the Expression Builder in Chapter 3, "Designing tables in a web app.") To the right of the word Then, Access displays a green up arrow. You can click this button if you want to move the position of the If block. (If there are actions below the If block, Access also displays a green down arrow.) If you move a block in error, you can click the Undo button on the Quick Access Toolbar. If you want to delete the If block, you can click the Delete button to the right of the up arrow. Below the arrow button are two links—Add Else and Add Else If. If you click the Add Else link, Access adds an Else branch to the If block, and if you click the Add Else If link, Access adds an Else If branch to the If block.

To test to see whether the VendorSortOrder variable defined in the On Load event currently has a value of Ascending, enter **[VendorSortOrder]="Ascending"** into the conditional expression box, as shown in Figure 8-19. With your completed conditional expression for the If block, Access executes actions after the Then keyword and before the End If keywords only if the variable value currently matches that text string.

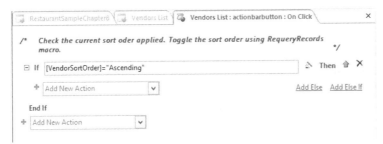

Figure 8-19 Enter a conditional expression to test the variable you defined in the On Load event.

The next step in our macro logic is to change the sort order of the displayed records in the view. To do this, tab or click into the Add New Action combo box that is inside the If block, type **RequeryRecords**, and press Enter to add this action inside the If block, as shown in Figure 8-20.

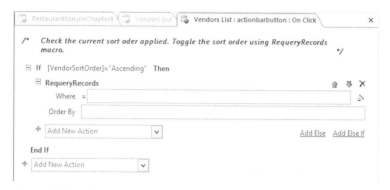

Figure 8-20 Add the RequeryRecords action inside the If block.

The RequeryRecords action takes two arguments:

- **Where.** Optional argument. The expression that Access uses to select records from the table or query.

- **Order By.** Optional argument. Use this argument to define the display sequence of records returned from the view's record source.

Both arguments for the RequeryRecords action are optional. If you provide no arguments for this action, Access Services requeries the view's record source and returns the latest values for all records. Access Services also navigates to the first record within the view. If you don't define an Order By argument, Access Services displays the records by the default order defined by the List Control (if you're using a List Details view), by any sort order in the query record source (if your view is based on a query), or by the AutoNumber ID field in the table. If you want Access to return a specific record or set of records in the view's record source, you must provide a valid Where clause expression to find the record. You can click the button with the magic wand on it to open the Expression Builder to assist you with creating a Where clause.

You don't need to define any Where clause for this RequeryRecords action, because you don't need to restrict the records returned; you want only to change the sort order. To do this, enter **[VendorName] DESC** in the Order By argument box, as shown in Figure 8-21. This statement instructs Access Services to sort the records returned by the VendorName field in the Vendors table in descending order. You must use DESC and not Descending here because DESC is a special command Access Services uses to interpret as descending order.

Chapter 8

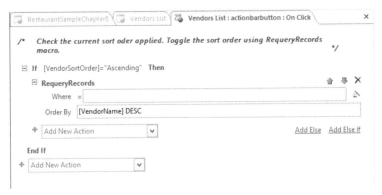

Figure 8-21 Enter a statement in the Order By argument to sort the records by VendorName in descending order.

After Access Services executes the RequeryRecords action, the current sort order on the view is no longer ascending, so you should modify the VendorSortOrder variable to a different value. Click the Add New Action combo box directly beneath the RequeryRecords action, type **SetVariable**, and then press Enter to add a new SetVariable action to the macro design surface. In the Variable argument box, enter **VendorSortOrder**, and in the Value argument box, enter **"Descending"**, as shown in Figure 8-22.

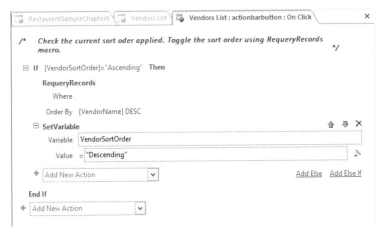

Figure 8-22 Use the SetVariable action to assign the variable to a different value.

Using the macro logic you've now defined, Access Services changes the sort order to descending in the runtime using the RequeryRecords action and then assigns a new value to the variable. This variable value stays in memory until you refresh your browser window or navigate to a different view and come back to the Vendor List view.

You're now halfway to our end goal of using this macro to continually toggle the sort order of the records. If you saved your macro changes at this point and clicked this custom Action Bar button in the view in your web browser, you'd see that Access Services changes the sort order of the vendor records. However, clicking the button a second or third time results in no change. To have this embedded macro attached to the On Click event continually change the sort order, you need to add an Else block inside the If block and then add actions to reverse the sort order. Click the Add Else link on the right side of the If block. Access adds a new Else block to the macro design surface.

Follow this procedure to add the remaining macro logic:

1. Add a RequeryRecords action inside the Else block. Leave the Where clause blank, and then enter **[VendorName]** in the Order By argument. When you want to sort records in ascending order, you don't need to specify a keyword command like you need to for descending order because ascending order is the default.

2. Add a SetVariable action beneath the RequeryRecords action from the previous step. In the Variable argument box, enter **VendorSortOrder**, and in the Value argument box, enter **"Ascending"** to complete this action. Make sure to include the quotation marks in the Value argument.

Your completed macro design surface should now look like Figure 8-23.

Chapter 8

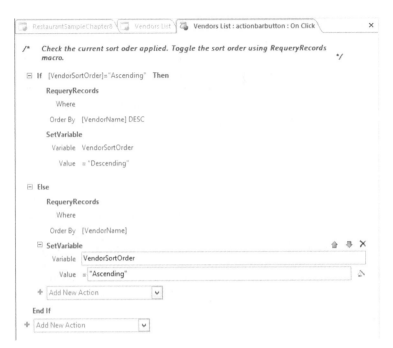

Figure 8-23 Your macro logic should now include actions in both the If and Else blocks.

Your macro logic now contains all the essential actions and arguments to toggle the sort order of the records in the Vendor List view each time you click this custom Action Bar button. The logic in the Else block is essentially the reverse of the actions inside the If block. Each time you click the custom Action Bar button, Access Services resets the VendorSortOrder variable and changes the sort order. The next time you click the button, Access Services branches off to the other block, because the variable value changed.

Save your changes to the macro design surface, and then close the Logic Designer. Access returns you to the Vendor List view with the Data property callout menu for the custom Action Bar button still open. You'll notice here that Access displays a green background color for the On Click event because you saved macro logic for this event.

While you have the Data property callout menu still open for the custom Action Bar, change the Control Name property to **ToggleActionBarButton**, change the Tooltip property to **Toggle Sort Order**, and change the Icon property to the Arrows Updown icon choice, as shown in Figure 8-24. These changes give the custom Action Bar button more meaning and help users understand the purpose of this control.

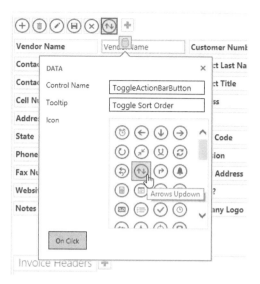

Figure 8-24 Update the properties of the custom Action Bar button before closing the view.

Close the Data property callout menu for the custom Action Bar button, and then save your view changes. We're finished with this view within Access, so you can close the view as well. To test out your macro logic attached to both the On Load event for the view and the On Click event for the custom Action Bar button, let's open the view in your web browser.

Click the Launch App button on the Home ribbon tab. After Access opens your default web browser and navigates to your Access web app, click the Vendor List view caption in the View Selector. If you already have the view open in your browser, you can refresh the page to see the changes you made. After Access Services opens the view, click the custom Action Bar button. Access Services changes the sort order of the records displayed in the List Control so that they are now sorted in descending order, as shown in Figure 8-25. Click the button again, and observe that the records are in ascending order. You can continue clicking the button, and each time, Access Services switches the sort order based on your defined macro logic embedded within a view and control event.

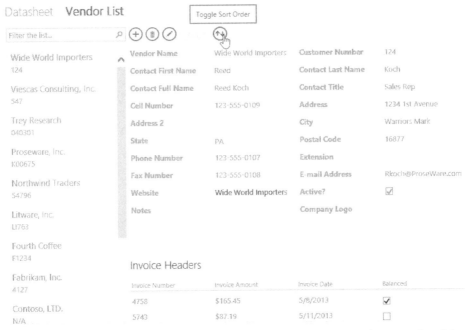

Figure 8-25 Your macro logic attached to a view and control event changes the sort order of the displayed records.

Controlling record navigation with macros

A common use for macros within bound Blank views is to control record navigation. Blank views do not contain a List Control element, which means you cannot navigate to different records. To navigate to different records within Blank views, you must attach embedded macro logic to control events. For example, you could use different command buttons and attach macro logic to their On Click events to navigate between records. You could also use the On Click event of label controls, text boxes, and even image controls.

Let's create custom Action Bar buttons for record navigation. Click the Invoices table name caption in the Table Selector, click the Invoice Blank view caption in the View Selector, and then click the Edit button in the middle of the view preview window. Access opens the Invoice Blank view in Design view, as shown in Figure 8-26.

Figure 8-26 Open the Invoice Blank view in Design view.

As you might recall, you created and customized this Blank view in Chapter 7. This view displays information from the Invoice Headers table and the Vendors table. (You defined an embedded query that joined those two tables for the view's record source.) The view also contains a subview control that displays related records from the Invoice Details table and a web browser control. Before we continue, delete the web browser control from the view, because you don't need it for this example. Select the web browser control in the lower-right corner of the design grid, and then press Delete.

If you look at this view in your web browser, Access Services displays only one invoice record. This view currently is of little use to you besides viewing data for one invoice record. To navigate between all the records in the view's record source, begin by adding four new custom Action Bar buttons to the design grid. Click the Add Custom Action button on the right side of the Action Bar four times. Access creates four new custom buttons and positions them along the right side of the Action Bar, as shown in Figure 8-27.

Figure 8-27 Add four new custom Action Bar buttons to the Invoice Blank view.

Access assigns the default star icon to each of these custom Action Bar buttons, so it's not easy to distinguish the purpose of each button. Make the following changes on the Data property callout menu for each of the new custom Action Bar buttons, starting from left to right:

- **Control Name.** Name the buttons **FirstActionBarButton**, **PreviousActionBarButton**, **NextActionBarButton**, and **LastActionBarButton**.

- **Tooltip.** Change the tooltip text to **Go to first record**, **Go to previous record**, **Go to next record**, and **Go to last record**.

- **Icon.** Change the icons to Track Back, Triangle Left, Triangle Right, and Track Forward.

Your custom Action Bar buttons now have their own unique look, as shown in Figure 8-28. The custom tooltips and icons help users understand the purpose of each button at runtime.

Figure 8-28 Your four new custom Action Bar buttons now have custom icons.

You've assigned properties for each custom Action Bar button, so let's create macro logic for the On Click event of each button. Click the first custom Action Bar button, named FirstActionBarButton, click the Data charm button that appears next to it, and then click the On Click button on the menu to open the Logic Designer. Add a Comment block to the macro design surface, and enter **Navigate to first record** in the box. Access provides the GoToRecord macro action to navigate to different records. Click the Add New Action combo box, and select GoToRecord from the drop-down list of actions. Access adds a GoToRecord action beneath the Comment block, as shown in Figure 8-29.

Figure 8-29 Select First for the Record argument of the GoToRecord action.

The GoToRecord macro action uses only one argument: Record. Access provides a drop-down list of four choices for the argument—Previous, Next, First, and Last. By default, Access selects Next for the Record argument whenever you add a GoToRecord macro action to the design surface. Click the Record argument, and select First from the drop-down list for this macro. Selecting First instructs Access Services to navigate to the first record in the view's record source when you click this custom Action Bar button at runtime. That's all the macro logic you need to define for this particular button. Save your macro changes, and then close the Logic Designer for this event.

Complete the macro logic for the remaining three custom Action Bar button On Click events by using the same technique as you did for the button you just completed. For each macro, provide appropriate text in the Comment block, and select the GoToRecord action. Select Previous for the Record argument when defining the PreviousActionBarButton, select Next for the NextActionBarButton (this argument option should be selected by default), and select Last for the LastActionBarButton one. Save your macro design changes for each event, and then save and close the view when you are finished.

To test out your record navigation macro logic, open the view in your web browser. Click the Launch App button in the Home ribbon tab, or click the Launch App button on the Quick Access Toolbar. After Access opens your default web browser and navigates to your Access web app, click the Invoices table name caption in the Table Selector, and then click the Invoice Blank view caption in the View Selector. After Access Services opens the view, click the next record custom Action Bar button. Access Services navigates to the next invoice record defined in the view's record source, as shown in Figure 8-30. Continue testing all of the custom Action Bar buttons, and observe how Access Services moves to the appropriate record. Access Services also updates the related invoice detail data shown in the subview control as you move between different main view records.

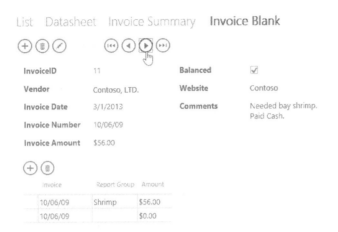

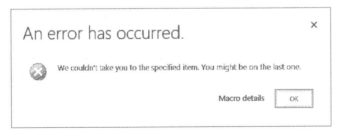

Figure 8-30 Clicking your custom Action Bar buttons for record navigation allows you to move to different records.

If you are currently viewing the first record in the view's record source and click the previous record custom Action Bar button, Access Services displays a macro error dialog, as shown in Figure 8-31. You'll see this error dialog because Access Services can't navigate to any other record before the first one when using Previous for the Record argument. You'll see the same error dialog if you are currently viewing the last record in the view and then click the next record custom Action Bar button. Click the Macro Details link on this error dialog to see another dialog that displays the macro name, condition (if applicable), action name, arguments, and error number where Access Services encountered the macro execution problem. Click OK to dismiss the error dialog.

Figure 8-31 Access displays this message when it can't navigate to a record.

Creating an On Start macro

Access web apps can contain a special type of macro called an On Start macro. Access Services runs the On Start macro each time you navigate to the web app or when you refresh your browser window while viewing your web app. You cannot run the On Start macro from a separate macro using the RunMacro action; Access Services controls when it runs. The On Start macro is useful when, for example, you want to define variables each time a user navigates to your web app. Variables defined in views last until you close your browser window or set the variable to a different value.

To create an On Start macro, switch back to Access, select the App Home View object tab, and then click the Advanced button in the Create group on the Home ribbon tab. Access displays a drop-down list of seven options, as shown in Figure 8-32. Click the On Start Macro option in the drop-down list. Note that Access does not enable the On Start Macro option under the Advanced command if you have any other objects open in your web app and your focus is on one of those objects. You must select (click) the App Home View object tab or have all other objects closed before Access enables the On Start Macro option under the Advanced command.

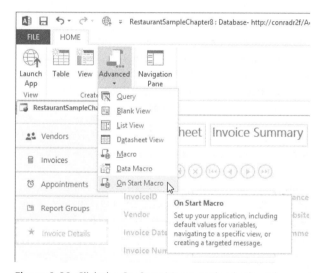

Figure 8-32 Click the On Start Macro option in the Advanced drop-list of commands.

Access opens the Logic Designer for the On Start macro, as shown in Figure 8-33. When you work with the On Start macro, Access collapses the Navigation pane and displays the macro design surface modally.

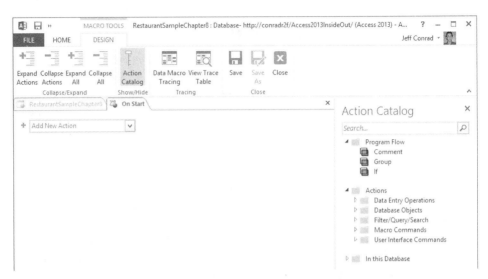

Figure 8-33 The Logic Designer for On Start macros displays modally.

All macro actions are available for use in the On Start macro; however, not all actions make sense to use within the On Start macro execution. For example, you should not use the ClosePopup action in the On Start macro, because no pop-up views should be open when you navigate to a web app. The primary use for the On Start macro is to set variables that you want to use throughout the app. If you reference a variable by name in a macro action or expression that you did not set previously, Access Services displays an error dialog indicating a control reference error. As a developer, you can be sure that Access Services initializes and assigns values to your variables by defining them in the On Start macro.

In the On Start macro you have open, let's define a variable that you'll use to track the name of the user currently using the web app. You'll then display the variable's value in a message box as a greeting to anyone navigating to the web app. Access provides two useful expressions you can use to know who currently is using the app—*UserDisplayName* and *UserEmailAddress*. The UserDisplayName expression returns a string representing the name of the user currently logged in and using the web app. The UserEmailAddress expression returns a string representing the current user's email address.

Follow this procedure to add the macro logic:

1. Add a Comment block to the macro design surface, and enter **Capture current user name** in the Comment box.

2. Add a SetVariable action beneath the Comment block from the previous step. In the Variable argument box, enter **CurrentUser**, and in the Value argument box, enter **UserDisplayName()** to complete this action.

3.   Add a MessageBox action beneath the SetVariable action. In the Message argument box, enter **="Welcome to the app" + [CurrentUser]** to complete this action. Make sure that you include the leading equal sign to denote to Access that this is an expression.

Your completed On Start macro design surface should look like Figure 8-34.

Figure 8-34 Your On Start macro logic should now include SetVariable and MessageBox actions.

Save your macro design changes, and then close the Logic Designer window. If you examine the list of object names in the Navigation pane, you'll notice no new object is listed for this On Start macro; Access attaches the On Start macro to the App Home View directly. You need to make sure to select the App Home View and then click the Save button on the Quick Access Toolbar, after closing the Logic Designer, for your On Start macro to execute in your web browser the next time you load the web app. If you need to edit or delete the macro logic for the On Start macro, click the Advanced command again on the Home ribbon tab and then click On Start macro from the drop-down list. Whenever you make changes to the On Start macro, you must always save the App Home View, because the On Start macro is attached directly to the App Home View.

Before you test out this On Start macro in your browser, let's make one final change to the web app. In the sample web app you have open, let's change the positions of the two view captions for the Vendors table. (If you recall, I had you swap these two view caption positions at the beginning of Chapter 6.) I prefer to use the Vendor List Details view as the first view that users see when navigating to the web app. Click the Vendor List view caption name in the View Selector, hold your mouse, and then drag the view name to the left of the Datasheet view caption name. After you release the mouse, Access places the Vendor List view caption to the left of the Datasheet caption name so that it is in the first position. Access Services displays the Vendor List view first now when you navigate to the app. Click Save on the Quick Access Toolbar one more time to save this latest change to the App Home View.

To see how the On Start macro works at runtime, click the Launch App button on the Home ribbon tab or refresh your web browser window, if you still have the web app open in the background. As Access Services loads your web app, you'll see a message box appear and display the welcome greeting before the first view finishes loading, as shown in Figure 8-35. Access Services displays your user name, which it determined by using the UserDisplayName expression and the variable you defined, at the end of the message. If you navigate to other views in your app, Access Services does not display the message box at any time. When you refresh your browser or close your browser and navigate back to your web app, Access Services fires the On Start macro logic again and displays your message box.

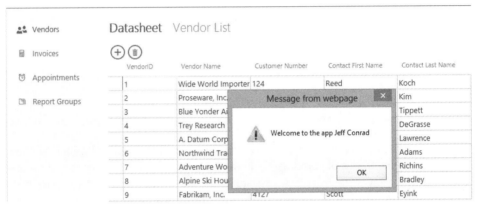

Figure 8-35 Access Services displays your message defined in the On Start macro.

This example showed you how to use the MessageBox action in the On Start macro, but you can use other actions in the On Start macro. You can test and verify that Access Services correctly assigned your CurrentUser variable to the current user's display name and then remove the MessageBox action if you want. Because you defined this variable in the On Start macro, you can reference that variable value at any other time in your web app with other macro actions and expressions.

You can close this sample web app now. Note that you can download a copy of the sample web app, called RestaurantSampleChapter8Completed.app, with the changes made in this chapter, from the book's catalog page.

Opening views with OpenPopup actions

Opening other views within your current view is a common scenario you'll find when designing your web apps. For example, you might want to open a pop-up view to display an informational message that includes data from the main view. You might also want to display more details about the specific record you're currently viewing, or you might want to display records confined to a set of criteria you define on a main view. In all of these cases, the OpenPopup macro action can help you automate these types of tasks within your web app. In the next few sections, you'll see examples of using the OpenPopup macro action.

To follow along with the examples in the next few sections, you'll first need to install the Back Office Software System sample web app (BOSS.app) in your SharePoint site and then download the app into Access. (You can download this sample web app from the book's catalog page.) After you install the sample web app, navigate to the app in your web browser to see the main Home view of the app, as shown in Figure 8-36. In the lower-right corner of this main view, you'll see a command button labeled About.

Figure 8-36 Click the About command button on the Home view of the BOSS sample web app.

The command button on the Home view contains macro logic attached to its On Click control event. Click the command button, and Access Services opens a pop-up view displaying general copyright information about the sample web app, as shown in Figure 8-37. Access Services opens the pop-up view on top of the main Home view, similar to how autocomplete, combo boxes, and related items controls use the Popup View control property to open a view and display related data. When Access Services opens a view as a pop-up view, you cannot interact with the main view controls, the Table Selector, or the View Selector. You must close the pop-up view to interact with the main view again. Click the command button labeled OK on the About view to close and dismiss this pop-up view.

Figure 8-37 Access Services opens the About view as a pop-up view on top of the main view.

Let's examine the macro logic behind the command button that opens the pop-up view. Open the sample web app within Access, if you haven't already, and then open the Home view in Design view. (Note that viewHome is the actual object name in the Navigation pane.) You can open it in Design view through the Navigation pane or through the view preview window. Now select the command button labeled About on the design grid, click the Actions charm button, and then click the On Click button on the Actions callout menu. Access opens the Logic Designer and displays the macro logic defined for this command button control event, as shown in Figure 8-38.

Figure 8-38 The On Click event uses the OpenPopup action to open the viewAbout view.

The embedded macro logic behind this command button is as follows:

```
Comment Block: Open the About view to display copyright information
OpenPopup
  View: viewAbout
  Where:
  Order By:
```

The OpenPopup macro action takes three arguments:

- **View.** Required argument. The name of a saved view within the web app.

- **Where.** Optional argument. The expression that Access uses to select records from the table or query to display in the pop-up view.

- **Order By.** Optional argument. Use this argument to define the display sequence of records returned from the pop-up view's record source.

The only required argument for the OpenPopup action is View. Access provides a drop-down list for this argument of all saved view objects within your web app. In this example, I chose the viewAbout view object to open. Both the Where and Order By arguments for the OpenPopup action are optional. If you provide no Where argument for this action, Access Services opens the view as a pop-up view and displays all records from the view's record source, if the view is bound. If you don't define an Order By argument, Access Services displays the records by the default order defined by the List Control (if you're using a bound List Details view), by any sort order in the query record source (if your view is based on a query), or by the AutoNumber ID field in the table.

The viewAbout view is an unbound stand-alone view, so the Where and Order By arguments are not applicable for this OpenPopup macro. This is the simplest example of using the OpenPopup macro, and you'll use it often when you need to open views as pop-up views.

> **CAUTION!**
>
> When you use an OpenPopup macro action, Access Services ignores all other macro logic after executing the OpenPopup action. Access Services designates the pop-up view as the active view and, therefore, stops executing any other macro logic after opening a view using an OpenPopup action. You'll see the same behavior when using a ChangeView or ClosePopup action.

Using Where clause syntax

Opening a pop-up view with no Where clause argument is fine for the simple case, but if you need to open the view and display a specific record, or set of records, from the view's record source, you need to provide an expression in the Where clause argument. Let's look at an example of using a Where clause to open a pop-up view to display a single record in the Back Office Software System sample web app.

Switch back to the web browser, click the Purchases table name caption in the Table Selector, and then click the Datasheet View caption name in the View Selector. When Access Services loads the view and displays each invoice record, click the command button labeled View for the first record. Access Services opens a List Details view that displays the invoice record information for just the one record you selected, as shown in Figure 8-39. If you close the pop-up view and click the View command button for a different record in the datasheet main view of invoice records, you'll see that Access Services opens the pop-up view and displays the specific selected record data only. Notice that if you click the command button labeled View on the new record row in the datasheet, Access Services does not open any pop-up view.

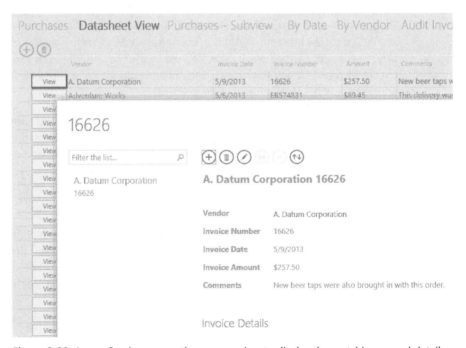

Figure 8-39 Access Services opens the pop-up view to display the matching record details.

Let's examine the macro logic behind the command button that opens the pop-up view. Switch back to Access, click the Purchases table name caption in the Table Selector, click the Datasheet View caption in the View Selector, and then click Edit in the view preview window to open this view in Design view. (Note that tblInvoiceHeaders Datasheet is the actual object name in the Navigation pane. You can open the view in Design view through the Navigation pane or through the view preview window.) After you open the view in Design view, select the command button labeled View on the design grid, click the Actions charm button, and then click the On Click button on the Actions callout menu. Access opens the Logic Designer and displays the macro logic defined for this command button control event, as shown in Figure 8-40.

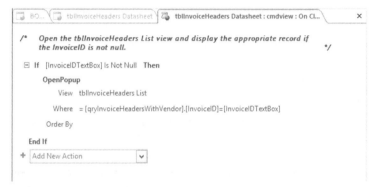

Figure 8-40 The On Click event uses the OpenPopup action with a Where clause to open a specific invoice record.

The embedded macro logic behind this command button is as follows:

```
Comment Block: Open the tblInvoiceHeaders List view and display the appropriate
record if the InvoiceID is not null.
If [InvoiceIDTextBox] Is Not Null Then
  OpenPopup
    View: tblInvoiceHeaders List
    Where:[qryInvoiceHeadersWithVendor].[InvoiceID]=[InvoiceIDTextBox]
    Order By:
End If
```

The If block, at the beginning of the macro logic, is a conditional expression that checks to see whether the control displaying the InvoiceID field value is Null. (The user of the app might click the command button labeled View on the new record row of the datasheet at runtime.) If the control is Null, the user is currently viewing a new unsaved record in the datasheet. In this case, I chose not to take any action, such as opening the pop-up view, by leaving off an Else block inside the If block. If you omitted the If conditional expression, in this scenario, Access Services opens the pop-up view and places the pop-up view into edit mode for a new record when you click the command button labeled View on the new record row in the datasheet. You might want that behavior in some cases in your web apps, but for this view, I want to open the pop-up view to display only existing records. Inside the If block is the OpenPopup macro action. In the View argument, I selected to open the tblInvoiceHeaders List view.

When you define a Where clause in an OpenPopup macro action, the general syntax you must use is as follows:

`[<name of table or query>].[<field name>]  <comparison predicate>  [<compare value>]`

In the first part of the expression, you need to identify the view's record source. You need to identify the record source of the view you want to *open* in the macro, not the view executing the macro. If the view you want to open uses a table name as its record source, you must list the table name here. If the view you want to open uses a saved query as its record source, you must list the query name here. If you leave off the table or query name in the first part of the Where expression, Access Services displays an error message at runtime.

> **Note**
>
> When you define a saved query object that joins two or more tables for your view's record source, you might encounter a situation where you have identical fields in two or more tables. In this case, you'll need to modify the first part of the Where expression to account for the identical field names. For example, assume that you have two tables named T1 and T2. Both tables include a field named F1, and you created a query (Query1) that joins these two tables and outputs all fields for a view record source. You'll need to use syntax such as [Query1].[T1.F1]=[<compare value>] to identify the field in table T1 and [Query1].[T2.F1]=[<compare value>] to identify the field in table T2.

In the second part of the expression, [<field name>], you need to enter the field name for which you're going to perform an evaluation. If your field name includes spaces, you must wrap the field name in brackets. In general, you should get in the habit of always wrapping the field name in brackets in these types of expressions even if the field name contains no spaces.

In the comparison predicate, you can use the common predicates you've used in other expressions in web apps, such as equal (=), less than (<), greater than (>), less than or equal to (<=), greater than or equal to (>=), or not equal (<>).

In the last part of the Where clause, [<compare value>], you need to provide a value that Access Services can evaluate against. The value could be a defined variable, a value you enter directly into the expression, or a value displayed within a view control. You can also create more complex expressions in the Where clause argument using mathematical operators, along with AND or OR operators for multiple evaluations.

In the Where argument box in this example, I used an expression that instructs Access Services to restrict the records displayed in the pop-up view to the one record where the InvoiceID field in a saved query object (qryInvoiceHeadersWithVendor) matches the value displayed in a control called InvoiceIDTextBox. The completed expression is as follows:

```
[qryInvoiceHeadersWithVendor].[InvoiceID]=[InvoiceIDTextBox]
```

You'll notice in this expression I used a control value—InvoiceIDTextBox. I could also use the InvoiceID field to achieve the same result or enter a specific ID number (for example, 5). However, if you use a defined static value, Access Services opens the pop-up view and displays the same invoice record each time. This type of static value is useful in some scenarios, but in most cases, you'll want to use a value that changes based on your context.

If you use a compare value that is dynamic, Access Services searches for the value in the web app in the following order: fields, view controls, properties, and then variable names. In the example expression for the Where clause, I used InvoiceIDTextBox. Access Services first searches for a field in the current view called InvoiceIDTextBox. Because there are no field names defined in the view's record source by that name, Access Services then searches for a control name called InvoiceIDTextBox within the current view. In this case, Access Services successfully finds a control by that name, inspects the current value, and then uses that value for the completed expression to find the appropriate invoice record in the pop-up view. If Access Services does not find a control on the view called InvoiceIDTextBox, Access Services continues checking for a matching property name and finally for a defined variable name. If Access Services cannot find a match in any of these cases, you'll see an error dialog at runtime, indicating a control reference error.

INSIDE OUT   Provide unique names for defined variables

Access Services searches across field names, view control names, property names, and variable names when evaluating the Where clause for the OpenPopup and other macro actions. To avoid potentially retrieving the wrong value based on fields, view controls, and variables using the same name, you should provide unique names for any defined variables in your web apps. For example, you might consider using a naming convention for your defined variables to avoid potential conflicts with field and view control names.

Troubleshooting

Why do I get an error trying to use a Where clause with an OpenPopup or ChangeView action when the view is based on an embedded query?

Access Services requires the Where clause to include the table or query name on which the view is based. When you define an embedded query as the record source for a view, Access Services creates a hidden system query that is not visible in the Navigation pane. Therefore, you cannot use a Where clause with the OpenPopup action or ChangeView action to open a view based on an embedded query. To work around this limitation, you can base your view on a saved query object. Note that Access Services creates a hidden system query as the record source also for Summary views. This means that you cannot use the Where clause argument to open a Summary view to a specific record or set of records. However, the workaround won't work for Summary views.

Referencing other view control values

In the previous example, you learned how to define a Where clause for an OpenPopup macro action that retrieves a value from the view on which the macro executes. In some cases, you might want to retrieve a value from a different view, such as a value displayed in a subview control. Close any open objects you might have within Access, and then switch back to your web browser. Navigate to the Home view in the Back Office Software System sample web app by clicking the Home table name caption in the Table Selector, and then click the Home view name caption in the View Selector. This main view, which you've seen previously, displays four subview controls. The subview in the lower-right corner of the view displays a datasheet with any appointments scheduled for the current date. Click the command button labeled View for one of the displayed appointment rows, and Access Services opens a pop-up view displaying the details for the selected appointment, as shown in Figure 8-41.

Note

You might not see any displayed appointments on the main Home view in Figure 8-41, because I entered a limited amount of sample data into the web app. If you don't see any appointments scheduled for the current date, you can create a new appointment record to follow along with this example. To do this, click the Appointments table name caption in the Table Selector and click the Full List view name caption in the View Selector. You can then click the Add Action Bar button on the displayed view to create a new appointment. Make sure you select the current date and save the record. When you navigate back to the main Home view, you'll see your new appointment record displayed within the subview.

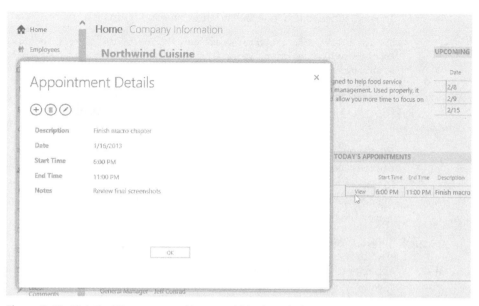

Figure 8-41 Click the View command button within the subview to open a pop-up view displaying the matching appointment record details.

Let's examine the macro logic behind the command button that opens the pop-up view. Switch back to Access, expand the Navigation pane, locate a view called viewTodaysAppointments, and then open it in Design view. This view is a Datasheet view displayed within the subview control on the main Home view. After you open the view in Design view, select the command button labeled View on the design grid, click the Actions charm button, and then click the On Click button on the Actions callout menu. Access opens the Logic Designer and displays the macro logic defined for this command button control event, as shown in Figure 8-42.

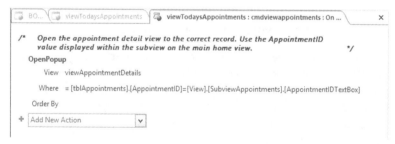

Figure 8-42 The Where clause for this OpenPopup action inspects the value of a subview control.

The embedded macro logic behind this command button is as follows:

```
Comment Block: Open the appointment detail view to the correct record. Use the
AppointmentID value displayed within the subview on the main home view.
OpenPopup
  View: viewAppointmentDetails
  Where:[tblAppointments].[AppointmentID]=[View].[SubviewAppointments].
        [AppointmentIDTextBox]
  Order By:
```

When you embed a view in another view, the view is contained in a subview control. You can reference a subview control by using the View property. The View property allows you to inspect the values of controls (including within subview controls) displayed within the main view currently loaded within your web browser. To refer to a value displayed in a control on the main view, use syntax as follows:

```
[View].[<control name>]
```

You refer to a value in a view control displayed within a subview control on a main view as follows:

```
[View].[<subview control name>].[<control on subview>]
```

Likewise, you can continue inspecting the values of a subview nested inside another subview on a main view as follows:

```
[View].[<subview control name 1>].[<subview control name 2>].[<control on subview 2>]
```

In the View argument for this OpenPopup macro, I chose to open the viewAppointmentDetails view, which is a custom Blank view I created to display individual appointment records. In the Where argument box for this example, I used an expression that instructs Access Services to restrict the records displayed in the pop-up view to the selected appointment record displayed within the subview using the View property. The expression uses the following syntax after the equal sign:

```
[View].[SubviewAppointments].[AppointmentIDTextBox]
```

SubviewAppointments is the name of the subview control displayed on the viewHome main view. Within the viewAppointmentDetails view, I have a control (hidden in runtime), called AppointmentIDTextBox, that contains the value of the AppointmentID from the view's record source. Using this expression, Access Services inspects the subview control at runtime, looks for the value displayed in the AppointmentIDTextBox, and then uses that value to look for the specific appointment record.

You can use these techniques from a pop-up view also to inspect and reference values displayed in the main view. Note that the View property references only the base main view controls and cannot be used to reference controls displayed on other pop-up views.

For example, assume that you had a main view called MainView1 displayed in your web browser. You open a pop-up view called Popup1 on top of MainView1. From the Popup1 view, you then open Popup2, which Access Services displays on top of Popup1. You can use the View property syntax from Popup2 (or Popup1) to reference control values displayed in MainView1; however, you cannot inspect the control values displayed on Popup1 from the Popup2 view, nor can you reference any control values displayed on Popup2 from MainView1 or Popup1.

> ## Note
>
> If you conduct your own testing on my example with the appointment subview, you'll probably discover that I could simplify the Where clause by excluding the extra reference to the View property. (The current context of the macro execution is the subview, and I need to inspect only a value on the same view instead of the main Home view.) Therefore, I can shorten the Where clause to the following:
>
> ```
> [tblAppointments].[AppointmentID]=[AppointmentIDTextBox]
> ```
>
> I included the View property here so that you can see a working example of referencing subview controls. Also, I prefer to fully qualify the context when I'm working with subview controls and macros.

In addition to Where clause arguments, you can also use the techniques outlined in this section for referencing control values in other areas of your web app. You can reference control values in other macro actions with arguments that accept an expression. For example, you can reference control values found on subviews and main views with the Message argument of the MessageBox action, or you could define variables referencing control values in the Value argument of SetVariable actions.

Troubleshooting

> **Why do I get an error when I try to use the UserDisplayName or UserEmailAddress expression values in an OpenPopup Where clause?**
> Access Services evaluates the expression entered into the Where clause of an OpenPopup action at the data layer; however, Access Services cannot interpret the UserDisplayName and UserEmailAddress expressions at the data layer. To use the values of those two expressions in the Where clause, you first need to use the SetVariable action to assign those expression values to defined variable names. You can then use the variable names in the Where clause of the OpenPopup action. You'll need to do the same type of procedure with the ChangeView and RequeryRecords actions. If you define variables once in the On Start macro to the values of the UserDisplayName and UserEmailAddress expressions, you can refer to those variables in Where clauses for other macro actions.

Passing parameters to views

In Chapter 4, you learned how the Logic Designer displays parameter boxes when you create and use named data macros. If you use parameters in a query for a view record source,
Access displays the parameters you defined in the query when you place an OpenPopup
action on the macro design surface. To show you an example of this behavior on the Logic
Designer, close any open object that you might have open in Access and then open the
viewPayrollTotals view in Design view from the Navigation pane. Now select the command
button labeled Open Report on the design grid, click the Actions charm button, and then
click the On Click button on the Actions callout menu. Access opens the Logic Designer and
displays the macro logic defined for this command button control event, as shown in Figure
8-43.

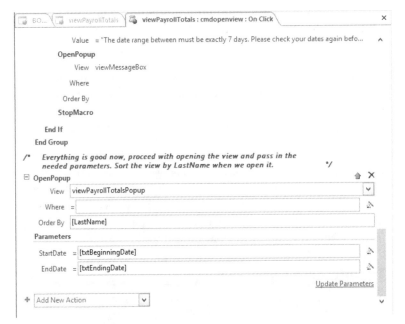

Figure 8-43 Access displays parameter boxes on the macro design surface for OpenPopup
actions when the view is based on a parameterized query.

The first part of the logic defined for this embedded macro is a Group block labeled
VerifyDateParameters. This macro logic verifies that the user entered beginning and ending dates for the pop-up view in the two text boxes displayed on this view. Using DatePart
expressions, I first verify that the starting date is a Monday and the ending date is a Sunday.
I then verify that the user provided both date values and did not enter an ending date that
is before the beginning date. Finally, I use the DateDiff expression to verify that the date
range the user provided is exactly seven days. If any of the conditions are not met, I set a

variable with a custom message and then use an OpenPopup action to open a small pop-up view and display that message text in a control on the pop-up view.

You can learn more about the DatePart and DateDiff functions in Article 5, "Function Reference," which you can download from the book's catalog page.

Scroll down the macro design surface until you see the last OpenPopup macro action at the bottom of the Logic Designer, as shown previously in Figure 8-43. This last action opens the viewPayrollTotalsPopup view based on the date range the user chooses on the main view. The viewPayrollTotalsPopup view uses the qryWeekTotalsLaborHoursFinalDisplay parameterized query as its record source. Remember, you learned how to create this parameter query in Chapter 5, "Working with queries in web apps."

Access displays the two parameters in the underlying query—StartDate and EndDate—as parameter boxes at the bottom of the action. You can enter a value you want to use for each parameter by typing the value into the parameter box or use an expression to derive that parameter value. In this example, I need to pass in the current date values displayed within the two unbound text boxes on the view—txtBeginningDate and txtEndingDate.

At runtime, when the user selects a beginning and ending date range in the date text boxes on the view and clicks the command button to open the pop-up view, Access Services passes in the values shown in the date controls to the query layer for processing. The query processor then uses the parameter values for the pop-up view that were obtained from the main view controls. Finally, Access Services sorts the records returned by the LastName field in the query, because I defined that field name in the Order By argument of the OpenPopup action.

INSIDE OUT   Click the Update Parameters link to update query parameters

If you add, edit, or delete parameters in the underlying query for a view record source, you can click the Update Parameters link on the OpenPopup macro action block on the macro design surface to update the parameters. Access evaluates the parameters in the query and then refreshes the parameters boxes to match the parameters in the query.

To show how these parameters function at runtime, close the Logic Designer you currently have open, close the viewPayrollTotals view you have open, and then switch back to your web browser. (If you are prompted to save any changes to the macro or view when you attempt to close the objects, click No.) Click the Labor Hours table name caption in the Table Selector, and then click the Payroll Totals view name caption in the View Selector. Access Services opens this unbound view and displays its controls, as shown in Figure 8-44.

Edit Labor Hours   List View   All Records   By Date   By Employee   **Payroll Totals**

Enter date range to view payroll totals. Time frame must be 7 days.

Start Date   End Date

5/6/2013   5/12/2013

Open Report

Figure 8-44 Enter a beginning and ending date, and then click the Open Report command button on the Payroll Totals view of the BOSS sample web app.

INSIDE OUT   Use the Format property with unbound controls to display Date Picker buttons

If you assign a date format for the Format property to an unbound text box control, Access Services displays the Date Picker button when you tab or click into the control. In Figure 8-44, you can see the Date Picker button displayed next to the End Date unbound text box control.

Enter **5/6/2013** in the beginning date control (May 6th, 2013), enter **5/12/2013** in the ending date control (May 12th, 2013), and then click the command button labeled Open Report. Access opens the viewPayrollTotalsPopup view as a pop-up view and displays the computed labor hour and wage information, including any overtime, for each employee within the date range you provided, as shown in Figure 8-45. By using parameters defined at the query level and binding a view to that query for its record source, Access displays the parameters needed for the view when you add an OpenPopup action to the macro design surface. You can pass parameter values from view controls in your macro action to the view you want to open. In this example, you can dynamically display labor hour and wage data from different date ranges by changing the supplied dates on the main view.

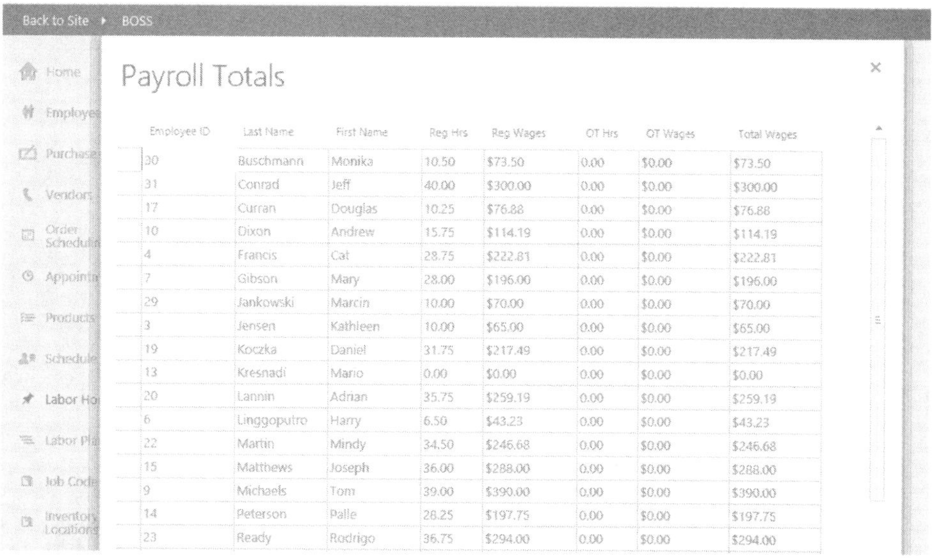

Figure 8-45 Access displays the pop-up view with record information contained within the two date parameter values passed from the main view.

Exploring the audit invoices macros

In the following sections, you'll explore one of the more complicated embedded macros used in the Back Office Software System sample web app (BOSS.app). I'll show you a complex macro that interacts with the data layer by calling named data macros and using return variables to display values returned back from the data layer to the users of the app. You'll also learn about the powerful SetProperty macro action and how to use it to dynamically change view control properties on your views while they are displayed in your web browser.

Switch back to Access, close any objects you might have open, and then open the viewAuditInvoices view in Design view from the Navigation pane. This view, shown in Figure 8-46, allows users of the web app to audit the invoice records stored in this restaurant management app. Before an app user opens a view of invoice totals, or perhaps creates a desktop database report based on the invoice data, the user might want to verify that all invoices in the app are balanced. For an invoice record to balance, the invoice detail line item totals stored in the tblInvoiceDetails table must add up to the correct invoice amount total stored in the parent invoice record in the tblInvoiceHeaders table.

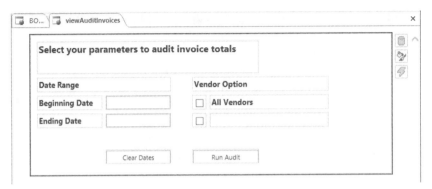

Figure 8-46 You can audit the invoice records in the web app through the viewAuditInvoices view.

Using the SetProperty action with view controls

When you're automating a web app, you'll probably find yourself using the *SetProperty* macro action quite often. The SetProperty macro action is a powerful macro, because it allows you to dynamically change several view control properties across different control types at runtime in your web browser. You can also change the values of certain control types by using the SetProperty action.

On the viewAuditInvoices view, shown previously in Figure 8-46, I provide two text boxes for the app users to enter a date range for invoices they want to audit. Under Vendor Option, the user can choose to audit the invoices from all vendors or from one specific vendor in the application. The command button, labeled Clear Dates, clears any selected dates in the text boxes. (We'll discuss the command button labeled Run Audit in the next section.)

Select the command button labeled Clear Dates, click the Actions charm button, and then click the On Click button on the Actions callout menu. Access opens the Logic Designer and displays the following embedded macro logic defined for this command button control event:

```
Comment Block: Clear the date fields
SetProperty
   Control Name: txtStartDate
   Property: Value
   Value:
SetProperty
   Control Name: txtEndDate
   Property: Value
   Value:
Comment Block: Move focus to the start date field
GoToControl
   Control Name: txtStartDate
```

The SetProperty macro action has three arguments—Control Name, Property, and Value. In the Control Name argument, you provide the name of the view control, which you can find displayed on the Data property callout menu. (In this example, I used txtStartDate and txtEndDate for control names.) In the Property argument, you can choose from one of six control properties to change—Enabled, Visible, ForeColor, BackColor, Caption, and Value. Note that you cannot set all six properties for any control type. (I'll discuss the supported properties for each control type in a moment.) In the Value argument, you can enter the value you want to set for the control property. Do not confuse the Value argument with the Value control property option for the Property argument. Although they are both named *value*, they have different purposes.

To set the Enabled and Visible properties, you enter Yes when you want the Value argument to contain a True value. Enter No when you want the Value argument to contain a False value. In the ForeColor and BackColor properties, you can enter a color value (such as #000000 for black) in the Value argument. In the Caption and Value properties, you can enter the text you want to use for the new control property in the Value argument. If you want to use an expression for the Value argument, enter an equals sign (=) first in the Value box.

See Article 6, "Color names and codes," which you can download from the book's catalog page, for a reference guide to the color values you can use for the ForeColor and BackColor properties.

I use the control name for each of the two text boxes, selected Value for the Property argument, and left the Value arguments empty in the embedded macro attached to the cmdClearDates command button. By leaving the Value arguments empty, Access clears any values in the text box controls. I use the GoToControl macro action as the last action in the macro to put the focus in the txtStartDate text box so that users can immediately enter a new date if they want. Close the Logic Designer for the embedded macro you have open, and then close the Actions callout menu for the cmdClearDates command button.

Click the Launch App button on the Home ribbon tab to open the viewAuditInvoices view in your web browser. You can leave the view open in Design view in Access, because you'll return to it in just a moment. Access opens your default web browser, navigates to your Access web app, and then attempts to navigate directly to the Audit Invoices view. If Access Services navigates you to the Home view, click the Purchases table caption name in the Table Selector and then click the Audit Invoices view caption name in the View Selector to see the view in your web browser, as shown in Figure 8-47.

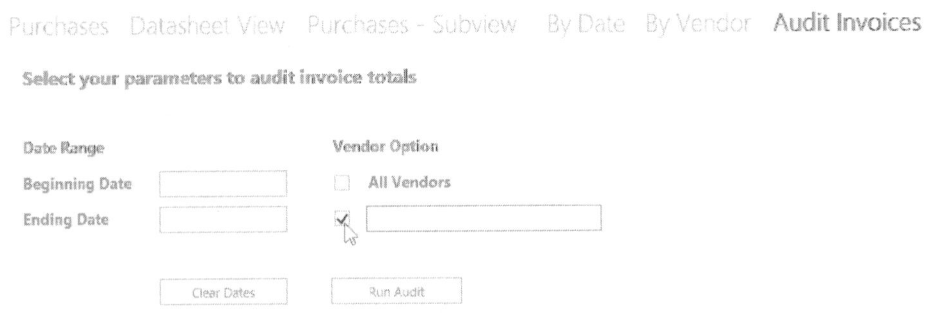

Purchases   Datasheet View   Purchases – Subview   By Date   By Vendor   **Audit Invoices**

Select your parameters to audit invoice totals

Date Range   Vendor Option

Beginning Date [   ]   ☐ All Vendors

Ending Date   [   ]   ☑ [   ]

[Clear Dates]   [Run Audit]

Figure 8-47 When you select a check box, Access Services clears the other check box.

Under the label with Vendor Option as the caption text, you'll see two check boxes, a label control, and an autocomplete control. If you select either of the two check boxes, you'll see that Access Services clears the other check box. You'll also notice that Access Services clears any values in the autocomplete control and selectively enables or disables the control to correspond to the selected check box. I accomplish all of this dynamic view control manipulation through SetProperty macro actions. You can use the autocomplete control on this view to select a specific vendor and audit their invoice records only.

INSIDE OUT   Use SetProperty with built-in Action Bar buttons

You can dynamically change the visibility and enabled state of any of the built-in Action Bar buttons on your views using the SetProperty action. For example, you might find this useful to selectively hide or show the buttons based on conditions within the view. To reference the built-in Action Bar buttons in the SetProperty action, use addActionBarButton, deleteActionBarButton, editActionBarButton, saveActionBarButton, or cancelActionBarButton for the Control Name argument. You can use Enabled or Visible for the Property argument.

Let's examine the embedded macro logic behind one of these check boxes. Switch back to Access, select the first check box (named chkAllVendors), click the Actions charm button, and then click the After Update button on the Actions callout menu. (Remember that check box controls support only After Update control events.) Access opens the Logic Designer and displays the following embedded macro logic defined for this check box control event:

```
If [chkAllVendors] = Yes Then
   Comment Block: Clear the check box for one vendor
   SetProperty
      Control Name: chkOneVendor
```

```
      Property: Value
      Value: No
    Comment Block: Clear any autocomplete value and disable the control
    SetProperty
      Control Name: AutoCompleteVendor
      Property: Value
      Value:
    SetProperty
      Control Name: AutoCompleteVendor
      Property: Enabled
      Value: No
Else
    Comment Block: Select the one vendor check box
    SetProperty
      Control Name: chkOneVendor
      Property: Value
      Value: Yes
    Comment Block: Enable the vendor autocomplete control and set focus to it
    SetProperty
      Control Name: AutoCompleteVendor
      Property: Enabled
      Value: Yes
    GoToControl
      Control Name: AutoCompleteVendor
End If
```

In the AfterUpdate event of this check box, I first check to see the current value of
the chkAllVendors check box. If the check box is selected (Yes), I clear any value in the
chkOneVendor check box, clear any value selected in the AutoCompleteVendor autocomplete control, and then disable the AutoCompleteVendor autocomplete control. If the
chkAllVendors check box is cleared (No), the macro executes the actions after the Else
keyword. Under Else, Access selects the chkOneVendor check box, enables the
AutoCompleteVendor autocomplete control, and then sets the focus to the
AutoCompleteVendor autocomplete control using the GoToControl action. If you examine
the embedded macro logic behind the second check box on the view—chkOneVendor—
you'll notice that the macro logic is essentially the reverse of the macro logic behind
chkAllVendors. Using SetProperty actions, you can effectively guide the user as they use
the web app and selectively hide, enable, or change view controls, as needed.

Table 8-3 lists the SetProperty behavior for the six possible Property arguments against
each of the view control types. You cannot use the SetProperty macro action with related
items controls. If the cell in the table displays the word Supported, Access Services changes
the property of the control at runtime in your web browser. If the table cell is empty, Access
Services displays a macro error message at runtime in your web browser when you attempt
to execute the action against the selected control with the provided Property argument.
The error message indicates that the property is not supported.

When you use the Value argument, your view must be in edit mode at runtime; otherwise, you'll receive an error message when you are in view mode in your web browser and try to execute the SetProperty action. Also, you must use Yes and No values when working with check boxes for the Value argument. If you are working with combo boxes or autocomplete controls, you need to provide a valid value when using the Value argument. For example, you'll need to provide the AutoNumber ID value from the related table if you bind your control to a Lookup data type or provide a valid value if you're using Value List for the Row Source Type property.

TABLE 8-3 SetProperty action behavior for view controls

Control Type	Enabled	Visible	ForeColor	BackColor	Caption	Value
Action Bar buttons	Supported	Supported				
Autocomplete	Supported	Supported	Supported	Supported		Supported
Check Box	Supported	Supported				Supported
Combo Box	Supported	Supported	Supported	Supported		Supported
Command Button	Supported	Supported	Supported		Supported	
Hyperlink	Supported	Supported	Supported	Supported		Supported
Image		Supported		Supported		
Label		Supported	Supported	Supported	Supported	Supported
Multiline Textbox	Supported	Supported	Supported	Supported		Supported
Subview	Supported	Supported				
Text Box	Supported	Supported	Supported	Supported		Supported
Web Browser		Supported				

INSIDE OUT   Changing a view caption

You can dynamically change the Caption property of a view by using the SetProperty macro action. For example, you might find this useful to display an employee's name as the view caption when you open the view as a pop-up view. To set the Caption property of the view at runtime in your web browser, leave the Control Name argument blank, select Caption for the Property argument, and enter the text, field name, or expression you want to display in the Value argument. You can see examples of this technique in many of the views for the Back Office Software System web app. You can study how I dynamically change the view caption in the On Open and On Current events for the tblEmployees List, viewEmployeeDetailsAll, viewInvoiceMainSubview, viewInvoicesPopup, viewInvoicesUnbalanced, and viewVendorListAll views.

Calling named data macros and using return variables

In Chapter 4, you learned how to define return variables in named data macros in web apps. In this section, you'll learn how to call a named data macro from an embedded macro attached to a view or view control event and then return data back to the calling macro by using return variables. You'll also learn how you can then use the values in the return variables in messages and other macro actions.

On the viewAuditInvoices view you've been studying, the user first selects a beginning and ending date range to audit invoices and then selects to edit either the invoices for all the vendors or a specific vendor within the given date range. The real magic for this view happens behind the command button labeled Run Audit.

If you have the Logic Designer still open from the previous section, close it, select the command button labeled Run Audit on the view design grid, click the Actions charm button, and then click the On Click button on the Actions callout menu. Access opens the Logic Designer and displays the embedded macro logic behind this command button. Scroll down the macro design surface until you see the CheckAllowedRange Group block, as shown in Figure 8-48.

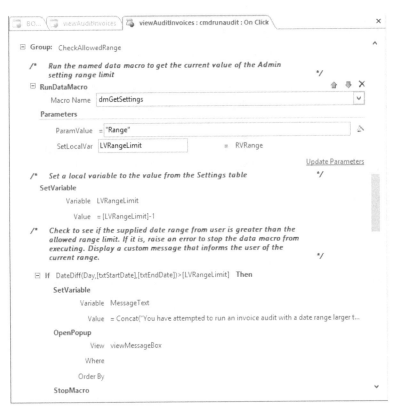

Figure 8-48 The macro logic behind the cmdRunAudit command button calls named data macros.

The first part of this embedded macro (not shown in Figure 8-48) verifies that the user entered a date range within the two text box controls, verifies that the ending date is after the beginning date, and then verifies that the user selected a vendor from the AutoCompleteVendor autocomplete control if the user chose to audit only one vendor. If any of the above conditions are false, the macro displays a message to the user by opening a pop-up view. Because I added a StopMacro action after each failure, the macro then halts further execution. If the initial test conditions pass, Access proceeds to the Group block called CheckAllowedRange, shown previously in Figure 8-48.

Auditing invoice records can be a time-consuming operation to perform, especially if you have many invoices and invoice detail records to verify. I purposely created a field in the tblSettings table that I could use to limit the number of days selected in a date range for different app operations. The default setting I defined in the tblSettings RangeLimit field is seven days. The RunDataMacro action takes only one required argument—Macro Name. Access provides a drop-down list of all saved named data macros within the web app for this argument. Within the CheckAllowedRange Group block, I use the RunDataMacro action to execute the dmGetSettings named data macro.

You previously studied the dmGetSettings named data macro in Chapter 4 and learned that I use this named data macro to fetch values from the one record in the administrative table called tblSettings. The dmGetSettings named data macro takes one parameter value, called ParamValue. When you select a named data macro for the Macro Name argument of the RunDataMacro action, Access examines the named data macro to see whether it contains any defined parameters. Access displays a parameter box for each defined parameter within the RunDataMacro action on the macro design surface. In this example, Access displays ParamValue as a parameter box. You can enter a value that you want to use for each parameter by typing the value into the parameter box, or you can use an expression to derive that parameter value. In this embedded macro, I pass in the text value Range as the parameter value ParamValue needed for the dmGetSettings named data macro.

Access also examines named data macros listed in RunDataMacro actions to see whether they contain any return variables. Access displays a SetLocalVar action for each return variable in the dmGetSettings named data macro beneath the parameter box. When Access returns the variable back to this macro, I assign a local variable called LVRangeLimit to the return variable. I can then use that value stored in the local variable during the execution of the remaining actions within the macro. Access Services executes the named data macro and returns the value stored in the RangeLimit field in the tblSettings table to this embedded macro.

After the named data macro finishes executing, Access continues with the next action in the embedded macro: Access subtracts one integer from the local variable just returned in the named data macro. (The expression I use in the next step requires this action.) Before starting the process of auditing invoices, the embedded macro compares the number of days the user selected to the maximum value allowed in the RangeLimit field. I accomplish this test by using the DateDiff function to calculate the number of days between the beginning and ending date range and seeing whether that value, in number of days, is greater than the local variable defined in the previous step. The conditional expression for this test in the If block is as follows:

```
DateDiff(Day,[txtStartDate],[txtEndDate])>[LVRangeLimit]
```

You'll notice I can use the return variable, just returned from the named data macro, by referencing the local variable assigned to that value. If the user selected a range of dates greater than the default of seven days, the macro displays a custom message passed into a view using an OpenPopup action and then stops the macro. In Figure 8-48, you cannot see the entire expression I use for the custom message. The expression is as follows:

```
= Concat("You have attempted to run an invoice audit with a date range larger than
the allotted number of days. Please restrict your date range to ",
([LVRangeLimit]+1)," days.")
```

Here again, I reference the variable value, originally obtained from the data macro return variable, and display that value in a custom message. I use the Concat function to concatenate the final display message shown at runtime. Users of the app have an easier time understanding why Access Services does not run the macro if they see a message that tells them exactly the maximum number of days they can select for the audit procedure.

If the user selected a date range less than or equal to my default of seven days, Access Services continues with the remaining actions defined in the embedded macro. If the user selected to audit all vendors, Access Services executes the dmAuditInvoiceTotalsAllVendors named data macro. If the user selected to audit only a single vendor, Access instead executes the dmAuditInvoiceTotalsOneVendor named data macro. In both cases, I pass the beginning date and ending date as parameters to the named data macros. If the user selected only one vendor, I also pass in the VendorID from the AutoCompleteVendor autocomplete control to the dmAuditInvoiceTotalsOneVendor named data macro. You can see both of these RunDataMacro actions in Figure 8-49.

Figure 8-49 The macro logic runs one of two named data macros, depending on the user's choice of vendor range.

After the named data macro completes auditing the invoices, Access Services returns the number of unbalanced invoices found in a return variable called RVUnbalanced. I assign that value to a local variable called NumberOfUnbalanced. Access Services could find either no unbalanced invoices or at least one unbalanced invoice within the given parameters. Access Services also returns the number of invoices audited in a return variable called RVAuditedInvoices. I assign that value to a local variable called NumberOfInvoices.

In Figure 8-50, you can see that I use an If conditional expression to test the value of the NumberOfUnbalanced variable returned from the named data macro. (Scroll down the macro design surface so that you can see the macro actions I'm discussing here.) If the variable NumberOfUnbalanced is 0, there are no unbalanced invoices, so the macro displays a custom message indicating that Access Services did not find any unbalanced invoices. The message uses the Concat function to include the number of invoices audited stored in the NumberOfInvoices variable. The macro is effectively finished at this point if Access Services finds no unbalanced invoices, because the remaining actions are within an Else block.

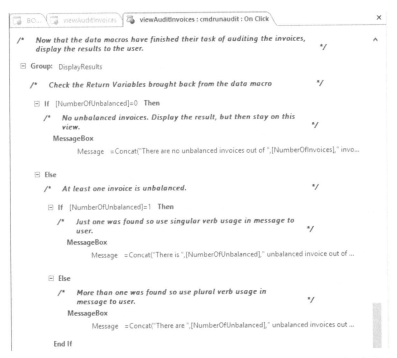

Figure 8-50 This macro uses return variables to display the number of unbalanced records found in message boxes.

The macro then uses another If condition expression inside the Else block to see whether the variable NumberOfUnbalanced is 1. If the value is exactly 1, the macro displays a message to the user with a singular tone in the sentence structure for the message. If the value is not 1, this means Access found more than one unbalanced invoice, so the macro then executes the actions in the nested Else block. Access displays a message to the user indicating the number of unbalanced invoices found but, in this case, uses a plural tone in the sentence structure. In both instances, I also include the number of invoices audited stored in the NumberOfInvoices variable. Finally, the macro browses to another view to display the list of unbalanced records Access Services found after executing the named data macros. (You'll learn about navigating to another view in the next section.) As you can see, using the RunDataMacro macro action in conjunction with named data macros and return variables allows you flexibility to pass data from the view level to the data layer and back.

Navigating to different views using ChangeView actions

Near the bottom of the embedded macro in the On Click event of the cmdRunAudit command button you've been studying so far, you'll notice that I use a macro action called ChangeView. You can use the ChangeView action to browse to a different view displayed in the View Selector for any associated table displayed in the Table Selector.

The ChangeView macro action and argument values I use in the cmdRunAudit embedded macro are as follows:

```
ChangeView
  Table: tblInvoiceHeaders
  View: viewInvoicesUnbalanced
  Where:
  Order By:[InvoiceDate]
```

In the required Table argument, provide the name of the table in the web app to which the view is associated in the Table Selector. For the Table argument, you must provide the actual table name listed in the Navigation pane, not the table caption name displayed in the Table Selector. In the View required argument, provide the name of the view to navigate to with this action. Note that you cannot use the ChangeView action to navigate to a stand-alone view not displayed in the View Selector for any tables. You must use a view name displayed in the View Selector, because Access Services navigates first to the table name caption in the Table Selector and then to the appropriate view in the View Selector. In the optional Where argument, you can use an expression to filter the records in the view. In the optional Order By argument, you can have Access Services sort the records returned by providing a field name with which to sort any returned records in the view's record source.

In this example, I want Access Services to navigate to a view object, called viewInvoicesUnbalanced, that is associated with the tblinvoiceHeaders table. The view caption name in the View Selector for this view is Unbalanced. The viewInvoicesUnbalanced view is a custom view I created to display unbalanced invoices only. After Access Services navigates to the view, I want the records sorted by the InvoiceDate field so that I can see oldest invoices first.

> **Note**
>
> The Table and View argument boxes for the ChangeView action on the macro design surface do not provide drop-down lists of the respective object names in your web app. You'll need to type in the exact object names in the argument boxes for this action.

If you'd like to see how this ChangeView action works in your web browser, close the Logic Designer, if you still have it open, and then close the viewAuditInvoices view. (If you are prompted to save any changes to the macro or view when you attempt to close the objects, click No.) Click the Launch App button on the Home ribbon tab to open your web browser. After Access Services opens your web app, click the Purchases table name caption in the Table Selector and then click the Audit Invoices view name caption in the View Selector. After the view opens, enter **5/6/2013** in the beginning date control (May 6th, 2013), enter **5/12/2013** in the ending date control (May 12, 2013), leave the vendor option set on the defaults, and then click the Run Audit command button. Access Services runs the macro actions you just studied and then displays a message box indicating that it found one unbalanced invoice among the 20 invoices audited (assuming you have not changed any of the sample data in this web app). After you click OK in the message box, Access navigates to the viewInvoicesUnbalanced view and displays the one unbalanced invoice record, as shown in Figure 8-51. You'll notice that Access Services selects the Unbalanced view name caption in the View Selector for the Purchases table name caption.

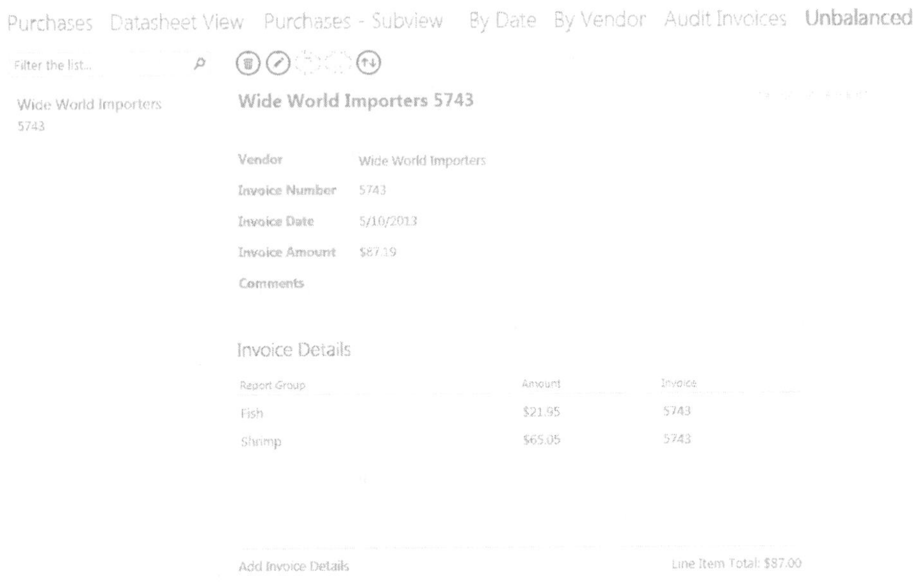

Figure 8-51 Access Services navigates to the viewInvoicesUnbalanced view using the ChangeView action defined in a different view.

INSIDE OUT   Navigate to hidden views

You can use the ChangeView action to navigate to views attached to the View Selector for tables hidden in the Table Selector. At runtime, Access Services navigates to the view but does not select any table name caption in the Table Selector. If there are other views attached to the View Selector for the same hidden table, Access Services displays those view name captions as well.

When should you use ChangeView instead of OpenPopup?

When you're working with views in your web browser, you can open views as pop-up views displayed on top of other views only when you use the OpenPopup macro action. You cannot open multiple main parent views using the OpenPopup action. For example, if you use the OpenPopup action, you cannot open a main parent view and then close the one you just opened. If you need this type of automated interface functionality in your app, you'll need to use the ChangeView macro action to open (or browse, in the web context) a new main parent view. If you need to open a stand-alone view, you must use the OpenPopup action, because stand-alone views cannot be opened using the ChangeView action. When you want to open a view based on a parameterized query, you must use the OpenPopup macro action.

Exploring other named data macro parameter examples

In the previous section, you've seen an example of a macro calling named data macros, passing parameters to the named data macros, and then using values returned from the named data macros at the user interface layer using return variables. I'd like to highlight a few other macro examples that you can study on your own in the Back Office Software System web app (BOSS.app) and the Auctions web app (Auctions.app), which you can download from the book's catalog page. I encourage you to open up the example views mentioned here to see how the macros are set up behind the view and view control events. You'll no doubt get some more ideas and learn some new tricks to using macros to communicate with the data layer by calling named data macros.

If you still have your web browser open to the Back Office Software System web app from the previous section, click the Inventory Locations table name caption in the Table Selector and then click the Change Sort Order view name caption in the View Selector. Access Services loads this Datasheet view in your web browser, as shown in Figure 8-52. (The name of this view object in the Navigation pane is viewSwapSortOrder.)

Figure 8-52 Navigate to the Change Sort Order view in the BOSS.app sample web app.

I created the Change Sort Order view to provide a method for users to change the sort order positions of the inventory locations defined in the web app. Clicking the command buttons labeled Move Up and Move Down execute embedded macros that call the dmSwapSortOrders named data macro. The named data macro takes three parameters from the user interface layer and swaps field values defined in the SortOrder field in the tblInventoryLocations table. Depending on which command button you click in the view, Access Services swaps the SortOrder values from the record either above or below the selected row displayed in the view. The named data macro uses a query that makes use of the Top Values query property to find the lowest current value in the SortOrder field.

Listed below are more view object names in the Back Office Software System sample web app that include macros calling named data macros. You can explore the embedded macros attached to these view and control events for additional examples.

- **viewCompanyInformation.** This view includes a command button that clears all records in the Trace table using the dmClearOutTraceTableRecords named data macro.

- **viewCopySchedules.** This unbound view allows users to dynamically create records in bulk in the tblSchedule table. The macros here utilize the dmApplyLaborPlanDetails, dmCopySingleDateRecords, and dmCopyDateRangeRecords named data macros.

- **viewDeleteScheduleRecords.** This unbound view allows users to dynamically delete records in bulk from the tblSchedule table. The macros here utilize the dmDeleteSingleDateScheduleRecords and dmDeleteDateRangeScheduleRecords named data macros.

For the next examples, let's look at a different sample web app, called Auctions, included with this book. You can use this sample web app to study other macros as well as other view and design elements. Close the Back Office Software System sample web app, if you have it open. Download the Auctions.app sample web app from the book's catalog page, and install the app within your SharePoint site running Access Services. Now navigate to the web app using your web browser. The first view you'll navigate to is the Home view, as shown in Figure 8-53.

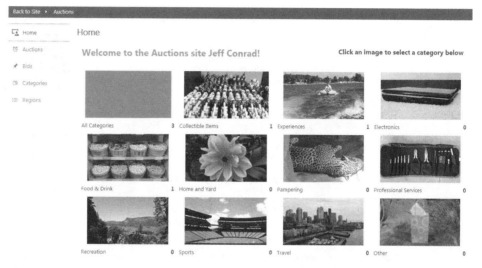

Figure 8-53 The Auctions sample web app Home view displays pictures and the number of open auctions in each category.

The Auctions app tracks items donated for auctions and includes the ability for users to submit bids for the active auction items. The Home view for this app is a Blank view type that displays a picture for each of the defined auction item categories. Beneath each picture, you'll see a number designating the total number of active auction items available in each category. In the On Load event for this view, I call a named data macro— dmGetOpenAuctionNumbers—to calculate the number of open auction items in each category. The named data macro returns 12 values to the calling embedded macro through return variables. I then use SetProperty actions to set the auction totals in the appropriate view controls beneath the pictures.

Click the picture displayed for the All Categories on the Home view, and Access Services opens the Active Auctions view, as shown in Figure 8-54. Note that I use ChangeView actions attached to the picture image control On Click events to navigate users to the Active Auctions view and display the appropriate auction items. The Active Auctions view displays information about each donated item, and the related items control at the bottom of the view displays all the bids submitted for the selected auction item.

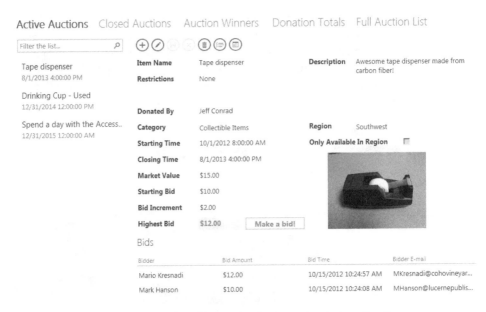

Figure 8-54 The Active Auctions view displays details about donated auction items.

Next to the text box that displays the current highest bid for the selected auction item, you'll see a command button labeled Make A Bid! (I use a SetProperty action to provide a different back color for the highest bid text box control.) Click the command button, and Access Services opens a pop-up view so that you can submit a bid for the auction item, as shown in Figure 8-55. I use a named data macro, called dmNextSuggestedBidAmount, within this app to identify the current highest bid for the selected auction and then add that value to the suggested bid increment for the selected auction item. Access Services returns the end result value to the embedded macro through a return variable and then opens the pop-up view. In the pop-up view's On Load event, I use a SetProperty action to fill in the next suggested bid amount, from the variable set on the main view, into the Bid Amount text box control. When the user submits their bid, Access Services displays the new highest bid in the main Active Auctions view and displays the saved bid record in the related items control.

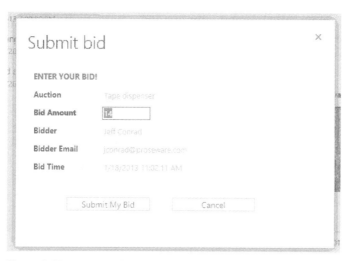

Figure 8-55 Access Services uses a named data macro to display the next suggested bid amount on the pop-up view

Although you've seen only a sampling of various macros in the Back Office Software System and Auctions web apps, I encourage you to explore the other macros attached to the various view and view control events in these apps as well as the Training Tracker sample web app, which you can also download from the book's catalog page.

This concludes our discussion of creating and working with Access web apps. Throughout the remainder of this book, you'll learn how to create and use Access desktop databases. You'll first learn about the user interface differences when you work with desktop databases as compared to web apps. You'll then learn about the different types of objects available in desktop databases and how to design and use them within Access.

Chapter 8

PART 2

Creating tables in a desktop database

Exploring the Access 2013 desktop database interface

B EFORE you explore the many features of desktop databases in Microsoft Access 2013, it's worth spending a little time becoming familiar with the user interface. The user interface for desktop databases is much different than the user interface in Access web apps. Although desktop databases and web apps share several common user interface elements, such as the ribbon and Navigation pane, there are many differences even with these common elements. In this chapter and the next, we'll explore the user interface for desktop databases, show you how to navigate through the Backstage view, and discuss the various components of an Access desktop database and how they interact.

Getting started with desktop databases

On first starting Access, you'll see a new Office Start screen on the Backstage view, as shown in Figure 9-1. We will discuss all the elements of this New tab and the Backstage view as it pertains to desktop databases in greater detail in "Exploring the Microsoft Office Backstage view," later in this chapter.

> **Note**
>
> The examples in this chapter are based on the TasksSample.accdb desktop database which can be downloaded from the book's catalog page at *http://aka.ms/Access2013IO/ details*. For more information about the sample files, see the section titled "Using the sample files" in the book's introduction.

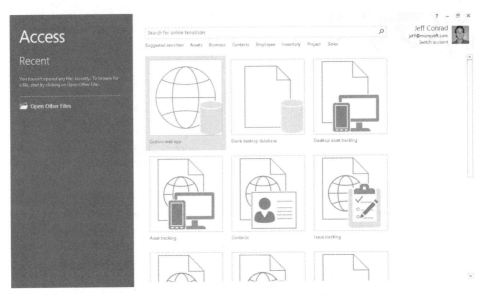

Figure 9-1 When you open Access 2013, you can see the new Office Start screen.

Opening an existing desktop database

To showcase the user interface for desktop databases, let's take one of the desktop template databases out for a test drive. Using the TasksSample.accdb desktop database, which can be downloaded from the book's catalog page, based on the Microsoft Tasks desktop database template, I will highlight some specific areas of Access 2013. First, follow the instructions in the Appendix of this book for downloading and installing the sample files on your local hard drive. Click the Open button on the left side of the Backstage view to see the Open dialog box shown in Figure 9-2.

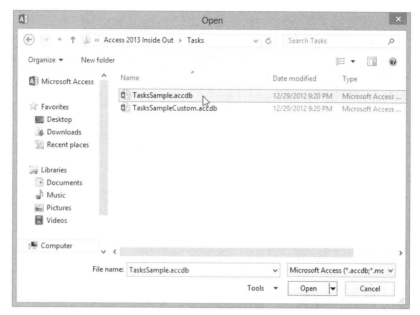

Figure 9-2 You can use the Open dialog box to find and open any existing desktop database file.

In the Open dialog box, select the TasksSample.accdb file from the Tasks subfolder inside the Access 2013 Inside Out folder where you installed the sample databases and files, and then click OK. You can also double-click the file name to open the desktop database. (If you haven't set options in Windows Explorer to show file name extensions for registered applications, you won't see the .accdb extension for your database files.) The Tasks sample application will start, and you'll see the startup form for the Tasks Sample desktop database along with all the various database objects listed on the left side, as shown in Figure 9-3.

Chapter 9

Backstage view

Quick Access Toolbar

Ribbon

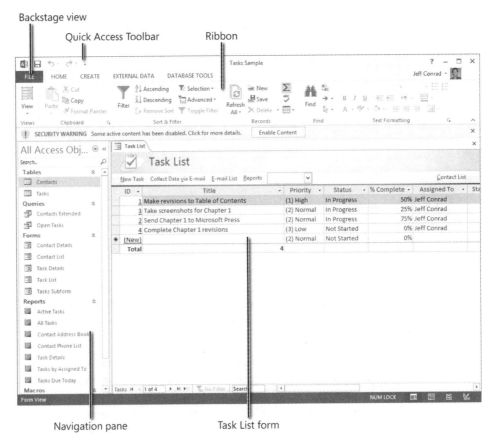

Navigation pane

Task List form

Figure 9-3 When you open the Tasks Sample desktop database, you can see the user interface for desktop databases.

We will discuss each of the user interface elements for desktop databases in greater detail in the following sections, but for now, here is a brief overview of the different elements. The upper-left corner of the screen contains a tab called File, which is the Backstage view. Above this tab are a few smaller buttons on what is called the Quick Access Toolbar. This toolbar holds frequently used commands within Access desktop databases. Beneath the Quick Access Toolbar is a tab called Home that contains many commands, options, and drop-down list boxes. This tab and other contextual tabs that appear based on your current context are located on what Microsoft refers to as the Office Fluent Ribbon. You will inter-act heavily with the ribbon when developing and using desktop databases because most of the commands you need are contained on it. The Backstage view, Quick Access Toolbar, and ribbon function the same in desktop databases as they do in web apps. However, in desktop databases, you'll see many more commands and options.

Beneath the ribbon is a small message that says "Security Warning." This Message Bar informs you if Access has disabled potentially harmful content in this database. See "Understanding content security," later in this chapter, to learn what this message means and what you can do to avoid it.

On the left side of the screen is the Navigation pane. In the Navigation pane, you can find all the various database objects for this desktop database (tables, queries, forms, and so on). Note that in desktop databases you have more options available for changing the display of objects in the Navigation pane. You'll learn more about these options later in this chapter.

To the right of the Navigation pane is where your database objects open. In Figure 9-3, you see that the Task List form is open. All possible views of your database objects appear in this area. Just beneath the Navigation pane and main object window is the status bar. The status bar displays text descriptions from field controls, various keyboard settings (Caps Lock, Num Lock, and Scroll Lock), and object view buttons.

Exploring the Microsoft Office Backstage view

The Microsoft Office Backstage view in desktop databases displays a collection of commands by clicking the File tab from within any desktop database. Figure 9-4 shows you the available commands on the Info tab of the Backstage view for desktop databases.

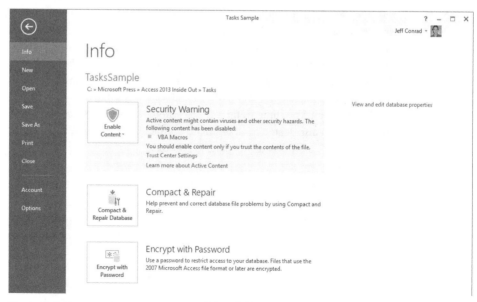

Figure 9-4 You can view many commands by clicking the File tab to open the Backstage view.

Chapter 9

The Backstage view contains information and commands that apply to an entire database. The nine main tabs and commands of the Backstage view for desktop databases are Info, New, Open, Save, Save As, Print, Close, Account, and Options. Commands and information displayed on these tabs can change depending on the current state of your application.

Info tab

Let's first explore the Info tab shown previously in Figure 9-4. The Info tab displays the name of your database and the full path to its location. Beneath the file path, you'll see an Enable Content button and security information about your database. You'll learn more about these settings in "Understanding content security," later in this chapter. The button below it, Compact & Repair Database, compacts and repairs your database file. The last button on the Info tab, Encrypt With Password, creates an encrypted version of your database with a password. On the far right of the Info tab, you'll see the View And Edit Database Properties link. Click this link to open the Database Properties dialog box to review and change properties specific to this database.

New tab

The New tab, shown in Figure 9-5, is the second tab shown in the Backstage view when you open desktop databases. This tab displays the Office Start screen where you can create new web apps, new desktop databases, or a new application using one of the templates available from Office.com. Access provides a scroll bar for you to scroll up and down to see the complete list of online templates. (You must be connected to the Internet to see and download any templates shown in the Office Start screen.) These templates were created by the Access development team and developers in the Access community. The templates represent some of the more common uses for a database and are therefore presented to you first. Microsoft is continually adding and modifying the selections available on the Office Start screen, so the list you see might be different from that shown in Figure 9-5. Be sure to check this screen from time to time to see whether a new template exists for your specific needs. You can also search for a template on the Office.com website by typing your search criteria in the Search Online Templates text box.

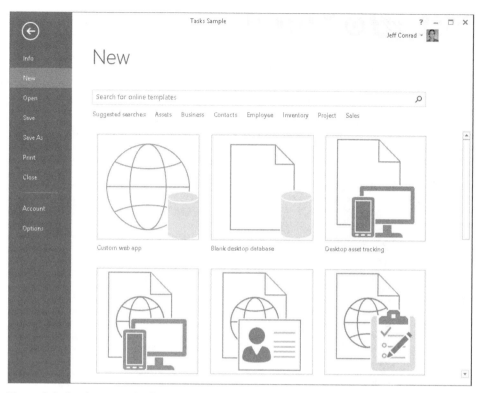

Figure 9-5 On the New tab of the Backstage view in Access, you can create a database from a template, create a new blank desktop database or web app, or search for a database file to open.

Just below the Search Online Templates text box, in the middle of the screen, are two buttons to create new blank applications. The first button on the left is labeled Custom Web App. You learned how to use this button to create new web apps in Chapter 3, "Designing tables in a web app." The next button to the right, Blank Desktop Database, starts the process of creating a new empty desktop database with no objects. (See Chapter 10, "Designing tables in a desktop database," for details about how to create a new blank desktop database.) The remaining buttons on the Office Start screen are web app and desktop database templates that you can download to get a jump-start on creating your next application. When you highlight a template file name, you'll see a pushpin button to the right of the template file name. Click this toggle button to alternatively pin or unpin that specific template file to the displayed list of templates on the Office Start screen. When you unpin the template file, you're not deleting the template from your computer; you are only unpinning its relative displayed position in the list of templates on the Office Start screen.

Open tab

The Open tab, shown in Figure 9-6, displays a list of the web apps and desktop databases you previously opened. If the number of apps and databases you open exceeds the space to display them, Access provides a scroll bar for you to scroll up and down to see the complete list. The Open tab also displays your recent web apps and desktop databases in different categories—Recent, <Your Company Name>, SkyDrive, and Computer. The last option in the left pane of the Open tab, Add A Place, allows you to add locations to make it easier to save applications to cloud services, such as Office 365.

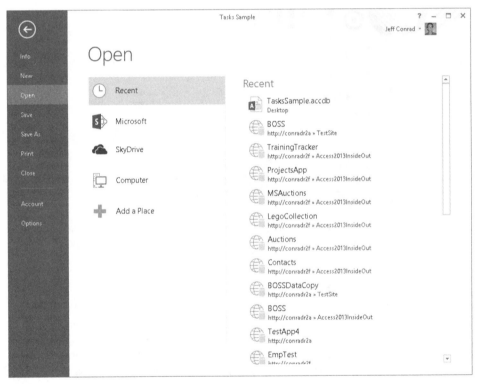

Figure 9-6 The Open tab of the Backstage view displays a list of recent web apps and desktop database files you opened from various locations.

To the right of each database file name, you'll see a pushpin button. Click this toggle button to alternatively pin or unpin that specific database file to the displayed list of recent databases displayed. Right-click any of the recent desktop databases displayed, and Access provides a shortcut menu with five options, as shown in Figure 9-7. Select Open from the list, and Access opens the highlighted desktop database. Select Copy Path To Clipboard, and Access copies the full file path of the selected desktop database to the Windows clipboard. When you select the Pin To List option, Access pins that specific desktop database file to the displayed list of recent databases. When you select the fourth option, Remove From List, Access removes that desktop database file from the list of recent databases. (When you remove the database file from the list, you're not deleting the desktop database from your computer; you are removing it only from this list on the Backstage view.) When you select the last option on the list, Clear Unpinned Items, Access prompts you for confirmation that you want to remove all unpinned items from the list. Click Yes in the confirmation dialog box, and Access removes all desktop database files and web apps from the list of recent database files that you have not pinned. You can use this option to quickly clear files that you might have deleted and no longer want to use from your list of recent databases.

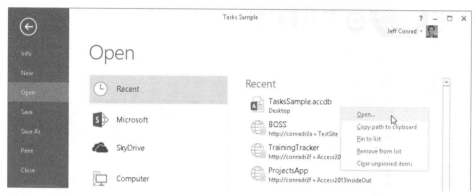

Figure 9-7 Right-click a desktop database file to see additional options you can use to manage your list of recent databases.

Save command

The Save option is not actually a tab like the other Backstage tabs; it is a direct command. Clicking the Save command here on the Backstage saves any pending design changes for the database object that is open and has the focus in the Navigation pane.

Save As tab

The Save As tab, shown in Figure 9-8, displays commands to save your desktop database and objects in other formats. In the center of the Save As tab, you'll see two commands under the File Types category—Save Database As and Save Object As. If you click one of these commands, additional commands appear in submenus under the Save Database As category to the right.

Click Save Database As under the File Types category, and you'll see two subcategories for this option—Database File Types and Advanced. Under Database File Types, you can choose to save a copy of your entire desktop database in default format (.accdb), 2002/2003 (.mdb), or 2000 (.mdb) Access format. If you choose to save the entire database,

Access closes the database you have open so that it can create the copy. You can use the last option under Database File Types, Template (.accdt), to save your database as an Access database template. To start these commands, you can either double-click the command you want or highlight the command and then click the Save As button at the bottom of the screen. Under the Advanced category, the first option, Package And Sign, packages your database as a Cabinet file (CAB) and digitally signs it. Double-click the Make ACCDE command to make an execute-only version (.mde or .accde) of your database. When you double-click the Back-up Database command, Access creates a complete backup of your desktop database file with the current date in the file name. You can choose the last command under the Advanced category, SharePoint, to publish your desktop database to a document manager server.

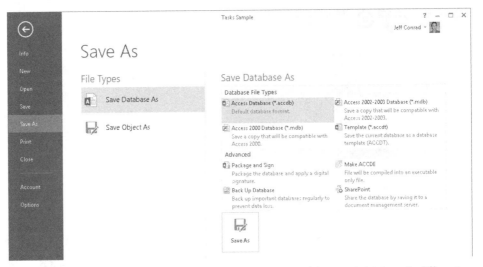

Figure 9-8 The Save As tab contains commands to save your objects and database in different formats.

Click Save Object As under File Types on the Save As tab, and Access displays a different set of commands on the right, as seen in Figure 9-9. When you double-click Save Object As on the right side, the default is to save a copy of the current open object that has the focus or the object that has the focus in the Navigation pane. Double-click PDF Or XPS to publish a copy of the current open object as a Portable Document Format (PDF) or XML Paper Specification (XPS) file. The last command for Save Object As, Save As Client Object, saves a copy of the current open web object to a client object format if you are using an older 2010-style web database.

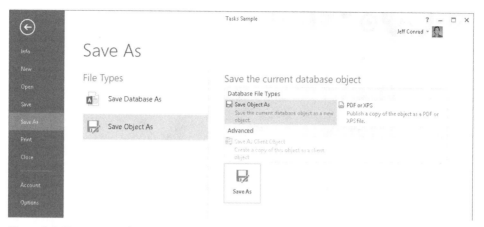

Figure 9-9 You can use the Save Object As command to save a copy of your database objects into different formats.

Print tab

The Print tab, shown in Figure 9-10, displays three commands—Quick Print, Print, and Print Preview. Click Quick Print to send the selected database object to the printer immediately. Be careful here, because the object that has the focus might not be the one currently on the screen. If the focus is on an object in the Navigation pane, that object is printed instead of the object currently open. When you click Print, Access opens the Print dialog box to print whatever object currently has the focus. Here again, be careful about which object has the focus. Click Print Preview to preview the printed appearance of what you are about to print on your monitor or device screen.

Chapter 9

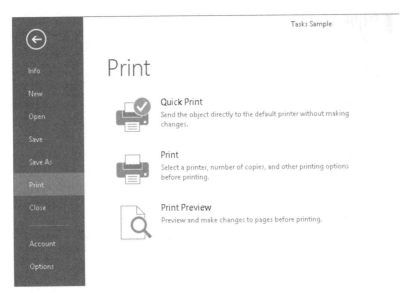

Figure 9-10 The Print tab of the Backstage view displays commands to print objects in your database.

Close command

The Close command, like the Save command, is not actually a tab like the other Backstage tabs; it is a direct command. Clicking the Close command closes the currently open desktop database.

Account tab

The Account tab of the Backstage view, shown in Figure 9-11, displays helpful information concerning Access 2013 and the Office 2013 software as well as connections to other online services and application backgrounds and themes. The connection options listed under Connected Services might differ from what you see in Figure 9-11, based on your Office installation and your organization's internal settings.

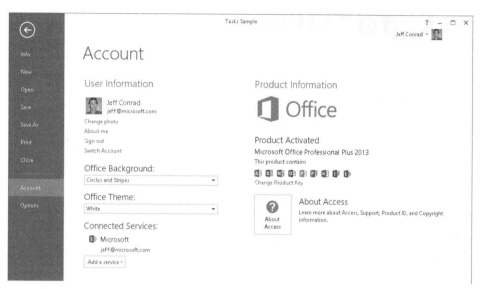

Figure 9-11 The Account tab on the Backstage view displays information about Access and Office 2013 applications.

Under the User Information category, you'll see your user name and email address for the account you are currently using. Click the Change Photo link to change the photo and name on your account. Click the About Me link to view your account information. To remove your account, click the Remove link. To log in to Access under a different account, click the Switch Account link. Access then opens the Sign In To Office dialog, as shown in Figure 9-12. Click the Microsoft Account button to sign into Access using a Microsoft account, or click the Organizational Account button on the Sign In To Office dialog to sign in to Access using an ID provided by your business or school. Click the Learn More link at the bottom of this dialog to open a webpage on Microsoft's website that discusses the sign-in process. Click the Privacy Statement link at the bottom of the Sign In To Office dialog to open a webpage that discusses Microsoft's privacy information concerning Office 2013. After you sign in under a different account, Access refreshes the user name and email address displayed on the Account tab of the Backstage view. You can also log in under a different account by clicking your user name link in the upper-right corner of the Access application window and then clicking Switch Account.

Chapter 9

Figure 9-12 Click your user name link on the Account tab to sign in to office under a different account using this dialog box.

Beneath the user information on the Account tab, you can select a background to use for Access and your other Office applications from the Office Background combo box and a White, Light Gray, or Dark Gray theme from the Office Theme combo box. Under Connected Services, Access displays different services that you are connected to from your current account. Click the Add A Service button, and Access displays three categories of services—Storage, Other Sites, and Office Store—as shown in Figure 9-13. You can select from these various options to connect to other online services for your Office applications. Note that the services options listed in this menu might differ from what you see in Figure 9-13, based on your Office installation and your organization's internal settings.

Figure 9-13 Click Add A Service to connect your Office applications with online services.

On the right side of the Account tab, you'll see information about your Access 2013 and Office 2013 installed programs. Click the Change Product Key link, previously shown in Figure 9-11, to open the Microsoft Office setup dialog box to change your product key for your installation. Click the About Access button to open the Access About dialog box to view the copyright information of your Access and Office installations.

INSIDE OUT   Closing the Backstage view

You can close the Backstage view quickly by pressing the Esc key. When you do this, Access returns focus to where you were before opening the Backstage view.

Modifying global settings via the Access Options dialog box

In addition to all the various commands and options available on the Backstage view, Access has one central location for setting and modifying global options for all your Access desktop database files or for only the desktop database currently open—the Access Options dialog box. Click the Options command at the bottom of the Backstage view, and Access opens the Access Options dialog box, as shown in Figure 9-14.

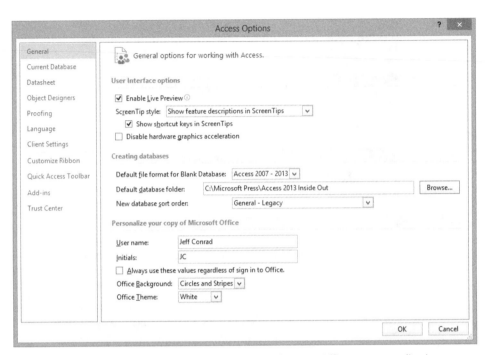

Figure 9-14 The General category has general settings for your Office system applications.

The Access Options dialog box contains 11 categories in the left pane to organize the various options and settings. The first category, General, has settings that apply not only to Access but also to any other Office system programs you might have installed. From here, you can choose to enable Live Preview, display ScreenTips, and enter a user name for use in all your Office system applications. In the Creating Databases section, you can choose a default file format for new databases that you create in Access. By default, the file format is set to create all new databases in Access 2007-2013 format. The Default Database Folder box displays the folder where Access will save all new database files unless you select a different folder when creating the database.

The Current Database category, shown in Figure 9-15, has many settings that apply only to the database currently open. This category groups the options into these areas: Application Options, Navigation, Ribbon And Toolbar Options, Name AutoCorrect Options, Filter Lookup Options, and Caching Web Service And SharePoint Tables.

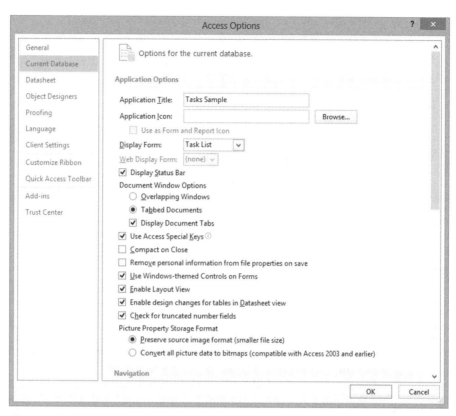

Figure 9-15 The Current Database category has general settings for the database currently open.

You can define a title for your desktop database in the Application Title box. Access displays this title at the top of the application window. You can define a form that you want Access to open each time you open the desktop database by selecting the form name in the Display Form combo box. You'll learn about the settings under Document Window Options in "Using the single-document vs. the multiple-document interface," later in this chapter. The remaining options in the Current Database category will be discussed throughout the remainder of this book in appropriate chapters.

The Datasheet category, shown in Figure 9-16, has settings that control the appearance of the datasheet views in your database. This category has options grouped in the following sections—Gridlines And Cell Effects and Default Font—which allow you to modify the look of your datasheets with different colors, gridlines, and cell effects. You can also select a default font and size under Default Font. You'll learn more about applying these settings to datasheets in "Working in query datasheet view," in Chapter 12, "Creating and Working with Simple Queries," in Chapter 15, "Using forms in a desktop database," and in Chapter 16, "Building a form." You can download these chapters from the book's catalog page.

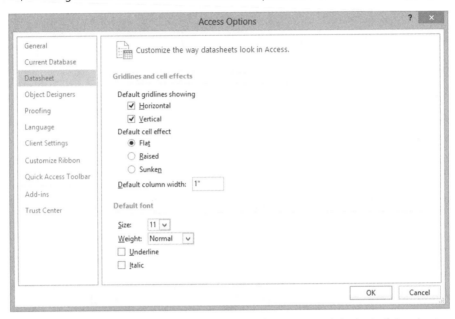

Figure 9-16 The Datasheet category has general settings to control the look of datasheets.

The Object Designers category, shown in Figure 9-17, includes settings for creating and modifying desktop database objects in all databases. The Object Designers category is divided into four sections: Table Design View, Query Design, Form/Report Design View, and Error Checking In Form And Report Design View. The Table Design View section has settings for Default Field Type, Default Text Field Size, and Default Number Field Size. You'll learn more about the impact of these settings in Chapter 10. The Query Design section lets you select a default font and size for working in the query design grid. You'll learn more about the impact of these settings in Chapter 13, "Building complex queries." The Form/Report Design View section has options that allow you to use the existing form and report templates or choose a custom template that you have created. You'll learn more about these settings in Chapter 16. The Error Checking In Form And Report Design View section has several default options that Access looks for when checking for errors in your database file. You'll learn more about these settings in Chapter 24, "Understanding Visual Basic fundamentals," which you can download from the book's catalog page.

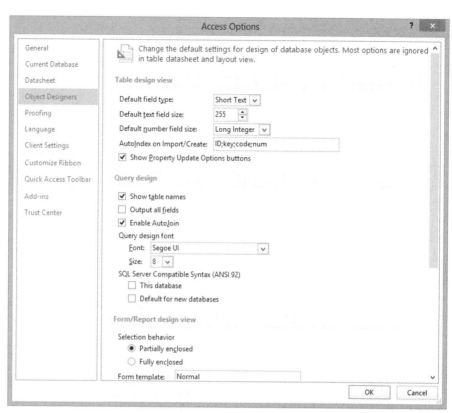

Figure 9-17 The Object Designers category has settings for working with database objects.

The Proofing category, shown in Figure 9-18, includes options for controlling the spelling and AutoCorrect features. You can click AutoCorrect Options to customize how Access helps you with common typing mistakes. You can also click Custom Dictionaries to select a custom dictionary to use when working with Access and the other Office system applications.

Chapter 9

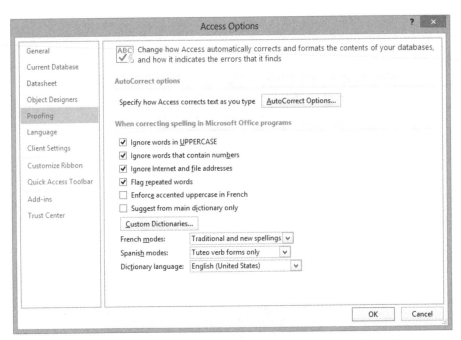

Figure 9-18 The Proofing category has settings for checking spelling and AutoCorrect.

The Language category, shown in Figure 9-19, contains options for controlling the language settings for your Access and Office installed programs. Under Choose Editing Languages, you can select a default editing language for Access. If you have installed additional language packs, you can choose to change your default language to a different language. Under Choose Display And Help Languages, you can change what display language and Help language to use when working with Access. Note that you will need to close your current session of Access and reopen to see these changes. If you click the arrow next to View Display Languages Installed For Each Microsoft Office Program, a list expands beneath the arrow that lists all of the Office applications that you have installed and their display languages.

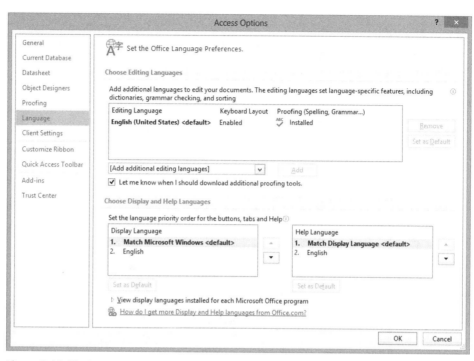

Figure 9-19 The Language category has settings for changing your editing, display, and Help language for Access and other Office programs.

The Client Settings category, shown in Figure 9-20, contains a wide variety of settings for Access. This category has options grouped in the following sections: Editing, Display, Printing, General, Advanced, and Default Theme. Each of the settings on this category applies to all desktop database files that you use in Access. Many of these settings are discussed later in various parts of this book. See Chapter 12, "Creating and working with simple queries," for more information.

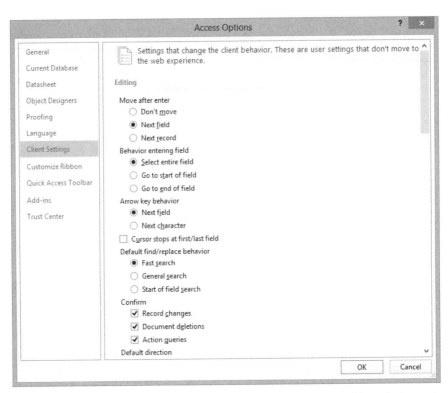

Figure 9-20 The Client Settings category has options for controlling editing, display, and printing.

The Customize Ribbon category, shown in Figure 9-21, allows you to customize the ribbon. You can make modifications to the built-in ribbon tabs or create your own custom ribbon tabs and groups. For example, if you do not like the order of the groups on the four default ribbon tabs, you can easily change the order to your liking.

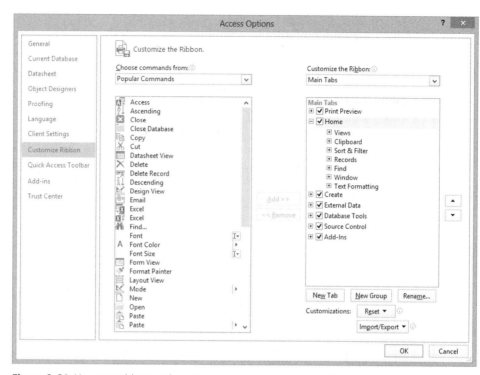

Figure 9-21 You can add new tabs, groups, or commands to the ribbon and change their sequence using the Customize Ribbon category in the Access Options dialog box.

On the left, you can see a list of built-in Access commands that you can select to add to groups on the ribbon for desktop databases. By default, the list shows commands from the Popular Commands category—commands that are used very frequently. You can change the list of commands by selecting a different category from the Choose Commands From list. The All Commands option displays the entire list of Access commands available in alphabetical order.

The list on the right side of the screen displays a list of the built-in Access ribbon tabs—Print Preview, Home, Create, External Data, Database Tools, Source Control, and Add-Ins. You can change the list of tabs by selecting a different category from the Customize The Ribbon list. The All Tabs option displays the entire list of Access ribbon tabs, and the Tool Tabs option displays only the list of Access contextual ribbon tabs. Next to the name of each tab in the list below Customize The Ribbon is a plus symbol. Click the plus symbol, and Access expands the list beneath the tab to show you all the groups and commands within that specific tab. Click the minus symbol, and Access collapses the list to show you only the name of the tab itself. Similarly, you'll see a plus symbol next to each of the group names underneath the tab name. Click the plus symbol here, and Access expands the group to show you all the commands on that specific group. Click the minus symbol to collapse the group. Next to the plus and minus symbols for each tab, you'll see a check box. Clear this check box to not display that tab on the ribbon. Note that clearing this check box does not delete the tab and all its contents; it merely tells Access not to show this tab on the ribbon. Select the check box, and Access displays that tab in the ribbon.

You'll notice that all the commands listed on the default tab groups are dimmed. You cannot rename or reorder the commands listed on the default tab groups; however, you can rename and reorder the group names on the default tabs, rename and reorder the names of the default tabs, add new custom groups to the default tabs, and add commands to these custom groups on the default tabs. You can also create your own custom tabs and add groups and commands by clicking the New Tab and New Group buttons near the lower-right corner of the screen. To change the name of a custom tab you create, highlight it and then click the Rename button.

To add a command to your custom group, find a command in the list on the left, and then either double-click it or click the Add button in the middle of the screen to add this command to your custom ribbon group. If you make a mistake and select the wrong command, select the command in the list on the right and click Remove to eliminate it from your custom group.

If you want to restore one of the built-in ribbon tabs to the default set of groups and commands, highlight the tab name in the list on the right, click the Reset button in the lower-right corner of the screen, and then click Reset Only Selected Ribbon Tab from the drop-down list. To remove all ribbon customizations, click Reset, and then click Reset All Customizations. Access resets the ribbon, as well as the Quick Access Toolbar, back to the defaults.

You can export your ribbon customizations to a file that can be imported to another computer running Access 2013. Click the Import/Export button at the lower-right corner of the screen, and then click Export All Customizations.

> **Note**
> When you choose to export ribbon customizations, Access also exports any Quick Access Toolbar customizations you created for all databases.

The Quick Access Toolbar category, shown in Figure 9-22, allows you to customize the Quick Access Toolbar for desktop databases. You can make modifications to the Quick Access Toolbar for this specific database only or to the Quick Access Toolbar for all Access databases.

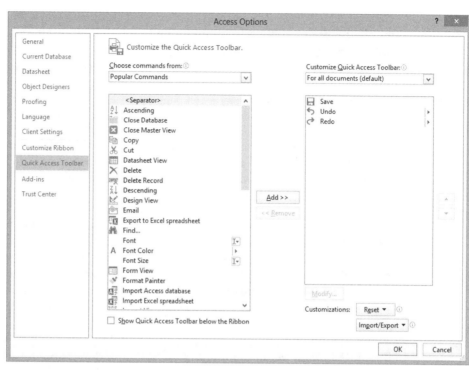

Figure 9-22 The Quick Access Toolbar category allows you to customize the Quick Access Toolbar.

On the left, you can see a list of built-in Access commands that you can select to add to the Quick Access Toolbar. By default, the list shows commands from the Popular Commands category—commands that are used very frequently. You can change the list of commands by selecting a different category from the Choose Commands From list. The All Commands option displays the entire list of Access commands available in alphabetical order. Just below the list of available commands is a check box that you can select to show the Quick Access Toolbar below the ribbon. Clear the check box to show the Quick Access Toolbar above the ribbon.

The list on the right side of the screen displays what options are available on every Quick Access Toolbar by default for all your desktop database files. If you add, remove, or modify the commands shown in the list on the right when you have chosen For All Documents (Default) in the Customize Quick Access Toolbar list, the changes are reflected in every desktop database you open with Access. To customize the Quick Access Toolbar for only the specific desktop database you currently have open, click the arrow in the drop-down list and select the database file path for your current database from the list.

When you select the current database, the command list below it is now empty, awaiting the changes you request. Find a command in the list on the left, and then either double-click it or click the Add button in the middle of the screen to add this command to your custom Quick Access Toolbar. If you make a mistake and select the wrong command, select the command in the list on the right and click Remove to eliminate it from your custom list. From top to bottom in the list on the right, the commands appear from left to right on the Quick Access Toolbar after the commands assigned to all databases.

In addition to the built-in commands, you can select any macros you have defined in this current desktop database. To do this, select Macros in the Choose Commands From list on the left. A list of all your saved macro objects appears, and you can add these macros directly to your custom Quick Access Toolbar.

After you have all the commands and macros that you want on your custom Quick Access Toolbar, you might decide that you do not like the order in which they appear. Access allows you to modify this order easily using the Move Up and Move Down arrow buttons at the far right of the dialog box. (You can rest your mouse pointer on either button to see the button name.) Select a command you want to move in the list on the right, and click the up arrow to move it up in the list. Each successive click moves that command up one place in the custom list. Likewise, the down arrow shifts the selected command down in the list.

To remove an item from your custom Quick Access Toolbar, select it in the list on the right and click Remove, and Access removes it from your list of commands. If you inadvertently remove a command that you wanted to keep, you can click the Cancel button in the lower-right corner to discard all changes. You can also find the command in the list on the left and add it back. Keep in mind that you can remove commands for all desktop databases or for only the current desktop database.

If you want to restore the Quick Access Toolbar for all desktop databases to the default set of commands, select For All Documents (Default) in the Customize Quick Access Toolbar list, click the Reset button in the lower-right corner of the screen, and then click Reset Only Quick Access Toolbar from the drop-down list. To remove all custom commands for the current database, select the database path in the Customize Quick Access Toolbar list, click Reset, and then click Reset Only Quick Access Toolbar. Access resets the Quick Access Toolbar for this current database back to the defaults.

If you modify the Quick Access Toolbar for all databases, you can export your customizations to a file that can be imported to another computer running Access 2013. Click the Import/Export button at the lower-right corner of the screen, and then click Export All Customizations.

The Add-Ins category, shown in Figure 9-23, lists all the various Access add-ins that might be installed on your computer. You can manage COM add-ins and Access add-ins from this area, and each add-in has its various properties listed. COM add-ins extend the ability of Access and other Office system applications with custom commands and specialized features. You can even disable certain add-ins to keep them from loading and functioning.

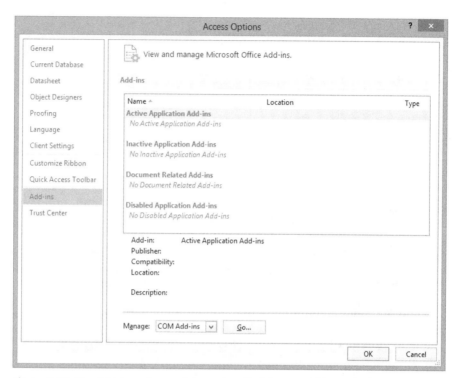

Figure 9-23 The Add-Ins category lists any installed Access add-ins and COM add-ins.

The Trust Center category, shown in Figure 9-24, is the last category in the Access Options dialog box. This category is where you access all Trust Center options for handling security. You'll learn all about the options in the Trust Center category in "Understanding content security," later in this chapter. This category also includes links to online privacy and security information.

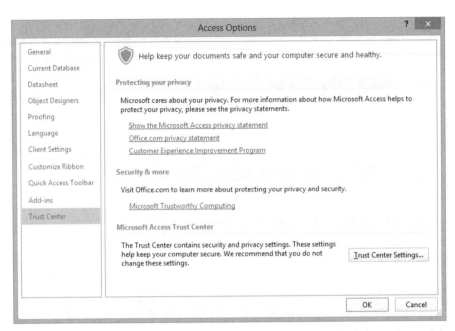

Figure 9-24 The Trust Center category has links to privacy and security information and the Trust Center Settings button, which allows you to view more options.

Click Cancel on the Access Options dialog box to return to the main application window.

Taking advantage of the Quick Access Toolbar

Above the Backstage view is the Quick Access Toolbar. You worked with the Quick Access Toolbar when you designed web apps earlier in this book. This toolbar has three default commands (Save, Undo, and Redo) for desktop databases. However, you can customize the toolbar to display many other command options.

At the right end of the Quick Access Toolbar is a small arrow. Click that arrow, and you'll see the Customize Quick Access Toolbar menu, as shown in Figure 9-25.

Figure 9-25 The default Quick Access Toolbar contains the Save, Undo, and Redo commands for the current object, and the command to customize the toolbar.

The upper section of the menu displays common commands that you might want to add to the Quick Access Toolbar. The three default commands have check marks next to them. You can click any of these to clear the check mark and remove the command from the Quick Access Toolbar. You can click any of the other ten commands (New, Open, Email, Quick Print, Print Preview, Spelling, Mode, Refresh All, Sync All, and Touch/Mouse Mode) to add them to the right end of the Quick Access Toolbar. When you click More Commands, near the bottom of this menu, Access opens the Access Options dialog box (discussed in the previous section) with the Quick Access Toolbar category selected. You can fully customize what commands are available and how those commands appear on the Quick Access Toolbar on this dialog box. The Show Below The Ribbon option on the menu allows you to move the Quick Access Toolbar above or below the ribbon, depending on your preference.

Chapter 9

INSIDE OUT   **Adding a command to the Quick Access Toolbar with two mouse clicks**

If you notice that you are using a command on the ribbon quite often, Access provides a very quick and easy way to add this command to the Quick Access Toolbar. To add a command on the ribbon to the Quick Access Toolbar, right-click the command and click Add To Quick Access Toolbar. This adds the command to the Quick Access Toolbar for all desktop databases. Alternatively, you can remove an item from your custom Quick Access Toolbar quickly by right-clicking the command and clicking Remove From Quick Access Toolbar.

Understanding content security

Access uses an interface component called the Trust Center for its security model. Access desktop databases can be considered unsafe because they could have some type of macros, Visual Basic for Applications (VBA) code, or calls to unsafe functions embedded in their structure. Any desktop database with queries is considered unsafe by Access because those queries could contain expressions calling unsafe functions. Depending on where your database is located on the local computer drive or network share, Access silently disables any malicious macros or VBA code unless your database is considered a Trusted Document or stored in a Trusted Location.

Note

The sample databases included with this book are not digitally signed, because they will become unsigned as soon as you change any of the queries or sample code. I designed all the sample applications to open successfully, but each displays a warning dialog box if the database is not trusted. If you have installed the database in an untrusted location, the application displays instructions in the warning dialog box that you can follow to enable the full application. See "Enabling content by defining trusted locations," later in this chapter, for information about defining trusted locations.

Enabling a database that is not trusted

When you open an existing desktop database or template, you might see a Security Warning message displayed in the Message Bar, just below the Quick Access Toolbar and ribbon, as shown in Figure 9-26. This message notifies you that Access has disabled certain features of the application because the file is not digitally signed, the file is not a trusted document, or the file is located in a folder that has not been designated as trusted.

Message Bar

Figure 9-26 The Message Bar alerts you if Access has disabled certain content.

To ensure that any restricted code and macros function in this desktop database, you must manually tell Access to enable this content by clicking the Enable Content button on the Message Bar. After you click this button, Access closes the database and then reopens the file to enable all content. Access does not display the Message Bar after it reopens the file, and all functions, code, and macros are now allowed to run in this specific database. Access also adds this database to its list of trusted documents.

If your database is not currently trusted, Access displays the Security Warning information on the Info tab of the Backstage view, as shown in Figure 9-27. If you have enabled the content of the database you are viewing or if the file is located in a folder that has been designated as trusted, Access does not display the Security Warning information on the Info tab of the Backstage view.

Chapter 9

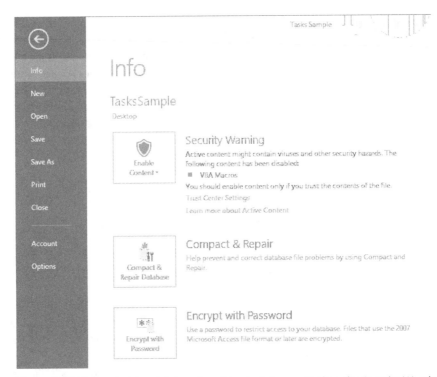

Figure 9-27 If your desktop database is not trusted, Access displays the Security Warning on the Backstage view.

When you click the Enable Content button under Security Warning, Access displays two options—Enable All Content and Advanced Options, as shown in Figure 9-28. When you click Enable All Content, Access adds this desktop database to its list of trusted database files. Each time you open this database from this point on, Access does not disable the content for that database. However, if you move this database to a different file location on your computer, Access disables the content again when you open the database.

Figure 9-28 Click Enable Content to enable all the content of your database or open advanced security options.

Click Advanced Options under Enable Content, and Access opens a dialog box, called Microsoft Office Security Options, as shown in Figure 9-29. This dialog box warns you that this file's content cannot be verified because a digital certificate was not found.

Figure 9-29 You can enable blocked content from the Microsoft Office Security Options dialog box.

You can choose to have Access continue to block any harmful content by leaving the default option set to Help Protect Me From Unknown Content (Recommended). By having Access block any harmful content, you can be assured that no malicious code or macros can execute from this database. However, you also have to realize that because Access blocks all Microsoft Visual Basic code and any macros containing a potentially harmful command, it is quite possible that this application will not run correctly if you continue to let Access disable potentially harmful functions and code. To have Access discontinue blocking potentially harmful content, you must select the option Enable Content For This Session. After you select that option and click OK, Access closes the database and then reopens the file to enable all content. Access does not display the Message Bar after it reopens the file, and all functions, code, and macros are now allowed to run in this specific database.

> **Note**
>
> When you enable content after opening an untrusted database, the database becomes trusted only for the current session. If you close the database and then attempt to reopen it, Access displays the warnings again on the Message Bar.

Understanding the Trust Center

You might have noticed a link to the Trust Center in the lower-left corner of the Microsoft Office Security Options dialog box. You can also open the Trust Center from the Info tab of the Backstage view by clicking the Trust Center Settings link beneath Security Warning, as discussed earlier.

Click Open The Trust Center in the Microsoft Office Security Options dialog box to view the advanced security settings. If the Security Warning on the Info tab of the Backstage view is not currently available, click the File tab and then click Options on the Backstage view. In the Access Options dialog box, click the Trust Center category on the left and then click Trust Center Settings. In the Trust Center dialog box, shown in Figure 9-30, you see eight categories of security settings.

Figure 9-30 The Trust Center dialog box displays various categories, from which you can select trust and privacy options.

Briefly, the categories are as follows:

- **Trusted Publishers.** Use to view and remove publishers that you have designated as being trustworthy. When applications are digitally signed by one of these trusted publishers, Access does not disable any content within the database and the Message Bar does not display any warning. By default, digitally signed applications from Microsoft are trusted. You might see one or more additional trusted publishers if you have ever tried to download and run a signed application and have indicated to Windows that you trust the publisher and want to save the publisher's certificate.

- **Trusted Locations.** Use to designate specific folders and subfolders as trusted locations. Access considers any database files within this folder as trustworthy, and all content in these folders is enabled. In the Trusted Locations dialog box, each designated trusted folder is listed with the file path, an optional description, and the date the entry was last modified. See "Enabling content by defining trusted locations," later in this chapter, for details about using the options in this category.

- **Trusted Documents.** Use to allow databases on a network share to be trusted, disable the Trusted Documents feature, or clear all trusted databases. By default, Access allows you to trust database files on a network share. Clearing this check box disables your ability to trust individual database files on network shares. If you select the option to disable trusted documents, Access disables all content in databases that you previously designated as trusted. If you click Clear, Access removes all database files from its internal list of trusted documents.

- **Add-Ins.** Use to set specific restrictions on Access add-in files by selecting or clearing the three check boxes in this category. An add-in is a separate program or file that extends the capabilities of Access. You can create these separate files or programs by using VBA or another programming language such as C#. You can require that add-in files be signed by a trusted publisher before Access will load and run them. If you select the option to require that add-ins be signed, you can disable notifications for add-ins that are unsigned. For added security, you can disable all application add-in functionality.

- **ActiveX Settings.** Use to configure how Access handles ActiveX controls in databases. Five options are available with this feature, but only one of the first four options can be active at any time. Table 9-1 discusses the purpose of each option.

TABLE 9-1 ActiveX settings

Option	Purpose
Disable All Controls Without Notification.	Access disables all harmful ActiveX controls but does not notify you through the Message Bar.
Prompt Me Before Enabling Unsafe For Initialization (UFI) Controls With Additional Restrictions And Safe For Initialization (SFI) Controls With Minimal Restrictions.	If a VBA project is present, Access disables all ActiveX controls and displays the Message Bar. If no VBA project is present, Access enables SFI and disables UFI ActiveX controls. In this case, Access displays the Message Bar. If you enable the content for a UFI ActiveX control, it will be initialized, but with restrictions.

Chapter 9

Option	Purpose
Prompt Me Before Enabling All Controls With Minimal Restrictions.	This is the default option for new installations of Access. If a VBA project is present, Access disables all ActiveX controls and displays the Message Bar. If no VBA project is present, Access enables SFI and disables UFI ActiveX controls. In this case, Access displays the Message Bar. If you enable the content for a UFI ActiveX control, it will be initialized, but with restrictions.
Enable All Controls Without Restrictions And Without Prompting (not recommended; potentially dangerous controls can run)	Access enables any and all potentially harmful ActiveX controls with minimal restrictions without prompting you. Setting this option could leave your computer at risk.
Safe Mode (helps limit the control's access to your computer)	This option, selected by default, enables SFI ActiveX controls in safe mode.

- **Macro Settings.** Use to configure how Access handles macros in databases that are not in a trusted location. Four options are available with this feature, only one of which can be active at any given time. Table 9-2 discusses the purpose of each option.

TABLE 9-2 Macro settings

Option	Purpose
Disable All Macros Without Notification	Access disables all harmful content but does not notify you through the Message Bar.
Disable All Macros With Notification	Access disables all harmful content but notifies you through the Message Bar that it has disabled the content. This is the default option for new installations of Access.
Disable All Macros Except Digitally Signed Macros	Access allows only digitally signed macros (code in digitally signed databases). All other potentially harmful content is disabled.
Enable All Macros (not recommended; potentially dangerous code can run)	Access enables any and all potentially harmful content. In addition, Access does not notify you through the Message Bar.

- **Message Bar.** Use to configure Access either to show the Message Bar when content has been disabled or not to display the bar at all.

- **Privacy Options.** Use to enable or disable actions within Access regarding computing privacy, troubleshooting system problems, and scanning suspicious website links. The first check box under Privacy Options tells Access to scan Microsoft's Office.com Help site when you are connected to the Internet. If you clear this check box, Access scans only your local hard drive when you conduct a search in Help. Selecting the second check box instructs Access to download and activate a special file from Microsoft's site that helps you troubleshoot Access and Office program installation and program errors. The third check box allows you to sign up for the Customer Experience Improvement Program. Microsoft uses this program to track statistics of the features you use most frequently and gather information about your Office system configuration. These statistics help determine changes in future program releases. The fourth check box under Privacy Options allows Access to scan Office documents automatically for possible links to and from suspicious websites. This option is turned on by default to help safeguard your computer against documents containing harmful web links. The fifth check box, Allow The Research Pane To Check For And Install New Services, allows Access to automatically check for new updates to research services and install them. The final check box turns on the Office Feedback Tool (Send a Smile) feature. You can use this feature to provide feedback to Microsoft concerning your experience using Access and other Office programs you have installed.

Enabling content by defining trusted locations

You can permanently enable the content in a database that is not trusted by defining a folder on your hard drive or network that is trusted and then placing the database in that folder. Alternatively, you can define the folder where the database is located as trusted. You define trusted locations in the Trust Center dialog box.

CAUTION

> If you are in a corporate network environment, you should check with your IT department to determine whether your company has established guidelines concerning enabling content on Access databases.

To define a trusted location, click the File tab on the Backstage view and then click Access Options. In the Access Options dialog box, click the Trust Center category and then click Trust Center Settings. Access displays the Trust Center dialog box. Click the Trusted Locations category to see its options, as shown in Figure 9-31.

Chapter 9

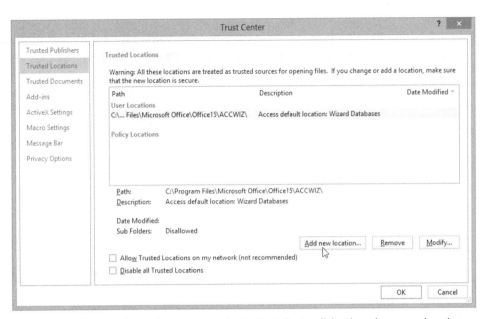

Figure 9-31 The Trusted Locations category in the Trust Center dialog box shows you locations that are currently trusted.

Click Add New Location. Access now displays the Microsoft Office Trusted Location dialog box, as shown in Figure 9-32.

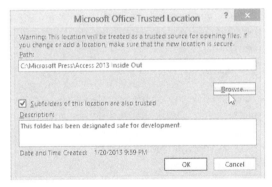

Figure 9-32 Creating a new trusted location from the Microsoft Office Trusted Location dialog box.

Click Browse, and locate the folder that you want to designate as trusted. You have the option of designating any subfolders in that directory as trusted without having to designate each individual folder within the hierarchy. Enter an optional description you want for this folder, and click OK to save your changes. The new location you just specified now appears in the list of trusted locations. Microsoft recommends that you do not designate the root folder for your Windows installation (for example, C:\ on a standard installation) as a trusted location. You should instead designate only the individual folders you want trusted. If you later decide to remove this folder as a trusted location, select that location, as shown in Figure 9-31, and then click Remove. Any Access desktop databases in that folder are now treated as unsafe. Figure 9-31 also shows two check boxes at the bottom of the dialog box. The first check box allows you to define network locations as trusted locations. Microsoft recommends that you not select this check box because you cannot control what files others might place in a network location. The second check box disables all Trusted Location settings and allows content only from trusted publishers.

> **Note**
>
> To ensure that all the sample desktop databases you download from the book's catalog page operate correctly, add the folder where you installed the files (the default location is the Microsoft Press\Access 2013 Inside Out folder on your C drive) to your Trusted Locations.

Understanding the Office Fluent Ribbon

The Office Fluent Ribbon, shown in Figure 9-33, is a context-rich strip displaying all the program functions and commands, with large icons for key functions and smaller icons for less-used functions. Access displays a host of different controls on the ribbon to help you build and edit your desktop database. Lists, command buttons, galleries, and Dialog Box Launchers are all on the ribbon and offer a rich user interface for Access and the other Office system products. When you studied web apps earlier in this book, you worked with the ribbon commands available in the web app environment. When you work with desktop databases, Access provides many more ribbon options.

Figure 9-33 The ribbon interface displays program functions and commands.

The ribbon in Access desktop databases consists of four main tabs—Home, Create, External Data, and Database Tools—that group together common tasks and contain a major subset of the program functions in Access. These main tabs are visible at all times when you are working in Access because they contain the most common tools you need when working with any database object. Other tabs, called contextual tabs, appear and disappear to the right of the Database Tools tab when you are working with specific desktop database objects and in various views. (In the following chapters, we will discuss in detail the various database objects and the contextual tabs that appear when working with each.)

INSIDE OUT   Scrolling through the ribbon tabs

If you click one of the ribbon tabs, you can then scroll through the other tabs using the scroll wheel on your mouse.

Each tab on the ribbon has commands that are further organized into groups. The name of each group is listed at the bottom, and each group has various commands logically grouped by subject matter. To enhance the user experience and make things easier to find, Microsoft has labeled every command in the various groups. If you rest your mouse pointer on a specific command, Access displays a ScreenTip that contains the name of the command and a short description that explains what you can do with the command. Any time a command includes a small arrow, you can click the arrow to display options available for the command.

Home tab

Let's first explore the Home tab, shown in Figure 9-34.

Figure 9-34 The Home tab provides common commands for editing, filtering, and sorting data.

The Home tab for desktop databases has the following groups:

- **Views.**   Most objects in an Access database have two or more ways to view them. When you have one of these objects open and it has the focus, you can use the View command in this group to switch easily to another view.

- **Clipboard.**   You can use the commands in this group to manage data that you move to and from the Clipboard.

- **Sort & Filter.**   You can use these commands to sort and filter your data.

- **Records.**   Use the commands in this group to work with records, including deleting records and saving changes.

- **Find.**   The commands in this group allow you to search and replace data, go to a specific record, or select one or all records.

- **Window.**   Use the commands in this group to resize windows or select one of several windows that you have open. Access displays this group only when you have set your database to display Overlapping Windows rather than Tabbed Documents. For more details, see "Using the single-document vs. the multiple-document interface," later in this chapter.

- **Text Formatting.**   You can change how Access displays text using the commands in this group. You can also design fields in your database to contain data formatted in Rich Text. (See Chapter 10 for more details about data types.) You can use the commands in this group to format text in a Rich Text field.

INSIDE OUT   Adding a group to the Quick Access Toolbar with two mouse clicks

If you notice that you are using commands found in a group on the ribbon quite often, Access provides a very quick and easy way to add the entire group to the Quick Access Toolbar. To add a group on the ribbon to the Quick Access Toolbar, right-click the group and click Add To Quick Access Toolbar. This adds the group, including all commands, to the Quick Access Toolbar for all databases. Alternatively, you can quickly remove a group from your custom Quick Access Toolbar by right-clicking the group and clicking Remove From Quick Access Toolbar.

Create tab

The Create tab, shown in Figure 9-35, contains commands that let you create new desktop database objects. Each group on this particular tab arranges its specific functions by database object type.

Figure 9-35 The Create tab provides commands for creating all the various types of database objects.

The Create tab contains the following groups:

- **Templates.** Use the commands in this group to create new template parts such as fields, tables, forms, and other objects. You can learn more about template parts in Chapter 10.

- **Tables.** Use the commands in this group to create new tables or link to a Share-Point Services list.

- **Queries.** Use the commands in this group to create new queries. You can learn more about creating queries beginning in Chapter 12.

- **Forms.** You can create new forms using the commands in this group, including Split Forms and Datasheet Forms. You can learn more about creating forms beginning in Chapter 15.

- **Reports.** The commands in this group allow you to create new reports using available wizards, start a new report design from scratch, or build web reports.

- **Macros & Code.** Use the commands in this group to build macros or modules to automate your application.

> ## INSIDE OUT   Opening the Access Options dialog box quickly to customize the ribbon
>
> Right-click any part of the ribbon, and then click Customize The Ribbon to open the Access Options dialog box quickly with the Customize Ribbon category selected.

External Data tab

The External Data tab, shown in Figure 9-36, provides commands to import from or link to data in external sources or export data to external sources, including other Access desktop databases or SharePoint lists.

Figure 9-36 The External Data tab provides commands for working with external data sources.

This tab has the following groups:

- **Import & Link.** The commands in the Import group let you link to data or import data or objects from other sources such as other Access desktop databases, Access web apps, Microsoft Excel spreadsheets, Windows SharePoint Services lists, and other data sources such as Microsoft SQL Server.

- **Export.** You can use these commands to export objects to another Access desktop database or to export data to Excel, SharePoint, Microsoft Word, and more.

- **Web Linked Lists.** Commands in this group allow you to synchronize offline data with an active SharePoint site, cache list data, and relink SharePoint lists.

Database Tools tab

The last tab that is always available on the ribbon for desktop databases is the Database Tools tab, shown in Figure 9-37. The upper part of Figure 9-37 shows the Database Tools tab when using an Access 2007-2013 database (.accdb), and the lower part shows the Database Tools tab when using Access 2000, 2002, or 2003 databases (.mdb).

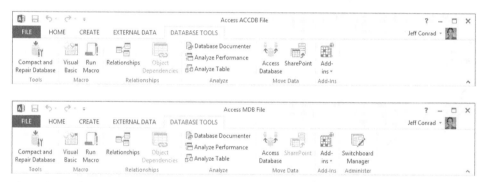

Figure 9-37 The Database Tools tab gives you access to miscellaneous tools and wizards.

The Database Tools tab on the ribbon includes the following groups:

- **Tools.** This group has one command: Compact And Repair Database. Use this command to compact and repair your desktop database file.

- **Macro.** Commands in this group let you open the Visual Basic Editor or run a macro.

- **Relationships.** Commands in this group activate useful information windows. Use the Relationships command to view and edit your table relationships. (See Chapter 10 for details.) Click the Object Dependencies command to see which objects are dependent on the currently selected object.

- **Analyze.**   Use the commands in this group to print a report about your objects or run one of the two analysis wizards.

- **Move Data.**   The two wizards available in this group allow you to either move some of or all your tables to a separate Access desktop database and create links to the moved tables in the current desktop database or move some or all of your tables to a SharePoint site.

- **Add-Ins.**   You can manage add-ins from this group or start the Add-In Manager to install new add-ins for your Access installation.

- **Administer.**   Access displays this group on the Database Tools tab only when you open an Access database file created in Access 2000, 2002, or 2003 (.mdb). The Switchboard Manager command starts the Switchboard Manager to assist you with building a switchboard form for navigating through your application.

INSIDE OUT   Collapsing the entire ribbon

If you need some additional workspace within the Access window, you can collapse the entire ribbon by double-clicking any of the tabs. All the groups disappear from the screen, but the tabs are still available. You can also use the keyboard shortcut Ctrl+F1 to collapse the ribbon or click the Minimize The Ribbon button in the lower-right corner of the ribbon. To see the ribbon again, simply click any tab to restore the ribbon to its full height, press Ctrl+F1 again, or click the Expand The Ribbon button.

Understanding the Navigation pane

The Navigation pane is a window that is located permanently on the left side of the screen that displays a list of all the objects, grouped together by type, in your desktop database, as shown in Figure 9-38. (You worked with the Navigation pane when you designed web apps earlier in this book.) Any open objects appear to the right of the Navigation pane. This means that you still have easy access to the other objects in your database without having to shuffle open objects around the screen or continually minimize and restore object windows. If the list of objects in a particular group is quite extensive, Access provides a scroll bar in each section so that you can access each object. When you work with the Navigation pane in desktop databases, you'll find that you have more options available to customize the display than when you work with the Navigation pane in web apps.

To follow along in the rest of this section, open the Tasks Sample desktop database (TasksSample.accdb) located in the Tasks subfolder where you downloaded and installed the sample files. (You should already have this database open if you've been following along with the examples so far in this chapter.) Unless you have previously opened this desktop database and changed the Navigation pane, you should see the Navigation pane on the left side of the screen, exactly like Figure 9-38.

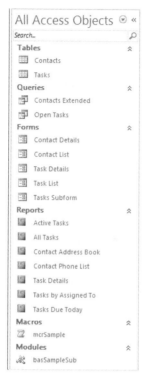

Figure 9-38 The Navigation pane displays all the objects in your desktop database.

INSIDE OUT   Jumping quickly to a specific object in the Navigation pane

Click an object in one of the groups in the Navigation pane to highlight it, and then press a letter key to jump quickly to any objects that begin with that letter in that particular group.

«

Shutter Bar
Open/Close
button

You can expand or contract the width of the Navigation pane easily by positioning your pointer over the right edge of the Navigation pane and then clicking and dragging the edge in either direction to the width you want. Keep in mind that the farther you expand the width, the less screen area you have available to work with your database objects because all objects open to the right of the Navigation pane. To maximize the amount of screen area available to work with open objects, you can collapse the Navigation pane completely to the far-left side of the application window by clicking the double-arrow button in the upper-right corner, called the Shutter Bar Open/Close button. When you do this, the Navigation pane appears as a thin bar on the left of your screen, as shown in Figure 9-39. After you have "shuttered" the Navigation pane, click the button again to reopen the Navigation pane to its previous width. Access remembers the last width that you set for the Navigation pane. The next time you open an Access desktop database, the width of the Navigation pane will be the same as when you last had the database open. Pressing the F11 key alternately toggles the Navigation pane between its collapsed and expanded views.

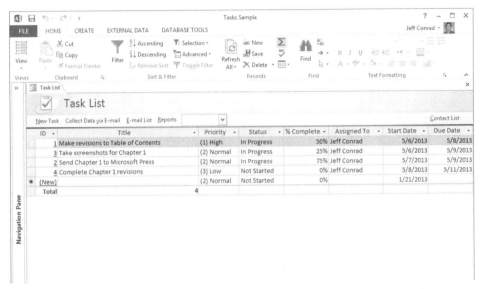

Figure 9-39 You can collapse the Navigation pane to give yourself more room to work on open objects.

Exploring Navigation pane object views

When you first open the TasksSample.accdb sample database, the Navigation pane shows you all the objects defined in the database grouped by object type and sorted by object name. You can verify this view by clicking the menu bar at the top of the Navigation pane, as shown in Figure 9-40, which opens the Navigation Pane menu. Under Navigate To Category, you should see Object Type selected, and under Filter By Group, you should see All Access Objects selected. This is the view I selected in the database before saving it. By default, all new blank desktop databases created in the Access 2007-2013 format display the object list in the Navigation pane in this view.

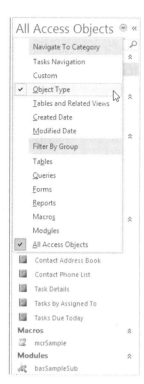

Figure 9-40 You can change the display in the Navigation pane by selecting a different category or filter from the Navigation Pane menu.

This view displays each object by object category and sorted by object name. The objects in each of the six object types—Tables, Queries, Forms, Reports, Macros, and Modules—are grouped together. When the list of objects is longer than can be displayed within the height of the Navigation pane, Access provides a scroll bar.

You can customize the Navigation pane to display the object list in many different ways. Access provides a set of predefined categories for the Navigation pane that you can access with a few mouse clicks. You can see these available categories by clicking the top of the Navigation pane to open the menu, as shown previously in Figure 9-40.

Notice that this Tasks Sample database lists six categories under Navigate To Category: Tasks Navigation, Custom, Object Type, Tables And Related Views, Created Date, and Modified Date. The first category in the list, Tasks Navigation, is a custom category specific to this database that I created. Access always provides the other five categories in all desktop databases to allow you to view objects in various predefined ways.

INSIDE OUT   Collapsing an entire group in the Navigation pane

If you click the header of each object type where the double arrow is located, Access collapses that part of the Navigation pane. For example, if you want to hide the tables temporarily, you can collapse that section by clicking the double arrow next to the word Tables. To bring the table list back to full view, simply click the double arrow that is now pointing downward, and the tables section expands to reveal all the table objects.

The Navigation pane menu also provides commands under Filter By Group to allow you to filter the database object list. The filter commands that are available change depending on which Navigate To Category command you select. Notice in Figure 9-40, where Navigate To Category is set to Object Type, that the Filter By Group section in the lower half of the Navigation Pane menu lists each of the object types that currently exist in your desktop database. When you have the menu categorized by object type, you can filter the list of objects further by selecting one of the object types to see only objects of that type. Click one of the object types (Forms, for instance), and Access hides all the other object types, as shown in Figure 9-41. This feature is very useful if you want to view and work with only a particular type of database object. Click the All Access Objects filter command to see all objects by object type again.

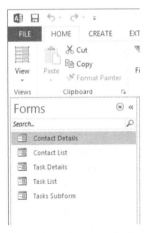

Figure 9-41 You can display only the Forms group of objects in the Object Type view by applying a filter in the Navigation Pane menu.

By default, new blank databases created in the Access 2007-2013 format also include a Navigation Pane category called Tables And Related Views. You can switch the Tasks Sample database to this category by opening the Navigation Pane menu that contains categories and filters and then clicking the Tables And Related Views command, as shown in Figure 9-42.

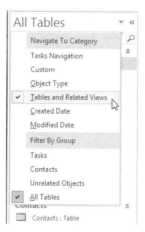

Figure 9-42 The Tables And Related Views category on the Navigation Pane menu offers a different way to view your database objects.

After you click Tables And Related Views, the Navigation pane should look similar to Figure 9-43. This particular view category groups the various database objects based on their relation to a common denominator—a table. As you can observe in Figure 9-43, each group of objects is the name of one of the tables. Within each group, you can see the table as the first item in the group followed by all objects that are dependent on the data from the table. Therefore, Access lists all database objects dependent on the Tasks data table together in the Tasks group, and similarly, it lists all objects dependent on the Contacts table in the Contacts group. At first glance, you might be a bit confused as to the purpose of each object, but notice that the various types of objects each have their own unique icon to help you differentiate them. For example, the Tasks table is listed first, with the icon for a table before the name and the word Table next to it. The remaining objects in the group are the various objects that are dependent on the Tasks table in alphabetical order by name, and each object has an icon before the name that identifies the type of object.

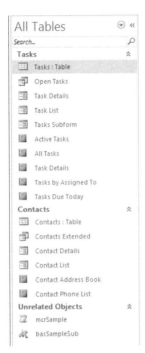

Figure 9-43 The Tables And Related Views category in the Navigation pane groups objects under a table.

Some objects appear in a category called Unrelated Objects, such as the macro called mcrSample and the module called basSampleSub, in this Tasks Sample database. Macros and modules contain code that you can reference from any object in your database. They always appear in the Unrelated Objects category of Tables And Related Views because Access does not search through the macro arguments and module code to see whether any table references exist.

INSIDE OUT When to use the Tables And Related Views category

This particular view category can be quite useful if you are making some changes to a table and want to see what objects might be affected by the change. You can check each query, form, and report that is related to this table one at a time in this view to ensure that no functionality of the database is broken after you make a change to the underlying table.

Now that you have changed to Tables And Related Views, open the Navigation Pane menu again. Notice that the names of both data tables in this database are listed beneath Filter By Group, as shown previously in Figure 9-42. Click Tasks, and Access reduces the Navigation pane to show only the objects related to the Tasks table, as shown in Figure 9-44. By filtering the Navigation pane to one table, you have reduced the number of objects displayed and you can focus your attention on only a small subset of database objects. You can open the Navigation Pane menu again and click All Tables to restore the complete list.

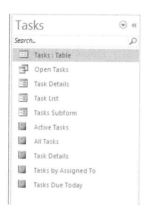

Figure 9-44 You can filter Tables And Related Views to show only the database objects dependent on one table.

Access provides two related types of object view categories on the Navigation Pane menu, called Created Date and Modified Date, as shown in Figure 9-45. These categories list all the objects in descending order based on when you created or last modified the object. These views can be quite useful if you need to locate an object that you created or last modified on a specific date or within a range of dates. When you click either of these commands, the Filter By Group options on the Navigation Pane menu offers to filter by Today, Yesterday, one of the five days previous to that (listed by day name), Last Week, Two Weeks Ago, Three Weeks Ago, Last Month, Older, or All Dates.

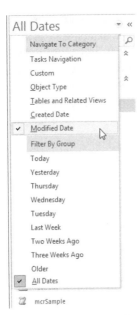

Figure 9-45 The Created Date and Modified Date categories display objects in the order you created or last modified them.

> **Note**
> You will not see the same options listed in Figure 9-45 when you open your copy of Tasks Sample, because all the Modified dates will be older than three weeks. The only two options you will see are Older and All Dates.

Working with custom categories and groups

We have not yet discussed the remaining two object categories available in the Navigation Pane menu of the Tasks Sample database: Custom and Tasks Navigation, as shown in Figure 9-46. Whenever you create a new desktop database, Access creates the Custom category that you can modify to suit your needs. Initially, the Custom category contains only one group, Unassigned Objects, containing all the objects defined in your database. You can change the name of the Custom category, create one or more custom groups, and assign objects to those groups.

When you create a new desktop database using one of the many templates provided by Microsoft, nearly all these databases contain an additional predefined group designed to make it easier to run the sample application. I created the Tasks Sample database using the Tasks template, and the Tasks Navigation category is predefined in that template. As with any custom category, you can create new groups, modify or delete existing groups, assign additional objects to the groups within the custom category, or delete both the category and all its groups.

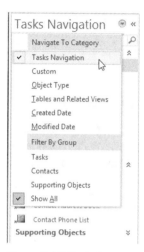

Figure 9-46 Both Custom and Tasks Navigation are custom categories available in the Tasks Sample database.

To see an example of a finished custom category in this database, open the Navigation Pane menu and select Tasks Navigation. The Navigation pane changes to display the object list shown in Figure 9-47. This custom category contains three custom groups called Tasks, Contacts, and Supporting Objects. There is actually a fourth group called Unassigned Objects, which you cannot see.

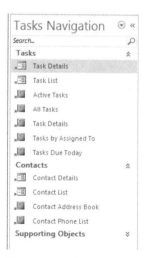

Figure 9-47 The Tasks Navigation category displays a custom view of the various database objects.

In Figure 9-47, notice that each object icon has a small arrow in the lower-left corner. This arrow indicates that you are looking at a shortcut or pointer to the actual object. These shortcuts act similarly to shortcuts in Windows—if you open the shortcut, you're opening the underlying object to which the shortcut points. When you view custom categories and groups in the Navigation pane, you are always looking at shortcuts to the objects. If you delete one of these shortcuts, you are deleting only the pointer to the object and not the object itself.

Exploring the Navigation Options dialog box

To create your own custom categories and groups for the Navigation pane, you need to open the Navigation Options dialog box. To open the Navigation Options dialog box, right-click the menu bar at the top of the Navigation pane and click Navigation Options on the shortcut menu, as shown in Figure 9-48.

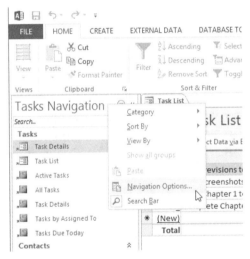

Figure 9-48 Right-click the top of the Navigation pane, and click Navigation Options to open the Navigation Options dialog box.

Access opens the Navigation Options dialog box, as shown in Figure 9-49.

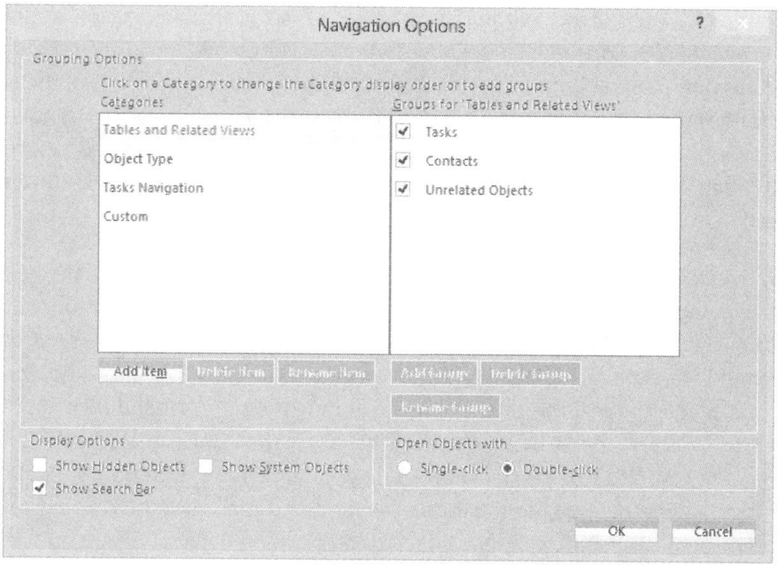

Figure 9-49 The Navigation Options dialog box lets you create and edit grouping and display options.

The Categories list under Grouping Options lists all the categories that have been defined in this desktop database. In this list, you can see two built-in categories—Tables And Related Views and Object Type—that you cannot delete. The list also shows the Tasks Navigation category that was defined in the template and the Custom category that Access defines in all new desktop databases. When you select a different category in the list on the left, the list on the right displays the groups for that category.

Next to each of the groups for the selected category is a check box. When you clear the check box next to any group on the right, Access does not display that group in the Navigation pane. As you might recall, when you looked at the Tasks Navigation category in the Navigation pane, you could see only Tasks, Contacts, and Supporting Objects. Because I cleared the check box next to Unassigned Objects in the Navigation Options dialog box, you are unable to view it in the Navigation pane.

> **Note**
>
> The Tables And Related Views category by default includes one group for each table defined in the current database and one additional group called Unrelated Objects. The Object Type category includes one group for each of the six object types—tables, queries, forms, reports, macros, and modules.

In the lower-left corner of this dialog box, the Display Options section contains three check boxes—Show Hidden Objects, Show System Objects, and Show Search Bar. We'll discuss these options later in this chapter. The last section in the lower right of the Navigation Options dialog box is called Open Objects With. When you select the Single-Click option, each object listed in the Navigation pane acts like a hyperlink, so you need only one click to open the object. Double-Click, the default option, opens objects in the Navigation pane with a double click.

To create a new navigation category, click the Add Item button. To delete a custom navigation category, select the category and then click the Delete Item button. To rename a custom category, select it and then click the Rename Item button. Access places the category name in rename mode where you can enter a new name. To create a new group for a custom category, select the category name in the list on the left and then click the Add Group button. Access creates a new group in the list on the right and places the group name in rename mode so that you can enter a unique name for the group. To delete an existing group, select the group in the list on the right and then click the Delete Group button. To rename an existing group, select it and then click the Rename Group button.

Click the Tasks Navigation custom group from the list on the left to see the custom groups defined for this category, as shown in figure 9-50. Next to whichever custom group is selected on the right is a Move Up arrow and a Move Down arrow, which you can click to change the display order of the groups in this category. When you select this category from the Navigation Pane menu, Access displays the groups in the Navigation pane based on the display order that you set in the Navigation Options dialog box. In Figure 9-50, you can see arrow buttons next to the Tasks Navigation category and the Tasks group within that category.

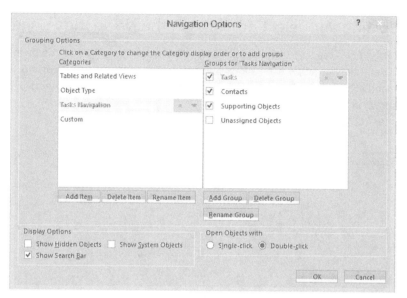

Figure 9-50 Access displays Move Up and Move Down arrows next to custom category and group items.

INSIDE OUT
Understanding display order rules for categories and groups

In the Categories list of the Navigation Options dialog box, you cannot change the display order of the Tables And Related Views and Object Type categories. All custom categories you create must appear below these two built-in categories.

The Unassigned Objects group in all custom groups you create can be displayed only at the bottom of the list of groups. You cannot place any custom groups below this built-in group. Similarly, the Unrelated Objects group within the Tables And Related Views category always appears at the bottom of the list.

When you are finished creating custom categories and groups, click OK to save your changes. You'll see your options displayed in the Navigation pane menu and the Navigation pane itself when you select your custom category. For now, click Cancel to close the Navigation Options dialog box without making changes. Switch back to displaying the objects in the Navigation pane by object type before continuing to the next section. Click the menu at the top of the Navigation pane, and then click the Object Type command.

Chapter 9

Sorting and selecting views in the Navigation pane

By default, Access sorts the objects in the Navigation pane by object type in ascending order. The Navigation pane allows for several other types of object sorting. Right-click the menu at the top of the Navigation pane, and move the mouse pointer over Sort By, as shown in Figure 9-51.

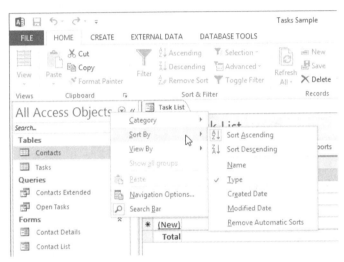

Figure 9-51 The Sort By submenu in the Navigation Pane menu allows for further Navigation pane sorting.

The Sort By submenu has options to sort the Navigation pane list by the name of the object, the object type, the created date, and the modified date. You can change the sort order from ascending to descending for any of these Sort By options by clicking Sort Ascending or Sort Descending at the top of the Sort By submenu. The last option on the Sort By submenu, Remove Automatic Sorts, lets you lay out your object list in any order you want within the Navigation pane when viewing custom navigation categories.

The View By submenu has three choices available—Details, Icon, and List—as shown in Figure 9-52. The Details view displays in the Navigation pane the name of each object, its type, and the creation and modified dates, as well as a large icon next to each name. The Icon view displays only the name of the object (or the shortcut name for custom groups) next to a large icon of the object type. The List view similarly displays only the name of the object or shortcut, but the object icon is smaller than in the other two views.

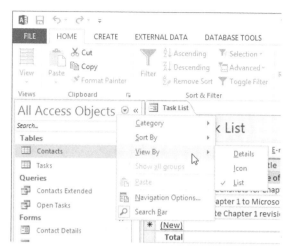

Figure 9-52 The View By submenu lists commands to view the Navigation pane objects by Details, Icon, or List.

Chapter 9

INSIDE OUT   Viewing categories from the Navigation pane submenus

You can choose one of the view categories—either a custom category or one of the built-in categories—by right-clicking the Navigation Pane menu and selecting the Category submenu.

Searching for database objects

In desktop databases with a large number of objects, locating a specific object can be difficult, so Access includes the Search Bar feature to make this task easier. By default, this feature is turned on; however, if the feature is turned off for your Access installation, you must turn it on through the Navigation pane. You can enable this feature in one of two ways. One method is to right-click the top of the Navigation pane and then click Search Bar, as shown in Figure 9-53.

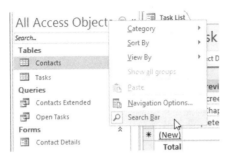

Figure 9-53 Click the Search Bar command on the Display Options menu to display the Search Bar.

Alternatively, you can right-click the top of the Navigation pane and then click Navigation Options on the shortcut menu to open the Navigation Options dialog box, shown in Figure 9-54.

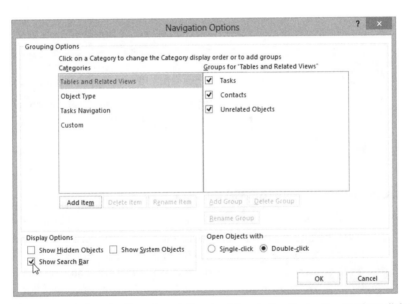

Figure 9-54 Select the Show Search Bar check box in the Navigation Options dialog box to display the Search Bar.

Select the Show Search Bar check box, and then click OK. Access displays the Search Bar near the top of the Navigation pane, as shown in Figure 9-55.

Figure 9-55 The Search Bar in the Navigation pane helps you find specific database objects.

INSIDE OUT   Moving focus to the Search Bar with a keyboard shortcut

You can quickly move the focus to the Search Bar from anywhere within the application window by pressing Ctrl+Alt+F.

I think the Search Bar is misnamed. Rather than "search" for objects that match what you type in the search box, Access filters the list in the Navigation pane. As you begin to type letters, Access filters the list of objects to those that contain the sequence of characters you enter anywhere in the name. For example, if you want to find an object whose name contains the word Today, type the word **today** in the Search Bar. As you enter each letter in the Search Bar, Access begins filtering the list of objects for any that contain the characters in your entered search string. With each successive letter you type, Access reduces the list of objects shown in the Navigation pane because there are fewer objects that match your search criteria. Notice that as soon as you have typed the letters *to*, Access has reduced the list to two objects—Tasks by Assigned To and Tasks Due Today—as shown in Figure 9-56. The names of both objects contain the letters *to*.

Figure 9-56 The Search Bar collapses any groups if it does not find any objects in that group that meet your search criterion.

Access collapses any group headers if it does not find any objects (or object shortcuts if you're using a custom category) that meet your search criterion. To clear your search string if you need to perform another object search, either delete the existing text using the Back-space key or click the Clear Search String button on the right side of the Search Bar. Clear-ing the search box or clicking the Clear Search String button restores the Navigation pane to show all displayable objects.

INSIDE OUT   Maximizing your search to include all objects

If you need to search through all your desktop database objects to find a specific named object, I recommend that you set the Navigation Menu category to one of the built-in categories such as Object Type or Tables And Related Views. Also, check to see that all groups are visible in the Navigation pane for that category to ensure that Access does not miss any objects when it conducts the search.

Using the single-document vs. the multiple-document interface

In versions of Access before Access 2007, all objects opened in their own windows where you could edit, view, or print them. This type of interface, multiple-document interface (MDI for short), was the cornerstone for working with objects in Access desktop databases. Access 2013 includes an interface model called single-document interface (SDI). In the SDI model, all objects open in a series of tabs along the top of the object window to the right of the Navigation pane. In the older MDI model, switching between open objects usually meant constantly minimizing, resizing, and maximizing the various objects to work with them. In Figure 9-57, you can see two forms, one table, and one report open using MDI format. To switch among these objects, you must move the objects around or minimize some of them, as shown near the bottom of the screen.

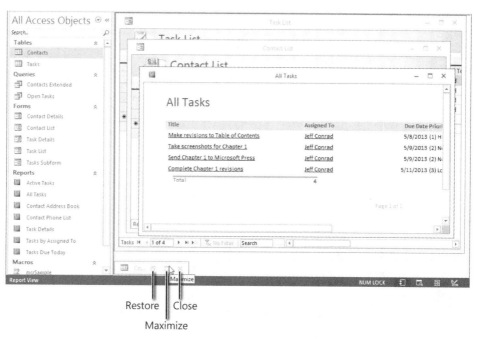

Restore   Close

Maximize

Figure 9-57 All open objects appear in their own separate windows when using the MDI.

In the SDI model, each open object appears on a tab to the right of the Navigation pane. In Figure 9-58, you can see the same four objects open as before, but here each open object has its name listed at the top of a tab next to an icon for that particular type of database object. Switching among open objects is as simple as clicking a different tab. The end result of this interface is that you can easily see the names of all open objects and find the ones that you need to work with much faster.

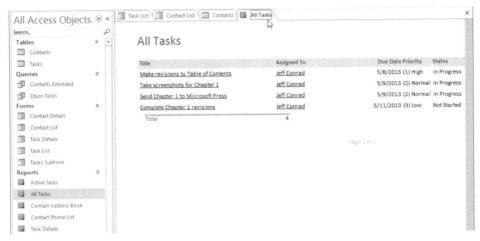

Figure 9-58 All open objects appear on their own tabs when using the SDI.

INSIDE OUT   Closing objects with one click

If you are using the SDI, you can close any window with a middle-click. Click the mouse wheel on the object tab at the top of the application window, even if the tab is not currently selected, and Access closes that object.

For new databases created in the Access 2007-2013 format, Access uses the SDI by default, but for older databases in the MDB/MDE type format, Access still opens those files in MDI mode. Access easily allows you to change the interface mode for any database through the Access Options dialog box. Click the File tab on the Backstage View, and then click Options. Click the Current Database category in the left pane to display a list of settings to tailor this current database. In Figure 9-59, note the section called Document Window Options in the Current Database category of the Access Options dialog box.

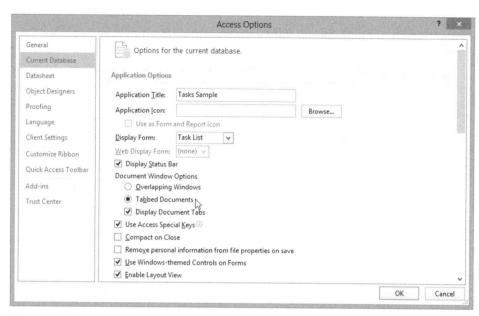

Figure 9-59 The Document Window Options section in the Current Database category of the Access Options dialog box controls the interface mode.

To work in MDI mode, select Overlapping Windows. For the SDI interface, with each object on its own tab, select Tabbed Documents. Under these two options is a check box called Display Document Tabs. You can select this check box only in conjunction with the Tabbed Documents option. When you select the Display Document Tabs check box, each object has a tab across the top of the object window with the object's name and an icon for the object type, as shown in Figure 9-58. If you clear Display Document Tabs, you do not see any tabs for open objects, nor do you see any Restore, Minimize, Maximize, or Close buttons for open objects.

After you make your selections in the Access Options dialog box, click OK to save your changes. Access applies these interface settings to this current database the next time you open the file. To see the interface change, you need to close and reopen the database.

Chapter 9

INSIDE OUT
Why you might want to use the Tabbed Documents setting with no tabs visible

If you're creating an application for novice users, you might want to set up the application so that the user can work with only one object at a time. Presenting a single object minimizes the choices for the user. However, you will have to be sure to include a method to allow the user to navigate to other objects, perhaps with command buttons that execute VBA code or macros to open and set the focus to other objects. You must design such an application carefully so that the user never gets "trapped" in one object, unable to get to others.

Perhaps the most important aspect of building an application is designing the database tables that will support your application. In the next chapter, you'll learn how to design your database application and its data structures through tables. Building a solid foundation with tables makes creating the forms and reports for your application easy.

CHAPTER 10

Designing tables in a desktop database

DEFINING tables in a Microsoft Access 2013 desktop database (.accdb file) is very easy. This chapter shows you how it's done. You'll learn how to:

- Create a new desktop database application using a database template.

- Create a new empty database for your own custom application.

- Create a simple table by entering data directly in the table.

- Get a jump-start on defining custom tables by using Application Parts.

- Create new fields by using Data Type Parts.

- Define your own tables from scratch by using Design view.

- Select the best data type for each field.

- Define the primary key for your table.

- Set validation rules for your fields and tables.

- Tell Access what relationships to maintain between your tables.

- Optimize data retrieval by adding indexes.

- Set options that affect how you work in Design view.

INSIDE OUT   Take time to learn about table design

You could begin building a desktop database in Access much as you might begin creating a simple single-sheet solution in a spreadsheet application such as Microsoft Excel—by simply organizing your data into rows and columns and then inserting formulas where you need calculations. If you've ever worked extensively with a database or a spreadsheet application, you already know that this unplanned approach works in only the most trivial situations. Solving real problems takes some planning; otherwise, you end up building your application over and over again. One of the beauties of a relational database system such as Access is that it's much easier to make midcourse corrections. However, it's well worth spending time up front designing the tasks you want to perform, the data structures you need to support those tasks, and the flow of tasks within your database application.

To teach you all you might need to know about table design would require another entire book. The good news is Access provides many examples of good table design in the templates available with the product and online. If you want to learn at least the fundamentals of table and application design, be sure to read Article 1, "Designing your database application," which you can download from the book's catalog page at *http://shop.oreilly.com/product/0790145367969.do*.

Creating a new desktop database

As you learned in Chapter 2, "Exploring the Access 2013 web app interface," when you first start Access 2013, you see the Office Start screen, as shown in Figure 10-1. If you've previously opened other databases, you also by default see a most recently used list of database selections on the left, under Recent.

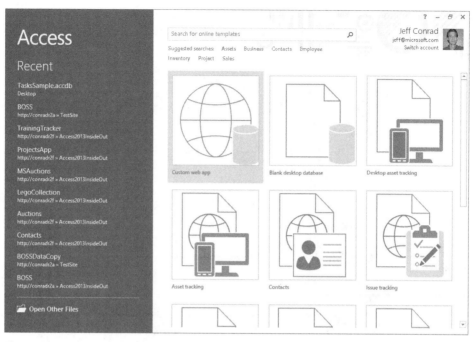

Figure 10-1 When you first start Access 2013, you see the Office Start screen.

Using a database template to create a desktop database

Just for fun, let's explore the built-in database templates first. If you're a beginner, you can use the templates included with Access to create one of several common applications without needing to know anything about designing database software. You might find that one of these applications meets most of your needs right away. As you learn more about Access, you can build on and customize the basic application design and add new features.

Even if you're an experienced developer, you might find that the application templates save you lots of time in setting up the basic tables, queries, forms, and reports for your application. If the application you need to build is covered by one of the templates, the wizard that builds an application with one of the templates can take care of many of the simpler design tasks.

On the Office Start screen tab of the Backstage view, you can access the built-in local desktop templates by clicking one of the template icons in the center of the screen. You can identify whether a template on the Office Start screen is a desktop database by looking for the text *Desktop* in the template name. When you click one of the desktop template graphics on the Office Start screen, Access displays additional detailed information about the purpose of the template in a pop-up dialog. Click the Desktop Task Management template in the middle of the screen to see detailed information about the template, as shown in Figure 10-2. You can work with all desktop templates from the Office Start screen in the same way. The following example will show you the steps that are needed to build a Task Management desktop database.

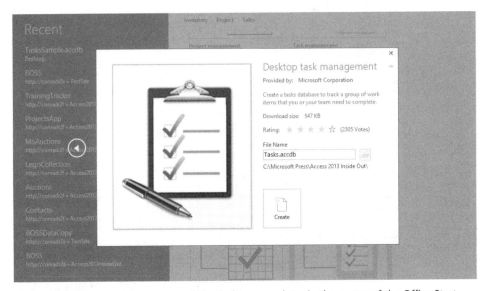

Figure 10-2 When you choose one of the desktop templates in the center of the Office Start screen, Access shows you information about the database in a dialog.

Access displays a preview graphic on the left side of the dialog and additional information about the purpose of the database on the right side of the dialog. If you decide at this point not to create the database, click the Close (X) button near the top right of this dialog to stop the process and return to the main Office Start screen. You'll also notice the left and right arrow buttons on either side of the pop-up dialog. (In Figure 10-2, you can see only a left arrow button.) When you click these buttons, Access displays the details about the previous or next desktop or web app template. You can shuffle through the various templates displayed on the Office Start screen using these buttons.

On the right side of the dialog, Access suggests a name for your new database in the File Name text box and a location to save the file beneath the File Name text box. You can modify the name of this database by typing in the File Name text box. If you want to change the suggested save location, click Browse to open the File New Database dialog box, as shown in Figure 10-3.

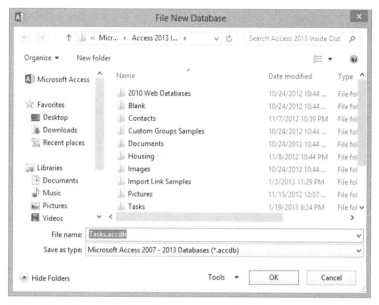

Figure 10-3 Use the File New Database dialog box to select a folder for saving the new local desktop database template.

You can select the drive and folder you want by clicking the links on the left and browsing to your destination folder. After you select the specific folder to which you want to save this new database, click OK to return to the pop-up dialog. Your new folder location is shown beneath the File Name text box. Click Create, and Access begins the process of creating this new desktop database template.

A progress bar appears on the screen asking you to wait while Access creates the template. After a few seconds of preparation, Access opens the new Tasks database and displays the Task List form, as shown in Figure 10-4. Close this new database for now by clicking the File tab on the Backstage view and then clicking Close.

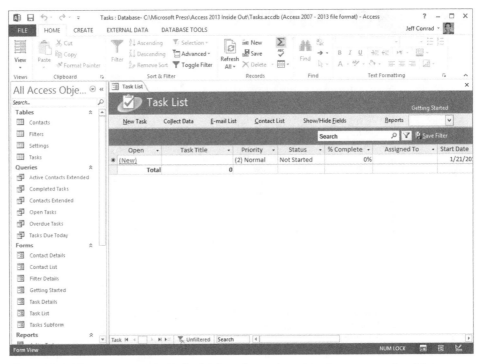

Figure 10-4 After you create the Tasks database from a template, Access opens the database and displays the Task List form.

Creating a new empty database

To begin creating a new empty database when you start Access, click the New tab of the Backstage view and click Blank Desktop Database. Access opens the Blank Desktop Database pop-up dialog, as shown in Figure 10-5. Access displays a generic preview graphic on the left side of the dialog when you create new blank desktop databases. If you decide at this point not to create the new database, click the Close (X) button near the top right of this dialog to stop the process.

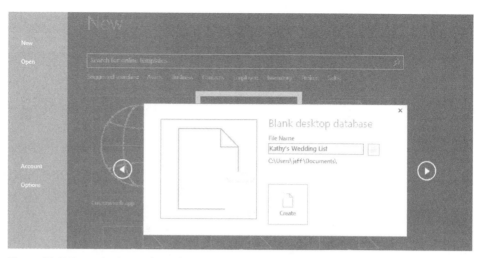

Figure 10-5 From the New tab on the Backstage view, click Blank Desktop Database in the center to open the Blank Desktop Database dialog box.

You can click Browse to open the File New Database dialog box, shown in Figure 10-3, to select the drive and folder that you want. In this example, I selected the Documents folder in Windows 8 for the current user. Next, type the name of your new database in the File Name text box—Access appends an .accdb extension to the file name for you. Access uses a file with an .accdb extension to store all your database objects, including tables, queries, forms, reports, macros, and modules. For this example, let's create a database with a table containing names and addresses—something you might use to track invitees to a wedding. Type **Kathy's Wedding List** in the File Name box, and click Create to create your database.

Access takes a few moments to create the system tables in which to store all the information about the tables, queries, forms, reports, macros, and modules that you might create. Access then displays the Navigation pane for your new database and opens a new blank table in Datasheet view, as shown in Figure 10-6.

Chapter 10

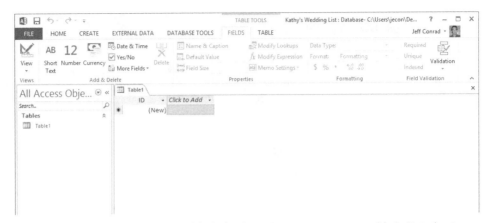

Figure 10-6 When you create a new blank database, Access opens a new table in Datasheet view for you.

When you open a database (unless the database includes special startup settings), Access selects the object you last chose in the Navigation pane for that database. For example, if you worked on a table the last time you opened this database, Access highlights that object (a table) in the Navigation pane. Access also remembers the view and filters you applied to the Navigation pane. For example, if Tables And Related Views was the last selected view applied to the Navigation pane, Access will remember this the next time you open the database.

Because this is a new database and no objects or special startup settings exist yet, you see a Navigation pane with only one object defined. For new databases, Access, by default, creates a new table in Datasheet view called Table1 with an ID field already defined. However, Access has not saved this table, so if you do not make any changes to it, Access will not prompt you to save the table if you close it. The following sections show you various methods for creating a new table.

Creating your first simple table by entering data

If you've been following along to this point, you should still have your new Kathy's Wedding List database open with Table1 open in Datasheet view, shown previously in Figure 10-6. (You can also follow these steps in any open database.) What you see is an empty datasheet, which looks quite similar to a spreadsheet. Access automatically created the first field, called ID, in the left column. Leave this field intact for now. In the second column, Access has placed another field with the Add New Field heading. You can enter just about any type of data you want in this field—text, dates, numbers, or currency. But unlike a spreadsheet, you can't enter any calculated expressions in a datasheet. As you'll see later in this chapter, you can easily display a calculated result using data from one or more fields by entering an expression in a Calculated data type.

Because we're starting a list of wedding invitees, we'll need columns containing informa-tion such as title, last name, first name, middle initial, street address, city, state, postal code, number of guests invited, number of guests confirmed, gift received, and a gift acknowl-edged indicator. Be sure to enter the same type of data in a particular column for every row. For example, enter the city name in the seventh column (named Field6 by Access) for every row.

You can see some of the data entered for the wedding invitee list in Figure 10-7. When you start to type in a field in a row, Access displays a pencil icon on the row selector at the far left to indicate that you're adding or changing data in that row. Press the Tab key to move from column to column. When you move to another row, Access saves what you typed. If you make a mistake in a particular row or column, you can click the data you want to change and type over it or delete it. Notice that after you enter data in a column, Access guesses the most appropriate data type and displays it in the Data Type box on the Fields tab on the ribbon.

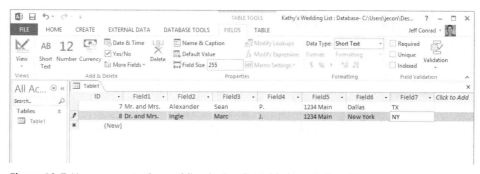

Figure 10-7 You can create the wedding invitee list table by entering data.

If you create a column of data that you don't want, click anywhere in the column and click Delete in the Add & Delete group of the Fields contextual tab on the ribbon. Click Yes when Access asks you to confirm the deletion. If you want to insert a blank column between two columns that already contain data, right-click the column header to the right of where you want to insert the new column and then click Insert Field on the shortcut menu that appears. To move a column to a different location, click the field name at the top of the column to select the entire column, and then click again and drag the column to a new location. You can also click an unselected column and drag your mouse pointer through several adjacent columns to select them all. You can then move the columns as a group.

You probably noticed that Access named your columns Field1, Field2, and so forth—not very informative. You can enter a name for each column by double-clicking the column's field name. You can also right-click a column header and then click Rename Field on the shortcut menu that appears. In Figure 10-8, I have already renamed one of the columns and I'm in the process of renaming the second one.

Figure 10-8 Double-click the column heading to rename a column in Datasheet view.

Save

After you enter several rows of data, it's a good idea to save your table. You can do this by clicking the Save button on the Quick Access Toolbar or by clicking the File tab and then click Save. Access displays a Save As dialog box, as shown in Figure 10-9. Type an appropriate name for your table, and then click OK. If you deleted the ID field by mistake, Access displays a message box warning you that you have no primary key defined for this table and offers to build one for you. If you accept the offer, Access adds a field called ID and assigns it a special data type named AutoNumber that automatically generates a unique number for each new row you add. See "Understanding field data types," later in this chapter, for details about AutoNumber. If one or more of the data columns you entered would make a good primary key, click No in the message box. In Chapter 11, "Modifying your table design," you'll learn how to use Design view to define your own primary key(s) or to change the definition of an existing primary key. In this case, Access should not display a message box because it already generated the field called ID to serve as the primary key. After you save the table, close this database for now by clicking the File tab on the Backstage view and then clicking Close.

Figure 10-9 Access displays the Save As dialog box when you save a new table so that you can specify a table name.

Creating a table using Application Parts

If you look in the Wedding List sample database (WeddingList.accdb), which you can download from the book's catalog page, you'll find it very simple, with one main table and a few supporting tables for data such as titles, cities, and groups. Most databases are usually quite a bit more complex. For example, the Proseware Housing Reservations sample database (Housing.accdb) contains six main tables, and the Conrad Systems Contacts sample database (Contacts.accdb) contains more than a dozen tables. If you had to create every table manually, it could be quite a tedious process.

> **Note**
>
> The examples in this chapter are based on the WeddingList.accdb, Housing.accdb, and Contacts.accdb sample desktop databases, which can be downloaded from the book's catalog page. For more information about the sample files, see the section titled "Using the sample files," in the book's introduction.

Fortunately, Access comes with a feature called Application Parts to help you build a few common tables and other database objects. Let's move on to a more complex task—building tables like those you find in Conrad Systems Contacts. To do this, click the File tab on the Backstage view and then click Blank Desktop Database. This returns you to the Blank Desktop Database dialog, ready to define a new blank database. For this exercise, create a new blank database and give it the name **Contact Tracking**.

To build a table using one of the Application Parts, close the table that Access created when you opened the database (Table1), click the Create tab on the ribbon, and then click the Application Parts button in the Templates group. Access displays a list of 10 form types under the Blank Forms category and five Application Parts under the Quick Start category, as shown in Figure 10-10. Microsoft also uses the term *Models* to refer to this one-click object creation feature. You'll learn more about using the 10 form Application Parts in Chapter 16, "Building a form."

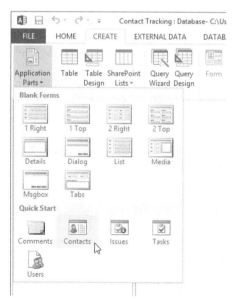

Figure 10-10 Application Parts help you create common types of database objects.

The five Application Parts under Quick Start, which represent some of the more common types of table structures and objects found in databases, are as follows:

- **Comments.** Use this Application Part when you need a table to track various comments. Clicking this option creates one table with a comment date and comment fields.

- **Contacts.** Use this Application Part when you need to track your personal or business contacts. Clicking this option not only creates a Contacts table but it also creates a query, three forms, and four reports to work with that Contacts table. With one click, you are well on your way to creating a functional application to track your contacts. Key fields in the Contacts table include the contact's company, job title, and phone numbers.

- **Issues.** Use this Application Part for recording various personal or business issues. Clicking this option creates an Issues table as well as two forms to work with that table. Some key fields in the Issues table include the title of the issue and the issue status.

- **Tasks.** Use this Application Part for keeping track of various tasks and projects needing completion. Clicking this option creates a Tasks table as well as two forms to work with that table. Key fields in the Tasks table include start and due dates for the task and percentage complete.

- **Users.** Use this Application Part for maintaining a list of users for your database. Clicking this option creates a Users table as well as two forms to work with that table. Key fields in the Users table include the email, full name, and login information.

Click Contacts in the Quick Start list, and Access builds a complete table structure for a contacts table as well as other supporting objects, as shown in Figure 10-11. Access creates a total of 20 fields to identify the data elements for this contacts table. Use the horizontal scroll bar or press Tab to see the field names to the right. This contacts table Application Part includes fields such as Company, First Name, Last Name, E-mail Address, Job Title, and so on to identify a single subject—a contact. The Quick Start command also automatically defines a data type for each of these fields.

See Table 10-1 for a full discussion of the various data types available within Access desktop databases.

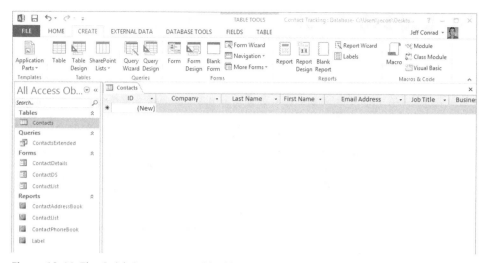

Figure 10-11 The Quick Start command builds a complete table with appropriate field types and supporting objects.

By default, Access assigned the name ID to the first field in this Contacts table. This field name is not very descriptive, so we will rename this field ContactID. There are several ways to rename a field using Access, but for now we will focus on one of the easiest methods— renaming the field directly from Datasheet view. Double-click the heading of the ID field, and then type **ContactID**, as shown in Figure 10-12. After you press Enter, Access immediately renames the field. Save the change to this table now by clicking the Save button on the Quick Access Toolbar.

Figure 10-12 You can double-click a column heading in Datasheet view to change the name of the field.

You will further change this Contacts table later in this chapter and in Chapter 11 so that it is more like the final tblContacts table in the Conrad Systems Contacts database. For now, close the Table window so that you can continue building other tables you need. Also, let's delete all the other supporting objects the Application Part command created so that we can concentrate just on the tables for now. Highlight the query called ContactsExtended in the Navigation pane, and then press Delete. Click OK in the confirmation dialog box when Access prompts you to delete the object. Continue deleting the remaining three forms and four reports until you are left with just the Contacts table in the Navigation pane.

Creating a table using Data Type Parts

Access includes another feature, called Data Type Parts, to assist you with creating tables and fields. Application Parts, as you just learned, help you build complete tables and other database objects, but Data Type Parts help you create individual fields or groups of fields. As you design more databases, you might find yourself needing to create similar field struc-tures in your tables. For example, you'll probably find yourself needing to have fields in at least one table that tracks address information such as street address, city, state, and ZIP code. With Access, you can now add a group of fields to track address information easily using Data Type Parts. You can also save your own custom field or groups of fields to be used in other Access applications that you create.

If you've been following along to this point, you should still have your new Contact Track-ing database open with just the Contacts table in the Navigation pane. (You can also follow these steps in any open database.) To build a table using one of the Data Type Parts, you first need to have a table opened in Datasheet view. Click the Create tab on the ribbon, and then click the Table button in the Tables group. Access creates a new table called Table1 with one field called ID and displays it in Datasheet view. Click the More Fields button in the Add & Delete group on the Fields tab, and Access displays a large list of field types grouped by category, as shown in Figure 10-13.

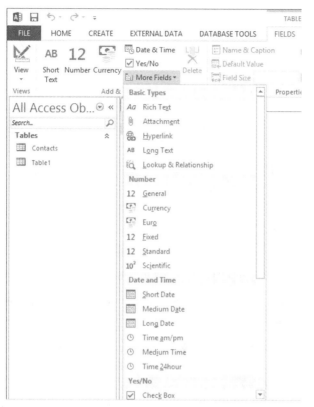

Figure 10-13 Click More Fields to see many field types and formatting choices you can use in your table.

Under the Basic Types, Number, Date and Time, and Yes/No categories, Access displays many options for different field types and field formats that you can use in your table. You can click any of the options in these categories, and Access creates a new field in your table. You'll learn more about the different field types and formats later in this chapter. Scroll down to the bottom of the list under the More Fields button, and Access displays a list of nine Data Type Parts under the Quick Start category, as shown in Figure 10-14.

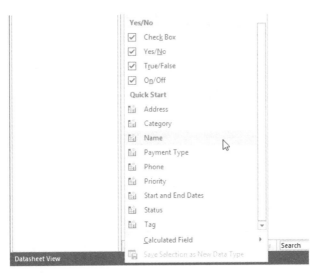

Figure 10-14 Data Type Parts help you create common types of fields.

The nine Data Type Parts under Quick Start, which represent some of the more common types of fields used in a database, are as follows:

- **Address.** Use this Data Type Part when you need fields to list address information. Clicking this option creates the following five fields—Address, City, State Province, ZIP Postal, and Country Region.

- **Category.** Use this Data Type Part when you need to create a list of categories. Clicking this option creates a list box with three generic category names.

- **Name.** Use this Data Type Part to create fields to store the names of people. Clicking this option creates two fields—Last Name and First Name.

- **Payment Type.** Use this Data Type Part when you need a list of payment types for order tracking or contribution tracking purposes. Clicking this option creates a list box called Payment Type with four options—Cash, Credit Card, Check, and In Kind.

- **Phone.** Use this Data Type Part when you need to create fields to store phone numbers. Clicking this option creates the following fields—Business Phone, Home Phone, Mobile Phone, and Fax Number.

- **Priority.** Use this Data Type Part when you need to create a list of priority levels. Clicking this option creates a list box with three generic priority levels—(1) High, (2) Normal, and (3) Low.

- **Start and End Dates.** Use this Data Type Part when you need fields to track start dates and end dates. Clicking this option creates two Date/Time fields.

- **Status.** Use this Data Type Part when you need to create a list of status levels. Clicking this option creates a list box with five generic status levels—Not Started, In Progress, Completed, Deferred, and Waiting.

- **Tag.** Use this Data Type Part when you need to create a list that allows you to select multiple items. Clicking this option creates a multivalue list with three generic items—Tag 1, Tag 2, and Tag 3.

Click Name under the Quick Start category, and Access creates two fields ready for you to use to track names of your contacts, as shown in Figure 10-15. You can add more Data Type Parts to this table by clicking another option under the Quick Start category.

Figure 10-15 Use the Name Data Type Part when you need to create fields to record the names of people.

To add the Address Data Type Part to this table, first click the Click To Add entry to move the focus to the right of the First Name field in the table Datasheet view. Access always adds new fields to the left of where the current focus is located in the Datasheet view grid. Now click the More Fields button in the Add & Delete group on the ribbon, and then click Address under the Quick Start category. Access creates five more fields in your table, as shown in Figure 10-16. Your table now has fields to track the address information for your contacts.

Figure 10-16 You can add fields to hold address information by clicking the Address Data Type Part.

When you're designing your tables in Access, using Data Type Parts can save you time by giving you a jump-start on creating common field types. Close the Table window now, and do not save the changes to this table when Access prompts you to save the changes.

Chapter 10

Creating a table in Design view

You could continue to use Application Parts and Data Type Parts to build some of the other tables in the Contact Tracking database to mimic those in the Conrad Systems Contacts sample desktop database. However, you'll find it very useful to learn the mechanics of building a table from scratch, so now is a good time to explore Design view and learn how to build tables without using Application Parts or Data Type Parts. Application Parts offer only a few choices for sample tables, and there is no way to pick and choose which fields to include or exclude. By working in Design view, you'll see many additional features that you can use to customize the way your tables (and any queries, forms, or reports built on these tables) work when creating a table from scratch.

To begin creating a new table in Design view, click the Create tab on the ribbon and then click the Table Design button in the Tables group. Access displays a blank Table window in Design view, as shown in Figure 10-17. You worked with tables in Design view when you created web apps earlier in this book. When you design tables using Design view within desktop databases, you'll see a familiar interface; however, Design view presents more options in desktop databases.

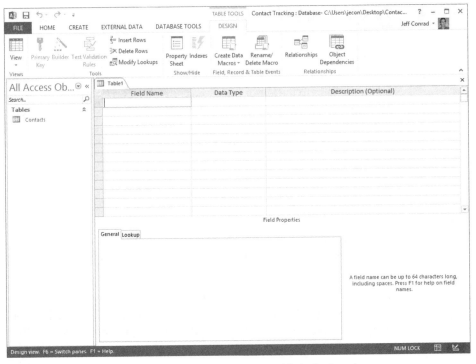

Figure 10-17 The Table Design command opens a new table in Design view.

In Design view, the upper part of the Table window displays columns in which you can enter the field names, the data type for each field, and a description of each field. After you select a data type for a field, Access allows you to set field properties in the lower-left section of the Table window. In the lower-right section of the Table window is a box in which Access displays information about fields or properties. The contents of this box change as you move from one location to another within the Table window.

Defining fields

Now you're ready to begin defining the fields for the Companies table that mimics the one you can find in the Conrad Systems Contacts sample database (Contacts.accdb). Be sure the insertion point is in the first row of the Field Name column, and then type the name of the first field, **CompanyID**. Press Tab once to move to the Data Type column. A button with an arrow appears on the right side of the Data Type column. Here and elsewhere in Access, this type of button signifies the presence of a list. Click the arrow or press Alt+Down Arrow to open the list of data type options, shown in Figure 10-18. In the Data Type column, you can either type a valid value or select from the values in the list. Select AutoNumber as the data type for CompanyID.

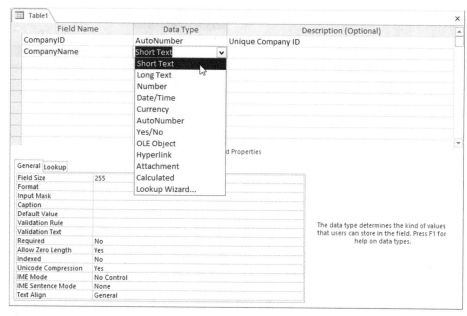

Figure 10-18 You can choose the data type of a field from a list of data type options.

In the Description column for each field, you can enter a descriptive phrase. Access displays this description on the status bar (at the bottom of the Access window) whenever you select this field in a query in Datasheet view or in a form in Form view or Datasheet view. For example, enter **Unique Company ID** in the Description column for the CompanyID field.

INSIDE OUT   Why setting the Description property is important

Entering a Description property for every field in your table helps document your application. Because Access also displays the description on the status bar, paying careful attention to what you type in the Description field can later pay big dividends as a kind of mini-help for the users of your database.

Tab down to the next line, enter **CompanyName** as a field name, and then choose Short Text as the data type. After you select a data type, Access displays some property boxes in the Field Properties section in the lower part of the Table window. These boxes allow you to set *properties*—settings that determine how Access handles the field—and thereby customize a field. The properties Access displays depend on the data type you select; the properties appear with some default values in place, as shown in Figure 10-18.

For details about the values for each property, see "Setting field properties," later in this chapter.

Choosing field names

Access gives you lots of flexibility when it comes to naming your fields in desktop databases. A field name can be up to 64 characters long, can include any combination of letters, numbers, spaces, and special characters except a period (.), an exclamation point (!), an accent grave (`), and brackets ([ ]); however, the name cannot begin with a space and cannot include control characters (ANSI values 0 through 31). In general, you should give your fields meaningful names and should use the same name throughout for a field that occurs in more than one table. You should avoid using field names that might also match any name internal to Access or Microsoft Visual Basic. For example, all objects have a Name property, so it's a good idea to qualify a field containing a name by calling it CustomerName or CompanyName. You should also avoid names that are the same as built-in functions, such as Date, Time, Now, or Space. See Access Help for a list of all the built-in function names.

Although you can use spaces anywhere within names in Access, you should try to create field names and table names *without* embedded spaces. Many Structured Query Language (SQL) databases to which Access can link (notably Oracle and Ingres) do not support spaces within names. Although Microsoft SQL Server does allow spaces in names, you must enclose such names in brackets, or use quotes and execute a Set Quoted Identifier On command. If you ever want to move your application to a client/server environment and store your data in a SQL database such as SQL Server or Oracle, you'll most likely have to change any names in your database tables that have an embedded space character. As you'll learn later in this book, table field names propagate into the queries, forms, and reports that you design using these tables. So any name you decide to change later in a table must also be changed in all your queries, forms, and reports.

If you use reserved words or function names for field names, Access catches most of these and displays a warning message. This message warns you that the field name you chose, such as Name or Date, is a reserved word and that you could encounter errors when referring to that field in other areas of the database application. Access still allows you to use this name if you choose, but take note of the problems it could cause. To avoid potential conflicts, I recommend that you avoid using reserved words and built-in functions for field names.

Understanding field data types

Access 2013 supports 11 types of data, each with a specific purpose. You can see the details about each data type in Table 10-1. Access also gives you a 12th option, Lookup Wizard, to help you define the characteristics of foreign key fields that link to other tables. You learned how to use the Lookup Wizard when you created tables in web apps earlier in this book.

TABLE 10-1 Access data types

Data Type	Usage	Size
Short Text	Alphanumeric data.	Up to 255 characters.
Long Text	Alphanumeric data—sentences and paragraphs.	Up to about 1 gigabyte (GB), but controls to display a Long Text are limited to the first 64,000 characters.
Number	Numeric data.	1, 2, 4, 8, or 16 bytes.
Date/Time	Dates and times.	8 bytes.
Currency	Monetary data, stored with 4 decimal places of precision.	8 bytes.
AutoNumber	Unique value generated by Access for each new record.	4 bytes (16 bytes for ReplicationID).
Yes/No	Boolean (true/false) data; Access stores the numeric value zero (0) for false, and -1 for true.	1 byte.
OLE Object	Pictures, graphs, or other ActiveX objects from another Windows-based application.	Up to about 2 GB.
Hyperlink	A link "address" to a document or file on the Internet, on an intranet, on a local area network (LAN), or on your local computer	Up to 8,192 (each part of a Hyperlink data type can contain up to 2048 characters).
Attachment	You can attach files such as pictures, documents, spreadsheets, or charts; each Attachment field can contain an unlimited number of attachments per record, up to the storage limit of the size of a database file.	Up to about 2 GB.
Calculated	You can create an expression that uses data from one or more fields. You can designate different result data types from the expression.	Dependent on the data type of the Result Type property. Short Text data type result can have up to 243 characters. Long Text, Number, Yes/No, and Date/Time should match their respective data types.
Lookup Wizard	The Lookup Wizard entry in the Data Type column in Design view is not actually a data type. When you choose this entry, a wizard starts to help you define either a simple or complex lookup field. A simple lookup field uses the contents of another table or a value list to validate the contents of a single value per row. A complex lookup field allows you to store multiple values of the same data type in each row.	Dependent on the data type of the lookup field.

For each field in your table, select the data type that is best suited to how you will use that field's data. For character data, you should normally select the Short Text data type. You can control the maximum length of a Short Text field by using a field property, as explained later. Use the Long Text data type only for long strings of text that might exceed 255 characters or that might contain formatting characters such as tabs or line endings (carriage returns).

When you select the Number data type, you should think carefully about what you enter as the Field Size property because this property choice will affect precision as well as length. (For example, integer numbers do not have decimals.) The Date/Time data type is useful for calendar or clock data and has the added benefit of allowing calculations in seconds, minutes, hours, days, months, or years. For example, you can find out the difference in days between two Date/Time values.

INSIDE OUT   Understanding what's inside the Date/Time data type

Use the Date/Time data type to store any date, time, or date and time value. It's useful to know that Access stores the date as the integer portion of the Date/Time data type and the time as the fractional portion—the fraction of a day, measured from midnight, that the time represents, accurate to seconds. For example, 6:00:00 A.M. internally is 0.25. The day number is actually the number of days since December 30, 1899 (there will be a test on that later!) and can be a negative number for dates prior to that date. When two Date/Time fields contain only a date, you can subtract one from the other to find out how many days are between the two dates.

You should generally use the Currency data type for storing money values. Currency has the precision of integers, but with exactly four decimal places. When you need to store a precise fractional number that's not money, use the Number data type and choose Decimal for the Field Size property.

The AutoNumber data type is specifically designed for automatic generation of primary key values. Depending on the settings for the Field Size and New Values properties you choose for an AutoNumber field, you can have Access create a sequential or random long integer. You can include only one field using the AutoNumber data type in any table. If you define more than one AutoNumber field, Access displays an error message when you try to save the table.

Use the Yes/No data type to hold Boolean (true or false) values. This data type is particularly useful for flagging accounts paid or not paid, or orders filled or not filled.

Chapter 10

The OLE Object data type allows you to store complex data, such as pictures, graphs, or sounds, which can be edited or displayed through a dynamic link to another Windows-based application. For example, Access can store and allow you to edit a Microsoft Word document, a Microsoft Excel spreadsheet, a Microsoft PowerPoint presentation slide, a sound file (.wav), a video file (.avi), or pictures created using the Paint application.

The Hyperlink data type lets you store a simple or complex "link" to an external file or document. (Internally, Hyperlink is a Long Text data type with a special flag set to indicate that it is a link.) This link can contain a Uniform Resource Locator (URL) that points to a location on the World Wide Web or on a local intranet. It can also contain the Universal Naming Convention (UNC) name of a file on a server on your LAN or on your local computer drives. The link can point to a file that is in Hypertext Markup Language (HTML) or in a format that is supported by an ActiveX application on your computer.

The Attachment data type is very similar to the OLE Object data type in that you can use it to store complex data. However, unlike the OLE Object data type, you can store *multiple* attachments in a single record. These files are stored in a binary field in a hidden system table. OLE objects usually result in database bloat because the files are not compressed, and Access also stores a bitmap thumbnail of the embedded file that can often be larger than the original file. For the Attachment data type, Access compresses each file, if it isn't already, and uses the original file rather than a generated thumbnail to minimize the amount of database bloat.

The Calculated data type allows you to create a calculated result using an expression. The expression can include data from one or more fields. For example, if you have a number field that holds quantity information for products purchased and a currency field that holds the price of a product, you can create a calculated field that multiplies the quantity and price fields and stores it with a result type of currency. You could also create a calculated field that concatenates first name, middle name, and last name fields and stores it with a result type of short text for a field called Full Name. Access recalculates the value of the calculated field any time the dependent fields are changed.

CAUTION!

You can use the Attachment and Calculated data types only with databases in the .accdb file type. If you plan to create a database in the older .mdb format and have users with previous versions of Access use this database, you cannot define any fields as Attachment or Calculated.

Setting field properties

You can customize the way Access stores and handles each field in desktop databases by setting specific properties. These properties vary according to the data type you choose. Table 10-2 lists all the possible properties that can appear on a field's General tab in a table's Design view for desktop databases, and the data types that are associated with each property.

TABLE 10-2 Field properties on the General tab

Property	Data Type	Options, Description
Field Size	Short Text	Text can be from 0 through 255 characters long, with a default length of 255 characters.
	Number	**Byte**. A 1-byte integer containing values from 0 through 255.
		Integer. A 2-byte integer containing values from -32,768 through +32,767.
		Long Integer. A 4-byte integer containing values from -2,147,483,648 through +2,147,483,647.
		Single.[1] A 4-byte floating-point number containing values from -3.4×10^{38} through $+3.4 \times 10^{38}$ and up to 7 significant digits.
		Double.[1] An 8-byte floating-point number containing values from -1.797×10^{308} through $+1.797 \times 10^{308}$ and up to 15 significant digits.
		Replication ID.[2] A 16-byte globally unique identifier (GUID).
		Decimal. A 12-byte integer with a defined decimal precision that can contain values from approximately -7.9228×10^{28} through $+7.9228 \times 10^{28}$. The default precision (number of decimal places) is 0, and the default scale is 18.
New Values	AutoNumber only	**Increment**. Values start at 1 and increment by 1 for each new row.
		Random. Access assigns a random long integer value to each new row.

Property	Data Type	Options, Description
Format	Short Text, Long Text	You can specify a custom format that controls how Access displays the data.
	Number (except Replication ID), Currency, AutoNumber	**General Number (default)**. No commas or currency symbols; the number of decimal places shown depends on the precision of the data.
		Currency.[3] Currency symbol (from Regional And Language Options in Windows Control Panel) and two decimal places.
		Euro. Euro currency symbol (regardless of Control Panel settings) and two decimal places.
		Fixed. At least one digit and two decimal places.
		Standard. Two decimal places and separator commas.
		Percent. Moves displayed decimal point two places to the right and appends a percentage (%) symbol.
		Scientific. Scientific notation (for example, 1.05E+06 represents 1.05×10^6).
		You can specify a custom format that controls how Access displays the data.
	Date/Time[4]	**General Date (default)**. Combines Short Date and Long Time formats (for example, 7/1/2013 5:30:10 PM).
		Long Date. Uses Long Date Style from the Regional And Language Options item in Control Panel (for example, Monday, July 1, 2013).
		Medium Date. 1-Jul-2013.
		Short Date.[5] Uses Short Date Style from the Regional And Language Options item (for example, 7/1/2013).
		Long Time. Uses Time Style from the Regional And Language Options item (for example, 5:30:10 PM).
		Medium Time. 5:30 PM.
		Short Time. 17:30.
	Yes/No	**Yes/No (default)**
		True/False
		On/Off
		You can specify a custom format that controls how Access displays the data.

Property	Data Type	Options, Description
	Calculated	Format options for calculated fields depend on the Result Type. The format options and defaults for the Result Type align with the other data types.
Precision	Number, Decimal	You can specify the maximum number of digits allowed. The default value is 18, and you can specify an integer value between 1 and 28.
Scale	Number, Decimal	You can specify the number of digits stored to the right of the decimal point. This value must be less than or equal to the value of the Precision property.
Decimal Places	Number (except Replication ID), Currency, Calculated	You can specify the number of decimal places that Access displays. The default specification is Auto, which causes Access to display two decimal places for the Currency, Fixed, Standard, and Percent formats and the number of decimal places necessary to show the current precision of the numeric value for General Number format. You can also request a fixed display of decimal places ranging from 0 through 15.
Input Mask	Short Text, Number (except Replication ID), Date/ Time, Currency	You can specify an editing mask that the user sees while entering data in the field. For example, you can have Access provide the delimiters in a date field, such as __/__/__, or you can have Access format a U.S. phone number as (###) 000-0000. See "Defining input masks," later in this chapter, for details.
Caption	All	You can enter a more fully descriptive field name that Access displays in form labels and in report headings. (Tip: If you create field names with no embedded spaces, you can use the Caption property to specify a name that includes spaces for Access to use in labels and headers associated with this field in queries, forms, and reports.)
Default Value	Short Text, Long Text, Number, Date/Time, Currency, Hyperlink, and Yes/No	You can specify a default value for the field that Access automatically uses for a new row if no other value is supplied. If you don't specify a Default Value, the field will be Null if the user fails to supply a value. (See also the Required property.)

Chapter 10

Property	Data Type	Options, Description
Validation Rule	All (except OLE Object, Replication ID, Attachment, Calculated, and AutoNumber)	You can supply an expression that must be true whenever you enter or change data in this field. For example, **<100** specifies that a number must be less than 100. You can also check for one of a series of values. For example, you can have Access check for a list of valid cities by specifying **"Chicago" OR "New York" OR "San Francisco"**. In addition, you can specify a complex expression that includes any of the built-in functions in Access. See "Defining simple field validation rules," later in this chapter, for details.
Validation Text	All (except OLE Object, Replication ID, Attachment, Calculated, and AutoNumber)	You can specify a custom message that Access displays whenever the data entered does not pass your validation rule.
Required	All (except Calculated and AutoNumber)	If you don't want to allow a Null value in this field, set this property to Yes.
Allow Zero Length	Short Text, Long Text, Hyperlink	You can set the field equal to a zero-length string ("") if you set this property to Yes. See the sidebar "Nulls and zero-length strings," later in this chapter, for more information.
Indexed	All except OLE Object, Calculated, and Attachment.	You can ask that an index be built to speed access to data values. You can also require that the values in the indexed field always be unique for the entire table. See "Adding indexes," later in this chapter, for details.

Property	Data Type	Options, Description
Unicode Compression	Short Text, Long Text, Hyperlink	As of version 2000, Access stores character fields in an .mdb and .accdb file using a double-byte (Unicode) character set to support extended character sets in languages that require them. The Latin character set required by most Western European languages (such as English, Spanish, French, or German) requires only 1 byte per character. When you set Unicode Compression to Yes for character fields, Access stores compressible characters in 1 byte instead of 2, thus saving space in your database file. However, Access will not compress Long Text or Hyperlink fields that will not compress to fewer than 4,096 bytes. The default for new tables is Yes in all countries where the standard language character set does not require 2 bytes to store all the characters.
IME Mode, IME Sentence Mode	Short Text, Long Text, Hyperlink	On machines with an Asian version of Windows and appropriate Input Method Editor (IME) installed, these properties control conversion of characters in kanji, hiragana, katakana, and hangul character sets.
Text Align	All data types except Attachment	**General (default)**. Text aligns to the left, but numbers and dates align to the right.
		Left. All data aligns to the left.
		Center. All data aligns to the center of the field.
		Right. All data aligns to the right.
		Distribute. The data is evenly distributed throughout the field.
Text Format	Long Text only	**Plain Text (default)**. The text in the Long Text field is stored and displayed as plain text.
		Rich Text. You can specify that the data in the Long Text field can be formatted as rich text. Access applies HTML formatting tags to your data.
Append Only	Hyperlink and Long Text	You can specify to see column history for this field. When you change the field's data, the data change and time stamp are recorded and appended to the version history of the field.

Chapter 10

Property	Data Type	Options, Description
Show Date Picker	Date/Time only	**For Dates (default)**. Displays the built-in date picker control to select a date when the field receives focus in a table datasheet or query.
		Never. The built-in date picker control is not shown when the field receives focus in a table datasheet or query.
Expression	Calculated	The expression used to calculate the value for this column. The expression can use the value of one or more fields in the same table and can be up to 65,000 characters in length.
Result Type	Calculated	For calculated fields, you need to provide the data type that results from the expression you use for the field. The result type can be Double, Integer, Long Integer, Single, Replication ID, Decimal, Short Text, Date/Time, Long Text, Currency, or Yes/No.

1 Single and Double field sizes use an internal storage format called floating point, which can handle very large or very small numbers, but it is somewhat imprecise. If the number you need to store contains more than 7 significant digits for a Single or more than 15 significant digits for a Double, the number will be rounded. For example, if you try to save 10,234,567 in a Single, the actual value stored will be 10,234,570. Likewise, Access stores 10.234567 as 10.23457 in a Single. If you want absolute fractional precision, use Decimal field size instead.

2 In general, you should use the Replication ID field size only in an Access 2003 format and earlier database that is managed by the Replication Manager.

3 Note that Currency, Euro, Fixed, and Standard formats always display two decimal places regardless of the number of actual decimal places in the underlying data. Access rounds any number to two decimal places for display if the number contains more than two decimal places.

4 You can also specify a custom format in addition to the built-in ones described here. See Chapter 17, "Customizing a form," for details.

5 To help alleviate problems with dates spanning the start of the century, I recommend that you select the Use Four-Digit Year Formatting check box in Access. To do this, click the File tab on the Backstage view, click Options, and then scroll to the General section in the Client Settings category to find this option. You should also be sure that your Short Date Style in the Regional And Language Options dialog box uses a four-digit year. (This is the default in Windows 7 and Windows 8; you can double-check your settings by accessing Regional And Language Options in Control Panel.)

INSIDE OUT   Don't specify a validation rule without validation text

If you specify a validation rule but no validation text, Access generates an ugly and cryptic message that your users might not understand:

"One or more values are prohibited by the validation rule '*<your expression here>*' set for '*<table name.field name>*'. Enter a value that the expression for this field can accept."

Unless you like getting lots of support calls, I recommend that you always enter a custom validation text message whenever you specify a validation rule.

Nulls and zero-length strings

Relational databases support a special value in fields, called a Null, that indicates an unknown value. In contrast, you can set Short Text and Long Text fields to a zero-length string to indicate that the value of a field is known but the field is empty.

Why is it important to differentiate Nulls (unknown values) from zero-length strings? Here's an example: Suppose you have a database that stores the results of a survey about automobile preferences. For questionnaires on which there is no response to a color-preference question, it is appropriate to store a Null. You don't want to match responses based on an unknown response, and you don't want to include the row in calculating totals or averages. However, some people might have responded "I don't care" for a color preference. In this case, you have a known "no preference" answer, and a zero-length string is appropriate. You can match all "I don't care" responses and include the responses in totals and averages.

Another example might be fax numbers in a customer database. If you store a Null, it means that you don't know whether the customer has a fax number. If you store a zero-length string, you know the customer has no fax number. Access gives you the flexibility to deal with both types of "empty" values.

You can join tables on zero-length strings, and two zero-length strings will compare to be equal. However, for Short Text, Long Text, and Hyperlink fields, you must set the Allow Zero Length property to Yes to allow users to enter zero-length strings. Otherwise, Access converts a zero-length or all-blank string to a Null before storing the value. If you also set the Required property of the Short Text field to Yes, Access stores a zero-length string if the user enters either "" (two double quotes with no space) or blanks in the field.

Nulls have special properties. A Null value cannot be equal to any other value, not even to another Null. This means that you cannot join (link) two tables on Null values. Also, the question "Is A equal to B?" when A, B, or both A and B contain a Null, can never be answered "Yes." The answer, literally, is "I don't know." Likewise, the answer to the question "Is A not equal to B?" is also "I don't know." Finally, Null values do not participate in aggregate calculations involving such functions as Sum or Avg. You can test a value to determine whether it is a Null by comparing it to the special keyword NULL or by using the IsNull built-in function.

Chapter 10

Completing the fields in the Companies table

You now know enough about field data types and properties to finish designing the Companies table in this example. (You can also follow this example using the tblCompanies table from the Conrad Systems Contacts sample database.) Use the information listed in Table 10-3 to design the table shown in Figure 10-19.

TABLE 10-3   Field definitions for the Companies table

Field Name	Data Type	Description	Field Size
CompanyID	AutoNumber	Unique Company ID	
CompanyName	Short Text	Company Name	50
Department	Short Text	Department	50
Address	Short Text	Address	255
City	Short Text	City	50
County	Short Text	County	50
StateOrProvince	Short Text	State or Province	20
PostalCode	Short Text	Postal/Zip Code	10
PhoneNumber	Short Text	Phone Number	15
FaxNumber	Short Text	Fax Number	15
Website	Hyperlink	Website address	
ReferredBy	Number	Contact who referred this company	Long Integer

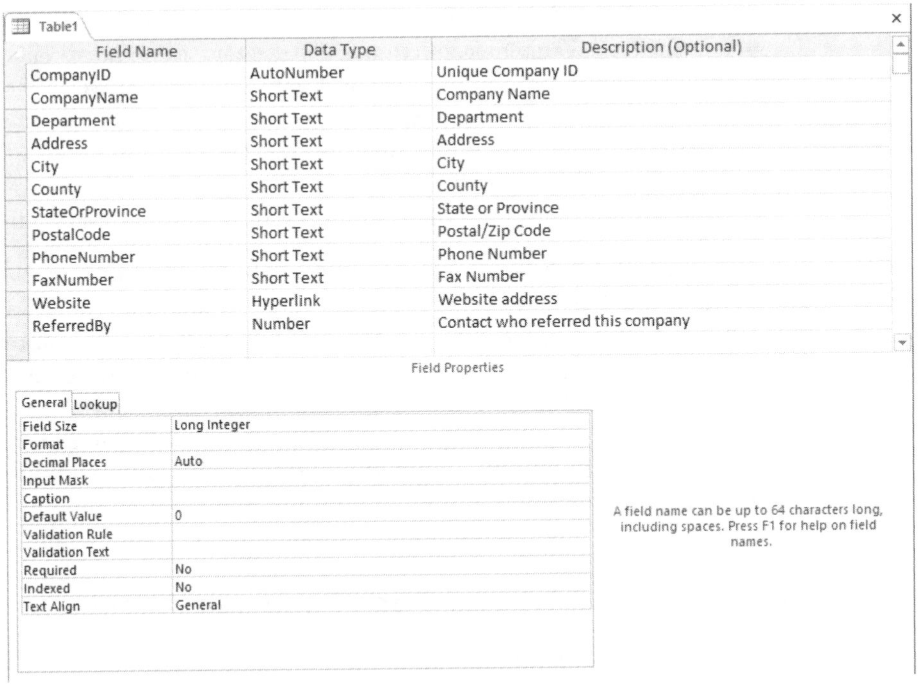

Figure 10-19 Your fields in the Companies table should look like this. You'll learn how to define validation rules in the next section.

Defining simple field validation rules

To define a simple check on the values that you allow in a field, enter an expression in the Validation Rule property box for the field. Access won't allow you to enter a field value that violates this rule. Access performs this validation for data entered in a Table window in Datasheet view, in an updatable query, or in a form. You can specify a more restrictive validation rule in a form, but you cannot override the rule defined for the field in the table by specifying a completely different rule in the form.

In general, a field validation expression consists of an operator and a comparison value. If you do not include an operator, Access assumes that you want an "equals" (=) comparison. You can specify multiple comparisons separated by the Boolean operators OR and AND.

It is good practice to always enclose text string values in quotation marks. If one of your values is a text string containing blanks or special characters, you must enclose the entire string in quotation marks. For example, to limit the valid entries for a City field to the two largest cities in the state of California, enter **"Los Angeles" OR "San Diego"**. If you are comparing date values, you must enclose the date constants in pound sign (#) characters, as in #07/1/2013#.

You can use the comparison symbols to compare the value in the field to a value or values in your validation rule. Comparison symbols are summarized in Table 10-4. For example, you might want to ensure that a numeric value is always less than 1000. To do this, enter **<1000**. You can use one or more pairs of comparisons to ask Access to check that the value falls within certain ranges. For example, if you want to verify that a number is in the range of 50 through 100, enter either **>=50 AND <=100** or **Between 50 AND 100**. Another way to test for a match in a list of values is to use the IN comparison operator. For example, to test for states surrounding the U.S. capital, enter **In ("Virginia", "Maryland")**. If all you need to do is ensure that the user enters a value, you can enter the special comparison phrase **Is Not Null**.

TABLE 10-4   Comparison symbols used in validation rules

Operator	Meaning
NOT	Use before any comparison operator except IS NOT NULL to perform the converse test. For example, NOT > 5 is equivalent to <=5.
<	Less than.
<=	Less than or equal to.
>	Greater than.
>=	Greater than or equal to.
=	Equal to.
<>	Not equal to.

Operator	Meaning
IN	Test for equal to any member in a list; comparison value must be a comma-separated list enclosed in parentheses.
BETWEEN	Test for a range of values; comparison value must be two values (a low and a high value) separated by the AND operator.
LIKE	Test a Text or Memo field to match a pattern string.
IS NOT NULL	Requires the user to enter a value in the field.

INSIDE OUT   A friendlier way to require a field value

When you set the Required property to Yes and the user fails to enter a value, Access displays an unfriendly message:

"You must enter a value in the '<*tablename.fieldname*>' field."

I recommend that you use the Validation Rule property to require a value in the field and then use the Validation Text property to generate your own specific message.

If you need to validate a Short Text, Long Text, or Hyperlink field against a matching pattern (for example, a postal code or a phone number), you can use the LIKE comparison operator. You provide a text string as a comparison value that defines which characters are valid in which positions. Access understands a number of *wildcard characters*, which you can use to define positions that can contain any single character, zero or more characters, or any single number. These characters are shown in Table 10-5.

TABLE 10-5   LIKE wildcard characters

Character	Meaning
?	Any single character
*	Zero or more characters; use to define leading, trailing, or embedded strings that don't have to match any specific pattern characters
#	Any single digit

You can also specify that any particular position in the Short Text or Long Text field can contain only characters from a list that you provide. You can specify a range of characters within a list by entering the low value character, a hyphen, and the high value character, as in [A-Z] or [3-7]. If you want to test a position for any characters *except* those in a list, start the list with an exclamation point (!). You must enclose all lists in brackets ([ ]). The following table shows examples of validation rules using LIKE.

Validation Rule	Tests For
LIKE "#####" or	A U.S. 5-digit ZIP Code
LIKE "#####-####"	A U.S. 9-digit ZIP+ Code
LIKE "[A-Z]#[A-Z] #[A-Z]#"	A Canadian postal code
LIKE "###-##-####"	A U.S. Social Security Number
LIKE "Smith*"	A string that begins with Smith[1]
LIKE "*smith##*"	A string that contains smith followed by two numbers, anywhere in the string
LIKE "??00####"	An eight-character string that contains any first two characters followed by exactly two zeros and then any four digits
LIKE "[!0-9BMQ]*####"	A string that contains any character other than a number or the letter B, M, or Q in the first position and ends with exactly four digits

1 Character string comparisons in Access are case-insensitive. Therefore, smith, SMITH, and Smith are all equal.

Defining input masks

To assist you in entering formatted data in a desktop database, Access allows you to define an input mask for Text, Number (except Replication ID), Date/Time, and Currency data types. You can use an input mask to do something as simple as forcing all letters entered to be uppercase or as complex as adding parentheses and hyphens to phone numbers. You create an input mask by using the special mask definition characters shown in Table 10-6. You can also embed strings of characters that you want to display for formatting or store in the data field.

TABLE 10-6   Input mask definition characters

Mask Character	Meaning
0	A single digit must be entered in this position.
9	A digit or a space can be entered in this position. If the user skips this position by moving the insertion point past the position without entering anything, Access stores nothing in this position.
#	A digit, a space, or a plus or minus sign can be entered in this position. If the user skips this position by moving the insertion point past the position without entering anything, Access stores a space.
L	A letter must be entered in this position.
?	A letter can be entered in this position. If the user skips this position by moving the insertion point past the position without entering anything, Access stores nothing.

Mask Character	Meaning
A	A letter or a digit must be entered in this position.
a	A letter or a digit can be entered in this position. If the user skips this position by moving the insertion point past the position without entering anything, Access stores nothing.
&	A character or a space must be entered in this position.
C	Any character or a space can be entered in this position. If the user skips this position by moving the insertion point past the position without entering anything, Access stores nothing.
.	Decimal placeholder (depends on the setting in the Regional And Language Options item in Control Panel).
,	Thousands separator (depends on the setting in the Regional And Language Options item in Control Panel).
: ; - /	Date and time separators (depends on the settings in the Regional And Language Options item in Control Panel).
<	Converts to lowercase all characters that follow.
>	Converts to uppercase all characters that follow.
!	Causes the mask to fill from right to left when you define optional characters on the left end of the mask. You can place this character anywhere in the mask.
\	Causes the character immediately following to be displayed as a literal character rather than as a mask character.
"literal"	You can also enclose any literal string in double quotation marks rather than use the \ character repeatedly.

An input mask consists of three parts, separated by semicolons. The first part defines the mask string using mask definition characters and embedded literal data. The optional second part indicates whether you want the embedded literal characters stored in the field in the database. Set this second part to **0** to store the characters or to **1** to store only the data entered. The optional third part defines a single character that Access uses as a placeholder to indicate positions where data can be entered. The default placeholder character is an underscore (_).

Perhaps the best way to learn to use input masks is to take advantage of the Input Mask Wizard. In the Companies table of the Contact Tracking database you are building, the PhoneNumber field could benefit from the use of an input mask. Click the PhoneNumber field in the upper part of the Table window in Design view, and then click in the Input Mask property box in the lower part of the window. You should see a small button with three dots on it (called the Build button) to the right of the property box.

Build button

Click the Build button to start the Input Mask Wizard. If you haven't already saved the table, the wizard will insist that you do so. Save the table, and name it **Companies**. When Access warns you that you have not defined a primary key and asks whether you want to create a primary key now, click No. We'll define a primary key in the next section. On the first page, the wizard gives you a number of choices for standard input masks that it can generate for you. In this case, click the first one in the list—Phone Number, as shown in Figure 10-20. You can type something in the Try It box below the Input Mask list to test the mask.

Figure 10-20 You can choose from several built-in input masks in the Input Mask Wizard.

Click Next to go to the next page. On this page, shown in Figure 10-21, you can see the mask name, the proposed mask string, a list from which you select the placeholder character, and another Try It box. The default underscore character (_) works well as a placeholder character for phone numbers.

Chapter 10

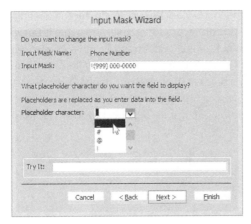

Figure 10-21 You can choose the placeholder character in the Input Mask Wizard.

Click Next to go to the next page, where you can choose whether you want the data stored without the formatting characters (the default) or stored with the parentheses, spaces, and hyphen separator. In Figure 10-22, I'm indicating that we want the data stored with the formatting characters. Click Next to go to the final page, and then click the Finish button on that page to store the mask in the property setting. Figure 10-23 shows the resulting mask in the PhoneNumber field. You'll find this same mask handy for any text field that is meant to contain a U.S. phone number (such as the phone number fields in the Contacts table).

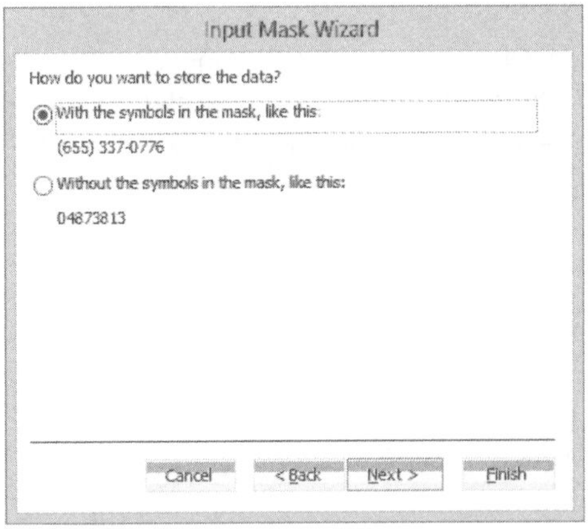

Figure 10-22 You can choose to store formatting characters.

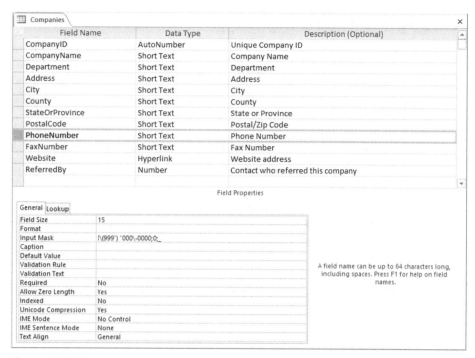

Figure 10-23 The wizard stores the input mask for the PhoneNumber field based on the criteria you selected.

Note

If you look closely at Figure 10-23, you can see a backslash before the area code and quotation marks around the second parenthesis. When you complete the Input Mask Wizard, Access initially does not display these extra characters. After you click off that field or save the table, Access adds the missing characters. The mask generated by the wizard is incorrect, but the table editor fixes it before saving.

CAUTION

Although an input mask can be very useful to help guide the user to enter valid data, if you define an input mask incorrectly or do not consider all possible valid values, you can prevent the user from entering necessary data. For example, I just showed you how to build an input mask for a U.S. telephone number, but that mask would prevent someone from entering a European phone number correctly.

Defining a primary key

Every table in a relational database should have a primary key. Telling Access how to define the primary key is quite simple. Open the table in Design view, and click the row selector to the left of the field you want to use as the primary key. If you need to select multiple fields for your primary key, hold down the Ctrl key and click the row selector of each additional field that you need.

For details about designing primary keys for your tables, see Article 1, "Designing your database application," which you can download from the book's catalog page.

After you select all the fields you want for the primary key, click the Primary Key button in the Tools group of the Design contextual tab on the ribbon. Access displays a key symbol to the left of the selected field(s) to acknowledge your definition of the primary key. To eliminate all primary key designations, see "Adding indexes," later in this chapter. When you've finished creating the Companies table for the Contact Tracking database, the primary key should be the CompanyID field, as shown in Figure 10-24. Be sure to click the Save button on the Quick Access Toolbar to save this latest change to your table definition, and then close the table.

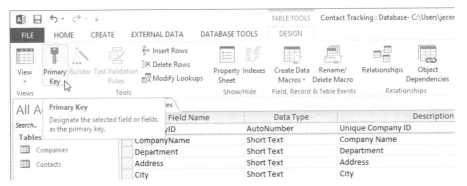

Figure 10-24 You can define the primary key for the Companies table easily by selecting the field in Design view and clicking the Primary Key button on the ribbon.

Defining a table validation rule

The last detail to define is any validation rules that you want Access to apply to any fields in the table. Although field validation rules get checked as you enter each new value, Access checks a table validation rule only when you save or add a row. Table validation rules are handy when the values in one field depend on what's stored in another field. You need to wait until the entire row is about to be saved before checking one field against another.

One of the tables in the Contact Tracking database—Products—needs a table validation rule. Define that table now using the specifications in Table 10-7. Be sure to define ProductID as the primary key, and then save the table and name it **Products**.

TABLE 10-7   Field definitions for the Products table

Field Name	Data Type	Description	Field Size
ProductID	AutoNumber	Unique product identifier	
ProductName	Short Text	Product description	100
CategoryDescription	Short Text	Description of the category	50
UnitPrice	Currency	Price	
TrialVersion	Yes/No	Is this a trial version?	
TrialExpire	Number	If trial version, number of days before expiration	Long Integer

To define a table validation rule, be sure that the table is in Design view, and then click the Property Sheet button in the Show/Hide group of the Design contextual tab on the ribbon, shown in Figure 10-25.

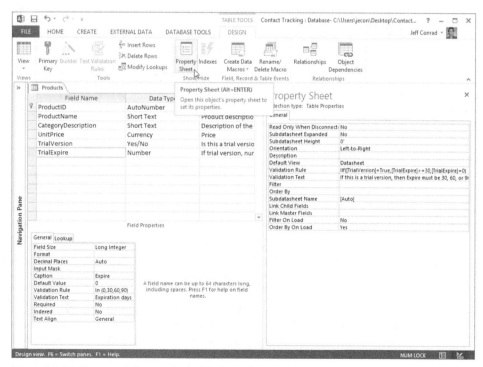

Figure 10-25 You can define a table validation rule in the property sheet for the table.

On the Validation Rule line in the table's property sheet, you can enter any valid comparison expression, or you can use one of the built-in functions to test your table's field values. In the Products table, we want to be sure that any trial version of the software expires in 30, 60, or 90 days. Zero is also a valid value if this particular product isn't a trial version. As you can see in Figure 10-25, I've already entered a *field* validation rule for TrialExpire on the General tab to make sure that the TrialExpire value is always 0, 30, 60, or 90—IN (0, 30, 60, 90). But how do we make sure that TrialExpire is zero if TrialVersion is False, or one of the other values if TrialVersion is True? For that, we need to define a *table-level* validation rule in the table's property sheet.

To refer to a field name, enclose the name in brackets ([ ]), as shown in Figure 10-25. You'll use this technique whenever you refer to the name of an object anywhere in an expression. In this case, I'm using a special built-in function called Immediate If (or IIF for short) in the table validation rule to perform the test on the TrialExpire and TrialVersion fields. The IIF function can evaluate a test in the first argument and then return the evaluation of the second argument if the first argument is true or the evaluation of the third argument if the first argument is false. As you will learn in Chapter 24, "Understanding Visual Basic fundamentals," which you can download from the book's catalog page, you must separate the arguments in a function call with commas. Note that I said *evaluation of the argument*—this means that we can enter additional tests, even another IIF, in the second and third arguments.

In the Products table, you want to make sure that the TrialVersion and TrialExpire fields are in sync with each other. If this is not a trial version, the TrialExpire field value should be zero (indicating that the product never expires), and if it is a trial version, TrialExpire must be set to some value greater than or equal to 30. The expression I used to accomplish this is as follows:

```
IIf([TrialVersion]=True,[TrialExpire]>=30,[TrialExpire]=0)
```

Therefore, the first argument uses IIF to evaluate the expression `[TrialVersion] = True`—is the value in the field named TrialVersion True? If this is true (this is a trial version that must have a nonzero number of expiration days), IIF returns the evaluation of the second argument. If this is not a trial version, IIF evaluates the third argument. Now all we need to do is type the appropriate test based on the true or false result on TrialVersion. If this is a trial version, the TrialExpire field must be 30 or greater (we'll let the field validation rule make sure it's exactly 30, 60, or 90), so we need to test for that by entering **[TrialExpire] >= 30** in the second argument. If this is not a trial version, we need to make sure TrialExpire is zero by entering **[TrialExpire] = 0** in the third argument. If TrialVersion is True, then `[TrialExpire] >= 30` must be true or the validation rule will fail. If TrialVersion is False, then `[TrialExpire] = 0` must be True. As you might imagine, when you become more familiar with building expressions and with the available built-in functions, you can create very sophisticated table validation rules.

On the Validation Text line of the table's property sheet, enter the text that you want Access to display whenever the table validation rule is violated. You should be careful to word this message so that the user clearly understands what is wrong. If you enter a table validation rule and fail to specify validation text, Access displays the following message when the user enters invalid data: "One or more values are prohibited by the validation rule '< *your vali-dation rule expression here* >' set for '<*table name*>'. Enter a value that the expression for this field can accept."

Understanding other table properties

As you can see in Figure 10-25, shown previously, Access provides several additional table properties that you can set in Design view. You can enter a description of the table in the Description property, and you'll see this description in the Navigation pane if you choose to view objects by Details. Access defines Datasheet as the Default View property.

The Filter property lets you predefine criteria to limit the data displayed in the Datasheet view of this table. If you set Filter On Load to Yes, Access applies the filter that you defined when you open the datasheet. You can use Order By to define one or more fields that define the default display sequence of rows in this table when in Datasheet view. If you don't define an Order By property, Access displays the rows in primary key sequence. You can set the Order By On Load property to Yes to request that Access always applies any Order By specification when opening the datasheet.

> **Note**
>
> If you apply a filter or specify a sorting sequence when you have the table open in Datasheet view, Access saves the filter in the Filter property and the sorting sequence in the Order By property. If you have Filter On Load or Order By On Load set to Yes, Access reapplies the previous filter or sort sequence criteria the next time you open the datasheet.

You can find five properties—Subdatasheet Name, Link Child Fields, Link Master Fields, Subdatasheet Height, and Subdatasheet Expanded—that are all related. The subdatasheet feature lets you see information from related tables when you view the datasheet of a table. For example, in the Contacts Tracking database you have been building, you can set the Subdatasheet properties in the definition of Contacts to also show you related information from ContactEvents or ContactProducts. In the Proseware Housing Reservations sample desktop database, you can see Departments and their Employees, or Employees and their Reservation Requests. Figure 10-26 shows you the Departments table in the Housing.accdb file open in Datasheet view. (You can find this sample in the Housing subfolder where you installed the sample files.) For this table, I defined a subdatasheet to show related employee information for each department.

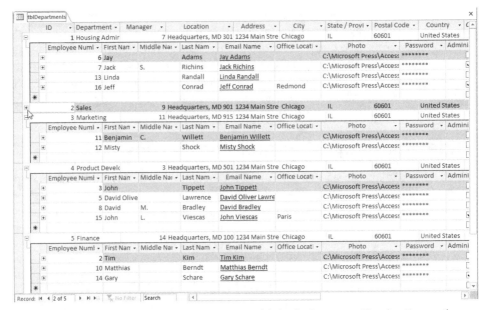

Figure 10-26 The datasheet for the Departments table in the Proseware Housing Reservations sample desktop database shows an expanded subdatasheet.

Notice the small plus and minus signs at the beginning of each department row. Click a plus sign to expand the subdatasheet to show related employees. Click the minus sign to shrink the subdatasheet and show only department information. Table 10-8 explains each of the Table Property settings that you can specify to attach a subdatasheet to a table.

TABLE 10-8   Table properties for defining a subdatasheet

Property	Setting	Description
Subdatasheet Name	[Auto]	Creates a subdatasheet using the first table that has a *many* relationship defined with this table.
	[None]	Turns off the subdatasheet feature.
	Table.*name* or Query.*name*	Uses the selected table or query as the subdatasheet.
Link Child Fields	Name(s) of the foreign key fields(s) in the related table, separated by semicolons	Defines the fields in the subdatasheet table or query that match the primary key fields in this table. When you choose a table or query for the Subdatasheet Name property, Access uses an available relationship definition or matching field names and data types to automatically set this property for you. You can correct this setting if Access has guessed wrong.

Property	Setting	Description
Link Master Fields	Name(s) of the primary key field(s) in this table, separated by semicolons	Defines the primary key fields that Access uses to link to the subdatasheet table or query. When you choose a table or query for the Subdatasheet Name property, Access uses an available relationship definition or matching field names and data types to set this property automatically for you. You can correct this setting if Access has guessed wrong.
Subdatasheet Height	A measurement in inches	If you specify zero (the default), each subdatasheet expands to show all available rows when opened. When you specify a nonzero value, the subdatasheet window opens to the height you specify. If the height is insufficient to display all rows, a scroll bar appears to allow you to look at all the rows.
Subdatasheet Expanded	Yes or No	If you specify Yes, all subdatasheets appear expanded when you open the table datasheet. No is the default.

INSIDE OUT   Don't set subdatasheet properties in a table

For a production application, it's a good idea to set Subdatasheet Name in all your tables to [None]. First, when Access opens your table, it must not only fetch the rows from the table but also fetch the rows defined in the subdatasheet. Adding a subdatasheet to a large table can affect performance negatively.

Chapter 10

You can use the Orientation property to specify the reading sequence of the data in Datasheet view. The default in most versions of Access is Left-to-Right. In versions that support a language that is normally read right to left, the default is Right-to-Left. When you use Right-to-Left, field and table captions appear right-justified, the field order is right to left, and the tab sequence proceeds right to left.

The Read Only When Disconnected property by default is set to No, which means that you can still update or add new records to a table that is linked to a Microsoft SharePoint Services site when you are offline.

Defining relationships

After you have defined two or more related tables, you should tell Access how the tables are related. You do this so that Access will be able to link all your tables when you need to use them in queries, forms, or reports.

Thus far in this chapter, you have seen how to build the main subject tables of the Contact Tracking database—Companies, Contacts, and Products. Before we define the relationships in this sample desktop database, you need to create a couple of *linking* tables that define the many-to-many relationships between the Companies and Contacts tables and between the Products and Contacts tables. Table 10-9 shows you the fields you need for the Company Contacts table that forms the "glue" between the Companies and Contacts tables.

TABLE 10-9   Field definitions for the Company Contacts table

Field Name	Data Type	Description	Field Size
CompanyID	Number	Company/organization	Long Integer
ContactID	Number	Person within company	Long Integer
Position	Short Text	Person's position within the company	50
DefaultForContact	Yes/No	Is this the default company for this contact?	

Define the combination of CompanyID and ContactID as the primary key for this table by clicking the selection button next to CompanyID and then holding down the Ctrl key and clicking the button next to ContactID. Click the Primary Key button in the Tools group of the Design tab on the ribbon to define the key, and then save the table as **CompanyContacts**.

Table 10-10 shows you the fields that you need to define the Contact Products table that creates the link between the Contacts and Products tables.

TABLE 10-10   Field definitions for the Contact Products table

Field Name	Data Type	Description	Field Size
CompanyID	Number	Company/organization	Long Integer
ContactID	Number	Related contact	Long Integer
ProductID	Number	Related product	Long Integer
DateSold	Date/Time	Date product sold	
SoldPrice	Currency	Price paid	

The primary key of the Contact Products table is the combination of CompanyID, ContactID, and ProductID. You can click CompanyID to select it and then hold down the Shift key while you click ProductID (if you defined the fields in sequence) to select all three fields. Click the Primary Key button in the Tools group of the Design tab on the ribbon to define the key, and then save the table as **ContactProducts**.

You need one last table, the Contact Events Table, to define all the major tables you'll need for Contact Tracking. Table 10-11 shows the fields you need. The primary key for this table is the combination of ContactID and ContactDateTime. I took advantage of the fact that a Date/Time data type in Access can store both a date and a time, so we don't need the two separate date and time fields. Save this last table as **ContactEvents**.

TABLE 10-11   Field definitions for the Contact Events table

Field Name	Data Type	Description	Field Size
ContactID	Number	Related contact	Long Integer
ContactDateTime	Date/Time	Date and time of the contact	
ContactNotes	Long Text	Description of the contact	
ContactFollowUpDate	Date/Time	Follow-up date	

Now you're ready to start defining relationships. To define relationships, first close any Table windows that are open, and then click the Relationships command in the Relationships group of the Database Tools tab on the ribbon to open the Relationships window. If this is the first time you have defined relationships in this database, Access opens a blank Relationships window and opens the Show Table dialog box, shown in Figure 10-27.

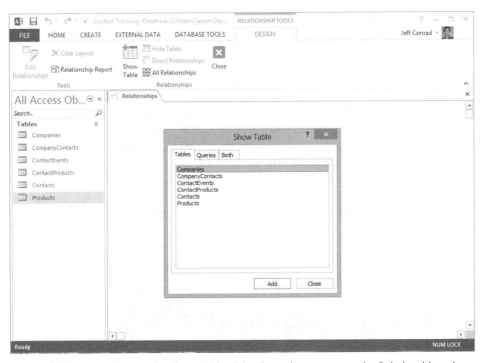

Figure 10-27 Access displays the Show Table dialog box when you open the Relationships window for the first time.

In the Show Table dialog box, select each table and click Add in turn. Click Close to dismiss the Show Table dialog box.

Defining your first relationship

A company can have several contacts, and any contact can belong to several companies or organizations. This means that companies have a many-to-many relationship with contacts. Defining a many-to-many relationship between two tables requires a linking table. Let's link the Companies and Contacts tables by defining the first half of the relationship—the one between Companies and the linking table, CompanyContacts. You can see that for the CompanyID primary key in the Companies table, there is a matching CompanyID foreign key in the CompanyContacts table. To create the relationship you need, click in the CompanyID field in the Companies table and drag it to the CompanyID field in the CompanyContacts table, as shown in Figure 10-28.

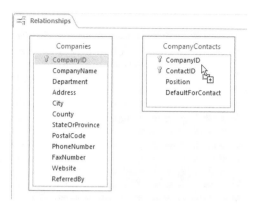

Figure 10-28 Drag the linking field from the "one" table (Companies) to the "many" table (CompanyContacts) to define the relationship between the tables.

You can read about determining the type of relationship between two tables in Article 1, "Designing your database application," which you can download from the book's catalog page.

When you release the mouse button, Access opens the Edit Relationships dialog box, shown in Figure 10-29.

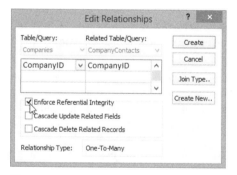

Figure 10-29 The Edit Relationships dialog box lets you specify the linking fields in two tables.

INSIDE OUT   Creating relationships from scratch

You can also click the Edit Relationships command in the Tools group of the Design contextual tab on the ribbon to create a new relationship, but you have to fill in the table and field names yourself. The dragging operation does some of this work for you.

You'll notice that Access has filled in the field names for you. If you need to define a multiple-field relationship between two tables, use the additional blank lines to define those fields. (We'll do that in just a second.) Because you probably don't want any rows created in CompanyContacts for a nonexistent company, select the Enforce Referential Integrity check box. When you do this, Access ensures that you can't add a row in the CompanyContacts table containing an invalid CompanyID. Also, Access won't let you delete any records from the Companies table if they have contacts that are still defined.

After you select the Enforce Referential Integrity check box, Access makes two additional check boxes available: Cascade Update Related Fields and Cascade Delete Related Records. If you select the Cascade Delete Related Records check box, Access deletes child rows (the related rows in the *many* table of a one-to-many relationship) when you delete a parent row (the related row in the *one* table of a one-to-many relationship). For example, if you removed a company from the table, Access would remove the related company contact rows. In this database design, the CompanyID field has the AutoNumber data type, so it cannot be changed after it is set. However, if you build a table with a primary key that is Short Text or Number (perhaps a ProductID field that could change at some point in the future), it might be a good idea to select the Cascade Update Related Fields check box. This option requests that Access automatically update any foreign key values in the *child* table (the *many* table in a one-to-many relationship) if you change a primary key value in a *parent* table (the *one* table in a one-to-many relationship).

You might have noticed that the Show Table dialog box, shown earlier in Figure 10-27, gives you the option to include queries as well as tables. Sometimes you might want to define relationships between tables and queries or between queries so that Access knows how to join them properly. You can also define what's known as an *outer join* by clicking the Join Type button in the Edit Relationships dialog box and selecting an option in the Join Properties dialog box. For example, with an outer join, you can find out which companies have no contacts or which products haven't been sold.

For details about outer joins, see "Using outer joins," in Chapter 13, "Building complex queries."

INSIDE OUT   Avoid defining a relationship with an outer join

I recommend that you do not define an outer join relationship between two tables. As you'll learn in Chapter 13, Access automatically links two tables you include in a query design by using the relationships that you have defined. In the vast majority of cases, you will want to include only the matching rows from both tables. If you define the relationship as an outer join, you will have to change the link between the two tables every time you include them in a query.

I also do not recommend that you define relationships between queries or between a table and a query. If you have done a good job of naming your fields in your tables, the query designer will recognize the natural links and define the joins for you automatically. Defining extra relationships adds unnecessary overhead in your desktop database application

Click the Create button to finish your relationship definition. Access draws a line between the two tables to indicate the relationship. Notice that when you ask Access to enforce referential integrity, Access displays a 1 at the end of the relationship line, next to the one table, and an infinity symbol next to the *many* table. If you want to delete the relationship, click the line and press the Delete key.

You now know enough to define the additional one-to-many simple relationships that you need. Go ahead and define a relationship on ContactID between the Contacts and CompanyContacts tables to complete the other side of the many-to-many relationship between companies and contacts, a relationship on ContactID between the Contacts and ContactEvents tables, and a relationship on ProductID between the Products and ContactProducts tables. For each relationship, be sure to select the Enforce Referential Integrity check box.

Creating a relationship on multiple fields

There's one last relationship you need to define in the Contact Tracking database between CompanyContacts and ContactProducts. The relationship between these two tables requires multiple fields from each table. You can start by dragging the CompanyID field from the CompanyContacts table to the ContactProducts table. Access opens the Edit Relationships dialog box, shown in Figure 10-30.

Chapter 10

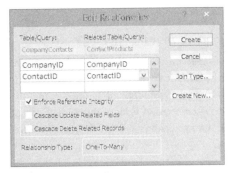

Figure 10-30 Select multiple fields in the Edit Relationships dialog box to define a relationship between two tables using more than one field.

When you first see the Edit Relationships dialog box for the relationship you are defining between CompanyContacts and ContactProducts, Access shows you only the CompanyID field in the two lists. To complete the relationship definition on the combination of CompanyID and ContactID, you must click in the second line under both tables and select ContactID as the second field for both tables, as shown in Figure 10-30. Select the Enforce Referential Integrity check box, as shown, and click Create to define the compound relationship.

Figure 10-31 shows the Relationships window for all the main tables in your Contact Tracking database. Notice that there are two linking lines that define the relationship between CompanyContacts and ContactProducts.

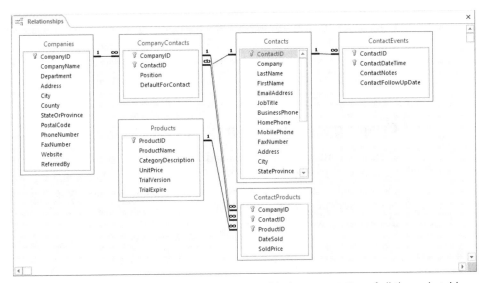

Figure 10-31 The Relationships window shows a graphical representation of all the main tables in your Contact Tracking database.

If you want to edit or change any relationship, double-click the line to open the Edit Relationships dialog box again. If you want to remove a relationship definition, click on the line linking two tables to select the relationship (the line appears highlighted) and press the Delete key. Access presents a warning dialog box in case you are asking it to delete a relationship in error.

After you define a relationship, you can delete the table or query field lists from the Relationships window without affecting the relationships. To do this, click the table or query list header and press the Delete key. This can be particularly advantageous in large databases that have dozens of tables. You can also display only those tables that you're working with at the moment. To see the relationships defined for any particular table or query, include it in the Relationships window by using the Show Table dialog box, and then click the Direct Relationships button in the Relationships group of the Design contextual tab on the ribbon. To redisplay all relationships, click the All Relationships button in the Relationships group.

When you close the Relationships window, Access asks whether you want to save your layout changes. Click Yes to save the relationships you've defined. That's all there is to it. Later, when you use multiple tables in a query in Chapter 12, "Creating and working with simple queries," you'll see that Access builds the links between tables based on these relationships.

INSIDE OUT   Additional features in the Relationships window

You can right-click any table in the Relationships window and then choose Table Design from the shortcut menu to open that table in Design view. You can also click Relationship Report in the Tools group of the Design contextual tab on the ribbon to create a report that prints what you laid out in the window.

Chapter 10

Adding indexes

The more data you include in your tables, the more you need indexes to help Access search your data efficiently. An *index* is simply an internal table that contains two columns: the value in the field or fields being indexed and the physical location of each record in your table that contains that value. Access uses an index similarly to how you use the index in this book—you find the term that you want and jump directly to the pages containing that term. You don't have to leaf through all the pages to find the information you want.

Let's assume that you often search your Contacts table by city. Without an index, when you ask Access to find all the contacts in the city of Chicago, Access has to search every record in your table. This search is fast if your table includes only a few contacts but very slow if the table contains thousands of contact records collected over many years. If you create an index on the City field, Access can use the index to find more rapidly the records for the contacts in the city you specify.

Single-field indexes

Most of the indexes you'll need to define will probably contain the values from only a single field. Access uses this type of index to help narrow the number of records it has to search whenever you provide search criteria on the field—for example, City = Chicago or PostalCode = 60633. If you have defined indexes for multiple fields and provided search criteria for more than one of the fields, Access uses the indexes together to find the rows that you want quickly. For example, if you have created one index on City and another on LastName, and you ask for City = Redmond and LastName = Conrad, Access uses the entries in the City index that equal Redmond and matches those with the entries in the LastName index that equal Conrad. The result is a small set of pointers to the records that match both criteria.

Creating an index on a single field in a table is easy. Open the Contacts table (that you created earlier using an Application Part) in Design view, and select the field for which you want an index—in this case, City. Click the Indexed property box in the lower part of the Table window, and then click the arrow to open the list of choices, as shown in Figure 10-32.

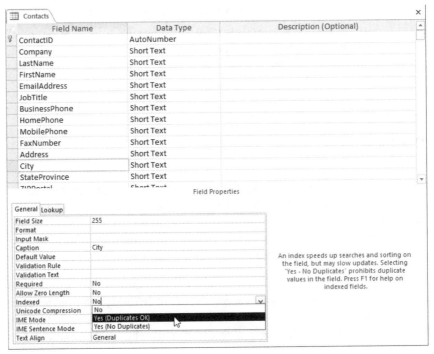

Figure 10-32 You can use the Indexed property box to set an index on a single field.

When you create a table from scratch (as you did earlier in this chapter for the Companies table), the default Indexed property setting for all fields except the primary key is No. If you use an Application Part or a Data Type Part to help create a table (as you did for the Contacts table in this chapter), the Application Part or Data Type Part indexes fields that might benefit from an index. If you followed along earlier using an Application Part to build the Contacts table, you will find that the template built an index only for the ContactID and ZipPostal Code fields. Any tables created using an Application Part or Data Type Part could obviously benefit from some additional indexes.

If you want to set an index for a field, Access offers two possible Yes choices. In most cases, a given field will have multiple records with the same value—perhaps you have multiple contacts in a particular city or multiple products in the same product category. You should select Yes (Duplicates OK) to create an index for this type of field. By selecting Yes (No Duplicates), you can have Access enforce unique values in any field by creating an index that doesn't allow duplicates. Access always defines the primary key index with no duplicates because all primary key values must be unique.

> **Note**
> You cannot define an index using an OLE Object, Attachment, or Calculated field.

Multiple-field indexes

If you often provide multiple criteria in searches against large tables, you might want to consider creating a few multiple-field indexes. This helps Access narrow the search quickly without having to match values from two separate indexes. For example, suppose you often perform a search for contacts by last name and first name. If you create an index that includes both of these fields, Access can satisfy your query more rapidly.

To create a multiple-field index, you must open the Table window in Design view and open the Indexes window by clicking the Indexes button in the Show/Hide group of the Design contextual tab on the ribbon. You can see the primary key index and the index that you defined on City in the previous section as well as the index defined by the Application Part (ZipPostal Code). Each of these indexes comprises exactly one field.

To create a multiple-field index, move the insertion point to an empty row in the Indexes window and type a unique name. In this example, you want a multiple-field index using the Last Name and First Name fields, so FullName might be a reasonable index name. Select the Last Name field in the Field Name column of this row. To add the other field, skip down to the next row and select First Name without typing a new index name. When you're done, your Indexes window should look like the one shown in Figure 10-33.

Chapter 10

INSIDE OUT Inserting new rows in the Indexes window

To insert a row in the middle of the list in the Indexes window, right-click in the Index Name column and then choose Insert Rows from the shortcut menu.

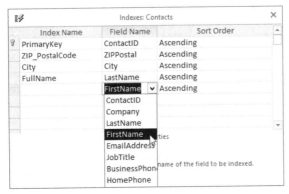

Figure 10-33 The FullName index includes the Last Name and First Name fields.

You can remove an existing single-field index by changing the Indexed property of a field to No on the field's property list. The only way to remove a multiple-field index is via the Indexes window. To remove a multiple-field index, select the rows (by holding down the Ctrl key as you click each row selector) that define the index and then press Delete. Access saves any index changes you make when you save the table definition.

Access can use a multiple-field index in a search even if you don't provide search values for all the fields, as long as you provide search criteria for consecutive fields starting with the first field. Therefore, with the FullName multiple-field index shown in Figure 10-33, you can search for last name or for last name and first name. There's one additional limitation on when Access can use multiple-field indexes: Only the last search criterion you supply can be an inequality, such as >, >=, <, or <=. That is, Access can use the index shown in Figure 10-33 when you specify searches such as these:

Last Name = "Smith"
Last Name > "Franklin"
Last Name = "Buchanan" And First Name = "Steven"
Last Name = "Conrad" And First Name >= "Jeff"

But Access will not use the FullName index shown in Figure 10-35 if you ask for

Last Name > "Davolio" And First Name > "John"

because only the last field in the search (First Name) can be an inequality. Access also will not use this index if you ask for

First Name = "John"

because the first field of the multiple-field index (Last Name) is missing from the search criterion.

Setting table design options

Now that you understand the basic mechanics of defining tables in your desktop database, it's useful to look at a few options that you can set to customize how you work with tables in Design view. Close any open tables so that all you see is the Navigation pane. Click the File tab on the Backstage view, and then click Options to see all the custom settings offered.

You can find the first options that affect table design in the Client Settings category, as shown in Figure 10-34. One option that I highly recommend you use is Use Four-Digit Year Formatting, found in the General section. When you enable four-digit year formatting, Access displays all year values in date/time formats with four digits instead of two. This is important because when you see a value (in two-digit medium date format) such as 15 MAR 12, you won't be able to tell easily whether this is March 15, 1912 or March 15, 2012. Although you can affect the display of some formats in your regional settings in Control Panel, you won't affect them all unless you set four-digit formatting in Access.

Chapter 10

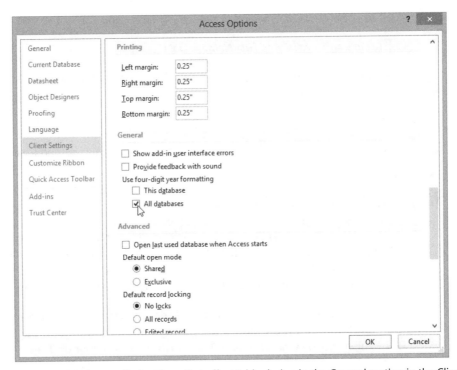

Figure 10-34 You can find settings that affect table design in the General section in the Client Settings category of the Access Options dialog box.

As you can see in Figure 10-34, you have two options under Use Four-Digit Year Formatting in the General section. If you select the This Database check box, the setting creates a property in the database you currently have open and affects only that database. If you select the All Databases check box, the setting creates an entry in your Windows registry that affects all databases that you open on your computer.

In the Current Database category of the Access Options dialog box, you can configure an option, called Name AutoCorrect, that asks Access to track and correct field name references in queries, forms, and reports. If you select the Track Name AutoCorrect Info check box in the Name AutoCorrect Options section, Access maintains a unique internal ID number for all field names. Selecting this option allows you to select the next check box, Perform Name AutoCorrect, as shown in Figure 10-35.

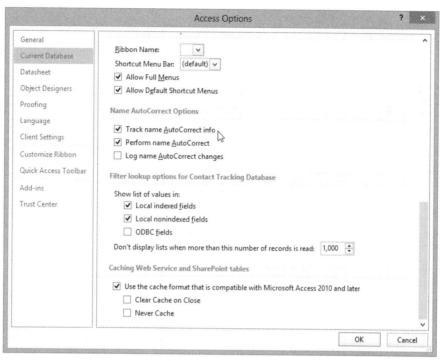

Figure 10-35 You can set Name AutoCorrect options in the Current Database category of the Access Options dialog box.

If you select the Perform Name AutoCorrect check box, when you change a field name in a table, Access automatically attempts to propagate the name change to other objects (queries, forms, and reports) that use the field. However, Track Name AutoCorrect Info requires some additional overhead in all your objects, so it's a good idea to choose names carefully as you design your tables so that you won't need to change them later. Note that Access does not attempt to propagate the name change to any Visual Basic code you created in your database. Finally, if you select the Log Name AutoCorrect Changes check box, Access logs all changes that it makes in a table called AutoCorrect Log. You can open this table to verify the changes made by this feature. (Access doesn't create the table until it makes some changes.)

The next category that contains useful settings affecting table design is Object Designers. Click that category to see the settings shown in Figure 10-36.

Chapter 10

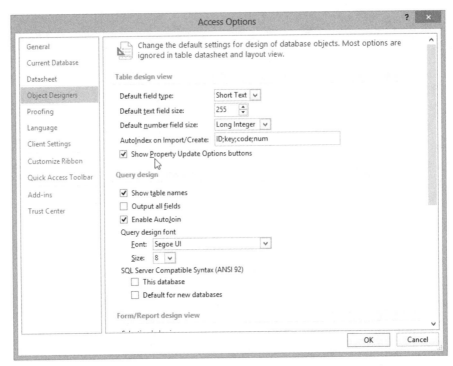

Figure 10-36 You can find settings that affect table design in the Object Designers category of the Access Options dialog box.

In the Table Design View section, you can set the default field type and the default field size for Short Text and Number fields. The Default Field Type setting allows you to choose the default data type that Access selects when you type a new field name in table design and then tab to the Data Type column. When you select a data type of Short Text (either because it is the default data type or you select the Short Text data type in a new field), Access automatically sets the length you select in the Default Text Field Size box. When you select a data type of Number, Access sets the number size to your choice in the Default Number Field Size box of Byte, Integer, Long Integer, Single, Double, Decimal, or Replication ID. Use the AutoIndex On Import/Create box to define a list of field name prefixes or suffixes for which Access automatically sets the Index property to Yes (Duplicates OK). For example, in the default list, any field that you define with a name that begins or ends with ID will have an index automatically.

If you select the Show Property Update Options Buttons check box, a button appears that offers to update related properties automatically in queries, forms, and reports when you change certain field properties in a table design. You can see more details about this option in the next chapter.

You can find the last option that affects how your tables are stored (and, in fact, all objects in your database) in the General category, as shown in Figure 10-37. When you create a new desktop database in Access, you actually have a choice of three different file formats. These options also appear in the File New Database dialog box, but this setting in the Access Options dialog box controls which file format appears as the default. You should use the Access 2000 format if others with whom you might share this database are still using Access 2000, or you should use the 2002-2003 format if others sharing this database are still using Access 2002 or Access 2003. Selecting the Access 2007-2013 format—used by Access 2007, Access 2010, and Access 2013—ensures maximum compatibility of what you build in Access with future versions of the product. If you choose to use an older file format, you won't be able to use some of the new features found only in the .accdb file format, such as Attachment, Multi-Value Field, and Calculated data types.

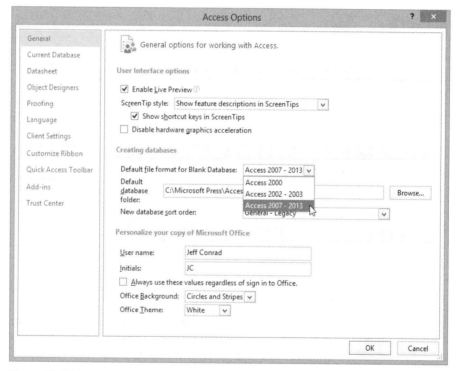

Figure 10-37 You can select your default database file format in the Creating Databases section of the General category in the Access Options dialog box.

Database limitations

As you design your desktop database, you should keep in mind the following limitations:

- A table can have up to 255 fields.

- A table can have up to 32 indexes.

> **Note**
>
> Keep in mind that defining relationships with Referential Integrity turned on creates one additional index in each participating table that counts toward the 32-index limit per table.

- A multiple-field index can have up to 10 fields. The sum of the lengths of the fields cannot exceed 255 bytes.

- A row in a table, excluding Long Text fields and ActiveX objects, can be no longer than approximately 4 kilobytes (KB).

- A Long Text field can store up to 1 GB of characters, but you can't display a Long Text larger than 64 KB in a form or a datasheet.

> **Note**
>
> Clearly, if you try to store a 1-GB Long Text (which requires 2 GB of storage because of double-byte character set support) or a 2-GB ActiveX object in your desktop database file, your file will be full with the data from one record.

- An ActiveX object can be up to 2 GB in size.

- There is no limit on the number of records in a table, but an Access desktop database cannot be larger than 2 GB. If you have several large tables, you might need to define each one in a separate Access database and then attach it to the database that contains the forms, reports, macros, and modules for your applications. For details see Article 3, "Importing and linking data," which you can download from the book's catalog page.

Now that you've started to get comfortable with creating databases and tables, you can proceed to Chapter 11 to learn how to make modifications to existing tables in a desktop database.

N o matter how carefully you design your desktop database, you can be sure that you'll need to change it at some later date. Here are some of the reasons you might need to change your database:

- You no longer need some of the tables.

- You need to perform some new tasks that require not only creating new tables but also inserting some linking fields in existing tables.

- You need to perform some new tasks that require not only creating new tables but also inserting some linking fields in existing tables.

- You find that you use some fields in a table much more frequently than others, so it would be easier if those fields appeared first in the table design.

- You no longer need some of the fields.

- You want to add some new fields that are similar to fields that already exist.

- You discover that some of the data you defined would be better stored as a different data type. For example, a field that you originally designed to be all numbers (such as a U.S. ZIP Code) must now contain some letters (as in a Canadian postal code).

- You have a number field that needs to hold larger values or needs a different number of decimal places than you originally planned.

- You discover that the field you defined as a primary key isn't always unique, so you need to change the definition of your primary key.

- You find that some of your queries take too long to run and might execute more quickly if you add an index to your table.

> **Note**
>
> The examples in this chapter are based on the tables and data in the Housing.accdb and Contacts.accdb sample desktop databases, which you can download from the book's catalog page, and the Contact Tracking database you built in Chapter 10, "Designing tables in a desktop database." If you did not create the Contact Tracking database, you can download ContactTracking.accdb from the book's catalog page and use it to follow along in this chapter. You can find the Housing.accdb database in the Housing subfolder of the sample files and the Contacts.accdb and ContactTracking.accdb databases in the Contacts subfolder. The results you see from the samples you build in this chapter might not exactly match what you see in this book if you have changed the sample data in the files.

This chapter takes a look at how you can make these changes easily and relatively pain-lessly with Microsoft Access 2013. If you want to follow along with the examples in this chapter, you should first create the Contact Tracking database described in Chapter 10.

> **Note**
>
> You might have noticed that the Contacts table you defined for the Contact Tracking database in Chapter 10 is different from the tblContacts table in the Conrad Systems Contacts database (Contacts.accdb). In this chapter, you'll modify the Contacts table you built in Chapter 10 so that it is more like the tblContacts table in the Contacts.accdb sample file.

Before You Get Started

Access makes it easy for you to change the design of your desktop database, even when you already have data in your tables. However, you should understand the potential impact of any changes you plan and take steps to ensure that you can recover your previous design if you make a mistake. Here are some things to consider before you make changes:

- Access does not automatically propagate changes that you make in tables to any queries, forms, reports, macros, or modules. You must make changes to dependent objects yourself or configure Access to propagate the changes for you. To do so, click the File tab on the Backstage view, click Options, and then in the Current Database category, select the Perform Name AutoCorrect check box. See "Setting table design options," in Chapter 10, for more details.

- You cannot change the data type of a field that is part of a relationship between tables. You must first delete the relationship and then change the field's data type and redefine the relationship.

- You cannot change the definition of any table that you have open in a query, a form, or a report. You must close any objects that refer to the table you want to change before you open that table in Design view. If you give other users access to your database over a network, you won't be able to change the table definition if someone else has the table (or a query or form based on the table) open.

INSIDE OUT   Access always prompts you to save your work

Before saving any changes that permanently alter or delete data in your database, Access always prompts you for confirmation and gives you a chance to cancel the operation.

The safest way to make changes to the design of your desktop database is to make a backup copy of the database before you begin. If you expect to make extensive changes to several tables in your database, you should also make a copy of the .accdb file that contains your database. You could use a utility such as Windows Explorer, but Access includes a handy feature for making backups easily. When you have the database open that you want to back up, click the File tab on the Backstage view, click the Save As tab, and then click Back Up Database, as shown in Figure 11-1. Access offers to create a copy of your database with the current date appended to the file name.

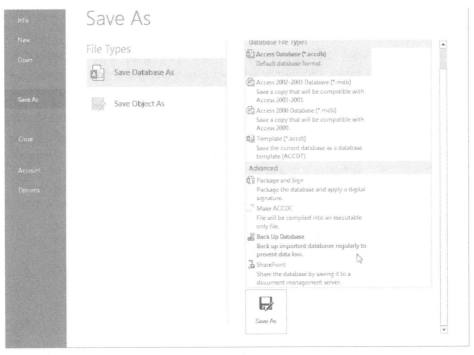

Figure 11-1 The Back Up Database command creates a backup of your entire desktop database file.

If you want to change a single table, you can make a backup copy of that table easily, right in your database. Use the following procedure to copy any table—the structure and the data together.

1. Open the database containing the table you want to copy. If the database is already open, make sure the list of tables is showing in the Navigation pane. Click the top of the Navigation pane to open the Navigation Pane menu, and click Object Type beneath Navigate To Category. Click the top of the Navigation pane again, and then click Tables under Filter By Group, as shown in Figure 11-2, to display only the tables contained in your database.

Figure 11-2 Click Object Type and Tables on the Navigation Pane menu to display only the tables in your database.

2. Select the table you want to copy by clicking the table's name or icon in the Navigation pane. Access highlights the table name.

3. Click the Copy command in the Clipboard group on the Home tab on the ribbon, as shown in Figure 11-3. This copies the entire table (structure and data) to the Clipboard.

Figure 11-3 Click the Copy command to copy a table from the Tables list.

4. Click the Paste command in the Clipboard group on the Home tab on the ribbon. Access opens the Paste Table As dialog box, shown in Figure 11-4. Type a new name for your table. (When naming a backup copy, you might simply add Backup and the date to the original table name, as shown in Figure 11-4.) The default option is to copy both the structure and the data. (You also have the option of copying only the table's structure or of appending the data to another table.)

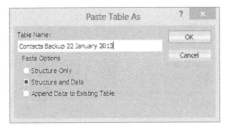

Figure 11-4 Enter the new name for the copied table in the Paste Table As dialog box.

Deleting tables

You probably won't need to delete an entire table very often. However, if you set up your application to collect historical information—for example, total product sales by year— you'll eventually want to delete information that you no longer need. You also might want to delete a table if you've made extensive changes that are incorrect and it would be easier to delete your work and restore the table from a backup.

To delete a table, select it in the Navigation pane and press the Delete key (or click the Delete command in the Records group on the Home tab of the ribbon). Access opens the dialog box shown in Figure 11-5, which asks you to confirm or cancel the delete operation.

INSIDE OUT   Access is forgiving when you delete something by mistake

Even if you mistakenly confirm the deletion, you can click the Undo command on the Quick Access Toolbar to get your table back. In fact, you can undo up to the last 20 changes that you made in a window—either in the table's Design view or in the Navigation pane. However, after you save changes to a table design, you will not be able to undo those changes.

Figure 11-5 This dialog box gives you the option of canceling the deletion of a table.

INSIDE OUT   Using Cut to move an object to the Clipboard

You can use the Cut command in the Clipboard group on the Home tab on the ribbon to delete a table. This method moves a copy of the table to the Clipboard. If you open another instance of Access, you can paste the table into a different database from the Clipboard into it. However, if you close the database you deleted the table from, you cannot paste the table into a different database.

If you have defined relationships between the table you want to delete and other tables, Access displays another dialog box that alerts you and asks whether you want to also delete the relationships. If you click Yes, Access deletes all relationships between any other table and the table you want to delete and then deletes the table. (You can't have a relationship defined to a nonexistent table.) Even at this point, if you find you made a mistake, you can click Undo on the Quick Access Toolbar to restore both the table and all its relationships.

CAUTION!

When you undo a table deletion, Access might not restore all the previously defined relationships between the table and other tables. You should verify the table relationships in the Relationships window.

Renaming tables

If you keep transaction data (such as receipts, deposits, or checks written), you might want to save that data at the end of each month in a table with a unique name. One way to save your data is to rename the existing table (perhaps by adding a date to the name). You can then create a new table (perhaps by making a copy of the backup table's structure) to start collecting information for the next month.

To rename a table, right-click it in the Navigation pane and click Rename on the shortcut menu. Access places the name in edit mode in the Navigation pane so that you can type in a new name, as shown in Figure 11-6. Type the new name, and press Enter to save it.

Chapter 11

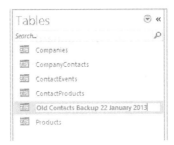

Figure 11-6 After clicking Rename on the shortcut menu, you can rename a table in the Navigation pane.

INSIDE OUT   Using the keyboard to rename an object

You can also edit the name of the object by selecting it in the Navigation pane and pressing the F2 key. This puts the object name in edit mode so that you can type a new name.

If you enter the name of a table that already exists, Access displays a dialog box that asks whether you want to replace the existing table, as shown in Figure 11-7. If you click Yes, Access deletes the old table before performing the renaming operation. Even if you replace an existing table, you can undo the renaming operation by clicking the Undo command on the Quick Access Toolbar.

Figure 11-7 This dialog box asks whether you want to replace an existing table with the same name.

INSIDE OUT   Renaming other Access objects

You can use the techniques you just learned for copying, renaming, and deleting tables to copy, rename, and delete queries, forms, reports, macros, or modules.

Changing field names

Perhaps you misspelled a field name when you first created one of your tables, or perhaps you've decided that one of the field names isn't descriptive enough. As you learned in Chapter 10, you can change the displayed name for a field by setting its Caption property. But you won't necessarily want the hassle of giving the field a caption every time it appears in a query, a form, or a report. Fortunately, Access makes it easy to change a field name in a table—even if you already have data in the table.

> **Note**
>
> The next several examples in this chapter show you how to change the Contacts table that you created in the previous chapter to match the tblContacts table in the Conrad Systems Contacts sample database more closely.

You created the first draft of the Contacts table by using an Application Part. Now you need to make a few changes so that it will hold all the data fields that you need for your application. The Contacts Application Part does not give you the option to rename the fields before creating them, but now you decide to rename one of the fields before beginning to work on the rest of your application.

Renaming a field is easy. For example, the Application Part created a field called Address, but you've decided that you want to have two address fields because a contact could have a work address and a home address in this database. It makes sense to change the field name to reflect the actual data you intend to store in the field, so let's change Address to WorkAddress. To do this, open the Contacts table in the Contact Tracking database in Design view, use the mouse to move the insertion point to the beginning of the Address field name, and then type **Work**. You can also click in the field name, use the arrow keys to position the insertion point just before the letter A, and type **Work**. As you learned in Chapter 10, I recommend that you not have any spaces in your field names, so do not put a space between the words Work and Address. Your field should now be called WorkAddress. Press F6 to move down to the Field Properties section of the window, tab down to the Caption property, and change the field caption to **Work Address**. Your result should look like Figure 11-8.

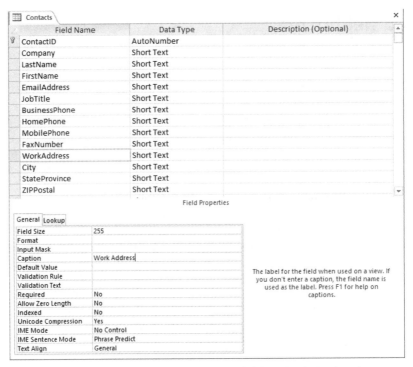

Figure 11-8 You can change a field name and a field caption in Design view.

Comparing the two Contacts tables

As you follow along with the examples in this chapter, it might be useful to compare the structure of the Contacts table you built in Chapter 10 and the actual tblContacts table in the Conrad Systems Contacts sample database (Contacts.accdb). If you exactly followed the instructions in Chapter 10, your Contacts table in the Contact Tracking database should look like Table 11-1. You can see the actual design of tblContacts in Table 11-2.

TABLE 11-1   Contacts

Field Name	Type	Length
ContactID	AutoNumber	
Company	Short Text	255
LastName	Short Text	255
FirstName	Short Text	255
EmailAddress	Short Text	255
JobTitle	Short Text	255
BusinessPhone	Short Text	255
HomePhone	Short Text	255
MobilePhone	Short Text	255
FaxNumber	Short Text	255
Address	Short Text	255
City	Short Text	255
StateProvince	Short Text	255
ZipPostal	Short Text	255
CountryRegion	Short Text	255
WebPage	Hyperlink	
Notes	Long Text	
Attachments	Attachment	
ContactName	Calculated	
FileAs	Calculated	

TABLE 11-2   tblContacts

Field Name	Type	Length
ContactID	Auto Number	
LastName	Short Text	50

Field Name	Type	Length
FirstName	Short Text	50
MiddleInit	Short Text	1
Title	Short Text	10
Suffix	Short Text	10
ContactType	Short Text	50
BirthDate	Date/Time	
DefaultAddress	Integer	
WorkAddress	Short Text	255
WorkCity	Short Text	50
WorkStateOrProvince	Short Text	20
WorkPostalCode	Short Text	20
WorkCountry	Short Text	50
WorkPhone	Short Text	30
WorkExtension	Short Text	20
WorkFaxNumber	Short Text	30
HomeAddress	Short Text	255
HomeCity	Short Text	50
HomeStateOrProvince	Short Text	20
HomePostalCode	Short Text	20
HomeCountry	Short Text	50
HomePhone	Short Text	30
MobilePhone	Short Text	30
EmailName	Hyperlink	
Website	Hyperlink	
Photo	Attachment	
SpouseName	Short Text	75
SpouseBirthDate	Date/Time	
Notes	LongText	
CommissionPercent	Number	Double
Inactive	Yes/No	

As you can see, we have a lot of work to do—renaming fields, moving fields, inserting fields, adding new fields, and changing data types and lengths—to make the two tables identical.

Before we go any further, you should rename the remaining fields and add captions so that they more closely match the fields in the tblContacts table in the Conrad Systems Contacts sample database. Following the preceding steps for renaming fields and changing the Caption property, go through each of the fields and change them as shown in the following table.

Old Name	New Name	Caption
EmailAddress	EmailName	Email Name
JobTitle	Title	Title
BusinessPhone	WorkPhone	Work Phone
FaxNumber	WorkFaxNumber	Fax Number
City	WorkCity	Work City
StateProvince	WorkStateOrProvince	State/Province
ZIPPostalCode	WorkPostalCode	Postal Code
CountryRegion	WorkCountry	Work Country
WebPage	Website	Website
Attachments	Photo	

Your table should now look like Figure 11-9. Click the Save button on the Quick Access Toolbar to save the changes to the table when you are finished.

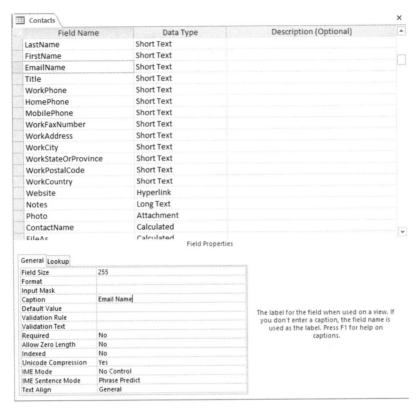

Figure 11-09 After renaming the fields in the Contacts table created from the template, it is beginning to look more like the table in the Conrad Systems Contacts sample database.

Moving fields

You might want to move a field in a table definition for a number of reasons. Perhaps you made an error as you entered or changed the information in a table, or perhaps you've discovered that you're using some fields you defined at the end of a table quite frequently in forms or reports, in which case it would be easier to find and work with those fields if they were nearer the beginning of your table definition.

INSIDE OUT   How important is the sequence of fields in your table?

The actual sequence of field definitions in a table is not all that important. In the relational database model, there really is no defined sequence of fields in a row or rows in a table. Access, like most databases that implement the relational model, does allow you to define a field order when you create a table. This order, or sequence of fields, becomes the default order you see in a table datasheet or in a list of field names when you're designing a query, form, or report.

I like to group fields together in some reasonable order so that they're easy to find, and I like to place the primary key fields at the top of the list. There's really no hard and fast rule that you must follow for your database to work efficiently.

You can use the mouse to move one or more rows. Simply follow these steps:

1. To select a row you want to move, click its row selector.

   If you want to move multiple contiguous rows, click the row selector for the first row in the group and scroll until you can see the last row in the group. Hold down the Shift key, and click the row selector for the last row in the group. The first and last rows and all rows in between will be selected. Release the Shift key.

2. Click and drag the row selector(s) for the selected row(s) to a new location. A small shaded box attaches to the bottom of the mouse pointer while you're dragging, and a highlighted line will appear, indicating the position to which the row(s) will move when you release the mouse button.

In the design for the tblContacts table in the Conrad Systems Contacts database (Contacts.accdb), the EmailName field appears after all the address fields and before the Website field. It certainly makes sense to place all the web-related fields together. Select the EmailName field by clicking its row selector. Click the row selector again, and drag down until the line between the WorkCountry field and the Website field is highlighted, as shown in Figure 11-10.

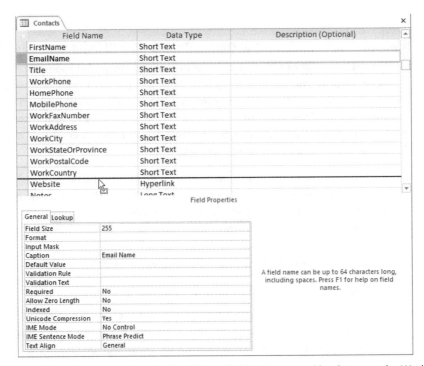

Figure 11-10 You can drag the EmailName field to a new position between the WorkCountry and Website fields.

INSIDE OUT
Using the keyboard instead of the mouse in Table Design view

When it comes to moving fields, you might find it easier to use a combination of mouse and keyboard methods in Table Design view. Use the mouse to select the row or rows you want to move. Then activate Move mode by pressing Ctrl+Shift+F8, and use the arrow keys to position the row(s). Press Esc to deactivate Move mode. As you experiment with Access, you'll discover more than one way to perform many tasks, and you can choose the techniques that work the best for you.

In Figure 11-11, the fields are positioned correctly.

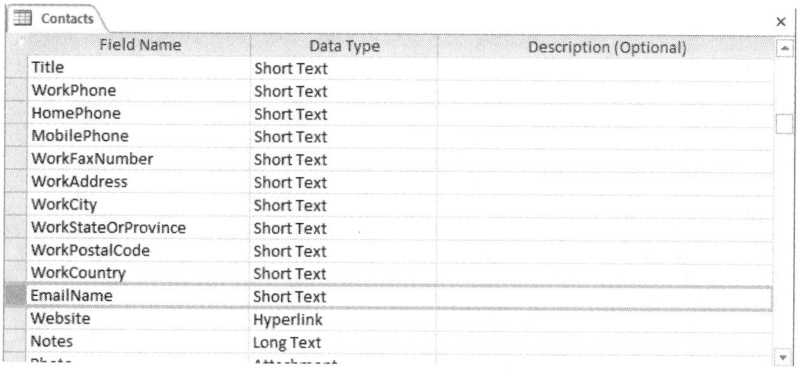

Field Name	Data Type	Description (Optional)
Title	Short Text	
WorkPhone	Short Text	
HomePhone	Short Text	
MobilePhone	Short Text	
WorkFaxNumber	Short Text	
WorkAddress	Short Text	
WorkCity	Short Text	
WorkStateOrProvince	Short Text	
WorkPostalCode	Short Text	
WorkCountry	Short Text	
EmailName	Short Text	
Website	Hyperlink	
Notes	Long Text	

Figure 11-11 The EmailName field now is placed correctly.

In this exercise, we'll move a couple of additional fields to make the design of Contacts more similar to tblContacts. In the tblContacts table, the HomePhone and MobilePhone fields appear just before the EmailName field. Click the row selector for HomePhone, hold down the Shift key, and click the row selector for MobilePhone to select both fields. Drag the two fields to just above the EmailName field. Now that you've moved HomePhone and MobilePhone out of the way, you can select both WorkPhone and WorkFaxNumber and drag them to where they belong after the WorkCountry field. Finally, move the Notes field after the Photo field. After you've done this, your table should look like Figure 11-12.

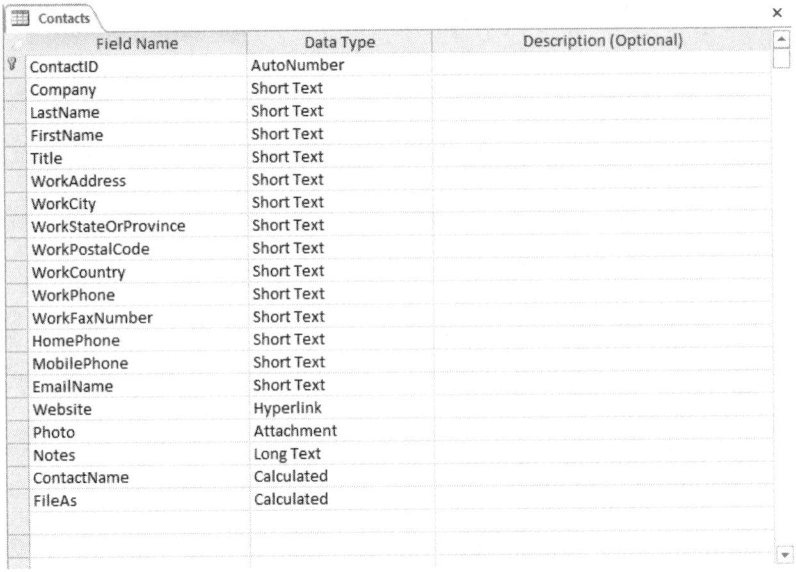

Figure 11-12 After moving several fields, the sequence of fields in your Contacts table is similar to that in tblContacts.

Inserting fields

Perhaps one of the most common changes you'll make to your database is to insert a new field in a table. Up until now, we've renamed and moved the available fields to match tblContacts more closely. If you take a look at the comparison of the two tables again (Tables 11-1 and 11-2), you can see that we need to add several more fields. Now you're ready to insert fields to store the middle initial, suffix, contact type, default address indicator, and more. As you go through adding these new fields, be sure to enter a description for each new field as well as the existing fields.

First, select the row or move your insertion point to the row that defines the field after the point where you want to insert the new field. In this case, if you want to insert a field for the middle initial between the FirstName and Title fields, place the insertion point anywhere in the row that defines the Title field. You can also select the entire row by using the arrow keys to move to the row and then pressing Shift+Spacebar or by clicking the row selector. Next, click the Design contextual tab, which is located below Table Tools on the ribbon. Finally, click the Insert Rows command in the Tools group, as shown in Figure 11-13. (You can also click a field row and press the Insert key to insert a row above your selection.)

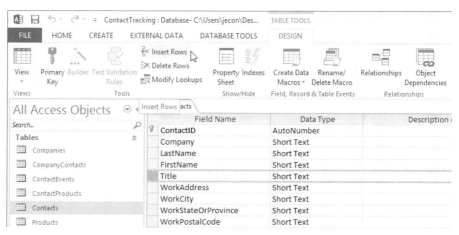

Figure 11-13 The Insert Rows command inserts a new row above a selected row or above the row in which the insertion point is located.

Access adds a blank row that you can use to define your new field. Type the definition for the MiddleInit field. Choose the Short Text data type, and set the Field Size property to **1**. Now move down to the WorkAddress field, and insert another row above it. Enter a Suffix field that has the Short Text data type with a field size of **10**. Finally, insert a ContactType field between Suffix and WorkAddress, set its data type to Short Text, and set its length to **50**. Insert a field between ContactType and WorkAddress, name it **BirthDate**, and set its data type to Date/Time. Insert another field between BirthDate and WorkAddress, name it **DefaultAddress**, set its data type to Number, and set the field size to Integer. The actual Conrad Systems Contacts application uses this field to indicate whether the work or home address is the default mailing address.

Move down to WorkFaxNumber, and insert a field above it. Enter a field name of **WorkExtension**, set its data type to Short Text, and set the field size to **20**. Now move down to the bottom of the field list, and insert another new field above Notes. Enter a field name of **SpouseName**, set its data type to Short Text, and set the field size to **75**. Insert another row between the SpouseName and Notes fields, enter a field name of **SpouseBirthDate**, and set its data type to Date/Time. Move down to the ContactName field, and insert a field above it. Create a field named **CommissionPercent** with a data type of Number and a field size of Double. Finally, insert another new field above ContactName named **Inactive**, and set its data type to Yes/No.

At this point, your Table window in Design view should look something like the one shown in Figure 11-14. (I entered information in the Description properties of all fields we're going to keep. You can change your descriptions to match the figure.) Don't worry about setting other properties just yet. As you can see, we are getting closer to the exact design specifications of tblContacts in the Conrad Systems Contacts database, but we still have more things to change.

Field Name	Data Type	Description (Optional)
ContactID	AutoNumber	Unique Contact ID
Company	Short Text	
LastName	Short Text	Last name
FirstName	Short Text	First name
MiddleInit	Short Text	Middle initial
Title	Short Text	Person Title
Suffix	Short Text	Person Suffix (Jr., Sr., II, etc.)
ContactType	Short Text	Description of the contact type
BirthDate	Date/Time	Birth date
DefaultAddress	Number	Specify work or home as default address
WorkAddress	Short Text	Address
WorkCity	Short Text	City
WorkStateOrProvince	Short Text	State or Province
WorkPostalCode	Short Text	Postal/Zip Code
WorkCountry	Short Text	Country
WorkPhone	Short Text	Work phone
WorkExtension	Short Text	Phone extension
WorkFaxNumber	Short Text	Fax number
HomePhone	Short Text	Home phone
MobilePhone	Short Text	Mobile phone
EmailName	Short Text	Email name
Website	Hyperlink	Website address
Photo	Attachment	Photo of contact
SpouseName	Short Text	Spouse name
SpouseBirthDate	Date/Time	Spouse Birth date
Notes	Long Text	Notes
CommissionPercent	Number	Commission when referencing a sale
Inactive	Yes/No	Contact is inactive
ContactName	Calculated	
FileAs	Calculated	

Figure 11-14 The Contacts table with additional fields inserted and descriptions defined.

INSIDE OUT   Using the keyboard to move between windows

You can move the insertion point between the upper part and the lower part of any Table or Query window in Design view by pressing F6.

Copying fields

As you create table definitions, you might find that several fields in your table are similar. Rather than enter each of the field definitions separately, you can enter one field definition, copy it, and then paste it as many times as necessary.

To finish defining our Contacts table, we need five additional fields—HomeAddress, HomeCity, HomeStateOrProvince, HomePostalCode, and HomeCountry. You could insert a new row and type all the properties as you just did in the previous section, but why not copy a field that is similar and make minor changes to it?

For this part of the exercise, select the row for the WorkAddress field definition by clicking the row selector at the left of the row. Click the Copy command in the Clipboard group on the Home tab, as shown in Figure 11-15.

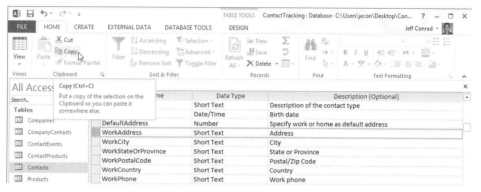

Figure 11-15 Select the WorkAddress field, and click the Copy command on the Home tab on the ribbon to copy the field to the Clipboard.

Move the insertion point to the row that should follow the row you'll insert. (In this case, move the insertion point to the HomePhone field, which should follow your new field.) Insert a blank row by clicking Insert Rows in the Tools group of the Design contextual tab below Table Tools on the ribbon. (In this procedure, you switch back and forth between the Home tab and the Design contextual tab.) Select the new row by clicking the row selector. Click the Paste command in the Clipboard group on the Home tab on the ribbon, as shown in Figure 11-16.

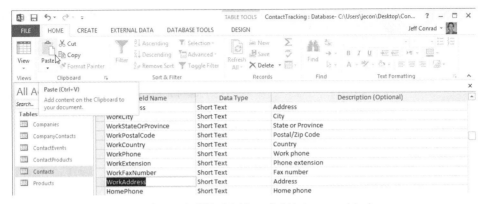

Figure 11-16 You can paste the copied WorkAddress field into a new blank row.

CAUTION

If you click the Paste command when a row containing data is selected, the copied row will replace the selected row. Should you make this replacement in error, click the Undo command on the Quick Access Toolbar to restore the original row.

You can use the Paste command repeatedly to insert a copied row more than once. Remember to change both the name and the description of the resulting field or fields before you save the modified table definition. In this case, it's a simple matter to change the name of the copied row from WorkAddress to HomeAddress and to correct the description and caption accordingly. This procedure also has the benefit of copying any formatting, default value, or validation rule information.

If you're careful, you don't actually have to insert a blank row to paste a field definition from the Clipboard. You can also copy and paste multiple fields at a time. After you fix the HomeAddress field name in the upper part of the window and the caption in the lower part of the window, select the WorkCity field, hold down the Shift key, and select the WorkCountry field. Click the Copy command to copy all four fields to the Clipboard. Move down to the HomePhone field again and click in the row, but *do not select the row*. Click the Paste button in the Clipboard group of the Home tab to insert the four fields just above HomePhone. Change the name of the first one to **HomeCity**, the second to **HomeStateOrProvince**, the third to **HomePostalCode**, and the fourth to **HomeCountry**, and then correct the captions. You should now have a table that's almost identical to the tblContacts table in the Conrad Systems Contacts sample database, as shown in Figure 11-17. Be sure to save your changed table.

Field Name	Data Type	Description (Optional)
ContactID	AutoNumber	Unique Contact ID
Company	Short Text	
LastName	Short Text	Last name
FirstName	Short Text	First name
MiddleInit	Short Text	Middle initial
Title	Short Text	Person Title
Suffix	Short Text	Person Suffix (Jr., Sr., II, etc.)
ContactType	Short Text	Description of the contact type
BirthDate	Date/Time	Birth date
DefaultAddress	Number	Specify work or home as default address
WorkAddress	Short Text	Address
WorkCity	Short Text	City
WorkStateOrProvince	Short Text	State or Province
WorkPostalCode	Short Text	Postal/Zip Code
WorkCountry	Short Text	Country
WorkPhone	Short Text	Work phone
WorkExtension	Short Text	Phone extension
WorkFaxNumber	Short Text	Fax number
HomeAddress	Short Text	Home address
HomeCity	Short Text	Home city
HomeStateOrProvince	Short Text	Home State or Province
HomePostalCode	Short Text	Home Postal/Zip Code
HomeCountry	Short Text	Home Country
HomePhone	Short Text	Home phone
MobilePhone	Short Text	Mobile phone
EmailName	Short Text	Email name
Website	Hyperlink	Website address
Photo	Attachment	Photo of contact
SpouseName	Short Text	Spouse name
SpouseBirthDate	Date/Time	Spouse Birth date
Notes	Long Text	Notes
CommissionPercent	Number	Commission when referencing a sale
Inactive	Yes/No	Contact is inactive
ContactName	Calculated	
FileAs	Calculated	

Figure 11-17 The Contacts field list is now almost identical to tblContacts.

Deleting fields

Removing unwanted fields is easy. With the Table window open in Design view, select the field that you want to delete by clicking the row selector. You can extend the selection to multiple contiguous fields by holding down the Shift key and pressing the Up and Down Arrow keys to select multiple rows. You can also select multiple contiguous rows by clicking the row selector of the first row and, without releasing the mouse button, dragging up or down to select all the rows you want. After you select the appropriate fields, click Delete Rows in the Tools group of the Design tab below Table Tools on the ribbon. Or, press the Delete key to delete the selected fields.

We have three extra fields in our current Contacts table that we do not need—the Company, ContactName, and FileAs fields that were created by the Contacts Application Part.

(Remember that in Chapter 10, you created a Company Contacts table to link contacts to their respective companies.) To delete the Company field, click the row selector next to the Company field and then click the Delete Rows button in the Tools group of the Design tab on the ribbon. Access prompts you that calculated columns depend on the Company field. Click Yes to confirm that you want to delete the field. Now move down to the last two fields, and also delete the ContactName and FileAs fields from your contacts table. Your Contacts table now matches the tblContacts table from the Conrad Systems Contacts database in terms of the correct number of fields and field names. Save these latest changes to the Contacts table by clicking the Save button on the Quick Access Toolbar.

If a table contains one or more rows of data, Access displays a warning message when you delete field definitions in Design view, as shown in Figure 11-28. Click No if you think you made a mistake. Click Yes to proceed with the deletion of the fields and the data in those fields. Keep in mind that you can still undo this change up to the point that you save the table.

Figure 11-18 This dialog box asks you to confirm a field deletion.

If you want to test this in the sample table you have been building, make sure that you have saved your latest changes and then switch to Datasheet view by clicking the small arrow below the View button in the Views group on the Home tab and then clicking Datasheet View. Type your name in the Last Name and First Name fields, and switch back to Design view by clicking the small arrow below the View button again. Try deleting any field in the design, and Access will warn you that you might be deleting some data as well.

Changing data attributes

As you learned in the previous chapter, Access provides a number of different data types. These data types help Access work more efficiently with your data and also provide a base level of data validation; for example, you can enter only numbers in a Number or Currency field.

When you initially design your desktop database, you should match the data type and length of each field to its intended use. However, you might discover that a field you thought would contain only numbers (such as a U.S. ZIP Code) must now contain some letters (perhaps because you've started doing business in Canada). You might find that one or more number fields need to hold larger values or a different number of decimal places.

Access allows you to change the data type and length of many fields, even after you've entered data in them.

Changing data types

Changing the data type of a field in a table is simple. Open the table in Design view, click in the Data Type column of the field definition you want to change, click the arrow button at the right to see the available choices, and select a new data type. You cannot convert an OLE Object, an Attachment, Calculated, or a ReplicationID data type to another data type. With several limitations, Access can successfully convert any other data type to a different data type, even when you have data in the table. Table 11-3 shows you the possible conversions and potential limitations when the table contains data.

CAUTION

When the field contents don't satisfy the limitations noted in Table 11-3, Access deletes the field contents (sets it to Null) when you save the changes.

TABLE 11-3   Limitations on converting one data type to another in desktop databases

Convert To	From	Limitations
Short Text	Long Text	Access truncates text longer than 255 characters.
	Hyperlink	Might lose some data if the hyperlink string is longer than 255 characters.
	Number, except ReplicationID	No limitations.
	AutoNumber	No limitations except ReplicationID.
	Currency	No limitations.
	Date/Time	No limitations.
	Yes/No	Yes (-1) converts to Yes; No (0) converts to No.
Long Text	Short Text	No limitations.
	Hyperlink	No limitations.
	Number, except ReplicationID	No limitations.
	AutoNumber	No limitations.
	Currency	No limitations.
	Date/Time	No limitations.
	Yes/No	Yes (-1) converts to Yes; No (0) converts to No.

Convert To	From	Limitations
Hyperlink	Short Text	If the text contains a valid Hyperlink string consisting of a display name, a # delimiter, a valid link address, a # delimiter, and optional bookmark and ScreenTip, Access changes the data type without modifying the text. If the text contains only a valid link address, Access surrounds the address with # delimiters to form the Hyperlink field. Access recognizes strings beginning with *http://*, *ftp://*, *mailto:*, *news:*, *\\servername*, and *d:* as link addresses. Access also assumes that a text string in the form *text@text* is an email address, and it adds *mailto:* to the beginning of the string before converting it. If Access does not recognize the text as a link, it converts the text to *[text]#http://[text]#*, where *[text]* is the original contents of the field; the result is probably not a valid link address.
	Long Text	Same restrictions as converting from Short Text.
	Number, except ReplicationID	Possible, but Access converts the number to a text string in the form *[number]#http://[number]#*, where *[number]* is the text conversion of the original numeric value; the result is probably not a valid link address.
	AutoNumber	Possible, but Access converts the AutoNumber to a text string in the form *[number]#http://[number]*, where *[number]* is the text conversion of the original AutoNumber; the result is probably not a valid link address.
	Currency	Possible, but Access converts the currency value to a text string in the form *[currency]#http://[currency]*, where *[currency]* is the text conversion of the original currency value; the result is probably not a valid link address.
	Date/Time	Possible, but Access converts the date/time to a text string in the form *[date/time]#http://[date/time]#*, where *[date/time]* is the text conversion of the original date or time value; the result is probably not a valid link address.
	Yes/No	Possible, but Access converts the yes/no to a text string in the form *[yes/no]#- http://[yes/no]*, where *[yes/no]* is the text conversion of the original yes (-1) or no (0) value; the result is probably not a valid link address.
Number	Short Text	Text must contain only numbers and valid separators. The number value must be within the range for the Field Size property.
	Long Text	Long Text must contain only numbers and valid separators. The number value must be within the range for the Field Size property.
	Hyperlink	Not possible.
	Number (different field size or precision)	Number must not be larger or smaller than can be contained in the new field size. If you change precision, Access might round the number.

Convert To	From	Limitations
	AutoNumber	The number value must be within the range for the Field Size property.
	Currency	Number must not be larger or smaller than can be contained in the Field Size property.
	Date/Time	If the Field Size is Byte, the date must be between April 18, 1899,[1] and September 11, 1900. If the new Field Size is Integer, the date must be between April 13, 1810, and September 16, 1989. For all other field sizes, there are no limitations.
	Yes/No	Yes (-1) converts to -1; No (0) converts to 0.
AutoNumber	Short Text	Not possible if the table contains data.
	Long Text	Not possible if the table contains data.
	Hyperlink	Not possible.
	Number	Not possible if the table contains data.
	Currency	Not possible if the table contains data.
	Date/Time	Not possible if the table contains data.
	Yes/No	Not possible if the table contains data.
Currency	Short Text	Text must contain only numbers and valid separators.
	Long Text	Long Text must contain only numbers and valid separators.
	Hyperlink	Not possible.
	Number, except Replication ID	No limitations.
	AutoNumber	No limitations.
	Date/Time	No limitations, but value might be rounded.
	Yes/No	Yes (-1) converts to $1; No (0) converts to $0.
Date/Time	Short Text	Text must contain a recognizable date and/or time, such as 18-Jul-13 5:15 PM.
	Long Text	Long Text must contain a recognizable date and/or time, such as 18-Jul-13 5:15 PM.
	Hyperlink	Not possible.
	Number, except Replication ID	Number must be between -657,434 and 2,958,465.99998843.
	AutoNumber	Value must be less than 2,958,466 and greater than -657,433.
	Currency	Number must be between -$657,434 and $2,958,465.9999.
	Yes/No	Yes (-1) converts to 12/29/1899; No (0) converts to 12:00:00 AM.
Yes/No	Short Text	Text must contain only one of the following values: Yes, True, On, No, False, or Off.

Convert To	From	Limitations
	Long Text	Text must contain only one of the following values: Yes, True, On, No, False, or Off.
	Hyperlink	Not possible.
	Number, except Replication ID	Zero or Null converts to No; any other value converts to Yes.
	AutoNumber	All values evaluate to Yes.
	Currency	Zero or Null converts to No; any other value converts to Yes.
	Date/Time	12:00:00 AM or Null converts to No; any other value converts to Yes.

1 Remember, Access stores a date/time value as an integer date offset and fraction of a day. April 18, 1899, happens to be -256 internally, which is the smallest number you can store in a Byte.

If you want to see how this works in the Contacts table you have been building, open the table in Datasheet view and enter any last name and first name in one or two rows. We want to change the EmailName field from the Short Text data type that the Contacts Application Part provided to Hyperlink. Scroll right, and enter an invalid email address in one of the rows in the form: **Proseware email address**. In another row, add the correct URL prefix in the form: **mailto:jeffc@proseware.com**.

Now switch to Design view, and change the data type of the EmailName field from Short Text to Hyperlink and save the change. Notice that Access gives you no warning about any conversion problems because it knows it can store any text field that is not larger than 255 characters in a hyperlink, which can be up to 8,192 bytes. Save this change to the table, switch back to Datasheet view, and scroll to the right to find the changed field. You should see a result something like Figure 11-19.

Figure 11-19 Access can convert the Short Text data type to Hyperlink correctly, but only if the text contains a recognizable protocol string.

Both entries look fine. However, if you click the first one, Access attempts to open your browser because the full text stored in the hyperlink is
Proseware email address#http://Proseware email address#. Because the link address portion indicates http://, your browser attempts to open instead of your email program. Access displays a message box that says it cannot follow the hyperlink. When you click the second link, it should open a blank message in your email program with the To: line filled in correctly. Access recognized the *mailto:* prefix and converted the text correctly.

I show you how to make sure that Access correctly recognizes an email name typed into a hyperlink field in Chapter 25, "Automating your desktop database with Visual Basic," which you can download from the book's catalog page.

Changing data lengths

For Short Text and Number fields, you can define the maximum length of the data that can be stored in the field. Although a Short Text field can be up to 255 characters long, you can restrict the length to as little as 1 character. If you don't specify a length for Short Text, Access normally assigns the length you specify in the Table Design section in the Object Designers category of the Access Options dialog box. (The default length is 255.) Access won't let you enter text field data longer than the defined length. If you need more space in a Short Text field, you can increase the length at any time; but, if you try to redefine the length of a Short Text field so that it's shorter, you will get a warning message (like the one shown in Figure 11-20) stating that Access will truncate any data field that contains data longer than the new length when you try to save the changes to your table. Note also that it warns you that any validation rules you have designed might fail because of the changed data.

Figure 11-20 This dialog box informs you of possible data truncation problems.

INSIDE OUT   Setting field defaults through Access options

Remember, you can change the default data type for a new field and the default length of new text and number fields by clicking the File tab on the Backstage view, clicking Options, clicking the Object Designers category of the Access Options dialog box, and then selecting your defaults in the Table Design View section.

If you want to try this in your Contacts table, open it in Design view, change the length of the MiddleInit field to **10**, and save the change. Switch to Datasheet view, and type more than one character in MiddleInit. Now switch back to Design view, and set the length of MiddleInit to **1**. When you try to save the change, you should see the error message in Figure 11-20 (because you're shortening the length of the MiddleInit field). Click Yes to allow the changes, and then switch back to Datasheet view. You should find the data that you typed truncated to one character in MiddleInit. Review Table 11-2, verify that each field's length in your Contacts table matches tblContacts in the Conrad Systems Contacts database, and make any necessary adjustments before proceeding further.

Sizes for numeric data types can vary from a single byte (which can contain a value from 0 through 255) to 2 or 4 bytes (for larger integers), 8 bytes (necessary to hold very large floating-point or currency numbers), or 16 bytes (to hold a unique ReplicationID or decimal number). Except for ReplicationID, you can change the size of a numeric data type at any time, but you might generate errors if you make the size smaller. Access also rounds numbers when converting from floating-point data types (Single or Double) to integer or currency values.

Dealing with conversion errors

When you try to save a modified table definition, Access always warns you if any changes to the data type or field length will cause conversion errors. For example, if you change the Field Size property of a Number field from Integer to Byte, Access warns you if any of the records contain a number larger than 255. (Access deletes the contents of any field that it can't convert at all.)

If you examine Table 11-3, you'll see that you should expect some data type changes to always cause problems. For example, if you change a field from Hyperlink to Date/Time, you can expect Access to delete all data. You'll see a dialog box, similar to the one shown in Figure 11-21, warning you about fields that Access will set to a Null value if you proceed with your changes. Click Yes to proceed with the changes. You'll have to examine your data to correct any conversion errors.

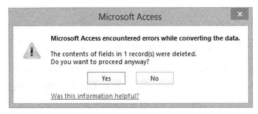

Figure 11-21 This dialog box informs you of conversion errors.

If you click No, Access opens the dialog box shown in Figure 11-22. If you deleted any fields or indexes, added any fields, or renamed any fields, Access will save those changes. Otherwise, the database will be unchanged. You can correct any data type or field length changes you made, and then try to save the table definition again.

Figure 11-22 This dialog box appears if you decide not to save a modified table definition.

Changing other field properties

As you learned in Chapter 10, you can set a number of other properties that define how Access displays or validates a field that have nothing to do with changing the data type. These properties include Description, Format, Input Mask, Caption, Default Value, Validation Rule, Validation Text, Required, Allow Zero Length, and Indexed.

If you have data in your table, changing some of these properties might elicit a warning from Access. If you change or define a validation rule, or set Required to Yes, Access offers to check the new rule or requirement that a field not be empty against the contents of the table when you try to save the change. If you ask Access to test the data, it checks all the rows in your table and opens a warning dialog box if it finds any rows that fail. However, it doesn't tell you *which* rows failed. If you changed the rules for more than one field, you'll see the error dialog box once for each rule that fails.

As you'll learn later, when you define queries, forms, and reports, these objects inherit several of the properties that you define for your table fields. In previous versions of Access before Access 2007, the catch was that after you defined and saved another object that used table fields, any subsequent change that you made to properties in table design didn't change automatically in other dependent objects. You had to go find those properties and fix them. You would get the new property settings in any new objects you created, but the old ones remained unchanged.

The good news is that there's a feature in Access 2013 that takes care of this problem for some properties. To see how this works, you must first make sure that you have this option selected in Access Options, as I showed you in the previous chapter. Click the File tab on the Backstage view, click Options, click the Object Designers category, and verify that you have selected the Show Property Update Options Buttons check box. Click OK to close the Access Options dialog box.

Next, open the Contacts table in Design view in the Contact Tracking database you have been building. Remember from the previous chapter that Access displays the description on the status bar when the focus is on the Description field in any datasheet or form. Click in the Description column next to the ContactID field, and change the description from

Unique contact ID to just **Contact ID**, and then press Tab. As soon as you do this, you'll see an AutoCorrect button that looks like a lightning bolt. If you rest your mouse pointer near the button, it tells you that it offers property update options. Click the arrow next to the tag to see the options you can choose from, as shown in Figure 11-23. Access offers you these options whenever you change the Description, Format, or Input Mask properties.

Figure 11-23 When you change a field description, you see a button offering property update options.

You can click Update Status Bar Text Everywhere ContactID Is Used to ask Access to change this property wherever the ContactID field is used in other objects as well. Of course, you don't have anything but tables in your sample database right now, so clicking this command won't do anything. You can select Help On Propagating Field Properties to open the Help window to read how this works.

CAUTION !

> You must click the Update Status Bar Text Everywhere ContactID Is Used command immediately after you make the change in your table definition. If you move to another field or move to another property and make another change, the button disappears. You can make it reappear by returning to the property you changed and changing it again. If you choose to make changes, Access opens an Update Properties dialog box that lists all the objects it plans to change. You can reject all changes or selectively apply the change to only some of the objects.

Reversing changes

If you make several changes and then decide you don't want any of them, you can close the Table window without saving them. When you do this, Access opens the dialog box shown in Figure 11-24. Simply click No to reverse all your changes. Click Cancel to return to the Table window in Design view without saving or reversing your changes.

Figure 11-24 This dialog box gives you the option of reversing unsaved changes to a table.

INSIDE OUT   Reversing multiple changes

You can always reverse up to the last 20 changes you made since you last saved the table design by clicking the Undo button. You can also open the list next to the Undo button to undo a series of changes selectively.

Taking a look at Lookup properties

As you have been working with table design, you've probably noticed that there's a Lookup tab available in the lower part of the Table window in Design view. You might have also noticed that Access offers you a Lookup Wizard entry in the drop-down list of data types and a Modify Lookups option in the Tools group on the Design tab. This feature allows you to predefine how you want the field displayed in a datasheet, form, or report. For example, if you have a DepartmentID field in an Employees table that stores the primary key value of the department for which the employee works, you might want to display the department name rather than the number value when you look at the data. If you're displaying a Yes/No field, you might want to provide a drop-down list that shows options for *invoiced* and *not invoiced* instead of *yes* and *no* or *true* and *false*.

In the sample desktop databases, I defined Lookup properties for only a few fields—ones for which we knew that we would later need a combo box with the relevant available choices on one or more forms or reports. (You will also see combo boxes described as drop-down lists.) One such example is in the Housing Reservations sample database (Housing.accdb). Close the Contact Tracking database you've been working with so far in this chapter. Now, open the Housing Reservations sample desktop database from the Housing subfolder where you installed the sample files, view the table objects, select tblEmployees, and open it in Design view. Click the DepartmentID field, and then click the Lookup tab to see the settings, as shown in Figure 11-25.

Chapter 11

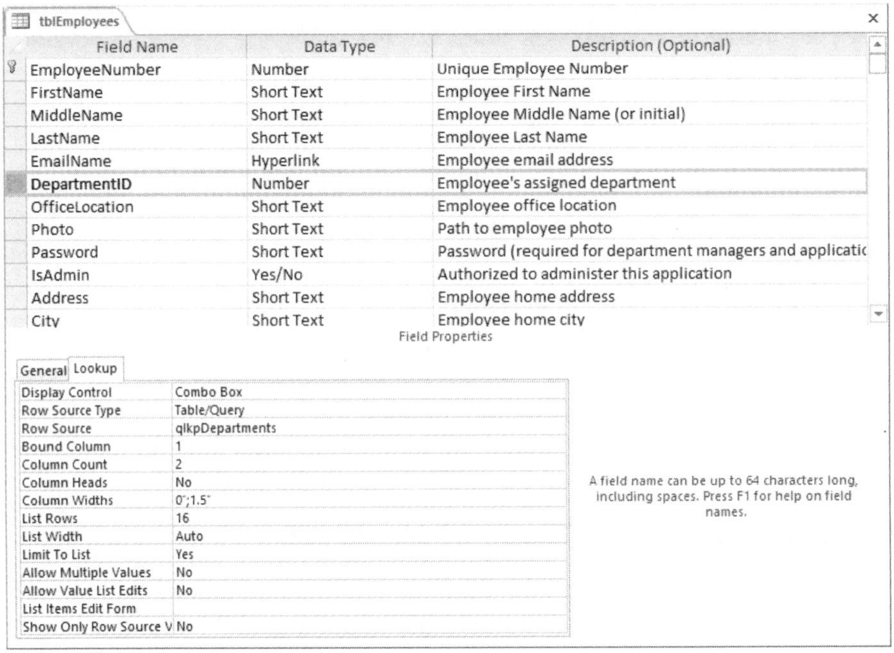

Figure 11-25 The DepartmentID field in tblEmployees in the Housing Reservations sample database has Lookup properties defined.

As you can see, I have set the Display Control property to Combo Box. You see combo boxes in Windows applications all the time. It's a box that you can type in, with a button on the right that you can click to drop down a list of values to select. In Access, you tell the combo box what type of list you want (Row Source Type) and specify the source of the list (Row Source). Access is a bit unusual because it lets you define a list that contains more than one column that you can display (Column Count), and it requires you to specify which of the columns (Bound Column) actually supplies the value to be stored when you pick an item from the list. This means that you might see a text value, but the combo box stores a number.

You can see this combo box in action by switching to Datasheet view. You can click in the Department field and type a name from the list, or click the arrow on the right and select an item from the list, as shown in Figure 11-26. Remember, DepartmentID is actually a number. If you didn't define the special settings on the Lookup tab, you would see a list of numbers in the Department column. For details about these settings, see Table 11-4.

Figure 11-26 The Lookup tab settings show you a combo box in Datasheet view.

I decided to define these properties in this table because I knew was probably going to use a combo box in one or more forms that I would build later to display related department information while editing an employee record. By setting the values in the table, I can avoid having to define the combo box settings again when I build the forms. If you want to see how this works on a form, you can open frmEmployeesPlain in the Housing Reservations database. (Although you can open the "production" version of frmEmployees from the Navigation pane, code in that form prevents you from updating any data unless you are signed in to the application.) Locate the frmEmployeesPlain form object in the Navigation pane and then double-click it. You can see the result in Figure 11-27.

Figure 11-27 The table Lookup tab properties were inherited by the combo box on frmEmployeesPlain.

Table 11-4 gives you an overview of what the lookup settings mean. When you study combo box controls in Chapter 16, "Building a form," you'll see how you can also use Lookup properties to display lists from related tables in a form. In Chapter 16, we'll also explore the Combo Box Wizard, which makes it easy to correctly define these settings.

Chapter 11

TABLE 11-4 Lookup properties

Lookup Property	Setting	Meaning
Display Control	Check Box (Yes/No fields only), Text Box, List Box, or Combo Box	Setting this property to Text Box or Check Box disables lookups. List Box shows a list of values in an open window. Combo Box shows the selected value when closed and shows the available list of values when opened.
PROPERTIES AVAILABLE WHEN YOU SET DISPLAY CONTROL TO LIST BOX OR COMBO BOX		
Row Source Type	Table/Query, Value List, or Field List	Table/Query specifies that you want rows from a table or query to fill the list. If you select Value List, you must enter the values you want displayed in the Row Source property, separated by semicolons. The Field List setting shows the names of the fields from the table or query you enter in Row Source—not the data in the rows.
Row Source	Table Name, Query Name, or a list of values separated by semicolons	Use a table name, query name, or enter the text of the query in Structured Query Language (SQL) that provides the list values when Row Source Type is Table/Query. For details about SQL, see Chapters 12 and 13 for details about building queries, and Article 2, which you can download from the book's catalog page, for details about SQL. Enter a list of values separated by semicolons when Row Source Type is Value List. Use a table or query name when Row Source Type is Field List.
Bound Column	An integer value from 1 to the number of columns in the Row Source	Specify the column in the Row Source that provides the value stored by the list box or combo box.
Column Count	An integer value from 1 to 255	This determines the number of columns available to display. (See Column Widths.) When Row Source Type is Value List, this setting determines how many consecutive values that you enter in Row Source make up a logical row.
Column Heads	No (default) or Yes	Choose Yes to display the field name at the top of any displayed column when you open the list.
Column Widths	One width value per column, separated by semicolons	Specify a zero width if you do not want the combo box or list box to display the column. It is common not to display an AutoNumber ID field, but you might need that field in Row Source as the bound column.
Allow Multiple Values	No (default) or Yes	Choose Yes to allow the user to select multiple values from Row Source for each record. Caution: If you set this property to Yes and save the table definition, you cannot change the value back to No later.

Lookup Property	Setting	Meaning
Allow Value List Edits	No (default) or Yes	Choose Yes to allow the user to add and edit items in the underlying Row Source.
List Item Edit Form	Form Name	Specify the name of a form that Access will open for the user to add items to the Row Source when the user enters a new value that is not in the list specified in Row Source.
PROPERTIES THAT APPLY TO COMBO BOXES ONLY		
List Rows	An integer value between 1 and 255 (default is 16)	Specify how many rows the combo box displays when you open the list. If this setting is less than the number of rows in Row Source, the combo box makes a scroll bar available to move through the list.
List Width	Auto or a specific width	Specify the width of the list when you open it. Auto opens the list the width of the field display.
Limit To List	No (default) or Yes	Choose No to allow the user to enter a value that's not in the list. When the bound column is not the first displayed column, the combo box acts as though Limit To List is Yes regardless of the setting.

INSIDE OUT   Allowing space for the scroll bar

When I'm designing a combo box that displays multiple columns when dropped down, I always specify a List Width value that's the sum of the Column Width values plus 0.25 inch to allow for the vertical scroll bar.

Working with Multi-Value Lookup Fields

In Chapter 1, "What is Access?", I introduced you to the concept of complex data. Access desktop databases include a feature called Multi-Value Lookup Fields, to handle complex data. The purpose of lookup fields, as you just learned, is to *display* one value in a field but actually *store* a different value. For example, a lookup field could store the company ID in a field for an invoice but display the company name to the user for easier data entry on a form or to show the name on a printed invoice report. Lookup fields in this scenario take the guesswork out of trying to remember a specific company ID number. Multi-Value Lookup Fields take this concept a step further by allowing you to store multiple values in a single lookup field. When you define a field as a Multi-Value Lookup Field, Access provides a special control in the Datasheet view of the table similar to a combo box to display the list of valid values. When you drop down the combo box list, you'll see what looks like a list box that has a check box next to each of the available value choices. Selecting the check box next to one or more of the values stores the selected values in the field.

Figure 11-28 shows an example of a Multi-Value Lookup Field in the Conrad Systems Contacts database. Close the Housing Reservations database you have open. Open the Contacts.accdb sample desktop database in the Contacts subfolder where you installed the sample files, and then open the tblContacts table in Datasheet view. Any specific contact could be one or more contact types. The Contact Type field is designated as a Multi-Value Lookup Field, so the user can select from any of the contact types in the database and mark them as related to the current record. In Figure 11-28, you can see that Jeff Conrad is both a developer and a distributor. By selecting the check boxes next to the available contact types, you tell Access to store multiple values for this single record. Notice that after you tab away from this field, Access separates the values with commas.

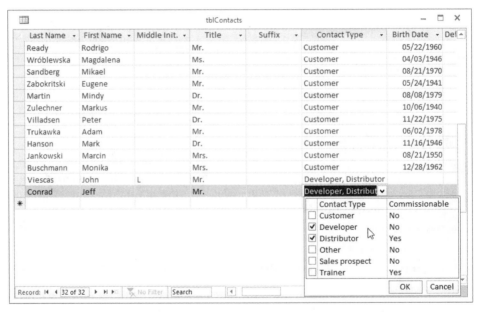

Figure 11-28 A Multi-Value Lookup Field control allows you to select more than one value for a particular field.

Access also provides the list box control that you see in a table in Datasheet view on a form object in Form view. Close the tblContacts table, and then open the frmContactsPlain form object in Form view from the Navigation pane. In Figure 11-29, you can see the Contact Type field, which displays an arrow on the right side. Clicking the arrow drops down the list with the available choices of contact types.

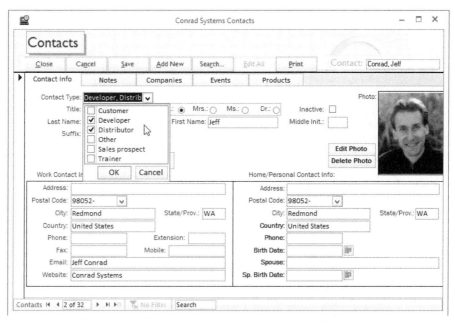

Figure 11-29 Access also provides a Multi-Value Lookup Field control in the frmContactsPlain form of the Conrad Systems Contacts database.

To set up a Multi-Value Lookup Field, you must set the properties in the table in Design view. Close the frmContactsPlain form, and then open the tblContacts table in Design view. (Because this is a linked table, Access will warn you that you cannot modify the design. Click Yes in the warning dialog box to open the table design and view the field properties.) Click the ContactType field, and then click the Lookup tab under Field Properties to see the settings, as shown in Figure 11-30. The Allow Multiple Values property has been set to Yes, which tells Access that it can store multiple values in this field.

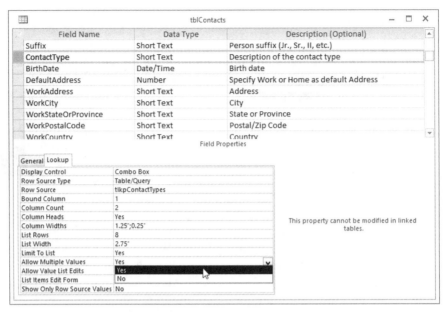

Figure 11-30 Set the Allow Multiple Values property to Yes to enable a field as a Multi-Value Lookup Field.

How do Multi-Value Lookup Fields maintain data normalization rules?

If you are familiar with data normalization rules, you might be asking yourself how it is possible to store multiple values into a single field and still follow normalization rules. Under the covers and hidden from the standard user interface, Access actually creates a many-to-many relationship with a hidden join table. All the work of creating this join table and establishing the relationship rules is handled by Access when you set the Allow Multiple Values property to Yes or choose to allow multiple values in the Lookup Wizard. To ensure that only possible related values can be entered into the Multi-Value Lookup Field, Access displays a combo box or list box control containing only the valid related values for data entry. These Multi-Value Lookup Fields allow for better integration with Microsoft SharePoint complex data structures.

However, you cannot upsize any table that has a Multi-Value Lookup Field to Microsoft SQL Server. If you import a Multi-Value Lookup Field into a web app, Access imports a list of values of the data, separated by semicolons, into a Long Text field. Although Multi-Value Lookup Fields can help novice developers create applications that deal with complex many-to-many relationships in a simple way, I recommend that you learn to create such relationships properly when you need them in your desktop database, using the appropriate linking table.

Compacting your database

As you delete old desktop database objects and add new ones, the space within your .accdb file can become fragmented. The result is that, over time, your database file can grow larger than it needs to be to store all your definitions and data.

To remove unused space, you should compact your database periodically. No other users should be accessing the database you intend to compact. You can compact the database you currently have open by clicking the File tab on the Backstage view and then clicking Compact & Repair Database on the Info tab. If you want to compact another database, you must close your current database and then click the Compact & Repair Database command in the Tools group on the Database Tools tab. Access opens the dialog box shown in Figure 11-31.

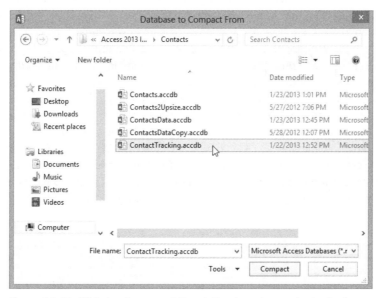

Figure 11-31 Click the Compact & Repair Database button in the Tools group on the Database Tools tab to open the dialog box for specifying a database to compact.

Select the database you want to compact, and then click Compact. Access asks you for a name for the compacted database. You can enter the same name as the database you are compacting, or you can use a different name. If you use the same name, Access warns you that the original database of the same name will be replaced. If you proceed, Access compacts your database into a temporary file. When compaction is completed successfully, Access deletes your old database and gives its name to the new compacted copy.

INSIDE OUT   Compacting a database when you close it

You can also set an option to compact the database each time you close it. Open your database, click the File tab on the Backstage view, and then click Options. In the Access Options dialog box, select the Current Database category and then select the Compact On Close check box under Application Options. If multiple users are sharing the same database, Access compacts the database when the last user closes it.

At this point, you should have all the information you need to modify and maintain your desktop database table definitions. This also concludes the printed chapter portion of *Microsoft Access 2013 Inside Out*. However, you can download the remaining sixteen additional chapters from the book's catalog page. In Part 3, "Building queries in desktop databases," you'll learn how to build desktop database queries to analyze and update data in your tables. In Part 4, "Creating forms," you'll learn how to create and customize forms for data entry in your applications. In Part 5, "Working with reports," you'll learn how to design reports to view and print the data in your applications. In Part 6, "Automating a desktop database using macros," you'll learn about event processing, data macros, and user interface macros in desktop databases. In Part 7, "Automating a desktop database using Visual Basic," you'll learn how to use Visual Basic for Applications (VBA) and see many examples of how I automated the sample databases using Visual Basic code. In Part 8, "After completing your desktop database," you'll learn how to create custom ribbons for your applications, create database templates, understand how run-time mode works, as well as many other topics. You'll also find seven reference articles on the book's catalog page that you'll find essential for increasing your knowledge about building applications using Access.

Installing your software

Tʜɪꜱ book assumes that you have installed Microsoft Access 2013 as part of Microsoft Office Professional Plus 2013 from an installation media. You can also install Office 2013 programs through an online installation procedure with Office 365, if you have purchased a plan that includes Office 2013. To install Office and related software for a single user, you need a computer that is compatible with Microsoft Windows or a device that is configured as follows::

- One gigahertz (GHz) or faster x86-bit or x64-bit processor with Streaming SIMD Extensions 2 (SSE2) instruction set.

- Microsoft Windows 7 (32-bit or 64-bit), Microsoft Windows 8 (32-bit or 64-bit), Windows Server 2008 R2, or Windows Server 2012 operating systems.

- At least 1 gigabyte (GB) of random access memory (RAM) for 32-bit operating system environments or 2 GB of RAM for 64-bit operating systems.

- A hard drive with at least 3.0 GB available.

- A DirectX10 graphics card and 1024 x 576 resolution for graphics hardware acceleration.

- Microsoft Internet Explorer 8, 9, or 10; Mozilla FireFox 10.x or a later version; Apple Safari 5; or Google Chrome 17.x or a later version.

- Microsoft .NET version 3.5, 4.0, or 4.5.

- A touch-enabled device for using any multitouch functionality in Windows 8. (However, all features and functionality are always available by using a keyboard, mouse, or other standard or accessible input device.)

Note
Apart from the following system requirements, Microsoft recommends installing Silverlight together with Office 2013 to improve the online experience.

> **Note**
>
> MSI and Click-to-Run installations of Office 2013 require that Task Scheduler be enabled on the client computers. If your network administrator set up Group Policy to disable Task Scheduler or if an individual client computer has Task Scheduler disabled, attempts to install Office 2013 will fail. You'll need to contact your corporate network administrator if you are encountering problems installing Office 2013.

Installing the Office system

Before you run the Office system setup program, be sure that no other applications are running on your computer.

If you're installing from the Office Professional Plus 2013 DVD-ROM, insert the disc. On most systems, the Office system setup program starts automatically. If the setup program does not start automatically, click the Run command on the Start menu. In the Run dialog box, type ***x:\setup.exe*** (where *x* is the drive letter of your DVD-ROM drive), and click OK. If you see the User Account Control dialog box and you're logged on as a non-administrative user, specify the user name and password for an administrative account and click Continue. If you're logged on as an administrator, click Continue.

To install from a network drive, use Windows Explorer to connect to the folder in which your system manager has placed the Office system setup files. Run Setup.exe in that folder by double-clicking it. If you're installing the Office system from a Master License Pack, click Run on the Start menu, and include a PIDKEY= parameter and the 25-character volume-license key in the open box, as in the following example:

```
x:\setup.exe PIDKEY=1234567890123456789012345
```

The setup program might take several minutes after it displays its opening screen to examine your computer and determine what programs you currently have installed. If you didn't supply a license key on the command line, the setup program asks for a valid product key. If you're installing from a DVD, you can find the product key in the materials included with the Office 2013 installation package. Enter a valid key, and click Continue to go to the next page. The setup program asks you to confirm that you accept the license agreement. Select the I Accept The Terms Of This Agreement check box, and then click Continue. The setup program asks whether you want to install now or to customize your installation.

Choosing options when you have no previous version of the Office system

When you install Office 2013 on your computer or device, you can choose between two options—Install Now or Customize, as shown in Figure A-1. If you click Install Now, the setup program installs all the programs and components that Microsoft considers most useful to the majority of users. The fastest way to complete an install is to click Install Now. If you don't want to tailor the installation to your specific needs by clicking Customize, click Install Now to include Access 2013 so that you can work through the examples in this book.

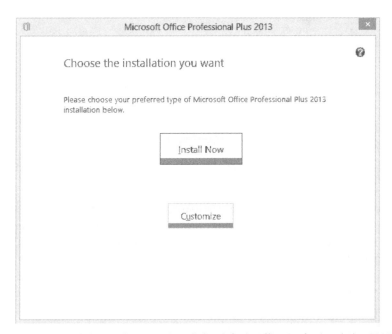

Figure A-1 Click Install Now to install the default Office Professional Plus 2013 programs.

I like to click Customize to pick the options I need. The Customize install option allows you to choose only some applications or include additional features that Microsoft considers optional. When you click Customize, the setup program displays a window with three tabs—Installation Options, File Location, and User Information, as shown in Figure A-2.

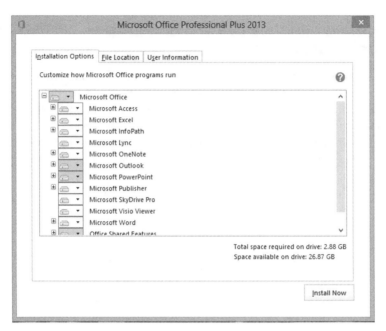

Figure A-2 The Installation Options tab allows you to choose which programs and options to install.

The setup program shows you the available options for the Office system and each program in a hierarchical view. By default, the setup program selects all programs, but it selects only some of the features for several of the programs. Click the plus sign (+) next to any category to expand it and see the options in subcategories. When you see a category that interests you, click the arrow next to the disk drive icon to choose options for all items in that category and its subcategories. To work through all the examples in this book, you should select the Run All From My Computer option for Microsoft Access, as shown in Figure A-3. Choosing this option selects the Run From My Computer option for all subcategories. When you select Installed On First Use, the installation program creates a shortcut for the program on your Start menu, but you'll be prompted to install the application when you select the shortcut the first time. Choosing Not Available causes the installation program to neither install the program nor provide a shortcut.

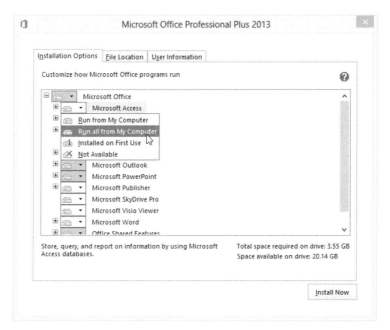

Figure A-3 Choose Run All From My Computer to have the setup program install Access 2013 components.

I personally like to begin by selecting the Run All From My Computer option for the top-level item, Microsoft Office. I then go through each of the major categories and selectively choose Installed On First Use or, for options that I do not want, Not Available. For example, you might want to go to the Office Shared Features category and remove some of the extra fonts under International Support. If you're unsure about any option, you can click the title of the option to see a brief description in the lower part of the window.

On the File Location tab, you see a box with a default location chosen, as shown in Figure A-4. You can enter a different program file location or click Browse to select a location on your hard drive. I recommend that you keep the default location. You'll see summary information on how much space is required and available on your hard drive in the middle of the window.

Figure A-4 Select an installation folder on the File Location tab.

On the User Information tab, you can enter personal information about yourself and your company, as shown in Figure A-5. Type your name in the Full Name text box, your initials in the Initials text box, and your organization or company name in the Organization text box. (If you do not fill in these boxes here, the first Office system program you open after installation prompts you for your full name and initials.)

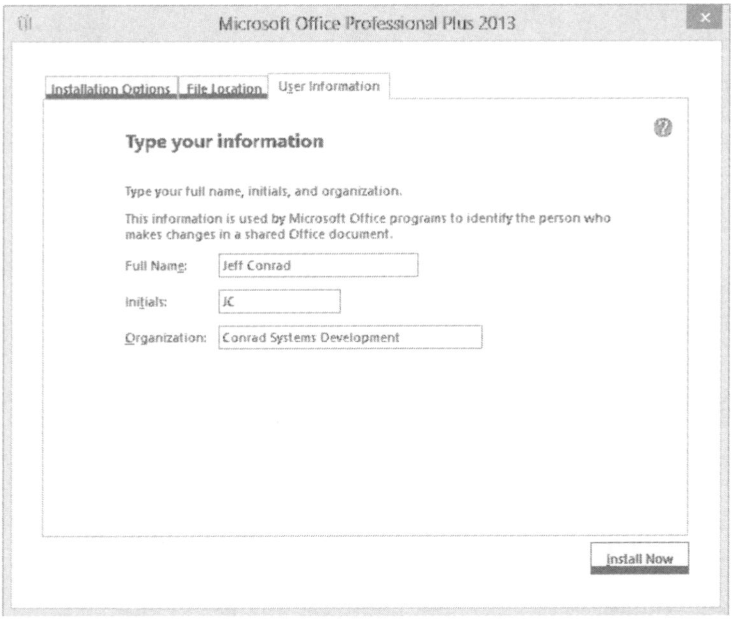

Figure A-5 Enter your personal information on the User Information tab.

After you have finished making your selections, click Install Now to proceed. If you're not sure, you can click any of the three tabs to verify the options you selected. When the setup program finishes, it shows you a setup completed window, as shown in Figure A-6. In this final window, you can select options to open your web browser to check for additional updates. You can click the Help icon in the upper-right corner of the window to display information about how to register your copy of the Office 2013 release. Click Close to close the setup program window.

Figure A-6 The setup program displays this message when the installation process completes.

Choosing options to upgrade a previous version of the Office system

When you have a previous version of any of the Office system programs installed on your computer, the setup program shows you different options after you accept the license agreement, as shown in Figure A-7. If you click Upgrade, the setup program installs all the programs and components that Microsoft considers most useful to the majority of users and removes any previous versions of the Office system programs. The fastest way to complete an install is to click Upgrade.

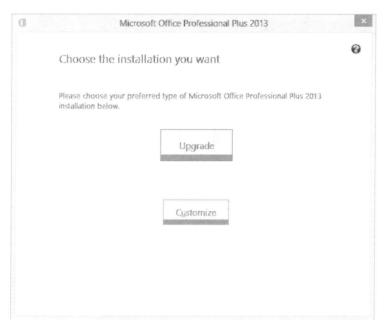

Figure A-7 When you have previous versions of the Office system programs installed, you can choose either Upgrade or Customize.

I like to click Customize to pick the options I need. The Customize install option allows you to choose only some of the applications to install and to not remove previous versions. When you click Customize, the setup program displays a window with four tabs—Upgrade, Installation Options, File Location, and User Information, as shown in Figure A-8.

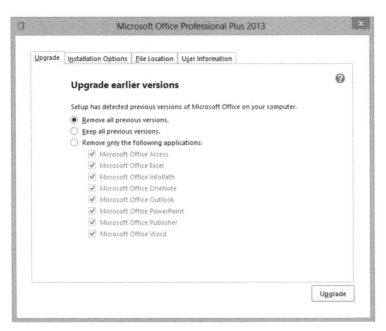

Figure A-8 On the Upgrade tab, you can choose to keep or remove existing Office system programs.

The Installation Options, File Location, and User Information tabs display the same options you learned about in the previous section. The setup program displays the Upgrade tab only when you have previous versions of Office system programs installed on your computer. If you select Remove All Previous Versions, the setup program removes any existing Office system programs before installing the Office 2013 programs. If you select the Keep All Previous Versions option, the setup program does not remove any existing Office system programs before installing the Office 2013 programs. If you select Remove Only The Following Applications, you can choose which existing Office system programs to keep.

As a professional Access developer, I keep several versions of Access installed on my primary development computers so that I can continue to support older applications that I created. You might also want to keep an older version of Microsoft Excel, Microsoft Power-Point, or Microsoft Word. To keep an older version, you must clear the appropriate check box for the application under Remove Only The Following Applications.

As you learned in the previous section, you can change which of the Office 2013 release components are installed on the Installation Options tab, change the installation folder on the File Location tab, and specify your user name information on the User Information tab. After clicking Upgrade, the setup program proceeds and displays the Setup Completed window, shown earlier in Figure A-6, when it is finished. You can click the Help icon in the upper-right corner of the window to display information about how to register your copy of the 2013 Office release. Click Close to close the setup program window.

Converting from a previous version of Access

Access 2013 (version 15 of Access) can work with the data and tables in a database file created by Access version 9 (Access 2000), version 10 (Access 2002), version 11 (Access 2003), version 12 (Access 2007), and version 14 (Access 2010). You can also open a version 9, version 10, version 11, version 12, or version 14 database with Access 2013 and modify any of the objects in the database.

You can convert a version 9 database file to either the Access 2002-2003 format (versions 10 and 11) or the Access 2007-2013 .accdb format (versions 12, 14, and 15). Before you begin the conversion process, make sure that all Access Basic or Microsoft Visual Basic for Applications (VBA) modules are compiled in your earlier version database. If you want to convert your database to the .accdb file format, start Access 2013, click the File tab on the Backstage view, click Save As, and then click Access Database (*.accdb) under Save Database As. Access opens the Save As dialog box. You must specify a different file name or location for your converted database because Access won't let you replace your previous version file directly. Click Save to convert the database. If you want to convert your database to the Access 2000 or Access 2002-2003 format, start Access 2013, click the File tab on the Backstage view, click Save As, and then click either Access 2000 Database (*.mdb) or Access 2002-2003 Database (*.mdb). Access opens the Save As dialog box. You must specify a different file name or location for your converted database because Access won't let you replace your previous version file directly. Click Save to convert the database.

Conversion issues

Access 2013 reports any objects or properties that it is unable to convert by creating a table called Convert Errors in your converted database. The most common problems you're likely to encounter are Microsoft Visual Basic libraries that were available in a previous version, but not in Access 2013, and obsolete code that you created in a user-defined function.

Other changes that might affect the conversion of your application code or how your converted application runs include the following:

- In versions 7 and earlier, you had to use macros to construct custom menus. Access 2013 no longer supports macros for custom menus, so you might want to rebuild custom ribbons using Extensible Markup Language (XML).

- As of version 8, DoMenuItem is no longer supported. The conversion utility replaces this command in all macros with the equivalent RunMenuCommand action or method. The DoMenuItem method in Visual Basic code is still supported for backward compatibility, but you should locate and change these statements after converting your database.

- In version 8, you could create a formatted Windows dialog box with the MsgBox action or function, separating the sections of the message with the @ character. Version 9 and later no longer support this feature. You should remove the @ character used in this way in code you wrote for version 8.

- Versions 7 and 8 supported the Microsoft Data Access Objects (DAO) 2.5/3.x compatibility library for databases converted from previous versions. Versions 9 and later no longer support this library. You will need to replace the reference to this library to the Microsoft Office 15.0 Access Database Engine Object Library after you convert the database, and you might need to change old Visual Basic statements that depended on the older version of DAO.

- If you convert a database by importing its objects, your new database might not compile or execute properly. The problem is most likely a reference to an obsolete Visual Basic code library. You can correct this by opening any module in the Visual Basic Editor and then clicking Tools, References. Remove any libraries marked MISSING, and attempt to compile the project.

- Unless you also have Office 2003 installed on your computer, you won't be able to open or edit any data access pages that you created in Access 2003.

- If your application includes the ActiveX Calendar Control that shipped with versions of Access before 2010, you'll need to remove the control from any forms that use it.

- You cannot open Access Data Project (.adp) files in Access 2013 that were created in previous versions of Access.

Installing the Office 64-bit version

The Office 2013 applications are also available in 64-bit versions. Before you run the Office system setup program, be sure that no other applications are running on your computer. You can install the 64-bit versions of Office 2013 only on a computer running a 64-bit Windows operating system.

If you're installing from the Office Professional Plus 2013 DVD-ROM, insert the disc. On most computers, the Office system setup program starts automatically. By default, the Office setup program wants to install the 32-bit versions of the Office 2013 applications. To install the 64-bit versions, you need to exit the default setup program. Using Windows Explorer (or File Explorer in Windows 8), browse to your DVD-ROM drive, open the x64 folder on the install disc, and then double-click the Setup.exe file located inside the x64 folder. If the setup program does not start automatically, click the Run command on the

Start menu. In the Run dialog box, type **y:\x64\setup.exe** (where *y* is the drive letter of your DVD-ROM drive), and click OK. If you see the User Account Control dialog box and you're logged on as a non-administrative user, specify the user name and password for an administrative account, and click Continue. If you're logged on as an administrator, click Continue.

If you have any previous 32-bit versions of Office applications already installed on your computer, you'll see the Setup Error dialog box shown in Figure A-9. You must uninstall all 32-versions of Office applications on your computer before you can install the 64-bit versions of Office 2013 applications. This rule applies even if you have 32-bit versions of Office 2013 applications installed. You cannot have mixed versions of 32-bit and 64-bit Office applications installed on the same computer.

Figure A-9 You must uninstall all previous versions of 32-bit Office programs before installing 64-bit versions of the Office 2013 applications.

The setup procedures for installing the 64-bit Office 2013 applications after this point are the same as the 32-bit versions of Office 2013. You can follow the steps outlined in the previous sections for customizing the application options you'd like to install.

Here are some caveats to using the 64-bit version of Access 2013 that you should be aware of before deciding to install the 64-bit version:

- Existing 32-bit ActiveX controls will not work with the 64-bit version of Access 2013. If you open a form or report that contains a 32-bit ActiveX control, you'll see a red "X" within the box where the control should be. You'll need to update those 32-bit ActiveX controls to work within 64-bit environments.

- Microsoft did not update the ComCtl collection of controls to work within 64-bit environments. If you open a form or report that contains a ComCtl control, you'll see a red "X" within the box where the control should be. You'll need to update those 32-bit ComCtl controls to work within 64-bit environments.

- Existing 32-bit Access add-ins will not work in 64-bit Access 2013. You'll need to obtain a version of the add-in that works in 64-bit environments from the supplier of the add-in.

- Existing Access .mde and .accde files compiled with 32-bit versions of Access will not work with the 64-bit version of Access 2013. You'll need to create a new .mde or .accde from the original database and compile it in the 64-bit version of Access 2013.

- You'll need to update some existing VBA code for it to work within the 64-bit version of Access 2013. In Chapter 25, "Automating your desktop database with Visual Basic," which can be downloaded from the book's catalog page at http://shop.oreilly.com/product/0790145367969.do, you'll learn what changes you need to make to your VBA code so that your application runs within a 64-bit environment.

For all the reasons mentioned above, Microsoft recommends using the 32-bit version of Access 2013 unless you have a specific reason for using the 64-bit version of Office 2013. The main reason for using the 64-bit versions of Office 2013 is the capacity to work with very large workbooks in Excel and very large projects in Microsoft Project. The maximum desktop database size for Access 2013—2 GB—is identical for both the 32-bit and 64-bit versions of Access 2013.

Installing the sample files

To install the sample files, which can be downloaded from the book's catalog page, you'll first need to create a new folder on your C drive called **Microsoft Press**. Next, download the Sample Files zip file from the book's catalog page locally to your desktop or documents folder. Finally, extract the zip folder contents into the Microsoft Press folder you created earlier. You should now have a folder structure like this on your C drive:

C:\Microsoft Press\Access 2013 Inside Out

Inside the Access 2013 Inside Out folder, you'll see additional subfolders that contain supporting files, as well as the main sample web apps and desktop databases used throughout the book. After you have your files downloaded from the book's catalog page and placed in the correct folder on your computer or device, make sure you set the Microsoft Press folder and all its subdirectories as a trusted location to enable all the content in the sample desktop databases. See the section, "Enabling content by defining trusted locations," in Chapter 9, "Exploring the Access 2013 desktop database interface," for information about creating trusted locations in desktop databases.

> **Note**
> The book's catalog page contains one Sample Files folder for use with 32-bit installations of the Office 2013 applications and one Sample Files folder for use with 64-bit installations of the Office 2013 applications. Make sure you download and extract the Sample Files folder that corresponds to your current Office installation environment. If you do not download the correct Sample Files folder corresponding to your Office installation environment, you will most likely encounter errors when working with the sample files and applications.

Index

About the author

Jeff Conrad started working with Access when he saw a need at his full-time position for a database solution. He bought a book on Access and began teaching himself how to use the program to solve his business's needs. He immediately became hooked on the power and ease of working with Access.

Jeff found a home in the Microsoft Access newsgroups asking questions as he was learning the ins and outs of Access and database development. He now enjoys giving back to a community that helped him when he was first learning how to use Access. He has been an active participant for many years in the Access newsgroups and online forums where he is best known as the Access Junkie.

Jeff also was awarded Microsoft's Most Valuable Professional award from 2005 to 2007 for his continual involvement with the online Access community. He maintains a website with a wealth of information and resource links for those needing guidance with Access (*http://www.AccessJunkie.com*). He co-authored *Microsoft Office Access 2007 Inside Out* with John Viescas and authored *Microsoft Access 2010 Inside Out*. Jeff is currently employed by Microsoft as a Software Design Engineer in Test working with the Access development team.

How To
Download
Your eBook

Thank you for purchasing this Microsoft Press® title. Your companion PDF eBook is ready to download from O'Reilly Media, official distributor of Microsoft Press titles.

To download your eBook, go to
http://go.microsoft.com/FWLink/?Linkid=224345
and follow the instructions.

Please note: You will be asked to create a free online account and enter the access code below.

Your access code:

GDZNJZN

Microsoft Access 2013 Inside Out

Your PDF eBook allows you to:

- Search the full text
- Print
- Copy and paste

Best yet, you will be notified about free updates to your eBook.

If you ever lose your eBook file, you can download it again just by logging in to your account.

Need help? Please contact:
mspbooksupport@oreilly.com
or call 800-889-8969.

Please note: This access code is non-transferable and is void if altered or revised in any way. It may not be sold or redeemed for cash, credit, or refund.

Now that you've read the book...

Tell us what you think!

Was it useful?
Did it teach you what you wanted to learn?
Was there room for improvement?

Let us know at http://aka.ms/tellpress

Your feedback goes directly to the staff at Microsoft Press,
and we read every one of your responses. Thanks in advance!

 Microsoft